Interconnections, Second Edition

Addison-Wesley Professional Computing Series

Brian W. Kernighan, Consulting Editor

Interconnections, Second Edition
Bridges, Routers, Switches, and Internetworking Protocols

Radia Perlman

ADDISON-WESLEY
An imprint of Addison Wesley Longman, Inc.
Reading, Massachusetts Harlow, England Menlo Park, California
Berkeley, California Don Mills, Ontario Sydney
Bonn Amsterdam Tokyo Mexico City

Many of the designations used by manufacturers and sellers to distinguish their products are claimed as trademarks. Where those designations appear in this book and Addison-Wesley was aware of a trademark claim, the designations have been printed in initial caps or all caps.

The author and publisher have taken care in the preparation of this book, but make no expressed or implied warranty of any kind and assume no responsibility for errors or omissions. No liability is assumed for incidental or consequential damages in connection with or arising out of the use of the information or programs contained herein.

The publisher offers discounts on this book when ordered in quantity for special sales. For more information, please contact:

Corporate, Government, and Special Sales Group
Addison Wesley Longman, Inc.
One Jacob Way
Reading, Massachusetts 01867

Visit AW on the Web: www.awl.com/cseng/

Library of Congress Cataloging-in-Publication Data

Perlman, Radia.
    Interconnections : bridges, routers, switches and internetworking
    protocols / Radia Perlman. — 2nd ed.
        p.   cm.
    Includes index.
    ISBN 0-201-63448-1
        1. Routers (Computer networks)   2. Computer network protocols.
    3. Local area networks (Computer networks)   I. Title.
    TK5105.543.P47   1999   99-37086
    004.6'2—dc21   CIP

Acquisitions Editor: Karen Gettman
Production Coordinator: Jacquelyn Doucette
Compositor: Octal Publishing, Inc.
Cover Designer: Simone R. Payment

ISBN 0-201-63448-1

Text printed on recycled and acid-free paper.

1 2 3 4 5 6 7 8 9 10—CRW—0302010099

First printing, September 1999

Praise for *Interconnections, Second Edition:*

"Many networking books are little more than condensations of product literature and standard documents. Radia's book goes into the concepts and principles behind the technology, and in some cases, the history. This information will be very useful to students learning the technology, networking managers trying to improve their networks and product developers hoping to avoid past mistakes. If network architects and standards developers absorb this book perhaps the next generation of networking will be less complex and more effective. The book includes historical anecdotes and controversial recommendations. These make it entertaining as well as informative."

—Tony Lauck

"While there are other books on routing, I can think of no other that covers bridging at any depth. And the fact that it deals with both in one book is helpful to show the relationship, strengths, and weaknesses of each technology."

—Paul Koning
Zedia Corporation

"*Interconnections, Second Edition* does an excellent job of presenting a wide variety of solutions to a common problem . . . allowing the reader to appreciate the trade-offs and key issues."

—Peter Memishian

Praise for *Interconnections:*

"No other book ever written is better suited to build a strong understanding of networking concepts. Radia Perlman has been intimately involved with networking during its evolution, and her experience carries over into this entertaining book. Radia's book is perfect for beginners who wish to build a strong base of networking knowledge. It's also a great book for experienced network professionals who have a difficult time finding books that have new information."

—Tony Northrup
GTE Internetworking

"This is one of the best sources of information on the design of network routing protocols that exists. The book is indispensable if you are involved in a software development project that benefits from routing, at any level."

—Thomas H. Ptacek
Sonicity, Inc.

"A wonderful and richly detailed introduction to bridging and routing from one of the creators of the field."

—Craig Partridge, author of *Gigabit Networking*,
Addison-Wesley, 1993

"This book is the one-stop introduction to the field. It explains in detail the transparent and source routing bridges, the spanning tree protocol, and the various IP/OSI routing protocols: RIP, OSPF, BGP, ISIS. This is a must read for anyone interested in gaining a good grounding in internetworking protocols."

—Great Mahershi

Contents

Preface

Interconnections, Second Edition is about what goes on inside the boxes that move data around the Internet. These boxes are variously called bridges, routers, switches, and hubs. The book also describes the devices that connect to the network.

There is considerable confusion in this area. Most of the terminology is ill defined and is used in conflicting ways. The terminology and the specifications tend to be daunting. Some knowledge is spread among many different documents; much is unwritten folk wisdom. Adding to the confusion is dogma. Beliefs are accepted as truth, and questioning any of the dogma is often greeted with hostility. But good engineering demands that we understand what we're doing and why, keep an open mind, and learn from experience.

In *Interconnections, Second Edition*, instead of diving right into the details of one protocol, I first focus on the problems to be solved. I examine various solutions to each of these problems and discuss the engineering trade-offs involved. Then I look at a variety of solutions that have been deployed and compare the approaches. I give technical arguments for any opinions, and if you think I have missed any arguments I welcome email discussion. My email address is at the back of the book, which I hope you will find after having read the book cover to cover.

In the first edition, my intention was to help people understand the problems and the general types of solutions, assuming that they would read the specifications to get the details of specific protocols. But people used the book as a reference in addition to using it to understand the issues. So in this edition I have documented many more of the protocols in detail.

I believe that to understand something deeply you need to compare it to something else. The first edition was "minimalist" in that I always used only two examples: two types of bridges, bridges versus routers, connection-oriented versus connectionless network layer protocols, and two examples of connectionless protocols (CLNP and IP). In this edition I add a lot more examples, including ATM, IPv6, IPX, AppleTalk, and DECnet. I did this in part because these protocols exist, and it is hard to get information about them. But mostly I did it because the protocols embody interesting ideas that should not be lost. When we design new protocols, we should learn from previous ideas, both good and bad. Also, it takes very little additional effort, after the problem is described generically, to describe several examples.

> **The Tao of network protocols: If all you see is IP, you see nothing.**
> —Greg Minshall

Roadmap to the Book

The first four chapters are not significantly different from their counterparts in the first edition, but the rest of the book has been largely rewritten. Chapters 1 through 4 cover general networking concepts, data link issues such as addressing and multiplexing, transparent bridges and the spanning tree algorithm, and source routing bridges. Chapter 5 is completely new and explains how the notion of a switch evolved into a rediscovery of the bridge. It also covers VLANs and fast Ethernet.

The remainder of the book concentrates on layer 3 (the network layer). Chapter 6 gives an overview of the network layer. Chapter 7 covers connection-oriented networks, including ATM and X.25. Chapter 8 discusses the issues in a generic connectionless network layer. Chapter 9 covers layer 3 addressing generically and gives a detailed comparison of IP, IPv6, CLNP, DECnet, AppleTalk, and IPX. Chapter 10 covers the information that should appear in a network layer header and contrasts the headers of several protocols.

Chapter 11 covers autoconfiguration and neighbor discovery, including protocols such as ARP and DHCP. Chapter 12 covers routing algorithms generically.

Chapter 13 discusses the problem of doing longest-prefix matching, which is required in order to forward IP packets quickly. Chapter 14 discusses the specifics of various routing protocols including RIP, IS-IS, OSPF, PNNI, NLSP, and BGP. Chapter 15 covers network layer multicast. Chapter 16 explains how to design a network that is invulnerable to sabotage, an idea whose time may come.

The final two chapters summarize the book, and I hope they will be mostly light and entertaining reading. Chapter 17 probes the mystery of what, if anything, distinguishes a router from a bridge. Chapter 18 attempts to capture folk wisdom about how to design a protocol.

Finally, there is an extensive glossary. I try to define terms when I first use them, but if I ever fail to do that, you will probably find them in the glossary.

Acknowledgments

Writing this section is scary because I am afraid I will leave people out. I'd like to thank the people who reviewed all or part of the book: Peter Memishian, Paul Koning, Tony Lauck,

Craig Partridge, Dan Pitt, Brian Kernighan, Paul Bottorff, Joel Halpern, Charlie Kaufman, Mike Speciner, Andy Tanenbaum, Phil Rosenzweig, Dan Senie, William Welch, Craig Labovitz, Chase Bailey, George Varghese, and Suchi Raman. Other people who have been helpful by answering questions are Ariel Hendel, Rich Kubota, Stuart Cheshire, Tom Maufer, Steve Deering, and John Moy. The first time I sent an email question in the middle of the night (when I did most of my work on this book) to Craig Partridge, the co-series editor for this book, the beep indicating incoming mail happened so immediately that I assumed it was an automatic mail responder informing me he was on vacation. But it was an answer to my question. I assume he doesn't have an automatic mail responder so clever that it can answer technical questions, so I thank him for being so prompt and available. Brian Kernighan, the other series editor, also had detailed and helpful comments on the entire book.

The people at Addison-Wesley have been amazingly patient with me for the many years in which I've been working on this edition. I'm not sure they had any alternative besides patience, but it was nice that they believed I'd finish even when I wasn't so sure. So thank you to Mary Hart, Karen Gettman, Jacquelyn Doucette, and Jason Jones. And I'd also like to thank my copy editor, Betsy Hardinger. She of all people will have read every word of the book, while maintaining the concentration to note inconsistencies and ways of removing excess words here and there. I know it's her job, but I'm still impressed.

Mike Speciner helped me figure out the mysteries of Framemaker. Ray Perlner made sure that I maintained some humor in the book and watched over my shoulder while I typed the last chapter to see that I had enough funny bad real-life protocols. Dawn Perlner has been terrifically supportive, convincing her friends and even strangers in bookstores to buy my books. She used to be my child. Now she's a wonderful friend.

Chapter 1
Essential Networking Concepts

This chapter introduces concepts that are essential to understanding the specific subfield of computer networking that includes bridges and routers. It covers the OSI reference model, including layering and service models, because this model is a useful basis for some vocabulary. It also discusses various dimensions along which network designs can differ, such as scope, scalability, robustness, and autoconfigurability. Chapter 1 also describes the typical techniques involved in providing reliable two-party communication because some of the techniques used by routers can interact with techniques used by other layers.

1.1 Layers

Understanding, designing, and building a computer network would be too difficult a task unless the problem were partitioned into smaller subtasks, traditionally by dividing the problem into layers. The idea behind layering is that each layer is responsible for providing a service to the layer above by using the services of the layer below.

Each layer communicates with its *peer* layer in another node through the use of a *protocol*. This communication is accomplished through direct communication with the layer below. The communication between layer n and layer $n-1$ is known as an *interface*.

The OSI (Open Systems Interconnection) Reference Model defines seven layers, as shown in Figure 1.1. There is nothing magic about the number seven or the functionality in the layers. The reference model was designed before the protocols themselves, and then committees were set up to design each of the layers. Many of the layers were subsequently subdivided into further layers. The distinction between the layers is not always clear. Bridges and routers are a good example of a case in which people should rightfully be confused about which layers are which. But semantic arguments about layers are not very productive. Instead, the layering should be viewed as a useful framework for discussion and not as a bible.

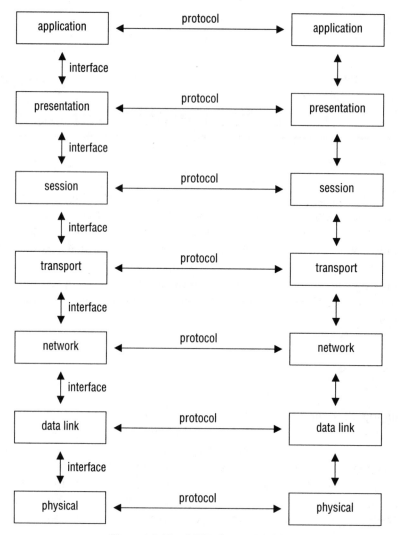

Figure 1.1 The OSI Reference Model

Layers defined by ISO:

1. *Physical layer:* The physical layer transmits bits of information across a link. It deals with such problems as size and shape of connectors, assignment of functions to pins, conversion of bits to electrical signals, and bit-level synchronization. It is usual for several different types of physical layers to exist within a network and even for multiple different types of physical layers to exist within a node, because each technology requires its own physical layer.

2. *Data link layer:* The data link layer (sometimes called the link layer) transmits chunks of information across a link. It deals with such problems as checksumming to detect data corruption; coordinating the use of shared media, as in a LAN (local area network); and addressing (when multiple systems are reachable, as in a LAN). Again, it is common for different links to implement different data link layers and for a node to support several data link layer protocols, one for each of the types of links to which the node is attached.

3. *Network layer:* The network layer enables any pair of systems in the network to communicate with each other. A *fully connected* network is one in which every pair of nodes has a direct link between its nodes, but this kind of topology does not scale beyond a few nodes. In the more typical case, the network layer must find a path through a series of connected nodes, and nodes along the path must forward packets in the appropriate direction. The network layer deals with such problems as route calculation, packet fragmentation and reassembly (when different links in the network have different maximum packet sizes), and congestion control.

4. *Transport layer:* The transport layer establishes a reliable communication stream between a pair of systems. It deals with errors that can be introduced by the network layer, such as lost packets, duplicated packets, packet reordering, and fragmentation and reassembly (so that the user of the transport layer can deal with larger-size messages and so that less-efficient network layer fragmentation and reassembly might be avoided). It is also nice if the transport layer reacts to congestion in the network by sending data more slowly in response.

5. *Session layer:* ISO had something in mind for this layer that doesn't seem useful to the Internet community. ISO's session layer offers services beyond the simple full-duplex reliable communication stream provided by transport, such as dialogue control (enforcing a particular pattern of communication between systems) and chaining (combining groups of packets so that either all or none of the packets in the group gets delivered). Whatever this layer is, it's irrelevant for bridges and routers.

6. *Presentation layer:* The goal of this layer is to agree on representations for data so that people defining structures don't have to worry about bit/byte order or what a floating point number looks like. ISO standardized on ASN.1 (Abstract Syntax Notation 1). Although I have yet to meet anyone who actually *likes* ASN.1—because it is complex and inefficient in both space and processing—a lot of the IETF (Internet Engineering Task Force) standards use it.

7. *Application layer:* As fascinating as bridging and routing is, it's actually because of applications that people want any of this stuff. Applications include file transfer, virtual terminal, Web browsing, and so on. It is common for multiple applications to be running concurrently in a node.

In this book, the data link layer is relevant because bridges operate within it and because the service provided by it is relevant to routers, which operate at the network layer, thereby making the network layer also relevant. The transport layer is somewhat relevant because it is a user of the network layer and because certain decisions that the network layer might make (such as whether to allow traffic to be split among several equivalent paths) affect the transport layer. The layers above transport are largely irrelevant to the study of bridges and routers.

Typically, the way layer n works is that it receives a chunk of data from layer $n+1$ along with additional information (such as the destination address) that might be required. Layer n must transmit the data to the layer n process in the destination node, which delivers it to the layer $n+1$ process in the destination node. Layer n often needs to include with the data certain information—for example, the address of the destination—that will be interpreted by other layer n entities. To get the information to the destination node, layer n hands down a buffer to layer $n-1$, including the data received from layer $n+1$ and the control information added by layer n. Additionally, layer n might pass other information in the layer $n/n-1$ interface along with the buffer.

Let's look at an example of how layering works. Assume that the physical layer allows a stream of bits to pass from one machine to another. The data link layer marks the bit stream so that the beginning and end of a packet can be found; it also adds a checksum to the packet so that the receiving machine can detect whether noise on the line introduced errors.

There are various interesting techniques to ensure that the marker indicating the beginning or end of the packet does not appear inside the data. In one technique, known as *bit stuffing*, the marker is a sequence of six 1's. To ensure that six consecutive 1's do not appear in the data portion of a packet, the transmitter adds an extra 0 after five consecutive 1's. The receiver knows that if the next bit after five consecutive 1's is a 0, then the 0 should be removed and ignored. If the next bit after five consecutive 1's is a 1, then it is a signal for the beginning or end of a packet. Another technique involves using different physical signals for data bits (1's and 0's) than for markers.

The network layer allows communication across multiple hops by cooperating with the network layers in all the connected machines to compute routes.

When the network layer receives a packet from the transport layer for transmission, the network layer adds an *envelope*, which consists of information glued onto the beginning (known as a *header*) and/or onto the end (known as a *trailer*). The envelope includes information such as the source and destination addresses. The network layer chooses an appropriate link on which to dispatch the packet and then hands the packet plus the network layer envelope to the data link layer process responsible for the outgoing link.

When the packet is received by an intermediate node, it is processed by the data link layer. Then the data link layer envelope is removed and the packet is passed up to the network layer, where the packet looks exactly the way it did when the previous network layer handed the packet to the data link layer—that is, it has everything transport sent down plus the network layer envelope. The network layer process at the receiving node looks at the network layer envelope, makes a decision as to the direction in which the packet should go based on that envelope, modifies the envelope as necessary (for example, incrementing a hop count to indicate how many nodes the packet has passed through), and gives the modified packet to the data link layer process responsible for the outgoing link (see Figure 1.2).

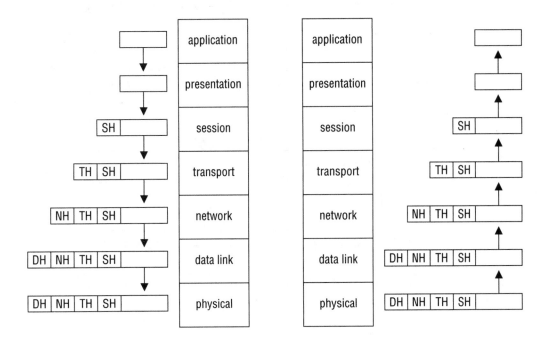

SH = session header
TH = transport header
NH = network header
DH = data link header

Figure 1.2 Envelopes added by lower layers

In the preceding description, words such as *packet* can be confusing. ISO has invented terminology that makes everything precise. Each layer communicates with its peer layer through a *protocol data unit*, or PDU. To make it clear which layer is being discussed, a single-letter prefix is added to PDU. The data link layer communicates with a peer data link layer by transmitting LPDUs. The network layer communicates with other network layers through NPDUs. The transport layer communicates with other transport layers through TPDUs.

When layer *n*+1 gives information to layer *n* for transmission, the information is known as an SDU, or *service data unit*. As with PDUs, a single-letter prefix is added to eliminate ambiguity. When the transport layer wishes to transmit a TPDU to another transport layer, it must do so by giving the network layer an NSDU. The network layer takes the NSDU, adds an envelope, and transmits it (through the data link layer) as an NPDU (see Figure 1.3).

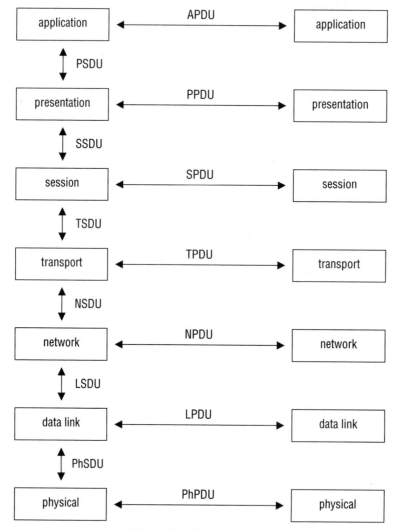

Figure 1.3 PDUs and SDUs

As a rule, the ISO terminology is not used in this book because it is wordy and hard to translate "in real time" until one has attended at least three standards meetings. However, the ISO terminology is used occasionally when it is necessary to be very precise.

1.2 Service Models

In general, the service provided by layer $n–1$ for layer n consists of transmitting data. Layer n provides layer $n–1$ with data (an SDU) plus extra information, such as the address of the destination. Layer n must also be able to receive data from a peer layer n, which it does by having layer $n–1$ inform it that data is available.

Layer $n–1$ can provide either connectionless or connection-oriented service. A *connectionless* service offers layer n two functions: it accepts packets for transmission from layer n, or it delivers packets to layer n.

With a *connection-oriented* service, a connection must be established before data can be transferred. Communication consists of three phases:

1. Connection setup

2. Data transfer (transmission or receipt of data)

3. Connection release

Associated with each of these phases are two functions: one in which layer n initiates the function and another in which layer $n–1$ informs layer n that its peer has initiated the function.

For connection setup, either layer n requests that a connection be set up to some destination address, or layer $n–1$ informs layer n that some layer n process in some other node is requesting a connection.

For connection release, either layer n requests that a connection be released, or layer $n–1$ informs layer n that the layer n process in the other node (or some other condition) requires release of the connection.

Various interfaces might provide other functions, but the preceding are the basic ones.

Services can also vary in their degree of reliability. A service that is purely *datagram* (also known as *best-effort*) accepts data but makes no guarantees as to delivery. Data may be lost, duplicated, delivered out of order, or mangled. A *reliable* service guarantees (or claims to guarantee) that data will be delivered in the order transmitted, without corruption (mangling of the bits), duplication, or loss. It is possible to build a connection-oriented network that is reliable (for example, X.25) or datagram (for example, ATM, Asynchronous Transfer Mode). A connectionless network layer only makes sense offering a datagram service because by definition nothing is keeping track of what gets delivered. IP, IPX, DECnet, CLNP, and AppleTalk are examples of connectionless network layers. Figure 1.4 shows examples of types of network layers.

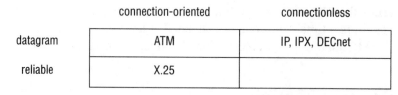

	connection-oriented	connectionless
datagram	ATM	IP, IPX, DECnet
reliable	X.25	

Figure 1.4 Examples of types of network layers

Intuitively, it might seem strange to want anything but a reliable service. However, reliability is not free. It usually makes layer $n-1$ more costly and less efficient. Although there are sometimes good reasons for providing reliability at more than one layer, it certainly need not be provided at every layer.

The trade-offs between connection-oriented and connectionless service and between datagram and reliable service are discussed in Chapter 6. In the world of the ISO and IEEE (Institute of Electrical and Electronics Engineers) standards, the advocates of connection-oriented, reliable service and the advocates of connectionless, datagram service can never convince each other, so both types of service tend to be offered at various layers in ISO and IEEE protocols. As you will see in the discussion of LANs in Chapter 2, this is why two flavors of data link layer are offered for running over LANs. The service is known as LLC, or *logical link control*. LLC type 1 is a connectionless datagram service; LLC type 2 is a reliable, connection-oriented service. ISO wound up defining two network layers: CONS (connection-oriented network service) and CLNS (connectionless network service).

Because there is no agreement about the kind of service provided by the network layer, five classes of transport are defined by ISO. They range from class 0, known as TP0, in which the assumption is made that the network layer does almost everything, to class 4, known as TP4, in which the assumption is made that the network layer is a datagram service.

In the TCP/IP protocol suite, the network layer (Internet Protocol, or IP) is connectionless. There are two transport layers. TCP (Transmission Control Protocol) offers reliable connection-oriented service, and UDP (User Datagram Protocol) offers datagram service.

ATM offers a connection-oriented, unreliable service that can be viewed as a network layer. But if there is another network layer—for example IP—running over ATM, then ATM is viewed by IP as a data link layer. As I said before, don't take the layering too seriously.

There is more discussion of service models in Chapter 6, including issues such as performance guarantees.

1.3 Important Properties of a Network

It is possible for network designs to seem as if they offer equivalent functionality. However, there are subtle ways in which they might differ. When you evaluate a network architecture, you should consider the following properties.

1. *Scope:* A network architecture should solve as general a problem as possible. It should be designed to support both a wide range of applications and a wide range of underlying technologies. If a network is either designed with a specific application in mind or designed to be built upon a particular technology, it may perform better for that one case. However, it is unlikely that a unique network can be designed and built for each specific case. Unless there is a reason that a general-purpose solution can't meet your needs, it is better to design a network that can handle a broad spectrum of applications and underlying technologies.

2. *Scalability:* The ideal network design would work well with very large networks and also be efficient with small networks. In the past, a network having thousands of nodes might have been considered "large." Now, in standardizing any design, we should be thinking in terms of its operating well with millions or even trillions of nodes. Ideally, efficiency would not be sacrificed if the same design were used on a very small network (say, 20 nodes), but meeting such a goal is unlikely. In such a case, a network designed for very few nodes could be more efficient, using, for example, smaller addresses. But we are willing to compromise somewhat to get a complete answer, provided that it is efficient enough in the special case.

3. *Robustness:* Some aspects of robustness are obvious, and most network designs take this into account. For example, the network should continue to operate even if nodes or links fail. Most networks have routing algorithms that adapt to changing topology. However, robustness also has certain more subtle aspects.

    Most networks will work properly in a theoretical world in which no undetected data corruption occurs, all nodes properly execute all the algorithms, parameter settings are compatible across all nodes, and all nodes have sufficient processor power to execute all necessary algorithms in a timely fashion.

    However, we do not live in a theoretical world. Undetected data corruption happens as a result of undetected data errors in transmission or in a node's memory, or during transfer of data internally across a bus. Defective implementations attach to the network. Hardware faults can cause unpredictable behavior. Implementations run out of memory or CPU and behave unpredictably instead of immediately ceasing operation or doing something compatible with the continued effective functioning of the network. Humans (notoriously unreliable components of a system) misconfigure things.

So robustness in the sense of computing alternative routes is not sufficient. A network should also have the following types of robustness.

a. *Safety barriers:* With most networks, malfunctions can cause widespread disruption. Some networks, however, are designed so that a fault does not spread beyond a safety barrier, and therefore a disruption affects only a portion of the network.

For example, LAN broadcast storms have been an annoyance with the TCP/IP (Transmission Control Protocol/Internet Protocol) network layer protocol. A *broadcast storm* is an event in which severe congestion is initiated; it is usually caused by bugs in implementations, ambiguous protocol specifications, or misconfigurations. The broadcast storms with IP can incapacitate a LAN. When two LANs are connected with a bridge, the bridge merges the LANs, and a broadcast storm on either LAN will incapacitate both LANs. If the LANs are instead connected with a router, the broadcast storm will be confined to the single LAN on which it started. Thus, the router acts as a safety barrier through which the LAN broadcast storm does not spread.

Another type of safety barrier is to design a routing protocol hierarchy in which the network is partitioned into *areas* or *domains*. Sometimes the routing protocol can be designed so that disruption in one piece, although it might disable that piece, does not spread to other pieces.

b. *Self-stabilization:* This concept means that after any sort of database corruption—due to such causes as malfunctioning hardware or undetected data errors—the network will return to normal operation without human intervention within a reasonable time, provided that the faulty hardware is disconnected from the network or repaired and no further data corruption occurs (for some time). Without this type of robustness, an error can cause the network to remain inoperative until every node in the network is simultaneously brought down and rebooted. As you will see in Chapter 12 when routing algorithms are discussed, the routing protocol implemented in the ARPANET (Advanced Research Projects Agency Network) was not self-stabilizing.

This type of robustness does not guarantee that a network will operate properly with a malfunctioning piece of equipment attached, but it makes the network easy to repair after the problem is diagnosed. You need only remove the offending device. Many pieces of equipment get into *wedged states*, and power-cycling them usually works as an instant repair. However, a network does not have an on/off switch and cannot easily be power-cycled. The network's very robustness, in the sense of its being distributed so that it can remain operational even if some parts of it are down, means that if the system is not self-stabilizing, all of it must be "killed" to eliminate any residues of a fault.

If a network is not self-stabilizing, a saboteur can inject a few bad packets and the network will remain down forever or until complex and costly human intervention occurs. If the network is self-stabilizing, a saboteur must inject bad data continually in order to keep the network disrupted. That is far riskier than surreptitiously connecting at some off-hour, injecting a few packets, and quietly slipping away.

Again, if the network is self-stabilizing, repair is simple. After the offending equipment is found, you simply remove it to restore the network to operational status.

c. *Fault detection:* Although none of today's networks will operate properly in the face of actively malfunctioning nodes (Byzantine failures, discussed next), it would be desirable for a network to have the ability to diagnose itself so that a faulty piece of equipment could be identified. All networks have some ability to detect faults, but none has a perfect ability to do so, and networks vary greatly in the degree to which faults can be identified.

d. *Byzantine robustness:* The term *Byzantine failure* is taken from a famous problem in computer science known as the *Byzantine generals problem.* A Byzantine failure is one in which a node fails not by simply ceasing operation but instead by acting improperly. Such failure can occur because of defective implementations, hardware faults, or active sabotage. A network with Byzantine robustness would be able to continue working properly even if some portion of the nodes had Byzantine failures. Although none of today's networks has this form of robustness, such networks are possible (see Chapter 16).

4. *Autoconfigurability:* Some network designs work well provided that very smart people do a lot of complex management and constantly tweak parameters. Such network designs greatly enhance the job security of the people who understand how to manage them. However, networks of that sort will not suffice in the future. Networks will become too large, they will be divided so that portions are managed by different organizations, and people will be too dependent on networks to rely on a very few experts to keep them running.

Tomorrow's networks must "run themselves" as much as possible. Ideally, naive users should be able to buy a piece of equipment from the local discount department store, plug it in to a network, and have an operational network. They should not have to configure complex parameters. They should not need to find the address guru to be given an address. (The address guru will be on vacation or will eventually quit, and the envelope on which the address guru scrawled the address assignments will be lost.) Users should not have to find the manager of other nodes to get information about their new node configured into databases.

5. *Tweakability:* Networks should come with reasonable defaults and should ideally be autoconfiguring. However, they should also come with timers and other parameters that adventurous network managers can play with to optimize performance for specific conditions. (Ideally, any setting of the parameters will result

in reasonable, if not optimal, performance, so even overly adventurous network managers will not be able to inflict much damage.)

6. *Determinism:* According to the property of determinism, identical conditions will yield identical results. For example, in a deterministic network design, routes would always be identical given identical physical topologies. In contrast, in a network design that is not deterministic, routes might differ depending on the order in which nodes were brought up in the network.

   Not all people feel that determinism is worth the price, which in some cases means disruptions if the highest-priority element keeps crashing and rebooting. But determinism advocates argue that by ensuring reproducible conditions, determinism makes network analysis much easier.

7. *Migration:* A network design will not last forever. It is therefore important to design network protocols so that new features can be added to nodes, one at a time, without disrupting current operations. It is also important to have a design that lets you make modifications, such as address changes, in a node-by-node fashion without disrupting network operations.

1.4 Reliable Data Transfer Protocols

All data link and transport protocols that provide reliable service tend to have the same general structure. This section introduces the basic ideas and brings up some of the deeper issues involved—issues that are explored in more detail later in the book.

The protocol must deliver a sequence of packets in the same sequence as was transmitted by the source. The protocol has failed if any packets are lost, damaged, misordered, or duplicated. The basic idea is that a packet is transmitted, and the recipient acknowledges its receipt. The packet has a checksum so that the recipient can detect (with high probability) whether the packet was damaged in transit.

In the overly simplified scheme, the transmitter sends a packet, waits for an acknowledgment (also known as an *ack*), and then transmits the next packet (see Figure 1.5). Let's assume that the data being transmitted is the message "1000 from acct A to acct B." Let's further assume that only three characters fit into each packet. If an acknowledgment does not arrive, the transmitter must retransmit the data. Because the transmitter has no way of knowing for sure whether an acknowledgment will arrive, the only thing it can do is to set a timer and assume that if the acknowledgment hasn't arrived within that time, the packet (or the acknowledgment) was probably lost.

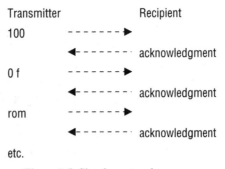

Figure 1.5 Simple protocol, no errors

Establishing the value of the timer is tricky. If the recipient is a busy server, its response time could be highly variable. When the system is heavily loaded, it might take so long to generate an ack that the transmitter will have given up and retransmitted. If the "link" over which the data is being transmitted is a computer network, some packets might take different paths, with the paths having different delays. Or the network might at times be congested (it takes longer to drive the same route at rush hour than at 3:00 A.M. in the U.S. highway network).

If the timer value is too small, packets will be needlessly retransmitted, adding to congestion in the network or adding processing burden to the recipient, which was already too overloaded to return an ack in time (see Figure 1.6). If the timer value is too large, throughput will be delayed after packet loss because the timer will need to expire before further progress can be made on data transmission.

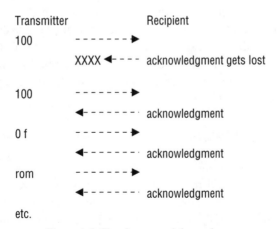

Figure 1.6 Simple protocol, lost ack

At this point, perhaps a more serious problem than optimizing the timer is that the protocol does not work. If an acknowledgment is lost or delayed, the recipient will get two copies of a packet and will not know that they are duplicates.

The result is that the recipient will assume the message was "1001000 from acct A to acct B." The owner of account B might be delighted to receive more than a million dollars instead of a thousand, but the owner of account A might object. Thus, the protocol must be modified somewhat.

The solution is to add packet numbers, and corresponding numbers in the acknowledgments, so that an ack can be matched with the packet being ack'ed (see Figure 1.7).

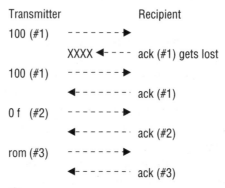

Figure 1.7 Adding packet numbers

The recipient receives 100 (#1) twice but, because both packets are marked with (#1), knows that they are duplicates and keeps only one.

Often, data is being transferred simultaneously in both directions. In this case, the packet numbers from right to left are totally independent of the packet numbers from left to right. There is no ambiguity. An ack number on an ack transmitted from right to left pertains to the stream of numbered packets being transmitted from left to right. An ack number on an ack transmitted from left to right pertains to the stream of numbered packets being transmitted from right to left.

If the transmitter had to wait for an acknowledgment after sending each packet, throughput would be needlessly low. Before the data transmitter can receive an ack, three things must happen after it finishes transmitting a packet. The packet must travel the route between the transmitter and receiver; the receiver must process the packet and generate an acknowledgment; and the acknowledgment must travel the route between the receiver and the transmitter. Because time is available after the transmitter finishes transmitting the packet and before the transmitter finishes processing the acknowledgment, it would be nice to use that time for transmitting more data.

Sending additional data before receiving an acknowledgment for earlier data is known as *pipelining*. The number of packets the transmitter is allowed to have "outstanding" (sent without yet having received an ack) is known as the *window*.

Another issue is the size of the packet number. Ideally the number would be of unlimited size. The first packet of a conversation would be numbered 1, and the 12 billionth would be numbered 12000000000. This would make the protocol very simple. The transmitter could transmit all the packets as quickly as it could. The recipient would then ack all the ones it received, and the transmitter could fill in the holes (noting that acks were not received for, say, packets numbered 17, 112, and 3178).

However, protocols are usually designed to use as few bits as possible for information other than data. (If that were not the case, a government agency responsible for truth in labeling might demand that instead of being called "datagram," the service be called "headergram.") Normally, a limited number of bits is set aside for the packet number; in this example (see Figure 1.8) we'll use 3 bits, although in real protocols a larger number would be desirable.

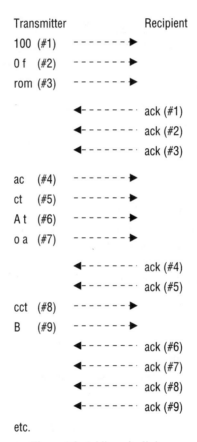

Figure 1.8 Adding pipelining

With a 3-bit packet number, what happens after packet 7 is transmitted? The answer is that the packet number *wraps around*. Packets are numbered 0, 1, 2, 3, 4, 5, 6, 7, 0, 1, 2, 3, 4. . . .

These types of protocols are usually designed so that an ack need not be transmitted for every packet. Instead, each ack is cumulative in the sense that an ack of packet 4 confirms that all packets through 4 have been received properly.

The finite packet number, together with pipelining and cumulative acks, can create problems unless implemented carefully. Following are some examples.

1. The transmitter transmits 0, 1, 2, 3, 4, 5, 6, 7, 0, 1, 2, 3. Assume that all packets after the first four are lost, so the recipient gets 0, 1, 2, 3 and returns ack (#3). The transmitter and receiver will assume that all packets arrived properly.

2. The transmitter transmits 0, 1, 2, 3, 4, 5, 6, 7, 0, 1, 2, 3, which are permuted into random order by a network that offers a datagram service. The recipient will have no way of knowing which packet 2 comes first and which packets may be duplicates.

3. The transmitter transmits packets 0, 1, 2, 3, 4, 5, 6, 7. The recipient receives them all and returns ack (#7), which gets lost in transit. The transmitter retransmits all eight packets, which the recipient accepts as new data and returns another ack (#7).

The solution to these problems is to design timers and window sizes carefully. It is important that the packet-numbering space be large enough so that the packet number cannot wrap around during the worst-case delay time. Thus, if it is conceivable that a network could delay a packet by 15 sec, it must not be possible for a transmitter, at maximum speed, to transmit enough packets so that a packet number will wrap around within 15 sec. If the recipient holds on to packets that arrive out of order (for example, if the recipient receives 1 and then 3, it holds on to 3 hoping that 2 will eventually arrive), it is also important that the window be no larger than half the packet number. On strictly sequential channels, packets might be lost but never reordered. If the recipient is guaranteed to discard any packet except the one with the next consecutive number, the window size can be as large as the packet number size minus 1.

Homework

1. Suppose that the session layer hands information down to the transport layer, which transmits that information (plus perhaps some control information) in a single packet. In ISO-ese, this would be stated, "A single SPDU results in a single TSDU, which results in a single TPDU."

   Suppose instead that the session layer gives the transport layer some information that is too large for the transport layer to send. The transport layer instead transmits it as a set of packets, with enough control information so that the transport layer at the destination can reassemble the session layer's information. How would this be expressed in ISO-ese?

2. Now suppose that the transport layer is capable, for efficiency reasons, of taking many little pieces of information handed down by the session layer and putting them all into one big "box" to be transmitted as a single packet. In this way, the transport layer at the destination can sort them back into individual pieces of information. Translate this situation into ISO-ese.

3. Now suppose that the network layer has a packet to send, but some intermediate router notices that the packet is too large to fit over the link on which it should be transmitted. The network layer at the intermediate node breaks the packet into smaller chunks so that they can be reassembled at the destination network layer. Translate this situation into ISO-ese.

4. Assume a packet number size of n and assume a sequential channel. Give an example of a protocol failure in which the transmitter has a window size of n and the receiver discards packets received out of order. Prove that no problems will occur if the window size is $n-1$ (assume that at start-up all old packets are removed from the channel).

5. Now assume that the receiver does not discard packets received out of order. In other words, the receiver holds on to packet number n, hoping that it will eventually receive packet $n-1$, and, when it does, it acknowledges them both. Give an example of a protocol failure in which the transmitter has a window size of $n/2+1$. Prove that no problems will occur if the window size is $n/2$.

6. Discuss the trade-offs of providing reliable versus datagram service at the data link layer. Assume that the transport layer will provide reliable connection-oriented service in either case.

   Consider the following points:

   a. The probability of a packet's making it across a sequence of links (which depends on the error rates of the links)

   b. The total number of packet hops required to successfully get a packet to the destination node and get an acknowledgment back to the source

   c. The desire to maximize throughput for the transport layer

   d. The need for the transport layer to estimate the round-trip delay in order to decide when to retransmit a packet that has not been acknowledged

Chapter 2
Data Link Layer Issues

This chapter discusses data link layer issues that affect bridges and routers. One issue is whether service provided by the data link layer should be reliable or datagram-oriented. Another is how to have multiple network layer protocols coexist on a link. When a node receives a packet, how can it tell which protocol suite originated the packet? Although the chapter also discusses many aspects of LAN technology, a fascinating topic, it is not meant to be a detailed reference on LANs. Rather, it explains those aspects of LANs in general, or of specific LAN technologies, that affect the bridging and network layer protocols.

2.1 Generic LANs

2.1.1 What Is a LAN?

When people use the term LAN, they may refer to any of a number of technologies that have the properties usually associated with LANs. Following are some of those properties.

- Multiple systems attached to a shared medium.

- "High" total bandwidth (the total bandwidth is shared by all the stations).

- "Low" delay.

- "Low" error rate.

- Broadcast capability, also known as multicast capability (the ability to transmit a single message and have it received by multiple recipients).

- Limited geography (several kilometers).

- Limited numbers of stations (hundreds).

- Peer relationship among attached stations (as opposed to a group of slaves with a master). In a peer relationship, all attached stations are equivalent. In a master/slave relationship, one special station, called the *master*, polls the *slaves*, giving each one a turn to transmit.

- Being confined to private property and not subject to PTT (a common abbreviation for Post, Telegraph, and Telephone, a government agency in many countries) regulation.

Note that the meaning of terms such as *low*, *high*, and *limited* is relative and changes with time. For the purposes of this book, we do not need a definition of a LAN that would distinguish it from a MAN (metropolitan area network) or a WAN (wide area network). (This is fortunate because as LAN technology improves to expanded geographies and WAN technology improves to increased bandwidth, the distinction between LANs and WANs becomes even less clear, and trying to figure out where a MAN fits in is hopeless.)

Basically, a LAN (as well as a WAN) can be viewed as a "cloud" to which stations can be attached (see Figure 2.1). If a station attaches to the cloud, it can transmit packets to, and receive packets from, every other station attached to the cloud.

Figure 2.1 Network cloud

2.1.2 Taking Turns

In a shared medium, only one station can successfully transmit at a time. Some mechanism must exist to allocate bandwidth among the stations so that

- Each station gets a fair share of bandwidth

- Each station gains access to the medium within a reasonable time

- The waste of bandwidth due to arbitration mechanisms is minimized

The two most popular bandwidth-arbitration mechanisms used on LANs are token schemes and contention.

In a token scheme, each station is granted permission to transmit in some round-robin fashion. In the case of a *token ring*, a particular sequence of bits known as a *token* travels around the ring (see Figure 2.2). A station is allowed to transmit when it sees the token.

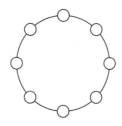

Figure 2.2 Token ring

In the case of a *token bus*, the token is a special packet that is sent from station to station (see Figure 2.3). Each station is required to know the identity of the station to which it should transmit the token.

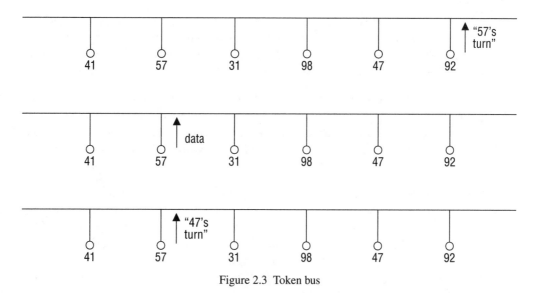

Figure 2.3 Token bus

In a *contention* scheme, stations transmit at will, and if two stations transmit simultaneously there is a *collision* and neither station's transmission is successful. Mechanisms are built in to minimize the probability of collisions. Contention schemes are *probabilistically fair*. This means that theoretically, some station might never succeed in transmitting because whenever it tries, some other station transmits at the same time. However, contention LANs are carefully designed to make this situation highly unlikely.

Relying on probability instead of a scheme that guarantees a desired outcome might seem worrisome, but you must realize that we rely on probability every day. It is only probably true that enough oxygen atoms will remain in the room in which you are sitting to enable you to continue breathing. It is theoretically possible that through random motion, all oxygen atoms will leave the room and you will asphyxiate.

Even schemes that seem to provide guarantees are actually probabilistic. The token is merely a sequence of bits, which can become corrupted. In a token scheme, it is theoretically possible that one particular station will never succeed in transmitting because the token always gets lost before that station gains access. Or it is possible that every time a station succeeds in acquiring the token, its transmitted packet will get corrupted.

2.2 IEEE 802 LANs

IEEE has a committee known as "802" whose purpose is to standardize LANs. It has standardized not one but several LANs.

LAN protocols cover the bottom two layers of the OSI Reference Model (the physical and data link layers). The 802 committee has chosen to subdivide the data link layer into two sublayers.

1. MAC, which stands for *medium access control*, addresses issues specific to a particular type of LAN. For example, it deals with channel management algorithms such as token passing (802.5 and 802.4), binary backoff after collision detection (802.3), priorities (802.5 and 802.4), error detection, and framing.

2. LLC, which stands for *logical link control*, defines the fields that allow multiple higher-layer protocols to share the use of the data link. Because some people thought that it was not enough for the data link layer to provide a simple datagram service, they pushed for additional functionality. The decision was to provide several flavors of LLC. The following two types are in wide use.

    a. *LLC type 1* is simply a datagram protocol, meaning that a packet is delivered with *best-effort* service by the data link layer. There is no protocol at the data link layer to alert the source as to whether the packet was successfully received. Instead, error control of that sort, if needed, is assumed to be carried out at a higher layer. Note that LLC type 1 doesn't actually do anything because the LAN already gives best-effort service. (That's not a criticism of LLC type 1. It's better to have a protocol that does nothing than a protocol that does something you don't need. Even better would be not to have a protocol at all when one is not needed. It would make the specs easier to read and would save paper.)

    b. *LLC type 2* is a reliable connection-oriented protocol on top of the basic datagram. This means that in addition to the fields required by LLC type 1, there are fields to number packets, provide a piggybacked acknowledgment field, and provide for differentiating data packets from control packets such as acknowledgments and resynchronization messages. LLC type 2 is basically running the connection-oriented data link protocol HDLC (high-level data link control), which was designed for point-to-point links, on top of the LAN datagram-oriented protocol.

The other types of LLC attempt to provide extra reliability without the overhead of LLC type 2. To demystify what the different types of LLC might provide, this book describes LLC types 1 and 2 in detail, but the details of all the types of LLC are not really relevant to bridges and routers.

The IEEE 802 committees relevant to this book are as follows.

- *802.1:* This committee deals with issues common across all 802 LANs, including addressing, management, and bridges.

- *802.2:* This committee defines LLC. MAC and physical layers are defined for a specific type of LAN by the committee that defines that type of LAN.

- *802.3:* This committee deals with the CSMA/CD (carrier sense multiple access with collision detection) LAN. This is derived from the Ethernet, which was invented by Xerox and developed by Digital, Intel, and Xerox.

- *802.4:* This committee deals with the token bus LAN.

- *802.5:* This committee deals with the token ring LAN.

Other 802 committees deal with such issues as metropolitan area networks and security.

Another type of LAN is FDDI (fiber distributed data interface), which is a 100Mb token ring. It is not simply a faster version of 802.5 but rather is very different from 802.5. (Although the technical differences between them are fascinating, they are not relevant to this book.) FDDI was standardized by ANSI rather than IEEE.

2.3 Names, Addresses, Routes

Considerable confusion exists regarding the terms *name*, *address*, and *route*. Shoch[1] defines these terms as follows.

- *Name:* what something is

- *Address:* where it is

- *Route:* how to get there

The Shoch paper seems to be referenced whenever any mention is made of names, addresses, or routes. However, I have never found these definitions helpful, in the sense of enabling one to look at a string of bits and decide, based on the preceding taxonomy, whether the string should be classified as a name, an address, or a route.

[1] J. Shoch, "Internetwork Naming, Addressing, and Routing," *Compcon* (Fall 1978), 72–79.

A helpful alternative method of defining the three concepts is as follows. Suppose a particular string of bits refers to a particular station. We want to decide whether that string of bits should be considered a name, an address, or a route. In the following definitions, the *destination* is the station referred to by the string of bits, and the *source* is the station that is using the string of bits to refer to the destination.

1. *Name:* A name is location-independent with respect to both the source and the destination. If something is the name of a destination, it will remain unchanged even if the destination moves, and it is valid regardless of which source is attempting to reach the destination. An example of a name is a Social Security number, which remains unchanged even if the number's owner moves. Sometimes, fields that are names are referred to as *identifiers*, or *IDs*.

2. *Address:* An address is valid regardless of the location of the source station, but it may change if the destination moves. An example of an address is a postal address. The same destination postal address works regardless of the location from which a letter is mailed. However, if the destination moves, it is assigned a new address.

3. *Route:* A route is dependent on the location of both the source and the destination. In other words, if two sources specify a route to a given destination, the routes are likely to differ. And if the destination moves, all routes to it are likely to change. An example of a route is the statement "To get to my house, go west three miles and take a right turn at the first light. It's the last house on the left."

Note that with the preceding descriptions, the entities known as "addresses" in 802 would be classified as "names" rather than "addresses." Especially with globally assigned 48-bit "LAN addresses," the LAN address will not change if a station moves to a different LAN. There are probably several reasons that these fields are referred to as addresses.

- Some people like to refer to something as a "name" if it is human-friendly—an ASCII string rather than a bunch of bits. Because 48-bit quantities are certainly unpleasant to type, remember, or look at, those who equate the word *name* with human compatibility prefer to refer to them as addresses. I would rather refer to a human-hostile quantity that is location-independent as an identifier, or ID.

- From the viewpoint of a higher-layer process that may move from node to node, its "LAN address" actually becomes an address because when the higher-layer process moves to a different node, its LAN address changes.

- If the 48-bit "LAN address" is stored in the interface to the LAN rather than in the node, then a node with multiple attachments to LANs has multiple LAN addresses. But then the 48-bit quantity is addressing not the node but rather one of the interfaces of the node, and I would therefore claim that the 48-bit quantity is an identifier of the interface.

Because everyone in the industry refers to the 48-bit elements as "addresses," I do so in this book. It is important to realize, however, that most terms (*layer, address, route, node, network, LAN,* and so on) are at best vaguely defined in the industry and are used in conflicting ways by various communities.

2.4 LAN Addresses

In many LAN technologies, every station on a LAN hears every packet transmission, so it is necessary to include a **destination** field in each packet. So that the destination can identify which station transmitted the packet, a **source** field is also included. To prevent software interrupts with every packet, LAN adapters can filter out packets not addressed to the station.

The 802 committee needed to standardize addresses for its LANs. The first decision was to set the length of the address field. The committee apparently thought that if standardizing on one size was a good thing, standardizing on several sizes would be even better. The 802 committee gave the option of running a LAN (other than 802.6) with 48-bit addresses or 16-bit addresses. It gave the option of running 802.6 with 16-, 48-, or 60-bit addresses. Luckily, 16-bit addresses have not caught on and can safely be ignored.

The argument for 16-bit addresses is that this size is sufficient for any single LAN provided that the manager of the LAN is capable of assigning addresses to the stations. Also, 802.4 used addresses to resolve an initial contention phase prior to building a logical ring and would come up or restart faster with 16-bit addresses.

The argument for 48-bit addresses is that they enable stations to be provided with a globally unique identifier at the time of manufacture. This allows networks to be truly *plug and play*, in the sense that a customer could buy an off-the-shelf system, plug it in to the network, and have it operate, without having to first assign it an address.

The way globally unique addresses work is that a global authority is responsible for handing out blocks of addresses. Originally, Xerox was the global authority; now the official global authority is IEEE. When a vendor wishes to manufacture equipment that will plug in to a LAN, it first contacts the global authority to obtain a block of addresses. The current cost of a block of addresses is $1,250, for which the vendor is given 2^{24} addresses. In other words, the vendor is given three fixed-value octets, with the remaining three octets being for the vendor to allocate. The fixed-value portion of the address is sometimes referred to in the industry as the *vendor code* or OUI (*organizationally unique identifier*), but that is really a misnomer (misaddresser?) because a vendor can purchase more than one block of addresses as well as donate addresses to other vendors.

The three fixed-value octets actually have additional structure (see Figure 2.4). One bit represents *group/individual*. If that bit is 0, the address refers to a particular station; if that bit is 1, the address refers to a logical group of stations. Thus, the global authority does not really give 24 bits of fixed value but rather gives 23 bits of fixed value, with the remaining bit being the group/individual bit. An entire address is 6 octets long. The 3 octets of constant leave an additional 3 octets (24 bits) that can be assigned by the vendor. Therefore, when a vendor purchases a block of addresses, it gets 2^{24} station addresses and 2^{24} group addresses.

	OUI				
1st octet	2nd octet	3rd octet	4th octet	5th octet	6th octet
10111101	01110101	11001111	01011111	01000101	01111010

G/I (group/individual) bit

G/L (global/local) bit

Figure 2.4 IEEE address

The 802 committee was not sure that everyone would want to go to the trouble (and expense) of obtaining a block of addresses from the global authority. Therefore, it designated another of the 48 bits to indicate whether the address was globally or locally assigned. If a vendor purchases a block of addresses from the global authority, the global/local bit will be set to 0. People are free to use any addresses with the global/local bit set to 1. However, if local addresses are used, it is up to the network manager to assign addresses and make sure that there are no *address collisions* (which occur when two stations use the same address). Address collision becomes an important issue when two networks are merged.

Group addresses are also sometimes referred to as *multicast addresses*. The most common use of multicast addresses is for discovering appropriate neighbors (nodes on the same link) by one of the following two methods.

1. *Solicitation:* Suppose the network contains one or more of a certain type of station—for example, a naming server, a router, or a file server—that station A is likely to want to contact. Management could configure station A, with the addresses of all those stations. However, it would be more desirable if station A did not need to know about specific servers a priori. Instead, it would know a single group address, ZSERVERS (where "Z" can be any type of service such as those just suggested).

   When station A wishes to find a Z server, it transmits a packet with the destination address ZSERVERS. All the Z servers listen for, and respond to, packets directed to that address.

2. *Advertisement:* A different way to use group addresses is to define an address to be used for stations listening for a service. Instead of having service Z clients ask for help by transmitting to ZSERVERS, Z servers would periodically transmit packets to the address ZCLIENTS. A Z client would listen for packets addressed to ZCLIENTS until it heard such a packet. Then, based on the source address of

the packet or on some other field explicitly contained in the data portion of the packet, the Z client would now know the address of a Z server.

The human counterpart of this method is commercial advertising. The advertising industry would love to be able to transmit an advertisement that would be received only by people interested in hearing it, but the best advertisers can do is to advertise in media whose audiences tend to match the type of people who might be interested in a particular product.

2.5 Multicast versus Unicast Addresses

Why is it that a multicast address looks different from an individual address? If a particular address is designated to mean "all Z servers" and if all Z servers are supposed to listen to that address in addition to their own, why can't just any address be used for a multicast?

The problem is that on a LAN there are a lot of packets, and it would seriously degrade the performance of an attached station if the software had to process an interrupt every time a packet for any destination was transmitted on the wire. The hardware will receive every packet, and it is possible to request that it deliver every packet. This is known as listening *promiscuously*.

Sometimes, as in the case of a bridge or a LAN-monitoring tool, it is appropriate for the hardware to deliver every packet, but for most applications, promiscuity is not desirable. Instead, it should be possible for the hardware to look at enough of a packet to decide whether the software might conceivably be interested in the packet. If the packet is of interest, the hardware should pass it up to the software. If it is not, the hardware should just drop the packet (*filter* it).

Theoretically, it is not necessary to reserve a bit in the address to differentiate group and individual addresses. Ideally, the software would tell the chip all the different addresses that the software was interested in receiving, and the chip would pass packets up to the software if and only if the "destination address" field in the data link header matched one of the addresses requested by the software.

The problem with having the software request a certain number of addresses is that the chip designer would need to pick a maximum number of addresses that could be requested. If the designer picked too large a number, the chip would be too expensive. If the designer picked too small a number, the chip would be useless for a station that required more addresses than were provided for in the chip.

Many chips were designed with the following compromise.

- A bit in the address designates the address as individual or group.

- A station informs the chip of the single individual address it wants to receive.

- The chip partitions the set of group addresses into a number of groups (the technical term is *hash buckets*). If the station wishes to receive a particular group address, it must request the bucket into which that address hashes. After a bucket is selected, the chip will send up all packets whose destination addresses hash into that bucket.

The theory is that a station will be interested only in a single individual address (its own) and some number of group addresses. The chip could have been designed to allow the software to specify exactly which multicast addresses to pass up, but again, the problem was to pick the right maximum number. So instead of exactly specifying group addresses, the chip has several hash buckets into which to sort group addresses, and the software specifies any subset of the hash buckets for the chip to pass up. This chip design means that a station cannot avoid software interrupts for group addresses in which it is not interested because the chip will pass up all group addresses that hash into a requested bucket.

An alternative chip design provides

- Some fixed number of exact addresses (either group or individual) that the station can request to receive

- Some number of hash buckets for addresses, with the provision that the station can request any subset of the hash buckets

With this design, if a station does not need to receive more than the number of addresses allowed for in the chip, it can get perfect filtering (it will not get software interrupts for addresses in which it is not interested). If the station needs to receive more than the specified number of addresses, it can fall back on the hashing scheme and hope that a foreign address with a lot of traffic does not happen to hash into a bucket containing an address that the station needs to receive.

2.6 The Broadcast Address

One particular group address has been named the *broadcast address*. It consists of all 1's. It is intended to mean "all stations," and, theoretically, all stations should receive any packet transmitted to the broadcast address. In the case of a protocol that must be implemented by every station on the LAN, it makes sense to use the broadcast address. But no such protocols exist, and they probably never will.

So it does not make sense for protocols to use the broadcast address because it really does not mean "all stations"; instead, it means "all stations that have implemented this particular protocol." Unfortunately, some protocols do use the broadcast address. To some extent they were forced to because of shortcuts that were taken in early LAN adapters—for example, ones that could not receive arbitrary multicast addresses unless they listened promiscuously. Because the hardware filtered only on the destination address and not on the multiplexing information (see Section 2.7), this meant that each packet addressed to the broadcast address, even if for a protocol not implemented in a station, would cause a software interrupt at that station.

2.7 Multiplexing Field

It is possible for multiple higher-layer protocols to be implemented in the same station. When a packet arrives addressed to that station, there must be a way to determine which protocol should receive the packet. Similarly, many different protocols (unfortunately) send packets to the broadcast address. When a station receives a packet, it must determine how to interpret the bits of the packet (that is, find out which protocol constructed the packet).

For example, it might be possible to examine the packet and determine that it could not possibly be a legal IP packet and thus must be a packet from some other network layer protocol. However, because most protocols were designed without attention paid to disambiguating valid packets from packets in other protocols, there is no effective way to determine from the data alone which recipient is intended.

We have the same problem in human language, which is fundamentally nothing more than a set of sounds. If you walk up to someone on the street and ask, "Can you please tell me how to get to the nearest subway stop?" the individual you've asked may be unable to speak English and may instead speak Martian. Worse yet, there is the danger that the sequence of sounds you uttered means something very rude in Martian—in which case, the creature, instead of directing you to a subway stop, may melt you with its ray gun.

To solve this problem, there should be a universally defined method by which, before delivering your message, you first identify the language in which you are about to speak. Although there is no such method for human speech, a method has been defined for LANs (see Figure 2.5). Included in the LAN header is a field that specifies the protocol being used. In the original Ethernet design, there was a 2-octet-long field known as the *protocol type*. The field was globally administered by Xerox, and anyone who wanted to define a protocol would negotiate with Xerox to obtain a number for the protocol.

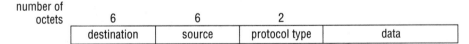

Figure 2.5 Protocol type multiplexing

When the 802 committee standardized LANs, it decided that a more flexible scheme would be to have separate fields for the source and the destination (see Figure 2.6). These fields were known as *service access points* (SAPs). Included in the 802 header are SSAP (*source service access point*) and DSAP (*destination service access point*). This arrangement gives the flexibility of assigning numbers to protocols differently in each machine.

number of
octets

Figure 2.6 SAP multiplexing

The SAP fields are 8 bits long. However, as with the LAN addresses, two of those bits are reserved. One of the reserved bits is for "global/local," which, as with the similar bit in the LAN address field, indicates whether the 802 committee has assigned the number (to guarantee its uniqueness) or whether the owner of the network or system manages the number.

The other reserved bit is for "group/individual." This lets you send a packet that would be received by multiple higher-layer protocols within a system. The reason for reserving a bit in the LAN address has to do with convenience in making chips. This reasoning is not applicable in the case of the SAP because filtering based on SAP is not done in the hardware. Another reason that the group/individual address makes sense in the LAN address but does not make as much sense in the SAP is that it seems likely that many different stations on the same LAN would implement the same protocol and thus would want to receive the same message. It seems less likely that a common protocol would be implemented by multiple upper-layer processes within the same station. However, with an entire 8 bits to play with, why not reserve one for the purpose, even though the justification for its need is slight? (Hint: The preceding statement is sarcastic, with a touch of bitterness. In fact, 8 bits are not nearly sufficient to make the scheme usable. Only because of the invention of the SNAP SAP kludge, described in the next few paragraphs, is it possible for protocols other than ISO or IEEE protocols to use the 802-defined LLC.)

The SAP consisting of all 1's is reserved to mean "all SAPs," as with the broadcast address. The SAP consisting of all 0's (except for the "G/L" bit) is reserved to mean the data link layer itself and not a user of the data link layer. Figure 2.7 shows the SAP structure.

Figure 2.7 Structure of SAP

With only 6 bits of globally assigned individual SAP numbers, the 802 committee cannot grant numbers to every organization that might want to design a protocol. Rather than assign numbers on a first-come, first-served basis until they are all gone, the 802 committee has strict rules for the sorts of organizations and protocols that can be granted a SAP number. To be eligible, a protocol must have been designed by a standards body approved by the 802 committee.

For those protocols privileged to receive a global SAP value, the SAP fields are used like a single protocol type field because the SSAP and DSAP will be equal (they will equal the global SAP value assigned to that protocol).

Other protocols (those without globally assigned SAP values) could use locally assigned SAP numbers, and the manager of a system could ensure that each protocol had a unique number within that system. However, this approach makes conversation start-up difficult because it is hard to send a protocol message to another machine when the SAP numbering within the foreign machine is unknown.

A plan to make the SAP system usable was proposed within 802. It consisted of requesting a single globally assigned SAP. When the DSAP was set to that value, it would indicate that the header was expanded to include a "protocol type" field. The protocol type field could then be large enough so that a global authority could ensure that every protocol was granted a globally assigned number.

Originally, the plan was that the protocol type field be 2 octets, on the theory that it was 2 octets in the original Ethernet, and Xerox must have known what it was doing. But then someone noticed that the 802 header contained an odd number of octets. If the protocol type field were an odd number of octets, it would make the entire header an even number of octets, and that would enhance performance on machines that like fields to be 16-bit aligned.

Then someone noticed that if the protocol type field were longer than 3 octets, the field could be administered "for free" by linking the administration of the protocol type field with the administration of the addresses. In other words, when a vendor bought a block of addresses, it received 3 octets of constant (including the group/individual bit), with the remaining 3 octets assignable by the vendor. The vendor could use those same 3 octets of constant as the higher-order portion of protocol types, which the vendor could then assign. So, for example, if the protocol type field were 4 octets long, then when a vendor purchased a block of addresses, it also received a block of 256 protocol types.

The agreed-upon size of the protocol type field was 5 octets because 5 is the smallest odd number greater than 3.

The globally assigned SAP value that indicates the presence of the protocol type field is known as the SNAP (*subnetwork access protocol*) SAP. It is equal to 10101010 (binary), which equals aa hex. When the SNAP SAP is used, both DSAP and SSAP are set to aa hex. The protocols that have a globally assigned SAP set DSAP and SSAP to the same value—namely, the value of the globally assigned SAP. And the protocols that do not have a globally assigned SAP also set DSAP and SSAP to the same value—in this case, the SNAP SAP, aa hex. (In my opinion, all the fields defined by 802.2—that is, the SAPs and LLC—are a waste of space in the header and make the specifications much longer and more difficult to understand. The only thing needed was a protocol type field.)

The structure of an address and the structure of the protocol type field are shown in Figure 2.8.

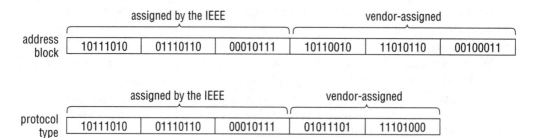

Figure 2.8 Structure of IEEE 802 address and protocol type field

When an organization purchases a block of addresses, it receives a 3-octet quantity such as XYZ, and its addresses have the form XYZ***. The organization can assign stations addresses having the form XYZ***. It can assign multicast addresses having the form X'YZ***, where X' is X with the G/I bit set. It can assign protocol types having the form XYZ**.

Note that after a protocol type gets assigned, it's irrelevant which organization assigned it. It's just a way of assigning a number to a protocol that does not conflict with a number assigned to another protocol. A protocol assigned the value XYZAB by the organization that happens to have the OUI=XYZ can be used by any organization and would always have the value XYZAB.

2.8 Bit Order

A serious problem with addresses is how they should be represented and transmitted. Different machines store bits and bytes in different ways. The 802.1 committee has defined a canonical format for writing addresses—namely, 6 octets separated by hyphens. Each octet is represented by two hex digits. For example, an address might be written as a2-41-42-59-31-51.

With 802.3 and 802.4, the least significant bit is transmitted first; with 802.5 (and FDDI), the most significant bit is transmitted first. This would not be an issue (adapters on the receiver and transmitter for a particular LAN would presumably be symmetric, and the order of transmission would be irrelevant) except that the group bit in addresses was defined not as "the most significant bit" or "the least significant bit" but rather as "the first bit on the wire." Thus, an address that was a group address on 802.3 would not necessarily look like a group address when transmitted on 802.5 because a different bit would be transmitted first.

The canonical format for addresses assumes least-significant-bit-first order. Therefore, the address a2-41-42-59-31-51 is not a group address because the least significant bit of the first octet (a2, which equals 10100010 binary) is 0.

When addresses are stored for transmission onto 802.5 or FDDI, which transmit the most significant bit first, they must be stored in a different format.

Figure 2.9 shows the address a2-41-42-59-31-51 as stored for transmission least significant bit first.

10100010	01000001	01000010	01011001	00110001	01010001

Figure 2.9 Address a2-41-42-59-31-51, least significant bit first

Figure 2.10 shows the address a2-41-42-59-31-51 as stored for transmission most significant bit first.

01000101	10000010	01000010	10011010	10001100	10001010

Figure 2.10 Address a2-41-42-59-31-51, most significant bit first

Therefore, bridges must shuffle the address fields when forwarding between 802.5 (or FDDI) and any of the other LANs.

An even more difficult problem is the inclusion of LAN addresses in higher-layer protocol messages (such as management messages or ARP [*Address Resolution Protocol*] messages, which are described in Chapter 11). If the implementers of the higher-layer protocol do not convert the LAN address into a canonical format before placing it into a protocol message, the destination cannot interpret the field that contains the LAN address without determining the type of LAN from which the protocol message originated—information that is not generally available to upper-layer protocols because it should be irrelevant.

The failure of the 802 committee to agree on a bit ordering for all the LANs has caused immense amounts of confusion and interoperability problems. For example, at least one protocol was implemented so that it broke if the address in the data link header was not identical to the address as represented in the higher-layer header. If bridges did the appropriate bit shuffling when forwarding between 802.3 and 802.5, the protocol would break. The solution that the bridge vendors were forced to adopt was to specifically check for the protocol type of this particular protocol and not shuffle the address bits in the data link header on packets having that protocol type. As a result, bridged packets from that protocol will have different addresses than they should. This can cause two major problems.

1. The station address—when the bits are in the flipped order—might appear on the LAN to be a multicast address. That may in turn confuse source routing bridges into misparsing the packet and cause transparent bridges to refuse to forward the packet.

2. The station address with the flipped order might turn into an address used by another station.

2.9 Logical Link Control

LLC is described in the specs as if it were a sublayer separate from the MAC sublayer. If people had agreed on a datagram model for LANs, the 802 committee might not have felt the need to subdivide the LAN data link layer into MAC and LLC.

As stated earlier in this chapter, several types of LLC are currently defined. Type 1 is datagram, and type 2 is connection-oriented. The other types are not in general use, and can be safely ignored.

The sublayering defined by the 802 committee has only the data link layer fields **DSAP, SSAP,** and **CTL** within LLC. The source and destination addresses are actually considered part of the MAC sublayer. Technically, this means that each individual LAN committee (802.3, 802.5, and so on) can define addresses as it chooses. It is lucky that addresses across various LANs are pretty much the same. Unfortunately, as described later in this chapter, they are not identical because of bit-ordering issues and problems in 802.5 with arbitrary multicast addresses. In fact, with 802.5, the addresses started out being different—they were originally hierarchical, with a portion of the 6 bytes indicating the ring number on which a station resided and the remainder of the address indicating the station number with respect to that ring. That has been changed to be 6 bytes of station address, as on the other LANs.

The **CTL** ("control") field in LLC type 1 (datagrams) is always 1 byte long and is always equal to one of three values.

1. UI, which stands for "unnumbered information." (This means it's a datagram.)

2. XID, which stands for "exchange identification." There are two types of XID: "response" and "command." *Command* informs the recipient of the identity of the transmitter of the XID command message and of the LLC types the transmitter supports. *Response* is the required reply to an XID command message. It contains the same information as the XID command: the identity of the transmitter of the XID response message and of the LLC types the transmitter supports.

3. TEST. As with XID, there are two types of TEST message: command and response. TEST is used to check whether a packet can be sent to the recipient and returned. Included in the command is any arbitrary data. The data in the TEST response is copied from the data in the TEST command.

Command and response packets in XID and TEST are distinguished based on a bit in the SSAP field. The 802.2 committee decided that there was no reason anyone would want to transmit a packet from a group SAP, so the bit in the SSAP designated to indicate group or individual actually indicates command or response.

In LLC type 2, the CTL field is either 1 or 2 bytes long depending on what type of packet it is. The packet types for which the CTL field is 2 bytes contain a sequence number. These packets are as follows.

1. I ("information") is a data packet. In this case, the CTL field is 2 bytes long and includes 7 bits of sequence number for the data packets being transmitted from source S to destination D plus 7 bits of sequence number for the acknowledgments for packets being received from D by S.

2. RR ("receive ready") is an acknowledgment. It contains a sequence number and indicates that all packets having lower sequence numbers have been received. It also indicates that the receiver is prepared to receive more data.

3. RNR ("receive not ready"), like RR, is an acknowledgment for previously transmitted packets (with numbers lower than the number in the receive sequence number field in the RNR). However, RNR also indicates that the receiver is temporarily busy and that further packets should not be transmitted until the receiver transmits RR to indicate it can accept new packets.

4. REJ ("reject") indicates that the receiver is requesting retransmission of packets starting with the number in the receive sequence number field.

The other LLC type 2 packet types, which use a 1-byte CTL field, are as follows.

1. SABME ("set asynchronous balanced mode extended"—aren't you sorry you asked?) requests that a connection be started. The bizarre name for the command is historical.

2. DISC ("disconnect") requests that a connection be ended.

3. DM ("disconnected mode") is transmitted in response to a DISC, indicating that the recipient has received the DISC.

4. FRMR ("frame reject") indicates receipt of an invalid packet—for example, one containing an out-of-order sequence number.

5. UA ("unnumbered acknowledgment") acknowledges a DISC or SABME message.

2.10 Issues in 802.3

The 802.3 LAN access is based on contention. The technology is known as CSMA/CD (carrier sense multiple access with collision detection). *Carrier sense* means that a station wishing to transmit first listens, and, if another station is transmitting, the first station does not transmit but rather waits until the medium is idle. *Multiple access* means that many stations share the same medium. *Collision detect* means that stations monitor the medium even while they are transmitting so that they can detect the occurrence of a collision—another station transmitting while they are transmitting.

A collision can occur if the medium is idle and two stations attempt to initiate transmission simultaneously. However, the transmission initiations need not be absolutely simultaneous. When one station starts transmitting, it takes time for its signal to be detected, especially if the second transmitter is far away. The shorter the wire, the lower the probability of collisions (see Figure 2.11).

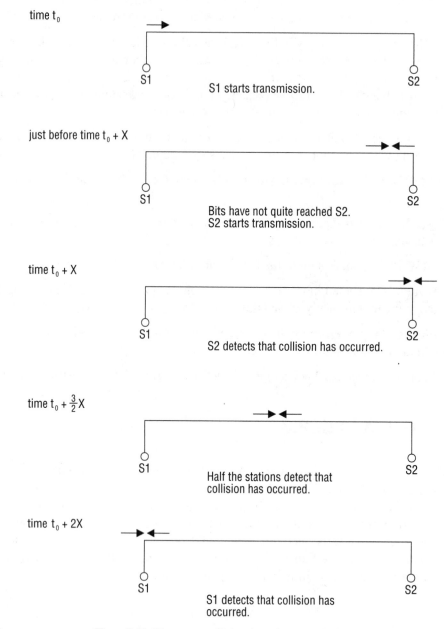

Figure 2.11 Worst case collision detection, round trip time

The original CSMA/CD LAN was designed at Xerox. Called the Ethernet, it was designed to guarantee that the transmitting station could tell whether its transmission had failed due to a collision. To meet the conditions of this guarantee, the length of the wire had to be limited and a minimum size had to be established for packet lengths. In the worst case, a station at one end of the wire initiates transmission. If a station at the other end initiates transmission just before the bits from the first station arrive, the first station will not detect that its packet has collided until twice the length of time it takes for a signal to go from one end of the wire to the other.

This time is known as a *slot time*. Given that the maximum length of the wire is set at 2.5 km, given the speed of electricity on the wire, and given the transmission speed of 10 Mb/sec, it might take as long as 512 bit times to detect a collision. Thus, each packet must be at least 512 bits long because if a station finishes transmitting a packet and does not discover during that time that a collision occurred, it will assume that its transmission was successful. Some protocols might want to issue shorter packets, but those packets must be padded to minimum length.

One problem specific to the 802.3 LAN is that the committee did not merely standardize the Ethernet. Instead, it made some modifications. Although 802.3-compliant hardware is compatible with Ethernet hardware—in that both types of stations can coexist on the same cable—header formats differ slightly.

The Ethernet and 802.3 headers are shown in Figure 2.12.

Ethernet

6	6	2	46–1,500	4
destination	source	protocol	data	FCS

802.3

6	6	2	1	1	1	43–1,497	4
destination	source	length	DSAP	SSAP	CTL	data	FCS

Figure 2.12 Ethernet and 802.3 headers

It was desirable to build stations that could receive packets in either format (Ethernet or 802.3). Luckily, these formats can be distinguished because of the 2-byte field that is *length* in 802.3 and *protocol type* in Ethernet. The maximum legal packet length in 802.3 is 1,500 bytes. Xerox made sure that none of the assigned protocol types used with the Ethernet format was smaller than 1,500. In fact, some protocol types assigned before the 802.3 standard had values smaller than 1,500, and they had to be reassigned as a result. Thus, if a station receives a packet and if the field following the source address has a value smaller than 1,500, the packet is assumed to be in 802.3 format; otherwise, it is assumed to be in Ethernet format.

Another difference between the two formats is the use of protocol type in Ethernet and two SAP fields in 802.3. Currently, the way the SAP fields are used in 802.3 is that (except for XID and TEST) either

- An 802-approved protocol is used—in which case, DSAP = SSAP and they equal the globally assigned SAP value

- Or DSAP = SSAP, they equal the globally assigned SNAP SAP value, and following the CTL field is a 5-byte protocol type field.

2.11 Issues in 802.5

Yes, but I'd rather go by bus. There is nothing nicer in the world than a bus.

—Charles, Prince of Wales, when asked whether he was excited about sailing to Tobruk on the royal yacht, news summaries of May 21, 1954.[2]

A token ring has the interesting property that each packet travels through every station. The source removes the packet from the wire. Thus, it is possible for the destination to mark the packet and thereby to indicate to the source that the packet was successfully received (at least by the hardware—congestion at the destination could force the packet to be dropped even though the hardware successfully received it).

In 802.5 there are 2 bits at the end of a packet, and they are used as an acknowledgment by the destination. One is the A bit, which means that the address was recognized. That, in turn, means that the destination is on the LAN. The C bit indicates that the packet was copied into the destination's buffer. If the A bit is on and the C bit is not on, it indicates that the destination was (presumably, only temporarily) congested; although the destination knew the packet was supposed to be copied, it could not copy the packet. Theoretically, if the source transmits a packet and if the packet successfully makes it around the ring back to the source, the source can examine the state of the A and C bits and surmise the following.

1. If the A bit is clear, the destination does not exist or is down, so there is no point in attempting to retransmit the packet.

2. If both the A and C bits are set, the destination has successfully received the packet, so no retransmission is necessary.

3. If the A bit is set and the C bit is clear, the hardware was temporarily congested at the destination, so an immediate retransmission will probably succeed.

---

[2] James B. Simpson, *Contemporary Quotations* (New York: Thomas Y. Crowell Company, 1964).

4. The case of the A bit's being clear and the C bit's being set was not originally assumed to be useful, and some implementations might have been built to handle this case as an error.

Although these bits seem to be a nice idea, it is difficult for bridges to do anything meaningful with them. A number of options for what bridges could do were discussed, including the following.

1. Always clear both bits.

2. Don't modify the bits at all.

3. Set A and C if the bridge decides to forward the packet.

4. Clear A and set C if the bridge decides to forward the packet.

The final option—that bridges should clear the A bit and set the C bit—was the one selected.

Note that the A and C bits have other uses. These bits help stations determine the order in which they physically appear in the ring. A station emits a packet with the ALL-STATIONS destination address. The next station in the ring will note that the A bit has not been set and that it therefore is the next station. It sets the A bit, and downstream stations do not conclude that they are the next station. Each station, in turn, emits a special packet to identify itself to the neighbor immediately downstream. But these other uses of the A and C bits, although interesting, are not relevant to bridges and routers.

Another issue in 802.5 is that the chips being used do not support true multicast addresses. Instead, they support *functional addresses*, of which there are only 31, because there are 17 bits of constant, followed by 31 bits, and an 802.5-style multicast address has only a single bit on. (Note: I would have called them "nonfunctional" addresses, which is more technically accurate, but I suppose the marketing people thought "functional" sounded better.) Because the 802.5 chips do not support receipt of true multicast addresses, a protocol that has been specified to use a particular multicast address must instead attempt to get one of the 31 functional addresses assigned to it. In addition, a bridge between 802.5 and some other LAN must know two things: the mapping between the multicast address that a protocol uses on a LAN other than 802.5 and the functional address assigned to that protocol for use on 802.5. If more than 31 multicast addresses are used, there must be a mechanism for multiplexing several multicast addresses onto a single functional address. The number of functional addresses (31) is not quite as large as the number of multicast addresses (2^{47}, which is greater than 100 trillion).

Even if new 802.5 chips are developed that support true multicast addresses, backward compatibility with existing devices will continue to make bridging 802.5 to other LANs more complicated as a result of the need to convert between multicast addresses and functional addresses.

2.12 Packet Bursts

Many stations are designed so that they cannot process packets at the rate of the LAN over a long period of time. The assumption is that if the total bandwidth of the LAN were, say, 10 Mb, a single station does not need to process packets that quickly because the amount of traffic destined for a particular station will be far less than 10 Mb.

Unfortunately, it is possible for a *burst* of packets to arrive, exceeding the station's ability to receive. Although some buffering is usually available, it can quickly be exceeded depending on the number of buffers and the speed with which the station can process the packets. If this situation occurs, the station will correctly receive and process the first few packets in the burst, and later ones will get lost.

It is important to understand this typical behavior because naive protocols might never work under these circumstances. Suppose that there were a query response protocol by which a station requested data from another station. If not all the data were received, the station would repeat the identical request. Suppose that the data required transmission of ten packets, the transmitter transmitted them all immediately, and the requester could buffer only two of the packets. Then every time the requester received the response, the first two packets would be accepted by the hardware and the remaining packets would be lost.

2.13 Reasons for Bridges

Each of the technologies discussed in the preceding sections has certain limitations.

1. *Limited number of stations:* In token rings, each station that is attached causes increased delay around the ring, even if it is not transmitting.

2. *Limited size:* In 802.3, the cable must be sufficiently short that when a station at one end of the cable transmits a packet of the legally minimum size, the transmitter will detect a collision.

3. *Limited amount of traffic:* In all LANs, the available bandwidth must be shared by all stations. The more stations that there are and the more stations that are attempting to transmit, the smaller the share of bandwidth for each station.

For these reasons, a single LAN is often insufficient to meet the requirements of an organization. If stations have been designed with the assumption that packets will need to get forwarded by routers in order to reach destinations in other locations, the stations will have implemented a network layer protocol that cooperates with routers. Then you could interconnect the LANs with routers.

However, if stations have been designed with the assumption that their entire world is a single LAN, they will not have implemented layer 3 (the network layer) and thus cannot use a router. Because many stations were designed without layer 3, it was deemed desirable to provide some sort of box that would allow LANs to be "glued" together so that packets could be forwarded from one LAN to another without any cooperation by the stations. These boxes, known as *bridges*, are discussed in Chapter 3. Although the original reason for the bridge was to accommodate stations designed without layer 3, they also proved useful because a bridge can support any layer 3 protocol, and for a while most organizations had many layer 3 protocols operating at once. Multiprotocol routers hadn't been widely deployed, but bridges could move traffic for any layer 3 protocol and served the function of a multiprotocol router. Then the world deployed multiprotocol routers, and people decided they didn't want to have to manage numerous layer 3 protocols, so the world pretty much converged on IP. But bridges are still popular because they are simple, attain high performance, and allow IP nodes to move within the bridged topology and maintain their layer 3 (IP) addresses.

2.14 Point-to-Point Links

Two of the issues relevant for LANs are also relevant for point-to-point links.

1. *Service:* Traditionally, data link layer protocols designed for point-to-point links provided reliable service. Hop-by-hop reliable service is vital if the error rate on each link is high. Otherwise, the probability of successfully transmitting a packet across many hops becomes very small, meaning that an unreasonably large number of retransmissions from the source would be required. Examples of data link protocols providing reliable service are HDLC[3] and DDCMP.[4]

   With improved technology, datagram service at the data link layer not only becomes acceptable but also improves performance. PPP (point-to-point protocol)[5] is a standard developed by the TCP/IP community for a datagram data link layer protocol for point-to-point links. It is basically a simplified HDLC. PPP as compared with HDLC is very similar to LLC type 1 as compared with LLC type 2.

   Figure 2.13 shows the HDLC format.

1	1	1	1	2	1
flag	address	control	data	checksum	flag

Figure 2.13 HDLC format

---

[3] International Organization for Standardization, ISO Standard 3309-1979. "Data Communication—High-level Data Link Control Procedures—Frame Structure," 1979.

[4] DNA Digital Data Communications Message Protocol (DDCMP) Functional Specification, Version 4.1.0, Order No. AA-K175A-TK., Digital Equipment Corporation.

[5] W. Simpson, editor, "The Point-to-Point Protocol" RFC 1661, July 1994.

Flag is a special bit pattern that indicates the start and end of a packet. *Address* is necessary when more than two stations share the link. On a LAN, two addresses are necessary: one to identify the source and a second one to identify the destination. However, HDLC was designed not for LANs but for multiaccess links with a master and several tributaries. *Tributaries* on that sort of link do not send packets to each other. Rather, packets are either transmitted by the master to a tributary or transmitted by a tributary to the master. In the former case, the address specifies which tributary is supposed to receive the packet; in the latter case, the address specifies the source. *Control* specifies the sorts of things that LLC type 2 specifies. The meanings of *data* and *checksum* are obvious.

2. *Multiplexing:* Just as on a LAN, multiple upper-layer protocols can be multiplexed over the same link. Unless all the protocols have been designed so as to make all packets unambiguous (incapable of being mistaken for a packet from a different protocol), there must be some field to disambiguate the packets. On a LAN, there is the protocol type field. Traditional data link layer protocols do not have a protocol type field. PPP has provided that functionality by adding a 16-bit *protocol* field. Figure 2.14 shows the PPP format.

1	1	1	2		2	1
flag	address	control	protocol	data	checksum	flag

Figure 2.14 PPP format

Address is set to the constant 11111111. *Control* is a single byte, set to the value 3, which would be considered "unnumbered information" by HDLC. *Protocol* is a 2-byte field, and the assigned values are listed in the "assigned numbers" RFC (currently, RFC 1700).

Homework

1. Is the address 53-21-ab-41-99-bb a group address? Has it been globally or locally assigned? Show bit-by-bit how it would be stored for transmission on 802.3. Show bit-by-bit how it would be stored for transmission on 802.5.

2. There are two methods of running a meeting. In the first approach, a moderator presides. People raise their hands when they have something to say and then wait until the moderator calls on them and gives them permission to speak. The second method is contention. Anyone who has attended such a meeting knows that certain people talk a lot and certain others never manage to get a word in edgewise. Assuming that 802.3 is fair (every station gets a chance to transmit if it has data), in what respects does 802.3 differ from a meeting of human beings?

3. Given that there is a "protocol type" field (or SAP fields), there is theoretically no need for group addresses. Instead, all protocols that wanted to send a multi-

cast packet could send packets to the broadcast address and differentiate their packets from packets originating with other protocols based on the protocol type field.

What is gained by using a group address specific to a particular protocol instead of using the broadcast address and specifying the protocol based on the protocol type field?

4. Assuming that every protocol uses a separate group address when transmitting multicast packets, why is it necessary to include a protocol type field in the packet header?

5. Assume that a particular station has limited buffering and loses all but the first few packets of a rapid packet burst addressed to it. What provisions should be made by a request/response protocol involving many packets in the response so that the requester will (with a reasonable probability) receive all the data?

6. Now suppose that the query/response is not something aimed at a particular destination but rather is something like an XID directed at the broadcast address, to which many destinations are expected to respond and the requester should receive all the replies. If we assume a high probability that some replies will get lost and that the requester will need to try several times, what provisions can be made in the protocol to ensure that the requester will eventually receive all the replies (so that the same ones don't always get lost)?

7. Organization A and organization B each apply for a block of addresses. Assume that you have the job of handing out addresses and that no addresses have previously been assigned. Assign a block of addresses to each organization.

Now assume that A and B each build a station. Give a possible address for A's station. Now give an address for B's station.

Now assume that organization A invents a wonderful protocol known as OZ that both organizations implement. Organization A is not a standards body recognized by the IEEE committee, so it must employ the SNAP SAP encoding when using its protocol.

Give an example of the destination, source, DSAP, SSAP, and protocol type fields when the station built by organization B transmits an OZ packet to the station built by organization A.

8. Suppose there were no SNAP SAP that you had to use DSAP and SSAP. Your protocol was one of the underprivileged ones that didn't have a globally assigned SAP. Furthermore, there were too many such protocols for some other organization to assign permanent values from the locally assigned space. In other words, each node speaking your protocol might have a different SAP value assigned to your protocol. How might you make this work? (Hint: Perhaps there could be one "well-known" SAP value that would be a protocol that could respond and tell you the SAP value for a particular protocol.)

Chapter 3
Transparent Bridges

Transparent bridges were originally developed by Digital Equipment Corporation and were adopted by the 802.1 committee. For clarity, I will "build" a transparent bridge by adding features.

The Digital bridges and the standardized 802.1 bridges have all the following features:

- The promiscuous listen and the store and forward capabilities of the "no-frills" bridge, as described in Section 3.1

- The station learning cache of the "learning" bridge, as described in Section 3.2

- The spanning tree algorithm of the "complete" bridge, as described in Section 3.3

Note: The intermediate forms of the bridge ("no frills" and "learning") are not standard bridges. To conform to 802.1d, a bridge must implement both learning and the spanning tree. Some early bridge implementations were built without these features, but they are presented here primarily because it is easier to understand bridges if each feature is described separately.

3.1 The No-Frills Bridge

The most basic form of transparent bridge is one that attaches to two or more LANs (each attachment to a LAN is known as a *port*). Such a bridge listens promiscuously to every packet transmitted and stores each received packet until it can be transmitted on the LANs other than the one on which it was received. I call this the no-frills bridge (see Figure 3.1).

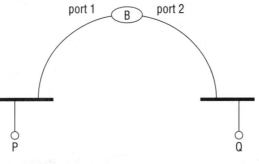

Figure 3.1 No-frills bridge

The transparent bridge was developed to allow stations that were designed to operate on only a single LAN to work in a multi-LAN environment. The stations expect to transmit a packet, exactly as they would in a single-LAN environment, and have the packet delivered. The bridge must therefore transmit the packet exactly as received. If the bridge modified the packet in any way—for example, by overwriting the source address portion of the header with its own address—then protocols in the stations might no longer work properly. The bridge does change the delay characteristics, something that might affect protocols having tight timers that expect a single-LAN environment. However, most protocols either don't have such tight timers or can be adjusted.

With just this basic idea, a no-frills bridge extends the capabilities of a LAN. For example, in the case of 802.3, it allows the length restriction necessitated by the 802.3 hardware to be exceeded. If the box connecting the two LANs were a repeater instead of a bridge, the repeater would forward each bit as it was received, and a station's transmission on one side of the repeater could collide with a station's transmission on the other side of the repeater.

However, with a no-frills bridge, the packet is not transmitted by the bridge while it is being received. Instead, the entire packet is first received by the bridge and then stored, waiting for the LAN on the other side to become idle. It is therefore possible for two stations on opposite sides of the bridge to transmit simultaneously without a collision.

Another example of how a no-frills bridge can extend the limits of a LAN is the ability to increase the number of stations in 802.5. In 802.5, the total number of stations in the ring is limited because clock jitter accumulates at each station; with enough jitter, the phase lock loop is unable to lock. A bridge solves this problem because it implements a completely independent instance of the ring MAC protocol on each ring to which it attaches (see Figure 3.2). Each ring has an independent token and a separate active monitor (the station on which all the stations synchronize their clocks).

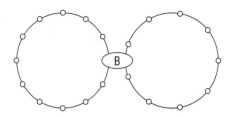

Figure 3.2 No-frills bridge connecting two rings

Regardless of the type of LANs involved, the no-frills bridge does not overcome the LAN total bandwidth limit. If each of the LANs connected by the no-frills bridge has a capacity of 10 Mb/sec (as in 802.3, 802.4, and 802.5), the total bandwidth that can safely be used will still be 10 Mb. This is because the no-frills bridge attempts to ensure that every packet transmitted on any LAN eventually winds up appearing on every LAN. Because each packet will appear on each LAN, the combined transmissions of all stations on all LANs cannot exceed 10 Mb (or whatever the speed of the LANs is).

Nit alert: The statement that "the combined transmissions of all stations on all LANs cannot exceed the bandwidth of any individual LAN" is not exactly true for two reasons.

1. A temporary traffic peak could occur for a short interval, and, as long as the buffer capacity of the bridge were capable of storing the excess packets, none of the packets would get lost.

2. If the buffering capacity of the no-frills bridge were exceeded and the bridge needed to drop packets, the bridge might be lucky enough to drop packets that didn't need to be forwarded because the source and destination were on the same LAN. Therefore, the throughput could theoretically exceed 10 Mb.

Therefore, in theory the total aggregate throughput could exceed the bandwidth of the LANs. However, in practice, since the no-frills bridge cannot distinguish between packets that can safely be dropped and those that must be forwarded, if total bandwidth exceeds the LAN speed, then packets will be dropped before reaching their destination.

The next enhancement to the bridge solves the problem of allowing the bridge to intelligently choose which packets to drop and also allows the aggregate bandwidth to exceed the LAN speed.

3.2 The Learning Bridge

Suppose a bridge were to "know" which stations were on which LANs. Here are some strategies that could be used (but are not).

1. The network manager could manually enter the addresses of all stations on each LAN into a database kept at the bridge (see Figure 3.3). (Some vendors made such bridges before 802.1 standardized the transparent learning bridge.)

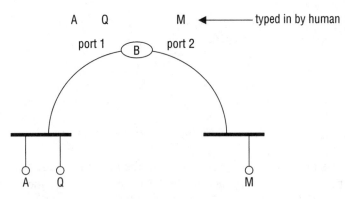

Figure 3.3 Station addresses individually configured

2. The network manager could place stations so that each LAN had only stations whose addresses were within a certain range. Figure 3.4 shows an example.

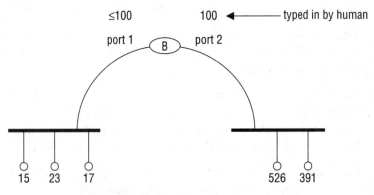

Figure 3.4 Station address ranges configured

3. The network manager could assign station addresses so that a portion of the address specified the LAN to which the station was attached. So, for example, an address could be partitioned into two parts (see Figure 3.5), one being the "LAN number" and the other indicating the station on the LAN.

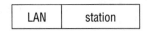

Figure 3.5 LAN number part of station address

For example, an address might read "5.21," which would mean station 21 on LAN 5.

All the preceding strategies involve difficult management. It would obviously be preferable if stations could use a globally assigned 48-bit ID stored in a ROM by the manufacturer and be plugged in to the topology in any location, and the bridge could just "figure out" where the stations were.

This turns out to be possible, based on the assumption that a station puts its address in the source address field in the packet header when it transmits a packet (see Figure 3.6). (Why do I call this an "assumption"? Wouldn't it violate "all sorts of standards" if a station put anything other than its own address into the source address field? Well, consider the fact that bridges do not put their address into the source address field when they forward packets. Luckily, it's a good assumption in general that the source address in the packet header identifies the transmitter of the packet.)

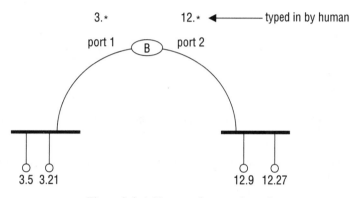

Figure 3.6 Address prefixes configured

The strategy used by the bridge is as follows.

1. The bridge listens promiscuously, receiving every packet transmitted.

2. For each packet received, the bridge stores the address in the packet's source address field in a cache (which I refer to as the *station cache*), together with the port on which the packet was received.

3. For each packet received, the bridge looks through its station cache for the address listed in the packet's *destination address* field.

   a. If the address is not found in the station cache, the bridge forwards the packet onto all interfaces except the one from which it was received.

   b. If the address is found in the station cache, the bridge forwards the packet only onto the interface specified in the table. If the specified interface is the one from which the packet was received, the packet is dropped (*filtered*).

4. The bridge ages each entry in the station cache and deletes it after a period of time (a parameter known as *aging time*) in which no traffic is received with that address as the source address. (Actually, the 802 spec spells the parameter "ageing" because the editor of 802.1d is British and the country seems to have a surplus of vowels.)

Assume the topology shown in Figure 3.7. B initially knows nothing about any of the stations.

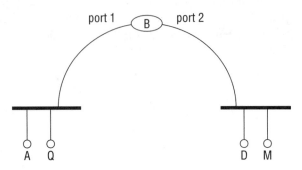

Figure 3.7 Initially the bridge B knows no station addresses

Now assume that station A transmits a packet with destination address D. The packet looks like Figure 3.8.

Figure 3.8 A sends to D

The bridge concludes, by looking at the packet's source address and noting that the packet was received on port 1, that A resides on port 1. The bridge does not know where D resides, so it forwards the packet onto all ports except port 1 (the one from which it received the packet), which in this case is just port 2 (see Figure 3.9).

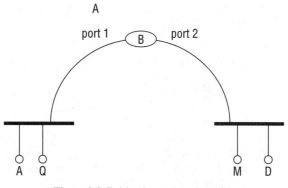

Figure 3.9 Bridge learns location of A

Now assume that D transmits a packet for A (see Figure 3.10).

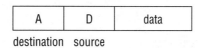

Figure 3.10 D sends to A

The bridge concludes, by looking at the packet's source address and noting that the packet was received on port 2, that D resides on port 2. The bridge has learned A's address, and, because it is on port 1, the bridge knows that it must forward the packet onto port 1 for A to receive the packet (see Figure 3.11).

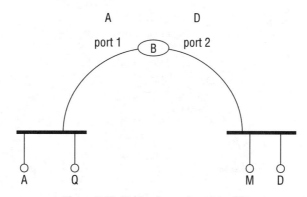

Figure 3.11 Bridge learns location of D

Now assume that Q transmits a packet for A (see Figure 3.12).

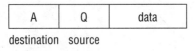

Figure 3.12 Q sends to A

The bridge concludes, by looking at the packet's source address and noting that the packet was received on port 1, that Q resides on port 1. The bridge has learned A's address, and, because it is on port 1, the bridge knows that it does not need to forward the packet because A also resides on port 1 (see Figure 3.13).

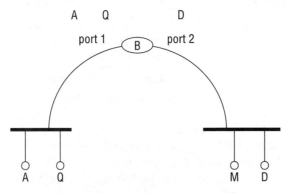

Figure 3.13 Bridge learns location of Q

The learning bridge concept is quite powerful and works for many topologies. For example, a bridge can have more than two ports (see Figure 3.14).

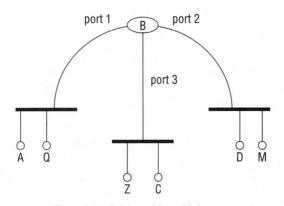

Figure 3.14 Bridge with multiple ports

Initially, B knows only that it has three ports. Assume that A transmits a packet with destination D. B will note that A resides on port 1. Since B does not know where D resides, B must forward the packet onto both ports 3 and 2.

After this initial packet, the state of B's learning is illustrated in Figure 3.15.

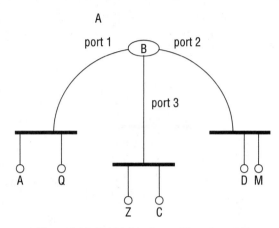

Figure 3.15 Bridge has learned location of A

Now assume that D transmits a packet with destination A. B will note that D resides on port 2, and, because B knows that A resides on port 1, B will forward the packet, but only onto port 1.

Now assume that Q transmits a packet with destination A. B will note that Q resides on port 1, and, because A also resides on port 1, B does not need to forward the packet (see Figure 3.16).

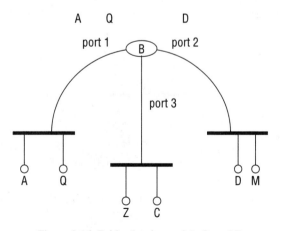

Figure 3.16 Bridge has learned A, Q, and D

Now assume that Z transmits a packet with destination C. B will note that Z resides on port 3, but because B does not know where C resides, it must forward the packet onto both ports 1 and 2.

Now that I've shown that the bridge concept works for any number of ports, let us examine multiple bridges. For example, consider the topology in Figure 3.17.

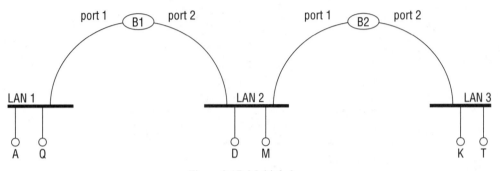

Figure 3.17 Multiple hops

Bridge B1 cannot distinguish stations on LAN 2 and LAN 3. As far as B1 can tell, it is connected to two LANs: the one on its port 1 and the one on its port 2. B2 connects LAN 2 and LAN 3 transparently, so B2's existence is hidden from B1, just as B2's existence is invisible to the stations.

After all the stations have transmitted something, the state of the caches in the two bridges will be as shown in Figure 3.18.

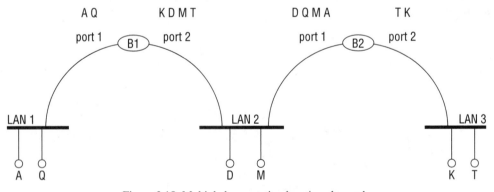

Figure 3.18 Multiple hops, station locations learned

Thus, to B1 the topology in Figure 3.18 looks like that shown in Figure 3.19.

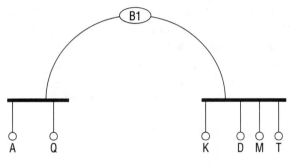

Figure 3.19 What it looks like to B1

To B2, the topology in Figure 3.18 looks like that shown in Figure 3.20.

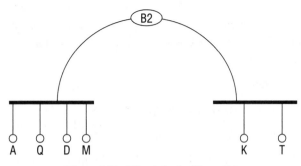

Figure 3.20 What it looks like to B2

The learning bridge concept works for any *tree* (loop-free) topology.
Does the concept extend to all topologies? Consider the network in Figure 3.21.

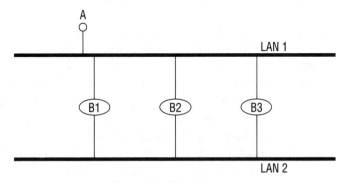

Figure 3.21 Multiple paths

What happens when station A transmits a packet? The destination to which A sends is irrelevant. Assume that it is a destination that has not yet transmitted anything and therefore the bridges do not have the destination in their station caches.

The first guess as to the behavior of this system is usually that three copies of the packet are transmitted to LAN 2. If that were indeed the way the system behaves, things wouldn't be so bad. However, the behavior is much worse than that. Infinitely worse, to be precise.

Initially, each of the three bridges

1. Receives the packet

2. Notes that A resides on LAN 1

3. Queues the packet for forwarding onto LAN 2

Then, by the laws of LANs, one of the bridges (let's say bridge 3) will be the first to succeed in transmitting the packet onto LAN 2. Because bridge 3 is transparent to bridges 1 and 2, the packet will appear, on LAN 2, exactly as if station A had transmitted the packet onto LAN 2. Thus, bridges 1 and 2 will

1. Receive the packet

2. Note in their tables that A now resides on LAN 2

3. Queue the packet for forwarding onto LAN 1

Next, suppose that bridge 1 succeeds in transmitting its first received packet onto LAN 2. Bridges 2 and 3 will also receive the packet. Bridge 2 will merely note that A is still on LAN 2, and bridge 3 will note that A has moved onto LAN 2; both will then queue the packet for transmission onto LAN 1.

Now suppose that bridge 1 succeeds in transmitting onto LAN 1. Bridges 2 and 3 will note that A has moved to LAN 1 and will queue the "new" packet for forwarding onto LAN 2.

Thus, not only do the packets loop, but they also proliferate. Every successful packet transmission results in two packets in the system. If you are familiar with routers, it is worth noting that although packet looping occurs with routers, it is not nearly so bad. With routers, each packet transmitted is directed to a specific router, and each router transmits a packet only onto a single interface. Therefore, with routers, a packet might be transmitted an infinite number of times, but it will not spawn additional copies at each hop. At any point, only a single copy of the packet will exist. And with routers there is generally a hop count in the packet so that a looping packet will eventually be dropped. But because bridges are supposed to be transparent, a packet looks the same on its 25-thousandth transmission as it did on its first transmission.

Now that it is clear how badly learning bridges will perform in a topology with loops, we have several options.

1. We can decide that bridges were a bad idea after all.

2.   We can document the fact that the topology must be kept loop-free. Then if someone accidentally plugs the topology together with a loop somewhere, we can smirk and tell the offender to read the documentation more carefully next time.

3.   We can design bridges to detect the existence of loops in the topology and complain. In this way, at least the customer doesn't have to learn about the problem from field service.

4.   We can design into the bridges an algorithm that prunes the topology into a loop-free subset (a spanning tree).

Option 1 is clearly not correct; in loop-free topologies, bridges are quite useful. Options 2 and 3 are undesirable because allowing loops in a topology is extremely useful. Without loops, the topology has no redundancy. If anything breaks, connectivity is lost. Loops should not be viewed as misconfiguration but rather as good design strategy. An additional drawback of option 2 is that it represents a poor customer relations strategy. Option 4 is clearly desirable if such an algorithm can be devised. Luckily, such an algorithm exists[1] and is quite simple (so simple, in fact, that it took me less time to invent the algorithm than write the poem in Section 3.3) (see Figure 3.22).

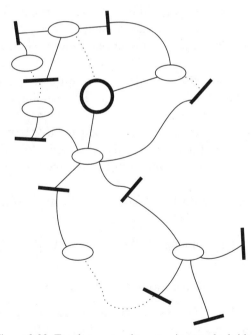

Figure 3.22 Topology pruned to spanning tree by bridges

[1] R. Perlman, "A Protocol for Distributed Computation of a Spanning Tree in an Extended LAN" Ninth Data Communications Symposium, Vancouver, 1985.

3.3 Spanning Tree Algorithm

Algorhyme

I think that I shall never see
A graph more lovely than a tree.

A tree whose crucial property
Is loop-free connectivity.

A tree that must be sure to span
So packets can reach every LAN.

First, the root must be selected.
By ID, it is elected.

Least-cost paths from root are traced.
In the tree, these paths are placed.

A mesh is made by folks like me,
Then bridges find a spanning tree.

—Radia Perlman

The purpose of the spanning tree algorithm is to have bridges dynamically discover a subset of the topology that is loop-free (a tree) and yet has just enough connectivity so that where physically possible, there is a path between every pair of LANs (the tree is *spanning*).

The basic idea behind the spanning tree algorithm is that bridges transmit special messages to each other that allow them to calculate a spanning tree. These special messages have been given the catchy name *configuration bridge protocol data units* (or *configuration BPDUs*) by 802.1. I was torn between using the ISO terminology and something friendlier. In this chapter, "configuration BPDU" is called a "configuration message," as a compromise between familiarizing you with the terminology in the specifications and making the chapter readable.

The configuration message contains enough information so that bridges can do the following.

1. Elect a single bridge, among all the bridges on all the LANs, to be the *Root Bridge.*

2. Calculate the distance of the shortest path from themselves to the Root Bridge.

3. For each LAN, elect a *Designated Bridge* from among the bridges residing on that LAN. The elected bridge is the one closest to the Root Bridge. The Designated Bridge will forward packets from that LAN toward the Root Bridge.

4. Choose a port (known as the *root port*) that gives the best path from themselves to the Root Bridge.

5. Select ports to be included in the spanning tree. The ports selected will be the root port plus any ports on which "self" has been elected Designated Bridge.

Data traffic is forwarded to and from ports selected for inclusion in the spanning tree. Data traffic is discarded upon receipt and is never forwarded onto ports that are not selected for inclusion in the spanning tree.

3.3.1 Configuration Messages

A configuration message is transmitted by a bridge onto a port. It is received by all the other bridges residing on the LAN attached to the port. It is not forwarded from that LAN.

A configuration message has an ordinary LAN data link layer header (see Figure 3.23).

destination	source	DSAP	SSAP	configuration message

Figure 3.23 Configuration message transmitted with data link header

The data link layer destination address is a special multicast address assigned to "all bridges." (A functional address is assigned for this purpose in 802.5 because of the inability of the 802.5 implementations to handle true multicast addresses.) The data link layer source address is the address on that port of the bridge transmitting the configuration message. (The bridge architecture requires a bridge to have a distinct data link layer address on each port.) The SAP value is 01000010, which is a wonderful value because there is no way to get the bit ordering incorrect.[2]

Although a bridge has a separate address on each port, it also has a single ID that it uses as its ID in the data portion of a configuration message. This bridgewide ID can be the LAN address on one of the ports, or it can be any unique 48-bit address.

Contained in the data portion of a configuration message (among other stuff to be described later) are the following:

- Root ID: ID of the bridge assumed to be the root

- Transmitting bridge ID: ID of the bridge transmitting this configuration message

- Cost: Cost of the least-cost path to the root from the transmitting bridge (at least, the best path of which the transmitting bridge is currently aware)

A bridge initially assumes itself to be the root and transmits configuration messages on each of its ports with its ID as root and as transmitting bridge and 0 as cost.

---

[2] It's also 42 hex. If you haven't done so already, read the wonderful *Hitchhiker's* books by Douglas Adams to discover another reason the committee picked that number.

A bridge continuously receives configuration messages on each of its ports and saves the "best" configuration message from each port ("best" is described in the next paragraph). The bridge determines the best configuration message by comparing not only the configuration messages received from a particular port but also the configuration message that the bridge would transmit on that port.

Given two configuration messages—C1 and C2—the following are true.

1. C1 is "better than" C2 if the root ID listed in C1 is numerically lower than the root ID listed in C2.

2. If the root IDs are equal, then C1 is better than C2 if the cost listed in C1 is numerically lower than the cost listed in C2.

3. If the root IDs and costs are equal, then C1 is better than C2 if the transmitting bridge ID listed in C1 is numerically lower than the transmitting bridge ID listed in C2.

4. There's an additional field in the configuration message known as *port identifier*. The transmitting bridge has some internal numbering of its own ports, and when it transmits a configuration message onto port *n*, it places *n* in the port identifier field. If the root IDs, costs, and transmitting bridge IDs are equal, then the port identifier serves as a tiebreaker. This field is useful primarily for detecting the case in which two ports of a bridge attach to the same LAN. This situation can be caused when two different LANs are connected with a repeater or when two bridge ports are attached to the same physical LAN. For simplicity, the port identifier field is ignored in the following examples.

In all three cases shown in Figure 3.24 (a, b, and c), the configuration message C1 is better than the configuration message C2. In case a, the root ID is lower in C1. In case b, the transmitting bridge ID is smaller, and the root ID and cost are the same. In case c, the root is the same, but the cost is better in C1.

	C1			C2		
	root ID	cost	transmitter	root ID	cost	transmitter
a.	29	15	35	31	12	32
b.	35	80	39	35	80	40
c.	35	15	80	35	18	38

Figure 3.24 Comparing configuration message

Note that with the preceding rules, configuration messages can be ordered by the multiprecision number consisting of root ID as the most significant portion concatenated with cost as the next most significant portion and transmitter's bridge ID as the least significant portion.

If a bridge receives a better configuration message on a LAN than the configuration message it would transmit, it no longer transmits configuration messages. Therefore, when the algorithm stabilizes, only one bridge on each LAN (the Designated Bridge for that LAN) transmits configuration messages on that LAN.

3.3.2 Calculation of Root ID and Cost to Root

Based on received configuration messages from all interfaces, each bridge B independently decides the identity of the Root Bridge. This is the minimum of B's own ID and the root IDs reported in any configuration message received by B on any of its ports.

Let us assume that B has an ID of 18. Suppose that the best configuration message B receives on each of its ports is as follows:

	Root	Cost	Transmitter
Port 1	12	93	51
Port 2	12	85	47
Port 3	81	0	81
Port 4	15	31	27

First, B selects the root. In this case, the best root heard about by B is 12. If B's ID had been smaller than 12, then B would be the root.

Now B calculates its own distance to the Root Bridge. If B is the Root Bridge, then B's distance to the root is defined to be 0. Otherwise (if B is not the root), B's cost to the root is the minimum, for each port that reports a cost to that selected root, of adding the cost of getting to the neighbor plus the cost reported by the neighbor to get from there to the root. Assume for now that the cost function is hops (a cost of 1 to traverse the link). Because B is not the root, its cost is 86 because it received a cost (to root 12) of 85 on port 2.

B also selects one of the ports from which it has a minimal cost path to the root to be its preferred path to the root. This port is sometimes referred to as the root port, or the *in-link*. B will choose port 2 as its root port. In the case of ties, the link with the numerically smallest transmitter ID is selected as the root port. If there's still a tie, the port ID (another field in the configure message, see Section 3.4.5) is compared.

After B determines the identity of the root and its own distance to the root, B knows what its own configuration message would contain and can compare that with the best received configuration message on each port to determine whether B should be the Designated Bridge on that port. In this case, B's configuration message would be 12.86.18. B's configuration message is better than the ones it has received on ports 1, 3, and 4, so B will assume (until it hears a better configuration message on one of those ports) that it is the Designated Bridge on ports 1, 3, and 4 and will transmit the configuration message 12.86.18 on those ports.

3.3.3 Selecting Spanning Tree Ports

After B calculates the root, its own cost to the root, and the Designated Bridge for each of its ports, B decides which ports are in the spanning tree and which are not. The following ports are selected for inclusion in the spanning tree.

1. B's root port. In the example we're working with, it would be port 2.

2. All ports for which B is the Designated Bridge. In our example, these would be ports 1, 3, and 4.

The ports selected by B for inclusion in the spanning tree are placed in the *forwarding* state, meaning that B will forward data packets to and from those ports. All other ports are placed in the *blocking* state, meaning that B will not forward data packets to or from those ports.

3.3.4 An Example

In Figure 3.25, the bridge with ID 92 has five ports. On port 1, the best configuration message it has received is 81.0.81, where 81 is the root ID, 0 is the cost to the root, and 81 is the ID of the bridge transmitting the configuration message, which, in this case, assumes at the moment that it is the root. On port 2, the bridge has received 41.19.125; on port 3, 41.12.315; on port 4, 41.12.111; on port 5, 41.13.90.

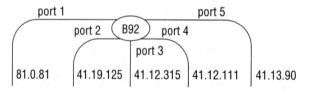

Figure 3.25 Configuration messages received

Bridge 92 will assume that the best known root is 41 and that the best cost to the root from bridge 92 is 12 + 1, or 13, via either port 3 or port 4. Bridge 92 must select one of these ports to be its root port. Because it uses the ID of the neighboring Designated Bridge as a tiebreaker, it will select port 4; the neighboring Designated Bridge's ID there is 111, which is numerically lower than 315.

The configuration message that bridge 92 can transmit—41.13.92—is a better configuration message than the ones received on ports 1 and 2. Therefore, bridge 92 will assume that it is the Designated Bridge on ports 1 and 2 and will discard the configuration messages it previously received on those ports (see Figure 3.26). Bridge 92's configuration message (still 41.13.92) is not better than the one received on port 5—namely, 41.13.90—because of the Designated Bridge ID tiebreaker.

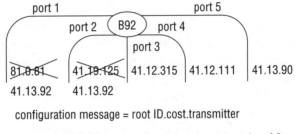

configuration message = root ID.cost.transmitter

Figure 3.26 Bridge overwrites message on ports 1 and 2

The result of this calculation is that bridge 92 will select port 4 (because 4 is its root port) and ports 1 and 2 (because bridge 92 is the Designated Bridge on those LANs) for inclusion in the spanning tree. Bridge 92 will classify ports 5 and 3 as in the blocking state—that is, bridge 92 will continue to run the spanning tree algorithm on those ports but will not receive data messages from those ports, learn the location of station addresses from them, or forward traffic onto them.

Note that if the example is changed so that the bridge's own ID is 15, then it will decide that the root ID is 15, the cost to the root is 0 (because it is the root), and it will be the Designated Bridge on all its ports, transmitting the configuration message 15.0.15.

3.4 Spanning Tree Algorithm Refinements

So far I've just discussed what happens when components start. This section describes how the algorithm deals with failures and changing topologies.

3.4.1 Failures

The algorithm presented in the preceding section describes how a network initially starts or how it adapts to the start-up of new bridges or links. However, it does not adapt to failures of bridges or links.

The stored configuration message for each port contains a *message age* field, which is incremented after each unit of time. If the message age reaches a certain threshold (known as *max age*), the configuration message is discarded and the bridge recalculates as if it had never received a configuration message from that port.

In the normal course of events, the Root Bridge periodically transmits configuration messages (every hello time). When the Root Bridge generates a configuration message, the message age field is set to 0. When bridges receive the root's configuration message, it causes them to transmit a configuration message on each of the ports for which they are designated, with a message age field of 0. Similarly, when the bridges downstream from any Designated Bridge receive a configuration message with message age 0, they transmit their own configuration message, on the ports for which they are designated, with message age 0.

If the root fails or if any component on the path between a bridge and the root fails, the bridge will stop receiving "fresh" (message age = 0) configuration messages on the root port, and it will gradually increase the message age on the configuration message stored for that port until it reaches max age. At that point, the bridge will discard that configuration message and recalculate the root, root path cost, and root port. For example, assume that the configuration message on port 4 times out (see Figure 3.27). If the configuration message on port 3 has not timed out, then bridge 92 will simply switch its root port from port 4 to port 3. Bridge 92's configuration message on ports 1 and 2 will not change.

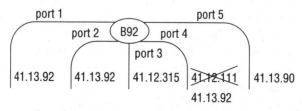

configuration message = root ID.cost.transmitter

Figure 3.27 Port 4's configuration message timed out

Now assume that the configuration message on port 3 also times out (see Figure 3.28). In that case, bridge 92 will choose port 5 as its root port. Switching to port 5 causes bridge 92 to change its configuration message to 41.14.92.

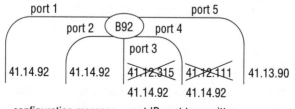

configuration message = root ID.cost.transmitter

Figure 3.28 Port 3's configuration message also timed out

If the configuration messages on all three ports—3, 4, and 5—time out, then bridge 92 will assume itself to be the root and will transmit 92.0.92 on all five ports until it receives fresh configuration messages from any of its ports regarding a better root (see Figure 3.29).

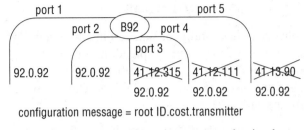

configuration message = root ID.cost.transmitter

Figure 3.29 Port 5's configuration message also timed out

The following events cause spanning tree calculation.

1. *Receipt of a configuration message on port X:* In this case, the bridge compares the received configuration message with the stored configuration message from port X. If the received configuration message is better or is the same but with a smaller age, the stored configuration message is overwritten and the bridge recalculates the root, root path cost, and root port.

2. *Timer tick:* In this case, the bridge increments the message age field in the stored configuration message for each port. If this causes the message age field in any stored configuration message to reach max age, the bridge discards that stored configuration message and recalculates the root, root path cost, and root port.

If the only time the Designated Bridge issued a configuration message were upon receipt of a configuration message from the direction of the root, there would be no reason to include the age field in the configuration message because upon transmission it would always be 0. However, there is another situation in which a Designated Bridge will issue a configuration message even if one has not been received recently from the root port.

Suppose that B is the Designated Bridge on a particular port. Suppose, too, that B has not recently received a configuration message from the direction of the root, so that the stored configuration message from the direction of the root now has age X (B has been aging the message while holding it in memory). If another bridge, B2, were to come up, it would issue its own configuration message because it would not have heard B's configuration message on that LAN. It would be dangerous for B to ignore this situation until B hears a new configuration message from the root because it would cause the new bridge to be very unsynchronized with respect to the rest of the network. If the new bridge does not hear B's configuration message, the new bridge will assume that it should become designated on that port, causing extra connectivity—a loop. If B retransmitted its configuration message without the age field (or with age field 0), then it would slow down discovery of any failure of the root in that subtree because B's retransmission of the configuration message would look like assurance that the root (and the path to the root) was still functioning at the time B retransmitted its configuration message.

So in this case, B must issue its configuration message but with age field X. The result will be the same as if the new bridge had heard B's configuration message when B transmitted it originally (X time units ago).

3.4.2 Avoiding Temporary Loops

After a topological change (a new bridge or link coming up or a bridge or link failing), it will take some time for news of the event to spread throughout the topology. Until news of the changed topology has reached all bridges, the bridges will operate on inconsistent data. This situation has two possible outcomes (both of which may occur simultaneously in various portions of the network).

1. There may be temporary loss of connectivity if a bridge port that was off in the old topology hasn't yet found out that it needs to be on in the new topology.

2. There may be temporary loops in the topology if a bridge port that was on in the old topology hasn't yet found out that it needs to be off in the new topology.

Although it was stated earlier, it is worth repeating that loops with bridges are far more frightening than loops with routers for two reasons.

1. There is no hop count in the data link header, so with bridges, packets will loop indefinitely until the topology stabilizes.

2. Packets can proliferate with bridges because a bridge might forward the packet onto several LANs, and several bridges might pick up the packet when it is transmitted onto a LAN. In contrast, routers forward the packet in only one direction and specify the router to which the packet is being forwarded. Therefore, a loop with routers will not cause packet proliferation.

Temporary partitions in a bridged topology are better than temporary loops. (Almost anything is better in a bridged topology than a loop.) You can minimize the probability of temporary loops by requiring that a bridge wait some amount of time before allowing a bridge port that was in the blocking state to transition to the forwarding state. Hopefully, the amount of time is sufficient for news of the new topology to spread. In that way, all bridge ports that should be off in the new topology have already heard the news and turned themselves off before any additional ports start forwarding data packets.

This timer should be at least twice the maximum transit time across the network. Suppose that bridge B1 is the root of the "old" topology. Suppose also that B1 issues one configuration message, which transits the network essentially instantaneously (no congestion). Then suppose that its next configuration message is maximally delayed by X sec. B1 then crashes. Bridges close to B1 will time out B1 and start to compute a "new" topology X sec before bridges maximally far from B1.

Now suppose that the root in the new topology is B2, which is maximally far from B1. And suppose that the first configuration message transmitted by B2 travels maximally slowly—that is, it takes X sec to reach the portion of the network that is near the ill-fated B1. Then bridges near B2 will find out about the new topology X sec before bridges that are close to B1.

In the worst case, news of the new topology will take twice time X to reach all bridges. Therefore, the algorithm does not allow a bridge to immediately transition a port from the blocking state to the forwarding state. Instead, the bridge temporarily puts the port into a different state: it still does not forward packets but does send Hello messages as if it were the Designated Bridge. After a timer expires, if the bridge still thinks the port should be in forwarding state, the port can be turned on. The purpose of this delay is to avoid adding extra connectivity until all bridges that might need to turn ports off in the new topology have had a chance to hear about the new topology.

The 802.1 standard actually calls for two intermediate states. This arrangement is designed to minimize learning of incorrect station locations while the topology has not yet stabilized. To minimize unnecessarily forwarded frames, the committee deemed it desirable not to allow a bridge to start forwarding until it has built up its learned cache. During the initial portion of the intermediate state, the bridge does not learn station addresses; then during the latter part, the bridge still does not forward packets over that port, but it does start learning station locations on that port. In other words, the intermediate state is subdivided into two substates: *listening* and *learning*.

Note: in the original spanning tree algorithm, I had only a single intermediate state, known as *preforwarding*. The committee asked whether bridges should learn station addresses in the preforwarding state. I said I didn't think it mattered. The committee decided to break preforwarding into the two aforementioned states. I believe that having two states is unnecessary and that bridges would work fine whether or not they learn station addresses in preforwarding. Breaking this period into two states makes the algorithm more complicated but does no harm. It would be an interesting project to study the trade-offs between the three strategies:

1. One intermediate state in which station learning is done

2. One intermediate state in which station learning is not done

3. Two intermediate states, as in the spec, in which learning is not done in the first half of the time and is done in the second half

3.4.3 Station Cache Timeout Values

Bridges learn and cache the location of stations. Because a station might move, it is important for a bridge to "forget" station locations unless it is frequently reassured that the learned information is correct. This is done by timing out entries that have not been recently verified.

Choosing a suitable timeout period is difficult. If an entry is incorrect for any reason, traffic may not be delivered to the station whose location is incorrectly cached. If an entry has been deleted, traffic for the deleted station will leak into other portions of the bridged network unnecessarily. If the timeout is too long, traffic will be lost for an unreasonably long time. If the timeout is too short, performance in the network will degrade because traffic will be forwarded unnecessarily.

If the only reason for a station's location to change is that the station moved, a timer on the order of minutes is reasonable for three reasons.

1. It would probably take someone 15 minutes or so to unplug a station, physically move it to a new location, and then plug it in.

2. Even if a station were moved more quickly than that, it is understandable that things might take a few minutes to start working again.

3. There are strategies that the moved station can employ to cause things to start working more quickly. For example, the moved station can transmit a packet to a multicast address. Packets transmitted to multicast addresses are forwarded throughout the spanning tree (unless it's a multicast address that the bridges have been explicitly configured not to forward). After all the bridges see a packet from source S, they will correct their entry for S. Because station S's multicast packet might get lost and not reach all parts of the extended LAN, S can either transmit a few multicast packets when it first comes up or live with the fact that most of the time things will work immediately when it moves, and occasionally it might take a few minutes. If indeed it takes at least 15 minutes to physically move a station, no special mechanisms are necessary.

However, a reconfiguration of the spanning tree can cause many station locations to change. It is unreasonable to have many stations become unreachable for as long as 15 minutes after a topology change. None of the aforementioned arguments holds for topological reconfiguration for the following reasons.

1. The spanning tree takes considerably less than 15 minutes to adapt to a new topology (if it didn't, bridges would be more useful as boat anchors than as LAN interconnection devices).

2. A station user would not understand why things mysteriously stop working every so often because a spanning tree reconfiguration happens without any action on the part of the user.

3. A station cannot correct its entry with a special mechanism such as transmitting a multicast packet because a spanning tree reconfiguration occurs without the station's being aware of it.

Therefore, a station cache timeout of 15 minutes is too long. What about a station cache timeout on the order of 15 seconds? I think that performance would not differ significantly with a station cache timeout on the order of 15 seconds as opposed to 15 minutes. My reasoning is that if a station has not transmitted anything for 15 seconds, it is probably not in the process of receiving a lot of traffic. After a gap of 15 seconds, it would probably not degrade network performance significantly if the first few packets destined for that station were sent unnecessarily to other portions of the network.

It would be interesting for someone to study the effect of shorter cache timeout values on network performance. If someone could positively identify the smallest cache timeout value before network performance degraded significantly and if that timeout were on the order of a few seconds, then bridges could simply use that timeout value.

Unfortunately, the question of timeout value cannot be answered definitively because it depends on the types of applications and the topology. It might be definitively shown that a cache timeout of, say, 3 seconds works fine in a particular network with a particular set of applications, but there might be other applications for which such a timeout would be unsuitable.

Because a suitable cache timeout value could not be definitively established, it was decided that the cache timeout value should be configurable. Furthermore, assuming that a cache timeout value longer than the spanning tree reconfiguration time would often be desirable, it was thought that there should be two cache timeout values:

1. A long value to be used in the usual case

2. A shorter value to be used following a reconfiguration of the spanning tree algorithm

Can bridges detect that the spanning tree has reconfigured? In all cases, at least one bridge can notice. However, in the general case, some bridges will not notice that the spanning tree has reconfigured. Many station entries can become incorrect in a bridge's station cache even when that bridge cannot detect that the spanning tree algorithm has reconfigured. (See homework problem 7.)

Therefore, the spanning tree algorithm had to be enhanced with a method for reliably advising all the bridges that the spanning tree has reconfigured. The enhancement should keep the "spirit" of the original spanning tree algorithm in that the required bandwidth should not grow with the size of the network. For example, having each bridge that noticed a topology change send a multicast message would cause the overhead to grow as the total number of bridges grew. The basic idea behind the enhancement is that when a bridge B notices that the topology has changed, B must inform the Root Bridge of the change. However, instead of having B inform the Root Bridge directly, B notifies the bridge on B's root port. That bridge, in turn, informs its parent, and so on, until finally the root has been informed that the topology has changed.

When the root has been informed of the change, it sets a flag in its configuration message, known as the *topology change flag*, indicating that the topology has changed. Bridges set the topology change flag in the configuration messages they transmit on the LANs for which they are the Designated Bridge as long as the flag is set in the configuration message from the root port.

The following steps occur.

1. A bridge notices that the spanning tree algorithm has caused it to transition a port into or out of the blocking state.

2. The bridge periodically transmits a topology change notification message on its root port, with the same period as the hello timer. It continues to do this until the parent bridge acks by setting a bit in its configuration message. The data link destination address of a topology change notification is the same multicast address as is used for configuration messages.

3. A bridge that receives a topology change notification on a port for which it is the Designated Bridge does two things.

   a. It performs step 2 (that is, it informs its parent bridge through topology change notifications).

   b. It sets the *topology change acknowledgment flag* in the next configuration message it transmits on the LAN from which the topology change notification was received.

4. The Root Bridge sets the topology change flag in its configuration messages for a period equal to the sum of the forward delay time parameter and the max age parameter if the Root Bridge either

   a. notices a topology change because one of its ports has changed state, or

   b. receives a topology change notification message.

5. A bridge that is receiving configuration messages with the topology change flag set (or the Root Bridge that is setting the topology change flag in its configuration messages) uses the short station cache timer until it starts receiving configuration messages without the topology change flag set.

Note that the long cache value is a network management parameter and that the short cache value is equal to the forward delay timer, which is also a network management parameter.

3.4.4 Networkwide Parameters

For the spanning tree algorithm to work properly, there are several parameters on which all bridges must agree. These parameters are configurable.

This approach might seem unworkable. What happens if the parameters are set incompatibly at different bridges? What happens if all bridges are set compatibly but someone then decides to change the networkwide value to a value that is incompatible with the first value? Will the network cease operating properly after a few bridges have been told to use an incompatible parameter value? And might the network become so nonfunctional that network management commands intended to fix the problem could not get through?

Luckily, there is a nifty solution. The Root Bridge includes in its configuration messages the values of the parameters on which all bridges must agree. If network management commands a bridge to set one of the parameters, that bridge notes the configured value in nonvolatile storage. If the bridge becomes the root, it uses its own values and puts them into its configuration messages. A bridge that is the Designated Bridge on some port copies the values it received in the configuration message from the root port into the configuration messages it transmits. Also, all bridges use the current root's values (as discovered through receipt of configuration messages from the root port) for the parameters.

The parameters dictated by the root in this way are as follows.

1. *Max age:* the time at which a configuration message is discarded

2. *Hello time:* the time interval between issuing configuration messages

3. *Forward delay:* the amount of time in the learning and listening states—that is, half the amount of time that must elapse between the time when it is decided that a port should become part of the spanning tree and the time when data traffic is allowed to be forwarded to and from that port.

3.4.5 Port ID

A configuration message also contains the *port ID*. This field has two purposes.

1. (Admittedly, a not very exciting purpose.) It allows the computed spanning tree to be *deterministic* in the sense that given the same topology the bridge will always select the same root port. For example, in Figure 3.30 B2 is faced with two ports, both of which have the same Designated Bridge, reporting the same root and the same cost to the root.

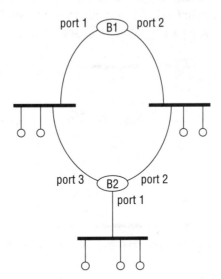

Figure 3.30 Two ports, same Designated Bridge

Assuming that B1 is the root, should B2 choose port 3 or port 2 as its root port?

Each bridge has an internal representation of the number of each of its ports. The Designated Bridge puts its internal value of the port number into its configuration message. On B2's port 3, B2 will receive the configuration message that B1 is the root, the cost to B1 is 0, the Designated Bridge is B1, and the port is 1.

On B2's port 2, B2 will get a similar configuration message, but with the port being 2. Because "1" is less than "2," B2 selects its own port 3 as the root port instead of its own port 2.

2. (A more exciting purpose.) It allows loops formed through means other than bridges to be dealt with properly. Suppose that a bridge has more than one port connected to what appears to the bridge to be a single LAN. This can happen for several reasons.

    a. Someone could hook two ports of a bridge onto the same LAN.

    b. Someone could hook two ports of a bridge onto two LAN segments connected with a repeater.

    c. Someone could hook two ports of a bridge onto different LAN segments but connect them with a "simple bridge"—one that does not run the spanning tree algorithm.

In Figure 3.31, B is the Root Bridge (because it's the only bridge). It will transmit (B, 0, B, port #) on each of its ports. However, on port 2 it will receive the configuration message it transmitted on port 1, and on port 1 it will receive the configuration message it transmitted on port 2. Because 2 > 1 the configuration message (B, 0, B, 1) (which it receives on port 2) is better than (B, 0, B, 2) (which it is transmitting on port 2). So B will defer to what it thinks is a better Designated Bridge on port 2.

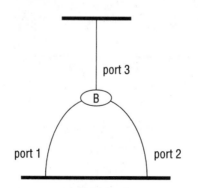

Figure 3.31 Two ports of bridge on same LAN

3.4.6 Assigning Port Numbers

Someone recently complained to me that bridges couldn't have more than 256 ports because of the spanning tree algorithm. I couldn't imagine why the spanning tree algorithm precluded lots of ports until I checked out the 802 standard. It says that the 2-byte port ID should be divided into two portions: the top byte should be "priority," and the bottom byte should uniquely specify the port. That would allow only 256 ports.

In the original spanning tree algorithm I hadn't bothered with a port priority at all. However, if people really want a port priority I suggest that they number the bridge ports appropriately within a priority level but not set aside a portion of the port number field for explicitly announcing the configured priority. So, for example, you could start with all the ports that have been configured with the lowest priority level. Assign them port numbers 1, 2, 3, and so on until all the ports configured with that lowest priority level have been assigned numbers. Now start on the next priority level. Suppose 14 ports have been assigned numbers. Start the next priority level by assigning 15, 16, and so on until you run out of ports assigned that priority level, and so forth. In this way you get full use of the 2 bytes of port priority and can have 64,000 ports. You also could have arbitrarily many levels of priority. Port numbers are purely a local matter to the bridge. The only constraint is that all of them have unique numbers. And unless there's some sort of conformance test that checks to make sure that when you configure priority 12, the number 12 appears as the top byte of the port ID, I'd advise vendors to ignore that part of the spec, especially if their bridges have more than 256 ports. I suggested this recently to the committee, and I think it may compromise on fewer bits for the priority but still have the port ID field explicitly announce the configured priority.

3.4.7 Performance Issues

The spanning tree algorithm has two properties that make performance critical.

1. Lack of receipt of messages causes bridges to add connectivity. For example, if a bridge does not receive any configuration messages on some port, it will take over as the Designated Bridge on that port.

2. Extra connectivity (loops) is potentially disastrous.

It is important to design the system so that if the network becomes congested, the spanning tree algorithm will run properly. Otherwise, the network's becoming temporarily congested might prompt the spanning tree algorithm to incorrectly turn extra bridge ports on, causing loops and dramatically increasing the amount of congestion to such a point that the algorithm never recovers.

A bridge must be engineered to have sufficient CPU power. If the bridge's CPU becomes a bottleneck, the bridge will start throwing away packets before it even looks at them. In this situation, there is no way for the bridge to avoid throwing away configuration messages because it can't distinguish a configuration message from a data message without looking at it.

Another requirement is that a bridge be able to transmit a configuration message no matter how congested the LAN is. All LANs enforce fairness, allowing each station at least a minimal amount of bandwidth. Therefore, no matter how congested the LAN, the bridge will be able to transmit a packet eventually. Because it is critical that configuration messages get sent in a timely fashion, a bridge should be engineered so that a configuration message can be put at the front of a queue.

The 802.1 standard does not require adequate performance. It is possible for a bridge to be underpowered and still fully conform to the standard. Extended LANs with under-powered bridges do not perform well and can become totally unstable in the face of congestion.

It is not necessary for a bridge to completely process every configuration message it receives in real time in order for the algorithm to work correctly. It might be possible for a bridge to have just enough processing power to receive every message on the LAN, worst case, and decide whether it is a data message or a configuration message but not have enough CPU to run the spanning tree algorithm until there is some idle time on the LAN. This is OK provided that the bridge keeps the "best" configuration message it has seen since it had sufficient CPU to process a configuration message. This can be done by simply looking at the multiprecision number consisting of the root ID as the most signif-icant part, the cost to the root as the next most significant, and the transmitter's ID as the least significant.

Note: I think that the bridge spec should have outlawed underpowered bridges. In practice, underpowered bridges are a problem. A temporary congestion situation causes lost configuration messages, which, in turn, causes loops. Then the congestion resulting from looping and proliferating data packets makes the situation worse.

Loops caused by congestion can occur if links have the property of being able to lose messages without the transmitter's knowledge. In such a case, the Designated Bridge on a link transmits configuration messages, but the link itself, because of congestion, loses them before they reach the other bridges. The 802 LANs do not behave this way, but there are technologies that have this problem. For such links, bridges are not an appropri-ate solution.

3.4.8 One-way Connectivity

It is possible for hardware to fail in such a way that connectivity between two bridges on a LAN becomes one-way; bridge A can hear bridge B, but bridge B cannot hear bridge A. This situation can be caused by bridge B's receiver being dead or weak, bridge A's transmitter being dead or weak, or some other component, such as a repeater, transmit-ting or receiving badly.

One-way connectivity between bridges is bad because a loop can be created. For example, assume that B1 cannot hear B2 (see Figure 3.32). If the cause is that B1's receiver is dead, B1 will not hear data packets on the LAN either. However, B1 might forward packets onto the LAN, creating a loop.

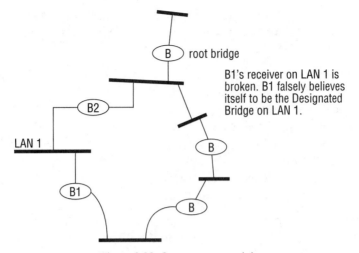

B) root bridge

B1's receiver on LAN 1 is broken. B1 falsely believes itself to be the Designated Bridge on LAN 1.

Figure 3.32 One-way connectivity

If the cause is that B2's receiver is dead, B2 will not be forwarding packets from the LAN; however, B2 will be forwarding packets onto the LAN, creating a loop.

The bridge standard does not say what to do in this case. One possibility is for any bridge that detects one-way connectivity on a LAN to stop forwarding packets to and from that LAN until the condition is no longer detected. One way to detect one-way connectivity is to notice that some other bridge is persistently sending configuration messages even though yours are better. This indicates that the other bridge is not receiving your messages. Perhaps your transmitter is faulty, or its receiver is faulty.

3.4.9 Settable Parameters

The following parameters can be set.

1. *Bridge priority:* a 2-octet value that allows the network manager to influence the choice of Root Bridge and the Designated Bridge. It is appended as the most significant portion of a bridge ID. A lower numerical value for bridge priority makes the bridge more likely to become the root.

2. *Port priority:* a 1-octet value that allows the network manager to influence the choice of port when a bridge has two ports connected in a loop. As I discussed in Section 3.4.6, I think the port priority should not appear in the configuration message but instead should only influence the assignment of port numbers. And in that case, priority could be 2-octets—large enough to assign a unique value to each port if desired.

3. *Hello time:* the time that elapses between generation of configuration messages by a bridge that assumes itself to be the root. The recommended time is 2 sec. Shortening the time will make the protocol more robust in case the probability

of loss of configuration messages is high. Lengthening the time lowers the overhead of the algorithm (because the interval between transmission of configuration messages will be larger).

4. *Max age:* the message age value at which a stored configuration message is judged "too old" and discarded. If the selected max age value is too small, then occasionally the spanning tree will reconfigure unnecessarily, possibly causing temporary loss of connectivity in the network. If the selected value is too large, the network will take longer than necessary to adjust to a new spanning tree after a topological event such as the restarting or crashing of a bridge or link.

   A conservative value is to assume a delay variance of 2 sec per hop. The value recommended in 802.1d is 20 sec.

5. *Forward delay:* a parameter that temporarily prevents a bridge from starting to forward data packets to and from a link until news of a topology change has spread to all parts of a bridged network. This parameter should give all links that need to be turned off in the new topology time to do so before new links are turned on.

   Because it is invoked twice, forward delay need only be half the time necessary for news of the new topology to have reached all parts of the network. When a bridge decides that a port should be switched from the blocking state to the forwarding state, it initially places the port in the listening state. In the listening state, the bridge continues running the spanning tree algorithm and transmitting configuration messages on the port, but it discards data packets received on that port and does not transmit data packets to that port. The bridge keeps the port in the listening state for forward delay and then moves the port into the learning state, which is like the listening state except that data packets are received on that port for the purpose of learning some of the stations located on that port. After forward delay, if the bridge still hasn't heard any information that would make it transition the port back to the blocking state, it transitions the port to the forwarding state.

   Setting the forward delay value too small would result in temporary loops as the spanning tree algorithm converges, so it is good to be conservative in setting this parameter. On the other hand, setting the forward delay value too large results in longer partitions after the spanning tree reconfigures. This can be sufficiently annoying to tempt people to be brave and set the value smaller.

   The value recommended in 802.1d is 15 sec. This means that a bridge will delay forwarding packets to or from a port that was in the blocking state in the previous topology and should be in the forwarding state in the new topology for 30 sec after that bridge discovers that the port should be included in the new spanning tree.

   Note that forward delay also serves as the value of the short cache timer, the one used following topology changes.

6. *Long cache timer:* a configurable value. The default recommended in the 802.1 spec is 5 min.

7. *Path cost:* the cost to be added to the root path cost field in a configuration message received on this port in order to determine the cost of the path to the root through this port. This value can be set individually on each port.

Setting this value to be large on a particular port makes the LAN reached through that port more likely to be a leaf or at least low in the spanning tree. The closer a LAN is to being a leaf in the tree, the less through traffic it will be asked to carry. A LAN would be a candidate for having a large path cost if it has a lower bandwidth or if someone wants to minimize unnecessary traffic on it.

Note: I would have called this parameter "link cost" or "port cost" so as not to confuse anyone into thinking that its value refers to an entire path.

3.5 Bridge Message Formats

There are only two types of messages used by the spanning tree algorithm: configuration messages and topology change notification messages.

3.5.1 Configuration Message Format

Figure 3.33 shows the format of the configuration message.

# of octets

2	protocol identifier
1	version
1	message type
1	TCA | reserved | TC
8	root ID
4	cost of path to root
8	bridge ID
2	port ID
2	message age
2	max age
2	hello time
2	forward delay

Figure 3.33 Bridge configuration message format

Protocol identifier: The constant 0.

Version: The constant 0.

Message type: The constant 0.

Flags:

> *TC*, the least significant bit, is the topology change flag. If set in the configuration message received on the root port, it indicates that the receiving bridge should use forward delay (a short cache timer) for aging out station cache entries rather than the aging timer (the normal, longer timer for station cache entries).

> *TCA*, the most significant bit, is the topology change notification acknowledgment. If set in the configuration message received on the root port, it indicates that bridges receiving this configuration message no longer need to inform the parent bridge that a topology change has occurred. The parent bridge will take responsibility for advising the root of the topology change.

> The remaining bits in the flags octet are unused.

Root ID: Each bridge is configured with a 2-octet priority, which is added to the 6-octet ID. The priority portion is the numerically most significant portion. The 8-octet root ID consists of the priority followed by the ID of the bridge that is the root.

Cost of path to root: 4 octets, taken as an unsigned binary number, which is the total cost from the bridge that transmitted the configuration message to the bridge listed in the root ID.

Bridge ID: 2 octets of configured priority followed by the 6-octet ID of the bridge transmitting the configuration message.

Port ID: The first, and most significant, octet is a configurable priority. The second octet is a number assigned by the bridge to the port on which the configuration message was transmitted. The bridge must assign a (locally) unique number to each of its ports. As I said before, the specification might change to have fewer bits set aside for priority so as to allow more ports or may change to not explicitly announce priority in the port ID, as recommended in Section 3.4.6.

Message age: estimated time, in 1/256ths of a second, since the root originally transmitted its configuration message, on which the information in this configuration message is based.

Max age: time, in 1/256ths of a second, at which the configuration message should be deleted.

Hello time: time, in 1/256ths of a second, between generation of configuration messages by the Root Bridge.

Forward delay: length of time, in 1/256ths of a second, that bridges should stay in each of the intermediate states before transiting a port from blocking to forwarding.

3.5.2 Topology Change Notification Format

Figure 3.34 shows the format of the topology change notification.

# of octets

2	protocol identifier
1	version
1	message type

Figure 3.34 Topology change notification format

Protocol identifier: The constant 0

Version: The constant 0

Message type: The constant 128 (decimal)

3.6 Other Bridge Issues

The remainder of this chapter covers advanced issues that arise with standard transparent bridges, including the implications of station behavior on bridge operations, bridged environments on stations, and configuration of bridge filtering. Section 3.7 discusses nonstandard extensions to transparent bridges that allow the use of routes other than spanning tree paths.

3.6.1 Multiply Connected Stations

The consequence of having an incorrect entry in a bridge's station cache is that traffic may not get delivered to the station. One particularly ironic example of how bridge caches can become incorrect is a station with multiple connections into an extended LAN. The problem does not occur if the station uses different data link addresses on each attachment, but some endnode implementations use the same address on multiple links.

Assume the topology shown in Figure 3.35, where station S is attached to two LANs: LAN 1 and LAN 7.

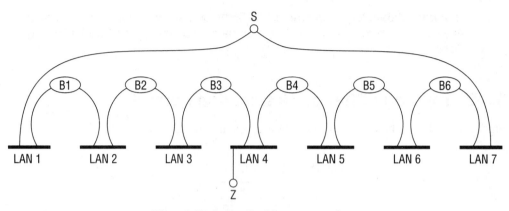

Figure 3.35 Station S with two connections

Suppose that S issues two packets at about the same time. Packet 1 is issued on LAN 1, and packet 2 is issued on LAN 7. Packet 1 travels toward the right, convincing each bridge that S resides on the left. Meanwhile, packet 2 travels toward the left, convincing each bridge that S resides on the right.

Assume that the two packets "cross" on LAN 4 as shown in Figure 3.36 (B4 has packet 2 queued for transmission onto LAN 4 while B3 has packet 1 queued for transmission on LAN 4). When B3 succeeds in transmitting the packet, it will cause B4 to change S's location from residing on the right to residing on the left, and B4 will forward the packet on, convincing B5 and B6 that S resides on the left. When B4 succeeds in transmitting the packet, B3 will become convinced that S resides on its right, and B3 will forward the packet on.

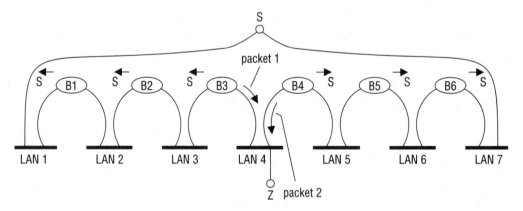

Figure 3.36 Packets 1 and 2 cross on LAN 4

Now the picture looks like the illustration in Figure 3.37.

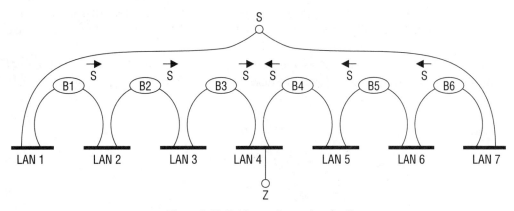

Figure 3.37 Bridge station caches for S

Now assume that Z, residing on LAN 4, transmits a packet for S. Because B3 thinks that S resides on its right, B3 will not forward the packet. Because B4 thinks that S resides on its left, B4 will not forward the packet either. Presumably, S is multiply attached into the extended LAN for increased availability, but indeed the multiple points of attachment make it possible for the bridges to become confused as to S's whereabouts and refuse to forward packets to S.

3.6.2 Configuration of Filtering

A bridge that discards a packet rather than forwarding it is said to *filter* the packet. The standard transparent bridge automatically learns station addresses and performs filtering in the sense that it does not always forward every packet throughout the spanning tree. After all bridges have learned the location of a particular station, traffic destined for that station should travel along the shortest path in the spanning tree from the source to that station and not "leak" to other parts of the spanning tree.

Filtering is useful for another reason. For example, it is sometimes desirable to keep certain kinds of traffic confined to portions of the topology. A case in point would be a time synchronization protocol that would not work with delays imposed by multiple hops and should therefore be kept confined to a single LAN. Or there might be terminal servers and hosts managed by different organizations in different portions of the spanning tree. It might be desirable to keep the terminal server protocol messages from leaking between the portions of the network.

The 802.1 standard specifies that network management have the ability to set certain addresses as being permanently in the filtering database of a bridge, with instructions as to which ports the bridge should allow the packets to traverse.

The mechanism specified in the standard is that a particular address is entered into the filtering database with an input port number, together with flags indicating the output ports on which a packet from the specified input port should be forwarded. Usually, the addresses that are manually entered into the filtering database are multicast addresses, but station addresses can also be configured.

First, let's look at a simple example. Suppose that you wanted a particular protocol to flow between ports 2, 4, and 5 and not flow on ports 1, 3, 6, and 7 (see Figure 3.38).

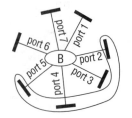

Figure 3.38 Desired scope of a multicast address

Assume that the multicast address used by the protocol is FOO. This would require management commands that look approximately like the following. The user interface is not standardized.

1. *Create filter address FOO:* Input port 2; outbound 1—no, 2—no, 3—no, 4—yes, 5—yes, 6—no, 7—no.

2. *Create filter address FOO:* Input port 4; outbound 1—no, 2—yes, 3—no, 4—no, 5—yes, 6—no, 7—no.

3. *Create filter address FOO:* Input port 5; outbound 1—no, 2—yes, 3—no, 4—yes, 5—no, 6—no, 7—no.

Now suppose that there are two domains for FOO running the same protocol and that traffic for these two domains should not commingle. For example, assume in the preceding example that in addition to having FOO flow between ports 2, 4, and 5, it should flow separately between 1 and 7 (see Figure 3.39).

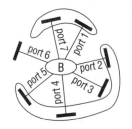

Figure 3.39 Desired scope of a multicast address

Then, in addition to the commands indicated earlier, the following commands must be given.

1. *Create filter address FOO:* Input port 1; outbound 1—no, 2—no, 3—no, 4—no, 5—no, 6—no, 7—yes.

2. *Create filter address FOO:* Input port 7; outbound 1—yes, 2—no, 3—no, 4—no, 5—no, 6—no, 7—no.

Many products offer vendor-specific additional filtering, such as

- Filtering based on SAP value rather than specific address

- Filtering based on source address

Note that setting up filtering can be tricky and counterintuitive because the boundaries that you can imagine with a particular physical topology might no longer work after the spanning tree defines the logical topology (see Figure 3.40).

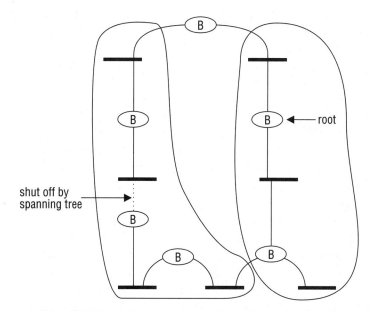

Figure 3.40 Confining protocols to regions of an extended LAN

3.6.3 Not Quite Transparent

Now that I've described the basic idea behind the transparent bridge, I'll discuss why it really should be called something like the "translucent" bridge.

One obvious way in which adding bridges alters the environment for the stations is that the following performance changes occur:

1. *The probability of packet loss increases.* Even if every bridge were engineered to have sufficient CPU to read every packet and determine the ports to which to queue it, links can become congested and thus packets may need to be dropped. Queues cannot become arbitrarily large because bridges do not have infinite buffering. Even if they did, as queue lengths increased indefinitely, so would delays.

2. *The delay increases.* At each hop, the bridge must wait until it acquires the channel. Also, a congested link along the path can cause a packet to be queued behind several others.

3. *The packet lifetime increases.* For the same reasons that delay increases, packet lifetime can increase when bridges are introduced. This has implications for higher-layer protocols. Counters set just large enough to avoid wrapping around during lifetimes on a LAN might wrap around during packet lifetimes across several bridged hops.

4. *The error rate increases.* There are two times when data corruption can occur. One is while data is being transmitted. The cyclic redundancy check (CRC) included in the data link layer protocol detects transmission errors. Data corruption can also occur in memory or while a packet is being transmitted across the bus inside a system. If bridges were to strip off the CRC upon packet reception (after checking it for correctness) and then regenerate a CRC upon transmission on the next hop, then errors introduced while the packet was inside the bridge would not be detected. For this reason, it is desirable for the bridge to keep the CRC that was received with the packet and use the same CRC upon transmission. Then data corruption errors occurring inside the bridge will be detected.

   However, bridges cannot always preserve the original CRC. In the case of 802 LANs, no two LANs have the same packet format, and 802.5 even has a different bit order. Thus, the CRC can be preserved only if a bridge is forwarding between two LANs of the same type.

   The standard doesn't *require* bridges to preserve the CRC when possible, so even if the extended LAN consists entirely of like LANs, some bridge implementations will not preserve the CRC. In the case of heterogeneous LANs in an extended LAN, bridges cannot preserve the CRC. Thus, the rate of undetected data corruption may increase by orders of magnitude when bridges are introduced.

5. *Packet misordering becomes possible (although very unlikely).* Although bridges go to great lengths to minimize the probability of out-of-order packets, packets can get misordered if spanning tree reconfigurations occur.

6. *The probability of duplicate packets increases.* Again, bridges go to great lengths to minimize the probability of duplicate packets, but it is still possible for packets to get duplicated in a bridged LAN. For example, if a repeater were to come up, joining two LANs that were previously separated within the spanning tree,

there would be a temporary loop, and packets on that loop would be duplicated, perhaps a dramatic number of times.

In addition to the quantitative performance-type changes that are introduced by bridges, certain qualitative functional differences result.

1. *Stations cannot use the LAN maximum packet size.* Suppose that different types of LANs having different maximum packet sizes are interconnected with bridges. Then a station emitting a maximum-size packet on its LAN will have a 100% probability of losing that packet if the packet needs to be forwarded by a bridge onto a LAN having a smaller maximum packet size.

   Stations can be configured to use smaller packet sizes, and one solution to the problem of differing LAN packet sizes is to configure all stations in the extended LAN to use the packet size of the LAN that has the smallest maximum packet size. This solution isn't totally satisfactory, though, because, in many cases, the source and destination might be on the same LAN and could converse with no problem using a large packet size. Mandating a smaller-than-necessary packet size degrades throughput. Another strategy involves having the transport layer in the stations attempt to discover a larger packet size, but that is not guaranteed for the lifetime of a transport connection because spanning tree reconfigurations can reroute the conversation. This scheme was facilitated by defining priority 0 on FDDI as the value filled in by a bridge when a packet is forwarded from 802.3. The details for using this information to determine packet size are left as homework problem 12.

   A "low-tech" method (one that doesn't use the FDDI priority field) of finding maximum packet size is to have the transport layer attempt to send a large packet to see whether it gets through. It keeps trying smaller packets until one succeeds.

   Chapter 4 discusses source routing, which solves the problem of determining the maximum packet size for a conversation. It is interesting that source routing solves the packet-size problem because even network layer protocols do not provide very satisfactory solutions. With network layer protocols, packets can be fragmented and reassembled at the destination, but this severely degrades performance. With transparent bridges, bridges cannot fragment a packet. They can't even issue an error report explaining that the packet needed to be dropped for being too large because no such protocol messages are defined for the data link layer.

2. *LAN-specific information in the data link layer may be lost.* Some LANs have LAN-specific information fields, such as priority. If a packet is transmitted from a LAN with a priority field onto a LAN without such a field and then onto another LAN with a priority field, there is no way to reconstruct the original priority because it cannot be carried in the intermediate LAN.

3. *Unexpected packet format conversion may occur.* There is a convention (RFC 1042) for an 802 format equivalent to the Ethernet format. This is done by using the SNAP SAP (see Section 2.7) as both the DSAP and SSAP and using 3 octets of 0 for the OUI, followed by the 2-octet Ethernet protocol type to form the 5-octet protocol type field (see Figure 3.41).

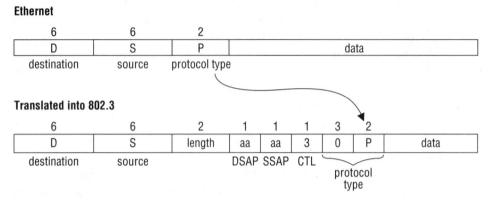

Figure 3.41 Translation from Ethernet to 802.3

After a packet is translated into 802 format, it can be forwarded onto other LAN types with minimal translation (for example, adding a priority field, deleting the length field). If the packet is eventually transmitted back onto an Ethernet and the first 3 octets of protocol type are 0, there is no way for the final bridge to know whether the packet was originally transmitted in Ethernet format or 802 format.

To keep compatibility with old stations that understand only Ethernet format, a bridge translates into Ethernet format a frame in which SNAP SAP is used and the top 3 octets of the protocol type are 0. For this reason, newer stations, if they use the SNAP SAP and 5-octet protocol type with OUI = 0 on 802.3, must be able to accept a packet in Ethernet format and treat it exactly as they would treat the 802.3 version. This rule is documented in RFC 1122. Unfortunately, the RFCs really apply only to IP implementations. There are protocols that use the SNAP SAP encoding with OUI = 0, and they get confused if the packet is received in a format different from the one in which it was transmitted.

In particular, bridge vendors became aware of one protocol (AppleTalk) that assumed the version number of its own protocol based on whether the packet was received in Ethernet or 802.3 format. It was essential for the correct operation of AppleTalk that if the transmitter emitted a packet with an Ethernet header, it ultimately be received in Ethernet format. Similarly, if the transmitter emitted the packet in 802.3 format, the packet ultimately had to be received in 802.3 format.

The bridge vendors got together and agreed to solve this problem by having bridges specifically check the protocol type for the value assigned to AppleTalk—say, X. If the packet was in Ethernet format, with protocol type = X, then instead of using the 5-octet protocol type field in 802 format normally used for translation—3 octets of 0 followed by X—they'd instead use a different value (which happens to be 00-00-f8). When forwarding onto an 802.3 LAN, a bridge checks the protocol type and translates into Ethernet format if

1. DSAP = SNAP SAP, the first 3 octets of protocol type = 00-00-00, and the last 2 octets of protocol type are anything other than X.

2. DSAP = SNAP SAP and the first 3 octets of protocol type = 00-00-f8.

Bridges also make certain assumptions about station behavior, which, if violated, can have consequences ranging from annoying to severe.

1. *They assume that a given data link source address can appear in only one location in the extended LAN.* Some implementations of stations with multiple links use the same data link layer address on all ports. This confuses bridge caches, as discussed in Section 3.6.1. As a result, packets might not be delivered at all to a station that presumably had multiple attachments for greater availability.

2. *They assume that a station receiving a lot of traffic will also be transmitting.* If a destination never transmits, packets destined for that station cannot be localized within the extended LAN but rather must be transmitted to all the LANs throughout the spanning tree.

3.7 Remote Bridges

When people wish to connect two geographically distant LANs, they cannot attach a single box to both LANs. Instead, they attach a bridge to each LAN and connect the bridges with a point-to-point link (see Figure 3.42). Bridges connected by point-to-point links are sometimes called *remote* bridges. They are also sometimes referred to as *half* bridges because the combination of the two bridges plus the point-to-point link can be thought of as a single bridge.

Figure 3.42 Two bridges connected with a point-to-point WAN link

The spanning tree algorithm works fine with point-to-point links. The two bridges on each side of the point-to-point link simply regard the link as a LAN.

One issue to consider is that the spanning tree algorithm makes sure that packets reach every LAN. One of the two bridges will be the Designated Bridge on the point-to-point link. That bridge will definitely consider the point-to-point link to be in the spanning tree and will forward data packets onto that link. The other bridge either will or will not consider the point-to-point link to be its root port. If the second bridge considers the link to be its root port, it will also forward data packets to and from the link, and the point-to-point link will be useful in the spanning tree. If the second bridge does not compute the link to be its root port, that bridge will not forward data packets to the point-to-point link and will ignore packets transmitted to that link.

On some point-to-point links, billing costs are traffic-sensitive. In such a case, it makes sense for the second bridge to alert the first bridge that it will be ignoring its data packets. The standard does not specify a means to do this. Instead, it assumes that remote bridges will be bought in pairs from the same vendor.

Another issue with remote bridges is the representation of the packet as it travels over the point-to-point link. Usually, the point-to-point link has some sort of header information that must be added to a packet. Bridges typically take the entire packet (including the LAN header) and treat it as the data portion of a packet on the point-to-point link (see Figure 3.43). In this way, it is possible to preserve the CRC.

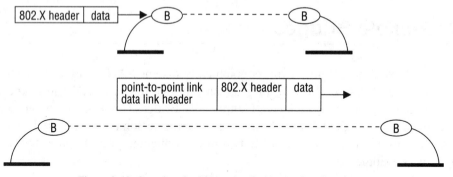

Figure 3.43 Carrying the 802 packet inside the data link frame

This same technique can be used if the point-to-point link is not a direct wire but rather is a *WAN cloud* to which both bridges connect (see Figure 3.44). RFC 1483 discusses the issues of doing this over ATM. RFC 1490 discusses how to do this over frame relay.

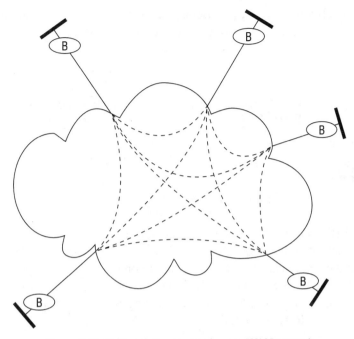

Figure 3.44 Bridges interconnected over a WAN network

Because most WANs do not provide multicast capability, a collection of bridges attached to a WAN cloud must be preconfigured with the network layer addresses of all the other bridges. Each bridge communicates with all the other bridges (see Figure 3.44).

Yet another issue with remote bridges is the need to pass the type of packet along with the packet (see Figure 3.45).

Figure 3.45 Mixture of frame types

If B1 merely packages a packet, as received from one of the LANs, and transmits it to B2, then B2 does not know whether the packet originated on 802.3 and can therefore be transmitted verbatim onto the 802.3 LAN attached to B2, or whether the packet originated on a different type of LAN and the header therefore requires modification. There are several solutions.

1. B1 and B2 could have a proprietary mechanism for passing along the type of LAN on which the packet originated (see Figure 3.46).

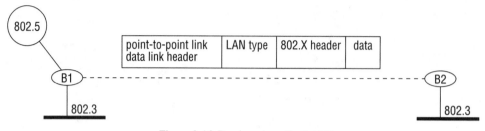

Figure 3.46 Passing along the LAN type

2. B1 and B2 could agree on a particular *canonical format* for packets and convert the packet into that canonical format before transmitting it on the point-to-point link. If the canonical format is not equal to one of the LAN types, then all packets will need to be reformatted both before and after transmission on the point-to-point link. The problem with reformatting packets is that there is no way to preserve the CRC end-to-end.

3. B1 and B2 could agree on a particular type of LAN—for example, 802.3—and then convert non-802.3 packets to that format before transmitting them on the point-to-point link. This enables 802.3 packets to be passed along unmodified. But a packet that originated on an 802.5 and needs to be transmitted back onto an 802.5 would have been needlessly reformatted, and the CRC will have been lost. Also, information specific to a particular type of LAN (such as priority) will get lost if the preferred format does not have the necessary field.

Homework

1. What problems occur if a bridge's cache is incorrect about the direction in which a station resides?

2. Suppose that the number of stations exceeds the capacity of a bridge's station cache. Will this cause problems? Should the bridge overwrite existing entries with new entries before the old entries have timed out, or should the new entries be ignored?

3. Despite careful configuration of timers, temporary loops can occur with bridges. For example, a repeater can come up, connecting two LANs that had not previously been connected. What design decisions in bridge implementation can ensure that the network will recover?

4. Why does using a smaller packet size degrade throughput on a long file transfer?

5. Suppose that someone built an "introduction" service to allow nodes to find other nodes' data link layer addresses. An "introduction server" has a well-known (unicast) data link address—say, "INTRO"—and it knows the data link addresses of all other nodes, but other nodes do not a priori know the data link addresses of other nodes. The protocol is as follows.

A node keeps a cache of data link layer addresses of nodes with which it is currently corresponding. This cache is learned based on the data link layer source address of received packets.

When a node—say, A (see Figure 3.47)—wants to talk to a node Z for which A does not know the data link address, A sends a packet to layer 2 address INTRO, with layer 3 destination address = Z. The intro server looks up Z's layer 2 address—say, "z"—writes z into the layer 2 destination address (leaving A's layer 2 address as the source address in the layer 2 header), and forwards the packet. Z will learn A's layer 2 address from the source address in the layer 2 header of the received packet. After Z replies, A will learn Z's layer 2 address as well. Although this protocol works fine on a LAN, why won't it work when there's a bridge separating A from Z and the intro server?

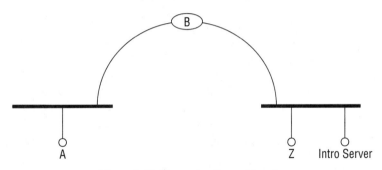

Figure 3.47 Illustration for problem 5

6. Consider the following alternative to the topology change notification protocol and the variable station timeout. When a bridge notices a topology change, it multicasts a special "flush cache" packet to all the other bridges. A bridge that receives a flush cache packet deletes its entire station cache.

How does this compare with the topology change notification protocol? Will all incorrect entries be deleted? Will the network's performance be any different if the station cache is completely deleted in one step rather than having the station cache slowly cleansed of incorrect entries by setting the cache timer smaller?

7. Demonstrate a topology in which the spanning tree can reconfigure without some particular bridge's being aware that the topology has changed (assuming the topology change notification protocol was not implemented). Demonstrate how portions of that bridge's station learning cache can become invalid as a result of that reconfiguration.

8. Assume that a bridge has seven ports and that there are three protocols using multicast addresses MULT1, MULT2, and MULT3, respectively. Suppose you want to allow MULT1 to travel freely between all ports; you want MULT2 to travel between ports 1, 2, and 3 and also between 5 and 7; and you want MULT3 not to travel between any of the ports. What network management commands would you give to the bridge to set up the filtering?

9. Where would filtering based on source address be useful? For example, a bridge might be configured with a set of source addresses and refuse to forward a packet unless the source was in the configured set. Also, a bridge might be configured with a set of disallowed source addresses—in which case, it would refuse to forward a packet whose source address was in the disallowed set.

10. Imagine a protocol in which clients and servers find one another based on multicast advertisements or solicitations. Suppose that for that protocol, there are specific regions of the extended LAN, and the person responsible for the extended LAN wants only clients and servers from the same region talking to one another. Assuming nonmalicious nodes, suppose that the manager configures bridges outside each of the regions to drop the multicast addresses used by the protocol. Furthermore, assume that the bridges do not filter based on protocol type. Will filtering based solely on the multicast addresses keep the separate regions segregated with respect to that protocol?

11. Discuss methods (both hardware and software) for organizing the station learning cache to speed the forwarding of packets. Adding entries to the cache based on newly learned source addresses should also be reasonably efficient but is not as critical as lookups of addresses already in the cache. The latter must be done at LAN speeds, whereas adding entries can be done in the background.

12. Assume for simplicity that there are only two types of LANs in the topology: FDDI and 802.3. FDDI allows 4,500-octet packets; 802.3 has a maximum packet size of 1,500 octets.

    FDDI has a priority field, which is not present in 802.3. The bridge spec states that when a bridge transmits a packet from 802.3 to FDDI, the bridge should transmit it at priority = 0. It is recommended that FDDI stations not originate traffic with priority 0. Use this information to devise a simple scheme that two FDDI stations can use to discover whether they can communicate with 4,500-octet packets or 1,500-octet packets. (Note that they must communicate with 1,500-octet packets if the path between them includes an 802.3 LAN.)

13. As stated in Section 3.4.2, the original spanning tree algorithm had only a single intermediate state between blocking and forwarding and did not indicate whether a bridge should perform learning of station addresses on a port in the intermediate state. The 802 bridge spec subdivides the intermediate state into two states. In the first, learning is not done; in the second, learning is done. Compare the following three strategies:

a. A single intermediate state, in which learning is done

b. A single intermediate state, in which learning is not done

c. As in the spec, two intermediate states

Consider the implications, such as unnecessarily forwarded frames and incorrect cache entries, of each strategy.

14. Compare the functionality of n-port bridges with two-port bridges. Can every configuration built with n-port bridges be built with two-port bridges? Suppose a topology consists of n LANs interconnected with a single n-port bridge; in that topology, a packet always requires just a single hop to get from any LAN to any other LAN. Can the same thing be accomplished with two-port bridges? If a customer wanted n LANs interconnected and only two-port bridges were available, what configuration of LANs and two-port bridges would you suggest?

15. Recently there was a proposal for a modification to the spanning tree algorithm to get rid of preforwarding delay in certain cases. The modification is that if the spanning tree algorithm tells you that link L should now be your in-link (path to the root), you are allowed to immediately start forwarding on L provided that you immediately stop forwarding on your previous in-link. The claim is that this modification will not introduce loops.

a. Can this modification ever introduce loops (even if multiple events occur in various portions of the network and different root candidates appear)? (Hint: I think the answer is no.)

b. Show that this proposal would introduce loops if the Designated Bridge adds the cost of the link into its Hello message—that is, the cost advertised is the cost to the LAN rather than the cost to the bridge. In other words, if B thinks it is 5 from the Root R and that link L has cost 2, B will advertise (R, 7, B, . . .) in its Hello. (Isn't it amazing that such a seemingly arbitrary choice of who adds in the link cost could make a difference here?)

c. Show a case in which this change causes a temporary partition when, with the original specification, no such delay was necessary. (Hint: The modification calls for instantaneously turning off the old in-link, whereas the original said you can keep a link forwarding if it was forwarding in the old topology.)

d. In what topologies does this modification speed forwarding of packets?

Chapter 4
Source Routing Bridges

Source route bridging was at one time a proposal before the IEEE 802.1 committee, competing against transparent bridging as the standard for connecting LANs in the data link layer. When the 802.1 committee decided to adopt transparent bridging, the proponents of source routing brought the concept to the 802.5 committee to standardize as a method of interconnecting 802.5 LANs.

For some time, transparent bridges and source routing bridges evolved independently. Then there arose the need to design a means of interconnecting extended LANs attached via source routing bridges with extended LANs attached via transparent bridges. This type of bridge was known as the SR-TB (*source routing to transparent bridging*) bridge. This approach proved complex, especially when people attempted to create networks in which both types of bridges attached to the same LAN.

It was subsequently decided that all standard bridges must support transparent bridging and that source routing would be an optional additional feature in a bridge. A bridge that does source routing in addition to transparent bridging is known as an SRT (*source routing transparent*) bridge.

Why do I bother to discuss source routing in this edition? There are many reasons. It hasn't completely died out as a technology, and some people still have to understand and manage it. The source route header is included in current standards, so the 802 standards seem to think it's very much alive. But mostly it's educational to learn about a different sort of approach. Whether it's a "good" or "bad" approach, it gives insight into protocols.

In this edition, I've added a section to the end of this chapter in which I suggest methods of eliminating what I consider the two major disadvantages of source route bridging: the need for configuration and the exponential overhead of route discovery.

4.1 Pure Source Routing

The basic idea behind source routing bridges is that a packet header contains a route and that route is inserted by the source end station.

For the source end station to know a route to the destination end station, it must *discover* a route by transmitting a special kind of packet that replicates itself as it reaches route choices, sending a copy over each possible path. Each copy collects a diary of its travels so that when the copies reach the destination station, a route can be selected.

When a station discovers a route to another station, it caches the route so that it can be used for subsequent packets to the same destination.

4.1.1 The Routing Header

Ordinarily, the data link layer header of a packet on a LAN looks roughly like that shown in Figure 4.1.

destination	source	data

Figure 4.1 Contents of layer 2 header

There are other fields—for example, the SAP and/or protocol type field, the checksum, and LAN-specific fields such as length or priority—but these fields are not relevant here.

A source routing packet requires additional information in the header, contained in a field known as the RI ("routing information") field. There must be a method for distinguishing packets that have the additional fields from those that don't since it could be unfortunate if a user's data were interpreted as source routing header information.

Distinguishing between packets whose headers include routing information and those whose headers do not was accomplished by taking advantage of an "otherwise useless" bit in the preceding packet format. (If you are unfamiliar with source routing, you should stop reading for a while at this point, examine the aforementioned packet format [the one with only three fields—destination, source, and data], and figure out where that magic bit might be.)

The magic bit is the multicast bit in the source address field. The reasoning is that nobody should be transmitting a packet *from* a multicast address. (Luckily, before the source routing bridge proposal, no applications used that bit.) If that bit in the source address is 0, the assumption is that the packet is ordinary; if that bit is set, the assumption is that the information following the regular data link layer header should be interpreted as a source routing header.

Thus, a packet without the RI field looks like that shown in Figure 4.2.

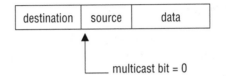

Figure 4.2 Header without the extra source routing information

A packet with the RI field looks like Figure 4.3.

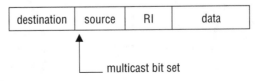

Figure 4.3 Header with the extra source routing information

The RI field contains the additional source routing information. It consists of the following fields.

- **Type** (3 bits): One of the following:

  a. *Specifically routed* (the route appears in the header)

  b. *All paths explorer* (the route gets collected as packet copies traverse the network)

  c. *Spanning tree explorer* (the route gets collected as packet copies traverse the network, just as with the all paths explorer, but the packet travels only along branches in the spanning tree)

- **Length** (5 bits): Specifies the number of bytes in the RI field

- **Direction** (1 bit): Specifies whether the route should be traversed from right to left or vice versa

- **Largest frame** (3 bits): A value representing one of a few popular packet sizes (516, 1500, 2052, 4472, 8144, 11407, 17800, 65535)

- **Route:** A sequence of 2-byte-long fields, called *route designators,* each of which consists of a 12-bit LAN number followed by a 4-bit bridge number (see Figure 4.4).

Figure 4.4 Route designator field

4.1.2 Bridge Numbers

Within an extended LAN, each LAN must be assigned a unique LAN number. To see why the 4-bit bridge number is needed, suppose that a route were designated as a sequence of LAN numbers and you have the topology shown in Figure 4.5.

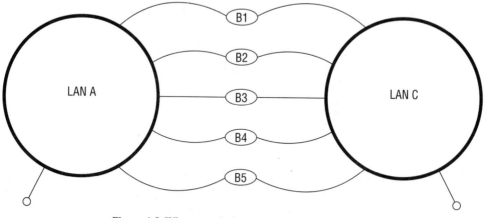

Figure 4.5 Why route designators need bridge numbers

If a packet were routed with the route "LAN A, LAN C," then five copies would arrive because each of the five bridges between LAN A and LAN C would assume that it should forward the packet. If there are multiple hops with parallel bridges, the number of copies grows exponentially with the number of hops (see Figure 4.6).

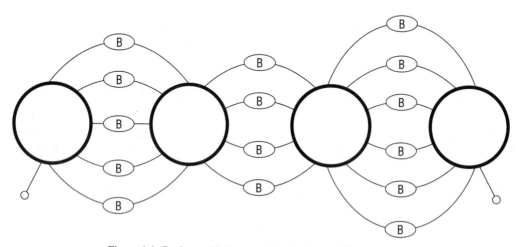

Figure 4.6 Copies multiply at each hop (without bridge numbers)

To solve this problem, each bridge is further assigned a 4-bit number to distinguish it from other bridges that connect the same pair of LANs. Each bridge must be configured with the LAN numbers for each port plus a bridge number. The assignment of the bridge number must follow the rule that no two bridges interconnecting the same two LANs are allowed to have the same bridge number.

Note: The standard calls for a single bridge number per bridge instead of a separate number with respect to each pair of LANs that the bridge connects. If bridges have many ports and if each bridge has only a single bridge number instead of one for each of its pairs of ports, then there may be topologies in which there is no way to assign bridge numbers. The "right" thing is for a bridge to have a separate number for each pair of LANs. But that can be a management nightmare, especially for a bridge that has hundreds of ports. (See homework problem 7.)

4.1.2.1 Internal LAN Number

An alternative to configuring a bridge with n ports with n^2 bridge numbers is to pretend that inside the bridge there is another LAN (see Figure 4.7).

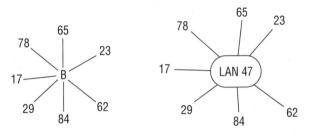

Figure 4.7 Internal LAN number

In this example, B has 7 ports. Rather than configure it with a carefully chosen bridge number for each pair of LANs that B connects, instead you can choose an unused LAN number, in this case 47, as B's *internal LAN*. The path from LAN 17 to LAN 78 looks as if it actually goes through three LANs: 17, 47, and 78. Bridge B is the only bridge that connects anything to 47, so you don't need to configure B with any bridge numbers. It can always be bridge 1 because the only pairs of LANs it connects consist of LAN 47 and one of its real LANs.

This scheme makes the paths look longer, but is really the only practical method of building a source route bridge with a lot of ports.

4.1.2.2 The Route

A route is really an alternating sequence of LAN and bridge numbers, always starting and ending with a LAN number. The fact that a LAN number and a bridge number are packaged together into a single route designator is merely an artifact of storing the information into octets. It is simpler to think of a route as (LAN, bridge, LAN, bridge, LAN, bridge, LAN). The final route designator's 4 bits indicating "bridge" are irrelevant. (They probably should be 0, but the standard has the bridges ignore that field, so a route would work no matter what the value of the final 4 bits.)

4.1.2.3 Reasons for Parallel Bridges

There are several reasons for having parallel bridges (two or more bridges interconnecting the same pair of LANs).

1. *Robustness:* If one bridge fails, another is available.

2. *Underpowered bridges:* If a single bridge cannot support full-bandwidth forwarding, it is possible that different conversations will choose different bridges so that the load might be shared between the bridges.

3. *Low-bandwidth links:* In Figure 4.8, B1 is attached to B4 with a slow point-to-point link, and B2 is attached to B3 in a like fashion. To bridge LAN 1 to LAN 2, traffic must traverse at least one of the slow links. If all traffic went via the link between B1 and B4, the amount of traffic would be limited to the capacity of the B1–B4 link. However, if some of the traffic were diverted to the B2–B3 link, the bandwidth between LAN 1 and LAN 2 would be increased.

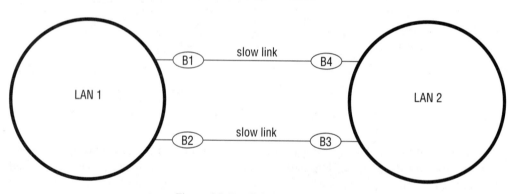

Figure 4.8 Parallel remote bridges

Note: If transparent bridges were used in Figure 4.8, the spanning tree would select one of the links (B1–B4 or B2–B3) as being in the spanning tree, and all traffic would flow on that single link, making load sharing impossible.

However, it is possible to implement an alternative topology (see Figure 4.9) to use multiple parallel low-speed links with transparent bridges. The alternative topology uses parallel links instead of parallel bridges.

In Figure 4.9, B1 and B2 use the parallel links as a logical single higher-bandwidth link. They must employ some sort of bridge-to-bridge protocol to put packets back into the correct order.

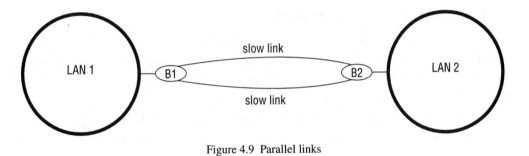

Figure 4.9 Parallel links

Parallel bridging (Figure 4.8) has an advantage over the parallel links link-sharing method (Figure 4.9) in that parallel bridging allows operation (with degraded service due to decreased bandwidth) in the event of bridge failures. However, the parallel links configuration has two advantages over parallel bridge configuration.

1. The bridges control how much traffic goes over each link, so they can equalize the loads on the multiple links. With parallel bridges, it can only be hoped that end stations happen to choose paths that distribute the load well.

2. Packets from a single large-bandwidth conversation can go over different links within the group of parallel links and can be put into the proper order afterward. With parallel bridges, all traffic due to a single large-bandwidth conversation must use the same path.

4.1.3 Bridge Algorithms

From the viewpoint of a bridge, there are four types of packets to be handled:

1. Packets without an RI field, known as *transparent packets*

2. Specifically routed packets

3. All paths explorer packets

4. Spanning tree explorer packets

This section discusses how a bridge handles each of these types of packet.

4.1.3.1 Transparent Packets

A pure source routing bridge explicitly ignores packets that do not have an RI field. To avoid confusion in case both source routing and transparent bridges attach to the same LAN, the transparent bridge standard requires that a transparent bridge ignore packets that have the RI field. So transparent packets are handled by the transparent bridges, and packets with the RI field are handled by the source routing bridges.

4.1.3.2 Specifically Routed Packets

Assume that bridge B receives a specifically routed packet on a port P1 attached to a LAN that B knows as "X." B checks the direction bit in the header and scans the route in the appropriate direction searching for LAN X. B forwards the packet onto port P2 if all of the following are true.

1. X appears in the route. Now assume that the bridge number following X is some number, B_n, and the LAN number following X is some number, Y.

2. The LAN number that B associates with port P2 is Y.

3. B's bridge number with respect to the pair of ports (P1, P2) is B_n. (Or the single bridge number that B uses for any pair of ports is B_n.)

4. Y does not appear anywhere else in the route. (Otherwise, a packet could be created that would loop. See homework problem 19.)

4.1.3.3 All Paths Explorer Packets

Assume that bridge B receives an all paths explorer packet on a port P1 attached to a LAN that B knows as "X."

An end system initially transmits the packet without any hops in the route. B must first check to see whether the packet has accumulated a route. If the RI field contains only the packet type and flags but no actual hops yet, B does the following for every port P other than port P1.

1. B initializes the route to "X, B_n, Y," where Y is the LAN number with which B has been configured for P and B_n is B's bridge number with respect to P1 and P (or simply B's bridge number if there's a bridgewide bridge number rather than a specific bridge number for each pair of ports).

2. B adjusts the value of the largest frame field to be the minimum of the value the end system placed in that field, the value configured into B as the largest frame possible on P1, and the value configured into B as the largest frame possible on P.

3. B recalculates the CRC (cyclic redundancy check) on the packet because the packet has been modified.

4. B transmits the packet onto P.

If the all paths explorer packet has been through other bridges (the *length* field is between 6 and 28 bytes, inclusive), B does the following for every port P except the port (P1) from which it received the all paths explorer packet. B forwards it onto port P (for which B has LAN number Y configured) if the following are true.

1. The final hop in the collected route is X. (If it isn't, B drops the packet and logs an error.)

2. Y does not appear anywhere in the route collected so far.

Before forwarding the packet onto port P, B does the following.

1. B adjusts the length of the RI field by adding 2 to the length field in the RI header.

2. B writes its bridge number into the bottom 4 bits of the route designator field that contains LAN number X.

3. B appends Y as the next LAN number.

4. B adjusts the largest frame field if the value configured into B as the largest frame possible on P is smaller than the value currently indicated in the largest frame field.

5. B recalculates the CRC because the packet has been modified.

If the route in the received all paths explorer packet is full, the packet is discarded.

4.1.3.4 Spanning Tree Explorer Packets

The spanning tree explorer packet has the same function as an ordinary transparent packet. It travels along the spanning tree. One obvious use of spanning tree explorer frames is in the transmission of multicast packets. Multicast packets cannot be specifically routed because they need to reach multiple destinations. It is undesirable for them to be sent via all paths explorer because multiple copies of each multicast packet would be delivered to each LAN.

Except for multicast situations, the standard has never been clear about when this type of packet is used. There are many possible scenarios for how an end system discovers a route. In one scenario, the conversation initiator sends the first packet of a conversation via spanning tree explorer and the destination replies with an all paths explorer. It is the source rather than the destination that chooses the route.

To support this type of packet, source routing bridges run the spanning tree algorithm, discussed in Chapter 3. The spanning tree that results is used only for spanning tree explorer packets.

A bridge handles a spanning tree explorer packet almost the same way as it handles an all paths explorer. There are only two differences.

1. The bridge does not check whether the output LAN already appears in the collected route.

2. The bridge accepts a spanning tree explorer packet only if it arrives on a port in the spanning tree and forwards it only to other ports in the spanning tree.

4.2　SR-TB Bridges

Assume that extended LANs are neatly partitioned into two kinds of portions: those connected solely via transparent bridges and those connected solely via source routing bridges. Devices that interconnect these portions are known as SR-TB bridges (see Figure 4.10). Although the concept seems to have died out, it is still interesting to understand how such a thing would have needed to work.

Figure 4.10　SR-TB bridge

Basically, such a device makes decisions about which packets should be forwarded and removes or adds a source routing header as appropriate (see Figure 4.11).

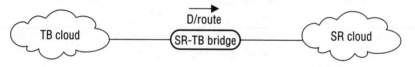

Figure 4.11　D known to be on SR side, and route to D cached

4.2.1　Packets from a TB Port

When a packet arrives from the transparent side, an SR-TB bridge must make a decision as to whether it should be forwarded (see Figure 4.12).

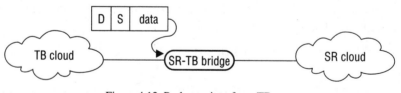

Figure 4.12　Packet arrives from TB port

If the destination is an address that the TB portion of the SR-TB bridge has learned is on the port on which the packet was received, the SR-TB bridge will not forward the packet (see Figure 4.13).

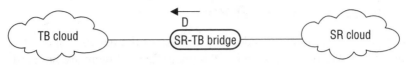

Figure 4.13 If location of D is known to be on TB side, SR-TB discards the packet

If a route to the destination address has been cached on the SR side of the bridge, the bridge will forward the packet, using the cached route, as a specifically routed packet. If no cache entry exists for the destination, the SR-TB bridge must forward the packet. It has several choices.

1. Forward the packet as an all paths explorer packet.

2. Forward the packet as a spanning tree explorer packet.

3. Cache the packet, go through a route discovery procedure, and forward the packet if or when a route is discovered to the destination.

4. Drop the packet (hope that the users will attribute the loss to congested LANs), go through some sort of route discovery procedure, and assume that the source will retransmit the packet if it was important. With luck, by the time the packet is retransmitted, a route to the destination may have been found.

The choice depends on how routes are being discovered, something that was never standardized. Two possible ways that the SR-TB bridge can learn a route to station S are

1. Record the route from received specifically routed packets from S

2. Choose routes based on received all paths explorer packets launched by S

After a route is stored, there is the problem of maintaining it. The SR-TB bridge does not necessarily know whether the packets it forwards along a route to station S actually reach that station. There can be no notification by the higher layer that a route is no longer working. Thus, there are only two possibilities for removing cache entries.

1. Remove the route to S if no packets from S (with a route identical to the stored route) are received within a specified amount of time.

2. Remove the route to S periodically, regardless of received traffic.

Neither of these schemes is particularly satisfactory. If routes are deleted quickly, the overhead increases greatly because of the need to rediscover routes frequently. Also, the more frequently routes change, the greater the probability of out-of-order packets. If the timers are very slow, a nonfunctional route will persist for a long time.

4.2.2 Packets from an SR Port

To deal with packets from the SR side, each portion of the network interconnected with transparent bridges will be assigned a LAN number. Even if there are hundreds of LANs within a TB portion, it is still assigned one LAN number and appears to the SR side as a single LAN (see Figure 4.14).

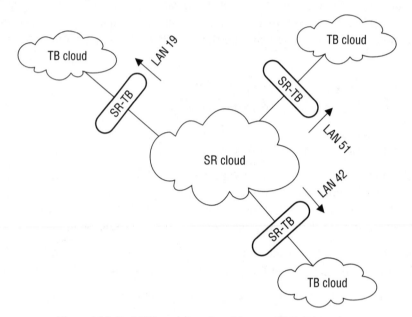

Figure 4.14 Each TB portion assigned its own SR LAN number

The SR-TB bridge can receive three types of packets:

1.   Specifically routed

2.   Spanning tree explorer

3.   All paths explorer

The first two cases are fairly straightforward. If the SR-TB bridge receives a specifically routed packet whose LAN number indicates that it should be forwarded onto the TB side, the SR-TB bridge forwards the packet, first removing the source routing header. If the SR-TB bridge receives a spanning tree explorer packet, it removes the source routing header when forwarding to ports into the TB portions of the network.

The third case is more difficult. If the SR-TB bridge receives an all paths explorer packet and if the launcher of the packet is expecting replies from the packet's target, the SR-TB bridge must respond on behalf of the target station. If the SR-TB bridge has learned that the target exists on the TB port, it can respond by adding the LAN number of the TB port and replying with a specifically routed packet along the reverse path. If the

SR-TB bridge has not learned the location of the target station, it could forward the all paths explorer packet, minus the source routing header, into the TB portion of the network and hope that the target station will transmit something in response. This would allow the SR-TB bridge to acquire a cache entry for the target, thereby enabling it to respond to a subsequent all paths explorer packet if one should arrive shortly.

The protocols for an SR-TB bridge are inherently confusing because the protocols for discovering routes have not been standardized. It is in no way obvious that all strategies interwork.

4.2.3 Loops

As Figure 4.15 indicates, it is possible for SR-TB bridges to create a loop. It is essential that one of the following strategies be employed to prevent this.

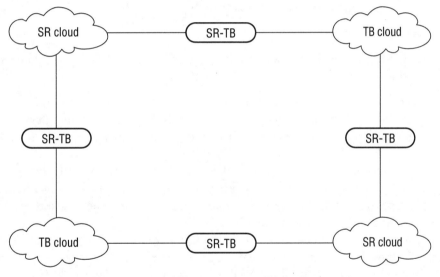

Figure 4.15 Loops of interconnected SR and TB domains

1. The entire extended LAN (SR bridges, SR-TB bridges, and TB bridges) can participate in one instance of the spanning tree. If that is done, there is the danger that the spanning tree would configure itself by breaking up a cloud. In addition, stations within the cloud would have to communicate via SR-TB bridges and clouds of different types, thereby degrading performance within the cloud.

2. The SR-TB bridges can run a separate instance of the spanning tree among only themselves. In this case, some SR-TB bridge will break the loop. The clouds will remain intact.

4.3 SRT Bridges

You can design a network so that independent sections of the network are tied together with source routing bridges and independent sections of the network are tied together with transparent bridges, and then those two types of sections are interconnected with SR-TB bridges. But this strategy proves unsatisfactory. SR-TB bridges have unsolvable problems (they function as "black holes" when their route caches have bad routes; their route finding strategy must be compatible with all possible source routing end-system implementations). And the restriction that no LAN can contain both types of bridges proved unworkable when both the transparent bridge community and the source routing community wanted to bridge to FDDI. The dramatic resolution was that the source routing proponents came to the standards body with the SRT proposal, which outlawed pure source routing bridges. Source routing was removed from the 802.5 standard and was made an optional "enhancement" to transparent bridges.

This means that there are only two standard types of bridges:

1. Transparent bridges

2. SRT bridges, which are transparent bridges that are also capable of doing source routing

However, just because pure source routing bridges were declared not to be standard doesn't make them disappear from the world. So the SRT proposal, rather than simplifying the world, meant that now there were four types of bridges: SR, TB, SR-TB, and SRT.

Once you understand transparent bridges and pure source routing bridges, SRT bridges are easy to understand. The SRT bridge handles packets having an RI field in the header exactly as a pure source routing bridge would, and it handles packets that do not have an RI field exactly as a transparent bridge would.

Customers can build networks with an arbitrary mix of the two standard types of bridges (TB and SRT). If an end system wants, for whatever reason, to employ source routing, it attempts to find a route to the destination using that approach. If that fails, it can always communicate with the destination through the spanning tree using transparent packets.

There is one potentially serious problem with an arbitrary mix of SRT and TB bridges. A station that goes to the trouble of attempting to find a route via source routing presumably does so to get a better route to the destination than the spanning tree path that it would otherwise use with transparent packets. If only some of the bridges are SRT bridges, the source routes that can be found must go through whatever SRT bridges happen to be available. Given that constraint, it is possible for the best source routing path to be vastly inferior to the spanning tree path.

4.4 End-system Algorithms

The source routing standard has always left end-system operation "open" in the sense that there are many methods an end system can use to establish and maintain routes. The rationale for not specifying a single strategy is that all the suggested strategies have their pluses and minuses. No one strategy is better than all others according to all measures.

In my opinion, although flexibility might sometimes be a good thing, in this case it would be better if the standard chose a single algorithm. Otherwise, each individual end-system implementer is forced to consider various strategies, and it is not obvious that independently chosen strategies will interwork. It is important for two source routing end systems designed by different organizations to have compatible route finding strategies.

If there is at least one strategy that works sufficiently well in all cases, it should be standardized. It doesn't matter whether some other strategy might be marginally better in certain circumstances. If no strategy works adequately for all end systems, it should cast suspicion on the viability of source routing as a bridging mechanism.

This section discusses and compares the suggested strategies. It does not definitively answer the question "How should my end system operate?" because the standards bodies have not specified end-system operation. Rather, this section raises the issues that should be considered when you design an end system capable of using source routing.

The basic idea is that an end system keeps a cache of routes for destinations with which it is currently having conversations. If no route for a particular destination is in the cache, the end system can employ a protocol to find a route or set of routes. If a route in the cache no longer works and the end system discovers this, the end system can either attempt to find another route or use one of the alternate routes it has stored for that destination.

It is important that any strategy allow an end station that is capable of source routing to communicate with an end station that uses only transparent packets. It is also important to realize that even though these two end stations are capable of communicating via source routing, if the only paths between them involve at least one transparent-only bridge, the two stations must in that case communicate with transparent packets.

4.4.1 When to Find a Route

When should an end system try to find a route to another end system? One possibility is for the end system to attempt to find a route when it needs to transmit a packet to a destination for which it has no cache entry. Assuming that only some of the bridges and end systems have implemented source routing (but that it is mandatory for all end systems and bridges to have implemented transparent bridging), there will be some destinations that can be reached only via transparent bridging. Thus, it is important that any strategy

1. Not declare a destination unreachable if source routing fails to find a route to the destination

2. Not continually (for example, on every packet transmitted to the destination)
    attempt to find a source route to a destination for which no route is cached

A natural time to attempt to find a route to a destination is when the end system wishes to
transmit a packet to that destination, the cache contains no route to that destination, and
the end system has not attempted to find a route to that destination very recently. Care
must be taken to note the failure of recent attempts to find a route to that destination. In
this way, the presence of stations reachable only via transparent bridging doesn't cause
the source to continually search for routes.

If the communication process in the end system is connection-oriented, it might be
natural to attempt to find a route every time a conversation is initiated. However, it might
also be desirable to keep a cache of routes found on previous conversations rather than
attempt to find a new route to a destination for which a route is still remembered.

If a connection is no longer working, it might be desirable to attempt to find a new
route before declaring the connection down because it is possible that the destination
itself remains reachable but the previous route to that destination is no longer working.

Now suppose that a route has been found to destination D, but a much better route
becomes available. Should an end system periodically attempt to find better routes, or
should it attempt to find a route only if the currently cached route stops working?

Suppose that an end system S is having a conversation with destination D and then
subsequently discovers a source route (or a new source route) to D. In this case, packets
from S to D can be delivered out of order because the ones transmitted on the previous
source route (or transmitted transparently and therefore routed on the spanning tree) are
traveling on a different route than the ones transmitted on the new source route. Depending on which applications are running, out-of-order packets might be a problem.

Suppose that a route is no longer working and the end system is using LLC type 1
(connectionless). There are three possible methods for making sure that the defunct route
is removed from the cache.

1. Assuming that a connection-oriented transport layer is running in the end sys-
    tem, provide an interface between the transport layer and the process P that
    maintains the route cache. This interface should allow the transport layer to alert
    P to delete the cache entry when a connection breaks or fails to come up.

2. Delete a route cache entry for destination D if no traffic from D has been
    received on that route for some time.

3. Delete a route cache entry for destination D after a specified amount of time has
    elapsed since the cache entry was originally made, regardless of use.

The first possibility is reasonable provided that

*   A connection-oriented transport layer is running

*   An interface exists between the transport layer and the process maintaining the route
    cache

This strategy will not find a better route if one exists, nor will it work if the traffic flow is one-way because the source would never know whether its packets were reaching the destination. Nor would the strategy work if the route cache is being maintained in a different node from that of the actual source. This is the case, for example, with the SR-TB bridge. That device must keep routes on behalf of all the end systems in the transparent extended LAN. Because there is no protocol from the end stations to the device to alert the device that a route is not working, the device does not know whether packets are failing to reach a particular destination.

The second strategy (deleting a cache entry if it is not periodically validated by receipt of traffic) must be used with care because the route from S to D may not be the same as the route from D to S. A route to D must not be assumed to be working based on receipt of traffic from D if the traffic to and from D uses a different route. However, it would slow the end system down if it had to check the route received against the route in the cache every time a data packet was received. Also, this strategy will not find a better route. Rather, after the end system finds a route that works, no matter how suboptimal it might be, the end system will continue using that route.

The third strategy (deleting a cache entry periodically, regardless of use) must also be employed with some care because it will cause the end system to find new routes in the middle of conversations, leading to the possibility of misordered packets. It is also difficult to select a reasonable timer value. If the value is short, the network will have a lot of overhead because of frequent route discoveries. If the value is long, a nonworking cache entry will cause traffic to a destination to "black hole" for an intolerably long time. Note that with the second strategy, a fairly short timer can be used. As long as packets for a conversation on a working route arrive faster than the cache value, the cache entry will not be deleted and will persist for the duration of the conversation.

4.4.2 How to Find a Route

It would be desirable if the protocol for finding routes could distinguish between the following scenarios, which require differing strategies as to the advisability of retrying, using the source route, or communicating transparently.

1. The destination might be down completely.

2. The destination might be up but reachable only via transparent bridging.

3. The destination might be reachable by source routing, and the source routing paths by which the destination can be reached are much better than the spanning tree path.

4. The destination might be reachable by source routing, but the source routing paths by which the destination can be reached are much worse than the spanning tree path.

Note that when source routing was an alternative to transparent bridging rather than an optional feature, a reasonable strategy was for an end system to first attempt to establish communication transparently (which would work if both stations were on the same LAN) and attempt to find a source route only if that failed. After transparent bridging became mandatory, this same strategy would continue to work, but it would never attempt to find a source route (unless the destination was down or completely unreachable) because a destination that was reachable would always be reachable transparently.

4.4.2.1 Route Finding Strategy 1

The source sends an all paths explorer packet to the destination. The destination receives multiple copies of the explorer packet and returns all these copies to the source as specifically routed packets, routed via the collected route (with the direction bit flipped). The destination does not store a route, nor does it modify its own route cache if it already has a route to the source. This strategy allows the source to choose the route (see Figure 4.16).

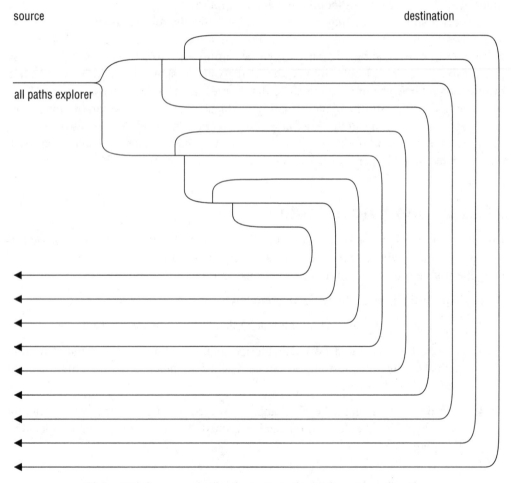

Figure 4.16 Source sends all paths explorer, destination returns all copies

This scheme has its disadvantages. If a single all paths explorer packet generates X packets, this strategy generates $2X$ packets because every copy of the all paths explorer that reaches the destination results in a packet from the destination to the source. Also, if the source is a client and the destination is a server with multiple clients, the many interrupts at the server for each client can be a performance problem.

There are several reasons that this scheme might fail to find a route: The destination might be down or reachable only via transparent packets, or the all paths explorer packet(s) and/or replies might have gotten lost in a congested network. The source must choose whether to try again with another all paths explorer, try to reach the destination with a transparent packet, or give up.

4.4.2.2 Route Finding Strategy 2

Strategy 2 is the same as strategy 1 except that the source first sends a special *need route* packet, transparently, to the destination and waits until it receives a *need route response* from the destination before launching the all paths explorer.

The advantage of this scheme over scheme 1 is that it enables the source to find out whether the destination is actually up before burdening the network with the overhead of an all paths explorer.

The paper submitted as a contribution to 802.1 that made this recommendation suggested using a special packet but left it up to end-system implementers to independently invent compatible need route packets. This is a clear example of a case in which the standard must specify the exact details of end-station operation to enable end stations from different vendors to interoperate. Allowing each implementation the flexibility to define its own special packets does not work.

4.4.2.3 Route Find Strategy 3

In this strategy (see Figure 4.17), the source S sends a special need route packet, transparently, to the destination D. D responds with an all paths explorer packet. S chooses a route.

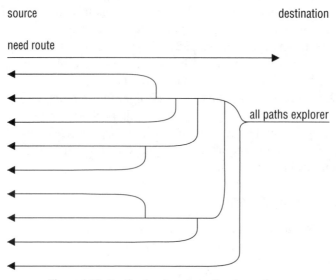

source   destination

need route

all paths explorer

Figure 4.17 Destination launches all paths explorer

An advantage of this strategy over the first strategy is that it generates only half as much traffic. Like strategy 1, it allows the source to choose the route.

A disadvantage of this scheme is that it fails to find a route if the need route packet is launched during a time when the spanning tree is reconfiguring. It also fails to distinguish between a destination's being down and a destination's being reachable but only via transparent packets.

4.4.2.4 Route Finding Strategy 4

The fourth strategy is the same as strategy 3, but the destination should reply to a received need route packet with two packets:

1. An all paths explorer packet

2. A transparent need route reply

This strategy allows the source to discover the case in which the destination is reachable but not via source routing.

This strategy requires that the destination transmit two packets as a result of receiving a single packet. This, in turn, requires that both source and destination implement compatible need route reply packets.

4.4.2.5 Route Finding Strategy 5

The source transmits an all paths explorer packet. The destination chooses a route and replies with a single specifically routed packet using that chosen route. The source stores the route from the received specifically routed packet (see Figure 4.18).

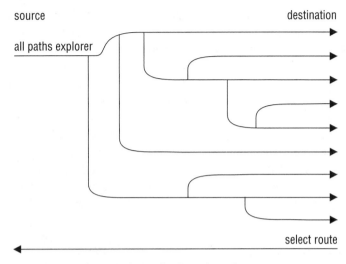

Figure 4.18 Destination selects the route

This scheme requires stations to store routes based on received specifically routed packets. It also burdens the destination with the task of selecting a route. It generates half as much traffic as strategy 1.

4.4.2.6 Route Finding Strategy 6

Strategy 6 is the simplest one possible (and is incidentally what I recommend). Always use transparent bridging. Do not maintain a route cache. This strategy offers the advantages of being simple, always working, and creating no overhead in the network due to route discovery. Its disadvantage is that if there exists a better source route to a particular destination, the source will not attempt to find it. However, I believe it is impossible for a station to determine whether the route discovered through source routing is better or worse than the route used by the spanning tree. Another disadvantage of using only transparent bridging is that the end station is not informed of the maximum packet size that can be used on the route to the destination, as it is with source routing. A third disadvantage is that data traffic cannot be spread over multiple paths, but all traffic instead traverses the spanning tree. However, I believe that these areas in which source routing offers advantages over transparent bridging do not warrant its increased complexity for the end stations or the bandwidth overhead required for discovering routes.

4.4.3 Route Discovery by the Destination

The various strategies presented in the preceding section do not specify how the destination finds a route. In some of the schemes, the destination sees the possible routes and could select and store one. But if it chooses a different path to reach the source than the source chose to get to the destination, then neither end system can be reassured, based on receiving packets from the other end system, that its cached route is correct.

Alternatively, the destination could wait until it has traffic to send to the source—at which point, it would reverse roles and obtain a route as the source. This scheme also results in asymmetric routes, and it generates a lot of traffic because both the source and the destination eventually issue all paths explorer packets.

Another possibility is for the destination to learn a route from received specifically routed packets. The advantage of this approach is that routes will be symmetric. A disadvantage is that the route discovery process must examine all incoming data packets. If the route cache already contains a route to end system S and a packet is received from S with a route that differs from the one in the route cache, the destination can either overwrite the cache entry or keep it.

4.4.4 Route Selection

Suppose that an end station receives multiple copies of an all paths explorer packet. What criteria should the station use to select a route? Again, the standard leaves it up to the end-station implementer. Some possibilities are as follows.

1. Select the first packet received, on the theory that it traveled on the fastest path.

2. Select the one that indicates a path with the maximum packet size.

3. Select the one with the fewest hops.

4. Select some combination of the preceding. For example, select the packet that arrived first, from among the ones with at least a certain packet size; or select the one that has the fewest hops, from among the ones that arrived within a certain amount of time.

5. Select the most recently received route. (Note: This is a bad idea. Why? See homework problem 4.)

4.5 Source Routing versus Transparent Bridging

Suppose that you were on a standards body evaluating the technical merits of source routing versus transparent bridging or that you were making a decision as to which scheme to adopt in your own network. What sorts of criteria could be used?

4.5.1 Bandwidth Overhead

The number of paths in a network is exponential. Theoretically, an all paths explorer packet will generate a copy of itself for each path through the network. Thus, theoretically, the number of copies of one all paths explorer packet that will be generated is exponential. Exponential grows very fast, especially with rich connectivity.

Basically, every time there is a choice (if many bridges are on a LAN or a bridge has many ports), the number of packets is multiplied by the number of choices. The maximum route length is 14 route designators, but there are actually 26 choice points in a path. (Each route designator contains both a LAN number and a bridge number, and that is why there are about twice as many choice points as route designators. The reason there are not 28 choice points in a route is that the first item is the source's LAN, which is fixed. The last item is the bridge portion of the final route designator, which is blank.) When an all paths explorer packet is transmitted on a LAN, all the bridges on that LAN receive a copy. Each bridge then generates a copy of its copy for each additional port to which the bridge attaches.

The number of packets spawned as a result of a single endnode's attempt to start a conversation with a single other endnode is on the order of the average number of bridges on each LAN to the 13th power multiplied by the average number of ports (more than two) on each bridge raised to the 13th power. Even if the destination can be reached with a route of length 2, after an all paths explorer packet is launched there is no way to stop it until it has spawned all its copies.

In my opinion, this exponential overhead, invoked every time any endnode wishes to communicate with any other endnode, is a fatal flaw of source routing. In small topologies that are simply trees, with bridges that have only two ports, the exponential factor might not be very serious. But people build transparent bridges with hundreds of ports, so it might not be unreasonable to imagine them building source route bridges with hundreds of ports. If there were two such bridges in a network, the proliferation of all paths explorer packets would be very serious.

Source routing bridges also use extra bandwidth because the headers must be larger, but that's hardly worth mentioning given the exponential proliferation of explorer packets.

Transparent bridges do not make optimal use of bandwidth either; they waste bandwidth by using only a subset of the topology, by not using optimal routes, and by forwarding packets needlessly before cache entries are established. But their bandwidth waste is not nearly as spectacular as with source routing.

4.5.2 Ease of Configuration

Transparent bridges are truly plug and play. Although there are plenty of parameters a network manager can use to fine-tune performance in a specific situation, there is no need to modify any parameters unless desired.

In contrast, source routing requires that every LAN be assigned a number and that every bridge be configured both with the LAN number for each of its ports and with a

4-bit bridge number for each pair of LANs it connects (although establishing restrictions on the topologies might enable a bridge to have only a single 4-bit number that would be unique for each pair of LANs it connects). Misconfiguration can cause problems such as loops or severe duplication of data packets.

4.5.3 Universality

Source routing requires support in the endnodes. Thus, any endnodes without source routing would be unable to have their packets routed through an (SR-only) source routing bridge. Such stations would still be able to communicate with other stations on their local LAN but could not communicate with any stations on remote LANs.

On the other hand, transparent bridges are not completely transparent, especially when used to connect different types of LANs. The packet size problem can be solved if the network manager configures all the endnodes to use the smallest maximum packet size allowed by any of the LANs. Alternatively, some sort of clever procedure in the end stations can be used to determine the best packet size. One such procedure, described in Section 3.6.3, employs the priority field on FDDI to signal that somewhere along the path between the source and the destination, the packet is bridged through an 802.3 LAN. Although admittedly such a procedure is an inelegant hack, it works, is useful, and is deployed in some FDDI stations to enable them to use large packet sizes when possible.

The source routing protocol does a fair job of solving the packet size problem because when a route is discovered, the maximum packet size on the path is also discovered. It is not necessarily easy to use the information about the maximum packet size on a route. It requires that the low-layer source routing process be able to share this information with the transport layer process, which makes decisions about packet sizes. If a source route changes in the middle of a transport connection, many end station implementations would not be able to change the packet size.

4.5.4 Cost and Performance of Bridges

It was originally asserted that source routing bridges would be cheaper and simpler and would offer higher performance than transparent bridges. Even if this were true, the number of endnodes in a network is vastly larger than the number of bridges, so an increase in a bridge's cost in order to ensure its adequate performance would likely be negligible compared with the cost of the network as a whole. Because source routing requires more complicated endnodes, it might increase the cost of the endnodes. When the additional endnode cost is multiplied by the number of endnodes, the resulting figure would probably far outweigh any increase in the cost of the bridge.

However, implementations of transparent bridges proved that transparent bridges with adequate performance could be built at a reasonable cost. People have stopped arguing that transparent bridges would be more expensive or slower.

4.6 Ideas for Improving Source Route Bridging

There are two disadvantages to source route bridging. One is the need for configuration, and the other is the exponential overhead of route discovery. Here are my suggestions for fixing those problems. Even if it's too late to bother implementing something like this, I think it's still an interesting concept. The strategy in Section 4.6.1 is a good general-purpose solution that would apply to other problems.

4.6.1 Autoconfiguration with Source Route Bridging

The items that must be configured are the LAN numbers as well as the parallel bridge numbers to differentiate among bridges between the same pair of LANs. We want one computer to take responsibility for assigning numbers. We want a new one elected if that one goes down. We want to preserve all the numbers handed out by the deceased number-hander-outer. Here's how to do it.

- Agree on who will hand out numbers. The spanning tree algorithm does the work for us of always having a single computer that everyone agrees on, and it elects a new one if the old one dies. That is the spanning tree root bridge.

- Agree on who will ask for a number for the LAN. Again, the spanning tree algorithm makes this easy. The logical choice is the designated bridge on that LAN.

- Make sure bridges can communicate with the root. It seems like a reasonable assumption that the root ID in the spanning tree configuration message is the root's MAC address. If for some reason the root wants to use a different ID than its MAC address, a new field *MAC address of root bridge* could be added to the spanning tree configuration message.

- Obtain a number for the LAN by having the designated bridge request a number from the root bridge. The request should specify the ID of the bridge making the request and the port number on that bridge. The port number is important because if a bridge is designated on more than one LAN, the root must assign separate LAN numbers to each of those LANs.

- Make sure that all bridges on the LAN know the LAN number. Because the designated bridge already periodically sends a configuration message, that would be a logical place to include the added field *LAN number.* Note that even without autoconfiguration, it would be useful to include that field to ensure that the LAN hasn't been misconfigured (the bridges have not all been configured with the same LAN number for that LAN). If it is too politically difficult to add a field to the configuration message, the designated bridge could periodically transmit a new message type on the LAN, which would tell the other bridges the LAN number.

- Have the root bridge keep a table of <ID,port,LAN number> mappings. Then the LAN number can be preserved if the designated bridge crashes and forgets the LAN number. (This would be a problem because endnode route caches are disrupted if LAN numbers change.)

- Have the designated bridge periodically reregister the assigned LAN number. This is important for two reasons. It allows the number to be recycled if it is no longer in use, and it ensures that the LAN number will not be given to another bridge in case the root bridge crashed and forgot the mapping or in case a new root bridge is elected. (The new root will not know the LAN mappings.)

- Have a newly elected root bridge wait for reregistrations to arrive before assigning LAN numbers. This is to prevent it from assigning a number already assigned to a LAN.

- Have a newly elected designated bridge register the old LAN number, including the ID and port number of the previous designated bridge. This allows that LAN to keep its old number because the root bridge will assume it is assigned to the previous designated bridge.

- If a bridge does not know of a previously assigned LAN number, have the root check its table and reassign the old number, if known. If the designated bridge crashed, forgot the number, and came back up, the root has a good chance of remembering the old number and assigning the same number again.

In most cases this scheme does exactly the right thing. The LAN number will remain constant even if the root bridge changes; or if the designated bridge changes, all bridges on a LAN will agree about the LAN number, and there will be no duplicate LAN numbers assigned in the network. There is one case in which this fails: if there is only a single bridge on the LAN, and it crashes, and then another bridge is brought up, there is no easy way to recognize that it is the same LAN as before and therefore it will get assigned a new number. Endnodes' source routes will be affected. But probably all the routes would have failed and been discarded anyway during the time when there was no bridge on the LAN.

The same mechanisms should work for autoconfiguration of parallel bridge numbers. The root bridge keeps the mapping of <LAN,LAN,ID,parallel bridge number>, which tells it which bridge ID has been assigned a particular parallel bridge number between a pair of LANs. Again, bridges should periodically reregister to keep the mapping fresh, and a bridge that crashed and forgot the old number is likely to get assigned the same number.

4.6.2 Fixing the Exponential Overhead

We want to allow routes used by data traffic to be good paths (to preserve the advantage that source routing can claim over transparent bridges, which confine routes to the spanning tree). We want a solution that will require no changes to stations that already use source route bridging. We must, however, modify all the bridges. For example, the bridges will need to run a link state routing protocol so that they can calculate optimal paths from each LAN to themselves and handle all paths explorer packets differently.

I'd propose the following.

- Have each bridge compute good paths between itself and each LAN. This can be done with a link state algorithm (see Section 12.2). The link state information in each link state packet includes the ID of the bridge generating the LSP, the LAN numbers that the bridge connects to, and the bridge's parallel bridge number between each pair of those LANs. Or you can avoid the parallel bridge numbers by including an internal LAN number (see Section 4.1.2.1).

- Have bridges handle all paths explorer packets differently. When a source transmits an all paths explorer, the route inside will be empty. Bridges other than the designated bridge should ignore all paths explorer packets, that is, they shouldn't forward them. The designated bridge should do the following.

  - Create a new packet, called the *optimal path finder* (OPF) packet, containing as data the source's MAC address, source LAN number, and original destination MAC address. The header of the OPF packet should indicate that it is a spanning tree explorer packet (rather than an all paths explorer) and should have a special destination multicast address to be processed by all the bridges.

  - Each bridge B will receive the OPF packet (once, via the magic of the spanning tree algorithm). In addition to forwarding the OPF on spanning tree ports, for each LAN L for which B is designated, B creates an all paths explorer into which B inserts the optimal path from the source LAN to L and forwards it onto L. To endnodes, this packet will look like a normal all paths explorer packet.

    Note that although the OPF arrived on the spanning tree, the path B computes from the source LAN to this LAN is not constrained to be the spanning tree path. It is instead the best path as computed by the link state routing algorithm.

  - Bridges that see an all paths explorer that is not empty must not forward the packet.

The result is that when S transmits an all paths explorer packet, a single filled-in explorer packet with a good path from the source LAN to that LAN will appear on each LAN.

Homework

1. Suppose that source routing were not allowed to use the multicast bit in the source address to flag that the LAN header contains the routing information field. What other encoding could have been used to signal that the header contains the extra field? The encoding must ensure that packets emitted by stations that have not implemented source routing will not accidentally get parsed as if they contained the RI field.

2. Assuming that the maximum packet lifetime is X seconds in an extended LAN, what strategy can an end system use to ensure that packets to a destination will not arrive out of order, even if in the middle of a conversation, the source changes source routes or switches from using transparent packets to using a source route?

3. How can it be possible for a destination to be reachable by source routing but for the source routing path to be much worse than the spanning tree path?

4. An end station that receives an all paths explorer packet giving a route from D could routinely overwrite the existing cache entry for D with the newly received route. Why is that a bad strategy?

5. Is it a good idea or bad idea for SRT bridges to learn the location of the source address, and forward based on the learned location of the destination address, in each of the following cases?

   a. Spanning tree explorer packets

   b. Specifically routed packets

   c. All paths explorer packets

6. How many copies of a spanning tree explorer packet (approximately) would arrive on a typical LAN in a topology in which every LAN had k bridges attached and every bridge had j ports? How many copies would arrive on the LAN from which the source station launched the packet?

   Now answer the preceding questions for an all paths explorer packet.

   Now assume that $k = 4$ and $j = 3$. What is the actual number of packets?

7. Can a bridge have only a single parallel bridge number? Assume the following topology.

   a. Between any pair of LANs, there are never more than 15 bridges.

   b. No bridge has more than one port onto the same LAN.

   Is it always possible to assign each bridge a single 4-bit parallel bridge number so that no two bridges between the same pair of LANs are ever assigned the same parallel bridge number? Prove that a single parallel bridge number per bridge will suffice even if the bridge connects to multiple LANs;

or show a topology in which (even though there are never more than 15 bridges between any two LANs) it is impossible to assign a single number per bridge without having multiple bridges between the same pair of LANs assigned identical numbers.

What happens if a bridge is allowed to have multiple ports on a LAN?

Assuming that the answer to the preceding questions is that it's not possible in all topologies to get by with a single bridge number, suppose that your job were to document which topologies will work with a single bridge number and also to explain how to assign bridge numbers. What would you do?

8. What problems can arise if two LANs are given the same LAN number?

9. What problems can arise if two bridges between the same pair of LANs are given the same bridge number?

10. What problems can arise if bridges don't agree about the LAN number? (For example, some bridges on a particular LAN think its LAN number is X, whereas others think it is Y.)

11. Bridges check whether the output LAN already appears in the collected route before forwarding an all paths explorer. Is it necessary for bridges to also check for duplicate LAN numbers when forwarding specifically routed packets?

12. Write code in your favorite language to handle forwarding of a specifically routed packet (make sure to take into account the direction bit and checking that the output LAN does not appear multiple times). Compare the processing required to route a specifically routed packet with that required to route a transparent packet (taking into account the need to efficiently search a station learning cache of 8,000 or so station addresses).

13. What happens if an end system launches a specifically routed packet with extra hops following the destination LAN and/or extra hops preceding the source LAN?

14. What procedure can a bridge B follow to determine whether there is another bridge between the same pair of LANs as B whose bridge number is identical to B's? If B has n ports, how many times would B need to carry out this procedure?

15. In a network in which only some of the bridges support the source routing option (but all the bridges support transparent bridging), compare the following two end-system strategies.

   a. The end system sends every packet transparently.

   b. The end system sends every packet using spanning tree explorer packets.

   Consider such factors as destination reachability and bridge forwarding speed.

16. Suppose that a network is interconnected with some SRT bridges and some TB bridges. Suppose, too, that stations A and B are both capable of using source routing and that they have successfully found a source route connecting them. As pointed out earlier in the chapter, it is possible for the source route to be much worse than the spanning tree path. Is there any way the stations can compare the spanning tree path with the source route they found? (Hint: Is the use of spanning tree explorer packets guaranteed to tell them the spanning tree path?)

17. Design several plausible end-system strategies for operation in a network with a mix of TB and SRT bridges and a mix of transparent and source-routing-capable end stations. Can you design two plausible end-station schemes so that an end station using one scheme will fail to establish communication with an end station using a different scheme?

18. In the topology in Figure 4.19, there are two extended LANs interconnected with pure source routing bridges and an extended LAN interconnected with transparent bridges. An SR-TB bridge connects the SR clouds to the TB cloud.

    Can the LAN numbers assigned to the LANs in the SR cloud on the left overlap with the LAN numbers assigned to the LANs in the SR cloud on the right?

Figure 4.19 Topology for problem 18

19. Why is step 4 in Section 4.1.3.2 necessary?

20. This is a research problem. What is the actual behavior of source routing in a richly connected topology? The potential number of packets is sufficiently astronomical that the vast majority will get lost. If the first few packets got through and the remainder got lost, the performance would not be particularly bad; in general, the first few will find better routes than later copies. However, when the network capacity is exceeded and most copies of an all paths explorer packet are being lost, data traffic and initial copies of all paths explorer packets for other station pairs will also be lost in the congestion.

21. In the scheme described in Section 4.6.1—for autoconfiguration of source route bridging—how much overhead is added for registration of LAN numbers? How much overhead is added for registration of parallel bridge numbers? Suggest a way of making parallel bridge number assignment reasonably efficient if a bridge has, say, hundreds of ports.

22. In the scheme described in Section 4.6.2, why does the first bridge send the packet as a spanning tree explorer rather than simply sending it to the destination's LAN?

Chapter 5
Hubs, Switches, Virtual LANs, and Fast Ethernet

I originally resisted adopting the term *switch*. Unlike *thing*, *switch* sounds like a word you'd apply to a well-defined concept, so it makes people assume that there is a crisp definition that everyone else knows. I thought the world was already confusing enough with the terms *bridge* and *router*. Unfortunately, people coined the word *switch* assuming they were inventing a new concept, somehow different from a bridge or a router. And there were various independent product concepts named switches. As "switch" vendors expanded the capabilities of their products, the products wound up being functionally the same as bridges and routers, usually a hybrid or superset. One cynical (and ungrammatical) definition I use for *switch* is "a marketing term that means *fast*." Almost all products these days are some hybrid or superset of bridges and routers. So maybe it's right for the industry to settle on a new word, *switch*, as a more generic term for a box that moves data.

In this chapter I talk about the various kinds of boxes that have evolved from the original repeaters, bridges, and routers.

5.1 Hubs

The Ethernet was originally conceived as a bus topology (a long wire with taps for plugging things in every so often). It turned out that this approach was often not the most convenient way of wiring a building. Also, certain types of faults would bring down the whole LAN.

A more convenient wiring strategy was a star topology, especially because buildings were already wired that way for telephones. To make things even more convenient, a variant of Ethernet was standardized that operated over ordinary telephone wire (twisted pair). The center of the star was called the *hub* (see Figure 5.1). It connected the segments (the spokes) together by acting as a repeater.

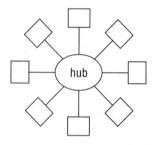

Figure 5.1 A star topology connected with a hub

Although the hub might look alarmingly like a single point of failure, it is less likely to fail than a bus because it can be kept locked in a safe place away from users who abuse hardware by spilling coffee or pulling wires out at random. And the bus really had many single points of failure. Removing the terminating resistor or having a single station babbling could bring down the whole LAN.

So we start with a hub, which is really just a multiport repeater. This means that when any station transmits, the hub simply acts as a repeater to every other link, forwarding the data one bit at a time. If two stations attempt to transmit at about the same time, there would be a collision, just as if it were all one long bus.

Sometimes a LAN built this way (with a hub and lots of point-to-point links as the spokes) is referred to as a *switched LAN*. But more commonly, especially today, the term *switched LAN* refers to the layer 2 switching described in Section 5.1.2. To unambiguously distinguish the cases, it would be more precise to call the multiport repeater product a "layer 1 switched LAN."

5.1.1 The Learning Hub and Security

In the classical (bus topology) Ethernet, everyone receives all transmissions whether or not they are the specified destination. Your computer's NIC (network interface card) does the software a favor by filtering packets that have destination addresses different from those that the software told the NIC it wants to receive.

With a star topology it is possible to have the hub be slightly more intelligent and forward unicast packets only to the port on which the specified recipient resides. Unfortunately, given that the hub is forwarding bits as soon as they are received, the hub will have already forwarded part of the packet (at least the destination address) before the hub can decide that the packet should not be forwarded on a particular port. One strategy might be to simply stop repeating the packet onto a port once the hub decided the packet didn't belong on that port. The station A on that port would receive the initial fragment of the packet and then silence. But that strategy would cause A to think that the LAN was idle during the remainder of the packet, and A might decide to transmit at that time, causing a collision. So instead, vendors typically have the hub pretend that there was a collision on all ports except the one on which the destination resides. The hub transmits the collision signal on those ports while transmitting the actual packet on the port on which the destination resides.

This is marketed as a security feature because the hub prevents stations on that hub from snooping on packets for other stations.

How does the hub know which stations are on which ports? It can learn, based on source addresses, just as a bridge can. When the destination address is unknown, however, the hub should forward onto all the ports (except the one it is receiving the packet from, of course). It might be tempting to assume that if station A is on port P, A is the only station on port P, and that a packet with destination C need not be transmitted on port P because that's A's port. Even if C's location were unknown, it couldn't reside on P because that's A's port. This assumption would be a mistake because a hub can be hooked into another hub so that stations A, C, and X would all appear to hub H1 to reside on port P (see Figure 5.2).

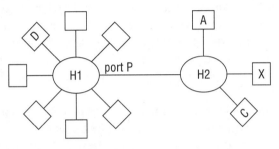

Figure 5.2 Multiple stations appear to H1 to reside on port P

Note that repeaters do not run the spanning tree algorithm. (Why would it be hard? See homework problem 5.) Therefore, you must take care when hooking hubs into other hubs. Things will not work (you'll get continuous collisions) if you plug hubs together into loops.

5.1.2 Store-and-Forward and Spanning Tree

Another enhancement to the hub is to note that if the hub stores the packet before forwarding it, there are several advantages.

- The hub can make intelligent decisions about where to forward the packet. Instead of forwarding a packet (or a collision signal) onto all ports, when the hub has learned that the destination resides on port p, it can forward the packet only onto port p.

- Collisions are no longer an issue. We don't have to worry about maximum distance or minimum packet size. (CSMA/CD requires a maximum distance and minimum packet size in order to detect collisions.)

- Ports can be different speeds. If the packet is stored before being forwarded, A and B can communicate even if A's port is 10 Mb/sec and B's is 100 Mb/sec.

- Aggregate bandwith is not limited by the port speeds. Assuming that H2 has already learned the locations of stations A, C, X, and D (see Figure 5.2), if A and C simultaneously transmit packets for destination X, hub H2 will forward the packets sequentially to X. However, if A is transmitting to X and C is transmitting to D, then H2 can simultaneously forward the packets onto the ports for which it has learned the locations of X and D, and both the A-X and C-D conversations can use full bandwidth.

Note that this is exactly the reasoning behind inventing a bridge rather than a repeater, and what we're doing is changing the hub from an n-port repeater into an n-port bridge. Often these store-and-forward n-port hubs are called *layer 2 switches*.

You might assume that delay is an issue because a layer 2 switch must store the entire packet before it forwards it, but it is possible to do what is called *cut-through* forwarding. This means that the layer 2 switch can forward as soon as it can make a fowarding decision, which is sometime after all the bits of the destination address are received (provided the port onto which it would like to forward is available). Cut-through forwarding is possible, but tricky, if the input port and output port are different speeds. (See homework problem 4.)

So now we've reinvented the simple learning bridge (see Section 3.2). All that's left is to note that because switches can be plugged in to switches, it is possible to form loops. Loops with bridges (even if the marketeers have renamed them "switches") are bad. So we need the spanning tree algorithm. At this point the so-called *layer 2 switches* really are just bridges. They are variously called *switches*, *layer 2 switches*, or *smart hubs*. When I try to pin people down about what's different about what they call a switch versus what they call a bridge I get various answers.

- "A switch has *n* ports, whereas a bridge has 2 ports." (Perhaps the first products tended to have limited numbers of ports, but there is nothing in the bridge concept that calls for limited numbers of ports.)

- "A switch is done in hardware and is fast, whereas a bridge is slow." (There were certainly fast bridges before anyone thought of calling them switches, and *fast* is a relative term.)

- "Ports on a switch are point-to-point links connecting to a single node, whereas a port on a bridge is an entire LAN." This may have been true for awhile, until people built LANs out of switches, and then plugging a switch in to another switch's port really is equivalent to having an entire LAN on that switch's port rather than a single station. Moreover, many switch vendors provide the capability of attaching to all types of link technologies, including token rings and buses.

I hate to spoil the suspense, but *layer 3 switches* are going to turn out to be just routers.

5.1.3 Mixing Layer 1 and 2 Switches

So let's call a multiport repeater a *layer 1 switch*, and a bridge a *layer 2 switch*. Some switches do both layer 1 and layer 2 switching. This means that on some ports they act as a repeater and on others they act as a bridge. This is similar to taking two LANs and bridging them together. Someone might want to do this for packaging convenience. In a *modular* switch, each line card has ports connected to it. Ports on the same line card are glued together at layer 1, whereas ports from different cards are bridged. The advantage of doing layer 1 switching within a card is that intracard packets do not need to use precious backplane bandwidth. If indeed stations can be positioned so that a lot of the traffic is between ports on a card, it allows a large aggregate bandwidth utilization. (This is true when backplane bandwidth is a bottleneck because the conversations that can be layer-1 switched are handled locally on the card and don't use backplane bandwidth.)

Of course, there's no reason that the intracard traffic can't also be store-and-forward and still avoid use of the backplane, but it would require fancier and more expensive hardware on the card to buffer packets.

The set of ports that are layer-1 switched are sometimes referred to as a *collision domain*. This means that stations on ports in the same collision domain will create a collision if they transmit at the same time, whereas this is not true of stations in different collision domains.

The total set of ports connected via layer 1 or layer 2 is sometimes referred to as a *broadcast domain* (see Figure 5.3). This means that layer 3 sees the entire collection as a single LAN. It's called a broadcast domain because if layer 3 transmits a broadcast packet, such as an ARP packet (see Section 11.2.2), the packet will be delivered to all ports in the broadcast domain.

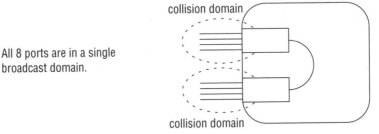

All 8 ports are in a single broadcast domain.

Figure 5.3 Two collision domains, one broadcast domain

5.1.4 Products versus Standards, Layer 1 versus Layer 2

Having the switch be layer 2 (store-and-forward) is clearly better than layer 1 (repeater) because it allows higher aggregate bandwidth and avoids the complexity caused by collisions. Worrying about collisions requires making minimum packet sizes or restricting the physical size. Also, if the switch is layer 2 the ports can be different speeds (for example, some ports can be 10 Mb/sec and others 100 Mb/sec). With a layer 1 switch all the ports must be the same speed. (See homework problem 3.)

Originally layer 2 forwarding was much more expensive than layer 1 forwarding (for example, about $1,000 per port instead of $300 per port), but switch manufacturers eventually figured out how to reduce the cost, making layer 2 forwarding comparable to layer 1 forwarding except at the very low end. So very few switches today are layer 1 rather than layer 2, especially for the higher-speed LANs (100 Mb/sec and gigabit).

But the 802 standards assume layer 1 forwarding. Why would that be? The reason is that the IEEE 802.3 committee wants to work within its charter of doing only CSMA/CD, and the feeling is that if the hub were to do store-and-forward it would really be a bridge and no longer in 802.3's charter. This is unfortunate because the 802.3 committee is therefore generating lengthy documents that are not what vendors should be building.

5.2 Faster LANs

The Ethernet protocol is designed so that stations can detect collisions. With the 10 Mb/sec speed (and original bus topology), a minimum legal packet size and a maximum legal cable length ensures that a station at one end knows that it has collided with a station at the other end.

So how can we make Ethernet faster? If we sped things up by a factor of 10, we could do one of the following:

*   Make the minimum legal packet size 10 times as large.

*   Make the maximum legal length one-tenth as big.

*   Use a mix of these first two.

*   Not worry about detecting collisions—that is, let collisions cause lost packets. Let some higher layer worry about it.

*   Have the switch be store-and-forward so that collisions do not occur.

In the 802.3 standard for 100 Mb/sec Ethernet, the maximum length was decreased by a factor of 10 (because the committee was assuming layer 1 forwarding). But this restriction is not necessary in products that are doing layer 2 fowarding.

In the gigabit Ethernet standard, to get an extra factor of 10 in speed the committee decided to extend packets to 512 bytes. That means a 64-byte packet is transmitted followed immediately by 448 bytes of *carrier extension* (so the total is 512 bytes). Note that this is not the same as requiring a minimum packet size of 512 bytes and creating a padded packet of size 512 bytes from a smaller packet (see Figure 5.4). In the gigabit standard, a

64-byte extended packet is still 64 bytes from the point of view of the layer above the MAC layer. If a bridge were to forward the packet onto a LAN other than gigabit Ethernet, the packet would be 64 bytes.

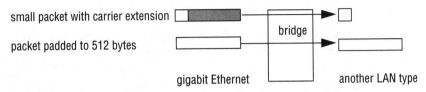

Figure 5.4 Carrier extension versus padded packet

If there are multiple little packets to transmit, they can be transmitted back to back except that the first packet must still be extended to 512 bytes (see Figure 5.5) to avoid creation of duplicate packets. If instead several packets were combined in the first 512 bytes and there was a collision, the destination might have received the first few packets correctly, but the transmitter would not be able to tell which packets in the first 512 bytes were successfully received. The transmitter would have to retransmit all of them, causing duplicates. After the transmitter has been transmitting for 512 bytes, all stations will have seen that the wire is busy, so packets after the initial 512 bytes will not experience collisions.

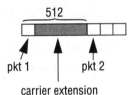

Figure 5.5 Carrier extension required so only one packet within first 512 bytes

Although the standard assumes that the hub is a repeater (layer 1 switch), in most products the hub is a bridge (layer 2 switch). In that case there is no need for the packet to be extended because there are no collisions.

Although the link between the hub and the station is always two links—one for each direction—the link pair can be treated either as *full duplex* (meaning that it is legal to be sending and receiving simultaneously) or *half duplex* (meaning that receiving while sending is treated as a collision). When the hub is a repeater, half duplex mode allows stations to react to collisions. If the link is full duplex, there is no need to do carrier extension.

When a link comes up there is a negotiation phase to determine the link speed and type of the link (full duplex or half duplex).

Although collisions are not an issue when doing layer 2 forwarding, the switch can still experience congestion. Here are two examples.

- The source's port might have a higher speed than the destination's port.

- Two sources might be transmitting at full speed to a single destination port.

In these cases the switch will run out of buffers because it cannot forward packets as quickly as it is receiving them. If a station is connected with a half duplex link, the switch can slow it down by using *backpressure*, which is done by sending collision signals on the reverse direction link. For full duplex operation the committee standardized (in 802.3x) a *pause frame*, in which the hub explicitly tells the station to slow down.

5.3 Virtual LANs (VLANs)

For those of you without prior knowledge of IP that are reading this book from beginning to end, you might want to skip this section and come back to it after you've read about IP and routing in the later chapters.

A wonderful question to start with is "What is a VLAN?" As usual, it's not well defined. Basically, a virtual LAN is really no different from a LAN. It is the territory over which a broadcast (or multicast) packet is delivered (also known as a *broadcast domain*). The difference between a VLAN and a LAN, if there is any, is in packaging. Virtual LANs allow you to have separate LANs among ports on the same switch. For example, a switch might be told that ports 1–32 are in VLAN A and ports 33–64 are in VLAN B. The switch would act as two separate bridges: one that forwarded between the first 32 ports and a second one that forwarded between the second group of ports (see Figure 5.6).

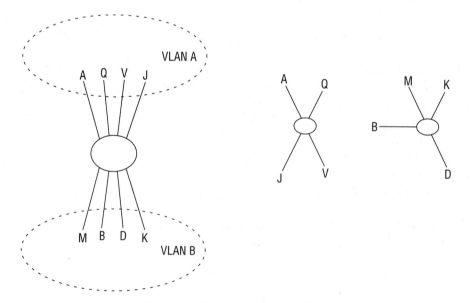

Figure 5.6 Virtual and physical LANs

To get from one VLAN to the other, you'd need a separate box, a router, that was connected to a port in each VLAN (see Figure 5.7) unless the switch were smart enough to act as a router between the VLANs (see Section 5.3.4). You could implement the same thing by using physically separate switches for each of the VLANs. Note that using a separate router to connect the VLANs involves using up a port on each of the VLANs.

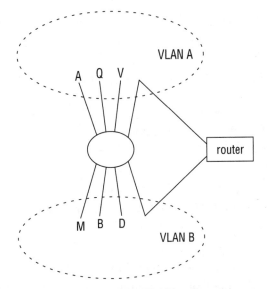

Figure 5.7 Connecting VLANs with a router

5.3.1 Why VLANs?

It is largely because of the idiosyncrasies of IP that people invented VLANs. The reasoning behind VLANs is as follows.

- IP requires that all nodes on a LAN share the same IP address prefix. Therefore, a node that moves to a different LAN must change its address.

- Changing an IP address is an annoying manual operation. (Note that DHCP [see Section 11.2.2.4] can make life easier, but VLANs predated widespread deployment of DHCP.)

- IP broadcasts traffic within a LAN, something that can cause congestion in a large LAN, especially if implementation or configuration bugs cause broadcast storms (see page 297).

- Routing IP (rather than bridging) was slow and expensive. (This is no longer true because people have risen to the challenge of building fast IP routers. There's really no reason that it should be significantly harder to make a decision based on an IP header than the Ethernet header.)

It might be tempting to bridge everything, making your whole topology one giant LAN from the perspective of IP. The advantage of this approach would be that IP nodes could move anywhere within your topology without changing their IP addresses. Also, you could interconnect everything with cheap, simple, fast layer 2 switches rather than what were at the time slow, more expensive routers.

The disadvantages of having your whole topology be one giant LAN are as follows.

- The broadcast traffic (such as ARP) grows in proportion to the number of stations on the LAN. It might be useful to isolate groups of users so that one group is not bothered by the broadcast traffic of the other group.

- Users can snoop on the traffic of other users on the same LAN, so it might be safer to isolate groups of users onto different LANs. (Note: I am not very sympathetic with this concern. With star topologies and with layer 2 forwarding, after the MAC address is learned the destination's traffic goes only to the destination's port. If it's a problem for the traffic to be read, the right solution is to use encryption. VLANs don't give significant security.)

- Some protocols are overly chatty, or they get into modes such as broadcast storms. Keeping the protocols on separate LANs can protect one protocol from the bad behavior of another.

So it seems desirable for users that need to talk to each other a lot to be in the same LAN (so that traffic between them can be bridged rather than routed) but to keep other groups of users in separate LANs (so that groups don't get bothered by each other's broadcast traffic). The assumption was that such groups of users might be scattered on ports of various switches.

This line of reasoning created the concept of VLANs, which let you make your broadcast domain exactly as large as you want it. A VLAN could be a subset of ports on a switch and/or it could consist of ports on multiple switches.

5.3.2 Mapping Ports to VLANs

The idea is to have a bunch of interconnected switches and define a mapping of VLANs to switch ports. The simplest example is a single switch, with some ports in VLAN A and others in VLAN B. How would you determine the scope of a VLAN? Here are some sample strategies.

- The switch always has ports 1 to k in one VLAN and has ports k+1 to 2k in a different VLAN.

- The switch can be configured with a port/VLAN mapping.

- The switch can be configured with a table of VLAN/MAC address mappings. It dynamically determines the VLAN/port mapping based on the (learned) MAC address of the station attached to the port.

- The switch can be configured with a table of VLAN/IP prefix mappings. It dynamically learns the VLAN/port mapping based on the source IP address in packets transmitted by the station attached to the port.

- The switch can be configured with a table of VLAN/protocol mappings. It dynamically learns the VLAN/port mappings based on the protocol type or SAP information in the data link header.

5.3.3 Example: VLAN Forwarding with Separate Router

Let's assume we have a switch with 16 ports, with each group of 8 ports considered a separate VLAN. Let's assume that the stations are talking IP. IP addresses must be assigned so that the stations on ports 1–8 have one prefix (say, a.b.c as shown in Figure 5.8) and stations on the other ports have a different shared prefix (f.g.k). The switch "bridges" ports 1–8; a packet transmitted by any station on those ports is forwarded to all the other stations on that group of ports unless the switch has learned the location of the destination address (in the layer 2 header). In other words, ports 1–8 are just like an ordinary LAN. Similarly, ports 9–16 are just like a LAN that is separate from the LAN composed of ports 1–8.

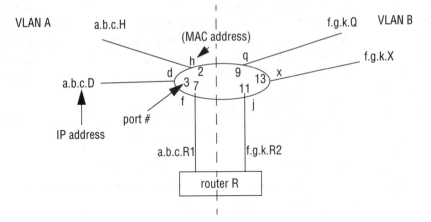

Figure 5.8 Router connects VLANs

If packets need to travel between the LANs, there must be a router. Some switches are capable of acting as routers between the VLANs, but for our first example let's assume that the switch cannot forward between VLANs. Therefore, to connect the VLANs there must be a router that connects the two VLANs by being connected to each of them.

In Figure 5.8, the ports on the left (2, 3, and 7) are in VLAN A and the ports on the right (9, 11, and 13) are in VLAN B. Router R is connected to two ports: port 7 in VLAN A and port 11 in VLAN B. For clarity I name a node by the fourth component of its IP address, so I refer to node a.b.c.H as H.

Let's say that node H wishes to transmit a packet to node D. The IP logic in node H notices that D's prefix (a.b.c) is the same as H's, so they are on the same LAN. Therefore, H issues an ARP request to discover D's data link address (d). Now that H knows that IP node a.b.c.D has data link address d, H communicates with D by issuing a packet with data link header source = c and destination = d, and IP header source = a.b.c.C and destination a.b.c.D. If the switch has not learned the location of data link address d it forwards the packet onto all the ports in VLAN A except for port 2 (from which it received the packet). If the switch has learned that d resides on port 3, it forwards the packet only onto port 3.

Now let's say that node H wishes to transmit a packet to node Q. Because Q's prefix (f.g.k) differs from H's (a.b.c), the IP logic at H tells H that it must transmit the packet to a router. Let's assume that H has discovered the IP address a.b.c.R1 of a router on its LAN (see Section 11.2.5.2 for several methods by which it might have done this). H issues an ARP to discover the router's data link address (in this case, f) and issues a packet to Q by having the data link header source = h, destination = f, and the IP header source = a.b.c.H, destination = f.g.k.Q.

Router R receives the packet and determines based on the prefix f.g.k in the IP header's destination address that it belongs in the LAN connected to its upper right port. Router R then issues an ARP to determine the data link address of IP node f.g.k.Q and is told q. Now to forward the packet R transmits it onto the port in VLAN B with data link header source = j and destination = q. The IP header is the same as it was before, namely, source = a.b.c.H, destination f.g.k.Q.

Note that from R's point of view as well as the endnodes' points of view, this entire scenario looks exactly as if there were two physical LANs (see Figure 5.9).

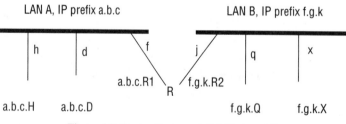

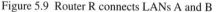

Figure 5.9 Router R connects LANs A and B

5.3.4 Example: VLAN Forwarding with Switch as Router

Now let's assume that the switch can act as a router. From the endnodes' point of view, everything looks the same, as shown in Figure 5.10.

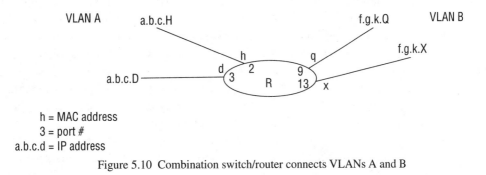

h = MAC address
3 = port #
a.b.c.d = IP address

Figure 5.10 Combination switch/router connects VLANs A and B

In this case the router R does not use up ports on the switch. If there are 8 ports allotted to VLAN A, there can be 8 stations attached to VLAN A. The switch must know that R's MAC address on VLAN A is f and on VLAN B is j. When the switch receives a packet from VLAN A (that is, it arrived on one of the ports 1–8), there are three possibilities.

- The destination data link address is unknown within ports 1–8. In this case the packet will be forwarded onto all the ports 1–8 except the one it was received from.

- The destination data link address is known to reside on port i, where i is within ports 1–8. The packet will be transmitted only onto port i.

- The destination data link address is f, in which case the packet is handled by the switch's IP router logic.

Note that if H transmits a packet with destination data link address q, it will be treated like an unknown destination within VLAN A because the switch does not bridge between the two VLANs.

5.3.5 Dynamic Binding of Links to VLANs

The standards committee did not attempt to standardize any dynamic binding of ports to VLANs. Any such solutions offered are proprietary. Some products attempt to learn the mapping by learning from received packets. If the VLAN mapping is based on IP address prefix, the learning must be based on the source address in the IP header (after the switch has determined that the packet is indeed an IP packet based on the protocol type indicated in the layer 2 header). If the VLAN mapping is based on protocol, the learning must be based on the protocol type or DSAP (destination service access point) in the data link header.

Learning the mapping is tricky. Until a station transmits a packet, the switch does not know which VLAN the port belongs to. If a packet is received from a port known to be in VLAN A with an unknown destination data link address or with a multicast or broadcast data link destination address, the switch would like to transmit that packet only onto ports that are in the same VLAN as the source. But it presumably should also transmit the packet onto ports with unknown VLAN mapping because they might be in VLAN A.

If the VLAN mapping is based on the protocol spoken, it becomes ugly to try to have the switch dynamically learn the VLAN/port mapping because a given station might speak multiple protocols and therefore be in multiple VLANs. For example, let's say that IP = VLAN A and AppleTalk is VLAN B. If a station on port x transmits an AppleTalk packet, it means that port x is in VLAN B. But unfortunately the switch cannot conclude that port x is *not* in VLAN A because the station might also speak IP.

To be safe, then, the switch would have to assume that all ports might be in all VLANs and transmit unknown and broadcast packets to all ports. But that would eliminate most of the advantage of VLANs. So undoubtedly, if any vendors attempt to provide dynamic binding of ports to VLANs, they make the assumption that a station will transmit packets for each protocol that it speaks. Until it transmits and the packet is correctly received by the switch, the switch simply does not forward packets properly to that station.

The same problem can occur if ports can have multiple stations. Multiple stations can occur if a switch is connected to another switch's port or if the port is a bus topology that has multiple stations on the same wire. Let's first discuss the case in which ports can have multiple stations (see Figure 5.11).

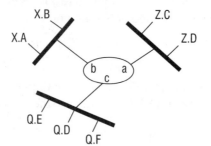

Figure 5.11 Ports with multiple stations

Initially, each port on the switch was intended to be a separate VLAN, and stations were assigned IP addresses accordingly. The switch is configured to know that VLAN1 has IP prefix X, VLAN2 has IP prefix Z, and VLAN3 has IP prefix Q, but it doesn't yet know which ports correspond to which VLANs. Eventually, it learns, by examining IP packets, that port a is VLAN2, port b is VLAN1, and port c is VLAN3.

Now let's make things more complicated. Let's move station Q.F to the LAN with prefix Z (see Figure 5.12).

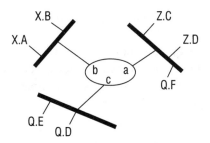

Figure 5.12 Move Q.F to LAN Z

The idea is not to force the user to reconfigure the moved station to have a new IP address. Because its IP address will not change, it must continue to function as part of the LAN whose prefix is Q even though it's physically on a different link. Somehow (in a proprietary way because it isn't standardized), the switch learns that now there are two VLANs on port a: VLAN2 and VLAN3. If a station on VLAN2 broadcasts a packet, the switch broadcasts it only on ports in VLAN2 (in this case, only port a). However, if a station on VLAN3 broadcasts a packet, the switch must broadcast it on all ports in VLAN3 (in Figure 5.12, ports a and c). If enough stations move around, broadcast traffic (mainly ARP packets) and unknown destination packets wind up having to be transmitted on all ports. You might as well have simply assumed the entire network was all one big LAN.

5.3.6 Dynamic VLAN Binding, Switch-Switch

Now let's look at the case when a switch can be attached to another switch (see Figure 5.13).

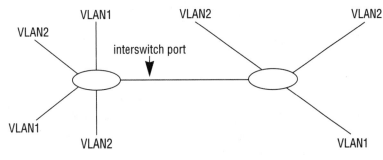

Figure 5.13 VLAN tagging needed on interswitch port

On the link between the two switches, packets can belong in either VLAN1 or VLAN2. So IEEE standardized a scheme for adding additional information, known as a VLAN *tag*, to a packet so that switches can know which VLAN a packet is intended for. A station would be confused if it received the packet with a VLAN tag, so the switches must be configured to know which ports contain switches and which ports contain stations.

A switch removes the VLAN tag from the packet before forwarding the packet onto a non-switch-neighbor port.

The VLAN tag is a 2-byte quantity containing 3 bits for *priority*, 12 bits for a VLAN ID, and 1 bit indicating whether the addresses are in canonical format. You define its presence by using the Ethernet type 81-00. For example, on 802.3 there might be a packet that looks like that shown in Figures 5.14 and 5.15.

6 octets	6	2	
destination	source	P	data

ptype

Figure 5.14 Ethernet packet without VLAN tag

6 octets	6	2	2	2	
destination	source	81-00	VLAN tag	P	data

ptype

Figure 5.15 Same packet with VLAN tag

An Ethernet type is used even if the original packet was in 802.3 format. For example, the packet in 802.3 format shown in Figures 5.16 and 5.17 is converted to one with a VLAN tag by adding the same 4 bytes (81-00 for Ethertype and 2-byte VLAN tag) as with an Ethernet packet.

6 octets	6	2	1	1		
destination	source	length	DSAP	SSAP	(etc.)	

Figure 5.16 802.3 packet without VLAN tag

6 octets	6	2	2	2	1	1	
destination	source	81-00	VLAN tag	length	DSAP	SSAP	(etc.)

Figure 5.17 Same packet with VLAN tag

On LANs other than 802.3 it is not possible to use Ethernet format, so SNAP encoding is used to insert the VLAN tag. An example is shown in Figures 5.18 and 5.19.

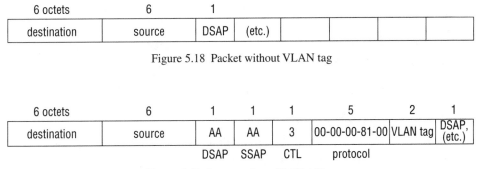

Figure 5.18 Packet without VLAN tag

Figure 5.19 Same packet with VLAN tag

Notice that in this format there is 10 bytes of overhead for the VLAN tag. If the committee had wanted to reserve one of the precious SAP values for VLANs, it could have done so much more compactly. For example, it could have reserved a SAP value—say, 97—and then if DSAP = 97 the VLAN tag would immediately follow. Then there would be only 3 bytes of overhead for the VLAN tag. Or if that would be considered unsavory (because the tagged packet doesn't have a proper SSAP and CTL field), the committee could set DSAP and SSAP to 97 and leave the ctl field, requiring only 5 bytes of overhead for the VLAN tag. The overhead for the tag is ignored in terms of maximum legal packet size. If the packet without the VLAN tag is of legal size, it's still considered of legal size with the tag inserted.

A switch can learn all the VLANs available on the port connecting it to another switch based on the VLAN tags in received packets on that port. Because stations are unlikely to understand the VLAN tag, the switch must be carefully configured so that it never transmits a packet with a VLAN tag on a port on which a station might reside.

Some switch vendors have a proprietary mechanism for having one switch tell another switch which VLANs are reachable on the switch-switch port. In that way, instead of learning the VLANs available through the switch-switch port based on received packets, the switch learns it through explicit protocol messages. But because there is no standard (as of the writing of this book) for a switch to tell its neighbor switch which VLANs it is connected to, the two switches would have to be from the same vendor.

Homework

1. Suppose A, B, C, D, and E are attached to a layer 2 switch. Suppose A and B are attached with 10 Mb/sec ports, whereas C, D, and E are attached with 100 Mb/sec ports. Furthermore, assume that the switch has unlimited bandwidth, although limited buffering, so that it applies backpressure or flow control as needed to prevent its buffers from overflowing. Ignore reverse traffic; that is, when I say,

"A is sending to B" assume a constant stream of traffic from A toward B. And assume that links are full-duplex. What is the total aggregate bandwidth in the following cases, assuming that each station sends as quickly as it can?

a. A is sending to B, C is sending to D.

b. A is sending to B, C is sending to B.

c. A is sending to C, B is sending to D.

d. C is sending to A, D is sending to B.

e. C is sending to D, E is sending to C.

2. Why are collisions (as with layer 1 switches) not an issue with a layer 2 switch that is doing cut-through forwarding?

3. Why is it possible to have ports with differing speeds on a layer 2 switch but not on a layer 1 switch?

4. How would you implement cut-through forwarding on a switch if ports are different speeds? What are the issues when forwarding from slow to fast links and from fast to slow links?

5. Why would it be difficult for layer 1 switches (repeaters) to run the spanning tree algorithm?

6. With a topology of multiple switches and multiple VLANs, many vendors choose to run separate instances of the spanning tree algorithm for each VLAN. In other words, each VLAN constructs its own spanning tree. Some links might belong to multiple VLANs and therefore belong to multiple spanning trees. What are the advantages of running a different instance of the spanning tree for each VLAN instead of running a single spanning tree?

Chapter 6
Network Interface: Service Models

This chapter discusses the endnode's view of the network and talks about various types of service models: connectionless versus connection-oriented, reliable versus datagram, classes of service, and various combinations.

6.1 What Is the Network Layer?

A network is made up of a bunch of packet switches connected through various types of technology such as point-to-point links or LANs. I'll call a packet switch a *router*, although other names are in use, including

- Intermediate system, or IS (used by ISO)

- Gateway (sometimes used by the IP community)

- Switch, or layer 3 switch

The purpose of a network is to enable users who attach their equipment to the network to transmit data to and receive data from other users' equipment. This is similar to the telephone network, in which you attach your phone to the network to communicate with other users who have attached their phones to the network. I call the equipment attached to the network an *endnode*, which is commonly used terminology, although other names are in use, including

- Host (used by the IP community)

- Data terminal equipment, or DTE (used by the X.25 standard)

- End system, or ES (used by ISO)

- Station

Thus, as far as an endnode is concerned, the network is one big "cloud" to which it attaches, thereby enabling itself to communicate with other endnodes that are also attached to the cloud.

Additionally, the term *node* is often used to mean both endnodes and routers.

6.2 Network Service Types

People argue about what a network should look like to the endnodes. There are really two different issues.

1. Should the network be *reliable* or *datagram (best effort[1])*?

2. Should the network be *connection-oriented* or *connectionless*?

A reliable service model is one in which the network guarantees to deliver every packet, in order, without duplication or loss. Datagram, otherwise known as best effort, delivers what arrives and lets the transport layer sort it out.

In a connectionless model, each small chunk of data (*packet*) is transmitted independently and carries a full source and destination address. This is similar to the postal system, in which each letter is deposited into the system with a complete address.

The connection-oriented (sometimes called *virtual circuit*) model is similar to the telephone network, in which a call must first be established, the network keeps track of the call, usually all packets travel on the same path from source to destination, and often the network assigns a small identifier to the conversation so that data packets need not carry the source and destination addresses. In this model, an endnode first informs the network that it wishes to start a conversation with another endnode. The network then notifies the destination that a conversation is requested, and the destination accepts or refuses. I use the term *call* to mean the virtual circuit set up by the network and the term *conversation* to mean the information flowing on the call, but the distinction is not important.

6.2.1 Performance Guarantees

There are also issues in terms of performance offered to or expected from the endnode. The network might offer the ability to request service guarantees such as minimum bandwidth, minimum delay, or minimum delay variance. The endnode might be limited to a certain bandwidth, and excess load might be dropped or carried only on a space-available basis. The bandwidth limit might be a limit that the endnode is never allowed to go

---

[1] The term *unreliable* is also used for this type of service, but it sounds derogatory so I prefer *best effort* or *datagram.*

beyond, or it might be an average (peaks are allowed as long as they don't overflow a certain threshold). If the endnode exceeds that threshold, the network might drop its excess data or mark the excess as a lower class: the first to be dropped in case of congestion.

Requesting a service guarantee from the network is usually done with connections. In a connectionless network, using a priority field accomplishes something similar. However, the difference occurs when there is too much high-priority traffic to give all of it the desired service guarantee. In the extreme, if all traffic is marked high priority, the priority field doesn't do anything at all. A connection-oriented network can lock out future connections when it has as much traffic as it can handle with the desired level of service; the lucky accepted connections get everything they want, and others get nothing.

Making *reservations* has the potential of wasting bandwidth. If endnodes reserve for their peak load and if the network must guarantee no congestion loss if all conversations simultaneously transmit at peak speed for long enough to use up all the buffering capacity, then the network will be underutilized because the unused bandwidth can't be used. Sometimes best-effort traffic can use bandwidth that was reserved but not used. Like airlines, networks can also overbook. At times, traffic might then need to be dropped, just as airlines occasionally bump passengers. (With data you can simply drop it, whereas airline passengers get grumpy. You have to apologize profusely, schedule them on the next available flight, and give them a coupon for a free round-trip ticket for their trouble.)

What should happen if a network says that it gives 100% reliable service, but it loses some of your data? Should it perhaps alert you with an "oops" notification—indicating that some of your data got lost—and then continue? Or should it simply hang up the call? Most implementations of X.25 hang up the call.

6.2.2 Sample Service Model Choices

ISO has never agreed on a service model. As a result, the ISO network layer designers have broken into two independent camps. The connection-oriented camp adopted the connection-oriented X.25 protocol of CCITT (International Telephone and Telegraph Consultative Committee.)[2] The connectionless camp designed CLNP (*Connectionless Network Layer Protocol*, ISO 8473). The IP community has traditionally been in the connectionless camp for the network layer, but various efforts to provide service guarantees—such as RSVP (resource reservation protocol, RFC 2205)—have led to connection-oriented proposals.

Although the X.25 designers chose a reliable connection-oriented service, it is possible to have a datagram connection-oriented service, and indeed ATM is a datagram connection-oriented service (in the sense that it does not guarantee delivery of data even though there are classes of service that guarantee bandwidth). The various choices are shown in Figure 6.1.

---

[2] The initials come from the French name Comité consultatif international téléphonique et télégraphique. These days the organization is known as ITU (International Telecommunication Union).

	datagram	reliable
connectionless	IP, IPX, DECnet, AppleTalk	not possible
connection-oriented	ATM	X.25

Figure 6.1 Examples of network layers with different service models

6.2.3 Hybrid Schemes

As always, it doesn't work to take the categories too seriously, because there are various types of designs that don't fit the image of a typical connection-oriented proponent's model of a network. Following are some examples.

1. A network in which a call-setup procedure is required before a conversation takes place. All packets are routed on the route established during the call setup, but there is not necessarily any guarantee as to bandwidth or packet loss.

   The purpose of designing a network this way is to enable the call setup to assign a small number to the call. This, in turn, enables routers to make the forwarding decision by performing a simple table lookup rather than by having to parse a general network layer header and deal with a large network layer address. The network could still offer datagram service, in the sense of allowing packet loss and providing no bandwidth or latency guarantees.

   ATM is an example of such a network. Additionally, it offers various types of service including guaranteed bandwidth.

2. A network in which a call-setup procedure is required before a conversation takes place, but only for the purpose of synchronizing an end-to-end connection between the first router and the final router. Packets are routed independently, but lost and reordered packets are recovered by handshaking between the first and final routers (using a protocol similar to a transport layer protocol); the packets as delivered to the destination endnode are in order, and no packets are lost. No bandwidth guarantees are provided.

   The purpose of designing a network this way is to support a connection-oriented interface. Not providing the uniform service normally associated with such an interface allows network resources to be shared.

   People have implemented X.25 networks this way, in which X.25 is carried over a datagram network such as IP, and it is only the routers at the edges that present an X.25 interface to the attached endnodes.

3. A network in which an explicit call-setup protocol is not required, but routers initiate a call-setup protocol on behalf of the endnodes when a new source-destination pair is encountered.

The purpose of such a network is to support a connectionless interface to the endnodes while allowing small numbers to be assigned to conversations so that intermediate routers can make quick forwarding decisions.

In the first edition of the book, I mentioned this as a possible method of building a network. Since then various schemes have been implemented along these lines (see LANE, Section 11.3.3). Some approaches use a connection-oriented data link layer such as ATM; they simply forward IP packets across an ATM virtual circuit to the exit router or create an ATM virtual circuit if one didn't exist. Others create a little extra header to tack on to the beginning of an IP header so that forwarding decisions can be based on the mini-header instead of the IP header. Currently the IETF has a working group, the MPLS (Multi Protocol Label Switching) working group, that is attempting to standardize a scheme.

6.2.4 Connectionless versus Connection-oriented

Is one type of service better than the other? Connection-oriented proponents argue as follows.

1. Connection-oriented service enables faster routers to be built. During call-setup time, the complicated address lookup can take place, and calls can be assigned small identifiers. Routers can then do a simple table lookup based on the small identifier when forwarding data packets.

2. If a network accepts a call, it is duty-bound to provide reasonable bandwidth. It is better to lock out new calls than to degrade the quality of service on current calls.

3. It is easier for the transport layer to deal with uniform service from the network. For example, if the network routes each packet independently (as is usually done in a connectionless network), it is difficult for the transport layer to calculate the round-trip delay to the destination. (This calculation is necessary in order to decide when a packet needs to be retransmitted because an ack has not yet been received from the destination.)

   Another example is packet size. It is desirable to send the largest packet possible, but different link types allow different maximum packet sizes. The maximum-size packet that can be transmitted on a route is equal to the smallest maximum packet size allowed on any of the links along the route. In a connectionless network, packets might get routed along routes having different packet sizes. In most connection-oriented networks, a single path is used for all packets, and the endnodes can be informed of the maximum packet size along the path.

4.   Interfacing to a connection-oriented network layer is easier than interfacing to a connectionless network layer because a connection-oriented network layer eliminates the need for a complicated transport layer.

5.   It might seem that a connection-oriented network is less reliable than a connectionless network because if anything along the path breaks, the connection breaks. However, in most datagram networks it takes sufficiently long for the routing protocol to notice a link has gone down and to compute an alternate path that the transport connection breaks anyway.

Connectionless proponents argue as follows.

1.   Most connection-oriented networks are built so that if anything along a call's route fails, the network hangs up the call automatically. It can no longer determine which packets have reached the destination and which have not, and it may be unable to recover packets "in the pipe" at the time of the failure. For this reason, a full-service transport layer is required even though the network layer claims reliable delivery. Therefore, rather than doing the endnode a favor, the connection-oriented network is only duplicating effort.

2.   Interfacing to a connectionless network layer is simpler than interfacing to a connection-oriented network layer, even when the need for a fully general transport layer is taken into account. But especially if the first argument is correct (that a full-service transport layer is required anyway), it is clear that the network layer code in an endnode is vastly simpler when the endnode is attached to a connectionless network layer.

3.   Many applications do not require sequential delivery of packets. For those applications, lost packets can be tolerated. One example is packet voice, where a modest percentage of lost packets can be tolerated but delayed packets are useless and might as well be dropped. A connection-oriented network sometimes delays otherwise deliverable packets because it refuses to deliver a packet until an earlier lost packet has been recovered.

     Another example of an application that does not require sequenced delivery of packets is an alternative design for file transfer. Each packet contains enough information so that the data can immediately be put into the proper place on disk when received by the destination. After a file transfer is completed, the application can determine which blocks are missing and specifically request them. The order in which packets are received is irrelevant. Such a protocol was standardized as 802.1e (multicast load protocol) based on work done at Digital.

4.   Network traffic is usually *bursty*, so it is wasteful to reserve resources. If an application tends to send data, then remain quiet for some time, and then send more data, the bandwidth reserved for that endnode is wasted when the endnode is not transmitting.

A lot of things that wouldn't seem as if they'd be bursty can turn out to be bursty. File transfer is usually assumed not to be bursty. However, if the transmitter is a busy server, the file transfer traffic can be quite bursty. Also, if bandwidth is really large, most file transfers would appear as bursts of short duration. Video and audio can be bursty because of compression.

Assuming that most traffic is bursty, it is better to budget resources optimistically and allow network resources to be shared (a practice that is similar to overbooking airline seats). If too many users request resources simultaneously, data will be dropped. However, this is not fatal because any application requiring loss-free service will be using a transport layer protocol that will retransmit lost data.

5. It is better to allow all users onto the network and have service degrade equally for everyone than to allow some lucky users onto the network and lock out others.

6. For many applications, particularly client-server request-response applications, maintaining state at the server (or at the router that services the server) regarding all current conversations would be difficult because the server might have hundreds or thousands of clients.

If "connection-oriented" means reliable and therefore something like X.25 (see Section 7.2), I am in the connectionless camp. However, I think it is reasonable to have connection-oriented datagram networks. I rather like ATM except for the tiny packet size (48 bytes). It is transport-friendly to have all packets for a conversation stay on a fixed path so that transport can know the round-trip delay and maximum packet size. It is nice to have a small connection identifier and forward based on that rather than a possibly complex layer 3 header. I also believe that traffic is almost always bursty, and therefore it is wasteful to reserve bandwidth. I also think it's better to degrade gracefully for everyone rather than lock out newcomers because all the bandwidth is reserved.

Ironically, both ATM and IP seem to be moving toward the same service. There is a proposal within ATM for supporting large (and variable-length) "cells." And the MPLS working group at IETF is working on standardizing what is basically an ATM header on an IP packet.

Homework

1. Sort the arguments in Section 6.2.4 to determine which ones apply to reliable and which ones apply to datagram networks.

2. What are the trade-offs between providing reliability at layer 3 versus layer 4?

3. For each of the following semireliable service variants, propose how a network might provide this service. Keep in mind limited buffering and memory capacity.

   a. All packets delivered (100% reliability), but out of order delivery is OK, so packets are delivered without waiting for previous lost packets

   b. Packets delivered in order, missing packets are OK (reliability is not 100%), but the network attempts to recover at least some packets that might get lost

   c. Packets delivered with enhanced reliability (not 100%, but better than pure datagram), with out-of-order delivery OK

Chapter 7
Connection-oriented Nets:
X.25 and ATM

This chapter covers connection-oriented networks, discussing X.25 and ATM in detail. Although X.25 may be dying out, I think it's worth studying as an example of a connection-oriented reliable network layer. There are all sorts of fascinating details—for example, that the sequence number when launched by the source can be different from the sequence number as received by the destination. And when you understand X.25 you can easily understand ATM.

7.1 Generic Connection-oriented Network

First, let's talk about a connection-oriented network generically before getting bogged down in the idiosyncrasies of X.25 or ATM. For A to talk to B, there must be a special call-setup packet that travels from A to B, specifying B as the destination. Each router along the path must make a routing decision, based on B's address, about how it should forward the call-setup packet. This is the identical problem that a router in a connectionless network, such as IP, faces.

In addition to simply forwarding the call-setup packet the goal is to assign the call a small identifier, which I call the connection identifier, or CI,[1] so that data packets do not need to carry the source and destination addresses. Instead, they carry only the CI. Addresses, as you'll see in Chapter 9, tend to be large so as to be easy to administer. CIs can be small because they are handed out dynamically and are significant only on a link. They need only be large enough to distinguish between the total number of calls that might simultaneously be routed on the same link, and they can be assigned densely.

---

[1] Note that CI is nonstandard terminology. I chose CI rather than a term such as VCI (in use by ATM) so as not to cause confusion with the specifics of ATM where there is subtlety with VPIs and VCIs, discussed in Section 7.4.2.

In Figure 7.1, A sets up a call to B. The call-setup packet launched by A says, "Source A wants to talk to B and use CI 57."

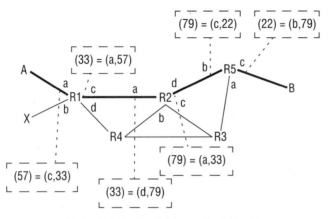

Figure 7.1 Router databases for A-B call

- R1 decides that it should forward traffic for B onto port c. R1 chooses a CI not currently in use on port c—say, 33—and sends a call setup to R2 saying, "A wants to talk to B and use CI 33." R1 also adds the entry (57) = (c,33) on its database for port a, meaning that data received on port a with CI 57 should be forwarded onto port c and the CI should be rewritten as 33. R1 also makes the entry in its port c database (33) = (a,57), meaning that data with CI received on port c should be forwarded onto port a and the CI should be rewritten as 57.

- R2 receives the call setup on port a, indicating that the call is CI 33 and the destination is B. R2 decides that it should forward traffic for B onto its port d. R2 chooses the CI 79 because it's not in use on port d. It makes the entry (33) = (d,79) on its port a and the entry (79) = (a,33) on its port d and sends "A wants to talk to B and use CI 79 on port d."

- R5 receives the call setup on its port b, decides traffic for B should be forwarded on port c, and chooses CI 22 for port c. It makes the entry (79) = (c,22) on the port b database and the entry (22) = (b, 79) on its port c database. It sends "A wants to talk to B and use CI 22" onto port c, where it is received by B.

After the path is set up, A launches data that needs to specify only the CI for its call to B, which is 57. When R1 receives it on port a, it looks in the port database for a and, seeing the entry (57) = (c,33), notes that data it receives on that port with CI 57 should be forwarded onto port c with CI 33. R2 receives the data on its port a and sees (33) = (d,79). It forwards the data onto port d and changes the CI to 79. R5, seeing the entry (79) = (c,22) in the database for the port on which it received the data marked with CI 79, forwards it onto port c, changing the CI to 22.

Why does the CI have to change hop by hop? The answer is that it would be very difficult to choose a CI that was unused on all the links along the path. And except for the bother of rewriting the CI field as a router forwards the data, there's no problem with making the CI link-specific.

Let's get rid of some of the clutter in the picture to illustrate what happens when B transmits to A, which works the same way (see Figure 7.2).

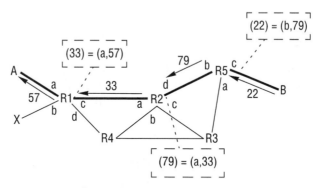

Figure 7.2 Data travels from B to A

B launches the data with CI 22. R5 receives it on port c, which has an entry (22) = (b,79), so R5 forwards the data onto port b, changing the CI to 79. R2 receives it on port d, which contains the entry (79) = (a,33), so R2 forwards it onto port a, changing the CI to 33. R1, seeing (33) = (a,57) in the database for the port on which it received data with CI 33, forwards the data onto port a, changing the CI to 57.

7.2 X.25: Reliable Connection-oriented Service

X.25, which was designed by CCITT, was adopted (except for minor modifications) by ISO as its connection-oriented network layer, with the name ISO 8208. X.25 does not specify how to build a connection-oriented service. Instead, it specifies the interface between an endnode (known in X.25 as a DTE) and a router (known in X.25 as a DCE).

This section discusses what the interface looks like to the endnode. Section 7.3 discusses implementation issues involved in building routers that support X.25 service.

The X.25 standard comes in three levels.

1. *Physical level:* This specifies the physical layer, including the size and shape of the connector, the voltage levels that appear on each pin, the meaning of signaling on the pins, and so on. It is not really relevant to network layer issues.

2. *Link level:* This specifies a data link layer protocol, including how to delimit the start and end of packets, number packets, acknowledge them, enforce flow control, and so on. The link level, like the physical layer, is not very relevant to network layer issues.

3. *Packet level:* This really is the network layer interface, which is described in the balance of this section.

7.2.1 The Basic Idea

The service as seen by the DTE involves the ability to carry on multiple simultaneous *calls* over a single link to a DCE (see Figure 7.3). Each call must first be established; then data can flow in both directions between the endpoints of the call, after which the call must be cleared.

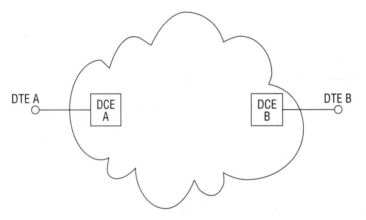

Figure 7.3 Picture of X.25 network

From DTE A's viewpoint, there are three ways to establish a call.

1. DTE A can initiate the call by informing DCE A of its desire to place the call (informing DCE A of the destination's *DTE address*—for example, DTE B). This is similar to dialing a telephone; the telephone number corresponds to the destination's DTE address. A call of this sort is known as an SVC (*switched virtual circuit*).

2. DCE A can notify DTE A that some other DTE—such as DTE B—has asked to place a call to DTE A (this is similar to having your telephone ring). This form of call is also an SVC. From DTE A's viewpoint, it is known as an *incoming call*.

3. The call can be permanently up. This is known as a PVC (*permanent virtual circuit*). PVCs are set up administratively. Data flows on a PVC in the same way as on the first two types of calls, but call setup and call clearing are not done, or at least are not visible to the DTEs.

Each call is assigned a *virtual circuit number* upon setup. This number is of significance only between the DTE and the DCE to which it is attached. The DTE that is the other endpoint of the call typically associates a different virtual circuit number with that call. Each data packet header carries the virtual circuit number rather than the source and destination DTE addresses. This is desirable because the virtual circuit number is generally shorter than a DTE address, and it is easier for the routers to make a high-speed forwarding decision based on a shorter field.

X.25 provides *multiplexing*, which means that multiple calls can take place simultaneously over the same connection to the DCE. Thus, for example, there might be several processes within the source DTE, each of which might be carrying on multiple conversations with different destinations. Each call has its own virtual circuit number. When the DCE gives the DTE a data packet, it contains a virtual circuit number so that the DCE can identify the call to which the packet applies. Similarly, when the DTE gives the DCE a data packet, the virtual circuit number in the header informs the DCE of the call to which the packet applies.

Again, X.25 specifies only what happens between a DTE and its local DCE. For a network to provide X.25 service, there must be protocols and algorithms between the DCEs so that paths can be established, data can be transmitted, and so on. However, these protocols are not standardized. They are proprietary to an individual X.25 network.

7.2.2 Virtual Circuit Numbers

Virtual circuit numbers are actually 12 bits long. In specifications of X.25, however, packet formats are written out byte-by-byte, making it pictorially awkward to represent a 12-bit field. So the virtual circuit number is actually written as though it consisted of two fields, which, concatenated together, form the virtual circuit number. One field, which the standard calls the *logical channel group number*, is 4 bits long; the other, the *logical channel number*, is 8 bits long. For brevity, I refer to the concatenation of the two fields as the *call number*.

By convention, call number 0 is reserved for control packets (such as restart packets and diagnostic packets) that refer to all virtual circuits. Then a block of call numbers is reserved for PVCs. Next, a block is reserved for incoming calls (calls for which the DCE must assign a call number and notify the attached DTE that a remote DTE is "ringing its phone"). Next, a block is reserved for either outgoing or incoming calls. Next, a block is reserved for outgoing calls—calls initiated by the DTE and for which the DTE must assign a call number. This convention avoids a *call collision*, which occurs when the DTE decides to initiate a call and chooses call number X, and, almost simultaneously, the DCE receives notification of an incoming call for the DTE and chooses call number X to alert the DTE to the incoming call.

Note that call collisions would not be an issue at all if there were independent VC numbers in the two directions on a link (see homework problem 3).

7.2.3 Call Setup

Assume that DTE A wishes to converse with DTE B. DTE A chooses a call number—say, *X*—which is not in use for any of DTE A's currently ongoing calls. DTE A issues a *call request* packet to DCE A. Figure 7.4 shows the format of a call request packet.

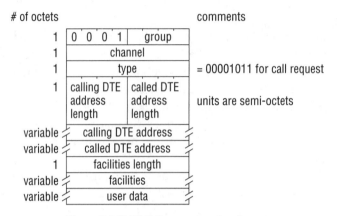

Figure 7.4 X.25 Call request packet format

DTE A writes its own address into the calling DTE address field, DTE B's address into the called DTE address field, and *X* into the call number field. (Actually, it puts 4 bits of the call number into **group** and the remaining 8 bits into **channel**.)

By some mechanism not specified in the standard, DCE A informs DCE B that DTE A wishes to talk to DTE B. DCE B chooses a call number—say, *Y*—that is not in use for any of DTE B's current calls and issues an *incoming call* packet to DTE B. The incoming call packet has the same format as the call request packet. The call number is almost always different because the call number in the incoming call packet has been selected by DCE B. (Only by coincidence would DCE B choose the same call number as DTE A chose, and it would never happen if all DCEs used the same convention as to which portion of the numbers the DTEs were allowed to assign [outgoing calls] and which portion of the numbers the DCEs were allowed to assign [incoming calls].) Other fields might also differ. For example, the packet size in the facilities might be different because the packet size between the source DTE and the source DCE might differ from the packet size between the destination DCE and the destination DTE.

If DTE B accepts the call, it sends a *call accepted* packet to DCE B. The call number on the call accepted packet transmitted by DTE B is the same as the call number received from DCE B in the incoming call packet.

When DCE B receives the call accepted packet, it somehow (in a manner not specified by the standard) informs DCE A, which notifies DTE A with a *call connected* packet. The latter is identical to the call accepted packet, but with *X* (the call number that was chosen by DTE A) rather than *Y* (the call number that was assigned by DCE B and that DTE B associates with the call).

Figure 7.5 summarizes an X.25 call.

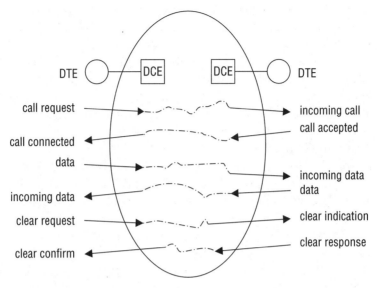

Figure 7.5 Overview of an X.25 call

7.2.4 Data Transfer

After the call has been established, data exchange is *full duplex*, which means that data can flow simultaneously in both directions (see Figure 7.6).

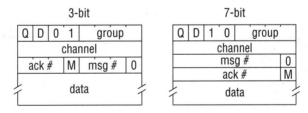

Figure 7.6 X.25 data packet formats

As shown in Figure 7.6, data packets have two formats. One format has 3-bit sequence numbers; the other has 7-bit sequence numbers. With some providers, the choice of 7-bit or 3-bit sequence number is made at the time of subscription. With others, the choice is made on a per-call basis. It is not possible to switch between 3- and 7-bit sequence numbers in the middle of a call.

The standard allows the DTEs to use the **Q** bit for any purpose. A data packet transmitted with the Q bit set will be delivered to the destination DTE with the Q bit set, and it is up to the application running in the DTEs to interpret the meaning of the Q bit. (For those who are curious, "Q" stands for "qualified.")

The **M** bit defines whether "more data follows." It is used to transmit a packet larger than the maximum packet size allowable on the DTE/DCE link. When a DTE wishes to transmit a packet larger than the maximum size allowable on the link to its DCE, the DTE breaks the packet into maximum-allowable-size pieces and sets the M bit on each piece except the last. By the time the data reaches the destination DTE, it may be fragmented still more if the destination DTE/DCE interface has an even smaller maximum packet size. The destination DTE receives data packet after data packet, finally receiving one with the M bit clear. It then treats the entire collection of data as if it were a single large packet transmitted from the source DTE.

The **D** bit determines whether an acknowledgment means that the packet was received by the destination DTE or only by the DCE. (It is network-specific whether an acknowledgment when the D bit is 0 indicates that the packet was received by the source DCE or by the destination DCE.)

When a DTE wishes to transmit data on a particular call, it sends a data packet—marked with the call number and with a sequence number—that increments for each packet on that call. If a DTE is transmitting data for several calls simultaneously, the sequence numbers for packets on different calls are unrelated (see Figure 7.7).

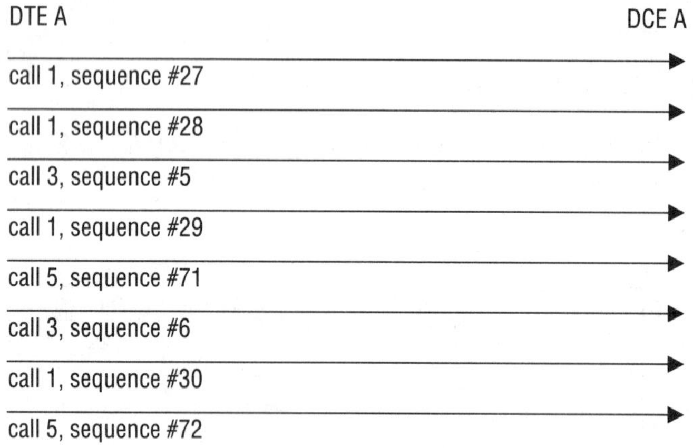

DTE A   DCE A

call 1, sequence #27 ⟶

call 1, sequence #28 ⟶

call 3, sequence #5 ⟶

call 1, sequence #29 ⟶

call 5, sequence #71 ⟶

call 3, sequence #6 ⟶

call 1, sequence #30 ⟶

call 5, sequence #72 ⟶

Figure 7.7 X.25, sequence numbers on different calls unrelated

On a particular call, it is possible for a single data packet to have one sequence number when it is transmitted by the source DTE and a different sequence number when it is received by the destination DTE.

First, assume that the application's data size can be carried within the packet size allowed by the DCE/DTE link at both the source and the destination. In this case, each packet transmitted by the source DTE is delivered as a single packet to the destination DTE (see Figure 7.8).

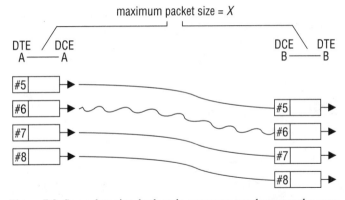

Figure 7.8 Same data size, both ends, sequence numbers stay the same

Now assume that the application's data size is bigger than the packet size at the destination DCE/DTE link. In this case, each packet transmitted by the source results in several packets delivered to the destination; every packet except the final one in each group has the M bit set. When the destination DTE receives a packet with the M bit clear, it transmits the data it has received on that call (since the last packet with a clear M bit) to the application as a complete packet (see Figure 7.9).

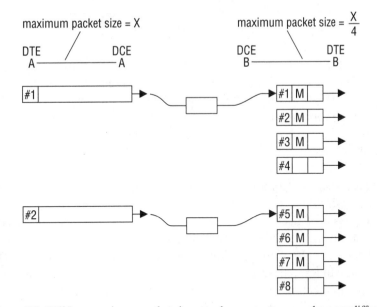

Figure 7.9 Different maximum packet size at ends, so sequence numbers are different

If the maximum packet size used by the source DCE/DTE link is smaller than the packet size used by the application, something similar happens, except it is the source DTE that transmits a sequence of packets to the source DCE (see Figure 7.10). All packets except the final one have the M bit set.

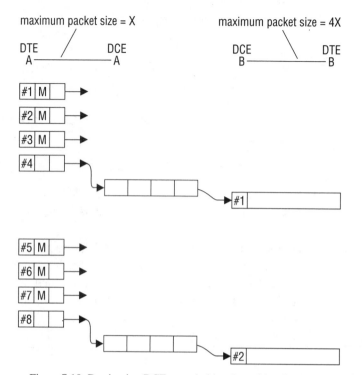

Figure 7.10 Destination DCE must hold and combine fragments

In general, if the maximum packet size at the source differs from that at the destination DCE/DTE links, a data packet will have a different sequence number when transmitted by the source DTE than when received by the destination DTE (see Figure 7.11).

An interesting problem arises because the standard does not allow the M bit to be set if the packet is not full (except if the D bit is set—see homework problem 5). Thus, if the DCE/DTE link allows a certain packet size—say, 1,024 bytes—a packet must contain 1,024 bytes if the M bit is set.

This creates a curious complication when the source DCE/DTE link has a smaller maximum packet size than that of the destination DCE/DTE link. When the source DTE transmits a sequence of packets, each with the M bit set, the destination DCE cannot transmit the data to the destination DTE until it has enough data for a maximum-size packet. Thus, for example, if the maximum packet size on the source DCE/DTE link is one-eighth the maximum packet size on the destination DCE/DTE link and if the packet size used by the application is at least as large as the size on the destination DCE/DTE link, the destination DCE must hold onto eight packets with the M bit set in order to accumulate enough data to transmit a maximum-size packet with the M bit set to the destination DTE.

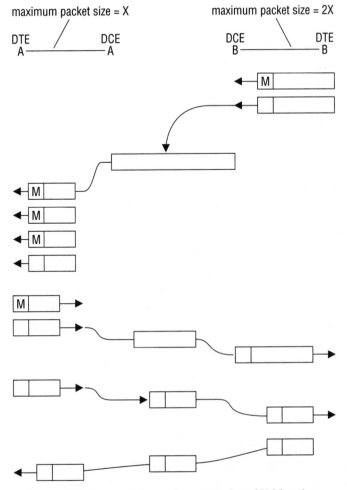

Figure 7.11 Fragmentation and concatenation of X.25 packets

7.2.5 Flow Control

In addition to a message sequence number (msg #), each data packet contains an acknowledgment number (ack #), whose purpose is to acknowledge received data. Assume a call between DTE A and DTE B. When DTE A transmits a packet to DTE B, it might have sequence number k when received by DCE A. When DTE A receives from DCE A a packet that originated from DTE B, it will have a totally unrelated sequence number—say, j. If DTE A has just received sequence number j from DCE A on that call and if DTE A is about to transmit data with sequence number k on the same call, it will set the msg # field in the data packet to k and the ack # field to j.

The protocol is symmetric. When DCE A is transmitting data to DTE A, it also transmits a msg # and ack # in each data packet.

The ack # field serves two purposes.

1. It acknowledges that the data packet with the indicated sequence number (as well as all previous ones) was received correctly.

2. It indicates that the receiver is ready to receive data packets beyond the indicated sequence number.

If the receiver does not have data to transmit and simply needs to acknowledge received data, it transmits a *receive ready* packet, which contains the sequence number of the packet being acknowledged.

Suppose that the DTE cannot receive more data on that call. Suppose, too, that the window for the call is w—that is, the transmitter is permitted to transmit w packets beyond the last one acknowledged. Assume that an application is transmitting data to a user's terminal and the user has typed "pause," gotten distracted, and gone to lunch. If the DTE has acknowledged sequence number j, either in the ack # of a data packet or in the acknowledgment sequence number included in a *receive ready* message, then the DCE will transmit up to sequence number $j + w$ and then not send any more data on that call until the user returns from lunch and types "resume."

There is another mechanism for flow control in X.25 in addition to the refusal to acknowledge further packets. A node (DTE or DCE) can transmit a *receive not ready* packet, which includes the sequence number, j, of the most recently received data packet. This indicates that packet j was received correctly but that the DTE cannot receive additional data packets. Later, the node can transmit a receive ready packet, with sequence number j. If the node transmits data after the receive not ready, it will have j in the ack # field, which, in this case, is not the same as a receive ready with j in the msg # field. It does not give the transmitter permission to transmit beyond sequence number j. After a receive not ready has been sent, the only way to give permission to transmit more data is to send a receive ready.

The receive not ready mechanism does not make very much sense. Suppose that the receiver sends a receive not ready with sequence number j but then gets sequence number $j + 1$ because the transmitter transmitted sequence number $j + 1$ before the receive not ready arrived. If the transmitter assumes that the receiver has discarded $j + 1$ and therefore retransmits $j + 1$ after it gets a receive ready, then the receiver might notice that it has gotten a duplicate of sequence number $j + 1$, causing it to reset the call (hang up).

The only way this mechanism can work properly is if the receiver realizes that an acknowledgment of j requires that it be willing to receive w packets beyond j even though it sends a receive not ready. But if the receiver realizes this and implements the procedure accordingly, a receive not ready is really a no-op. Merely not acknowledging sequence numbers beyond j would have the same effect as sending a receive not ready with sequence number j.

7.2.6 Facilities

Some facilities are contracted and therefore are set up manually at the DCE (not part of the X.25 protocol as seen by the DTE). Following are examples of these facilities.

1. Fixing the window size at some value or letting it be negotiated on a per-call basis.

2. Fixing the packet size at some value or letting it be negotiated on a per-call basis.

3. Allowing throughput to be negotiated on a per-call basis (with values between 75 bps and 64 Kbps).

4. Establishing a *closed user group*—a set of DTEs in which only members of the set can communicate with one another over the X.25 network. A DTE can be a member of multiple closed user groups. In that case, the DCE can determine whether an incoming or outgoing call should be allowed, based on the specification of the identity of the closed user group in the call request packet and the DCE's configured information regarding the closed user groups to which the DTE belongs.

   The numbering of a closed user group is local to a particular DTE/DCE interface. In other words, if DTE A and DTE B are in a closed user group, DTE A might refer to the closed user group as *n* and DTE B might refer to it as *m*.

5. Allowing no incoming calls.

6. Allowing only incoming calls.

7. Establishing the lowest outgoing virtual circuit number, which defines the boundary between virtual circuit numbers that can be chosen by the DTE and virtual circuit numbers that can be chosen by the DCE.

The following list provides examples of other facilities that are selected on a per-call basis. Note that in the first three cases, the facilities can be selected on a per-call basis only if the ability to do so has been contracted.

1. Window size for this call

2. Maximum packet size

3. Throughput

4. Closed user group, which specifies the closed user group to which the call applies

5. Reverse charging (the side other than the call initiator pays for the call)

7.2.7 Call Release

The standard method for releasing a connection is for one of the DTEs involved in a call to request that the call be cleared by transmitting a *clear request* to its DCE. That DCE will inform the network that the call is being cleared, and the other DCE will inform the other DTE that the call is being cleared. When the noninitiating DTE acknowledges that it knows the call has been cleared, its DCE informs the network, which informs the initiating DTE's DCE, which, in turn, informs the DTE that originally requested that the call be cleared.

When the network detects a problem with a call, it might do one of the following.

1. The DCE might issue a clear request, which causes the call to be disconnected with no guarantee regarding unacknowledged packets. They may or may not have been delivered to the destination.

2. The DCE might issue a reset, which also offers no guarantee regarding the fate of unacknowledged packets. It restarts the sequence numbers for the call at 0 but keeps the call up.

3. The network might recover transparently. (This is, unfortunately, not common.)

The sorts of problems that could trigger one of the preceding responses include the following.

1. A DCE or link along a call's route goes down. (X.25 networks can be designed so that a call could be rerouted when a route fails, but many of them are not.)

2. The DTE transmits a packet for a call with an unexpected sequence number, indicating that the DCE and DTE are no longer coordinated with each other regarding that call.

It is also possible for a DCE to inform a DTE that all the DTE's current calls have been torn down. This is usually the result of a restart by the DCE because it has lost state with respect to any calls that might have been in progress.

7.2.8 Interrupts

X.25 offers the ability for a DTE to transmit a single packet (with 1 to 32 bytes of data) on a call, which the network will deliver to the destination DTE as quickly as possible—that is, without having to wait for all previously transmitted data to be delivered to the destination. There is no flow control on *interrupt* packets, so even if the destination has transmitted a receive not ready the interrupt packet will be delivered. An *interrupt confirmation* packet is used to acknowledge an interrupt packet. A DTE can transmit a second interrupt packet only after the DCE informs the DTE (via an interrupt confirmation packet) that the destination DTE has acknowledged the previous interrupt packet.

7.3 Implementing X.25 Inside the Net

In this section, I discuss two methods of implementing a service interface with the X.25 guarantees: that all packets be transmitted in order with no duplication or loss, or else the call is disconnected. Some X.25 providers use the first strategy, and others use the second.

7.3.1 Circuit Method

In this method a call-setup procedure is done, just as in Figure 7.1, creating state in all the routers along the path. In X.25 nets built this way, the routers usually reserve a certain number of buffers for each call that has been set up through them. If a call request comes in and the call-mapping database is full or all the buffers are reserved, the call is refused by the network (as with "fast busy signal" in the U.S. telephone network).

Because the number of calls is limited, if the network completes a call a certain level of performance is guaranteed. When the network gets to a particular level of utilization, further calls are refused but service is not degraded for those calls already in progress. This is in contrast to a connectionless service, in which service for all users would be degraded democratically.

In an X.25 network built this way, a router usually holds on to a data packet only until the downstream router acknowledges it. Consequently, if any router along the path fails, there is no way for the network to recover lost packets. The network disconnects or resets the call under these circumstances because it can't guarantee 100% reliability.

7.3.2 Reliable Connections over Datagrams Method

Another way to provide an X.25 interface is to build a connectionless network but have additional code in routers with endnode neighbors. The additional code is a protocol similar to a full-service transport layer. When a router, R1, receives a call request packet from an attached endnode, E1, with destination address E2 and call number x, R1 consults its routing databases to find out the router, R2, to which endnode E2 is attached. R1 then sets up a connection to R2—an end-to-end service between the two routers that ensures that every packet transmitted by R1 gets received by R2 in order, with no loss, duplication, or misordering. Other than R1 and R2, no other routers keep state regarding the conversation between endnodes E1 and E2. Load splitting might be implemented within the network, and different packets of the conversation might travel different routes. R2 will hold on to data packets until all earlier ones have been received. R1 will hold on to packets until R2 has acknowledged them.

7.3.3 Comparison

With the second method for building an X.25 interface, no service guarantees are made. As long as the end routers have sufficient space to hold the state regarding the end-to-end connection, the call is accepted by the network. Buffers in intermediate routers are not reserved, and packets might be dropped en route (but the source router will be able to retransmit them).

A network built according to the second method can handle more calls because buffers and bandwidth can be shared. With the first method, if traffic is at all bursty, the resources reserved for a particular call are wasted when no data is being sent.

The first method enables routers to forward data packets more quickly and easily because the routing decision is based on a small call number rather than a larger network layer address.

With the second method, an alternate route can be found if an intermediate router or link fails. The routing algorithm adapts to the changed topology, and routes are recalculated. Although packets in transit are most likely dropped while the routing algorithm is adapting, the source router fails to receive acknowledgments for those packets and retransmits them.

7.4 Asynchronous Transfer Mode

ATM stands for Asynchronous Transfer Mode (aren't you glad you asked?). Why is it called that? The phone companies were accustomed to protocols that had data for each call occur at regular intervals in the data stream. If you stick enough header information on the data so that it is self-describing, the data can be transmitted as it exists rather than according to a fixed amount every unit of time. Although it takes more overhead to make the data self-describing, it's more flexible. Most applications do not operate at a constant bit rate. ATM allows data to be bursty and to be sent when needed. So that's why they call it asynchronous. Basically, ATM reinvented packet switching.

ATM people call the boxes that move cells *switches*, although they really are not conceptually different from routers. They need a routing algorithm. They make forwarding decisions. The main difference between something that moves ATM cells and something that moves, say, IP packets is that in ATM you set up the path first, assigning a virtual circuit number. Then the switches make forwarding decisions based on the virtual circuit number rather than the destination address. ATM is a connection-oriented datagram service.

There are other things to know about ATM, such as LANE (LAN emulation), MPOA (multiprotocol over ATM), classical IP over ATM, and the addresses that are used. These topics are discussed in Section 11.3.3.

7.4.1 Cell Size

Perhaps the weirdest thing about ATM is that packets (which it calls *cells*) carry only 48 bytes of data, with a 5-byte header. The number 48 made everyone unhappy. The French PTT claimed that it needed cells to be no more than 32 bytes, or else it would need echo suppressors. (Delay is caused by waiting for there to be enough data to fill a cell, followed by the propagation time across the country.) The data people wanted large cells, at least 128 bytes. They had two main arguments. One was that 5 bytes of overhead for small cells was excessive; for example, for a 48-byte payload there would be more than 10% overhead. The other argument was that switches couldn't make a decision fast enough, so with small cell sizes ATM networks would be limited in speed because of the switching speed rather than the transmission speed. If the speed of the switches really was the thing that limited the speed of the ATM network, you could get twice as much throughput by making the cells twice as large. The claim was that cells needed to be somewhere between 64 and 128 bytes long so that switching speed would not be the limiting factor.

So the committee compromised on 48, a number large enough that it requires echo suppressors and small enough to make the data people as unhappy as the French PTT.

7.4.2 Virtual Circuits and Virtual Paths

ATM is conceptually very similar to X.25. Virtual circuits are created as in Figure 7.1, creating the call-mapping database in the switches that specifies the port onto which to forward a cell and what the outgoing connection identifier should be.

The connection identifier in the ATM cell header has two complexities.

- It's hierarchical and divided into two subfields: VPI (*virtual path identifier*) and VCI (*virtual circuit identifier*). The VCI is 16 bits. The VPI is 12 bits.

- It looks different between an endnode and a switch than between two switches. Between the endnode and the switch there are 4 bits reserved for a field called *generic flow control,* which the committee thought might be useful someday. The generic flow control uses 4 bits of the VPI field, so to endnodes the VPI field is 8 bits long. Except for making the spec a little more complicated, reserving those 4 bits does no harm because the endnode doesn't need any more bits than the VCI field.

So what's a VPI? There might be a very high speed backbone carrying many millions of calls. This split between VPI and VCI saves the routers in the backbone from requiring that their call-mapping database keep track of millions of individual calls. Instead, the backbone routers use only the VPI portion of the call identifier. Thousands of VCs might be going on the same VP, but the switches inside can treat all the VCs for that VP as a unit. Outside the backbone, the switches treat the entire field (VPI and VCI) as one combined, nonhierarchical field. The term *VP-switching* refers to switches that are looking at only the VPI portion. *VC-switching* refers to switches that are looking at the entire field.

A way of comparing VPs and VCs is to think of each connection across the cloud as a logical port (see Figure 7.12). To forward onto the logical port, a physical port *and* the correct VPI must be selected.

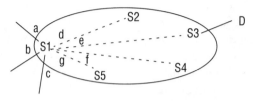

Figure 7.12 VPs as logical ports

In the "normal" VC-switching described in Section 7.1, if S1 were to receive a call setup on port b with CI 17 for destination D, S1 would decide which port it should use to forward to D and would pick a CI unused on the chosen outgoing port. In the case in Figure 7.12, it would be "port" e. The only complication is that forwarding onto "port e" involves selection of a physical port within the cloud, and a VPI. So there are three cases.

- Switches within the cloud do normal VP-switching, with the CI being the 12-bit VPI.

- Switches outside the cloud do normal VC-switching, with the CI being the 28-bit concatenated VPI/VCI field.

- Switches on the border do VC-switching, with the CI being the 28-bit concatenated VPI/VCI field; but the "port" that's internal to the cloud is defined by a combination of physical port and VPI, and the outgoing CI must be chosen so that the VPI portion of the outgoing CI is equal to the outgoing VPI.

In Figure 7.13, assume that S1 receives a call setup on port a with CI = 89, with a destination that is reachable through S6. Assume that S1 already has a virtual path set up to S6, which involves forwarding onto port c and using VPI 187 (if not, the VP gets created as the call setup is routed toward S6). The connection identifier within the backbone is the VPI. The VCI is ignored and not modified. The notation "x.y" is used to specify both VPI and VCI independently. This is relevant only at the ingress and egress switches from the backbone. The notation "x." is used for the CI in the databases of the switches internal to the backbone because they look only at the VPI portion. A number without a dot—for example, "z"—is used for switches outside the backbone that use the entire VPI+VCI field as a CI.

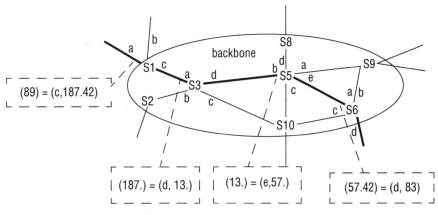

Figure 7.13 Within backbone, switch only on VPI

S1 receives the call setup with the VCI field being some value—say, 89. S1 looks at the destination address and determines that the packet should be routed out of the backbone via S6 and that S1 already has a path set up to S6 with VPI 187. S1 needs to choose a VCI unused within (port c, VPI 187) because (c, VPI 187) is the *outgoing port.* Say it chooses 42. Then S1 will map 89 to (c, 187.42). Now the VCI = .42 will stay constant throughout the backbone and will be ignored by the switches until exiting the backbone. But the VPI will change hop-by-hop. S1 and S6 must pay attention to both VPI and VCI.

The result is that 64,000 VCs (16 bits' worth) can be carried within a single VP, and the tables of the switches inside the backbone can therefore be dramatically smaller. They do not need to keep track of all the VCs but only the VPs.

In general, there are ATM networks belonging to the customer and ATM networks that serve as backbones. I call them *customer* and *provider*, respectively. The customer ATM nets tend to route based on the 28-bit VPI+VCI, and the provider ATM nets tend to route based on VPI. At the boundary, the switch connecting the two must map 28-bit CIs to (VPI, VCI) pairs, which really is the same as routing based on the 28-bit VPI+VCI.

When a link is brought up between two ATM switches, they negotiate a few things, including the following.

- Maximum number of active bits in VCI and VPI. Whichever switch wants to look at fewer of the bits wins the negotiation.

- Maximum number of VCs and VPs each can support. The one that can support fewer wins the negotiation, and no more than that number will be in use at any time on that link.

- Maximum allowable VPI number. This might be different from the maximum number of VPs you can support if you're willing to have "holes" in the assigned VP space. So, for example, you might be willing to support only 50 active VPs but allow a VPI as large as 1,000.

- Minimum and maximum VCI number for switched VCs. The numbers less than the minimum are reserved for well-known VCIs or for permanent virtual circuits. The switched VPs start at 1, so there's no need to negotiate the minimum for VPI.

As implemented in most provider ATM networks, VPs are not set up dynamically. Instead they are PVCs, which means that they are set up manually and are permanently up. The result is that the provider network looks to the customer network like a bunch of point-to-point links (each one a VP and using the VPI portion of the ATM cell header). It is up to the customer network to run a routing protocol or be configured with the mapping of destination addresses to VPs. I think it would be more civilized to have the provider run the routing protocol and figure out which VP should be used for a given destination address. PNNI (private network-to-network interface, a link state protocol for ATM similar to IS-IS), now being deployed, will solve this problem.

7.4.3 ATM Service Categories

ATM has defined several categories of service.

- *CBR:* constant bit rate. Data is accepted and delivered at a constant rate. That amount of bandwidth is reserved and guaranteed by the network.

- *UBR:* unspecified bit rate. Data is accepted with no constraints and carried if bandwidth is available or dropped if there isn't. No reservations or guarantees.

- *ABR:* available bit rate. Like UBR, but the network provides congestion feedback. The assumption is that if the endnode reacts appropriately to the feedback, there will be low data loss due to congestion.

- *VBR:* variable bit rate. Like CBR, bandwidth is reserved, but not for peak rate. It allows for peaks within limits (burst tolerance). VBR is further divided into RT (real time) and NRT (non real time), and the network is more careful about timely delivery with the RT-VBR class.

7.4.4 ATM Cell Header Format

Figure 7.14 shows the format of the 5-byte header of an ATM cell.

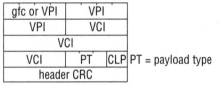

Figure 7.14 ATM cell format

- The first 4 bits are either part of the VPI (if the cell is traveling between two switches) or make up the reserved field called *generic flow control* (if the cell is traveling between an endnode and a switch).

- The next 24 bits are the VPI/VCI (see Section 7.4.2).

- The *payload type* is a 3-bit field. The top bit = 0 indicates data rather than ATM control information. For data, the middle bit indicates congestion experienced, and the bottom bit is used by AAL5 to indicate the last cell of a packet. The values are shown in Figure 7.15.

value	payload type
000	data, no congestion yet, not last cell
001	data, no congestion yet, last cell of pkt
010	data, congestion, not last cell
011	data, congestion, last cell
100	control info between nbr switches
101	control info between 1st and last switch on a path
110	ABR rate control information
111	reserved for future use

Figure 7.15 Values defined for payload type field in ATM cell

- CLP (cell loss priority) = 1 indicates this cell should be dropped before a cell with CLP = 0. This can be set by the endnode or by a switch. The switch might set the flag if that VC is sending at a higher rate than it should. The excess cells might be allowed on a capacity-available basis but might be marked for discard if the net does not have excess capacity.

- The final byte is a CRC of the first 4 bytes of the header.

7.4.5 Setting Up and Releasing Calls

ATM refers to this as *signaling*. The functions are very similar to those in X.25. The signaling messages are sent as ATM cells and are recognized as signaling messages because they use VCI = 5 (with VPI = 0). That VCI value (with VPI = 0) is reserved and would never be chosen for data. The signaling messages are longer than 48 bytes and so are transmitted over AAL5 (see Section 7.4.6.3).

- *setup:* This sets up a call and contains the source and destination addresses as well as information describing the traffic characteristics of this connection, quality of service requested (for example, whether we want to pay for a reservation or share unallocated bandwidth), and transit network (which is like dialing a prefix on a phone call to specify long distance carrier).

- *call proceeding:* This is sent by each switch to the preceding hop, and optionally by the destination, indicating receipt of the call setup and an attempt to process it.

- *connect:* This is sent by the destination and percolates back to the source, indicating that the destination has accepted the call.

- *connect acknowledge:* This is sent by the source and percolates to the destination, indicating that the source knows the call has been accepted by the destination.

- *release:* This is sent by either end to hang up the call, and it percolates across the network to the other end.

- *release acknowledge:* This is sent by the end that is informed of the release, and it percolates back to the side that initiated the release.

7.4.6 ATM Adaptation Layers

Because sending data in 48-byte chunks is inconvenient, various alternative interfaces to ATM can be implemented in a layer above ATM. This layer above is called the AAL, for ATM Adaptation Layer. The type of AAL to be used for a VC is announced in the call setup.

AAL0 is just direct ATM. AAL1 is for constant bit rate (CBR). AAL2 is similar to AAL1 but for variable rate, and the committee pretty much gave up on it before designing it completely. They "standardized" it in an incomplete state and declared victory, hoping nobody would notice that there was nothing implementable there. Recently a new AAL was proposed for multiplexing several voice channels into a single cell. Instead of being called AAL6, it's being called AAL2 and is under development. AAL3 and AAL4 were attempts at designing something that might be useful for data. Eventually they were combined into a single AAL called AAL3/4, but it was complex and inefficient. So the computer industry designed AAL5. AAL3/4 is used in some implementations done before AAL5 was defined, but most likely AAL3/4 will go away.

7.4.6.1 AAL1

AAL1 accepts a constant bit rate stream from the source and presents a constant bit rate stream to the destination. It must transmit these bits over the network as ATM cells that can incur delays, get lost, and so on.

AAL1 does this by buffering the data to smooth over delays and by numbering the cells so that lost data will be detected and not merely truncated out of the bit stream. It uses the first byte of the ATM payload for its control information, leaving 47 bytes for data in each ATM cell. That first byte contains the following.

- C: a somewhat mysterious bit that can be used for signaling—for example, marking points in the data stream for application-dependent reasons

- Seq: a 3-bit sequence number

- SNP: a 4-bit sequence number protection field that consists of a 3-bit CRC and a parity bit

Note that with only a 3-bit sequence number, AAL1 is somewhat dangerous because it's possible to lose 8 cells in a row.

7.4.6.2 AAL3/4

AAL3/4 attempts to provide a service that allows you to send a reasonable sized datagram. It was done in a complex and inefficient way, and people stepped in and designed AAL5, which is better in all ways, and AAL3/4 will eventually go away. Meanwhile, here's how it works.

- Take the datagram you'd like to send and add a header and a trailer. The header is 4 bytes long. It consists of a byte always set to 0; a tag of arbitrary value that will appear in both the header and the trailer and ensures that parts of different packets don't accidentally get concatenated; and a 2-byte length field indicating the number of bytes a buffer should be to hold the data plus all the overhead of headers, trailers, and padding. The trailer looks similar to the header. It contains a useless byte, followed by a 2-byte length (except this length is the number of bytes in the data), and a tag that should have the same value as the tag in the beginning of the packet. There's also padding between the data and the trailer to make sure that the trailer is 32-bit aligned.

- Now that you have added header, padding, and a trailer to the data, chop the data into 44-byte chunks. Each chunk is put into a cell along with 4 bytes of overhead: a 2-byte header and a 2-byte trailer. The header consists of a 2-bit field that indicates whether this cell is the beginning, the end, the middle of, or the complete packet. Then there's a 4-bit sequence number and a 10-bit field that the committee intended to allow multiplexing cells on a single virtual circuit, but it's unlikely anyone will think of a way to use it before AAL3/4 dies completely. The trailer consists of a 6-bit length field, which says how much data is in the cell (44 unless it's the last cell and isn't full), plus a 10-bit CRC covering this cell.

7.4.6.3 AAL5

The computer industry hated AALs 2 and 3/4. It stepped in and designed a new one, which the ATM forum then standardized as AAL5.

AAL5 has the same purpose as AAL3/4—namely, to allow the application to send a civilized sized datagram. The datagram you'd like to send is padded, and an 8-byte trailer is added. The amount of padding is such that the datagram plus padding plus trailer is an integral number of 48-byte chunks (ATM cells). The trailer has two unused bytes (the ATM forum seems to like having headers and trailers that are powers of 2 bytes in length), a 2-byte length field indicating the number of bytes in the data (not including padding and trailer), and a 4-byte CRC.

After the packet is padded and trailered, it is chopped into 48-byte cells and transmitted. It's nice that AAL5 doesn't take any overhead in ATM cells, in contrast to AAL1, which uses 1 byte, and AAL3/4, which uses 4 bytes out of the payload portion of every cell. However, AAL5 "cheats" a little by using 1 bit from the ATM cell header to indicate "end of packet."

You might think that AAL3/4 is better at detecting errors because there is a CRC on each cell. But it turns out that a 4-byte CRC is better than lots of 10-bit CRCs at detecting errors. Having individual CRCs on cells might be useful if you could transmit only the one damaged cell, but if a single AAL3/4 cell is damaged the entire packet must be retransmitted anyway.

So indeed AAL5 is superior in every way to AAL3/4. Because it supports variable bit rate, it can also do everything anyone would have wanted to do with AAL2. So almost certainly the only AALs that will survive are AAL1 and AAL5.

Homework

1. The link layer of X.25 includes flow control, in which the DTE can inform the DCE that it cannot receive any more packets. What is the difference in functionality between flow control performed at the link layer and flow control performed in X.25's network layer?

2. Design a connection-oriented net so that the VCI remains constant as it travels from source to destination. Compare this approach to having a virtual circuit number with only local significance.

3. Would it be possible in a connection-oriented network for neighbors to have a different VCI for a particular call in the two directions? In other words, if the path between A and B goes through R1 and then R2, would it be possible for R1 to assign a different VCI to that call on the R1-R2 link than the one R2 assigns?

   a. Explain how the call-setup protocol would need to handle this. Would it matter whether R1 chooses the VC number it wants to use when transmitting to R2, or whether it chooses the VC number R2 should use when sending to R1?

b. Does this arrangement require more memory in the routers for the call database? Modify the call-mapping database in Figure 7.1 as it would be if each end of each link were to independently choose a VCI for one direction of the call.

c. Would such a network have the potential for call collisions?

4. Would it be possible in a connection-oriented network to have different paths in the two directions (A to B and B to A)? What would the call-setup protocol look like?

5. The X.25 standard allows an exception to the rule that a packet must be maximum-size to have the M bit set—the exception being when the D bit is set. What problems could arise if this exception were not made? (Hint: consider S transmitting a packet much larger than the link size that S has between itself and its DCE, and a destination whose link size is very large.)

6. Suppose that the source DTE/DCE link allows a maximum packet size one-quarter the size allowed by the destination DTE/DCE link and that the source DTE has transmitted a packet to the source DCE with sequence number N. What can be said about the sequence number on that data when it is delivered by the destination DCE to the destination DTE?

7. Compare the strategies in Sections 7.3.1 and 7.3.2 for providing X.25 service to the DTE. Which one is more prone to call hangups?

8. Assume that an X.25 network is implemented using the method in Section 7.3.1. Assume that buffers are reserved in all the intermediate routers when a call is set up. Will delays on the path be constant?

9. What is the purpose of dividing the virtual circuit field into VPI and VCI in ATM?

10. Add the call-mapping entries that would get added in Figure 7.13 if S1 received two more call setups on port a, one of which would exit from S6 and the other of which would exit the backbone from S10.

11. How much overhead is involved in transmitting a 1,500-byte packet with AAL3/4 versus AAL5?

12. The VPI/VCI split in ATM allows two levels of hierarchy. How could you provide more levels of hierarchy? Let's use the term *call identifier* for the entire 28-bit field in the cell header. Divide it into, say, three levels of hierarchy and describe how this would be used and what portions of the field would get mapped at different parts of the hierarchy.

Chapter 8
Generic Connectionless Service

This chapter discusses generic issues in connectionless network layer service. Subsequent chapters go into the specifics of various connectionless network layer protocols such as IP, IPX, AppleTalk, CLNP, and DECnet, but the concepts are introduced here. Why do I bother describing protocols that are dying out? Why don't I just describe IP, which the world is basically converging on? There are a number of reasons.

- You will have a deeper understanding of IP if you also understand alternatives.

- A lot of interesting ideas, both good and bad, are in the other protocols. It's important to write them down so that future designers can use the good ideas and learn from the bad ones.

- Most protocols don't go away completely. Occasionally there is a need to learn about one of the rare protocols, so it's useful to have all of them summarized in one place.

- Historically it is nice to see where some ideas came from so that the inventors of the good ideas can be credited.

8.1 Data Transfer

A connectionless interface consists mainly of a header format for data because there is no need to do connection setup and release. You can still think of the interface as having three levels, just as in X.25. The endnode must attach to some sort of link, whether it be a point-to-point link, a LAN, or a full mesh network such as ATM. There is a physical layer (the kind of cable are you using), a data link layer (such as Ethernet, HDLC, FDDI, or ATM), and a network layer (such as IP or IPX).

A connectionless network layer is very simple—or rather does not need to be complicated—but a committee can create a complicated solution to any problem. The packet header contains addresses for the source and destination and a hop count to detect and destroy vagrant packets that are lost and wandering aimlessly. The header might also contain fragmentation and reassembly information and special service requests such as priority.

8.2 Addresses

The most interesting difference between various connectionless network layer protocols, such as IP, IPX, AppleTalk, and IPv6, is the size of the addresses. In general, larger addresses make it easier to assign addresses and minimize configuration, although AppleTalk, amazingly, as you will see in Section 9.10, manages to do a good job of auto-configuration with a tiny 3-byte address. Variable-length addresses are clearly the most flexible. They do not require choosing one size address that will suffice forever, and they save bandwidth in small networks where small addresses suffice. But they make the header more difficult to parse.

8.3 Hop Count

Unfortunately, when topologies change due to links and routers going up or down, it takes the routing protocol a certain amount of time to adapt to the new topology. During this time, databases in routers can be in an inconsistent state and packets can loop. For this reason it is a good idea to have a field in the header that can be used to detect and delete a packet looping. I think that getting rid of packets that are looping is the only reason for the field.

Unfortunately, the hop count is called *time to live* (TTL) in both CLNP and IP protocols. The theory when IP was developed was that the endnode might have some traffic (such as packet voice) that should be dropped if delayed beyond its time to live, and the network would have the capacity to measure elapsed time with sufficient accuracy. In practice, TTL fields do not have the granularity, nor can delays be measured with sufficient accuracy, for TTL to be any more useful than a simple hop count. It is common for implementations to treat the field as a hop count (that is, to have the value change by exactly 1 each time it is forwarded). CLNP basically copied the IP header but made the addresses larger and variable-length, so CLNP also calls the field "time to live," and the specification claims it really should represent time. The other protocols (IPX, AppleTalk, DECnet, IPv6) have only a hop count.

In IPX the hop count field increments, whereas in the other protocols it decrements. How could this possibly matter? If there were one universal value for "too many hops," it wouldn't matter. However, networks vary greatly in size, and over time a value such as 16, which might have seemed a reasonable limit a few years ago, is no longer large enough. So the limit would have to be a parameter, set independently at each router, if the hop count incremented. Then it would be difficult to debug when some router happened to have too small a value configured. Paths through that router would, inexplicably to a user, sometimes fail.

On the other hand, if the hop count decrements, the source can start the packet with whatever value the source thinks is reasonable, and the routers would not be making independent decisions. Calling a decrementing field "hop count" seems wrong. In IPv6 the terminology *hop limit* was adopted.

Having the source choose the hop limit has added benefits. If the source knows that the destination is nearby, it can set the hops to a smaller value, wasting less bandwidth if the routing algorithm has a temporary loop. And having the source choose the hop limit allows a cute utility used with IP called "traceroute." This useful debugging tool allows a source to find out the path being taken to a particular destination. First, the source issues a packet with the value 1 in the "time to live" field. The first router, R1, decrements the field, discovers the packet has expired, and sends back an error. The source now knows (based on who sent the error) that R1 is the first hop in the path. Then the source issues a packet, with the value 2 in the hop limit, to find out the next router in the path. This continues until the packet reaches the destination.

Note that traceroute wouldn't work very well if IP router implementations took the "time to live" field as anything but a hop count.

8.4 Service Class Information

Service class information advises the network of any special requirements pertaining to this packet. An example might be priority or a request for a route that does not incur per-packet charges. This is analogous to X.25's *facilities* field, which, in X.25, is carried only in the call request packet. In a connectionless network layer, such information would need to be carried in the header of every packet.

8.4.1 Priority

> **Priority is an attempt to implement the principles of jealousy and envy
> in computer networks.**
>
> —**Tony Lauck**

Priority raises all sorts of issues. Should high-priority traffic get absolute priority over lower-priority traffic? In other words, if there is sufficient high-priority traffic to use up all the bandwidth, should low-priority traffic get completely starved? If it should not, then a strategy is to reserve some percentage of the buffers for each priority class, with unused buffers being available to any priority class. So, for example, you might guarantee 20% of the bandwidth for high-priority traffic and 10% for low-priority traffic.

What's counterintuitive is that if there really is enough high-priority traffic to use 100% of the traffic and there is only enough low-priority traffic to use 10% of the traffic, then with this strategy low-priority traffic would get better service. That might indeed be what we want. It's not clear what people really want.

An even more difficult problem with priority is to make sure that people set it to a reasonable value. If networks do not impose disincentives (such as charging more money) for requesting better service, everyone would ask for highest priority.

8.4.2 Bandwidth Reservation and Service Guarantees

Bandwidth reservation should not be part of a connectionless network because it requires setting up the path and keeping state, something that makes the network connection-oriented. RSVP (RFC 2205) was an attempt to do just that, but network providers did not want to deploy it because of the amount of state they feared would be consumed if every conversation were allowed to set up state.

I'm not wild about bandwidth reservation. My intuition says that bandwidth is bursty and reserving bandwidth for the worst case would be wasteful. Also, most applications, such as video, that people cite as needing bandwidth reservation can do fine with some lost data. I'd rather see a network degrade for everyone rather than lock most people out and let the lucky few who got there first have excellent performance. People argue that for some applications you'd rather not bother at all if you can't get adequate service. But in that case I'd prefer to at least be able to be told when it would be possible to get that service—and make a reservation for the future—rather than constantly trying and getting busy signals. Ideally, the network should be keeping ahead of its customers by adding bandwidth before the network looks like the California highway system at rush hour.

8.4.3 Special Route Computation

Special route computation means having multiple metrics so that you can have your path optimized for something (say, delay) different from what someone else is attempting to optimize (say, bandwidth).

Paths are computed by minimizing the total cost of the path, usually by adding up the individual costs of the links. But what is the cost of the link? Is it based on delay, bandwidth, or something else? What if I want a route computed according to minimum delay, and you want one computed to maximize bandwidth?

IP defines three metrics: delay, bandwidth, and *residual error rate*, which in theory means how flaky the link is. CLNP, which basically copied IP and made a few additions here and there, added an additional metric, which was money.

All this sounds reasonable. Why should everyone have to have routes computed according to the same metric?

Let me explain why I don't like it.

1. Every metric requires configuring an extra number on the link. It also requires that extra information be passed in the routing protocol and extra computation be made (a whole set of paths must be computed for each metric). Separate forwarding databases must also be kept.

2. There really is very little difference between delay and bandwidth. A low-bandwidth link, if even slightly congested, will become a high-delay link. So there's no reason to bother having separate metrics for those two. The money metric sounds like a nice idea, but there are few situations when having the metric will make a difference. A simpler method is to place a high cost (according to the single metric I recommend using) on expensive links. And the residual error rate metric . . . what were they thinking? Nobody uses this. If the links are flaky, you should fix them or run a data link protocol that detects and retransmits damaged packets.

So, not enough is gained by allowing multiple metrics to warrant the extra configuration and bandwidth, memory, and CPU overhead.

8.5 Network Feedback

In addition to receiving and transmitting data packets, an endnode might receive certain types of advisory information from the network. The two most common instances of this are as follows.

1. Error reports, indicating that a packet could not be delivered for some reason. Usually, the error report gives a hint as to the reason. For example, the destination might have been unreachable or the packet might have been illegally formatted or too big.

2. Congestion information, indicating that the network is becoming overly utilized and that the endnode should reduce its use of the network by setting its transport layer window smaller.

8.6 Fragmentation and Reassembly

X.25 manages to perform fragmentation and reassembly with only a single bit in the header (the M bit; see Section 7.2.4). But this mechanism does not work in a datagram network, in which fragments can be lost, duplicated, or arrive out of order. Neither would a mechanism in which a router marked each fragment with a "fragment number"; a router could fragment a packet into fragments 1, 2, 3, and 4, and then, some hops later, fragment 2 could encounter a link that required fragment 2 to be fragmented further.

The common solution is for the network layer data packet format to contain an *offset* field. For example, if a packet whose size is 8,000 octets encounters a link that can handle only 4,000 octets, the router might fragment the packet into two pieces, each 4,000 octets long. (Each fragment must also carry header information, so the router must take into account the size of the header when it calculates the size of the fragment it will produce.) The first fragment will have the offset field set to 0. The second fragment will have the offset field set to 4,000. If the second fragment encounters a link on which it needs to be further fragmented—say, into 1,000-octet chunks—then the second fragment will become four fragments, with the offset fields set to 4,000, 5,000, 6,000, and 7,000, respectively.

It is essential for the destination to know when a packet has been completely reassembled. One issue is for it to be able to determine the total length of the packet before fragmentation. ISO's CLNP (connectionless network protocol) protocol provides this information in its **total length** field. IP instead provides a **more fragments** flag, which is set on all but the final fragment. Although IP has a field called **total length**, it does not give the same information as the CLNP **total length** field. The CLNP field gives the total length of the packet before fragmentation. The IP field gives only the size of that fragment (plus the header of that fragment).

When the destination knows that it has received the final fragment, it still does not know that the packet has been successfully reassembled, because some of the packet's intermediate fragments may have gotten lost. Nor can it simply count the number of octets received; some of the received fragments may be duplicates. Even if exact duplicates were discarded, a simple count of the octets received might not work because different copies of duplicated fragments may have taken different paths and may have been fragmented in different, overlapping places.

One possible solution is to allocate a bitmask, 1 bit per octet in the reassembly buffer. As data arrives, it is copied into the reassembly buffer and the relevant bits in the bitmask are marked off. This solution requires the bitmask to be 1/8th as big as the reassembly buffer. However, both the IP and the CLNP standards require reassembly on 8-octet chunks, so the bitmask can be 1/64th as big as the reassembly buffer.

Another possible solution is to keep pointers in the reassembly buffer itself, in locations that have not yet been filled with data (see Figure 8.1). Initially, a reassembly buffer of some size is allocated—say, 8,000 octets. (In CLNP, each fragment's header gives the prefragmentation size of the packet, so the size of the required reassembly buffer is known.) Associated with the reassembly buffer is a pointer that points to the first location within the reassembly buffer that has not yet been filled with data. Initially, the pointer points to the beginning of the buffer. At the location where the pointer points is written a pointer to the next such location in the buffer and the size of the current "hole." As fragments arrive, the pointers and lengths are modified accordingly. When the initial pointer points to the end of the buffer, the packet has been completely reassembled.

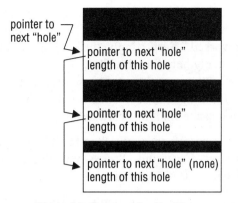

Figure 8.1 Reassembly algorithm

Another issue is for the destination to be able to determine when to discard partly reassembled packets. If a fragment has been lost in transit, the partly reassembled packet can never be successfully reassembled. Memory must be freed up for future packets. If all buffers are used for partly reassembled packets and a fragment arrives for a packet other than one of the packets currently being reassembled, various strategies can be employed. The destination can discard the most recently received fragment, the least recently received fragment, or a fragment chosen at random.

Network layer reassembly is CPU-intensive, especially because it usually involves copying data at the destination. High-bandwidth applications would be better served if the source transport layer chose a packet size so that packets would not need to be fragmented inside the network. Ideally, the source will want the largest possible packet size that won't require fragmentation because throughput is degraded both if the packet size is smaller than necessary and if the packet size is so large that network layer fragmentation is required.

With connectionless networks, maximum packet size is a difficult issue. Even if the appropriate size is found for a given path, the network may reroute packets in the middle of a conversation or do path splitting.

8.7 Maximum Packet Size Discovery

The standard term for figuring out the biggest packet you can send that won't require fragmentation is *MTU discovery* (MTU stands for *maximum transmission unit*). Both IP and CLNP have a flag in the header indicating whether it is legal to fragment the packet. If a router decides to forward a packet onto a link for which the packet is too large and if the flag indicates fragmentation should not be performed, the router returns an error message. The error message says that the packet had to be dropped because fragmentation was necessary but not allowed.

An IETF working group decided that the error message should include the size of packet that would work. It seems strange to say, "That was too big" without saying, "But 1,000 bytes would have worked." Surprisingly, the extra information (the size that would have worked) does not actually help find the MTU.

How many different packet sizes are there, really? Let's say 8. There's Ethernet (1,500), FDDI (4,500), and maybe 3 or 4 others, but probably no more than 8. What kinds of strategies can you use to find the best size?

1. Suppose the error message says only "too big." You could do a binary search of possible packet sizes. Given only 8 possible values, it would take three probes before the right size were pinpointed.

2. Suppose the error message says which size would work. The problem is, that's not the size that would work through the whole path. It's only the size that gets by the first bottleneck. The obvious strategy, with this added piece of information in the error message, is to try the largest size first, then try the size given in the error message, and then try it again until it gets through. But in the worst case, rather than trying log n probes (where n is the number of packet sizes on links in the network), you could wind up doing n probes. Extra information might lead you to a worse algorithm! Of course it's unlikely that the worst case would come up often, but it's still not obvious that the binary search scheme, ignoring the packet size hint in the error message, isn't the best strategy.

3. Suppose routers truncated the packet rather than returning an error message, and flagged that the packet was truncated, or allowed a special type of packet that would be legal for routers to truncate, and that packet could be used to find out the MTU on a path. In this case a single packet can make it to the destination, getting truncated as necessary. When it reaches the destination, the destination can inform the source what the MTU is, with only a single probe. I like this strategy, but I'm not aware of any network layers that do this.

4. Another strategy I've suggested (but I don't think has been deployed) is to have the routers perform fragmentation so that there is always a maximum-sized fragment. For example, if the maximum size on a link is 1,000 bytes and the packet is 1,200 bytes, the router fragments into 1,000 and 2,000. Then the destination can conclude that the maximum packet size is the size of the largest fragment received.

Note that all these schemes might give incorrect results if packets are being routed on different paths.

Homework

1. Discuss the relative merits of the three proposals for discarding partly reassembled packets (discard the oldest fragment, discard the newest fragment, discard a fragment chosen at random).

2. Discuss strategies for finding the maximum packet size to the destination in the following cases.

    • The network gives no feedback other than dropping large packets.

    • A router truncates packets, marking them as truncated.

    • A router returns an error "packet too large."

    • A router returns an error "packet too large, size n would have worked."

    • A router fragments packets into equal-sized fragments.

    • A router creates maximum-sized fragments plus remainder fragments.

3. Compare all the schemes in problem 2. Consider properties such as how long it takes to find the maximum packet size, whether data transfer can occur while the maximum packet size discovery process is being performed, how resilient it would be to path splitting, and so on.

Chapter 9
Network Layer Addresses

This chapter describes the structure of addresses in various network layer protocols, including IP, IPX, IPv6, CLNP, AppleTalk, and DECnet. Even if all you care about is IP, you will understand IP better if you can see contrasting solutions. There are also good ideas as well as mistakes in the other protocols (as well as in IP), and it is important to learn these lessons, both good and bad, for the sake of future protocols. For example, IPv6 benefited by using some of the ideas in IPX and CLNP. And although the world seems to have converged around IPv4, the other protocols exist, and it's good to have them documented somewhere.

The major difference among all the connectionless network layer protocols is the size of the addresses. Other than that, there's not much to a connectionless network layer protocol. You just put the destination and source addresses on the packet and launch it into the network, hoping for the best.

Another interesting issue about addresses is whether an address is of the node or of an interface to the node. For example, IP (and IPX, IPv6, and AppleTalk) are protocols in which addresses are not really the node itself but rather an interface to the node, so a node that has multiple links has a different address for each link. A packet addressed to one of the links arrives at that link. This case is analogous to a house built on a corner, with an entrance onto two streets—say, Router Road and Bridge Boulevard (see Figure 9.1). In theory, the house could then have two addresses, one for each street—say, 110 Router Road as well as 31 Bridge Boulevard.

In contrast, CLNP and DECnet have addresses for the nodes (within an area), so a node with multiple links can have a single network layer address (as long as all the links are in the same area).

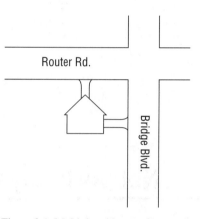

Figure 9.1 Multiple addresses for a node

Another difference is how addresses are constructed: whether they must be configured in the endnode or in an on-LAN server, or can be plug-and-play. I nominate Apple-
Talk for the most creative solution to the plug-and-play problem.

9.1 Hierarchical Addresses with Fixed Boundaries

When there are too many destinations for a network to keep track of, routing is designed
to be *hierarchical*, in the sense that the network is partitioned into pieces. Then one portion of the address indicates the "piece" of the network in which the destination resides,
and another portion of the address distinguishes destinations within that piece.

The postal service uses hierarchical addresses. A portion of the address indicates the
country in which the destination is located. The first step in routing is to get the letter to
the correct country. After the letter has reached the correct country (say, the United
States), the portion of the address that indicates the state in which the destination is
located becomes relevant. Then routing delivers the letter to the correct state, ignoring
the remainder of the address. Only when the letter has reached the correct state does the
city portion of the address become relevant, and then the street and number, and finally
the name.

Network layer addresses in all the protocols we are discussing here are also hierarchical. In contrast, for the purpose of routing, IEEE 802 addresses are not hierarchical.
Although IEEE 802 addresses seem hierarchical—because the top three octets are named
the OUI, these addresses are in fact hierarchical only for ease of address assignment. No
assumption can be made about the location of a LAN node based on its OUI. Any sort of
routing based on IEEE 802 addresses (such as bridge station learning) must treat each
address as an individual 48-bit quantity. If the 802 address were geographically hierar-

chical, bridges would be able to assume that all stations with an address whose first octet was equal to "X" would be located in the same place.

With fixed-boundary hierarchical addressing (as opposed to flexible-boundary addressing, described in Section 9.2), a large network is broken into chunks, which I call *level 1 subnetworks*. Within a level 1 subnetwork, routers keep track of all the individual links and nodes. The routers routing within a level 1 subnetwork are known as *level 1 routers*. *Level 2 routing* concerns itself with where all the level 1 subnetworks are but not with details internal to the level 1 subnetworks. If the size of the level 1 subnetworks is kept manageable, the job of level 1 routing is tractable. If there are not too many level 1 subnetworks, the job of level 2 routing is tractable. It is possible for a level 2 router to also participate as a level 1 router in one or more level 1 subnetworks. In this case the level 2 router would have to know about the internals of the level 1 subnetworks in which it resided in addition to knowing the internals of the level 2 subnetwork. If there are too many level 1 subnetworks, the network can be partitioned into *level 2 subnetworks*, with *level 3 routers* routing to the proper level 2 subnetworks.

In a network having three fixed levels of hierarchy, an address would look like the one in Figure 9.2.

level 2 subnetwork	level 1 subnetwork	endnode

Figure 9.2 An address with a three-level hierarchy

A three-level address would have three components and look something like 37.91.12, where 37 would indicate the level 2 subnetwork, 91 would indicate the level 1 subnetwork, and 12 would indicate the endnode within level 1 subnetwork 37.91 (see Figures 9.3 and 9.4).

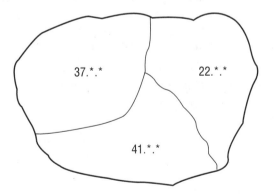

Figure 9.3 Level 2 subnetworks

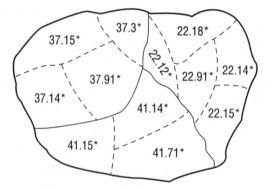

Figure 9.4 Level 1 subnetworks

9.2 Hierarchical Addresses with Flexible Boundaries

Some network layer protocols, including IP, IPX, and CLNP, can have arbitrary levels of hierarchy; they do not explicitly set aside portions of the address for each level, except for possibly having a fixed boundary at the lowest level. The basic idea is that you should be able to draw a circle around a portion of the network, and, assuming you have assigned addresses in a logical way, you should be able to summarize the addresses reachable within that circle. Then you should be able to take a bunch of these circles and draw a bigger circle. A router should not need to know whether it is operating at level 3 or level 17. And the address does not have fixed fields for "level 14 subnetwork," "level 13 subnetwork," and so on. Instead, an address summary is merely an address prefix. And in general, the shorter the prefix, the higher the level of hierarchy, because there are more addresses that match 5* than match 58493748*.

For example, let's start building a network from the inside out. There is a backbone that owns all the addresses. Let's assume the backbone allows various providers to hook up and gives each one a block of addresses to hand out to customers. A block of addresses is defined by a prefix, meaning that all addresses in the block start with the same number. Consider Figure 9.5.

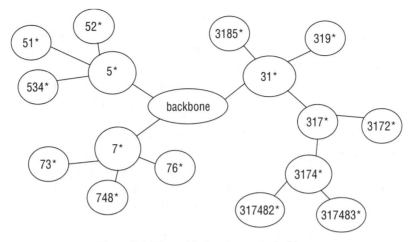

Figure 9.5 Hierarchical assignment of addresses

The backbone gives the address blocks 5*, 7*, and 31* to each of the three attached providers to hand out to their customers. The backbone has very small routing tables because it needs to know only about the three prefixes 5*, 31*, and 7*. Then the provider with the block 31* has customers and gives them blocks 3185*, 319*, and 317*, respectively. The customer 317* has such a large network that it assigns addresses hierarchically, with 3174* in one piece and 3172* in another. And 3174* further gets broken into pieces, one with addresses of the form 317482* and another with addresses of the form 317483*.

Note that there is no reason for a router to know how many levels of hierarchy are below it. And there is no fixed place in the address where level boundaries are. Prefixes can be whatever length is appropriate. For example, if a provider is expecting a lot of customers and therefore needs a large block of addresses, it will have a short prefix. More numbers of a fixed length, such as 6 digits, start with 5 than start with 51827.)

9.3 Owning versus Renting Addresses

To make routing tables small, your address must make sense for your location in the topology. This is similar to your telephone number. If you move to a different town, you must change your telephone number.

In the beginning, people obtained IP addresses by asking IANA for a block of addresses. (Internet Assigned Numbers Authority is the organization that had the administrative task of handing out IP addresses and numbers in various protocol fields.) They then assumed they could keep that block of addresses forever. However, the people running the Internet eventually realized that the routing tables were getting too large; it was unlikely that such blocks of IP addresses would be aggregatable—that is, having all addresses in a certain range conveniently located next to each other in the topology. The telephone analogy would be that everyone would apply for a telephone number to a central place that would give out the numbers in numerical order as it processed requests. So someone in Florida would get 1, someone in Colorado would get 2, someone in Wisconsin would get 3, someone in Albania would get 4, and so on because that was the order in which they requested numbers and not because the numbers made sense in the topology.

So the conclusion was that they'd use *provider based addressing*, which means you get a block of addresses from your ISP (Internet service provider).

People don't like provider-based addressing because it means that they have to change their addresses when they change providers, and with IP it is painful to renumber because IP involves a lot of configuration. But if you don't have a choice, you learn to cope, or you invent kludges such as NAT (network address translators; see Section 9.12).

9.4 Types of Addresses

People use the following terms when referrring to addresses.

- *Unicast:* A unicast address is intended to be destined for a single node.

- *Multicast:* A multicast address is intended to be destined for a group of nodes.

- *Broadcast*: A broadcast address is intended to be destined for all nodes. This is a nonsensical concept. Whatever you can do with broadcast you can do with multicast. If everyone happens to be listening to a particular multicast, then fine. There's no way to legislate that everyone listen to something, so there should only be multicast.

- *Anycast:* An anycast address is intended to be destined for one of a group of nodes, and it doesn't matter which one of them receives the packet. Usually the packet is delivered to the nearest node listening for that address. This type of address is useful for reaching one of a group of nodes that provides some sort of service.

9.5 IP

When I use the term IP, it indicates IPv4, the ubiquitous current protocol everyone knows as IP as defined in RFC 791. In IP, network layer addresses are 4 octets long. A portion of the address indicates a link number, and a portion indicates the system on the link, which in IP terminology is referred to as the *host*. (There is no IP terminology exactly corresponding to the *link*, except perhaps the word *subnet*, which does not exactly correspond because what I refer to as the *link number* is often referred to in IP as containing two fields: *net* and *subnet*. This should become clearer in a few paragraphs.)

An IP address looks like the illustration in Figure 9.6.

link	host

Figure 9.6 IP address

Which bits in the address belong in the *link* field and which bits belong in the *host* field is not fixed but rather can differ for each link in the network. It is important for a node to know, for each link to which it is attached, which bits correspond to the link portion of its address on that link and which bits correspond to the host portion.

For each link in an IP network, the person who is planning the network decides the value of the link number and which bits in the address will correspond to the link number. A link (such as a LAN) has a link number and a mask indicating which bits correspond to the link number. Figure 9.7 shows an example.

mask

11111111	11111111	11000000	00000000

link number

11101000	01010101	01000000	00000000

Figure 9.7 Link number and mask

In this case, the leftmost 18 bits of all addresses of nodes on that link equal 111010000101010101, and the rightmost 14 bits are used to distinguish attachments to the link.

In theory, IP allows the mask to have noncontiguous 1's. This means that the bits that indicate the link number need not be contiguous but can be sprinkled throughout the address. This is incredibly confusing and likely to create ambiguous addresses (addresses that could reside on more than one link). It also results in inefficient routing because it makes it computationally expensive for a router to identify the destination link toward which to route. And in fact none of the router vendors supports noncontiguous subnet masks, so we really can think of the link address as a prefix.

Each node on a link must know the mask for the link as well as its own IP address. An IEEE 802 address can be installed in ROM in a node and always be applicable no matter where the node is plugged in to a network. IP addresses cannot work that way because a node must acquire an IP address that matches the link's address (for the portion of the address that has 1's in the mask) and is different from the IP addresses of any other nodes on that link. Typically, IP nodes either are configured with their IP address and mask or use the BOOTP protocol (RFC 951),[1] DHCP protocol (RFC 1531),[2] or, less commonly, the RARP protocol (RFC 903)[3] to acquire the information. They must start

[1] B. Croft and J. Gilmore, "Bootstrap Protocol," RFC 951, September 1985.

[2] R. Droms, "Dynamic Host Configuration Protocol," RFC 1531, October 1993.

[3] R. Finlayson, T. Mann, J. Mogul, and Marvin Theimer, "A Reverse Address Resolution Protocol," RFC 903 (Network Information Center, SRI International, Menlo Park, Calif., June 1984).

with some information—generally, their LAN address (which can be stored in ROM at the node) and the address of a BOOTP server. Assuming that the BOOTP server has been configured to know that node's IP address on that link as well as the link's mask, the BOOTP server will inform the endnode of its IP address and mask.

Originally, in IP, the boundary between the link number and the host number was less flexible. Also, the link was known as the *network*. The boundary was after either the first, second, or third octet. If the leftmost bit in an address was 0, the boundary was after the first octet; the address was known as a *class A* address and had the form shown in Figure 9.8.

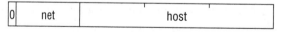

Figure 9.8 Class A address

If the leftmost 2 bits in an address were 10, the boundary was after the second octet; the address was known as a *class B* address and had the form shown in Figure 9.9.

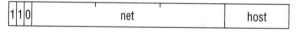

Figure 9.9 Class B address

If the leftmost 3 bits in an address were 110, the boundary was after the third octet; the address was known as a *class C* address and had the form shown in Figure 9.10.

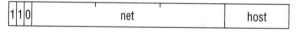

Figure 9.10 Class C address

The idea of making the boundary between net and host more flexible was known as *subnetting*. The original assumption was that a mask for a class A address would always have 1's for the highest octet (and an arbitrary mixture of 1's and 0's for the remaining octets), a mask for a class B address would always have 1's for the two highest octets, and a mask for a class C address would always have 1's for the three highest octets. The subnetting idea allows a mask with more 1's than 8 for class A, 16 for class B, and 24 for class C.

The portion of the class A address that had 1's in the bottom 3 octets of its mask was known as the *subnet*. For a class B address, the 1 bits in the bottom 2 octets of the address mask correspond to the subnet. And for a class C address, the 1 bits in the bottom octet correspond to the subnet. Usually, IP addresses are referred to as having three fields: the *net* number, the *subnet* number, and the *host* number. For example, in a class B address, the top 2 octets would be the net portion, any bits in the bottom 2 octets corresponding to

1's in the mask would be the subnet portion, and the remainder of the bottom 2 octets would be the host portion.

However, it turns out to be potentially useful to allow masks with 0's in what used to be known as the net portion of the address (to get more levels of hierarchy), and addressing conventions that made a distinction between net and subnet were not found useful. If all protocols provided a mask when reporting a reachable destination, knowing about class A, B, and C addresses would become unnecessary. Most modern IP routing protocols include a mask. Old ones (RIP, EGP, early versions of BGP) did not. When a protocol does not include a mask when reporting a reachable destination, the portion of the address corresponding to the link number must be calculated implicitly based on whether the address is class A (in which case, the "link number" is the first octet), class B (the first two octets), or class C (the first three octets).

The idea of allowing arbitrary length masks and doing away with the classes was given the name CIDR (Classless Inter-Domain Routing) and written up in RFC 1519.

The link portion of the IP address can be used in a flexible way to obtain arbitrary levels of hierarchy, as described in Section 9.2. Some routing protocols (such as OSPF—see Section 14.4.1.3) do not allow arbitrary hierarchy, but this constraint is not due to IP addresses but only to the design of the routing protocol. OSPF allows two levels of hierarchy within the link portion of the address. This means that if you count the node portion as another level of hierarchy, with OSPF you can obtain three levels of hierarchy. IS-IS (see Section 14.4.1.1), BGP (see Section 14.5.3), and PNNI (see Section 14.4.1.4) allow arbitrary levels of hierarchy (see Figure 9.11).

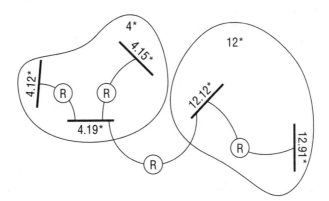

Figure 9.11 Hierarchical IP network

9.5.1 IP Address Conventions

IP addresses have the conventions that all 1's in a field means "all," and all 0's means "this." The uses for these conventions are as follows.

1. <link = 0><host = 0>

   This is employed when a host boots knowing only its data link address and uses RARP, BOOTP, or DHCP to find out its IP address.

2. <0><host>

   This would theoretically be employed by a host using RARP, BOOTP, or DHCP to determine the net and/or subnet portions of its address. This is not very useful because there is no rational reason that a host would know its host number relative to a link but would not know the link number.

3. <-1>

   The notation −1 means all 1's. This destination address indicates that the packet should be transmitted as a data link broadcast packet on the attached link. Using all 1's in the source address of an IP packet is illegal and a nuisance. (Just because it's illegal doesn't mean it isn't done, however, especially by implementations with bugs.)

4. <net = X><−1>

   This indicates that the packet should be transmitted as a broadcast packet to all of net X. If net X is actually partitioned into multiple subnet numbers, this address implies that the packet should be transmitted as a broadcast packet on all those subnets, but none of the routing protocols supports this functionality.

   Again, transmitting a packet with a network layer source address of this form is illegal and a nuisance.

5. <net = X><subnet = Y><−1>

   This indicates that the packet should be transmitted to the link known as <X> <Y>. When it arrives, it should be transmitted on that link as a broadcast packet.

   Again, an address of this form is legal only as a destination address.

An additional addressing convention is <127><X>, which is to be used as an internal host loopback address, regardless of the value of X. This form of address is illegal except when used internally.

A host's IP address cannot have 0 or −1 in any of the fields <net>, <subnet>, or <host>.

One additional convention for IP addresses has been established to support IP multicasting. (see Section 15.2). An IP multicast address has its top 4 bits equal to 1110 and is known as a *class D* address. In case IP ever invents some other form of address, its top 4 bits will be equal to 1111 (but not all the bits in the first octet will be 1's, or else this form would conflict with one of the broadcast conventions defined earlier in this section). This form of address, which is currently known as a *class E* address, is not yet defined for any purposes.

9.5.2 Text Representation of IP Addresses

The standard method of writing or displaying an IP address is as the decimal value of each of the four octets, separated by periods. For example, the IP address 15.29.13.4 would equal the one shown in Figure 9.12.

00001111	00011101	00001101	00000100

Figure 9.12 The IP address 15.29.13.4

A mask is written in the same way, so a 16-bit mask would be 255.255.0.0. Although I know 0 and 255, it takes some computation for me to figure out what, say, a 10-bit mask would equal (255.192.0.0), and I'd be likely to make mistakes. I can't imagine anyone consciously deciding this was a good representation for addresses. I haven't inquired about who invented this notation. It's probably better that I don't know.

9.6 IPX

IPX addresses are 10 bytes long. The top four bytes, called the *network* part, specify the link, and the bottom 6 bytes specify the node on the link. This is like having a 10-byte IP address rather than a 4-byte IP address, where the mask is 4 bytes of 1's.

Just as with IP, the network part of the address can have flexible multiple levels of hierarchy, provided the routing protocol supports it (see Figure 9.13).

Figure 9.13 IPX address

Why would IPX "waste" 6 bytes of address on the node portion? You'd never have a link with 2^{48} nodes on it. The reason is for autoconfiguration and protocol simplicity. The bottom 6 bytes are equal to the node's IEEE 802 address. Because every node that can plug in to a LAN comes with a ROM with a unique IEEE address, IPX is truly plug-and-play. The node starts out knowing only its IEEE address, broadcasts on the LAN to ask a router what the network number is for that LAN, and presto! The node now knows its IPX address.

Another advantage of IPX is that it does not need a protocol such as ARP (see Section 11.2.2). After the packet gets to the destination LAN you know its data link address—it's the bottom 6 bytes in the packet.

So IPX is autoconfiguring and has lower overhead because it does not need ARP packets on the wire and ARP caches in the nodes. And it is a larger address space than IP (10 bytes rather than 4).

9.6.1   Privacy Issue with Unique IDs

From a protocol perspective IPX is simple and elegant and has low overhead. But recently a privacy concern was raised about unique IDs on computer chips, and some of the arguments could apply to a protocol in which a system's unique ID is embedded in its layer 3 address. The concern is that if a person carries a laptop and plugs it in to a network, the laptop's unique ID can possibly be used to identify the person, and the rest of the address can be used to indicate the person's location. Almost all the same concerns apply to IP unless every time you power up you get a new address through DHCP (see Section 11.2.2.4). If your layer 3 address remains constant, it is as much a unique ID as your IEEE 802 address or your computer chip's ID. If you move locations your IP address will change, but if you don't then the IP address is a unique ID. If you acquire a new IP address each time you power up (through DHCP), only the low-order part of your address will change (because the link address must be constant). For most nefarious purposes, tracing you back to a LAN, if not a specific machine on the LAN, is sufficient.

If people really want privacy on a network, they should use an *anonymizer.* You connect to this proxy machine and then connect from it to machines on which you would like to be untraceable. It gives you an untraceable name and address, either for the session or longer term if desired. A NAT or NAPT box (see Section 9.12) can be thought of as an anonymizer for network addresses.

9.6.2   Ugly Rumors about IPX

People believe, for some reason, that IPX is "unroutable", "doesn't work on WANs" or "doesn't scale." IPX is actually a wonderful network layer protocol, better than IP in almost every way (except for little things such as having a hop count that increments rather than decrements). Why do many people believe bad things about it?

The answer is that there is a germ of truth in what they are saying, but it has nothing to do with IPX. IPX is, as I said, quite wonderful: it has large addresses, it is autoconfiguring, it is simple to implement, and it requires low overhead. But unfortunately, IPX hangs out with some unsavory company, such as SPX, a protocol just like TCP but with a window size of 1; RIP, a routing protocol as bad as its namesake for routing IP; and SAP (Service Advertisement Protocol), a protocol for finding services, which we discuss more in Section 11.4.3. Of course you don't get high performance on large delay links with a transport protocol that can have only a window of 1. Of course the routing protocol has a lot of overhead if it's RIP! And SAP is also a spectacularly chatty protocol.

All this can be fixed. RIP can be replaced by a civilized routing protocol (NLSP, which is basically an IPX-specific version of IS-IS). SPX can be replaced by TCP (and there are implementations of TCP on top of IPX). SAP can be replaced by advertising services in a directory. But people either have continued to run networks with the old protocols with IPX or have just remembered the bad old days, and IPX has never gotten the respect it deserves.

9.6.3 Administering IPX Addresses

From the start with IP, there was a registry (the IANA) where you could get a block of IP addresses. As it turned out, that was the wrong way to get addresses, and IP eventually moved to provider-based addresses (you must get a block of addresses from your service provider so that your addresses make sense in the topology). But until the Internet got really large the registry approach worked, and the unique addressing already in place encouraged interconnection of IP networks.

IPX, on the other hand, did not have a registry. So although there were many more nodes running IPX than IP in the mid-90s, nobody thought of it as an Internet protocol because you didn't have one big IPX internet; you just had zillions of little IPX networks. Because IPX was plug-and-play, it shouldn't have been very hard to combine networks because only the routers would have to be reconfigured. But people who had experience renumbering with IP whimpered if you mentioned renumbering. A short-lived registry was created at about the same time that people were starting to realize that obtaining permanent, globally unique blocks of addresses was not the right thing. The registry also defined a way to map global blocks of IP addresses into global blocks of IPX addresses.

The real answer, if a true IPX Internet had taken off, was to force people either to renumber based on a block of addresses they'd be given by their ISP or use IPX+ (see Section 9.7).

9.6.4 Internal IPX Network Numbers

When people found out I worked at Novell, the second question everyone seemed to ask me was "What's an internal network number?"

First, I'll explain the problem that is solved by internal network numbers. IPX, like IP, assigns an address to each interface. So a server that has two links has two addresses (see Figure 9.14).

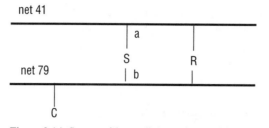

Figure 9.14 Server with two links and two addresses

On net 41, S must have an address of the form 41.something. Let's say that S's Ethernet address on the top LAN is a, and on the bottom LAN is b. So S's two IPX addresses would be 41.a and 79.b. Server S chooses one of its addresses—say, 41.a—and advertises itself as that address.

The way IPX works, the client, wanting to reach the service at IPX address 41.a, broadcasts a message on its LAN asking which router can help it reach net 41. A router that is a good path to that network replies. Both R and S are good paths to 41, so both reply. C chooses the first reply and uses that router to reach service 41.a. C is as likely to choose R as S. If C chooses R, all its packets to S will be one-hop suboptimal because C will send it to R, which will transmit it onto the top LAN, where it will reach S. (When told this problem, my immediate reaction was "So?" I never get very excited about sub-optimal routes. I think people should be grateful if their packets get there at all.)

The solution was to assign S an *internal network number*—say, 92. To the outside world the picture in Figure 9.14 becomes the one shown in Figure 9.15.

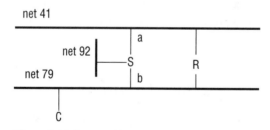

Figure 9.15 Server with two links and two addresses

The server advertises the address of its service as 92.something, usually a low num-ber such as 92.1. Now when C asks who is the best path to net 92, only S replies.

This technique solves the one-hop-suboptimality problem. But it eats up network numbers, and there is only a 4-byte network number space. IP has a 4-byte space, but that space must be shared between the net and the node. IPX might seem to have a lot more addresses for LANs because the 4-byte network number is only for LANs. But because all the servers wind up using network numbers, there really aren't very many more IPX network numbers than IP network numbers.

But the real problem is that this approach requires extra configuration. I liked IPX so much because it was plug-and-play for the clients. And I was surprised to find that all servers must be assigned an internal network number, even those with only a single link and for which therefore there is no one-hop-suboptimality problem. I suggested making configuration of an internal network number optional, not only for the single-link server case but also when customers prefer living with one-hop suboptimality sometimes and saving configuration (and network numbers). But I was told that customers did not mind configuring the internal network number. Loved it, in fact. And that it would be more confusing for them to have to sometimes configure it and sometimes not need to configure it.

OK. But then in a later release, the implementation gave the option of having the server choose its own internal network number. Yikes! It picks one at random, looks at the routing table, and assumes that if the random number it chose for a network number is not currently reachable in the routing table it's safe to use for its own internal network number. So much for aggregatable addresses! So much for routing hierarchy, in which you don't see the addresses reachable in other parts of the network. Why would anyone consider putting in such a feature if customers really enjoyed configuring the internal network number?

Anyway, don't use the option of letting the server choose its own internal network number.

Incidentally, IP has the problem that nodes having multiple links have multiple addresses. It is a nuisance, not only for the one-hop suboptimality but because also sometimes a service might be unreachable at one address but reachable at a different address. So the internal network number is helpful in these cases.

CLNP and DECnet do not have the problem (unless a node has links in multiple areas) because level 1 routing in CLNP and DECnet routes to the node and not to the link. Therefore, a node having multiple links can still have a single address.

9.7 IPX+

IPX+ was intended both as an enhancement to IPX and a migration path to 16-byte IPv6 addresses, while keeping the simplicity and plug-and-play nature of IPX. It solved the site renumbering problem and expanded the size of the address, and it did not require modifying the routers in the customer's network. It was approved in about 1994 by the now-defunct IPX advisory committee, a short-lived open standards body that worked on IPX. Originally the IPX advisory committee consisted of e-mail lists and occasional short, focused meetings of implementers. Then the IPX advisory committee was folded into a larger organization run by marketeers. Then the length and frequency of meetings, as well as the quality of the food, increased immensely, but the focus and technical content got lost. In addition, the world was convinced that what it really wanted was IP, so people decided to stop working on IPX.

IPX+ may have been implemented but certainly has not been widely deployed. Still, the ideas are worth learning, and IPv6 is evolving so that one of its modes of operation will resemble IPX+.

To review IPX, the endnode starts out knowing its IEEE 802 address and uses that as the bottom 6 bytes of its address (on 802 LANs). The top 4 IPX bytes represent the *network number*, which must be configured into the routers but is learned by the endnodes.

IPX+ expands the IPX address by 6 bytes, making the total address 16 bytes (see Figure 9.16). The top 6 bytes are obtained from the service provider and are learned automatically by the nodes in the customer network. In that way, the 4-byte "network" portion of the IPX address need only be configured into the routers once, but the whole customer net can be moved to a different part of the Internet and automatically adjusts to a new block because only the top 6 bytes change. The top 6 bytes are called the *domain number*.

6 bytes	4 bytes	6 bytes
domain number	net	node

Figure 9.16 IPX+ address

The basic IPX header does not change for IPX+. Rather, an additional header is added after the basic header. Old routers do not look beyond the basic header and they route solely based on the net portion of the address as they always have. To talk outside the domain, the source must be smart enough to know about the extra header and the expanded addresses.

At least one network number is used for reaching boundary routers, and the number FFFC is reserved for that purpose. The boundary routers advertise reachability to FFFC. The basic header contains FFFC as destination net (when the destination is outside the domain). The expanded header (which old routers assume is part of the packet's payload) contains the real destination network number in the foreign domain, the source domain number, and the destination domain number.

Within the domain, routers need only route based on a 4-byte field (the network number). After it reaches a boundary router they need only route based on a 6-byte number (the domain number). After it reaches the destination domain, the real destination net number is copied from the expanded header into the basic header and routers again route based solely on the destination net field.

9.8 IPv6

IPv6 was designed by the IETF as an intended replacement for IP. The "v6" means that the *version* field at the beginning of the IP packet is 6, whereas for IP it's 4. You might think that if it were really a version field the next number after 4 would be 5. But it's more like a "protocol type" field than a version number, because 5 is assigned to something totally different: a multicast protocol called ST2 (for "streams, version 2"). Because of IPv6 (also sometimes referred to as IPng, for IP next generation, after the TV show that tends to be admired by the same types of people that enjoy going to IETF meetings), people sometimes refer to IP as IPv4. Whenever I use the term IP, I mean IP version 4. At any rate, the terms IPv4 and IP are currently used interchangeably.

IPv6 addresses are similar in spirit to IPv4 addresses except that they are 16 bytes long. In theory, they have a totally flexible boundary between the *link* and the *node* portion of the address, as with IP. However, the specification says that "typically" the bottom 8 bytes will be a unique ID based on EUI-64, an IEEE effort to expand the 6-byte MAC addresses to 8-byte addresses (see Section 9.8.4). IPv6 supports plug and play, and the committee is working on a protocol to do automatic site renumbering similar to that of IPX+. Unfortunately, as is typical both when something is designed by committee and when there are backward-compatibility considerations (there was a desire for a smooth transition from IPv4, IPX, and CLNP addresses), almost any way people might imagine using addresses is possible with IPv6. So an IPv6 address can be thought of as a 16-byte IP address. Although equivalent, prefixes are expressed as a *prefix length* (as is done in CLNP) rather than a mask (as is done in IP) because a prefix length is more compact and readable.

9.8.1 The IPv6 Version Number Story

What's the difference between a new protocol and a new version of an old protocol? The IAB realized that it needed a replacement for IP that would have bigger addresses. It also knew that CLNP was an international standard already implemented by all the routing vendors and that it looked for all practical purposes just like IP except for having larger addresses. When the IAB recommended replacing IP with CLNP, various very vocal people protested that IP was the heart of the Internet and that we couldn't *replace* IP. But it was OK to migrate IP to a new version.

Anything can be modified into anything else, so there isn't a clear distinction between a new protocol and a new version of an old protocol. IPv6 is certainly no more similar to IP than CLNP is to IP. However, there was one way in which IPv6 is more of a new version rather than a new protocol, and that's because it uses the same initial 4 bits of the IP packet, the version number field. Theoretically, IPv6 and IP can be considered the same "protocol" at layer 2 and can use the same Ethertype.

Unfortunately, it was discovered that using two protocols having the same Ethertype does not work in practice because bridges (and perhaps other devices) assume that if the Ethertype indicates IP, the packet must be IP, and they look in specific places for fields. They do not check the version field. Theoretically, bridges shouldn't have been looking inside the packet, but various bridge vendors made their bridges clever enough to do things such as IP fragmentation but not clever enough to check the version number field first.

So IPv6 wound up using a different Ethertype anyway. At this point a version number field wasn't really needed at all. But because everyone was calling it IPv6, it was easier to leave the field there so that there could be a 6 to point to when people asked where the 6 was in IPv6.

9.8.2 Written Representation of IPv6 Addresses

The written representation for IPv6 addresses consists of hex values of each of the 16-bit chunks, separated by colons (:). For example:

> 3A57:0:0:9CD5:3412:912D:6738:1928

Because many addresses contain a lot of 0's, a more compact way of representing such addresses was devised. You take any substring that looks like :0:0:0: and replace it with "::". You can put the double colon at the beginning, so that ::1938:A5CD would be the address that started with 96 zero bits. You can put the double colon at the end, so that 2938:: would be the address that starts with the 16-bit hex value 2938, and the rest all zeroes. Or you can have it in the middle, as in 1928::0482:AB39, which is an address with 1928 as the top 16 bits, 0482AB39 as the bottom 32 bits, and zeroes in between.

Another representation was invented for embedded IPv4 addresses. The reasoning was that the bottom 32 bits, in which the IPv4 address would reside, should be represented as an IPv4 address. So for embedded IPv4 addresses another legal representation is to use IPv4 notation for the bottom 32 bits and IPv6 notation for the top 96 bits. The way to recognize this notation is that "." rather than ":" is used at the bottom of the address. An example is 0:0:0:0:0:0:109.71.47.8, which in compressed format would be ::109.71.47.8. Another example is 0:0:0:0:0:FFFF:109.71.47.8, which in compressed format would be ::FFFF:109.71.47.8. Luckily, only the prefix 0:0:0:0:0:0 and 0:0:0:0:0:FFFF have embedded IPv4 addresses. I think it would be mind-bogglingly confusing to read addresses with arbitrary IPv6 prefixes with IPv4 notation on the bottom.

9.8.3 Written Representation of IPv6 Prefixes

A prefix is represented as IPv6-address/prefix length, where *IPv6-address* is an IPv6 address in the notation of Section 9.8.2, and *prefix length* is the number of bits (from the left) of the prefix, expressed in decimal. For example, all IPv6 addresses that start with the first byte equal to 73 hex could be represented as 73::/8, or 73:0:0:0:0:0:0:0/8.

9.8.4 EUI-64

IEEE has defined an 8-byte address space similar to the 6-byte address space for IEEE LANs. It is intended to be used in "next generation" LANs defined by IEEE. It's not clear at this point whether anything using EUI-64 addresses will be widely deployed.

The 6-byte addresses (which are called EUI-48 addresses) are widely deployed and popular in the 802 LANs. The rationale for expanding them was that unique addresses might wind up manufactured into things such as lightbulbs and therefore there would be much more demand for unique addresses.

Fair enough. But where should the split be? The 802 address has a 3-byte OUI, and owning an OUI gives you 3 bytes of assignable addresses, or 2^{24} addresses, or approximately 16 million addresses. What if you use up all the 16 million addresses in your OUI? You can then obtain another OUI.

Now let's expand the address to 8 bytes. If it were me, I'd expand the OUI to be 5 bytes long so that there would now be 2^{38} OUIs, a virtually unlimited number of OUIs. (It's not 2^{40} because two bits of the OUI are used for global/local and group/individual.) Each manufacturer would get 2^{24} addresses (as with 6-byte addresses) per OUI in my recommended scheme. If the manufacturer ran out, it would have to get another OUI. If an occasional manufacturer realized it was going to need a lot of OUIs, it could ask for and be given a whole block of OUIs, essentially by giving the OUIs a prefix smaller than 40 bits. Perhaps manufacturers could get a "volume discount" if it seems outrageous to make them pay so much for a 5-byte OUI. If every manufacturer asked for 64,000 OUIs, we'd run out as quickly as we would with 3-byte OUIs. But I think the majority of manufacturers would not need more than a very small number of 5-byte OUIs.

However, what IEEE did was to continue having OUIs be 3 bytes. It did start calling it *company_id* rather than OUI. But there is no difference between a company_id and an OUI except for the name. The IEEE Web page asks you whether you want an OUI (to be used with 6-byte addresses) or a company_id (for use with 8-byte addresses). But in either case you get a 3-byte quantity that can be used for either purpose. In other words, it's perfectly legal to ask for a company_id and then use it in 6-byte addresses.

So where should the split be between assigned prefix and assignable address block? Suppose we guess too big on the prefix and allocate too many bits to the OUI. The result is that some manufacturers will run out of addresses and have to go back and ask for more OUIs. Suppose we guess too small on the prefix. Then we run out of OUIs, and the world comes to an end.

I'm surprised that IEEE chose to stick with the 3-byte OUI. There are only 2^{22} OUIs because 2 of the bits are used for global/local and multicast/unicast. So there are really only 4 million OUIs. They cost \$1,250 apiece. Anyone with \$1,250 can buy one until IEEE runs out of them.

The following appears on the on-line form for requesting an OUI or company_id:

> **The IEEE Registration Authority will assign an additional OUI to any organization requesting one, providing they submit a letter to the IEEE Standards Department, stating that their company will not "ship" product in the new block assignment until well after they have reached (shipped) at least 90% of the block assignment, in the context of a specified standard. Your company should ensure that large numbers of derived identifiers are not left unused.**

That is supposed to discourage people from wasting addresses. I asked one person on the committee why it chose to keep the OUI at 3 bytes even with an expanded address. I was told that it would be too expensive and error-prone for a manufacturer to have to retool with a different OUI when it ran out of addresses with the first OUI. That makes no sense to me. It's more likely it would make mistakes on its first OUI than its 17th. One possible reason for sticking with 3-byte OUIs is for backward compatibility and to allow a manufacturer to use an OUI it had already acquired in EUI-64. And indeed it can. But it also could have done so with a 5-byte OUI. It would simply create a 5-byte OUI by padding with a defined constant—say, two bytes of 0's. In that way, only one 64 thousandth of the 5-byte OUIs would be taken up even if all the 3-byte OUIs had already been handed out.

My belief is that if the world does not run out of OUIs, it could have lived forever with 6-byte addresses. I suppose that if they do use EUI-64 and people run out of OUIs, there could then be a "recycling" campaign in which people would buy subblocks from OUI owners that were not planning to use all 2^{40} addresses in their block.

9.8.5 EUI-64 As Used by IPv6

Several types of IPv6 addresses use EUI-64 but modify it slightly. An OUI or company_id acquired from IEEE has the global/local bit set to 0, whereas a locally defined EUI-64 or EUI-48 address is supposed to have that bit set to 1. The global/local bit is the seventh bit in the top byte. (The bottom bit in the top byte is the unicast/multicast bit.) Thus, instead of being able to legally define your own local EUI-64 addresses (in IPv6 notation) as ::1, ::2, ::3 and so on, you'd have to define them as 0200:0:0:1, 0200:0:0:2, and so on in order for them to come from the locally assigned space rather than the globally assigned space.

So the IPv6 committee decided that because it wished that the global/local bit were the opposite (0 for locally defined addresses), the rule is that an EUI-64 address should have that bit complemented when used in an IPv6 address. So if a node actually had a globally assigned EUI-64 of, say, (in IEEE notation) 34-A4-29-15-F3-81-02-9C, that globally assigned EUI-64 address would have to be modified by flipping the global/local bit, resulting in 36-A4-29-15-F3-81-02-9C.

In fact, until LANs using EUI-64 addresses become popular (I'm not holding my breath, and I don't recommend that you do either), nodes will start out with EUI-48 addresses. The IPv6 committee has defined how to take a globally assigned EUI-48 address (that is, an IEEE 802 address) and map it into the modified EUI-64 for use by IPv6. Let's say the EUI-48 address the node has is 28-9F-18-1C-82-35. The global/local bit must be inverted, changing the first byte from 28 to 2A. Then you must add 2 bytes (to create an 8-byte quantity out of a 6-byte quantity) by inserting the 2 bytes between the OUI and the rest of the address. IEEE says that the inserted bytes should be FF and FE. So the resulting modified EUI-64 address for use by IPv6 would be 2A-9F-18-FF-FE-1C-82-35.

9.8.6 IPv6 Address Conventions

In RFC 2373 (IPv6 Addressing Architecture) a number of addressing conventions are defined.

- ::0 (all zeroes): The *unspecified* address, which should never be assigned as an actual address. It is used in protocols such as DHCP to indicate an unknown address.

- ::1 (bottom bit 1, rest zeroes): The *loopback* address, which should appear only internal to a node.

- ::IPv4 address (all but bottom 32 bits are zero, bottom 32 bits are an IPv4 address): an *IPv4-compatible* address, which would be used by a node that can speak both IPv6 and IPv4. The node would use the same address when speaking either protocol rather than have separately assigned IPv4 and IPv6 addresses (see transition strategy, Section 9.8.7).

- ::FFFF:IPv4 address (all but bottom 48 bits are zero, bottom 32 bits are an IPv4 address, and next higher 16 bits are FFFF): *IPv4-only* address. This indicates a node that can speak only IPv4, but for some reason the packet must be translated into IPv6 in order to reach that node.

- 2000::/3 (any address that starts with binary 001): This is a *normal aggregatable unicast* address, where the bottom 8 bytes is the *node,* using modified EUI-64 (see Section 9.8.5), and the rest contains three levels of hierarchy.

- FE80::/10 (any address whose top 10 bits is binary 1111 1110 10): This is *link-local*, where the bottom 8 bytes is supposed to be the *node*, using modified EUI-64 (see Section 9.8.5). This is intended to be used before the remainder of the address is known or in the case of a link having no routers. A link-local address must never be forwarded. (Forwarding by a bridge is OK. That's not forwarding from the point of view of IP because bridges are invisible to IP.)

- FEA0::/10 (any address whose top 10 bits is binary 1111 1110 11): This is *site-local*, where the bottom 8 bytes is supposed to be the *node*, using modified EUI-64, and the 2 bytes next to the node is the *subnet ID*. This is intended to be used within a "site" (yes, that's vague) when the site does not know its high-order prefix. Such addresses should be filtered by routers on the boundary of the site so that they do not escape into or out of the site.

- *Anycast* for a router on this LAN: This is the address formed by taking the link prefix and using zeroes for the rest of the address.

- FF00::/8 (any address whose top 8 bits are 1's): *Multicast* address. Following the mandatory FF in the top 8 bits are 4 bits of flags, in which only the bottom bit is defined, indicating whether the multicast address is a well-known address or dynamically assigned. The next 4 bits specify *scope*, of which five values are currently defined: node-local, link-local, site-local, organization-local, and global. The bottom 112 bits gives the actual multicast address. The currently defined well-known values for the bottom 112 bits are 1 (for "all IPv6 nodes") and 2 (for "all IPv6 routers").

9.8.7 Transition from IPv4 to IPv6

Will the transition ever happen? That I can't say. I believe an IP with bigger addresses would have been more likely to happen if the IETF had agreed to accept the IAB's recommendation of moving to CLNP. At that time, CLNP had been implemented in all the routers and a lot of endnodes, and IPv4 was creaking at the hinges. CLNP would have been just fine. But because the IETF wanted to invent something new, this delayed transition by several years. Customers had real, immediate needs. As a result, during the years the committee was designing IPv6 several critical improvements were made to IPv4, resulting in increasing its useful lifetime by a lot, perhaps even forever. The improvements were as follows.

- CIDR provides saner address allocation to reduce router table size.

- DHCP (dynamic host configuration protocol), although not as good as the plug and play of IPX, CLNP, or IPv6, certainly provides a much improved ability to configure IPv4 addresses.

- NAT (network address translator) is a box that translates addresses within an intranet into global IP addresses. It enables an entire corporate network to look to the outside like a single IP address, or small set of IP addresses, thus allowing many more than 2^{32} hosts to be connected in a 32-bit address space.

Assuming that the world will move toward IPv6, what is the best transition strategy? It's tempting to temporarily assign IPv4-translatable addresses to the IPv6 nodes, thus allowing mixing of IPv4 and IPv6, with translation between the packet formats. The problem with this strategy is that if you are forced to use IPv4-translatable addresses, you gain no advantage from IPv6. You are still stuck with a 32-bit address that is padded to fit into a 128-bit field. And how long would you have to stick with IPv4-translatable addresses? Until the last IPv4-only node that you want to talk to has been upgraded to IPv6. When will that happen? Probably never.

The alternative transition plan is *dual stacks*. This means that new nodes speak both IPv4 and IPv6 and have two addresses. That is the simpler scheme. IPv4 could be shut off at a node if and when there was no IPv4-only node to be spoken to. Actually, with NAT devices to translate addresses, it would be possible for IPv4-only nodes and IPv6-only nodes to communicate. A NAT box is capable not only of translating IPv4 addresses to IPv4 addresses but also of translating any sort of address into any other sort of address. For example, IPX to IPv4, or IPv6 to IPv4.

9.9 CLNP Network Layer Addresses

CLNP (Connectionless Network Layer Protocol) addresses are defined by ISO and used by DECnet Phase V, ATM, and CDPD (cellular digital packet data). CLNP could be explained in complex detail. Luckily, most of the details are unimportant for understanding the network layer, and I therefore refrain from discussing them.

ISO network layer addresses are variable-length, with a maximum of 20 octets. Because they are variable-length, any packets that contain an address must contain an additional octet specifying the address's length (in octets). An ISO address can be thought of as shown in Figure 9.17.

Figure 9.17 CLNP address

An *area* in CLNP is larger than a single link, and all nodes in the area share the same prefix (the *area* portion of the address). You can't tell, within an area, which link a node is on because all the nodes share the same prefix. This has the advantage that the address can be of the node rather than the interface. In other words, a node with multiple links has a single address provided that all the links are in the same area.

CLNP has two types of routing. *Level 1* routes based on the ID field, and there is no hierarchy in the ID portion of the address. The ID field is assumed to be a flat address space with no topological significance. *Level 2* routes based on longest prefix of the area portion of the address, and can have arbitrarily many levels of hierarchy. It is perhaps confusing to call it "level 2" when it can be many levels of hierarchy. Level 2 routing is similar to IP or IPX routing. IP and IPX do not have the concept of level 1 routing as in CLNP because the bottom level in IP or IPX is always confined to a single link. The bottom level of routing is highly desirable, so that a node can move and retain its address. Bridging is what saves IP, since it provides the equivalent for IP of CLNP's level 1 routing.

If the area portion of a CLNP packet's destination address matches the address of the area in which the packet exists, the packet is routed via level 1 routing, based on exact match of the contents of the ID field in the destination address to an entry in the forwarding database. Level 2 routing, in contrast, is based on prefixes rather than exact matches, and it routes to the longest matching prefix.

Originally, the ID field was 6 octets, which is a convenient number because it is the same length as an 802 address. A 6-octet ID field enables an endnode to automatically figure out its network layer address based on a globally assigned 802 address as the ID portion. The remainder of the address can then be obtained by copying the portions of the address other than ID from a router's address.

Endnodes built to attach to an 802 LAN automatically have a globally assigned 802 address. (I suppose some vendors might build equipment not preconfigured with a unique address ROM for the 802 attachment, but anyone buying such a beast deserves all the joys of figuring out how to configure addresses.) Endnodes not built to attach to an 802 LAN can also be preconfigured with a globally assigned 802 address because obtaining 802 addresses is not very difficult. Vendors can (and, in my opinion, should) obtain a block of 802 addresses for their systems and configure each system at the time of manufacture with a ROM containing a unique 802 address; then even endnodes that are not attached to an 802 LAN can have a globally unique ID.

Some members of the ISO committee objected to standardizing the size of the ID field. Some members thought that 6 octets were far too many; others felt that 6 octets were not enough. The committee compromised by allowing each routing domain (a portion of a network under the same administrative control) to use whatever size ID field it wanted (from 0 to 8 octets). Theoretically, routers could be configured with an ID size to use (but in practice, many products are likely to support only the 6-octet size). Because routing would be highly confusing if routers within a routing domain disagreed on the size of the ID field, a field was added to various routing control packets indicating the size of the ID field as understood by the router generating the packet. This technique enables misconfiguration to be detected. Because the configurable ID length was added late in the standards process, the **ID length** field, which appears in the appropriate routing control packets, is encoded so that the value 0 means that the ID is 6 octets. Values between 1 and 8 correspond to ID lengths from 1 to 8 octets (which means that an ID length of 6 can be encoded as either 0 or 6). The value 255 indicates that the ID length is 0.

(In my opinion, failing to establish a single ID size has economic and/or performance implications for CLNP routers. To do efficient data packet forwarding, level 1 routers must have specialized data structures and algorithms, and perhaps even specialized hardware assistance for address lookups, to deal with whatever ID size is implemented. It is unlikely that a vendor will be able to implement a high-performance router that can be configured at the last minute with the proper ID size for the routing domain. But almost nobody cares about CLNP anymore, so it doesn't matter.)

The purpose of the **SEL** octet is to differentiate among multiple network layer users. It is like the DSAP and SSAP octets in 802.1.

The area field actually has more structure and can yield many levels of routing hierarchy. The next level of complexity involves dividing the field into two parts (see Figure 9.18).

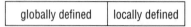

Figure 9.18 Structure of CLNP area field

The globally defined portion is variable-length (of course—it's a standard!). The locally defined portion is also variable, but the global addresses are assigned so that there is always room for at least another 2 octets of area. Someone in charge of a routing domain can get a single globally defined number for the entire routing domain, and, if the routing domain is so large that it must be hierarchical, the locally defined portion of the area field can be used to identify the level 1 subnetworks within the routing domain. The locally defined field can even be assigned hierarchically—for example, by having the upper octet signify the level 2 subnetwork and the lower octet signify the level 1 subnetwork within the level 2 subnetwork.

ISO calls the globally defined portion an IDP, which stands for *initial domain part* (see Figure 9.19). ISO does not administer all of the IDP values directly but rather assigns various authorities to define their own addresses. The first octet of the IDP is known as the AFI, which stands for *authority and format identifier*. The remainder of the IDP is known as the IDI, or *initial domain identifier*. The portion of the address that is not globally defined is known as the DSP, or *domain-specific part*.

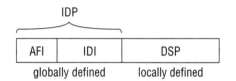

Figure 9.19 Structure of CLNP address

The globally defined portion of the address is hierarchical for the purpose of address assignment. However, in practice, a great deal of geographic information can be inferred from the IDP. This gives even more levels of routing hierarchy, allowing ISO networks to scale, in practice, to arbitrary sizes.

Someone skilled in ISO network layer addresses could examine the first several bits and say, "That's a telephone number in the United States," because one of the ways of getting an IPD is based on phone numbers. The person could then examine a few more bits and say, "That telephone number is in area code 617." A few more bits, and the person could say, "The telephone number is (617) 555-1234." This makes for very efficient routing when pieces of your corporate network are attached over a public net, since the address of the attachment point can be embedded in the IDP, and then no explicit routing or configuration is required over the backbone (see Section 9.9.2).

9.9.1 Autoconfiguration

CLNP was designed to enable autoconfiguration. As with IPX, the idea is to take the IEEE address, find out the upper portion of the address from a router (through the ES-IS protocol), and thereby form the entire address. But since standards committees don't seem to want to actually tell you how to do something, you didn't have to autoconfigure, and indeed could not assume that the ID field in someone's CLNP address matched their IEEE address.

9.9.2 Embedded DTE Addresses

Another feature of ISO addresses is the ability to embed a DTE address in the area address. For example, a common type of network is shown in Figure 9.20. Pieces of the network are interconnected via a big common-carrier network, such as the phone company or an X.25 network. I call each piece a *network fragment* because the word *subnet*, which I'd rather use, has too many other meanings.

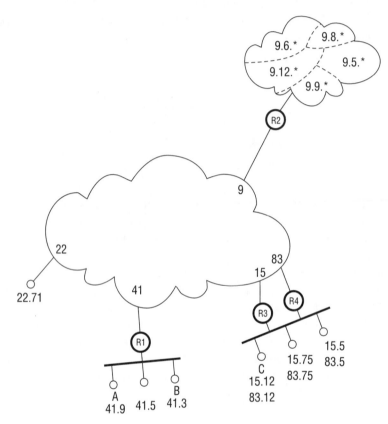

Figure 9.20 Using embedded DTE addresses

Assume that the area address of each of the network fragments shown in Figure 9.20 contains the DTE address of the point of attachment of the fragment to the X.25 network. This approach eliminates the need for a potentially expensive routing protocol operating on the X.25 network designed to keep the fragments aware of one another.

Assume that endnode A wants to talk to endnode B. The area address portion of A matches the area address portion of B. The level 1 routers within that fragment route the packet correctly. Now assume that A transmits a packet with destination address C. The level 1 routers within A's fragment recognize that the destination does not reside in that fragment and thus route the packet toward a level 2 router—in this case, R1, which attaches directly to the X.25 network. R1 has no previous knowledge of C's area address (other than having been configured to know that any packet whose address prefix indicates that the address is on that X.25 network can be routed over the link by extracting the DTE address from the area address). R1 thus knows (based on its having matched the configured address prefix) that the packet should be forwarded over the X.25 network. R1 then extracts the DTE address from C's area address and places a call to that DTE address, whereupon the packet magically gets delivered to a router that knows how to reach C.

A network fragment can be composed of multiple level 1 subnetworks and still have the DTE address of its attachment embedded in the area address of each of the level 1 subnetworks. This is possible because the DTE address is embedded in the *globally defined* portion of the area address, and the area address can be expanded by at least another 2 octets.

Assume that the fragment containing D is sufficiently large that it must be broken into multiple level 1 subnetworks. Assume, too, that the IDP corresponding to R2's DTE address is X. Then the area address of each of the level 1 subnetworks has the form X.y (X concatenated with a locally assigned field to distinguish the level 1 subnetworks within that network fragment). Note that the fragment containing C is reachable via either R3 (DTE address 15) or R4 (DTE address 84). In this case it is convenient to allow that fragment to have two area addresses.

Again, this sort of magic no-overhead routing cannot be accomplished with IP because the addresses are too small for a DTE address to be embedded.

9.10 AppleTalk Network Layer Addresses

Before I saw AppleTalk, I would have told you that autoconfiguration requires large addresses. However, AppleTalk manages to do autoconfiguration based on tiny addresses!

An AppleTalk address is 3 bytes long. The first two bytes specify the net, and the last byte specifies the node. So it's similar to a 3-byte IP address. But because you might want to have more than 256 nodes on a LAN, the LAN can be specified by a whole range of numbers rather than a single number. So, for example, the network number for a particular LAN might be anything in the range 135–141. This is similar to a shorter IP mask, although it's more flexible. The AppleTalk ranges can start and end on any number, whereas with masks, the size of the range must be a power of 2 and the start of the range must be a multiple of the size of the range.

In Section 11.2.5 we talk about how AppleTalk manages to do autoconfiguration with such tiny addresses.

9.11 DECnet Phases III and IV

DECnet Phase V supports both CLNP and IP. Usually when people say "DECnet" they mean Phase IV or earlier.

9.11.1 A Bit of History

DECnet Phase III had a 2-byte address but no hierarchy. The routing algorithm and router implementations at the time (the late 70s) couldn't handle a network with 65,000 nodes. In fact, the DECnet Phase III spec recommended that "networks" be no larger than 32 nodes! Luckily, nobody noticed that in the spec and they built reasonably large Phase III nets (perhaps a few thousand nodes). That was when I became the routing architect at Digital. I wanted to make the following changes to DECnet.

- Expand the address space. (At the time, I recommended an 8-byte address with 2 bytes for area and 6 bytes for node, to be autoconfigured from the IEEE 802 address. This predated IPX and XNS, the protocol from which IPX was derived.)

- Convert to a link state routing protocol.

- Efficiently incorporate Ethernets into the routing protocol (routing algorithm changes such as Designated Routers on LANs).

The implementers thought this was too great a change because DECnet customers needed larger networks right away. So I agreed, as a compromise, to do an intermediate phase, Phase IV, that kept the 2-byte address space but made it hierarchical and that kept the distance vector routing algorithm. So in Phase IV, a DECnet address consisted of 6 bits for area and 10 bits for node. I got no end of grief from people complaining that 6 bits was not enough for area and that 10 bits was not enough for node. But, hey! All I had was 16 bits! And besides, Phase IV was only going to last for a year or so until the ultimate 8-byte hierarchical address, plus link state routing, could be implemented.

Unfortunately, there was the decision to use CLNP as the data packet format for Phase V, which delayed us for eight years or so until ISO could finish the standards process. So Phase IV lived a lot longer than I expected.

9.11.2 DECnet Phase IV Address

The top 6 bits of the 16-bit address specified the area. An area could be larger than a single link, so it was not possible (as it is in IP, IPX, IPv6, and AppleTalk) to tell from an address whether two nodes were on the same link; you could tell only whether they were in the same area. This meant that there were two types of routing: level 1 routing, which found the correct node within an area, and level 2 routing, which found the correct area.

Again, it makes sense for a protocol such as DECnet or CLNP to have two distinct types of routers that route based on different portions of the address, because the "level 1" routing is looking at a different portion of the address. However, for protocols such as IP and IPX, there should be only one type of routing—based on longest address prefixes—and that single type of routing should allow arbitrarily many levels of hierarchy.

9.11.3 Mapping DECnet Address to Ethernet Address

The weirdest part of DECnet Phase IV was something I agreed to in order to make peace with the implementers. Ethernet addresses were 6 bytes long. DECnet addresses (for Phase IV) were 2 bytes long. The implementers did not want to have to keep a cache of (DECnet, Ethernet) address correspondence (similar to an ARP cache). They wanted to be able to algorithmically map from DECnet address to Ethernet address. In protocols such as IPX, you do this by having the Ethernet address embedded in the network layer address. You might assume that the network layer address would have to be larger than the Ethernet address to map from a layer 3 address to a layer 2 address. But amazingly, the implementers came up with a scheme that allowed a node to figure out someone's Ethernet address from the DECnet address. Pause for a second and think of how you might do that. You know someone's 2-byte DECnet address, and you need to figure out its 6-byte Ethernet address.

Give up? Well, the way it worked was that Digital came up with a 4-byte constant—consisting of an OUI owned by Digital plus another byte—and appended that to the DECnet address to form the node's Ethernet address. That 4-byte constant, called HIORD, happens to be AA-00-04-00.

The Ethernet chips can be told to use a different address than the one in ROM. So you buy your Ethernet adapter with some globally unique IEEE address in it—say, 02-00-00-45-92-31—but when DECnet starts up, having been configured as DECnet node number 2B-79, DECnet tells the chip to use AA-00-04-00-2B-79 as its Ethernet address.

This would have been less annoying if the chips had the ability to simultaneously use multiple addresses; in this way, when DECnet transmitted a packet it would use address AA-00-04-00-2B-79, and when something else transmitted, it used the address that came in ROM with the adapter. And it should receive packets transmitted to either address, perhaps being clever enough to multiplex based on the data link destination address as well as protocol types and SAPs.

But unfortunately, the chips could use only one address at a time. So let's say IPX comes up first. IPX figures out that its address is net.02-00-00-45-92-31. Then DECnet comes along and changes the Ethernet address of the node. Someone talking to that IPX node will expect to be able to reach it with Ethernet address 02-00-00-45-92-31, but it won't work. Similar problems would occur with IP because ARP caches would be wrong if the node's Ethernet address changed. So basically DECnet had to come up first.

It's partially the fault of the chip vendors. If they were able to receive at two Ethernet addresses, nobody would have been annoyed by the DECnet Phase IV kludge.

Another little bit of ugliness is that an implementation of DECnet on token ring (where the bit order is different) did not flip the bits in HIORD. So when transmitted on token ring, the first byte, AA, turned into a multicast address.

9.12 NAT/NAPT

A NAT (network address translator) is an (admittedly useful) kludge that sits between your network and the Internet and translates network layer addresses so that your intranet can survive without globally unique addresses. A NAPT (network address port translator) translates (address, port) pairs.

Why wouldn't your network have globally unique addresses? Perhaps you've changed providers and you don't want the hassle of renumbering. Perhaps you are using a different address space, such as IPX, inside your network and IP on the Internet. Or perhaps globally unique IP addresses are scarce or expensive.

The NAT box (see Figure 9.21) has a set of globally unique IP addresses that it can assign as nodes from inside ("inside" means your private network) initiate conversations with nodes outside (in the global Internet). It is possible to assign these statically or have the NAT box assign them dynamically.

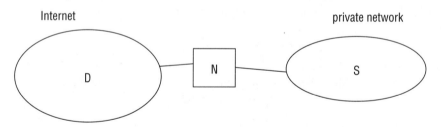

Figure 9.21 N is address (and possibly port) translator

D is on the Internet, so it has an address with global significance. S launches a packet with destination address D and with source address something that has significance only within the private network. The NAT box keeps a mapping table. If S is not already associated with a global address from the pool of addresses the NAT box has, then S is assigned a global address S_G and the NAT box modifies the source address from S to S_G as it forwards the packet across to the Internet. As traffic returns from D to S_G, the NAT box rewrites the destination address from S_G to S.

Assuming that most nodes in the private network are not simultaneously talking to nodes on the Internet, the NAT box can have a pool of global addresses smaller than the number of nodes inside the private network. However, there's another way of conserving global addresses: using a NAPT. In this case N translates from (address, port) pairs to (address, port) pairs. This allows potentially thousands of simultaneous connections with only a single global address representing the entire private network. To the outside world it looks as if all nodes inside the private network are processes within N. They all have the same address but different port numbers.

A lot of people passionately hate NAT, in part because they'd like to see IPv4 die sooner so as to force deployment of IPv6 and in part because although NAT works in the simple case, there are many cases in which things get ugly. If there are multiple NAT boxes in parallel between the private net and the Internet, they must make sure they maintain consistent mappings. Also, some protocols carry addresses. An example is FTP (file transfer protocol). The NAT (or NAPT) box not only has to be clever enough to know the FTP protocol and to know where it carries addresses so that it can translate them, but the way addresses are carried in FTP is as the text string representation. Suppose the internal address was 10.7.54.192 and the NAT box mapped that to the global address 105.197.183.114. That means the message would be 4 bytes bigger after the address in FTP was replaced. The problem is, TCP numbers bytes, so now the NAT/NAPT box has to also remember that it has to adjust the TCP sequence number on every subsequent packet of that FTP connection. That would be particularly difficult to coordinate across NAT/NAPT boxes.

End-to-end encryption would make it impossible for the NAT/NAPT box to look inside and replace addresses.

Another idea being introduced is called *host* NAT or *host* NAPT. The idea is that the host inside must first request a global address from the NAT/NAPT box before initiating a connection, but it is the host that does all the necessary translation of the packet. I think this is a more promising approach.

Homework

1. With IP addressing (and noncontiguous subnet masks), find two different (value, mask) pairs and an IP address that would match either link. Make sure that each mask has at least one 1 where the other mask has a 0.

2. (research) Suppose that a router had a list of destination links, as a table of (value, mask) pairs, with instructions for each entry about how to route a packet given a destination address matching that entry. Assuming noncontiguous subnet masks, is there, in the general case, any algorithm (including any way of organizing the table), other than trying each (value, mask) pair in turn, that will indicate which entry matches the destination address? (I think the answer is no. It would be of great interest if someone were to devise an efficient algorithm.)

3. Assuming that noncontiguous masks in IP are disallowed, IP routing becomes similar to ISO level 2 routing—the (value, mask) pairs become address prefixes and can be expressed as a (mask length, value) pair.

   How many bits must be allocated to the mask length? Is an encoding of (mask length, value) more efficient than an encoding of (mask, value)?

4. Some people have attempted to get noncontiguous IP subnet masks banned, but there are those who defend noncontiguous subnet masks as being useful. Can you think of anything that can be done with noncontiguous subnet masks that cannot be done without them?

5. Assume a problem that requires finding, from a table of entries, the entry that is the longest matching initial substring of a given quantity. Devise an algorithm to do this efficiently.

6. Suppose you are told that you must implement a high-performance ISO level 1 router and that the customer must be able to set a management parameter indicating which size ID field is to be used. What kind of strategies could be employed? Keep in mind that high-performance forwarding usually requires specialized hardware. What kinds of economic trade-offs can be made? For example, the router might theoretically support all address sizes but attain higher performance on some. Also keep in mind that your product should be competitive both economically and in terms of performance.

7. The rule in IP is that none of the three fields (net, subnet, host) in an IP address is allowed to be all 1's or all 0's. Why does this rule exclude a single-bit host or subnet field?

8. At $1,250 per OUI, what percentage of Bill Gates's net worth would be consumed by buying up all OUIs?

9. Compare the addressing schemes of IPv4, IPv6, CLNP, and IPX. Consider ability to autoconfigure, bandwidth use, simplicity, interconnection over public networks, and anything else of importance.

Chapter 10
Connectionless Data Packet Formats

This chapter covers the data packet formats of various connectionless network layer protocols, including IP, CLNP, IPX, DECnet, AppleTalk, and IPv6. Again, you might think that all you care about is IP, but it's interesting to compare approaches. Also, you'll understand IP at a deeper level if you compare it to other things, and there is no other reference for seeing all the packet formats in one place.

10.1 Pieces of a Connectionless Network Layer

Connectionless network layer protocols tend to be described in several documents. The more or less separable pieces consist of the following.

1. *Basic connectionless service:* This part of the network layer consists of the format for data packets and certain error messages or other notifications that the network can send to an endnode.

   In CLNP (ConnectionLess Network Protocol), this part of the protocol is defined in ISO 8473, "Protocol for Providing the Connectionless-mode Network Service." I refer to the ISO protocol by its common nickname, CLNP. In the Internet protocol suite the equivalent protocol is defined in RFC 791, known as "The Internet Protocol," or IP. IPv6 is defined in RFC 1883. I found the specification for DECnet Phase IV at the following URL:

   http://ftp.digital.com/pub/DEC/DECnet/PhaseIV/route20.txt

   AppleTalk is nicely documented in the book *Inside AppleTalk*, by Gursharan S. Sidhu, Richard F. Andrews, Alan B. Oppenheimer, and Apple Computer, published by Addison-Wesley.

2. *Neighbor greeting:* This aspect of the protocol enables neighbors to discover each other. It allows endnodes to know which routers are available on their LAN and to find out that it is possible to communicate directly with other endnodes on the same LAN. It also allows routers to find their endnode neighbors. In this way, the routers can tell all the other routers how to reach those endnodes, and the neighbor routers know the data link layer destination addresses needed to deliver packets across the final hop to destination endnodes.

   I talk about this part of the network layer in Chapter 11.

3. *Routing:* This aspect of the network layer concerns the protocol and algorithms that routers should use so that they can cooperate to calculate paths through a mesh topology. I talk about this aspect of the network layer in Chapter 12.

This chapter is about the first aspect: the data packet format.

10.2 Data Packets

CLNP and IP data packet formats are remarkably similar. In part, this is because the information to be carried in a data packet is fairly simple (source, destination, fragmentation information, special requests, and data). In part, it's because ISO basically started out with the IP data packet, expanded the addresses, and made minor changes. IPv6 got rid of some unnecessary fields (which were in both CLNP and IP because CLNP basically copied IP). It's ironic that the people who treated IP as a "religion" were so offended at the idea of "replacing" IP with CLNP, when CLNP is more similar to IP than IPv6 is. In fact, none of it is rocket science and none of it should be religion.

IPX and AppleTalk are basically identical except for the size of the address. DECnet (Phase IV) probably gets the prize for simplest—certainly for shortest.

10.3 Summary of Packet Formats for Easy Reference

This section shows the packet formats with quick descriptions of the fields. Following the formats, Section 10.4 compares and discusses technical issues involved in all the data formats.

10.3.1 IP

Figure 10.1 shows the IP header format.

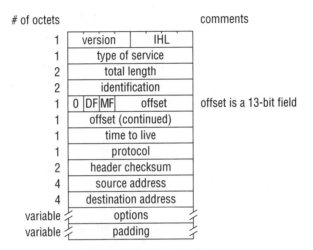

Figure 10.1 IP header format

The 4-bit **version** field is set to 4 (that is why it's also OK to call IP "IPv4").

IHL is the length of the header in 32-bit units.

TOS is "type of service," and the world pretty much agrees that its original definition is not very useful (see Section 10.4.19.4).

Total length is the length of the data in this fragment plus the header.

Identification helps in reassembly of a fragmented packet because it identifies fragments of the same packet between the same source/destination pair.

DF = don't fragment.

MF = more fragments.

Offset is the offset of this fragment in 64-bit chunks.

Time to live (TTL) was intended as a measure of real time before the packet might as well get dropped, but in practice is mostly (and properly in my opinion) used as a decrementing hop count.

Protocol is like the Ethernet "protocol type" field and identifies the transport protocol (for example, UDP, TCP).

Header checksum is a checksum of the header.

Options are things such as source routing that can be tacked on.

10.3.2 IPX

Figure 10.2 shows the IPX format.

# of octets

2	checksum
2	packet length
1	"transport control" (hop count)
1	packet type
4	destination net
6	destination node
2	destination socket
4	source net
6	source node
2	source socket

Figure 10.2 IPX header format

IPX is such a simple packet format that it's difficult to find much to say about it. The **checksum** is not implemented and is set to FFFF (see Section 10.6.1). The hop count counts upward, and router R deletes the packet if the **hop count** exceeds the default value 16 or a threshold individually configured into R. It is confusing to have multiplexing based on **sockets** as well as **packet type**, but this can be thought of as combining IP and UDP, or IP and the ports from TCP.

10.3.3 IPX+

Figure 10.3 shows the IPX+ header format.

# of octets

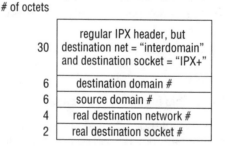
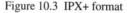

30	regular IPX header, but destination net = "interdomain" and destination socket = "IPX+"
6	destination domain #
6	source domain #
4	real destination network #
2	real destination socket #

Figure 10.3 IPX+ format

IPX+ is designed to solve the renumbering problem, to increase the size of IPX addresses to 16 bytes, and to be backward-compatible with old routers. The additional 6 bytes are called the *domain* number and are automatically learned. The 4-byte IPX network number no longer need be globally unique, only unique within a corporate network. The idea is that when your corporate network is attached to the IPX Internet, the router(s) on the boundary are told the domain number.

The only routers that need to be IPX+ aware are the ones attached to the backbone (the portion of the IPX network that routes between domains). Those boundary routers advertise (within the domain) that they can reach the special network number (−3, or FF FF FF FC), which means "other domains." The routers within the domain need not know that FF FF FF FC is special in any way; they just route to that as they route to any other 4-byte IPX network number.

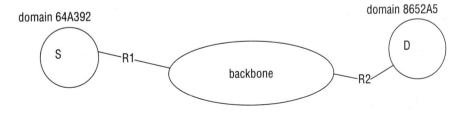

Figure 10.4 IPX+ routing

In Figure 10.4, an IPX+ aware node, S, talking to IPX+ aware node D, fills in the IPX header with destination network = −3 and destination socket = a value defined to be IPX+. (A new socket number is used to make sure that if the destination is not IPX+ aware it will not be confused by receiving an IPX+ packet. Instead, it merely drops the packet because there is no process listening on that socket.) R1 announces within the source domain that it can reach IPX network number −3. Within the domain, the packet is routed like any other IPX packet, toward R1, because it has announced reachability to net −3. After it reaches R1, the packet is routed within the backbone based solely on the 6-byte domain numbers in the IPX+ header. After it reaches R2, R2 copies the "real destination network number" from the IPX+ portion of the header into the destination network number in the IPX portion of the header, so the routers within D's domain route the packet as if it were an ordinary IPX packet.

It might seem like a kludge to have the address split into two pieces (net number inside IPX header, domain number in the IPX+ header). Although we defined IPX+ this way because of the need to be backward-compatible with routers that were not IPX+ aware, it has important technical advantages (and no disadvantages) over treating the address like a 16-byte quantity with longest prefix routing (as IPv6 is). The routers within a domain need only look at a 4-byte quantity. Hardware can be cheaper if it's known that the longest prefix needed is 4 bytes. Interdomain routers only need to route based on a 6-byte quantity.

Endnodes that are not IPX+ aware can talk only to other endnodes inside their own domain (unless there are address mapping gateways). An IPX+ aware endnode looks up the destination's domain number in a directory. If an endnode does not know the source domain number, it fills in "0"; when the packet reaches the boundary router, it corrects the source domain number in the packet and sends a report back to the source telling it the real source domain number. Similarly, if the source fills in the wrong source domain number (perhaps remembering an old value), the boundary router corrects the source domain number in the packet and sends a report back to the source informing it of the real source domain number.

IPX+ was designed and approved by the intervendor IPX Advisory Committee around 1994 but was not implemented (to my knowledge). Still, it is worth learning about. Later, IPv6 adopted the idea of having the high-order portion of the address automatically learned by routers. An interesting difference between the IPX+ method and the IPv6 method is that in IPv6, all the routers within the domain need to know the domain number, whereas in IPX+ there is really no reason for any nodes except the boundary routers and those nodes that talk to other domains to know the domain number.

10.3.4 AppleTalk

Figure 10.5 shows the AppleTalk header format.

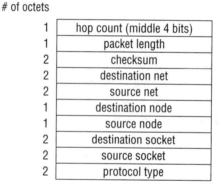

Figure 10.5 AppleTalk header format

AppleTalk is also very simple. Like IPX, it has both a **protocol type** and **sockets**. The **hop count** field, which counts up, is documented as being only 4 bits long, so the maximum length path is 16 hops. The routing protocol, RIP, limits computed IP paths to 16 hops, but this is a RIP limitation and not an IP limitation. With AppleTalk, the size of the hop count field in the data packet limits the length of paths to 16. But because the bits next to the hop count are unused, it would seem easy (except for backward compatibility with old routers) to expand the size of the hop count field.

10.3.5 IPv6

Figure 10.6 shows the IPv6 header format.

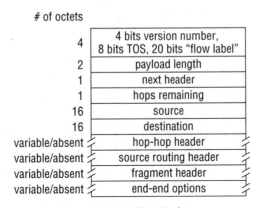

Figure 10.6 IPv6 header format

The first 4-byte field consists of the 4-bit **version** number (set to 6 for IPv6); 8 bits of **TOS** (type of service), of which 1 bit is used to indicate "congestion experienced" (see Section 10.4.18), another bit indicates whether you'll do something appropriate if you see that congestion was experienced, and the remaining 6 bits are being fought over by the IETF Differentiated Services working group (see Section 10.4.19.4); and 20 bits of **flow label,** which someone might figure out something to do with. The **payload length** is the length of the data (does not include all the headers). The **next header** field is like a protocol type field. **Hops remaining** is a hop count that decrements. The remaining "headers" are similar to "options" in IP or CLNP.

10.3.6 DECnet

Figures 10.7 and 10.8 show the two DECnet Phase IV header formats.

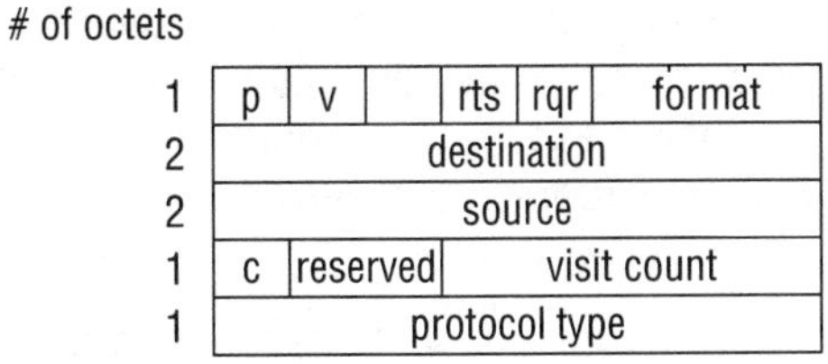

Figure 10.7 DECnet Phase IV short format

# of octets

1	p	v	i-l	rts	rqr	format	
8	destination						
8	source						
1	reserved						C
1	visit count						
2	reserved						
1	protocol type						

Figure 10.8 DECnet Phase IV long format

Phase IV DECnet has a pesky two-format situation. How did this happen? It was around 1980, a long time ago. We were planning for the future. We thought 8 bytes would be the perfect address size, but we needed to quickly add Ethernet support to DECnet. Someone thought it would be easier to have only one format of DECnet packet on Ethernets. The idea was that for Phase IV (which was supposed to be a short-lived steppingstone to the Perfect Network Layer), the packet format would look just like Phase III on point-to-point links but would start using the Ultimate Packet Format on Ethernets. And presumably Phase V would use the new format.

Then, shortly after Phase IV was complete, we decided that the next-phase DECnet packet format would be CLNP, so the Phase IV long format was never used except as an annoying alternative format for the short format. It is easy to map between them if you have plenty of time on your hands as you are forwarding packets.

The bits in the first byte are as follows.

P = 1 on first byte indicates that padding is added to the beginning of the packet; the low-order part of that octet indicates the number of bytes of padding.

V = version number.

I-L = "intra-LAN," meaning that this packet originated on this LAN (that is, the source is your neighbor, so send directly in the future).

RTS ("return to sender") means that the packet could not be delivered and is being returned from whence it came. The router swaps the source and destination fields, so the packet is routed like an ordinary packet. The RTS field is used by routers so that if this packet needs to be dropped it doesn't get returned to the other side (because an error packet should not generate an error packet).

RQR ("request return") means that if the packet needs to be dropped, please return it to the sender so that it knows the packet can't be delivered.

Format indicates whether the packet is in "long" or "short" format.

Visit count is a hop count that counts up.

Protocol type, like the protocol type field in IP or Ethernet, indicates the type of packet inside the DECnet header.

The **C** bit in both formats is the congestion-experienced flag.

10.3.7 CLNP

Figure 10.9 shows the CLNP header format.

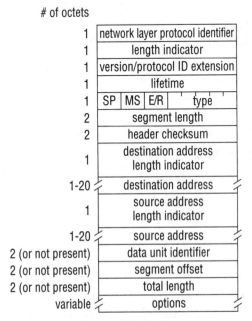

Figure 10.9 CLNP

Network layer protocol ID: Allows differentiation among various ISO packets so that all the ISO packets can share the same layer 2 SAP value.

Length indicator: The length of the header.

The 8-bit **version** field: = 1.

Lifetime: Like the **TTL** field in IP, it is intended to have something to do with time but in reality is treated like a decrementing hop count.

SP = segmentation permitted.

MS = more segments.

E/R: An error report is requested (rather than a silent discard) if the packet needs to be dropped.

Type has two defined values: 28 = data packet, and 1 = error report.

Segment length: The length, in octets, of the header plus the data in this fragment.

Header checksum: For detecting errors in the header.

Length indicator octets: Used in measuring variable-length addresses.

Data unit identifier: Helps the destination reassemble a fragmented packet by identifying fragments of the same packet.

Segment offset (in units of octets, although the bottom 3 bits are required to be 0 so that fragmentation occurs on 8-octet boundaries): Indicates where in the reassembly buffer this fragment belongs.

Total length: The length of the data before it was fragmented.

The final three fields are absent if **SP** = 0 because they are needed only for reassembling packets that were fragmented.

10.4 Technical Issues and Comparisons in Data Packet Formats

In the following subsections, I go through the fields you might find in these protocols and explain how they fit into each of the protocols.

10.4.1 Destination Address

All the protocols have a field indicating the address of the destination. The structure of addresses differs among the protocols, though, as discussed in Chapter 9. Because of the variable-length addresses, CLNP requires a **destination address length indicator**, a 1-octet field that specifies the number of octets in the destination address. IPX and AppleTalk split the address into two parts—**net** and **node**—which are not adjacent in the header. But because the routers look only at the **net** portion, this is just fine.

Note that both IPv4 and IPv6 have the source address first. For cut-through forwarding, in which a packet is forwarded before it is completely received, it is preferable if the destination address comes first so that the forwarding decision can be made more quickly.

10.4.2 Source Address

All the protocols have a field indicating the source address. Again, in CLNP it is variable-length, with a 1-octet **source address length indicator** field. And in IPX and Apple-Talk, it is split into two pieces: **net** and **node**.

10.4.3 Destination and Source Sockets

These fields are only in IPX and AppleTalk. Like SAPs in the 802 header, it is a way of doing multiplexing within the node. In the rest of the protocols (IPv4, IPv6, CLNP, and DECnet), the function is instead done by having sockets at the transport layer. The best way to understand this is to think of IPX and AppleTalk as being a combination of the functionality of IP and UDP in the TCP/IP protocol suite.

10.4.4 Header Length

This field is called **IHL** (Internet Header Length) in IP and **length indicator** in CLNP. In IP, the unit is in 32-bit words; in CLNP, the unit is in octets. In IP, the field is 4 bits long; in CLNP, the field is 1 octet long. Thus, the maximum header length in CLNP is 254 octets (the value 255 is reserved), whereas in IP the maximum header length is 60 octets (15 32-bit words). In IP, the header must be constructed as a multiple of 4 octets because the header length unit in IP is in 4-octet chunks. That is why the IP header requires the **padding** field—to allow the header to be a multiple of 4 octets.

Forcing the header to be a multiple of 4 octets is not unreasonable. Some implementations might be more efficient if the data always started on a 4-octet boundary.

The fact that the IP header cannot be larger than 60 octets can be viewed either as a disadvantage (long source routes and other options might be impossible to specify) or as an advantage (we really don't want people spending all the bandwidth on the header).

IPX, AppleTalk, and DECnet have no header length field because the header is always fixed-size. IPv6 also lacks a header length field. It could be argued that IPv6 doesn't need one because the IPv6 header is fixed-length (except for the extra headers that can be tacked on). But the IPv6 "extra headers" really are options, so a header length field might be useful in IPv6 for the same reason it might be useful in IPv4 and CLNP.

10.4.5 Packet Length

All the protocols except DECnet have a field that indicates the total length, in octets, of either the header plus data (IPv4, AppleTalk, IPX, and CLNP) or only the data (IPv6). In CLNP the field is called **segment length**. In IP it is called **total length** (which is confusing because this field indicates only the fragment's length and not the length of the original packet before fragmentation). The field is called "total length" in IP because it includes the length of the header in addition to the length of the data in the fragment. In IPv6 it is called **payload length**. In AppleTalk and IPX it is called **packet length**.

This field was introduced because of the Ethernet idiosyncrasy of having a minimum legal packet size. Packets smaller than that must be padded. There are other data links in which errors can damage the length of the packet, so the field might have wound up in layer 3 even without Ethernet. DECnet assumed it was the job of layer 2 to hide such ugliness from layer 3. The DECnet Ethernet driver pads and unpads the packet so that DECnet's layer 3 can always assume that layer 2 will deliver exactly what is given to it.

10.4.6 Header Checksum

IP, CLNP, AppleTalk, and IPX all have a 16-bit **header checksum** field, but they use different algorithms.

In IPv4 and AppleTalk, the header checksum is computed by doing a 1's complement addition of all the 16-bit words and then taking the 1's complement of the result. A 1's complement addition of two numbers consists of a normal addition followed by an increment of the total if the addition resulted in a carry. This is more robust than an unsigned addition because with a normal addition, two bit errors in the most significant bit would cancel out, whereas with 1's complement, the carry from the most significant bit carries over into the least significant bit. Thus, all bit positions are equally protected by the checksum.

In CLNP, the checksum is different. It can be thought of as two 8-bit checksums. The least significant octet is similar to the IP checksum but is performed by doing 1's complement sums based on octets rather than on 16-bit words. The second octet, known as a *Fletcher's checksum*, is also calculated using 1's complement arithmetic on octets. Fletcher's checksum is the sum of the value of each octet multiplied by that octet's offset from the end of the header. This might seem expensive to compute, but it can be computed and verified with additions or table lookups and is not significantly more expensive to compute than the IP checksum. (Some people argue that with cleverness it can be no more expensive to compute.)

Note that routers modify fields in the header—most obviously, the **time to live** field, but also many other fields if the packet must be fragmented. Thus, in addition to verifying the checksum, a router must recompute the checksum before forwarding a packet.

If a router recomputes the checksum from scratch after modifying the header, then the checksum doesn't give very much protection. The main purpose of a network layer checksum is to guard against corruption by a flaky router. The checksum provided by almost all data link layer protocols guards against transmission errors. A flaky router might mangle the packet and then recompute a good checksum for the mangled packet. To reduce the likelihood of a flaky router's introducing undetected errors, CLNP requires routers to incrementally modify, rather than recompute, the checksum. (Though I wonder how that can ever be checked in a conformance test.) IP does not require (but certainly allows) incremental modification of the checksum.

Dealing with the checksum makes it considerably more difficult to forward packets, especially if the router is required to incrementally modify a packet and if several fields have been changed (as in the case of fragmentation). IP always requires routers to verify and modify the checksum. CLNP allows the source to specify in a packet that the checksum is not being used, and that allows the routers to spend their cycles on tasks other than verifying and incrementally modifying checksums. In CLNP, if the 2 octets of checksum are 00-00 (all 0's), it means that the checksum is not being used and should not be checked or modified. Reserving the value 00-00 for this purpose is possible because in 1's complement arithmetic, 00-00 and FF-FF (all 1's) are equivalent. Thus, if the checksum computation results in the value 00-00, the value FF-FF is used instead.

There's a great story to tell about the IPX checksum. The value FF-FF (all 1's) meant that the checksum field should be ignored. Indeed, at the time, nobody had implemented the IPX checksum, so it was always set to FF-FF. The fact that nobody had implemented the checksum really saved the day. How could that be? Read all about it in Section 10.6.

I don't believe that the header checksum accomplishes enough to be worth the work during forwarding time. It might be nice to delete mangled packets earlier so that they don't waste bandwidth, but not at the expense of slowing down forwarding on every hop. Note that the header checksum was removed in IPv6.

10.4.7 Fragmentation Allowed

Both IP and CLNP have a 1-bit flag indicating whether fragmentation is allowed. In IP, the flag is the middle bit of the 3 bits set aside for **flags** and is called **DF**, for "don't fragment." If this bit is 0, fragmentation is permitted. In CLNP, the flag is called **SP**, for "segmentation permitted." Thus, it is the opposite of IP. In CLNP, if the flag is 0, fragmentation is not permitted.

In CLNP, if the SP flag is 0, the fields **data unit identifier**, **segment offset**, and **total length**, which are useful only for reassembly, are omitted. Although this saves bits by decreasing the size of the header, it introduces yet another case in which the header fields are in different places. That makes building high-performance CLNP routers more challenging.

None of the other protocols bothers with fragmentation. IPv6, though, has made a strange choice. It has fragmentation information in the header but claims that this would be done only by the source. But the source would be better off just sending the correct size rather than fragmenting. The claim is that the source transport layer can send the right size if it's TCP, but can't if it's UDP. Fair enough, but why would the source network layer know the right size to send? TCP can do maximum packet size discovery as described in Section 8.7. But UDP cannot because it is connectionless. It is hard to imagine how the source IP layer would know the correct size to send. If it did, it would be better off telling the application what size to send.

As of the writing of this book, IPv6 fragmentation isn't being used anyway. My guess is that either nobody will use the fragmentation in IPv6 or routers will wind up doing the fragmentation. (Or, as some people believe, IPv6 won't ever be widely enough used for us to find out whether fragmentation at the source IP layer and not in the routers makes sense.)

10.4.8 Packet Identifier

The packet identifier is another field that is useful only for fragmentation, so it does not exist except in IP, CLNP, and IPv6 (which allows fragmentation, but only at the source). This field consists of a number assigned by the source to the original unfragmented packet. Its purpose is to enable the destination to perform reassembly. Successful reassembly requires that the destination know which fragments belong together. The rule is that two fragments belong to the same original packet if the packet identifier field and the source address, destination address, and protocol fields match.

In IPv4 and IPv6, the field is called **identification**; in CLNP it is called **data unit identifier**. In CLNP the packet identifier field is present only if the **SP** flag is set. In IP the field is always present. In IPv6 it is present only if the source has fragmented the packet, and then it is in the fragment header.

The packet identifier field should be long enough so that it will not wrap around within a packet lifetime. IP and CLNP have a 16-bit packet identifier field. Now that technology allows gigabit speeds, this field is too small. In IPv6 the packet identifier field is 32 bits long.

The consequence of an insufficiently large packet identifier field is that multiple distinct packets having the same packet identifier can exist in the network simultaneously (with the same source/destination pair). If they have been fragmented, the destination can be fooled into combining fragments from different packets. If the transport layer has a checksum, the checksum will probably not match and the incorrectly reassembled fragments will be discarded. There is a small possibility that the checksum would not detect the error, in which case garbled data would be delivered to the application. There is also the possibility that the transport layer may not have a checksum (which means either that it can tolerate some garbage data or that it deserves what it gets).

The problems associated with a too-small packet identifier field may not be as frightening as they sound because they occur only when packets are fragmented. If the transport layer uses a packet size that does not require network layer fragmentation, the packet identifier field is irrelevant (and can be excluded in the case of CLNP).

10.4.9 Fragment Offset

IPv4, IPv6, and CLNP have a field indicating the offset at which this fragment belongs in the reassembled packet. This field is 0 in a packet that has not (yet) been fragmented.

To allow efficient reassembly algorithms, all three protocols require fragmentation to occur on 8-octet boundaries. In IPv4 and IPv6, this field is called **fragment offset** and is 13 bits long, with the unit being 8-octet chunks. In CLNP this field is called **segment offset** and is 16 bits long, with the unit being single octets. Because CLNP requires fragmentation on 8-octet chunks, the bottom 3 bits of the segment offset field in CLNP are always 0. Thus, the fields are equivalent. Each is essentially a 13-bit field indicating the offset in 8-octet chunks. CLNP puts in the extra 3 bits, "daring" you to commit the protocol crime of setting them to anything but 0.

In CLNP, the **segment offset** field is present only if the **SP** flag is set. In IPv6, it is present only if the fragmentation header is placed there by the source, which would use it only if it has fragmented the packet "at birth."

10.4.10 Prefragmentation Length

Only CLNP indicates the prefragmentation length, with a 2-octet field called **total length** (unfortunately allowing confusion with the badly named IP **total length** field). The prefragmentation length shows the length of the original packet, including both header and data, before any fragmentation occurred. The existence of this field allows the destination to know, upon receiving any fragment of a packet, how big a buffer to set aside for reassembly. If the segmentation permitted flag is 0, this field is not in the header because it is not needed (it is equal to CLNP's **segment length** field when a packet has not been fragmented).

IPv4 and IPv6 have no equivalent field. Thus, the destination must guess at a buffer size. If it guesses too small it must either copy the packet into a bigger buffer or use chains of buffer fragments.

10.4.11 More Fragments Follow

IPv4, IPv6, and CLNP have a 1-bit flag to distinguish the final fragment of a packet from the other fragments. In IPv4 and IPv6, this bit is called **MF**, for "more fragments"; it is set on all fragments except the last and is 0 on the last fragment. In CLNP, it is called **MS**, for "more segments," and is otherwise identical to the IP flag.

In CLNP the **MS** flag serves no useful function because its state can be determined from CLNP's **total length** field. If the offset plus the length of the fragment equals the total length, then it is the last fragment. This flag exists in CLNP because CLNP's designers started out with the IP packet format and did not notice that the flag was no longer necessary when the **total length** field was added. The **MS** flag in CLNP does no harm except that it will confuse implementers wondering what it is supposed to be useful for. It also raises the question of what a router or the destination should do if the flag is incorrectly set (indicating that a fragment is the last one when it is not or that it is not the last one when it is).

10.4.12 Lifetime

Despite all the hard work of the routing protocol, sometimes packets loop. Routers do not discover topological information simultaneously. Therefore, it is nice to have a field that changes (in a monotonically increasing or decreasing way) at each router so that a looping packet can eventually be noticed and discarded. All the protocols have such a field, but there are interesting differences in its use.

In IP it is called **time to live**, or **TTL**; in CLNP, it is called **lifetime**. In both these protocols, the field is initially set to a value by the source and is decremented by routers until it reaches 0—at which point, the packet must be discarded.

The time unit in IP is seconds. In CLNP, it is half-seconds. Both protocols specify that every router must decrement the field by at least 1. CLNP specifies that routers must overestimate rather than underestimate the amount by which the field should be decremented. I think that the field should simply be a hop count—that is, each router should modify it by 1.

There are four reasons for having a **lifetime** field.

1. While routing information is propagating, routing decisions can be inconsistent among routers, and packets can loop. The lifetime field enables looping packets to be deleted. A simple hop count field (one in which every router decrements the field by 1) would suffice for the elimination of looping packets.

2. Assuming that the network layer provides the equivalent of network layer multicast addresses or simply that many servers of a certain type might all advertise a well-known network layer address, a source might want to do an expanding search to find the closest station that answers a particular address. For this use, again, a simple hop count field would suffice. The source might first issue the packet with a very small count, and then, if no reply was received, the source might reissue the packet with a larger count, continuing the process until it either finds something or decides that the search is too expensive.

3. The traceroute utility is a clever hack designed to force each router along the path, in turn, to return an error report. It works by setting the **TTL** first to 1 (causing the first router to send an error report back to the source) and then setting it to 2 (causing the next router to send an error report) and so forth until the packet reaches the destination. A hop count field is preferable to a timer for this use.

4. To reuse connection identifiers and similar fields, certain transport protocols need assurances from the network layer that packets will not live in the network longer than a certain amount of time. A hop count would not solve this problem because a packet might be delayed a very long time at one router.

The granularity of the lifetime field in both IP and CLNP, along with the difficulty of estimation, makes this field not very useful for purpose 4. For example, it is impossible to estimate this field when a router transmits a packet onto a bridged extended LAN. After the router has successfully transmitted the packet onto its local LAN, the packet can be delayed for as long as 2 seconds per bridge. With the stipulation in CLNP that every router overestimate rather than underestimate, this implies that a router would need to decrement the CLNP lifetime field by 30 (half-seconds) each time the packet was forwarded onto a LAN.

In another example, it is not feasible to estimate an absolute upper limit on the delay when you're transmitting onto FDDI (fiber distributed data interface). Usually, there is a very small delay before a station gets permission to transmit on FDDI, but in the worst case the delay can be as long as 150 sec. Thus, theoretically, to comply with the CLNP overestimate constraint a router would need to decrement the lifetime field by 300 (half-seconds), which is larger than the maximum value of the field (255).

I believe that the only reasonable solution to the problem of guaranteeing the transport layer a maximum packet lifetime is to have the transport layer use large enough fields so that, given the natural characteristics of the network, there is an acceptable probability that they will not be reused. Pretending that the lifetime field is accurate enough, or that it gives sufficient granularity to be useful and safe, is not realistic. In fact, most router implementations treat the field as a simple hop count.

In IPX, DECnet, AppleTalk, and IPv6, the field is specified as a hop count (rather than a time) and is decreased or increased by exactly 1 at each router hop. As discussed in Section 8.3, it is preferable to count down rather than to count up. IPX, DECnet, and AppleTalk all count up. IPv6 counts down.

In AppleTalk the field is 4 bits long. That is definitely not big enough, although the two adjacent "reserved" bits can potentially be used as an extension to the field at some future time (although backward compatibility may be awkward). In DECnet it is 6 bits long. In IPX, IPv4, and IPv6 it is 8 bits long. Perhaps there might be paths longer than 256 hops, in which case it would be better to have a larger field. One argument against making it bigger (which was discussed for IPv6) is that then a looping packet would take longer to get discovered. But refuting this argument is easy. The field can be arbitrarily large, but it's not necessary to use the full value. Especially given that IPv6 counts down, it is easy to have endnodes, by default, set the "hops remaining" field to something reasonable in today's networks (say, 100) but have the field large enough and have packet sources configurable to be able to launch packets with larger hops-remaining fields if necessary. The other argument against making the field bigger is that it wastes room in the header. But a single extra bit doubles the possible path lengths, so this hardly seems like a strong argument.

10.4.13 Version

IPv4, IPv6, CLNP, and DECnet have a "version" field. The others do not. The lack of a version field in IPX forced us to be creative in order to add features. We wound up defining a new destination socket number to mean that extra header information followed the old IPX header. AppleTalk did the annoying thing of using the frame format (Ethernet versus 802.3) to decide the version of the AppleTalk packet, which caused problems for bridges (see Section 3.6.3).

In IPv4 and IPv6, this field is 4 bits long. However, it's not really a version number in the usual sense because version = 5 is not a newer version of IP. In CLNP, the version field is 8 bits long. In IPv4, the value is 4; in IPv6, the value is 6; in CLNP, the value is 1.

DECnet has a 1-bit version field! The designers did that on purpose because they never wanted to have to be compatible with more than one old version.

If **version** is not the expected value, the packet is supposed to be discarded without an error packet's being generated. (Theoretically, the packet cannot necessarily be parsed to find the source address, to which an error report would be transmitted.)

There is no clear distinction between a new version of a protocol and a new protocol. Instead of changing the version field, the standards body could achieve the same effect by assigning a new data link layer protocol type to the new protocol, so a version number field is really not necessary.

10.4.14 Padding

IPv4, CLNP, and DECnet make provision for **padding** in the header. In IP, the header must be a multiple of 32 bits because the header length is specified as the number of 32-bit chunks. If the IP header does not end on a 32-bit boundary, the remainder of the 32-bit chunk is filled with 0's. The IP header is variable-length because of the **options** field.

In CLNP, padding is encoded as one of the options. Unlike in IP, padding is never necessary in CLNP, but if it is convenient for the implementation to have the header end on a 16-bit or 32-bit boundary, the padding option can be used.

In DECnet, padding is put on the front of the header and is indicated by having the top bit set in the first byte and the length of the padding indicated by the remainder of the first byte (allowing as many as 128 bytes of padding). Thus, if the first byte were 85 hex, there would be 5 bytes of padding (including the first byte), and the 6th byte would be the real beginning of the packet.

10.4.15 Protocol

IPv4, IPv6, DECnet, AppleTalk, and IPX all have a 1-byte **protocol** field that indicates the type of the next protocol, much like the protocol type field in Ethernet. In all of them the field is 1 byte long.

DECnet Phase III did not have a **protocol** field. We managed to add it to Phase IV by clever "specsmanship." The field called **protocol type** in Phase IV DECnet actually was the first byte of the layer 4 header in Phase III DECnet. We found all the values used by DECnet's layer 4 (which was called NSP), declared all those to mean NSP, and defined other values for other layer 4 protocols running on top of DECnet.

The **protocol** field allows the network layer at the destination endnode to know which protocol running within the endnode should receive the packet. For IPv4 and IPv6, the "assigned numbers" RFC (RFC 1700) documents which numbers are to be used for which protocols. The most obvious user of IP is TCP, but the routing protocols and other essential parts of the network layer (such as ICMP, Internet Control Message Protocol) are specified as if they were separate protocols running on top of IP. As such, they also have protocol numbers, and their data is carried inside an IP datagram. In IPv6 the things that would have been options in IPv4 are instead lumped into groups, and each group (such as end-to-end versus hop-by-hop options) is considered a different "header" and given a different "protocol type" value. Within each header the options to be included in that header are encoded as TLV (type, length, value).

> An anecdote. When I arrived at Digital, DECnet called layer 3 the transport layer, and layer 4 the Network Services Layer (which is why the protocol was called NSP, for Network Services Protocol). I think "transport" is a much better name for layer 3 because it is the layer that carries the packet through the network. I can't imagine why ISO thought that "transport" was a reasonable name for layer 4. But even though DECnet had much better names, it was clear that the industry was getting very confused, and so was I. We considered changing DECnet's layers to ISO terminology but decided that would be too confusing to people used to DECnet terminology. So we changed the terminology to neutral descriptive terms: "routing layer" for layer 3 and "end communication layer" for layer 4.

TLV encoding allows you to add information to a protocol in a flexible and forward-compatible way. You can add new options by defining new types. Unknown types can be skipped because of the length field.

CLNP does not officially have a comparable **protocol** field. One reason is that a lot of the types of packets that IP assumes are separate protocols running on top of IP (such as ICMP) are considered an integral part of CLNP (and are differentiated from data packets by the **type** field, discussed in the following subsection). Another reason is that CLNP assumes that the network layer address actually specifies the process within the destination machine and not simply the destination machine. Thus, if there are n protocols running within an endnode, all using CLNP, the endnode will have n network layer addresses.

The specification for IS-IS (see Section 14.4) specifies the following addressing convention for CLNP. The n network layer addresses in a machine running n protocols on top of CLNP are all identical except for the final octet. Therefore, the final octet of the CLNP destination address serves the same function as the protocol field in IP but in a syntax similar to the DSAP value in the 802 header.

10.4.16 Type

CLNP has a 5-bit field called **type**, which distinguishes the type of network layer packet. An ordinary CLNP data packet is type *28* (binary 11100). An error report packet is type *1*. The ES-IS protocol uses types 2, 4, and 6. The IS-IS protocol uses more. Why the CLNP committee chose the number *28* for the first packet format it invented, and the number *1* for the second, is one of life's mysteries. (I asked most of the members of the committee, and their answers ranged from "Why do you care?" to "Oh, yes, I remember there was a big discussion about that, but I don't remember what was said.")

DECnet is the only other protocol that has a similar mechanism. In DECnet, an "error report" consists of sending the data packet back to the source. DECnet has the flags **RTS** and **RQR**. If the destination is unreachable and **RQR** is set (indicating "request return" in case of error), then the router clears **RQR** and sets **RTS** (indicating "return to sender," meaning that this is an error report rather than a regular data packet). It then switches destination and source and sends the packet back toward the source.

10.4.17 Error Report Requested

E/R is a 1-bit flag in CLNP that, if set, indicates that the source would like notification, if possible, if the packet cannot be delivered. This is basically the same as the **RQR** flag in DECnet.

Typically, a transport layer will set this bit on the connection-setup packet. After a transport connection is successfully established, the source might no longer set the **E/R** bit. In this way, it will not use the network resources that would be required to keep it informed about lost packets.

IPv4 and IPv6 have no such field. They assume that the source would always like to know if there is a problem with delivery of its packets. The IP router requirements document allows, but does not require, routers to limit the number of notification messages sent. For example, a router might generate a report only after each nth packet.

IPX and AppleTalk do not have error reports defined, so there wouldn't be much point in having a flag in the header asking for an error report.

10.4.18 Congestion Feedback: Source Quench versus DEC Bit

One method of finding out that the network is getting congested is to notice that some of your packets are getting lost and assume congestion is a likely cause. Another mechanism, known as *source quench*, was implemented in IP in the form of an ICMP message (see Section 10.7.2). This message is generated by a router that has dropped a packet due to congestion and is sent to the source. Another mechanism is known as the *congestion-experienced* bit; it is also known as the *DEC bit* because the inventors and vocal advocates of the scheme (K.K. Ramakrishnan and Raj Jain) were from DEC (Digital Equipment Corporation). The congestion-experienced flag is set in the header of the packet that encountered congestion and is received by the destination. The congestion-experienced bit appears in CLNP as **C** in the "quality of service" option, in the **TOS** (type of service) field in IPv4 and IPv6, and in DECnet Phase IV.

Why should you care if the network is getting congested? It enables you (and hopefully everyone else) to be a good citizen and lower your demand on the network by decreasing the rate at which you send traffic. Also, even if you are the only user of a congested link, it is in your interest to stop generating more traffic before the queue for that link is exceeded and packets are dropped. Your throughput will be lower if you have to notice and retransmit lost packets. This is especially true for TCP-type streams, in which a lost packet must be recovered before the subsequent data can be delivered.

The **C** bit allows the destination to discover that the path is congested and, through some means, to notify the source transport layer that it should decrease its window and thereby place less demand on the network. There are interesting trade-offs between the two schemes (the C bit versus source quench messages). The C bit approach avoids adding traffic to an already congested network (assuming that the destination can tell the source about the congestion by piggybacking it on other traffic). The C bit also requires fewer resources in the router because it involves only setting a bit (and modifying the checksum).

However, the C bit must first be transmitted all the way to the destination; after that, news of that event must somehow be conveyed to the source. As a result, the information in the source quench message is likely to reach the source more quickly than the information that the C bit was set.

Usually, a source quench message is sent because a data packet needed to be discarded because of congestion. The C bit will be set before the network becomes so congested that it must drop packets. It's possible in theory, of course, to generate source quench messages before queues are full and packets need to be dropped, that is, at the same point as the C bit would have been set.

A disadvantage of the C bit is that if the network is forced to drop the packet, the C bit will not reach the destination.

Routers that generate source quench are required to limit the rate at which they generate them. You can do this, for example, by limiting them to 1 per n packets dropped (either for all packets dropped or packets from a particular source) or 1 per unit time (again, this could be overall, or per source, or per source/destination pair).

Researchers are (still) investigating algorithms to determine when to set the C bit or generate a source quench message as well as algorithms for reacting to the information.

In the most recent router requirements RFC (RFC 1812), the source quench mechanism is listed as a SHOULD NOT, meaning that the current sentiment favors the C mechanism.

10.4.19 Type of Service

IPv4, IPv6, and CLNP have a **type of service** field, which is theoretically supposed to indicate something special about the packet that is desired by the source and can intelligently be supplied by the routers. This field has not proven very useful, and currently the group Differentiated Services IETF is experimenting with the field to see whether it can find anything useful for it to do. So the definition of the bits may change. First, for historical reasons, I describe the original definition of the **TOS** fields. Then, in Section 10.4.19.4, I discuss what it might look like in the future.

10.4.19.1 TOS Field in IPv4

In IP, the field is 1 octet and is defined as shown in Figure 10.10.

Figure 10.10 IP's type of service field

1. *Precedence:* A 3-bit number from 0 ("normal" priority) to 7 ("highest" priority)

2. *D:* A flag indicating whether the source would like low delay (0 is defined as "normal" delay; 1 is defined as "low" delay)

3. *T:* A flag indicating whether the source would like "normal" throughput (0) or "high" throughput (1)

4. *R:* A flag indicating whether the source would like "normal" reliability (0) or "high" reliability (1)

Note the interesting use of the word *normal*—high delay, low throughput, low priority, and low reliability. Would you buy a network from someone who defined *normal* that way? (Don't take that comment seriously. I'm trying to keep an entire chapter devoted to packet formats from being deadly dull.)

Although the **precedence** portion is somewhat useful, **D**, **T**, and **R** are not very useful. So recently people have tried to come up with a better use of the 8-bit **TOS** field (see Section 10.4.19.4).

10.4.19.2 TOS in CLNP

In CLNP, two options—**quality of service maintenance** (also known as **QOS**, for "quality of service") and **priority**—provide the equivalent function. As is described in the following subsection, any particular option may or may not appear in a packet. In ISO, the "globally defined" quality of service option (option code 201) is 1 octet long and has the definition shown in Figure 10.11.

format	R	S/D	C	D/C	E/D	E/C

Figure 10.11 CLNP's QOS option

Format: 2 bits. Set to "11" to indicate that this is the "globally defined" type of service.

R: 1 bit—reserved (it is an unused bit).

S/D: 1 bit—"sequencing versus delay." If this flag is set, it indicates that the source is requesting that insofar as possible, its packets should be delivered to the destination in the order in which they were transmitted. You implement this by having the routers transmit all packets for a particular destination with this bit set along the same path, rather than doing load splitting, when there are multiple equivalent paths to that destination. Not doing load splitting can affect throughput; hence, the "sequencing versus delay" terminology.

C: 1 bit—"congestion experienced." This flag is transmitted as 0 by the source and is set by a router along a packet's path if the packet needs to be transmitted on a congested link.

D/C: 1 bit—"transit delay versus cost." This flag, if set, indicates that the source regards low delay as more important than the expense of the path.

E/D: 1 bit—"residual error probability versus delay." This flag, if set, indicates that the source prefers that none of its data be corrupted and is willing to have the routers send the packet on a slower path if that path is more reliable.

E/C: 1 bit—"residual error probability versus cost." This flag, if set, indicates that the source is willing to have the routers send the packet on a more expensive path if that path is more reliable.

The final 3 bits in the preceding list have always mystified me. They were standardized without any hint as to how they should be used. There are lots of possibilities that are circular. For example, setting **E/C** and leaving the other 2 bits clear indicates that cost is more important than delay, delay is more important than error rate, and error rate is more important than cost. This is discussed further in Section 12.8.2.

> **Edible, adj.** Good to eat, and wholesome to digest,
> as a worm to a toad, a toad to a snake, a snake to a pig,
> a pig to a man, and a man to a worm.[1]
>
> —**Ambrose Bierce**

In CLNP, the **priority** option is the equivalent of the IP **precedence** field. **Priority** is option 205 (binary 11001101) and has a length of 1 octet, with a value between 0 (lowest priority, which CLNP also euphemistically refers to as *normal*) and 15.

Although the congestion-experienced bit really has nothing to do with type of service, this field was a convenient place to stick the bit.

---

[1] Ambrose Bierce, *The Devil's Dictionary* (Mattituck, N.Y.: River City Press, 1911).

10.4.19.3 TOS in IPX, AppleTalk, and DECnet

None of these protocols bothered with a TOS field.

10.4.19.4 New Ideas for TOS

I've been arguing for years that having multiple metrics is not useful for several reasons.

*   Delay is close enough to bandwidth (a low-bandwidth link is a high-delay link), and error rate is a very weird metric. We don't need more than one metric. A single metric in which you set your undesirable links to fairly high values and your more desirable links to fairly low values will compute fine routes. (Though there is one case in which bandwidth and delay differ significantly. A high-bandwidth satellite link is also high-delay.)

*   Multiple metrics require extra configuration (costs for each metric for each link).

*   Multiple metrics require additional bandwidth (to carry around each cost's metric in the routing messages).

*   Multiple metrics require additional computation because routers must compute paths according to each metric.

So people have pretty much given up on metrics and are now wondering what to do instead.[2] There is an 8-bit **TOS** field in both IPv4 and IPv6. As of my writing this edition of this book, nothing is stable enough to take very seriously, but I'll let you know some of the ideas.

The congestion control people have managed to convince the world to let them have 2 bits: one to indicate "congestion has been experienced" and one to indicate whether the endnodes understand how to react to that bit; the idea is that if they don't, the router should drop the packet rather than set the congestion-experienced bit.

So there are 6 bits left over. The Differentiated Services working group at IETF is trying to decide what to do with them. Some people have affectionately referred to the working group as "200 bald men fighting over 6 combs," meaning that it's not clear whether anyone has any actual use for the bits. But because there are only 6 of them, they're precious and therefore worth fighting over.

In 1981 I published a paper called "Incorporation of service classes into a network architecture." In it I described three categories of service classes:

*   Handling directives (for example, use link encryption, priority, try not to reorder, use hop-by-hop error recovery to increase the reliability)

*   Metrics (for example, delay, bandwidth)

---

[2] I'm talking about the IP community here. The PNNI routing protocol for ATM takes metrics and service constraints seriously.

- Constraints (for example, don't go through a particular domain—perhaps it's in an unfriendly country or a domain that does not want to carry traffic between you and the destination for some reason—don't go on links that cost money, go only through links that can reserve me a particular chunk of bandwidth)

Constraints can be considered a special case of metrics, where the cost is binary.

People are confused about service classes, and they use terminology in conflicting ways. Basically, it is easy to implement handling directives. It doesn't affect the computed routes, but each switch does what it can to provide that special handling for your special packet. Metrics are more difficult, and it's not clear that they are worth the effort. Constraints might unfortunately be necessary, although I suspect that if the world didn't provide them it would learn to live without them. They are difficult, and perhaps impossible to provide for if there are too many of them and if the network is hierarchical.

10.4.20 Options

IPv4, IPv6, and CLNP have a provision for "options." Each has several options defined, and any subset of them (including none) can appear in any packet. The other protocols (IPX, DECnet, AppleTalk) do not have options.

10.4.20.1 Options in CLNP

In CLNP, each option is defined as shown in Figure 10.12.

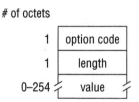

Figure 10.12 CLNP format for options

In CLNP, options can appear in any order, but no option is allowed to appear more than once.

For the CLNP options **security** and **quality of service**, the most significant 2 bits of the first octet of value have the following meaning.

- 00 = reserved (this combination is not used).

- 01 = *source-address-specific*. (Brace yourself for a mind-boggling definition!) This means that the interpretation of the option is not given in the spec but rather is defined by the authority from which the source got its address.

- 10 = *destination-address-specific*. (Why not?) This means that the interpretation of the option is defined by the authority from which the destination got its address.

- 11 = *globally unique*. This means that the interpretation of the option is given in the spec.

I am not aware of any implementations that use anything other than the globally unique options. The source- and destination-address-specific options are not useful unless the routers are coded to understand and implement them.

The source- and destination-address-specific options might be of use in a private network, with personalized routers (routers specially coded to handle options as specified by the customers). ISO, being a standards body, was reluctant to specify how to define options—thus, it provided this level of "flexibility." However, just to show that it does have the clout to make rules, it decreed that no option should appear twice. This restriction places a burden on routers (are they supposed to check that no option appears twice every time they forward a packet?) and reduces flexibility. For example, it precludes using padding in multiple places or using both the globally unique form of an option and the source-specified version in the same packet.

10.4.20.2 Options in IP

In IP, options are also coded as **code**, **length**, and **value** but with the following differences.

1. In the **code** octet, the **copy** flag specifies whether a router, upon fragmenting the packet, should copy the option into every fragment (if set) or only leave the option in the first fragment.

2. Instead of defining the bottom 7 bits as the code, the IP designers chose to subdivide these bits into two fields, giving the first octet of an option the format shown in Figure 10.13.

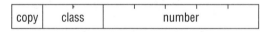

Figure 10.13 Format of first byte of IP option

For convenience, I refer to the **copy/class/number** octet as the "option code," even though it also contains the **copy** flag.

There is no particular reason that **class** and **number** could not be considered a single 7-bit field identifying the option. But the IP designers decided to mark options as being either *control* (class 0) or *debugging and measurement* (class 2). Classes 1 and 3 are reserved. Class 2 is used only for a single option: **Internet timestamp**. All the other defined options have the class field equal to 0.

3. Two options in IP are only a single octet long—that is, the only octet is the option code. Rather than waste an octet specifying that the option has 0 length, IP defines those options as not having the length octet because a length of 0 is implied by the option code.

The options that are just 1 octet long are as follows.

End of option list: IP option 0. (CLNP does not have, nor does it need, an equivalent option.) This indicates that the option list is ended. If the IP header length were in units of octets, this option would not be required; however, because the header length is in units of 32-bit chunks, this option indicates where the header ends. Note that because the padding is required to be transmitted as 0, the transmitter automatically adds this option when the header length is a nonintegral number of 32-bit chunks. This option may be introduced by a router after a packet is fragmented. (The router may fragment the packet, and the header length may change because of an option's not being copied; that might result in the header's being a nonintegral number of 32-bit chunks.) Also, if, after fragmentation, the header becomes an integral number of 32-bit chunks, this option can be omitted.

No operation: IP option 1. The equivalent option in CLNP is **padding**, option 204 (binary 11001100). In CLNP, the length octet must be present even if the length equals 0, which indicates that only the option type and option length octets are present. Thus, with CLNP, it requires at least 2 octets to include the padding option.

The **no operation** option can appear any number of times in IP and might be used, for example, to align the beginning of a subsequent option on a 32-bit boundary. In either IP or CLNP, this option can be deleted or introduced by a router eager to modify a packet in a nondestructive manner.

Other IP options require data in addition to the option number. The format for the other options in IP is that an option length octet follows the option code, indicating the number of octets in the option. The option code octet is counted, as well as the option length octet, so the smallest value possible for the option length octet is 2. Some options are variable-length. Others are fixed-length but still require the option length octet.

Both IP and CLNP have about the same options defined. These are as follows.

Security: This is intended to specify how sensitive the information in the packet is so that the routers can choose, for example, routes that stay within the country or routes upon which link encryption can be done. Of course, neither spec says what should be done about the security option. As long as the routers don't have special code enabling them to do something intelligent with it, the security option has no effect (other than possibly saving a spy some time by identifying interesting packets in which they might be interested). The CLNP spec does say that if the security option is specified in a packet but a router doesn't implement that option, the router should drop the packet. The only problem is that it doesn't specify what "implementing" the option means.

Source routing: Source routing is discussed in Section 10.5.

Route recording: This option is used to trace the path that a packet has taken. Each router that handles the packet adds its address to the route. Figure 10.14 shows the IP format, and Figure 10.15 shows the CLNP format.

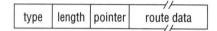

Type = 7.

Figure 10.14 IP route record option

| type | length | p/c | pointer | route data |

Type = 203. The p/c octet = 0 for "partial," 1 for "complete."

Figure 10.15 CLNP route record option

In CLNP, there are two types of route recording—partial and complete—just as with the source routing option. If complete route recording is specified, every router must add its address to the route. If a router receives a packet with complete route recording specified and if it does not implement route recording, it must drop the packet. If partial route recording is specified, a packet is allowed to arrive at the destination with only some of the route recorded because routers that do not implement partial route recording merely ignore the option if it is present. The missing hops are routers that do not implement this option.

In IP it is not mandatory for routers to implement route recording, and routers are not instructed to drop packets with this option if they do not implement route recording. As a result, IP specifies only one type of route recording, which is equivalent to CLNP partial route recording.

In both IP and CLNP, route recording has the same format as source routing. As in source routing, IP specifies that the router write its address on the outgoing link into the route. CLNP does not need to specify which address a router should write into the route because in CLNP routers are assumed to have only a single address.

In both IP and CLNP, the source makes the record route option **value** field as long as it thinks is necessary. Routers do not increase the length of the header as a result of adding their address to the route.

Both IP and CLNP specify that when the route is full, the packet is forwarded without modification to the route field, even if (in CLNP) complete route recording is specified. There is a subtlety in CLNP. Suppose that a packet is traveling the path shown in Figure 10.16.

Figure 10.16 Subtle route recording issue with variable-length addresses

Because CLNP addresses are variable-length, it could be that complete route recording is being done, and router R4 discovers that there is insufficient room in the route data to put its address. If it merely forwarded the packet on, it could be that R5, with a shorter address, might write its address into the route data. That would confuse someone trying to make sense of the supposedly complete, but in fact truncated, route. Thus, when R4 discovers that it cannot fit its address into the route, it sets the **pointer** octet to all 1's, indicating that no more route recording is to be done.

In IP, route recording is option 7; in CLNP, it is option 203 (binary 1100 1011). Complete route recording is distinguished from partial route recording by the first octet of option **value**, which is 0 for partial route recording and 1 for complete route recording.

4. **Internet timestamp:** This option, offered by IP, is option 4, class 2. CLNP has no equivalent. The format is shown in Figure 10.17.

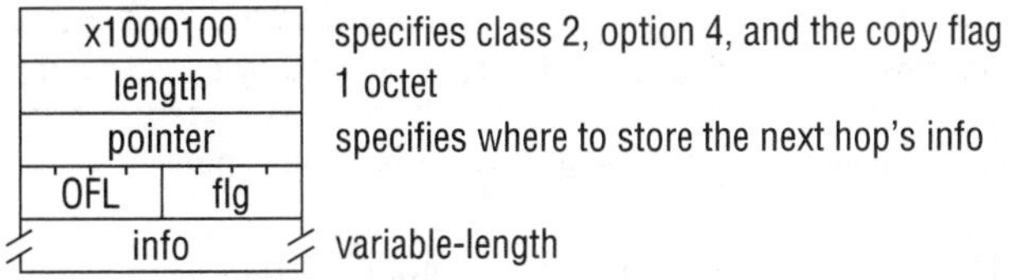

x1000100	specifies class 2, option 4, and the copy flag
length	1 octet
pointer	specifies where to store the next hop's info
OFL | flg	
info	variable-length

Figure 10.17 IP Internet timestamp option

The **info** field either is a sequence of 32-bit timestamps, marking the local time at each router at which the packet was received, or is a sequence of (address, timestamp) pairs, with each router recording its address as well as the timestamp.

If **flg** is 0, the routers just record the timestamp. If it is 1, they record their address plus the timestamp. If it is 3, it indicates that the source specified the addresses of the routers that should store their timestamps, with space in between for the timestamps to be stored.

As with route recording, the source allots whatever size it wishes for the timestamp recording. When it fills up, routers increment the **OFL** ("overflow") field, indicating how many timestamps—or (address, timestamp) pairs—were not stored because of lack of space.

The timestamp is a 32-bit timestamp in milliseconds since midnight universal time.

10.5 Source Routing

In IPv4 and CLNP, there are actually two source routing options (see Figures 10.18 and 10.19). In the first, *strict source routing*, the entire list of routers is specified. In the other, *loose source routing*, the source specifies several intermediate addresses along the route that the packet must not miss visiting, in the order specified, during its journey. In IPv6, there is a **type** field that implies that many variants on source routing might be defined at some point, but only type 0 is defined, which is loose source routing (see Figure 10.20).

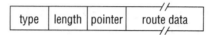

Type = 131 for "loose," 137 for "strict."

Figure 10.18 Format of IP source route option

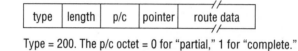

Type = 200. The p/c octet = 0 for "partial," 1 for "complete."

Figure 10.19 Format of CLNP source route option

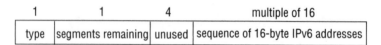

Figure 10.20 Format of IPv6 source route option

Both IPv4 and CLNP have a **pointer** field which indicates the offset into the route that has the next specified destination. IPv6 instead has a **segments remaining** field, so that it can support a route up to 256 hops with 1 byte (a pointer field equivalent to IPv4's would have only supported 16 hops since IPv6 addresses are 16 bytes). The remainder of the option value field consists of the sequence of addresses that the packet must visit. In IP, because addresses are fixed-length, the sequence of addresses is just that. In CLNP, because addresses are variable-length, each address consists of a length field (giving the length of the address) followed by the address.

In IPv6 the **unused** field is 4 octets long and must be there so that the addresses are on 8-octet boundaries. Remember that 2 octets are not shown in Figure 10.20. As with the other "headers" in IPv6, there is an initial octet that specifies the "type" of the next header and the length of this one (in units of 8 octets).

10.5.1 Loose versus Strict Source Routing

Strict source routing is useful[3] when the source does not trust the routers to route properly (as when the network is broken). It is also useful when, for security reasons, the source wishes to make sure that the packet does not stray from the specified path—for example, because the source suspects some router of having been compromised by the enemy.

Loose source routing is useful[4] when not all of a network recognizes all addresses. For example, suppose a packet originates in a portion of the network in which the routers would not recognize the destination address. If the packet is first directed to an intermediate address, with a "smarter" router that recognizes the destination address and whose address is recognized in the first portion of the network, the packet can proceed. Several intermediate destinations may be required in order for the packet to reach the final destination.

Loose source routing also allows the source to control some aspects of the route. This is similar to our ability to select a long-distance carrier when making a phone call.

In IP, loose source routing is option 3; strict source routing is option 9. In CLNP, both are option 200 (binary 11001000), and loose and strict are distinguished by the first octet of the option value, which is 0 for "partial" source routing (ISO's word for "loose" since "loose" probably offended someone) and 1 for "complete" source routing ("strict" was probably also deemed objectionable). In IPv6, type 0 is loose source routing and maybe later someone will bother defining strict source routing or some other variant. In an earlier version of IPv6 there was a bit vector that indicated, for each hop, whether that hop was loose or strict, but people decided that it was too inefficient to implement and too difficult to define what a "neighbor" was.

Note that anything that can be accomplished with loose source routing can be accomplished with tunneling (see homework problem 9).

10.5.2 Overwriting a Source Route with an Outgoing Link Address

In IP, a node has a different address for each link upon which it resides. Thus, a router (which presumably resides on multiple links; otherwise, it wouldn't be very useful as a router) has several addresses. In IP, the source routing options specify that when an intermediate destination is reached, the router overwrites the hop in the route that specified its address with its address on the outgoing link. For example, suppose the source route consisted of A–B–C. When router B is reached, B makes a decision as to which link it should forward the packet on in order to route to C. If B's address on the outgoing link is not "B," then it modifies the route with its alias on the outgoing link, which might be "D." Then the route will be A–D–C.

---

[3] But apparently not all that useful, since nobody has used it for anything in all these years.

[4] Still not breathtakingly useful.

10.5.3 Overwriting a Destination Address with a Next Source Route Destination

There is an interesting mechanistic difference between the handling of source routing in IPv4 and IPv6 versus the way it's handled in CLNP. In IPv4 and IPv6, the next hop in the source route is overwritten onto the destination address field in the header. This would have been awkward in CLNP because addresses are variable-length. Thus, in CLNP the destination address field remains constant throughout the packet's journey, whereas in IP, it always points to the next place, as specified by the source, that the packet must visit. In both IP and CLNP, routers were not required to implement loose source routing, and they were supposed to process the packet normally (as if the option were not specified) if the option was specified in a packet. This can cause packet looping in CLNP (see homework problem 6). As a result, CLNP was modified to make implementation of partial source routing mandatory, and that fixed the problem.

IP does not have the problem because, as just indicated, it requires the next destination to be written into the destination address field. This allows source routing to work even when intermediate routers other than those specified in the source routing header ignore the source routing option.

10.5.4 A Security Flaw with the Source Route Option

Unfortunately, some systems still believe that looking at the source address in the IP header is a secure way of deciding whom you're talking to. Originally, the IP designers thought of source routing as a very important security feature that would enable you to route around routers that had been taken over by the enemy in a battlefield situation. It wasn't exactly clear how you'd know which routers were the bad guys. Anyway, in the original specification (the host requirements RFC), it was specified that if you received a packet with a source route, you were required to reply using the same source route. After all, the source must have discovered a sinister plot requiring the use of the source route, and because the source knows it isn't safe to go the usual way, you'd better use the same source route.

Unfortunately, this reasoning is completely wrong. It's easy to forge a source address in a layer 3 header. You can write whatever you want into the source address field when you launch a packet. However, it's difficult to carry on a conversation when you've forged the source address because the answer will go to the source address, and not to you, unless you figure out a way to intercept the reverse traffic. Many times it is possible to intercept the reverse traffic. You might be on the path between the source address and the destination or might have an accomplice on the path. Or you might subvert the routing protocol so that it delivers packets for that source address to you.

But with source routing, you don't have to bother. It helpfully delivers the packet right to your doorstep.

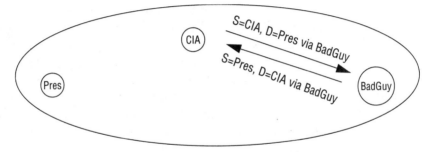

Figure 10.21 Source routing, security flaw

Suppose you (BadGuy) want to carry on a conversation with the CIA and have them think you are Pres (see Figure 10.21). You could just send a packet and fill in source = Pres, but the return traffic would go straight from CIA to Pres, and you wouldn't get it. So instead, you send a packet with a source route, claiming that the source = Pres, with source route BadGuy, CIA. CIA, of course, assumes the packet came from Pres, because that's what the IP header says, and an IP header would never lie. Furthermore, oh my, Pres seems to have discovered a nefarious plot that requires the secure path that goes through BadGuy. So the CIA returns the packet via the source route BadGuy, Pres.

Of course these days everyone realizes that looking at the source address in an IP packet is not a secure way to do authentication.[5]

10.6 The Great IPX Frame Format Mystery

Come gather 'round to hear a great tale.

Once upon a time, IPX was transmitted over Ethernet, with Ethertype 8137 hex. Then along came the 802.3 standard. The implementer of the IPX stack was told to make it work on 802.3. So that's what he set out to do.

Unfortunately, the IEEE committee did not make things easy. The 802 header was actually defined in two different documents. The 802.3 document defined the fields **destination**, **source**, and **length**. The rest of the header (**DSAP, SSAP, CTL**, and if SNAP SAP was used, **protocol-type**) was defined in the 802.2 document. So the implementer, using only the 802.3 specification, put the IPX packet right after the **length** field, on top of where **DSAP, SSAP,** and so on, were supposed to be! Admittedly, the 802 committee made things confusing. However, the implementer should have wondered what happened to the protocol type field. How could multiple protocols coexist on the same wire, and be implemented on the same machine, without such a field?

But the fact that nobody had implemented the IPX checksum saved the day because the first 2 bytes of the IPX packet were the checksum, which were set to FF-FF. The result was that IPX could be identified by the value FF-FF in the **DSAP** and **SSAP** fields.

---

[5] Sigh. I'm hoping that saying it will make it true. Unfortunately, there are systems that rely completely on the source address in the IP header for authentication.

This arrangement was rather unfriendly because FF is supposed to mean the "broadcast SAP," whatever that means (a bizarre and thankfully unused concept . . . a packet that should get delivered to all processes within a machine?). Maybe IPX did a great service to the world because there was so much IPX deployed that nobody got to invent and deploy a use for the broadcast SAP. (When I explained this once to someone he said, "Aha! Now I know why all the other processes in my machine crash when my node receives an IPX packet." He'd read the 802.2 spec faithfully, and when he received a packet with DSAP = FF, he delivered the packet to all the processes in the machine. What else could 802.2 have meant by the "broadcast SAP"?)

At this point, the state of the world was that the older version of the stack used Ethernet frame format, and the new version of the stack used an encoding that should be illegal. The official name given to this frame format was "raw 802.3." As long as people didn't implement the checksum, it worked. However, it wasn't quite "legal," so to fix things they implemented two new frame formats! One was called SNAP format, which used SNAP SAP for DSAP and SSAP and used the 5-byte protocol type 0.0.0.81.37 (as per the convention of translating from Ethernet format to 802.3 format). The other was called "802.2" and used E0 hex (a locally assigned SAP value) for DSAP and SSAP.

10.6.1 IPX's Four Frame Formats

Figures 10.22, 10.23, 10.24, and 10.25 show the four IPX frame formats.

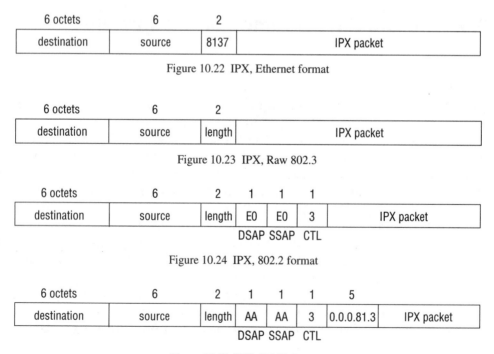

Figure 10.22 IPX, Ethernet format

Figure 10.23 IPX, Raw 802.3

Figure 10.24 IPX, 802.2 format

Figure 10.25 IPX, SNAP format

10.6.2 Dealing with Multiple IPX Frame Formats

The old version IPX endnodes (the ones that had been implemented using Ethernet format) did not understand any of the other formats. The next version (the ones that had implemented raw 802.3), were capable of understanding Ethernet format or raw 802.3. The newer ones could understand all four formats.

Remember that in IPX you assume someone is on the same LAN as you if the network number in their IPX address is the same as yours. If you think they are on the same LAN as you, you will transmit directly to them using their IPX node number as their data link address. But that would be a problem if someone transmitted a packet to an endnode that did not understand the data link format.

The chosen solution was to configure each endnode with exactly one format that it would receive and transmit. Even the endnodes capable of understanding all four formats would discard packets transmitted to them in a format other than the single format for which they were configured.

So now what would happen if some endnodes on a LAN were configured with one format and other endnodes were configured with another format? They would not be able to communicate. The solution was to force them to send their packets through a router, which would translate the formats.

This was accomplished by considering the LAN to consist of as many as four different LANs, one for each frame format in use. Each one would be assigned a different IPX network number. The router would be configured with a table such as the following, listing a network number for each frame format in use on that LAN:

- Port 7, frame format Ethernet = network number 92A6 (hex)

- Port 7, frame format 802.2 = network number 713B

- Port 7, frame format SNAP = network number 3C77

When an endnode boots up, it asks the router for the network number of the LAN. If the router receives the request on port 7 in frame format 802.2, it replies that the network number is 713B. If it receives the request on port 7 in frame format SNAP, it replies that the network number is 3C77.

In this way, two endnodes on the same LAN that use different frame formats will wind up with IPX addresses having different network numbers, and they will assume that to communicate they must transmit packets to a router for forwarding. And indeed the entire conversation between those two endnodes is transmitted through the router, which will transmit to the destination in the frame format that the destination understands.

The LAN in Figure 10.26 winds up looking like three distinct LANs connected with router R, as shown in Figure 10.27.

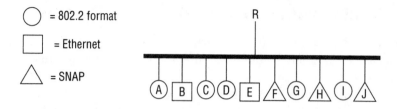

Figure 10.26 LAN with IPX clients configured with different formats

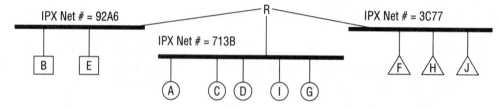

Figure 10.27 Acts like three separate LANs connected via R

10.7 Error Reports and Other Network Feedback to the Endnode

Although all the layer 3 protocols in this chapter provide datagram service, some are thoughtful enough to provide notification of trouble and other information to an attached endnode, if possible.

10.7.1 CLNP Error Messages

In CLNP, an error report has the same format as a data packet except that the **type** field (the bottom 5 bits of the fifth octet) is equal to 1, indicating that it is an error report, rather than 28 (binary 11100), which is a data packet.

When a router R cannot forward a packet from source S, R sends S an error report if S has set the **E/R** ("error report requested") flag in that packet's header. The source address is R; the destination address is S. The reason for discard is put into the error report's header, coded to look like the other options. It has code 1100 0001; its length is 2 octets. The value of the first octet is the type of error that is listed in Table 10.1. The value of the second octet is a pointer into the header where the error occurred. There are lots of error types, and it is not obvious what all of them mean. The error types were defined prior to the definition of any sort of routing protocol that would have provided a sensible context for them. Luckily, most of the defined error types make sense, and they include most errors that one would want reported.

Table 10.1 CLNP Error Types

Error Code	Meaning
0	Reason not specified
1	Protocol procedure error
2	Incorrect checksum
3	Congestion
4	Header syntax incorrect, header can't be parsed
5	Segmentation needed, but SP = 0 (segmentation not permitted)
6	Packet incomplete (header or total length doesn't match unfragmented packet size)
7	An option appeared twice
128	Destination address unreachable
129	Destination address unknown
144	Unspecified source routing error
145	Syntax error in source routing field
146	Unknown address in source routing field
147	Specified source routing path not acceptable
160	Lifetime expired while packet in transit
161	Lifetime expired at destination during reassembly
176	Unsupported option not specified (That's the wording in 8473, and it is supposedly self-explanatory. What it is intended to mean is that the packet contains an option that this router never heard of, and that option is such that it should be dropped by a router that doesn't support it. Unfortunately, 8473 says that if there's an option the router never heard of, the router should assume it is safe to ignore the option and forward the packet, so this error should never occur.)
177	Unsupported protocol version
178	Unsupported security option
179	Unsupported source routing option
180	Unsupported recording of route option
192	Reassembly interference

The data portion of the error report packet contains at least all of the doomed datagram's network layer header but may contain more. It is friendly of a router to provide at least enough more than the network layer header so that the entire transport header is included. This enables the source to match the returned datagram with the user process.

An error report packet has the **segmentation permitted** flag off. If an error report packet needs to be forwarded but is too long, a router will truncate the packet. Note that this is true only of error report packets. An oversized CLNP data packet will be fragmented (if possible) or discarded, but never truncated.

10.7.2 ICMP: IP Error Messages

In IP the error reports are provided by the ICMP (Internet Control Message Protocol), RFC 792. The ICMP packet is carried in the data portion of an ordinary IP packet. The **protocol** field in the IP header indicates ICMP. The basic format of ICMP messages is shown in Figure 10.28.

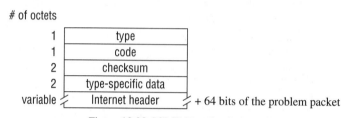

Figure 10.28 ICMP Message format

The ICMP message types are shown in Table 10.2.

Table 10.2 ICMP Message Types

Error Code	Meaning
0	Echo reply
3	Destination unreachable
4	Source quench
5	Redirect
8	Echo request
11	Time exceeded
12	Parameter problem
13	Timestamp request
14	Timestamp reply
15	Information request
16	Information reply
17	Address mask request
18	Address mask reply

Together, the message types "destination unreachable," "time exceeded," and "parameter problem" provide the functionality in CLNP error report packets.

The general format of these ICMP error report messages is as follows.

Type: 1 octet.

12	parameter problem
11	time exceeded
3	destination unreachable

Code: 1 octet.

In *time exceeded:*

0	died in transit
1	died while being reassembled by destination

In *destination unreachable:*

0	net unreachable
1	host unreachable
2	protocol unreachable
3	port unreachable
4	fragmentation required but not allowed by DF (don't fragment flag)
5	source route failed

In *parameter problem:* Code unused, set to 0.

Pointer: 1 octet. Used only in *parameter problem*. It is a pointer into the header indicating where a problem was found.

Unused: 3 octets.

Internet header + at least 64 bits of doomed datagram, and preferably as much of it as possible without the ICMP packet exceeding 576 bytes.

The other ICMP messages are as follows.

Echo: An echo request can be used to decide whether some destination is reachable. Any IP machine receiving an echo request is supposed to respond with an echo reply.

An echo request is known as a *ping. Ping* can also be used as a verb. To *ping* node X means to send X an echo request. This is a method of testing whether X is alive, well, and reachable.

Type: 1 octet.

8	echo request message
0	echo reply message

Code: 1 octet, set to 0.

Checksum: 2 octets. 16-bit 1's complement checksum of the ICMP message.

Identifier: 2 octets. A number that helps the echo requester match the reply to the request.

Sequence number: 2 octets. Another number that helps the echo requester match the reply to the request.

Data: Variable. Anything echo requester wants to put in. (It will be copied into echo reply.)

The **identifier** and **sequence number** fields can be thought of as a single 4-octet field that allows the echo requester to match the reply with the request. It was written as two fields because the suggested use was for the identifier to correspond to the TCP (transmission control protocol) or UDP (user datagram protocol) port number and for the sequence number to be incremented on each request.

Timestamp request or *timestamp reply as follows.*

Type: 1 octet.

13	timestamp request message
14	timestamp reply message

Code: 1 octet, set to 0.

Checksum: 2 octets. 16-bit 1's complement checksum of the ICMP message.

Identifier: 2 octets. A number that helps the requester match the reply to the request.

Sequence number: 2 octets. Another number that helps the requester match the reply to the request.

Originate timestamp: 4 octets. Timestamp put in by the requester to indicate the most recent known time before transmission of the timestamp request.

Receive timestamp: 4 octets. Timestamp put in by the replier to indicate the time that the request was received.

Transmit timestamp: 4 octets. Timestamp put in by the replier to indicate the time that the reply was transmitted.

Information request or *information reply as follows.*

Type: 1 octet.

15	information request message
16	information reply message

Code: 1 octet. Set to 0.

Checksum: 2 octets. 16-bit 1's complement checksum of the ICMP message.

Identifier: 2 octets. A number that helps the requester match the reply to the request.

Sequence number: 2 octets. A number that helps the requester match the reply to the request.

The information request message is used by a host that does not know the "network" number of the LAN on which it resides. The information request message is sent with the network portion of the source and destination addresses in the IP header equal to 0, and the reply has the addresses in the IP header fully specified.

The information request ICMP message is largely obsolete. A much more practical scheme for finding out the missing information is with the BOOTP and DHCP protocols.

Address mask request or *address mask reply as follows.*

Type: 1 octet.

17	address mask request message
18	address mask reply message

Code: 1 octet = 0.

Checksum: 2 octets. 16-bit 1's complement checksum of the ICMP message.

Identifier: 2 octets. A number that helps the requester match the reply to the request.

Sequence number: 2 octets. Another number that helps the requester match the reply to the request.

Address mask: 4 octets.

The address mask request message is used by a host that does not know its address mask. The reply contains the correct address mask. This message is described in RFC 950. It was added to ICMP after RFC 792 was published.

Source quench: as follows.

Type: 1 octet = 4.

Code: 1 octet = 0.

Checksum.

Unused: 4 octets.

IP header: at least 64 bits of the dead datagram.

The source quench message informs the source that the network is congested and that the source should attempt to lower its demand on the network. This message serves the same purpose as the congestion-experienced bit in the CLNP header. The IP method (sending a source quench message) has an advantage over the CLNP method in that a source quench is delivered to the source, which is where the information may be used. It has the disadvantage of causing an extra message to be generated in a congested network.

Redirect: This message is discussed in Chapter 11.

10.7.3 IPv6 Error Messages

IPv6 error messages are basically the same as in IPv4, using a modified ICMP. The **next header** value in the IPv6 header, indicating that the data is an ICMP message, is 58. The basic format of IPv6's ICMP protocol is as follows.

- An octet indicating **type** (where types 127 and lower are error messages, and those 128 and higher are informational, such as echo requests and replies).

- An octet of **code** indicating extra information specific to the type

- Two octets of **checksum**

In the case of an error report, as much of the original packet as will fit is returned, following the checksum and a 4-octet field which I'll call **extra info**, put there so that the returned packet will be on an 8-octet boundary. For some of the error messages there's actually information to put into that 4-octet field.

The error messages are as follows.

- type = 1; "destination unreachable," with **extra info** unused, and with code values as follows:

0	no route to destination
1	communication with destination administratively prohibited
2	not a neighbor
3	address unreachable
4	port unreachable

- type = 2; "packet too big" (with code value set to 0 and ignored), and **extra info** indicating the maximum packet size of the next hop.

- type = 3; "time exceeded," with **extra info** unused, and with code values as follows:

0	hops field went to 0
1	fragment reassembly time exceeded

- type = 4; "parameter problem," with **extra info** being a pointer into the offending packet, indicating the first place a problem was detected and code values as follows:

0	erroneous header field
1	unrecognized next header type
2	unrecognizeed IPv6 option

The IPv6 informational messages have the same format as IPv4 echo request and echo reply. They are .

- type = 128; "echo request"
- type = 129; "echo reply"

Homework

1. Suppose you are a router that needs to forward a fragment of size n onto a link that can handle only packets of size up to m (and assume $m < n$). Give the values of all the appropriate header fields, as a function of what they were in the received packet, as they should be transmitted for each outgoing fragment. Do this for both CLNP and IP.

2. Why is the **packet identifier** field not needed for X.25?

3. Both IP and CLNP specify that in addition to the packet identifier field, the **source address** and **destination address** fields (and in IP, the **protocol** field as well) should also be checked to determine whether two fragments belong to the same original packet. What does this imply about the algorithm for assigning packet identifiers?

   Suppose that the two protocols instead specified that only the **source address** and **packet identifier** fields were to be checked to determine whether two fragments belong to the same original packet. What advantages and disadvantages would this modification have? Take into account the probability of wraparound of the packet identifier field as well as CPU and memory in the source and destination stations.

   Suppose that this modification were made to the two protocols. Would stations implemented according to the old specification interwork properly with stations implemented according to the new specification?

   Suppose that the two protocols instead specified that only the **packet identifier** field was to be checked to determine whether two fragments belonged to the same original packet. Would this work?

4. IP does not have a "prefragmentation length" field. How can a destination reassemble packets without this field? If the field is not necessary, is it useful?

5. In the source routing options in IP, a router R that is one of the intermediate destinations overwrites the hop in the route that specifies R with its address on the outgoing link. Under what conditions will the router's overwriting of its specified address with its address on the outgoing link not cause the option value to be modified? Draw a picture of a network, specifying the routers' addresses on each link, and give a source route that would not be modified upon reaching the destination.

   If IP did not specify that routers must overwrite their address on the outgoing link, what would happen if the destination attempted to use the specified route (but in reverse order) when reaching the source?

6. How can a loop be created in CLNP as a result of a router's ignoring the partial source routing option? Why does mandating the implementation of partial source routing in CLNP fix the problem?

   Why doesn't IP have the same problem?

7. In IP route recording, would it be easier, harder, or neither easier nor harder to reconstruct a route if the routers recorded their address on the link from which the packet arrived rather than their address on the link on which they will forward the packet?

8. Suppose that a router implemented the **S/D** bit (see Section 10.4.19.2) by choosing the path to a particular destination based on the source address in the packet. In other words, if there are two equivalent paths to destination DEST, the router might send all packets with the **S/D** bit set on the first path if the source address was numerically even, and send all packets with the **S/D** bit set on the second path if the source address was numerically odd. Would this be a good or a bad idea? If some routers did it this way and others did it the "standard" way (sending all packets to DEST on the same path if the **S/D** bit was set), would there be any problems with the schemes interworking?

9. Suppose a packet had a loose source route specified of D1, D2, D3. Show how the packet would look if tunneling were used instead of source routing.

10. When might an IPv4 router add or delete the "end of option list" option?

Chapter 11
Neighbor Greeting and
Autoconfiguration

Neighbor greeting is one of three more or less orthogonal aspects of a network layer protocol. Neighbor greeting is the process by which endnodes find adjacent routers, distinguish adjacent nodes from those reachable only through a router, and find the data link layer address of adjacent nodes. It is also the process by which routers find the network layer address and data link layer address of adjacent endnodes. I also lump into this piece the ability for an endnode to find out its own layer 3 address.

This piece depends on the properties of the link. There are three basic types of links: point-to-point, LAN, and NBMA (nonbroadcast multiple access). The strategies are different for each type of link, as well as being done differently in each of the layer 3 protocols we're discussing.

We can think of this protocol as a layer between the network layer and the data link layer. In DECnet, we referred to this piece as the *subnet-dependent sublayer*, and the packet format, routing protocol, and so on as the *subnet-independent sublayer*. In this chapter I call it "neighbor greeting" even though "subnet-dependent sublayer" would probably be more accurate.

In ISO, this portion of the protocol is defined in document 9542, commonly known as the ES-IS protocol. In IP, most of this is defined in either BOOTP (RFC 951), DHCP (RFC 2131), or ARP (RFC 826). In DECnet, it is part of the routing specification. In IPX it's basically too trivial to write down. In AppleTalk, this functionality is provided by the AARP and ZIP protocols.[1] In IPv6, it is provided by ICMP for V6 (RFC 1885) and Neighbor Discovery for IPv6 (RFC 1970). However, as of the writing of this book there are newer versions of both in Internet draft form, so they are likely to be obsoleted by other RFCs.

---

[1] To get full details about AppleTalk, I highly recommend the book *Inside AppleTalk,* by Sidhu, Andrews, and Oppenheimer, published by Addison-Wesley.

A neighbor-greeting protocol is not present in X.25 (see Chapter 7) because X.25 makes the assumption that an endnode will be directly attached, via a point-to-point link, to a router, and the endnode's network layer address either contains the attached router's address, or the endnode's address is manually configured into the attached router.

Optimizations for NBMA have been done mostly in the context of IP over ATM.

11.1 Endnodes Attached via Point-to-Point Links

When an endnode E is attached to the network with a point-to-point link (see Figure 11.1), the neighbor-discovery protocol might enable the endnode to be assigned a layer 3 address by the router, and it might enable the router R to discover E's network layer address. This enables R to route packets to E and to announce E's network layer address to other routers so that they can direct packets destined to E toward R.

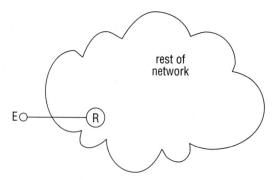

Figure 11.1 An endnode attached via a point-to-point link

In CLNP, the router finds out the network layer address of the endnode by having the endnode periodically transmit a packet known as an *end-system hello*, or ESH, that announces its network layer address. There is no reason for the endnode on a point-to-point link to know the identity of the adjacent router. When the endnode has a packet to transmit, all it needs to do is to transmit the packet with the destination's network layer address. Because there are only two nodes on a point-to-point link, there is no need for a data link layer address. ("Hey, you! Yes, of course, I mean you. Who else would I be talking to? The cable?")

Originally, in IP the router and the endnode had to be configured with the IP address and mask for each of its links. DHCP allows a router to dynamically hand out IP addresses and inform the endnode of its current IP address. IPv6 also allows a router to assign an address via IPv6's version of DHCP.

In IPX, a protocol called IPXWAN, run on point-to-point links, allows the router to assign an address to a neighbor endnode. It also measures the delay and bandwidth of the link upon start-up and uses these values to calculate a link cost (for use by the routing protocol), saving a human from having to configure a link cost.

In IP, the protocol PPP (point-to-point protocol), RFC 1661, adds a protocol type field (for carrying multiple protocols on the link), does authentication, and negotiates things such as data compression. The IETF PPP Extensions working group Web page lists about 50 relevant RFCs and more than 30 Internet drafts.

11.2 Endnodes Attached via LANs

Figure 11.2 shows a typical setup of endnodes attached via a Lan.

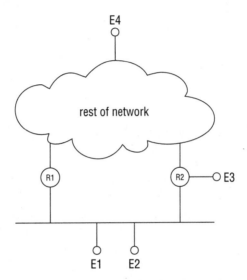

Figure 11.2 Endnodes attached via a LAN

As I discuss the mechanisms in the various schemes, I will refer to the following problems and show how each mechanism solves one of them.

1. Each endnode needs to know its own layer 3 address.

2. The routers on the LAN (R1 and R2) need to know the network layer addresses of their neighbor endnodes or some other information that they can announce to the rest of the network so that packets for E1 and E2 will be forwarded to the LAN.

3. The routers on the LAN need to know the data link layer addresses of their neighbor endnodes so that they can fill in the appropriate destination address in the data link layer header when forwarding a packet across the final hop to the destination endnode.

4. The endnodes on the LAN (E1 and E2) need to know the data link layer address of at least one router so that they can forward packets through the router when necessary.

5. When E1 needs to communicate with E2, it should be possible for E1 to send packets directly to E2 rather than having to transmit each packet initially to a router and then having the router forward the packet to E2. If this is not possible, forwarding packets via the router will still work, but it will result in a doubling of intra-LAN traffic.

6. When E1 needs to communicate with E3, it should be possible for E1 to find out that R2 is a better router to use than R1. If this is not possible, things will still work, but when E1 talks to E3, the LAN traffic will be doubled if E1 chooses R1 rather than R2 because each packet from E1 to E3 will result in two packets transmitted on the LAN: one from E1 to R1 and another one from R1 to R2.

7. If R1 and R2 are broken, it should still be possible for E1 and E2 to communicate. For that to happen, E1 and E2 need to find out each other's data link layer address.

11.2.1 ES-IS: The CLNP Solution

The protocol in CLNP for solving all these problems is known as ES-IS. It is defined in ISO 9542 and is officially titled by the catchy name of "End system to Intermediate system routeing exchange protocol for use in conjunction with the Protocol for providing the connectionless-mode network service." Somehow, nobody seems able to say or remember this title. Instead, this protocol tends to be called either 9542 or ES-IS, with ES meaning "end system" and IS meaning "intermediate system." Note that *routeing* is not a typo; rather, it was spelled that way at the insistence of the British delegation to ISO. I won't wantonly waste *e*'s when writing *routing*, except when quoting the title of an ISO document. Also note that the capitalization in the title is copied exactly from the ISO document, and I make no claim about understanding the capitalization rules.

In ES-IS, there are three types of messages.

1. *End-system hello, or ESH:* As with a point-to-point endnode, a LAN endnode periodically transmits an ESH, announcing its presence. On a LAN, the data link layer destination address is a special group address listened to by the routers (*intermediate systems,* in ISO terminology).

2. *Intermediate-system hello, or ISH:* This message is similar to the ESH except that it is periodically transmitted by a router and is transmitted to a special data link layer group address listened to by the endnodes.

3. *Redirect message:* This message is transmitted by router R to endnode E after E sends R a packet to forward that has network layer destination address D, and R notices that it forwards the packet back onto the same link from which it arrived, either directly to D or to a better router. The contents of the redirect inform E that for destination address D, E should send to the data link layer address that R used when R forwarded the packet back onto the LAN.

The periodic transmission of ESHs by the endnodes on the LAN enables the routers to learn the network layer addresses of the endnodes. In this way, they can announce these destinations to the other routers in the network (thus solving problem 2) as well as find out the data link layer address corresponding to the network layer address for each endnode (solving problem 3 from Section 11.2).

The periodic transmission of ISHs by the routers on the LAN enables the endnodes to learn the data link layer addresses of the routers (solving problem 4) and the routers' network layer addresses. It also allows the endnodes to autoconfigure because they can replace the ID field in the router's CLNP address with their own IEEE address (solving problem 1 from Section 11.2).

Following is the endnode algorithm (I'll explain in a minute the additional protocol needed).

1. Listen for ISHs. Store in a cache (the *router cache*) each data link layer address from which an ISH is received. Time it out if a new ISH is not heard within a specified period.

2. Keep a cache (the *destination cache*) of <destination network layer address, data link layer address> correspondence.

3. When transmitting to destination D, observe the following rules.

   a. If D is in the destination cache, with data link layer address X, transmit the packet with data link layer destination address X.

   b. If D is not in the destination cache and there is at least one router in the router cache, transmit the packet to a data link layer address (any of them) in the router cache.

      The final case, in which D is not in the destination cache and the router cache is empty, will be deferred for a moment so that the simple case can be explained.

   c. When transmitting to destination D, if D is not in the destination cache and the router cache is empty (the case I postponed discussing earlier), transmit the data packet to the group address ALL-ESs.

4. Upon receiving a redirect message with the information that data link layer address X should be used when transmitting to network layer address D, put <D, X> in the destination cache.

The way things work is that initially, E1 and E2 build up their router cache. When E1 wishes to transmit a packet to E4, it chooses the data link layer address of one of the routers. When E4 is the destination, either router will forward the packet through the network. One router might be slightly more optimal than the other, but unless the chosen router actually forwards the packet back onto the same link from which it was received, no redirect will be generated.

When E1 wishes to transmit a packet to E3, E1, as before, chooses the data link layer address of one of the routers. If it chooses R2, everything is fine. If it chooses R1, everything is still fine, but R1 forwards the packet over the LAN to R2 and sends E1 a redirect, telling E1 that in order to talk to E3, it should use R2's data link layer address (solving problem 6 from Section 11.2).

When E1 wishes to transmit a packet to E2, it again chooses the data link layer address of one of the routers. The data packet is forwarded by the chosen router, but that router also sends a redirect to E1 informing it to use E2's data link layer address when communicating with E2 (solving problem 5 from Section 11.2).

So far, problem 7 hasn't been solved. What happens when there is no router on the LAN? Maybe there never was, because the entire network consists of one LAN. Maybe there were routers, but they are all out to lunch. The topology then looks like that shown in Figure 11.3.

Figure 11.3 LAN with no routers

The additional endnode protocol rules for handling this case are as follows.

5. If you are an end system and receive a data packet addressed to the data link layer address ALL-ESs and if the network layer address matches yours, accept the packet (otherwise, discard it) and transmit your ESH to the data link layer source address in the received data packet.

6. If you are an end system and receive an ESH informing you that network layer address D corresponds to data link layer address X, put <D, X> in the destination cache.

These additional rules solve problem 7 from Section 11.2. If there is no router, E1 multicasts the data packet to E2, unfortunately bothering all the other endnodes on the wire with a "wrong-number" packet; but E2 responds with its ESH so that E1 will address future packets for E2 with E2's data link layer address. As the protocol is specified, when E2 responds with a data packet to E1, it goes through the same procedure, initially multicasting to ALL-ESs, receiving E1's ESH, and putting E1 in its destination cache.

When E1 wishes to communicate with E3 (an endnode not on the LAN), E1 also multicasts the packet to ALL-ESs because it does not know that E3 is not on the LAN. E3 does not receive the packet because no vendors to date have implemented an interface to the "ESP medium[2]." Hopefully, the upper-layer protocol at E1, upon not receiving a reply, will stop transmitting packets to E3 or will at least not retry frequently.

The cache timeouts are specified in the ISO protocol. All three protocol messages (ESH, ISH, and redirect) contain a *holding timer* indicating how long the corresponding cache entry should be kept in the cache. Each node on the LAN can have its own configured time for how long it thinks neighbors should remember it. If a node specifies a particular holding timer value, its period at which it transmits hellos should be about three times smaller than that holding timer value. In this way, a modest percentage of lost or delayed hello messages does not cause neighbors to assume that the node is down.

There is one additional subtle detail of the ISO scheme. When a redirect message points toward a router, the network layer address of the router is included in the redirect. This information allows an endnode, when it notices (through lack of received ISHs from router R) that R has gone down, to delete entries in the destination cache that are pointing toward R. Therefore, the destination cache contains an indication of whether the redirect is toward a router, and, if so, it also contains the router's network layer address (called *network entity title*).

Figure 11.4 shows the format of an ES-IS redirect message.

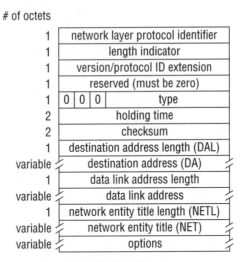

Figure 11.4 ES-IS redirect message

---

[2] Extra Sensory Perception

11.2.2 The IP Solution

In IP, the link number is a part of the network layer address and is recognizable by all the nodes attached to the link. As explained in Chapter 9, an IP node knows its 32-bit IP address as well as a 32-bit mask. The mask has 1's in the bits corresponding to the "link" portion of the address. If your IP address is X and your mask is Y, to determine whether a node with IP address Z is on the same link, you AND the mask Y with X and AND the mask Y with Z. If the result is the same, Z is on the same link.

Also, IP routing does not route to the destination endnode. Instead, it routes to the destination link. This is really the same as saying that there is no level 1 routing (the LAN provides the level 1 routing).

Again referring to the set of problems (from Section 11.2) that need to be solved by the neighbor-discovery mechanism, problem 2 (routers knowing the layer 3 address of endnodes on the LAN) is solved in IP by manual configuration of the routers attached on the LAN. Routers know the set of network layer addresses reachable on each of their links because they have been manually configured with the link number and mask of each of their links.

11.2.2.1 IP: Finding Neighbors' Layer 2 Addresses

So you know that the destination IP address is on your link. How do you transmit the packet—that is, what is the layer 2 address you put into the layer 2 header? The ARP protocol finds the layer 2 address corresponding to a layer 3 address. There are two messages.

1. *Address resolution protocol (ARP) query:* This is a message sent to the data link layer broadcast address indicating a network layer address for which the transmitter seeks a corresponding data link layer address.

2. *Address resolution protocol response:* This is a message transmitted in response to an ARP query by the node whose network layer address was queried. It contains the desired data link layer address and is transmitted to the unicast layer 2 address from which the ARP query was received.

When a node N on link L wishes to transmit a packet to a network layer address D that is also on link L, N first transmits an ARP query to the data link layer broadcast address, with data indicating that N seeks D's data link layer address. All nodes on L are bothered with the packet (even non-IP nodes because the ARP query is transmitted to the broadcast address). All of them except D throw it away after examining the data and discovering it is not their network layer address that is being queried. If D receives the ARP query and sees "D" inside, D replies with an ARP response transmitted to the data link layer source address in the received ARP query.

When N receives the ARP response, it makes an entry <D, DL address> in a cache known as the *ARP cache.*

11.2.2.2 ARP/RARP Message Format

ARP is defined in RFC 826. RARP (reverse ARP) is defined in RFC 903 and is used for autoconfiguration (see Section 11.2.2.4). An ARP/RARP message is carried directly inside an Ethernet packet (no IP header) using Ethernet protocol type 0806 (hex). Figure 11.5 shows the ARP/RARP message.

# of octets

2	hardware type	Ethernet=1
2	protocol type	IP=800 (hex)
1	length in octets of layer 2 address	6 for Ethernet
1	length in octets of layer 3 address	4 for IP
2	operation	see text
6	sender layer 2 address	
4	sender layer 3 address	
6	target layer 2 address	
4	target layer 3 address	

Figure 11.5 Format of ARP and RARP

The defined values for *Operation* are

- 1 = ARP request

- 2 = ARP reply

- 3 = RARP request

- 4 = RARP reply

11.2.2.3 Redirect Messages

The redirect message, which is specified in the ICMP (RFC 792) protocol, contains the layer 3 address of a better router. For example, in Figure 11.6, if A sends a packet for destination B to R1, R1 notices that it needs to forward the packet to R2, onto the same LAN from which the packet was received. So R1 sends a redirect to A, telling it that in the future, when sending to B, it should send via R2.

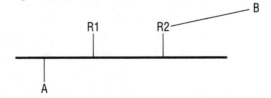

Figure 11.6 If A talks to B through R1, R1 sends redirect to A, pointing to R2

The format of the ICMP redirect message is shown in Figure 11.7.

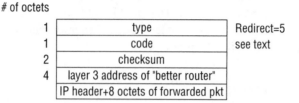

Figure 11.7 Format of ICMP redirect message

Note that the information you really want, which is the layer 2 address to fill in when forwarding to B, is not in the redirect message. To actually send a packet to B now you must do an ARP for R2's address to get back R2's layer 2 address. After R2 is in your ARP cache, of course, you don't need to do it again.

It would have been nice to have had R2's layer 2 address in the redirect. The reason it's not there is that ICMP (which describes the redirect message) was invented before LANs, so the concept of needing a data link layer address did not exist.

The code values defined in the **code** field are shown in Table 11.1.

Table 11.1 Values for ICMP Redirect **code** Field

Value	Meaning
0	Redirect datagrams for the network (obsolete)
1	Redirect datagrams for the host
2	Redirect datagrams for the type of service and network (obsolete)
3	Redirect datagrams for the type of service and host (should be obsolete)

The theory behind the code 0 redirect (for the network) is that a single redirect could apply to numerous destinations. The right way to have done this would have been to include 8 extra bytes of information in the redirect: the destination IP address and a mask. Then there would have been no need to include the IP header. But because there is no way of knowing how much of the address in the packet header is "network," it was easier to make code 0 obsolete. Unfortunately, this means that the endnode's destination cache must contain individual destinations rather than ranges of addresses.

The theory behind codes 2 and 3 is that different types of service might yield different routes, and therefore the redirect might apply only to the TOS in the packet. But because people have abandoned the TOS field in IP, codes 2 and 3 should also officially be considered obsolete.

11.2.2.4 IP: Endnode Autoconfiguration

Originally IP endnodes had to be individually configured. Then came the RARP protocol. An endnode comes up knowing only its layer 2 address. It sends a layer 2 broadcast asking for help. Hopefully, there is a RARP server on the LAN that is configured with (layer 2, layer 3) mappings for endnodes on that LAN. If such a server exists and if it has an entry in its database for the layer 2 address of the sender of the RARP request, it responds with a RARP reply containing the layer 3 address of the requester.

It is sort of cheating to call this "autoconfiguration" because someone must configure the RARP server. It also does not solve the problem of endnodes finding routers. There was no architected solution for this. One popular implemented solution is to simply require someone to configure at least one router address into the endnode, on the theory that it will find out about other routers through redirect messages. Another popular solution has endnodes listen for RIP messages (where RIP is one particular, not very good routing protocol). Which was kind of awkward when people wanted to replace RIP with better routing protocols, since there might be clients expecting to hear RIP messages in order to find the routers.

Later, the BOOTP protocol was invented. Unlike ARP/RARP, BOOTP is carried in an IP header so that it can be forwarded. Therefore, the BOOTP server does not need to be on the same link as the endnode requesting configuration information. Also, BOOTP contains much more information, such as the address of a router on the LAN and a file name to load, with a server name and address from which to load the file. This is useful for diskless operation.

BOOTP should have contained "options," TLV-encoded ("type, length, value," which allows you to add fields by defining new **Type** codes and allows skipping over unknown options because of the **Length** field). However, BOOTP was defined back in the Dark Ages (1985), so although the designers of BOOTP should probably have known better, we'll forgive them. Instead of "options," BOOTP has a field called **vendor-specific** that allows you to put whatever you want in it; it's up to you to make sure that what you define can't be confused with what other people define. Later (RFC 1048), the BOOTP **vendor-specific** field was "tamed" by defining its recommended use to be an options field with a coordinated way of administering option codes. The way to know that the **vendor-specific** field is used in this way is that the first 4 bytes of the field are set to the hexadecimal values 63, 82, 53, 63. These values are referred to as "the magic cookie." I asked everyone I could think of (including the author of the DHCP document) where those numbers came from. Did they flip coins at a working group meeting? Nobody remembered, except that they went to some effort to ensure that they did not conflict with any numbers in use. However, Mike Carney came up with an amazing theory, which might as well be considered true until someone comes up with a better one. His theory is that if you take the hexadecimal numbers 63, 82, 53, 63 and pretend they are decimal and convert to ASCII, you wind up with "?R5?", and the cookie was defined in BOOTP revision 5.

Later, BOOTP was extended and called DHCP. Although the distinction between a "new" protocol and a modification of an existing protocol is not well defined, DHCP certainly seems to me more like a simple extension of BOOTP than a new protocol, and it would have saved the world some brain cells to have merely called it BOOTP version $n+1$ rather than a whole new name. A strong indication that it's really the same protocol is that BOOTP and DHCP use the same UDP ports (67 decimal for server, and 68 for client) and compatible encodings. When a client requests help, the destination UDP port will be 67 (the server) and the source UDP port will be 68 (client).

The main capability introduced in DCHP is the ability to assign addresses dynamically and reuse them. Instead of telling a client an address that it can use forever, the address is "leased" to the client and is available for reassignment if the client does not renew the lease. The way to distinguish a DHCP packet from a BOOTP packet is that a DHCP packet must contain option 53.

Figure 11.8 shows the format for the BOOTP/DHCP message.

# of octets

1	operation	1=request, 2=reply
1	HTYPE (type of link)	Ethernet=1
1	HLEN (length of address for this like type)	Ethernet=6
1	HOPS	client sets to 0, relays increment it
4	transaction ID	for matching responses with requests
2	seconds since client started booting	see text
2	flags	see text
4	client IP address	
4	your IP address	see text
4	server IP address	where boot file stored
4	relay's IP address	
16	client hardware address	
64	server host name	null terminated string
128	boot file name	null terminated string
variable	options (beginning with magic cookie for DHCP and non-ancient versions of BOOTP)	

Figure 11.8 Format of BOOTP/DHCP message

Now I'll comment on some of these fields. The **seconds** field is rather weird. The BOOTP designers had two theories about the use of this field. One is that servers might feel sorry for clients that have been trying to boot for a long time and perhaps would service them ahead of clients that don't have as pitiful a hard-luck story. The other theory is that a relay agent might hope the client finds the server it wants on the LAN, and only after the **seconds** field gets higher than some threshold would the relay start forwarding the BOOTP packet off the LAN.

The **flags** field was unused in BOOTP. In DHCP only a single bit, the left-most bit, is defined. If set, it was set by the client and indicates that the client wants the response sent to the broadcast address in the IP header (all 1's). This is for clients that can't cope with receiving an IP packet sent to a specific IP address until their IP stack knows its own IP address.

If it were up to me, **client IP address** and **your IP address** would be the same field. Only one of them is used at a time. If the client knows its IP address, it fills it in the **client IP address** field. If it doesn't, it fills in 0's to **client IP address** and the server responds by filling in the client's IP address into **your IP address**.

Relay's IP address is filled in by a relay that forwards the BOOTP/DHCP packet off the LAN. If that field is nonzero in the request, the server responds to the relay's IP address.

The **server host name** and **boot file name** are for specifying a machine and file from which to download a boot image. After the BOOTP request and response, the client then invokes the TFTP (trivial file transfer protocol) on the specified server, asking to load the specified file name.

The options are defined in RFC 2132 and include such things as a set of IP addresses of routers on the LAN, the subnet mask of the LAN, a set of time server addresses, a set of DNS servers, values of parameters, and so on. An amazing kludge is that because BOOTP has these two really large and not terribly valuable fields (server name and boot file name), these fields can be used to put options into! There's an option called **overload**. If it has the value 1, it means that the **file name** field should be used for options. If it has the value 2, the **server name** field is used for options, and if it has the value 3, both are used for options.

Another problem is that the space for options is only 1 byte, so there are only 256 possible options. The IETF decided that only half of them (1–127) would be administered by IETF. The others would be up for grabs, usable by anyone, with no specific process to make sure people didn't step on each other's options. To get one of the administered values, you didn't need an RFC or anything. You just asked. So they got used up. Recently a committee attempted to figure out which ones were actually being used and tried to reclaim the others. The committee also hoped that it could use the option numbers 128–255, but the verdict was that there were proprietary uses of some of them and it would be impossible to know which ones were used. Another attempt to save option values is to move some of the options (such as finding the nearest "bizarro" server) to the Service Location Protocol.

With DHCP there does not need to be a configured database at the DHCP server of permanent layer 3/layer 2 address mappings. Instead, the DHCP server can have a block of addresses that it assigns dynamically and "leases" to clients upon request for a limited time. This approach saves configuration because the layer 3/layer 2 mappings are created dynamically rather than being configured by a human. Moreover, it enables there to be more nodes because nodes that are not attached to the net, or that are powered down, do not need to be using IP addresses. IP addresses are so precious that it is necessary to juggle them. The lease mechanism consists of having a client ask for an address and suggest a lease time; the server assigns an address, possibly telling the client a shorter lease time (if the DHCP server has been configured not to allow leases longer than a certain amount). Leases can be renewed so that a node can continue to use its address.

As if life isn't complicated enough, there's yet another mechanism in IP to discover routers. This is called "ICMP Router Discovery," documented in RFC 1256. It's similar to ES-IS. Routers advertise, but only every 7 to 10 minutes. So because it is too infrequent to be useful at start-up, there's an additional mechanism for an endnode to multicast a solicitation. I think that either routers should advertise more frequently (which also detects when routers go down) or they shouldn't advertise at all, relying simply on the solicitation mechanism. I asked why routers advertise so infrequently, mentioning that if it were more frequent "black holes" could be detected, and was told that the mechanism was only supposed to solve router discovery and not router aliveness detection.

When I wrote the first edition of the book, IP had no good mechanisms to do autoconfiguration or find routers. Now there are several awkward ones to choose from, although you don't get to choose. Routers really must support all of them because other things on the LAN might have implemented only some of the mechanisms. Several methods are also designed for IPv6. It wouldn't be fair for IPv6 to have fewer mechanisms for solving a problem than IPv4 had.

11.2.3 The IPX Solution

IPX gets the prize for simplicity and efficiency. Remember, an IPX address is 10 bytes long; the top 4 bytes define the link, and the bottom 6 bytes define the node on the link. On LANs, IPX uses the 6-byte layer 2 address in the node portion of the layer 3 address. The endnode discovers the top 4 bytes by broadcasting a message on the LAN asking a router to tell it the network number of the link. If there is no reply, the endnode uses network number 0. If there is a reply, the endnode uses the returned network number as the top 4 bytes of its own IPX address. This solves autoconfiguration, and there's no need for an ARP protocol because the layer 2 address is in the destination's layer 3 address.

To solve the problem of finding the best router to forward a packet off the LAN, IPX uses a mechanism interestingly different from redirect. Rather than choosing a random router and getting a redirect if it's the wrong router, IPX broadcasts a request to the routers asking which of them is the best one to use to get to a particular destination network number.

This mechanism uses two more messages than IP or CLNP when (in IP or CLNP) the endnode happens to choose the correct router. However, it has the useful property of avoiding sending into a "black hole" (a router that is dead) because the router must be alive in order to reply to the client's query.

A mechanism for detecting dead neighbors was approved by the IPX advisory committee but probably never implemented. It's worth mentioning here because it might be useful in some future protocol. The usual mechanism for detecting neighbor aliveness—periodic hello messages—can be very slow. Also, there might be links that charge money per packet, and therefore it is undesirable to send periodic hello messages.

The IPX solution is a flag in the data packet that indicates "Please send me a message to show you are alive." Thus, a neighbor can be assumed always to be alive, without the bother of periodic hello messages. But when there is traffic to send via that neighbor, having the flag set will cause the neighbor to send a hello message, and a black hole will be detected quickly. This mechanism can also be used on the final link, when endnodes do not need to send any sort of hello or ARP messages but it would be useful for the final router to know whether or not the destination was alive. In that way, the router could send a report back to the source and the source could learn more quickly that the destination was down.

11.2.4 The DECnet Solution

Remember, when we say "DECnet," we mean DECnet Phase IV. DECnet Phase V was either CLNP or IP. DECnet Phase IV gets the prize for boldness. Remember from Section 9.11.3 that DECnet requires the Ethernet address to consist of the 2-byte DECnet address appended to the 4-byte HIORD constant AA-00-04-00.

DECnet nodes must be configured with their 2-byte DECnet address; there is no autoconfiguration. The protocol by which endnodes discover routers and vice versa is similar to ES-IS. Endnodes periodically transmit *endnode hellos* to a multicast address listened to by routers, and routers periodically transmit *router hellos* to a multicast address listened to by endnodes. This is done frequently enough (the default is once every 10 seconds for router advertisements) so that at boot time routers are discovered quickly enough and dead routers can be eliminated from caches.

DECnet endnodes keep two caches.

- A router cache consisting of 2-byte DECnet addresses of routers on the LAN. This cache is filled in based on receipt of router hello messages.

- An on-LAN cache consisting of 2-byte DECnet addresses of destinations known to be on the LAN. This cache is filled in based on receipt of DECnet data packets with the *intra-LAN* flag set, which is a bit in the data packet header (see Section 10.3.6).

When an endnode E has a packet to send to destination D, E checks to see whether D is in its on-LAN cache. If D is in the on-LAN cache, E fills in the destination address in the layer 2 header with D's layer 3 address appended to HIORD. Otherwise, if there's at least one router R in the router cache, E chooses one and sends the packet to R by appending its DECnet address to HIORD. If there is no router in the router cache, E sends the packet to D appended to HIORD. If D is on the LAN, it will receive the packet. If it isn't, it won't, but nothing would have gotten the packet there anyway.

11.2.5 The AppleTalk Solution

AppleTalk gets the prize for cutest solution. It's somewhat similar to IP in that it has an address resolution protocol (which it calls AARP, for AppleTalk Address Resolution Protocol).

11.2.5.1 Knowing Who Is on Your LAN

AppleTalk addresses are 3 bytes long. Two bytes specify network number, and 1 byte specifies the node on the LAN. The problem is that 1 byte is often not enough. So Apple-Talk uses something equivalent to variable-length IP masks. Instead of giving a single network number to a LAN, the LAN is given a range of network numbers. This is like a mask but a little more flexible because with ranges the range can be an arbitrary size (not just a power of 2) and can start and end at any number, as in (131–136).

So you don't perform an AND operation with a mask, your address, and the destination address. Instead, to tell whether someone is on the same LAN as you, you look at the top 2 bytes of the address and see whether it's within the address range of your LAN.

11.2.5.2 Finding a Router

An endnode first discovers a router either by listening for RTMP (routing table maintenance protocol) messages (AppleTalk's version of RIP) or by broadcasting an RTMP query and getting a response from a router. Given that RTMP messages are transmitted every 10 seconds by each router, it probably isn't necessary to do the query to speed things up. The RTMP message broadcast by the router contains the router's address as well as the network number range for the LAN.

11.2.5.3 Acquiring an AppleTalk Address

After the endnode knows the network number range for the LAN it can attempt to acquire a layer 3 address for itself. It does this by choosing an appropriate address (one in the correct network number range) at random! Then it tests to see whether anyone else is using the layer 3 address it just chose at random. It tests this by sending an AARP message to the chosen address, hoping *not* to get a reply. If it gets a reply (meaning someone is using that address), it chooses a different address and tries again. If it does not get a reply, given that these are datagrams and the request or reply might have gotten lost, it tries several times. Only after failing to get a response in several attempts does it decide it is safe to use that address.

11.2.5.4 Seed Routers

Not all routers need to be configured with the network number range (and zone information, which we discuss in Section 11.4.2). At least one router must be configured with the necessary information (network number range and zone information). Such a router is known as a *seed* router. Other routers acquire the information from the seed router.

11.2.5.5 Some Wrinkles

The seed router concept is useful because it enables you to have some routers learn from others. Unfortunately, after a router learns the LAN information, it doesn't "unlearn" it unless the router is rebooted. So if the seed router is reconfigured with different information, the other routers must be rebooted all at once. If you rebooted one, it might learn the LAN information from a nonseed router with the old information rather than the seed router. It would depend on whom it heard from first.

The other interesting wrinkle is that there is a network number range known as the *start-up* range (FF00 to FFFE). When an endnode first boots, if it remembers the network number range that it was using before, it attempts to use that; it chooses another one if it turns out to be the wrong network number range or if the address is in use. However, if the endnode does not have a previous network number range stored, it starts out by choosing an address in the start-up range.

11.2.5.6 Finding the Best Router for a Given Destination

AppleTalk has an optional optimization in which an endnode can decide which router to use to forward off the LAN. There are no protocol messages, such as redirects, defined for this purpose. Instead, the endnode learns based on received data packets. If an endnode E receives a packet from network N and if N is not in E's LAN's network number range, E looks at the layer 2 source address, A, and makes an entry (N, A) in the "best router" cache. If E has a packet to send to destination net N and if (N, A) is in E's cache, E sends to layer 2 address A.

11.2.6 The IPv6 Solution

As of the writing of this book, IPv6 is still evolving. So the details aren't worth committing to something as permanent as a book, and you are referred to the relevant RFCs and Internet drafts. Basically, IPv6 is a combination of all previous protocols. An endnode can autoconfigure in a way very similar to CLNP and IPX: by getting the link prefix from a router advertisement and appending its IEEE 802 address. But instead of using the 6-byte IEEE address, it is padded to 8 bytes (see Section 9.8.5). Or it can be configured as IPv4 nodes are, using a DHCP server having a static database of mappings (the reasoning being that administrators want to control addresses). IPX mandates the use of the layer 2 address in the layer 3 address, so IPX has no need for an ARP-like protocol. In IPv6, although autoconfiguration on an IEEE LAN will almost certainly consist of using the IEEE address in the layer 3 address, it is not mandated, so ARP must still exist in order to map the layer 3 address to a layer 2 address. Routers can be discovered either through the ICMP-based neighbor-discovery protocol or through DHCP (both modified as necessary for the 16-byte IPv6 address). There are hundreds of pages of RFCs and Internet drafts dealing with this part of IPv6. So whatever IPv6 may bring for us, it is not simplicity.

The purpose of this book is to explain the concepts and not to be a reference for all the details of all the protocols. If you want the details, you must read the relevant RFCs. This book would be 9,000 pages long if I tried to explain all the relevant RFCs and Internet drafts, and the book would be out of date before it was published.

11.2.7 Review and Comparisons

Let's review each of the problems to be solved and discuss all the various approaches.

11.2.7.1 Endnodes Acquire a Layer 3 Address

In IPX, CLNP, and (one of the mechanisms in) IPv6, a router informs the nodes on the link of the link's prefix, and they fill in their IEEE 802 address to complete the layer 3 address. In AppleTalk, a router informs the nodes of the network number range for the link, and they pick layer 3 addresses at random (within the specified network number range) and do AARP to detect whether anyone else is using that address. In DECnet, addresses must be configured manually. In IPv4 and IPv6, they can be configured manually or discovered through a static database at a DHCP server, or they can be handed out dynamically by a DHCP server.

11.2.7.2 Router Finds Out Layer 3 Addresses of Endnode Neighbors

In CLNP and DECnet, this is done by having endnodes advertise periodically. In IPv4, IPv6, IPX, and AppleTalk, it is done by having routers configured with the layer 3 prefix that defines the link.

11.2.7.3 Router Finds Out Layer 2 Addresses of Endnode Neighbors

In CLNP, the router learns this from the endnodes' periodic advertisements. In IPv4, IPv6, and AppleTalk, it is done through an ARP mechanism. In DECnet, it is done by prepending HIORD to the 2-byte layer 3 DECnet address. In IPX it is done by extracting the 6-byte layer 2 address from the 10-byte layer 3 address.

11.2.7.4 Endnodes Find a Router

In CLNP and DECnet this is done through periodic advertisements by the routers. In IPX it is done by having endnodes solicit. In IPv4, IPv6, and AppleTalk, endnodes can either solicit or listen for periodic router traffic. IPv4 and IPv6 include both an ICMP-based neighbor-discovery protocol and DHCP to do this.

11.2.7.5 Endnode Neighbors Send Directly to Each Other

In AppleTalk, IPX, IPv4, and IPv6, a node can tell from the layer 3 address whether someone else is on the same link. In CLNP, a redirect message causes two endnode neighbors to talk directly to each other, although the initial packet is forwarded through a router. In DECnet, the intra-LAN flag in the data packet enables a receiver to know whether the sender is a neighbor and to cache that information.

11.2.7.6 Finding the Best Router

In IPv4, IPv6, and CLNP, this is done through redirects. In AppleTalk and DECnet, it is learned from received traffic, the assumption being that the router from which you receive traffic from X is probably the best router to use for traffic to X. In IPX it is done by having the endnode ask for the best router before it sends a packet to the destination LAN.

11.2.7.7 Routerless LAN

In AppleTalk, IPX, and IPv6, there is a LAN prefix that is used when no router is around to tell you something different. In IPv4, if an endnode is expecting to autoconfigure, it cannot do so without a router (really, a DHCP server). In DECnet, there's no problem. To send to 2-byte layer 3 address D, send to layer 2 address (HIORD.D). In CLNP, (if there is no router on the LAN) send to layer 3 address D by multicasting the packet to a multicast address listened to by all endnodes. D, noticing that the packet was sent to the multicast layer 2 address, sends its ESH to the source. The source puts D into its cache and thereafter sends to D's data link address.

In this one case, CLNP is similar in overhead to ARP because at the beginning of a conversation between S and D there is a packet that is multicast, bothering all nodes on the wire. The difference is that in CLNP it is the data packet that is multicast. In IP, a special packet (an ARP query) is broadcast, and it must get a response before the data can be sent. So there is an extra round trip delay with IP.

11.2.8 Comparisons

Now let's compare the approaches head to head.

11.2.8.1 ES-IS versus ARP

Both schemes require a certain amount of control traffic on a LAN. In ES-IS, the overhead is primarily caused by ESHs (there are so few routers that the overhead due to ISHs is insignificant). In IP, the overhead is caused by ARP queries and responses. Comparing the bandwidth usage in two schemes is an interesting research problem.

In IP, endnodes are forced to waste CPU cycles receiving and discarding ARP queries for other nodes. In ES-IS, endnodes are forced to waste CPU cycles when a node wishes to communicate with another node, but this waste occurs only when there are no routers on the LAN. In ES-IS, even if the entire topology is a single LAN and so no routers are needed, if the CPU cycles spent receiving and discarding data traffic destined for other nodes get to be a nuisance, a router can be added to the LAN. Although it never attaches to another link, the router can eliminate the need for multicasting data messages. If the router is known to be required only to stop the nuisance of multicast data messages, a simple box (which I call a *pseudorouter*) will suffice. It need not implement any routing protocol (because the entire network consists of only one link). All it needs to do is to listen to ESHs and transmit redirect messages.

ES-IS was designed the way it was because it was assumed that CPU cycles in end-nodes were precious. If this assumption is true, then the fact that ES-IS does not force endnodes to get software interrupts when two unrelated nodes start communicating (as ARP does) is an important advantage.

The people who hate ES-IS think that the bandwidth consumed by ESHs is too high and is much higher than ARP traffic. Theoretically, after ARP caches are built up, no further bandwidth use is required. However, if ARP cache timers are too long, then invalidating incorrect entries becomes a problem.

Furthermore, if a node wishes to communicate with a node that is down, it will need to do an ARP query because there is no way to distinguish an incorrect ARP entry from a dead destination. It could be argued that ES-IS uses *less* bandwidth, if assumptions are made about the frequency with which endnodes seek conversations with other endnodes and about reasonably small ARP caches in the endnodes.

My intuition says that the bandwidth used by the two schemes does not differ significantly and that neither scheme uses enough bandwidth to degrade network performance significantly. Thus, bandwidth should not be the criterion for choosing one scheme or the other.

Another argument used against ES-IS is that it consumes too much bandwidth and too much memory in the routers by forcing routers to keep track of every endnode instead of keeping track only of the links. I answer this by saying that ES-IS *allows* you to assign a different area number to each LAN—in which case, knowledge of the individual endnodes on the LAN would not be propagated off the LAN. ES-IS just doesn't *force* an area to be a single LAN. Thus, if several LANs and point-to-point links can be aggregated into an area and if level 1 routing can handle the area appropriately, keeping track of endnodes should not be an issue.

In fact IP in practice uses a level of routing that keeps track of individual endnodes. This is done today with bridges. But a protocol like ES-IS would be better than bridging so as to allow more optimal routing than spanning tree.

11.3 Endnodes Attached via Nonbroadcast Multiaccess Media

In NBMA (nonbroadcast multiaccess), there's a cloud with many nodes attached, but there is no multicast capability inherent in the cloud as there would be for a LAN. Really, NBMA is a layer 3 network, and what you're doing is treating it like layer 2 from the point of view of another layer 3 protocol. This is really tunneling (carrying protocol X over a network consisting of protocol Y).

As LANs have evolved from shared media to bridged point-to-point links, and as networks such as ATM attempt to add multicast capability, the distinction between a LAN and NBMA becomes blurred. Multicast came "for free" on a bus or ring topology, or, to look at it differently, it was unavoidable because packets had to go everywhere. When bridging gets introduced, switches must consciously forward multicasts.

11.3.1 Various Solutions

Before we discuss various solutions that have been deployed, let's discuss various alternative approaches. Let's assume we have protocol X nodes talking across a protocol Y cloud.

- Configure the X nodes with the Y addresses of their neighbors on the cloud, and treat the situation like a group of point-to-point links (not necessary fully connected), as shown in Figure 11.9. Each point-to-point link is known as a *tunnel,* and you implement communication over the tunnel by putting a protocol Y header on the protocol X packet. This is in a sense the most straightforward approach. It does not involve special protocols, but it involves a lot of configuration. And if full connectivity is not configured, multiple hops might be required for traversing the Y cloud.

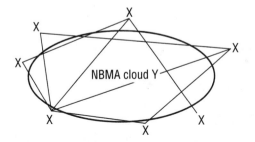

Figure 11.9 Configure point-to-point links

- Embed the layer Y address in the layer X address so that nodes on the cloud can talk to each other just by extracting the layer Y address. All layer X nodes attached via router R would have a prefix indicating R's point of attachment on Y. This could have been done with CLNP. It is a simple, low-overhead solution. It involves no configuration and no routing messages on the NBMA cloud. Multiple points of attachment to the protocol Y cloud can be accommodated by some media through the use of *hunt groups,* in which a single protocol Y address is shared by multiple routers, and whichever one answers first takes the call.

- Add multicast to the NBMA cloud and pretend you are on an Ethernet. Several types of clouds are attempting to do this, including ATM and IPX, and we discuss these in Section 11.3.2.

- Simulate multicast in the NBMA cloud by using a directory node, where nodes register and go to find each other. Then act as if you are on an Ethernet. This is basically the LAN emulation solution, which we discuss in Section 11.3.3.

- Simulate multicast in the layer above the NBMA cloud by doing something similar (a directory node that all nodes register with and find each other through). This is the classical IP over ATM solution, which we discuss in Section 11.3.4.

11.3.2 Providing Multicast in the Protocol Y Cloud

When protocol X is using a mesh network of protocol Y as a LAN, protocol Y must provide multicast.

11.3.2.1 Bridging

Bridging provides multicast by creating a spanning tree and delivering a single copy of each packet to all destinations. Manually configured filters can limit the range of a particular multicast. Sometimes bridges can attempt to be smart and figure out where a multicast will be of interest, and only deliver the packet to those portions of the network.

11.3.2.2 Multicast in IPX

A limited form of multicast is provided in IPX to accommodate carrying over IPX NetBEUI (NetBIOS Extended User Interface) and other protocols designed for a single LAN. This is done by setting the **packet type** field in the IPX header to hex 20. A packet of this type is supposed to be delivered to all LANs.

How did they implement it? Well, they copied source route bridging! Packets of this type collected a diary of LAN numbers visited, and each router that saw one copied the packet onto all its ports with IPX network numbers that were not already recorded in the packet header.

When I found out about this I suggested adding a bit more intelligence to the IPX forwarding algorithm to cut down on the exponential proliferation. It was too late to use spanning tree because upgrading some routers to use spanning tree while others did not use it would not work (at least I couldn't see how to make it work). But it was simple to do *reverse path forwarding,* which means that router R accepts a packet with source = S on link L only if link L is the link that R would use to forward to S. With reverse path forwarding, each router accepts the packet only once, so it cuts the overhead from exponential to $O(n^2)$ (one copy per link). Spanning tree would have reduced the overhead to $O(n)$.

When I suggested this at the IPX advisory forum, I found out that some of the other vendors had had the good sense to put in reverse path forwarding from the start, even though the IPX specification had not said to do it that way.

11.3.2.3 Multicast in ATM

Today ATM provides single-source multicast, which it calls *point-to-multipoint*. The sender creates a virtual circuit (VC) to one leaf, and when it wants to add new listeners it signals ATM to "add member." The result is a VC that branches out from the sender, in a tree, reaching all the members that the sender joined into the tree.

ATM did not do multiple sender multicast because it was assumed that the *cell interleaving* problem was difficult to solve.

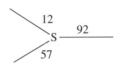

Figure 11.10 Cell interleaving problem

Referring to Figure 11.10, let's assume these ports are in a multicast switched virtual circuit (SVC). When S receives a packet on the rightmost port with VCI 92, it duplicates the cell, sending one copy to the top left port using VCI 12. It sends the other copy to the bottom left port using VCI 57. Now suppose S is simultaneously receiving cells from the left ports that all belong on this VC. Let's say it gets a 10-cell packet with VCI 12 from the top port, and an 8-cell packet from the bottom port with VCI 57. All the cells need to get forwarded onto the rightmost port with VCI 92 (in addition to being sent on the other left port). If S forwards them as they arrive, all the cells will get jumbled together and it will be impossible to sort out which ones came from which sources.

The solution is simple and is documented in a patent issued in 1995.[3] Simply have S avoid interleaving packets on a multipoint-to-multipoint VC. AAL5 indicates end of packet. When S receives the first cell for this VC—say, a cell from the top left port—S forwards the cell onto the other two ports but remembers that it's in the middle of a packet. If cells arrive on a different port for this VC, S queues them until it gets the end-of-packet indicator on a cell with VCI 12 from the top left port. Of course, in case that last cell gets lost, S must have a timer and give up eventually. If S gives up on a packet, it should add a bogus end-of-packet cell. This prevents the loss of two packets, which would result if there was no end-of-packet cell on the preceding packet and the next packet got concatenated onto the incomplete preceding packet.

Rumor has it that ATM may add multipoint-to-multipoint support using this solution to the cell interleaving problem. The only downside of this approach is that it requires buffering in the switches.

---

[3] US Patent 5,434,855. Radia Perlman, Charles Kaufman, Robert Thomas, William Hawe.

Without multipoint-to-multipoint support in ATM, using it to simulate an Ethernet can be awkward. There are basically two choices.

- Have a single node N that must forward all multicast traffic. N creates a point-to-multipoint SVC. Anyone who wants to participate as a sender must create a point-to-point SVC to N and send all packets on the point-to-point SVC to N. Then N sends them onto the point-to-multipoint SVC. This solution has the disadvantage of creating O(N) VCs, and it risks having N become a performance bottleneck.

- Have each node that wants to send create its own point-to-multipoint SVC. This has the problem that every node must know about every sender and must request each sender to add it to its SVC. If the point of all this multicast is to allow IP nodes to find each other, it defeats the purpose if they must know about each other in advance to participate in the multicast session in which they can discover each other.

11.3.2.4 Multicast in SMDS

SMDS (Switched Multimegabit Data Service) is a telephony offering similar to ATM and a precursor to ATM. I discuss it here because its solution to multicast is different from anything else.

SMDS provides multicast, of sorts. To use it, you must ask the telephone company to create a multicast group for you. It assigns you a special telephone number for the group. You tell the phone company all the members of the group. When someone sends a packet to a telephone number assigned to a multicast group, the packet is routed to a special node inside the SMDS net that the phone company has configured with the list of group members. That node creates a copy of the packet for each member of the group and sends out *n* individual copies. Not surprisingly, given how resource-intensive this solution is, "multicast groups" of this form are limited to about 100 members.

11.3.3 LAN Emulation

LAN emulation (LANE) was designed by the ATM forum so that any protocol (IP as well as IPX and so on) could use ATM as if it were a LAN. For more details on ATM, LANE, and IP over ATM I recommend *TCP/IP over ATM: A No-Nonsense Internetworking Guide*, by Berry Kercheval, published by Prentice Hall.

The basic idea is to configure all nodes with the ATM address of a special node that keeps track of all the nodes. You tell it you're alive and what your medium access control (MAC) address is (remember, we're simulating a LAN, so the assumption is that you want to think the thing is an Ethernet or token ring and use IEEE 48-bit MAC addresses), and what your ATM address is. If you want to reach someone else's MAC address, you ask the special node to let you know the corresponding ATM address. Similarly, there's a special node that simulates multicast. It creates a point-to-multipoint VC to all the client nodes. If you want to multicast something, you send it to that node, which then multicasts it out.

Because of the bottleneck at the special node, this solution would not be good for really large ATM clouds. Instead, LANE considers the cloud to be composed of a lot of limited-size ELANs (emulated LANs). Each client node is in one ELAN. To talk from a node in one ELAN to a node in another one requires a router, connected to both ELANs, that forwards the traffic.

11.3.3.1 Some LANE Jargon

Following is a list of terms associated with LANE.

- ELAN: Emulated LAN. A subset of the ATM cloud that looks like a LAN. All members of the ELAN seem like neighbors to each other, whereas members of other ELANs must be reached through routers.

- LEC: LAN emulation client. A node attached to an ELAN.

- LES: LAN emulation server. The node that keeps the mapping from MAC address to ATM address. A LEC registers its own (MAC, ATM) address with the LES and finds out the ATM address of other LECs by asking the LES. A LES supports one ELAN. A LES maintains a point-to-multipoint VC from itself to all LECs in the ELAN.

- LECS: LAN emulation configuration server. The node that tells you how to find the LES for your ELAN. A LECS in general supports multiple ELANs.

- BUS: Broadcast and unknown server. The node that maintains a point-to-multipoint VC to all LECs in the ELAN. To send a packet to a multicast address, you send it to the BUS that does the actual multicast.

Figure 11.11 shows an ATM cloud with a number of these elements.

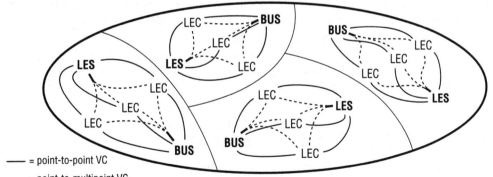

— = point-to-point VC

---- = point-to-multipoint VC

Figure 11.11 ATM cloud with multiple ELANs, each containing one LES and one BUS

11.3.3.2 A Client (LEC) Boots Up

The client's first step is to find the LECS because that machine is configured to know which client machines should be in which ELANs. There's a *well-known* ATM address for finding the LECS. So the client starts a connection to the LECS address and tells the LECS its ATM address and MAC address. The LECS looks it up and then tells the client all the information it needs in order to become part of the proper ELAN, including the ATM address of the LES associated with that ELAN.

11.3.3.3 Joining an ELAN

Now the client sets up a VC to the LES for its ELAN and tells the LES its ATM address and MAC address. The LES adds the new client to the point-to-multipoint VC that the LES maintains to keep in touch with all its clients.

11.3.3.4 Transmitting to Another LEC

Remember, we're simulating a LAN. The client machine thinks that it wants to send a packet to some MAC (layer 2) address D. Layer 3 thinks it wants to send a packet onto that LAN with layer 2 address D. LANE must make it happen somehow.

The way LANE does it is that the LEC asks the LES for the ATM address corresponding to layer 2 address D. When it finds out (from the LES), the LEC establishes a VC to that ATM address, and future packets for D are forwarded over that VC.

11.3.3.5 Sending a Multicast Packet

To send a multicast (or broadcast. . . remember, I consider these words interchangeable) packet, the LEC must find the ATM address of the BUS. It finds that out by asking the LES for the ATM address of FF:FF:FF:FF:FF:FF (just as it would ask the LES for any MAC address). The LES then tells it, and the LEC then establishes a VC to the BUS.

The BUS maintains a point-to-point VC between itself and each LEC in the ELAN. It also maintains a point-to-multipoint VC between itself and all the LECs. When a LEC sends it a packet to multicast, the BUS retransmits the packet onto the point-to-multipoint VC.

11.3.4 Classical IP and ARP over ATM

(I'm not sure what the word *classical* has to do with it, but that's the title of RFC 2225.) CIP (classical IP) is very similar to LANE but of course uses its own set of jargon. It's the same basic idea. The ATM cloud is divided into separate virtual LANs, each called a LIS (logical IP subnetwork) (much like an ELAN in LANE). The LIS looks like an IP subnet in that all nodes in the LIS share the same IP address prefix (the portion of the IP address corresponding to 1's in the mask). Each node is expected to know its own IP address and its own ATM address.

Each LIS has an ATMARP server (ATM ARP server). Each member of the LIS registers with the ATMARP server and requests IP-to-ATM mapping from the ATMARP server in order to create an SVC to another IP node in the same LIS. A node might also have permanent virtual circuits (PVCs) to other nodes. To figure out who is on the other end of a PVC, the node sends an InATMARP (inverse ATM ARP) request on the PVC, and whoever is on the other end responds with its IP address. To talk to another node on the ATM cloud, first you see whether you have a PVC to it, in which case you talk over the PVC. If you already have an SVC to it, you talk over the SVC. Otherwise, if it's on your LIS (which you know because its IP address prefix indicates it is on your LIS), you ask the ATMARP server for the ATM address and then establish an SVC to that ATM address. If it isn't on your LIS, you send it to a router on your LIS (either by sending over a PVC or SVC that you already have to the router or by creating an SVC to the router).

11.3.5 Cutting Out Extra Hops

If you partition a cloud into pieces (as LANE cuts ATM into ELANs and CIP cuts ATM into LISs) and you need a router to get to another piece, there is the likelihood that two nodes from different pieces will wind up talking to each other over a path that crosses the cloud several times. For example (using CIP terminology), see Figure 11.12.

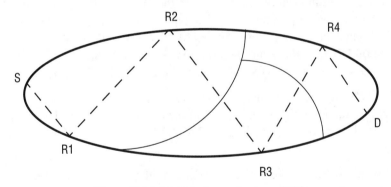

Figure 11.12 Multiple-hop path across ATM

Suppose S wants to talk to D. Because D's IP address indicates that D is in a foreign LIS, S sends traffic for D over a VC to a router, in this case R1. Theoretically, all routers on the cloud could be fully connected, in which case R1 would have a VC to R4 and the packet could go from S to R1 to R4 to D. But more likely there is not full connectivity between all the routers. So to the routers, the topology in Figure 11.12 looks like the one in Figure 11.13.

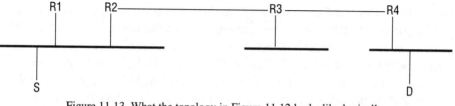

Figure 11.13 What the topology in Figure 11.12 looks like logically

There are various techniques one might imagine for getting rid of the extra hops and allowing S and D to talk to each other directly.

- When R1 forwards to R2 it notices that it is forwarding back onto the same cloud, and it could send a redirect (to R2) back to S. Then S could create a VC to R2, which would send another redirect (to R3). S would create a VC to R3, which would send a redirect (to R4). S would create a VC to R4, which would create a redirect (to D) so that S would create (finally) a VC to D.

- S could transmit a special packet that contained S's ATM address. When D received it, D could know it should create a VC to that address. Routers would have to know not to forward this type of packet off the cloud so as not to confuse two nodes on different clouds into attempting to talk directly.

- The routing algorithm run by the routers on the cloud could be sophisticated enough to know all the layer 3 prefixes reachable on the cloud as well as the ATM addresses of all the routers and perhaps even the ATMARP server. R1 could then know that R4 would be on D's LIS. R1 could then redirect S to R4, or query R4 (or the ATMARP server on D's LIS) for D's ATM address, and then redirect S all the way to D.

- S could transmit a special query packet that would travel across the cloud, with a reply sent by the node that exits the cloud (or the destination, if the destination is on the cloud). This is the approach taken by NHRP (Next Hop Resoloution Protocol, RFC 2332).

Although it would seem that such mechanisms should be straightforward, a few ugly, little problems make a real protocol more complicated. First, because such mechanisms weren't designed in from the start, they must be deployable incrementally—that is, not breaking things when some nodes implement the protocol and others don't. Another complexity is that an NBMA cloud may not really be logically fully connected. For example, a *closed user group* is one in which there is a subset of nodes on the cloud that can communicate only with other nodes in that subset. So although S might be able to talk to D over a routed path, they would not be able to communicate directly.

11.4   Finding Things

There are interesting mechanisms in IPX and AppleTalk for finding services or mapping names to addresses. These mechanisms are relevant to routers only because of the way they were done.

11.4.1   Finding Services, Generically

How do things on a network find each other? Think of a telephone network. The same mechanisms we use in life have similar mechanisms in computer networks.

- You use a telephone book. If you want to find your old friend Mary, you look up her name in the telephone book to get her network address (her telephone number). This is like using à name server or directory, such as DNS (domain name service).

- There could be a special *well-known* telephone number (information) that you call, and then you can ask for the telephone number associated with a particular name. In the computer network world, this might be provided by having a well-known address for the directory. Two mechanisms can provide this service. One is *anycast*, which finds the nearest thing listening on that address. The other is *multicast*, which finds all the things listening on that address. You can easily provide anycast by having multiple nodes claim they can reach that address. In Figure 11.14, both Q and C advertise that they can reach address 97. If X sends a packet to 97, the routers, finding the shortest path to "97," will route it toward Q. If Z sends a packet to 97, the routers will route it toward C. Anycast pretty much comes "for free" because to the routers it is indistinguishable from having a real node 97 that happens to be attached to Q and C. Multicast is discussed at length in Chapter 15.

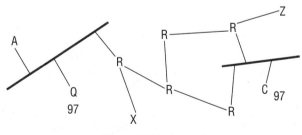

Figure 11.14 Anycast

- There could be a special well-known telephone number for each type of service. For example, 911 is the almost universal telephone number for emergencies in the United States. This service is similar to the one just discussed and can be provided in the same way, except that instead of needing only a single well-known number of the directory and using that to find everything else, each type of service needs its own well-known number.

- There could be a special telephone number that would ring all phones in the world. You could use it for querying for services. If you wanted to find Radia Perlman, you'd dial that number and say you were looking for Radia, and everyone who wasn't Radia would just hang up. This is similar to ARP and somewhat similar to AppleTalk. ARP works only on a LAN, but with bridges a LAN can be many hops. The AppleTalk mechanism (see Section 11.4.2) can be thought of as ARP at layer 3.

- Using the same (thankfully imaginary) telephone number that rings all phones in the world, you could use it for advertising. Periodically I could ring all the phones in the world and say, "In case you're interested, Radia Perlman's phone number is 97." This is somewhat similar to the NetWare version 3 scheme (see Section 11.4.3).

11.4.2 AppleTalk's Scheme

The AppleTalk mechanism is quite similar in concept to ARP, but instead of the ARP being confined to a LAN, routers forward the analogous AppleTalk query to all locations where the destination might be. ARP is used for mapping from layer 3 address to layer 2 address. The AppleTalk Name Binding Protocol (see Figure 11.15) is used for mapping from names to layer 3 addresses. It serves the same function as DNS but does it by broadcasting a query with a name being sought. The node with the sought-after name responds.

The routing protocol lets routers know about all the LANs in the network.

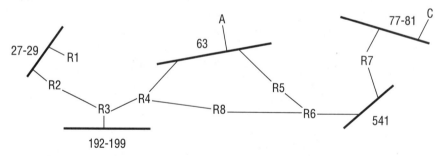

Figure 11.15 AppleTalk's Name Binding Protocol

Suppose A wants to talk to C, where "C" is a name. A can't send a packet to C until it finds out C's layer 3 address. So the following steps take place.

- A sends a packet to a router on the LAN—for example R4—saying, "I want to look up name C." The packet contains A's layer 3 address *a*.

- R4, through the magic of the routing protocol, knows the complete list of LANs: 27-29, 192-199, 63, 541, and 77-81. There are five LANs, so R4 creates five packets, one destined to any router on each of the five LANs. R4 uses the layer 3 address consisting of the lowest network number in the LAN's network number range as the "network" part of the AppleTalk destination address, and 0 as the node part. So R4 sends a packet to 27.0, 192.0, 63.0, 541.0, and 77.0, requesting each of them to ask the nodes on its LAN whether any of them happens to be C.

- Each of R3, R2, R6, and R7 receives a copy of the request. R2 queries the nodes on LAN 27; R3 on 192; R4 on 63, R6 on 541, and R7 on 77. They make the queries by multicasting a message on the LAN saying "If you are C, respond to *a*."

- C receives the query and responds to layer 3 address *a*.

One additional optimization cuts down on the number of LANs that need to be searched. A *zone* is a subset of the nodes (see Figure 11.16). The zone has a name—for example, ENGINEERS or MANAGERS. At least one router per LAN is configured with the set of zone names for that LAN. The routing protocol tells all routers not only about the network number range for each LAN but also which zones reside on which LANs. A zone can reside on multiple LANs, and multiple zones can reside on a LAN.

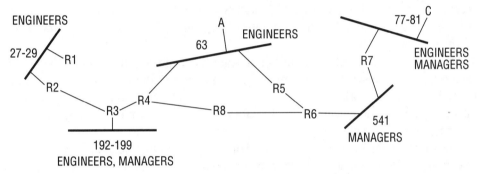

Figure 11.16 AppleTalk's Name Binding Protocol with zones

When a node asks to look up a name, it must also specify the zone in which the name is to be looked up. So, for example, in Figure 11.16, A might be searching for the name C in zone MANAGERS. In this case R4 does not send a message to every LAN. Instead, it sends it only to LANs 192-199, 541, and 77-81, the LANs that contain the zone name MANAGERS.

11.4.3 Service Advertising Protocol for NetWare

NetWare version 3 has a mechanism in which things that want to be found advertise themselves. The protocol is known as SAP (Service Advertisement Protocol; it has nothing to do with the SAP that means service access point). SAP looks very similar to the routing protocol RIP (see Section 14.2) except that instead of destinations being layer 3 addresses, they are names—for example, 3rd-floor-printer.

A service (something that wants to be found) periodically (every minute) broadcasts on the LAN a packet containing

- Its name

- Its service type (for example, printer, file server)

- Its layer 3 address

- The number of hops from where this advertisement originated (starts as 0)

Each router that hears a SAP advertisement also advertises it (on LANs for which it is the best path to the service), also every 60 seconds, but it increments the hops from the advertisement through which it learned of the service. Mercifully, not all routers on a LAN advertise the service. A router farther from the service does not advertise the service if a closer router is advertising it. But still, even with only a single router on each LAN advertising each service, this is like reading the phone book every 60 seconds. And people get annoyed with the traffic. Although SAP wasn't IPX's fault, and indeed Net-Ware version 4 deployed a directory, people still assumed IPX was "chatty" because of all the related SAP traffic.

Obviously, the SAP mechanism does not scale to a large network. But it is wonderful for easily deploying services. You simply attach a server to the network, and magically all the nodes in the network find out about it. That's much easier than finding the person who is authorized to add entries to the directory and wait for him or her to get around to adding the new service name.

There are mechanisms for taming SAP. You can filter it, that is, configure routers not to forward the SAP information. So, for example, you can configure all the routers with links outside a building not to bother to propagate any SAP information about printers from inside the building.

Replacing the RIP/SAP protocol with the routing protocol NLSP (NetWare Link Services Protocol) is another way to get rid of almost all the overhead of SAP advertisements. In NLSP, one router on the LAN announces all the services available on that LAN in its link state information, which gets propagated reliably. Then it need not advertise again unless things change (although, as a default, routers rebroadcast their routing information every 2 hours—much less frequently than once a minute). The ultimate answer is to stop learning of services through SAP and instead have the services listed in a directory.

Finding the directory is an interesting issue. SAP is a fine mechanism except that it doesn't scale to finding thousands of services. But it would be useful to keep a mechanism such as SAP for finding the directory, and then use the directory to find everything else.

Homework

1. Argue why the background traffic caused by ARP queries and responses would be more than, less than, or (relatively) equal to the background traffic caused by ESHs.

2. If the link number on which a node resides were standardized to be a recognizable portion of the CLNP address, what changes might be made to the ES-IS protocol? (Assume that ES-IS would not implement ARP because of the desire to avoid forcing endnodes to consume CPU cycles receiving and discarding ARP messages.)

3. A *broadcast storm* is an event causing a flurry of messages. Some storms last only a few seconds; others persist indefinitely or for such a long time that they might as well be never-ending. Broadcast storms have chiefly been observed with the IP protocols. One of the main implementation decisions that cause storms is the decision (in the Berkeley UNIX endnode IP implementation) that an endnode should attempt to forward a packet that it mysteriously receives with a network layer address of a different endnode. This is what you, as a good citizen, would do if you found a neighbor's letter wrongly placed in your mailbox. However, it is not a good thing for an endnode to do.

    Suppose an IP endnode is incorrectly configured and it thinks that its data link address is all 1's, that is, the data link layer "broadcast" address. What happens when someone attempts to transmit a data packet to that node? Give the sequence of events.

4. Refer to the set of problems to be solved in Section 11.2. Explain how each of them is solved in IP, CLNP, IPX, DECnet, and AppleTalk.

5. In the case of no router on the LAN, why does DECnet not need to multicast data packets (as CLNP needs to)?

6. Assume that IP is running on LANE. Describe the sequence of events that occur for each of the following scenarios:

    a. An IP node A wishes to talk to layer 3 address D, where D is on A's subnet and D is not in A's ARP cache.

    b. A wishes to talk to D, where D is on a different subnet (assume A knows the IP address of router R, but R is not in A's ARP cache).

7. Assume that IP is using Classical IP and ARP over ATM. Describe what happens in the scenarios presented in problem 6.

Chapter 12
Routing Algorithm Concepts

> More than any time in history mankind faces a crossroads. One path
> leads to despair and utter hopelessness, the other to total extinction. Let
> us pray that we have the wisdom to choose correctly.
>
> —Woody Allen[1]

In this chapter, I discuss the third piece in the network layer protocol: the routing algorithms and protocols. There are basically two types of distributed routing algorithms:

1. Distance vector

2. Link state

All the popular network layer routing protocols are based on one or the other. In this chapter, I consider these distributed routing protocols generically. In Chapter 14, I examine specific routing protocols derived from them.

I also discuss, generically, other problems that arise in routing, such as using levels of hierarchy, supporting multiple types of service, modifying routes to account for current traffic distribution, and supporting a connection-oriented interface.

12.1 Distance Vector Routing

Distance vector routing is sometimes known in the literature by other names. Probably the least sensible name for it is "old ARPANET routing." It is also sometimes referred to as Bellman-Ford, after the people who invented the algorithm from which distance vector routing is derived.

---

[1] Quoted in Robert Byrne, *1911 Best Things Anybody Ever Said* (New York: Ballantine Books, 1988), 82.

Distance vector routing requires that each node maintain the distance from itself to each possible destination. The distances are computed using the information in neighbors' distance vectors.

Imagine that you are sitting at the intersection of several roads, as shown in Figure 12.1.

Figure 12.1 Sitting in the middle of the intersection (don't try this at home!)

Your job is to post signs of the form shown in Figure 12.2.

Figure 12.2 Sign points the way, gives distance

You have been told that you must post a complete set of signs (one for each town), but you haven't even been told the names of all the towns. The only thing you have been told is the name of the town in which your intersection is located (for example, Hereville). You can start by constructing a sign such as in Figure 12.3.

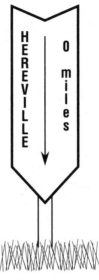

Figure 12.3 You are Hereville

How can you proceed? Luckily, you know that at every intersection, someone has been hired to do the same work you're doing. You can fulfill your obligation as follows.

1. Measure the distance to the nearest intersection down each of the roads radiating from your location.

2. Keep track of the set of signs posted at each of the neighboring intersections.

Now calculate the distance to each town independently by figuring out which direction will yield the smallest total distance. For example, in Figure 12.4, there are five possible ways to get to Littleton.

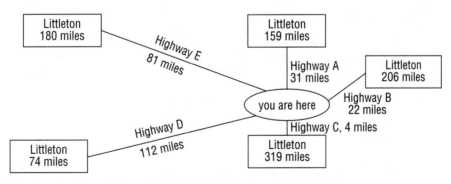

Figure 12.4 Which is the best way to Littleton?

If you go down Highway A, it will be 31 miles to the intersection, from which (according to the sign there), Littleton is an additional 159 miles, yielding a total distance of 190 miles. If you go down Highway B, the total distance will be 22 + 206, or

228 miles. Highway C yields a distance of 4 + 319, or 323. Highway D yields 112 + 74, or 186. And Highway E yields 81 + 180, or 261. Thus, the best way to get to Littleton is down Highway D. The sign you post should read "Littleton 186" and point down Highway D.

> **The trouble with our age is all signposts and no destination.**
> —**Louis Kronenberger**[2]

Now the question is, "How did your fellow sign painters get *their* information?" Amazingly, they can be doing the same thing you are—scouting down each of their roads to look at the signs at neighboring intersections and basing their information on those signs. The process will work. You must keep checking to make sure your neighbors have not changed anything on their set of signs, and you must keep modifying your signs if any of your neighbors change their signs, but this process will eventually converge to correct information.

In a computer network, the protocol is stated as follows.

1. Each router is configured with its own ID.

2. Each router is also configured with a number to use as the cost of each link. (Or a fixed value such as 1 is used as the cost of each link, or some sort of measurement is done to calculate a number to use as the cost.)

3. Each router starts with a distance vector consisting of the value "0" for itself and the value "infinity" for every other destination.

4. Each router transmits its distance vector to each of its neighbors whenever the information changes (as well as when a link to a neighbor first comes up and probably also periodically).

5. Each router saves the most recently received distance vector from each of its neighbors.

6. Each router calculates its own distance vector, based on minimizing the cost to each destination, by examining the cost to that destination reported by each neighbor in turn and then adding the configured cost of the link to that neighbor.

7. The following events cause recalculation of the distance vector.

   a. Receipt from a neighbor of a distance vector containing different information than before.

   b. Discovery that a link to a neighbor has gone down. In that case, the distance vector from that neighbor is discarded before the distance vector is recalculated.

---

[2] Quoted in James B. Simpson, *Simpson Contemporary Quotations* (New York: Thomas Y. Crowell Company, 1964), 314.

This algorithm seems somewhat magical, and it is. The intuition that explains why it works is that for a particular destination D, D knows the proper distance to D—that is, 0. When D sends its distance vector to its neighbors, they now have a good route to D. When they send their distance vectors to their neighbors, those nodes will have good routes to D. If the optimal route from D to A is D–C–B–A, then A will discover its best route to D after D sends a distance vector to C, followed by C's sending a distance vector to B, followed by B's sending a distance vector to A. Every destination is being calculated independently.

> **We are here and it is now. Further than that all human knowledge is moonshine.**
>
> **—H.L. Mencken**[3]

It might be hard to understand why distance vector routing works because my information depends on your information, which depends on my information, and so on. However, this algorithm is sufficiently robust that it works properly even if the implementers or network users do not understand or believe in it. It is easy to code and is therefore attractive.

12.1.1 Why Not Distance Vector?

If distance vector routing works, why is it the "old" ARPANET routing algorithm? The chief problem with distance vector routing is its slow convergence. While routing information has only partially propagated through a computer network, routing can be seriously disrupted. Because a single link change may affect many routes, it is important for routing to recover as quickly as possible after a topological change.

Distance vector routing can take a very long time to converge after a topological change. The reason for this can be seen in the simple topology shown in Figure 12.5.

Figure 12.5 Three-node network

Let us think only about everyone's distances to destination C. C calculates its distance to C as 0. To keep things simple, assume that the cost function is hops, so that the cost of each link is 1. B calculates its distance to C as 1. A calculates its distance to C as 2.

Now let us assume that C dies or that the link between B and C breaks. Noticing that a link has broken, B must discard the distance vector it received from that link and recalculate its distance vector. Unfortunately, B does not conclude at this point that C is unreachable. Instead, B decides that it is 3 from C, based on having a neighbor (A) at a distance of 1 from B that has reported a distance of 2 to C. Because B's distance vector

---

[3] Quoted in Byrne, *1911 Best Things,* 109.

has now changed, it transmits the changed vector to each of its remaining neighbors (in this case, only A). A, as a result of having received a modified distance vector from neighbor B, recalculates its own distance vector and concludes that C is now 4 away. A and B continue this process until they count to infinity. Furthermore, during this process, both A and B conclude that the best path to C is through the other node. Packets for C get bounced between A and B until they die of old age.

It might seem that counting by ones to infinity would take a very long time (try it sometime). It does, but not as long as you might imagine. First of all, computers keep getting faster. But more relevantly, "infinity" in distance vector routing is a parameter that can be set by network management. It is usually set to a value on the order of 20 (if the cost function is hops) or 20 times the largest link cost in the net (if the cost function is something other than hops).

A number of solutions have been proposed to fix the slow convergence in distance vector routing.

12.1.1.1 Hold-down

The idea of the hold-down solution is that if the path you are using to D goes down, you wait for some time before switching to another path. That time is known as the *hold-down time*, and during that time you advertise your cost to D as infinity. The hope is that news of that path breaking will spread throughout the network so that after the hold-down time expires nobody will remember the old broken path. The problem with this scheme is that it's a kludge based on a timer. The timer is arbitrary. It slows down convergence in many cases, and as people discovered when they applied it to the old ARPANET algorithm, it doesn't always prevent count-to-infinity behavior.

12.1.1.2 Reporting the Entire Path

In this scheme you don't just report your cost to the destination; rather, you report the path to the destination. This guarantees that there are no loops—because you can tell by looking at the path whether there are loops—but it's expensive.

12.1.1.3 Split Horizon

Another popular technique used to speed convergence of distance vectors is known as *split horizon.* It does no harm and speeds convergence in many cases. However, split horizon does not solve the count-to-infinity problem in some cases. The rule in split horizon is that if router R forwards traffic for destination D through neighbor N, then R reports to N that R's distance to D is infinity. Because R is routing traffic for D through N, R's real distance to N cannot possibly matter to N. N's distance to D cannot depend on R's distance to D. In the simple case of the three-node network in Figure 12.5, split horizon will prevent counting to infinity. A will have reported to B that A's distance to C is infinity. When B's link to C breaks, B has no alternative path to C and immediately concludes that C is unreachable. When B informs A that C is now unreachable, A now knows that C is unreachable.

However, split horizon does not work in some cases. Consider Figure 12.6.

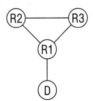

Figure 12.6 Count-to-infinity with split horizon

When the link to D breaks, R1 concludes that D is unreachable because both R2 and R3 have reported to R1 that D is unreachable because of the split horizon rule. R1 reports D's unreachability to R2 and R3. Now the scenario might differ slightly depending on the timing of events, but the results will be similar. When R2 receives R1's report that D is unreachable, R2 concludes that the best path to D is now through R3. R2 concludes that R2 is now 3 from D, reports D as being unreachable to R3 because of split horizon, and reports D as being reachable to R1 at cost 3. R1 now thinks that D is reachable through R2 at a cost of 4. The counting-to-infinity problem still exists.

12.1.1.4 Two Metrics

This trick is used by DECnet Phase 3 and by IPX RIP. The goal is to compute routes based on a more sophisticated cost function than hops. It would be nice to assign a larger cost to slow links than to fast ones so that a path going over several very fast links can be preferred over one that goes over a slow link. But if the cost function per hop is allowed to vary between 1 and, say, 100, then what can the value of infinity be? It can't be something such as 16. If the largest link cost is 100, you might want to set the maximum path length at, say, 300. But if the distance vector got into its unpleasant count-to-infinity mode in a loop of links with cost 1, it would take much longer to count to 300 than to 16. That's why IP's RIP uses a cost function of hops.

DECnet and IPX RIP manage to compute routes using a civilized cost function that can assign arbitrary costs to links, but they manage to count to infinity just as quickly as a distance vector protocol using hops. The way they do this is to compute two distances to each destination: one based on hops and one based on "cost." The cost function is used to pick the best path. The hops function is used to detect an unreachable destination.

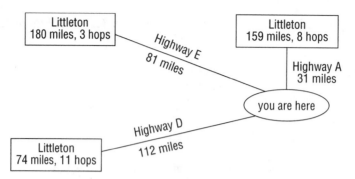

Figure 12.7 Two cost functions

So, referring to Figure 12.7, the path to Littleton through highway A would be 190 miles and 9 hops. The path through highway D would be 186 miles and 12 hops. The path through highway E would be 261 miles and 4 hops. The path chosen is the one with the best cost, in this case miles. So you'd choose highway D, with a cost of 186 miles and 12 hops. Even though you could reach Littleton in fewer hops, you advertise your distance as 186 miles, 12 hops.

12.1.1.5 Triggered Updates

In its initial implementation, RIP for IP sent distance vectors periodically and not when the vector changed. Of course that would slow down convergence. Suppose you're sending a distance vector once every minute. Right after you send one, you find out about a better path, or the link you were using dies. It's silly to wait until your periodic timer expires before telling your neighbors about the link. DECnet's distance vector protocol, implemented before IP RIP, sent information as soon as it changed. It would not have occurred to me to do otherwise.

But IP RIP didn't operate that way. Then someone noticed that the protocol could be sped up a lot by sending information as soon as it changed, and it got the fancy name of *triggered updates*. I would have preferred not even mentioning this—it merely fixes something that was done wrong in the first place rather than being a brilliant idea for speeding up distance vector protocols—but the term is used enough that people want to know what it means.

12.1.1.6 Poison Reverse

Poison reverse means reporting a value of infinity to explicitly report that you can't reach D rather than simply not mentioning D. Usually, the term is used together with split horizon, meaning that the destinations that you would forward to neighbor N are reported to N with a distance of infinity.

12.1.1.7 DUAL

Diffusing Update Algorithm (DUAL) was developed by J.J. Garcia-Luna-Aceves.[4] It notes that you can safely switch to an alternate path to D through neighbor N if N's reported distance to D is less than your previously reported distance to D. For example, if your previous path to D was through neighbor K, where K reported a cost of 10, and if your cost to K was 5, then your cost to D would be 15. If N reports a cost to D of 14 or less and if your path to D through K breaks, it is safe to switch to the path through N. The terminology is that N is a *feasible successor*. After that observation, the algorithm becomes much more complicated to understand. If you don't have any feasible successors you must poll your neighbors and must not switch to another path until they test whether they have any feasible successors. They won't if you were their best path to the destination and they have no other path short enough so they will need to poll their neighbors, and so on. This algorithm is like doing a hold-down; all the nodes on the other side of D from you are alerted to the broken path, and after that information travels all the way and news of that reaches you, then you can proceed. It's like doing hold-down, but instead of picking an arbitrary timer you are alerted when news of the broken path has reached the rest of the network.

This technique speeds convergence, but it is sufficiently complicated that it eliminates the main advantage of distance vector routing over link state routing, which is that distance vector protocols can be simpler to understand and implement. And DUAL still does not converge as quickly as a link state algorithm. And with messages being lost, nodes being slow to respond, simultaneous events occurring, routers failing, and other bad things that happen in practice, I've never really trusted this technique.

In Section 12.2 I examine link state routing and explain why it converges more quickly as well as discuss the other advantages it offers.

12.2 Link State Routing

The basic idea behind link state routing is simple.

1. Each router is responsible for meeting its neighbors and learning their names.

2. Each router constructs a packet known as a *link state packet*, or LSP, which contains a list of the names of and cost to each of its neighbors.

3. The LSP is somehow transmitted to all the other routers, and each router stores the most recently generated LSP from each other router.

---

[4] J.J. Garcia-Luna-Aceves, "Loop-free routing using diffusing computations," *IEEE/ACM Transactions on Networking* 1, Feb. 1993.

4. Each router, armed now with a complete map of the topology (the information in the LSPs yields complete knowledge of the graph), computes routes to each destination.

The following subsections examine each of these steps, some of which are nontrivial.

12.2.1 Meeting Neighbors

On a point-to-point link, neighbors can meet each other simply by transmitting a special packet over the link, identifying themselves. On a LAN, neighbor greeting is usually done by periodically transmitting the same sort of special packet to a predefined group address. Sometimes (as in IP, where a link is considered a neighbor), the set of addresses reachable over a particular interface is configured manually.

12.2.2 Constructing an LSP

After the identity of neighbors is known, constructing an LSP is not at all difficult. It is a simple matter of formatting.

A router R generates an LSP periodically as well as when R discovers that

- It has a new neighbor.

- The cost of the link to an existing neighbor has changed.

- A link to a neighbor has gone down.

12.2.3 Disseminating the LSP to All Routers

After router R generates a new LSP, the new LSP must be transmitted to all the other routers. This is the most complex and critical piece of a link state routing algorithm. If it isn't done correctly, various bad things can happen, including the following.

1. Routers will have different sets of LSPs. This means that they will calculate routes based on different information. Many routes can become nonfunctional as a result of a disagreement among routers about a single link.

   After a link changes state, any routing algorithm requires some short amount of time for updated knowledge of the link's state to propagate throughout the net. However, a faulty LSP distribution algorithm can cause knowledge of a link's state to propagate to only some of the routers, resulting in disruption of the routing for many orders of magnitude longer than necessary.

2. LSP distribution can become *cancerous*, a condition in which the number of LSPs rapidly multiplies until all network resources are spent processing LSPs. Section 12.2.3.3 examines an LSP distribution scheme used in the ARPANET that can get into this state.

Let's start by designing an LSP distribution scheme. Ordinarily, it would be possible in a network to distribute information using the information in the routing database. For example, when router S generates a new LSP, it could transmit a copy, as data, to each other router. However, LSPs cannot be transmitted based on the assumption that the routing database makes sense because it creates a chicken-or-the-egg problem (known more impressively as a *recursion* problem): LSP distribution relies on the routing database, but the routing database relies on the LSPs. So the distribution scheme cannot make any assumptions about the information in the routing databases. It must work no matter what kind of information is in those databases.

A simple scheme for routing that does not depend on having any routing information is *flooding*, in which each packet received is transmitted to each neighbor except the one from which the packet was received. Then, to prevent a single packet's spawning an infinite number of offspring, a packet could have a hop count (or a diary of the route—sound familiar?), and when the hop count reaches some threshold, the packet can be dropped. This creates an exponential number of copies of each packet. That can be an annoyance but is guaranteed to deliver a copy of the packet to every node provided that packets are not lost (which they undoubtedly will be in the congestion caused by exponential growth).

Luckily, when it is LSPs rather than data packets that are being distributed, we can do far better. Because each router R retains the most recently generated LSP from each router S, R can recognize when it is receiving a duplicate of S's most recently generated LSP, and R can refrain from flooding the packet more than once. If each router floods S's most recently generated LSP only once, then the flooding will not create an exponential number of copies. Instead, the LSP will travel over each link in the network only once.

A simple LSP distribution scheme is as follows. If an LSP is received from neighbor N with source S and if the LSP is identical to the one from S that is stored, then ignore the received LSP (it is a duplicate). If the received LSP is not identical to the one from S currently stored or if no LSP from S is stored, store the received LSP and transmit it to all neighbors except N.

The problem with this scheme is that R cannot assume that the LSP most recently received from S is the one most recently generated by S. Two LSPs from S could travel along different paths to R and might not be received in the order in which S generated them.

12.2.3.1 Timestamps

How can R know which of S's LSPs was generated most recently? One attractive possibility is to use a timestamp in the LSP. This would enable R to look at two LSPs and know that the one with the later timestamp was more recently generated. One possible problem is that if S accidentally generated an LSP with a timestamp 15 years in the future or if the timestamp on one of S's LSPs got corrupted and appeared to be from that far in the future, then none of S's LSPs for the next 15 years would be believed. All the nodes would assume that they had a more recent LSP from S.

If the timestamp has global meaning—that is, the routers' clocks are synchronized to within a few minutes—then R can do a *sanity check* on the timestamp in S's LSP. If R receives an LSP with a timestamp that appears to be too far in the future, R rejects the LSP. Similarly, if R receives an LSP with a timestamp too far in the past, R can delete the LSP to save memory because a node that hasn't issued a new LSP within some amount of time can be considered unreachable or dead.

However, if the timestamp does not have global meaning, R cannot do any sort of sanity check on the timestamp in S's LSP. If a timestamp became corrupted or if S, through temporary flakiness, issued an LSP with a bad timestamp (one in the future), S's real LSPs would be rejected by other nodes.

A globally synchronized timestamp would make LSP distribution a little simpler, but synchronizing clocks requires special hardware and is a more difficult problem than distributing LSPs. Thus, it is preferable to devise a solution to LSP distribution that does not depend on globally synchronized clocks. Currently deployed routing protocols do not rely on clocks and instead use a scheme involving a combination of a *sequence number* (a simple counter) and an *estimated age* field in each LSP.

12.2.3.2 Sequence Number/Age Schemes

A sequence number is a counter. Each router S keeps track of the sequence number it used the last time it generated an LSP; when S needs to generate a new LSP, it uses the next sequence number. When router R receives an LSP from S, router R compares the sequence number of the received LSP with the one from S stored in memory (if one is stored there) and assumes that the one with the higher sequence number is the more recently generated.

The sequence number approach has various problems that must be solved.

1. The sequence number field is of finite size. What happens if it reaches the maximum value?

   It is tempting to make the field large (say, 64 bits) and then assume that no node will ever issue enough LSPs to cause the field to reach the maximum value. The problem is that the sequence number on an LSP can become corrupted to a value near the maximum, or a router could mistakenly generate an LSP with a very large sequence number. So the protocol must provide a way to continue operating even if the sequence number for some router's LSP reaches the maximum value. If the sequence number reaches the maximum value, it must either *wrap around* or be reset. Early LSP distribution schemes assumed that the sequence number field would wrap around. Let us start by making that assumption.

   Wrapping around means that the sequence number starts at some value (say, 0), increases to some maximum value (say, n), and then goes back to 0. It is important to be able to compare two sequence numbers. Given two sequence numbers a and b, a is considered to be less than b if $|a - b| < n/2$ and $a < b$, or $|a - b| > n/2$ and $a > b$. Pictorially, the sequence number space can be considered a circle (see Figure 12.8). Given any point a on the circle, the numbers in the semicircle on one side of a are greater than a, and the numbers in the other semicircle are less than a.

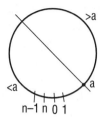

Figure 12.8 Comparing numbers in a circular sequence number space

2. What happens if router S goes down and forgets the sequence number it was using? If it starts again at 0, will its LSPs be believed by the network, or will they look older than the LSPs that S had issued before it crashed?

3. Suppose that the network partitions into two halves—say, East and West—with router S in the East. Suppose that the sequence number S used before the network partitioned was x and that the partition lasts long enough that S's sequence number used in the East partition wraps around and starts looking smaller than the last sequence number seen for S in the West partition. Some mechanism must exist so that when the network partition is repaired and East and West merge, the nodes in the West will believe S's current LSPs.

To solve the preceding problems, a second field, known as the *age* of the LSP, is added to each LSP. It starts at some value and is decremented by routers as it is held in memory. When an LSP's age reaches 0, the LSP can be considered too old, and an LSP with a nonzero age is accepted as newer regardless of its sequence number.

This is the general idea behind sequence number/age schemes for LSP distribution. Let us study the first such scheme, which was designed and deployed in the ARPANET. On the surface, it seems logical enough, but as we shall see, it has a spectacular failure mode.

12.2.3.3 The ARPANET LSP Distribution Scheme

An LSP contains the elements shown in Figure 12.9.

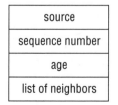

Figure 12.9 Contents of LSP

When router R generates an LSP, it sets the **source** to R, the **sequence number** to be 1 greater (mod n, the size of the circular sequence number space) than the sequence number of R's previously generated LSP, and the **age** to be the maximum value.

When a router other than R receives R's LSP, the router accepts it and overwrites any stored LSP from R provided that the sequence number of the received LSP is greater than the sequence number of the stored LSP (according to arithmetic in the circular sequence number space). If the age on the stored LSP is 0, the received LSP is accepted regardless of sequence number. (The received LSP will have a nonzero age because LSPs with 0 age are not propagated.) When a router accepts an LSP, it propagates the LSP to each neighbor except the one from which the LSP was received.

When a router holds on to an LSP for some specified time, it decrements the age field. When the age of an LSP reaches 0, the LSP is not propagated further, but it is kept in the database and used for routing calculations.

To get a feel for the actual parameter values used in the ARPANET, age was a 3-bit field, with units being 8 sec. The age started out as 56 sec (7×8) and was decremented every 8 sec.

Each router was required to generate a new LSP within 60 sec. Also, a router was required to wait for 90 sec before issuing its initial LSP upon start-up. This gave its old LSP a chance to age to 0 and gave the newly started router an opportunity to acquire a fresh LSP database because all the other routers would have issued new LSPs in that 90-sec interval.

On the surface, this scheme seems logical enough. But distributed algorithms can be tricky.

One night, the ARPANET stopped working. Diagnosis was difficult because, ordinarily, network management was done by sending and receiving messages over the network—which, at this point, was nonfunctional. In this case, a core dump indicated that the local router (at BBN, the site from which the ARPANET was maintained) had its queues filled with LSPs. Furthermore, all the LSPs were from some source router S, and S's LSPs had three different sequence numbers: a, b, and c, where $a < b < c < a$ (see Figure 12.10).

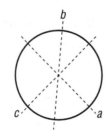

Figure 12.10 $a < b < c < a$

> **The world is round and the place which may seem like the end may also be only the beginning.**
>
> —**Ivy Baker Priest**[5]

When the network gets into such a state, there is no way for it to recover. If any router has a stored LSP from S with sequence number b, and if it sees an LSP from S with sequence number c, it will overwrite the one in memory and make copies of the LSP for each of its neighbors. Furthermore, a router will flood the LSPs in precisely the order that will cause its neighbors to accept every one (first a will be flooded, then b, then c, then a. . .).

Why didn't these LSPs age out? The reason is that a router decrements the age field on an LSP only after it sits in memory for 8 sec. These LSPs were not getting stored in memory long enough for the age field to be decremented but instead were being received and immediately propagated further. This is an excellent example of a network layer "virus."

After the problem was diagnosed, it was nontrivial to figure out how to fix the network. One possibility was to find a human at every router site to halt the router, and only after every router was manually halted bring the routers back up. This would not have been very practical. It would have required knowing the telephone number of someone at every site who would be able to manually halt the router, making a lot of phone calls, and hoping that someone responded at every site. Furthermore, if some sites had been overlooked, then when the network was restarted, S's LSPs might still have been lurking in some routers' memories, ready to reinfect the entire network. Also keep in mind that we are assuming the telephone network would have operated properly. Imagine if the telephone network had been the one with the network layer virus so that people could not even have been contacted by phone!

The approach chosen was to devise a patched version of the router code that specifically ignored LSPs from S. The local router was halted and rebooted with the patched version. Then its neighbors were halted and rebooted with the patched version—then their neighbors, and so forth, until the entire network was running the patched version of the code. Only after every router was running the patched version of the code was it possible to reboot the routers, one by one, with the real code.

In this case, it was particularly lucky that the people who designed the algorithm were also the implementers and the field service people. All routers were implemented on identical hardware and were running the same software. Is this true of the networks on which you depend today? The ARPANET "incident" (to borrow terminology from the nuclear power industry) occurred because of a single malfunctioning router. That router, instead of failing by stopping outright, failed by first emitting a few well-formed LSPs with random sequence numbers with its dying gasp and then stopping. The ARPANET was completely nonfunctional and would have remained nonfunctional forever (had there not been manual intervention), although all the remaining routers were functioning

---

[5] Parade (Feb. 16, 1958), quoted in Simpson, *Simpson Contemporary Quotations*, 324.

properly. It seems very unlikely that a router would fail in exactly that way, but it did happen. Furthermore, the same packets could as easily have been injected by a malicious node attached to the network. We should learn from this incident that distributed algorithms must be designed with care.

Section 12.2.3.4 describes the LSP distribution scheme accepted as the best known today. It is used in most of today's link state routing protocols, including DECnet Phase V (where it was originally developed and documented), IS-IS, OSPF, and PNNI. It has been proved self-stabilizing by Professor Nancy Lynch from MIT.

The basic improvements introduced are as follows.

1. *Self-stabilization:* No matter what sequence of events occurs, no matter how corrupted the databases become, no matter what messages are introduced into the system, after all defective or malicious equipment is disconnected from the network, the network will return to normal operation within a tolerable period of time (such as less than an hour).

2. *Efficiency:* The ARPANET scheme required every router to generate a new LSP every minute because the LSP lifetime was only on the order of a minute. The ARPANET parameters could not simply be increased because that would have required an even longer delay upon start-up (90 sec is already too long—it certainly couldn't have been cranked up to 90 min). The improved scheme still recommends periodic regeneration of LSPs, but it can be done on the order of once an hour. The periodic regeneration could be eliminated entirely, though it's helpful to recover from low-probability events such as undetected corruption (an LSP gets corrupted with a checksum that looks valid). (See homework problem 10.)

3. *Responsiveness:* The ARPANET scheme required a router to wait 90 sec before participating in the network. The improved scheme has no such requirement except in the very rare case in which the sequence number space for a router becomes exhausted. When that happens, only that single router must wait for its LSP to age out and be purged before it can participate in the network.

12.2.3.4 New, Improved LSP Distribution

As before, an LSP contains the elements shown in Figure 12.11.

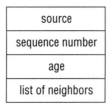

Figure 12.11 Contents of LSP

The sequence number is a linear space. It starts at 0, and, when it reaches its maximum value, no other LSP from that source will be accepted (until the LSP times out). The **sequence number** field should be large enough (say, 32 bits) that it will never reach the maximum value except as a result of malfunctioning nodes' generating bad sequence numbers.

The **age** field is set to a value (say, max age) by the router that generates the LSP. Max age should be on the order of an hour. Every router that handles an LSP must decrement the **age** field by at least 1 and should further decrement it as it sits in memory.

When a router receives a new LSP and determines that it should be transmitted on some of its links, it should not immediately queue the LSP. Rather, it should flag the LSP in memory as needing to be queued, with a separate flag for each link. In this way, fairness can be enforced for use of the bandwidth because the memory will be scanned round-robin for LSPs that need to be transmitted. Queues will not be permitted to be filled with multiple LSPs from the same source. If an LSP with a higher sequence number arrives before the preceding LSP is transmitted, the LSP with the higher sequence number will overwrite the LSP with the smaller sequence number, and the first LSP will never be transmitted (exactly the behavior desired).

In addition, we require that LSPs be acknowledged. We don't require an acknowledgment to be generated immediately but rather that a flag be set to indicate that an acknowledgment for that LSP should be sent to that link. Thus, each LSP in router R's memory has $2k$ flags associated with it, where k is the number of links connected to R. Half the flags are known as *send* flags, where the jth flag indicates that the LSP should be transmitted to the jth link. The other k flags are *ack* flags, where the jth flag indicates that an acknowledgment for that LSP should be transmitted to the jth link. At most, one of those flags would be set for a given LSP and link.

When bandwidth on a link becomes available, the LSP database is scanned round-robin for an LSP that has a send flag or an ack flag set for that link. If the flag found is a send flag, the LSP itself is transmitted on that link. If the flag found is an ack flag, an acknowledgment for that LSP is transmitted on the link, and the ack flag is cleared. (If the ack is lost, the neighbor will retransmit the LSP.)

When an LSP is initially accepted from the jth link, the LSP is written into the LSP database; all send flags except the jth are set, and all ack flags except the jth are cleared. The jth send flag is cleared, and the jth ack flag is set. If a duplicate LSP is received from link j, the jth send flag is cleared and the jth ack flag is set. If an ack is received from link j corresponding to an LSP in memory, the jth send flag and the jth ack flag are cleared for that stored LSP (see Figure 12.12).

LSPs	Flags	Neighbor 1	Neighbor 2	Neighbor 3	. . .	Neighbor k
R1 #27	send flag	✓	✓			✓
links	ack flag			✓		
R2 #15	send flag					
links	ack flag					
R3 #152	send flag		✓	✓		✓
links	ack flag	✓				
R4 #6	send flag	✓		✓		
links	ack flag		✓			✓
R5 #33	send flag	✓				
links	ack flag					
R6 #47	send flag					
links	ack flag			✓		

Figure 12.12 Flags for reliable dissemination of LSPs to neighbors

This improved scheme also tries to ensure that all routers will time out an LSP at about the same time. This is important because if one router had a much faster clock, it might time out an LSP much more quickly than other routers, and routing could be severely disrupted while the routers are making decisions based on different LSP databases. Thus, this scheme requires that an LSP be reflooded when its age becomes 0 and that a router receiving an LSP with 0 age that has the same source and sequence number as an LSP in memory overwrite the stored LSP with the newly received LSP.

When an LSP's age becomes 0, router R deletes the data associated with the LSP (the list of links), but R must hold the LSP header long enough to successfully transmit it to each of R's neighbors. The improved scheme allows R to delete an LSP with 0 age after all R's neighbors have acknowledged the LSP with 0 age or after some time (on the order of a minute) has elapsed since the LSP's age became 0.

This scheme further stipulates that R must not accept an LSP with 0 age if no LSP from the same source is already in R's memory. The reason for this is as follows (see Figure 12.13).

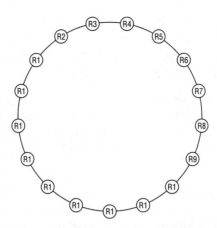

Figure 12.13 Why you shouldn't accept an LSP with age 0 if no LSP from that source is known

Never mistake motion for action.

—Ernest Hemingway[6]

Suppose that R1 has an LSP with 0 age and none of the other routers has that LSP. Perhaps R1 has just received the LSP from R17, which deletes it when R1 acknowledges it. Then R1 will transmit it to R2 and delete it when R2 acknowledges it, and so forth. The LSP will constantly be transmitted around the circle and never go away. The rule that a router merely acknowledges and does not store or propagate an LSP with 0 age when no corresponding LSP appears in the database prevents this. This example would not present a terrible problem because the protocol specifies that an LSP with 0 age not be used in the routing calculation. It is just a bit untidy to allow random LSPs to wander aimlessly about the net.

This new, improved protocol assumes that all links in the network are point-to-point links. When some routers are connected via LANs, the LSP distribution scheme must be modified to take that into account. This portion of the scheme is done differently in IS-IS and in OSPF, so it is explored in Chapter 14, when I discuss specific routing algorithms.

12.2.4 Computing Routes

When a router has a complete set of LSPs, it has complete knowledge of the network. There are straightforward algorithms to calculate routes, given a complete knowledge of the network. The algorithm that routers always seem to use is based on Dijkstra. The basic algorithm can be stated as follows.

First, there are several databases.

1. The link state database, which consists of the latest LSP from each other router.

---

[6] Quote 531 from Byrne, *1911 Best Things,* 378.

2. PATH, which consists of (ID, path cost, forwarding direction) triples. This is the set of nodes for which the best path from the computing router has been found. The triple contains the best path's cost and the direction in which the router should send packets to optimally reach the destination.

3. TENT, which has the same data structure as PATH—namely, triples of the form (ID, path cost, forwarding direction). The name comes from *tentative*, which signifies that the paths indicated in TENT are only possibly the best paths. After it is determined that a path is in fact the best possible, the node is moved from TENT to PATH.

4. The forwarding database, which consists of (ID, forwarding direction). This allows a router, when making a forwarding decision, to look up the ID of the destination and forward the packet along the specified direction. It is simply PATH minus the path cost element of the triples.

The Dijkstra algorithm is as follows.

1. Start with "self" as the root of a tree by putting (my ID, 0, 0) in PATH.

2. For the node N just placed in PATH, examine N's LSP. For each neighbor M of N, add the second item in N's triple in the PATH data structure (which is the cost from the root to N) to the cost of the link from N to M (as listed in N's LSP). If M is not already in PATH or TENT with a better path cost, put (M, computed path cost, direction to get to N) into TENT.

    (If N is self, with the special direction "0," then indicate that the packet should go directly to M.)

3. If TENT is empty, terminate the algorithm. Otherwise, find the triple (ID, cost, direction) in TENT with minimal cost. Move that triple to PATH and go to step 2.

Figures 12.14 and 12.15 show an example.

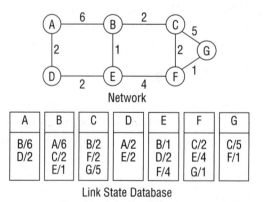

Figure 12.14 Sample network, with corresponding LSPs

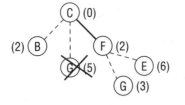

1. Place C in PATH.
   Examine C's LSP.
   Add B, G, F to TENT.

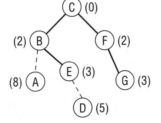

2. Place F in PATH.
   Examine F's LSP.
   Better path to G found.
   Add E to TENT.

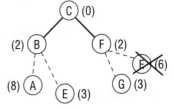

3. Place B in PATH.
   Examine B's LSP.
   Better path to E found.
   Add A to TENT.

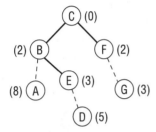

4. Place E in PATH.
   Examine E's LSP.
   Add D to TENT.

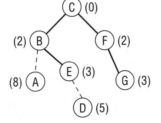

5. Place G in PATH.
   Examine G's LSP.

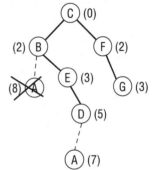

6. Place D in PATH.
   Examine D's LSP.
   Better path to A found.

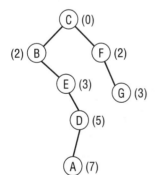

7. Place A in PATH.
   Examine A's LSP.
   No nodes left in TENT.
   Terminate.

Note: The number following the node
name represents the cost of the
best path known from C to that node.

Figure 12.15 Dijkstra computation as done by C

12.3 Comparison of Link State and Distance Vector Routing

In this section I compare link state routing and distance vector routing according to criteria such as resource utilization, robustness, speed of convergence, and other functionality.

12.3.1 Memory

Assume that every router in the net has k neighbors and that there are n nodes in the network. To run distance vector routing, a router must keep a distance vector from each of its k neighbors. Each distance vector is $O(n)$ because it contains information about all the n destinations. This yields a total memory requirement of $O(k * n)$.

In link state routing, each router must keep n LSPs: one from each node in the network. Each LSP contains information about each neighbor of the node that generated the LSP, so each LSP is proportional to k. This yields a total memory requirement of $O(k * n)$.

There are, however, some situations in which distance vector routing does give a significant memory savings. In the higher levels of hierarchical routing, it is not necessary to compute routes to each router. If there are significantly more level n routers than level $n - 1$ subnetworks—for example, s level $n - 1$ subnetworks, n level n routers, and each level n router having k neighbor level n routers—then the memory requirement for distance vector routing would be $O(k * s)$, whereas for link state routing, it would be $O(k * n)$. This is because in distance vector routing, the distance vectors would apply only to the s level n destinations. In link state routing, an LSP from each level n router must still be kept even if the routers themselves are not individually listed as destinations in the forwarding table.

12.3.2 Bandwidth Consumed

It is difficult to compare the bandwidth consumed by the two algorithms. Proponents of either type of protocol can demonstrate a topology in which their favorite uses far less bandwidth than the other.

For example, fans of distance vector routing point out that a link change propagates control messages only as far as the link change's routing effect. In the case of two parallel links, knowledge of the failure and recovery of one of the links while the other remains up will not generate any routing control traffic beyond the link, whereas in link state routing, the link change would trigger an LSP, which would be propagated to all the routers.

Fans of link state routing point out that a change in a single link can cause multiple control packet transmissions over a single link in distance vector routing because of the counting-to-infinity problem, in which the distance vectors must be tossed back and forth a few times. In link state routing, of course, each LSP travels on each link only once. Also, in link state routing, a change in a single link will cause a single LSP to be transmitted through the network, where the LSP is a fixed size independent of the network. With distance vector routing, a change in a single link can affect the cost of paths to a significant fraction of the nodes. This can cause many routers to have to transmit a large distance vector because the distance to all affected destinations must to be updated.

Although this issue deserves to be studied with more care than it has been, again I think that the bandwidth used in either algorithm is modest and should therefore not be the criterion by which one algorithm or the other is chosen.

12.3.3 Computation

Running Dijkstra's algorithm requires processing time proportional to the number of links in the net (there are $n * k$ links) times the log of the number of nodes in the net, so it is $O(n * k \log n)$. To run distance vector routing, the entire matrix of k distance vectors must be scanned, yielding an algorithm requiring $O(n * k)$. However, distance vector computation may require many passes before it is completed.

Often, the routing computation need not calculate routes from scratch. For example, if a distance vector from a neighbor is received that is identical to the preceding distance vector from that neighbor except for a change in cost to a single destination, the entire distance vector need not be recalculated. Instead, only the cost to that destination must be recalculated. Note, though, that a single link change can cause the cost of paths to many destinations to change simultaneously.

Similarly, in link state routing, if the only topology change is that an endnode has come up or gone down, a minimal amount of calculation can adjust the forwarding database accordingly. Less obviously, in link state routing, if a single link changes cost, even if it is a link between routers, there is a way of adjusting the calculated shortest-path tree rather than recomputing from scratch. This algorithm,[7] known as *incremental computation of the shortest-path tree*, was developed and deployed in the ARPANET. But its performance has never been formally studied, especially when additional questions are considered, such as the expected computation required when more than one link changes cost.

The true computational costs of link state routing versus distance vector routing have never been adequately studied and are a good area for research. In my opinion, the computation costs of the two algorithms are comparable and reasonably modest. Router boxes should be engineered with sufficient computation power to handle the routing computation, which need not be done at forwarding rates but rather can take a second or so in the background. An underpowered router is not as serious a problem as an underpowered bridge; however, because the cost of routers is a very small portion of the entire cost of a network, it is an unwise economy to use inadequate packet switches. They can cause unnecessarily lost packets, degrading throughput. They can also disrupt routing because they may be too slow to recompute routes after topology changes.

---

[7] McQuillan, Richer, and Rosen, "The New Routing Algorithm for the ARPANET," *IEEE Transactions on Communications,* May 1980, 711–19.

12.3.4   A Note about Computation Cost

An optimization to Dijkstra has been proposed by Anthony Lauck. It eliminates the factor of log n, which arises because of the step in the Dijkstra calculation when the element in TENT with the smallest path cost must be chosen. To eliminate the need to do a linear search through all the elements in TENT to find the one with the smallest path cost, TENT should be kept sorted. The factor of log n comes about because of the processing time involved in inserting a new entry into TENT using a binary search.

The optimization requires keeping the elements in TENT hashed according to path cost. This can be accomplished provided there are not too many possible values of path cost. Then the bins can be searched in numerical order to find all the elements in a particular bin, move them to PATH, and then move to the next bin when that bin has been emptied.

To allow for this optimization, we had a very small (6 bits) metric field in the routing protocol IS-IS (see Section 14.4). It could be argued that 64 bits for link cost is sufficient. Some people take costs too seriously, thinking that if link L1 (say, 1 Gigabit/s) has 20,000 times as much bandwidth as link L2 (say, 56 K/s), then L2's link cost should be 20,000 times as much as L1's. However, this implies that the routing protocol might need to make a choice between a single hop across L2 and 20,000 hops across Gigabit/s links. And which would you prefer, really? So for link costs, it would probably be fine to take the five or so different speed links in the network and give the fastest links a cost of 1, the next fastest a cost of 10, the next fastest a cost of 20, and so on.

However, when feeding reachable destinations from one area to another, the "link" cost is actually an accumulated path cost, and in that case 6 bits is not enough. The small metric in IS-IS is an annoyance. The world has lived with it for 10 years but has finally decided that it's annoying enough to fix. Recently the IETF has restarted the IS-IS working group to make a few minor changes to IS-IS such as increasing the cost of the metric field.

12.3.5   Robustness

Both algorithms (distance vector and link state) can be completely disabled by a single router that is not following the rules. This can be caused by incorrect software, incorrect configuration, hardware faults, or even a malicious attempt to sabotage the network. In link state routing, a malfunctioning router might

- Claim to have a link that does not exist

- Claim not to have a link that does exist

- Use a strange pattern of sequence numbers for its own LSPs

- Fail to forward data packets, forward them in the wrong direction, or incorrectly modify the TTL

- Fail to forward or acknowledge LSPs

- Corrupt the data in other routers' LSPs

- Corrupt the sequence number in other routers' LSPs

- Corrupt the age in other routers' LSPs

- Calculate incorrect routes

As a safeguard against nonmalicious corruption of LSPs, most link state routing algorithms include a checksum in the LSP that is inserted by the source and not modified by any other routers. Because the age field must be modified by other routers, it is not generally covered by the checksum, or, if it is, routers are required to incrementally modify the checksum as a result of modification to the age field (although enforcing this requirement through conformance tests is difficult).

Those sorts of failures, in which a router doesn't merely halt but rather behaves incorrectly, are known as Byzantine failures. I designed a method of routing that is resilient against Byzantine failures, and I describe it in Chapter 16. Adding my design to a link state protocol is fairly easy. I believe it would not be possible to design a distance vector protocol that would be resilient against Byzantine failures. That's not exactly proof that it can't be done, of course.

In the ARPANET experience with distance vector routing, a faulty router often transmitted a distance vector consisting of all 0's. This created a black hole with an enormous "gravitational field," which caused routers to send most of the packets to the single router in the network that was malfunctioning.

> **One hundred thousand lemmings can't be wrong.**
> **—Graffito[8]**

To truly compare the robustness of the two schemes, one would have to take into account how likely various error scenarios are and how profound a disruption each one might cause.

I believe that the difference in robustness between the two schemes is not great, but I think that link state routing (properly designed—without the ARPANET bug) is more resilient to nonmalicious malfunctions and that malfunctions are more likely to be detectable. This is another area in which careful study would be valuable.

12.3.6 Functionality

Link state routing provides more functionality for the following reasons.

1. It is easier to discover the topology of the network because you can acquire full knowledge of the topology by querying a single router. In contrast, with distance vector routing, mapping the network would be a difficult task, involving querying most, if not all, of the routers.

---

[8] Quote 558 from Byrne, *1911 Best Things*, 249.

2. Troubleshooting a network is easier in link state routing—again, because a single router can be queried, and, from its LSP database, all the broken links can be discovered (assuming that the original topology was known).

3. Source routing is more powerful with link state routing. I am not referring to the bridge style of source routing but rather to the network layer's feature of allowing the source to place a route in the packet header. Because the source can easily acquire the topology of the network, it can calculate routes based on such considerations as avoiding a particular router that it finds suspicious.

4. Implementation of really general types of service routing is more practical with link state routing.[9]

12.3.7 Speed of Convergence

Between the time a topology change occurs and the time all the routers have recomputed routes based on the new topology, routing in the network is disrupted—from minimally to severely, depending on the topological change. It is thus vital to keep the network in the "converged" state as high a percentage of the time as possible.

Link state routing converges more quickly than distance vector routing. For one thing, distance vector routing has the looping problem discussed earlier in the chapter. Even if that were solved, distance vector routing would still converge more slowly because a router cannot pass routing information on until it has recomputed its distance vector. In contrast, a router can recognize a new LSP and forward it before recalculating routes. Even in the schemes in which distance vector is enhanced to prevent temporary loops, the convergence is slowed by the enhancement. The enhancement delays a router from switching to another path for a round trip time because it must be reassured that news of the broken path has traveled to all downstream nodes.

I think that route convergence is the truly critical point of comparison between link state routing and distance vector routing. The chief argument in favor of distance vector routing is that it might require less memory. But because the cost of routers, and the cost of memory in routers, is an insignificant portion of the cost of a network, it seems ill advised to save a bit of money on routers at the expense of having the network broken a larger amount of the time.

[9]Radia Perlman, "Incorporation of Service Classes into a Network Architecture," ACM Sigcomm, 7th Data Communications Symposium, 1981.

12.4 Load Splitting

> Two roads diverged in a wood, and I—
> I took the one less traveled by,
> And that has made all the difference.
> —Robert Frost[10]

If the traffic load is spread among several paths, network capacity is increased. Both algorithms under discussion can easily be enhanced to allow keeping several paths to a destination.

With distance vector routing, if the paths through more than one neighbor are equally minimal (or close to equally minimal), then all such paths can be saved. The forwarding database consists of a set of neighbors (instead of a single neighbor) to which traffic for a particular destination can appropriately be sent.

With link state routing, it is also easy. As noted earlier, the data structures TENT and PATH are triples of the form (ID, path cost, forwarding direction). To keep track of multiple paths, "forwarding direction" should be a set of forwarding directions. Thus, TENT and PATH will be triples of the form (ID, path cost, {set of forwarding directions}).

When a new path to destination DEST is found or when a path better than any discovered so far is found, the entry in TENT will be as before. When a new path to DEST is found with the same cost as the one already in TENT, a set union is performed with the set of forwarding directions already stored with DEST and the set of forwarding directions stored with the node through which the new path to TENT was found.

For example, suppose that node A is being added to PATH, and its triple is (A, 35, {neighbor 5, neighbor 7}). One of A's neighbors is B, at a cost of 7. Thus, the path to B through A has a cost of 42. Suppose that B is already in TENT, with the triple (B, 42, {neighbor 1, neighbor 3, neighbor 7}). Then the set union of {neighbor 1, neighbor 3, neighbor 7} and {neighbor 5, neighbor 7} is performed, yielding {neighbor 1, neighbor 3, neighbor 5, neighbor 7}, and B's triple is modified in the data structure TENT to be (B, 42, {neighbor 1, neighbor 3, neighbor 5, neighbor 7}).

Now that the forwarding database contains a choice of neighbors for each destination, an algorithm must be devised for selecting among the choices when forwarding a data packet. One possibility is to always take the first-listed choice, but then we needn't have gone to the trouble of storing multiple choices in the forwarding database. Other possibilities are as follows.

1. Note the most recent choice made and move through the list of neighbors in the forwarding database round-robin as packets are forwarded to that destination.

2. Choose a neighbor at random from among those listed in the forwarding database.

---

[10] *New Enlarged Pocket Anthology of Robert Frost's Poems* (New York: Washington Square Press/Pocket Books, 1977), 233.

3. Do either 1 or 2, but enhance the process to make forwarding to neighbor N less likely if the link to N is more congested than the links to other neighbors listed in the forwarding database.

4. Have the routing protocol propagate congestion information, and use that to look ahead through each of the paths and choose more lightly loaded paths for sending most of the traffic.

Round-robin is simple and requires only a modest addition to the database to store the last-chosen neighbor for each destination. Random choice is attractive provided that the cost of choosing a random number is not high. Enhancing the schemes by taking congestion into account is also attractive, but without additional protocol traffic to propagate congestion information, this approach does not adjust to traffic that is more than one hop downstream; it adjusts only to the queues at the local router.

Although load splitting increases network capacity, it can be argued that load splitting is undesirable because it annoys the transport layer. The transport layer would prefer to get uniform service so that it can perform such calculations as round-trip delay and maximum packet size along the path. Load splitting also increases the number of out-of-order packets. Even though a self-respecting layer 4 protocol can handle out-of-order packets, it doesn't like its packets purposely shuffled because it requires more buffering.

However, this argument is relevant only if packets for a particular conversation are split among different paths. A router could keep multiple paths to each destination but ensure that packets for a particular conversation always go on the same path. In other words, it can do load splitting by using different paths for different conversations but always choosing the same path for a particular conversation. A router can recognize packets as belonging to the same conversation based on source and destination addresses and (if the router is really ambitious and wants to differentiate more conversations for more traffic spreading) layer 4 information as well, such as TCP ports. If the router has, say, five equal cost paths to D, it can do a hash of (source, destination, ports, and so on) and use that to select which path the packet should take.

12.5 Link Costs

Should the cost of a link be a fixed number, or should it be a quantity that varies with the utilization of the link?

If the cost is a fixed number, should it be automatically calculated at link start-up based on measured characteristics such as bandwidth and delay? Or should it be left solely to the discretion of the network manager to assign the number, based either on the characteristics of the link or on knowledge of the expected traffic matrix, so that traffic can be discouraged from using links that are likely to become congested with that matrix?

The alternative to establishing a fixed quantity is to have the routers measure the delay on each link and increase the link's cost as its utilization increases, thereby encouraging traffic to seek an alternate, and perhaps less congested, route.

These questions are important and interesting, and they have not been adequately studied.

The proponents of having link costs vary with traffic offer two major arguments.

1. Traffic is routed more optimally if the current traffic conditions are factored in to the link costs and thus in to the route calculations.

2. Having link costs assigned by network management requires additional configuration. That is undesirable both because it involves unnecessary work and because it introduces yet another place where human error can create problems.

The proponents of fixed link costs argue as follows.

1. If the cost of a link is a fixed quantity, routing information about the link needs to be generated only if the link goes down or recovers. This is a far less frequent event than changes in the traffic pattern on the link. Thus, with fixed link costs, there will be much less control traffic. That might more than offset the gain in network capacity that could be realized by using more-optimal routes.

2. Between the time a link changes cost and the time knowledge of that revised link cost has successfully reached all the routers and they have all completed their routing computations, routing is disrupted in the network because routers are making routing decisions based on different data. If link costs are frequently changing, the network is more often in an "unconverged" state, in which routing is disrupted to some degree, ranging from not at all to globally and severely. When the network is in an unconverged state, looping data packets consume a significant portion of the network capacity that was perhaps gained by more-optimal routing. The proportion of time that the network is in an unconverged state is also an annoyance because packets might be dropped and even transport layer connections might not survive the disruption. Although "network quality" is an intangible and hard-to-measure factor, it must be taken into account when the schemes are compared.

3. A fixed link cost need not be configured by a human. Instead, the attributes of the link can be measured at link start-up, and from that a link cost can be computed.

If the costs are human-assigned, another question is whether the costs should be a simple function of the characteristics of the link, such as its bandwidth and delay, or whether the costs should take into account the expected traffic matrix in the network.

The proponents of traffic-matrix-dependent costs argue that network capacity is increased if costs depend on the traffic matrix and are set to optimize flow. The opponents argue that attempting to optimize to that degree is a complex task, and it is likely to be done incorrectly. That's because the operating topology will differ from the topology on which link costs were optimized if new nodes are added to the network or if links or routers are down; furthermore, the actual traffic matrix might differ from the expected one. Simple link costs in which all equivalent links (all links of the same delay and bandwidth) are assigned the same value are safer.

An additional approach for optimizing traffic flow in a network is to have congestion information transmitted around the network in a manner that does not change the link costs but is used by routers only as advice for choosing among equivalent paths. This has the disadvantage of introducing more control traffic (the congestion information) but may enhance network capacity without creating instability in routing because no choice is "incorrect." This strategy does not create loops (see homework problem 9).

My opinion on all this is that attempting to increase network capacity a very small amount through complex and costly algorithms is a bad idea. I believe that there is little difference in network capacity between the simplest form of link cost assignment (fixed values depending on the delay and total bandwidth of the link) and "perfect routing" (in which a deity routes every packet optimally, taking into account traffic currently in the network as well as traffic that will enter the network in the near future). And the difference is probably negligible between simple routing and what you can gain by constantly monitoring delays on each link and adding control traffic to keep all the other routers informed, especially when the added bandwidth consumed by the routing information is taken into account.

If fixed costs are used, I do not think that fancy "traffic matrix" algorithms that are run on the assumed topology to optimize traffic flow are a good idea because the assumptions under which the numbers are generated are almost guaranteed to be incorrect (topology will evolve as nodes and links are added; topology will change as nodes and links fail; traffic patterns are not necessarily predictable). And I don't believe that the percentage of network capacity that could theoretically be gained is large enough to warrant the complexity and risk.

Having routers measure the characteristics of links and set the costs at link start-up seems like a good idea. It eliminates the possibility of human error, makes the network more plug-and-play, and does not add any control traffic or increase the time during which the network is unconverged. This strategy is used in NLSP, the link state protocol for routing IPX.

12.6 Migrating Routing Algorithms

An interesting problem is how to change the routing algorithm in an operational network. It is undesirable to require that the entire network be brought down while all the routers are simultaneously reloaded with code for the new algorithm. It is preferable to modify each router, one at a time, and somehow keep the network functioning.

If a network is hierarchical, the entire network need not be switched at once. Rather, each level 1 subnetwork can be switched at a different time, as can the level 2 subnetwork that connects the level 1 subnetworks. It is possible for a level 2 router to be running one algorithm at level 2 and a different algorithm at level 1.

In the following subsections, I describe strategies for migrating from one algorithm to another.

12.6.1 Running Both Algorithms

The strategy of running both algorithms was implemented in the ARPANET when the system was switched from distance vector routing to link state routing. The original ARPANET code ran only distance vector routing. An intermediate version of the code ran both distance vector routing and link state routing. It transmitted and processed distance vectors as well as LSPs. The two algorithms did not interact, in the sense that the link state algorithm computed routes based solely on the information received from LSPs. If only a single router, R, was running the intermediate version of the code while all the other routers were running the original code, the link state algorithm in R would conclude that the entire network consisted of R and its attached endnodes. Similarly, the distance vector computation was based solely on received distance vectors. The intermediate version of the code also contained a switch, settable by network management, that specified whether the routes chosen should be based on the forwarding database computed by the distance vector routing or by the link state routing. A third version of the code ran only link state routing.

At first, the network consisted solely of routers running the original code. Then, one by one, routers were modified to run the intermediate version of the code, all of them with the network-management-settable switch specifying that they should route based on distance vector routing. Only after every router was running the intermediate version of the code (so that the LSP database would compute correct routes) was it possible to modify the routers, one by one, by changing the setting of the network-management-settable switch to start using the link-state-computed forwarding database.

During the time when all routers were running the intermediate version of the code but forwarding based on distance vector routing, the sanity of the link state algorithm could be checked by comparing the forwarding databases computed by both algorithms.

When all the routers were running the intermediate version of the code but using the link-state-computed database, it was no longer necessary to run distance vector routing, and the third version of the code could be loaded into the routers one by one.

The disadvantage of this approach is that during the time when the intermediate version of the code was running, the memory, bandwidth, and computation requirements were doubled because both routing algorithms were running.

12.6.2 Manual Node-by-Node Switch

The strategy of doing a manual node-by-node switch is more disruptive of a network when the changeover from one algorithm to the other occurs, but the theory is that the changeover can be accomplished in an hour or so, and it is the simplest and lowest-cost strategy to implement.

The basic idea is that the code for the new algorithm should be designed so that nodes running the new algorithm look like endnodes to nodes running the old algorithm, and nodes running the old algorithm look like endnodes to nodes running the new algorithm. In this way, it is possible to migrate in both directions. If a level 1 subnetwork is running the old algorithm, then from one location, that router can be rebooted with the new algorithm. It will allow communication with its old-algorithm neighbors. After they are rebooted with the new algorithm, communication is possible with their neighbors, and so forth. If a portion of the network has been reloaded with the new algorithm and it is determined that the new algorithm is not behaving satisfactorily, a single site can be rebooted with the old algorithm, and then the neighbors of that site (which are accessible as endnodes), and so on.

This method is conceptually simple. It has the disadvantage of severely disrupting the network while the migration occurs, but it does not involve any intermediate code requiring twice the resources (enough memory, computation time, and bandwidth to run two algorithms). Also, implementing two routing algorithms to run simultaneously is more difficult than the sum of implementing each of the two algorithms individually; when they are running simultaneously, care must be taken to ensure that resources are shared fairly between the two processes.

This strategy is the one adopted for migrating DECnet from distance vector routing (used in Phase IV) to link state routing (used in Phase V).

12.6.3 Translation

The idea is that a router can simultaneously participate in both algorithms, on a per-link basis. For example, consider Figure 12.16.

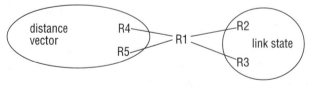

Figure 12.16 Running two routing protocols

Assume that R1 is capable of talking both protocols. It discovers which protocol to run based on negotiation with its neighbor on each link. R1 now must participate in both protocols because it has neighbors in each cloud. R1 conveys information from one cloud to the other. It learns all the destinations reachable in the left cloud and introduces them into the right cloud as if all the destinations in the left cloud were neighbors of R1. In other words, R1 reports all the left-cloud destinations in the link state information R1 injects into the right cloud. Similarly, R1 figures out all the reachable destinations in the right cloud (together with path cost to each) and reports that information in its distance vector reports injected into the left cloud.

This technique is the most complex, especially when the metrics in the two protocols are dissimilar. For instance, if the distance vector protocol has a maximum path cost of 16, metrics must be translated, which can lead to permanent loops if not done carefully. The best way for a routing protocol to behave is for paths to always increase in cost when further from the destination. But this will not be the case if the path cost has to be translated into a smaller number in order to be reported into a distance vector region.

12.7 LANs

In describing the routing algorithms, I assumed that all links in the network were point-to-point links. There are extra issues to be considered when some of the links are LANs.

12.7.1 Making the LAN a Node

A LAN is equivalent to full connectivity between every pair of nodes on the LAN. However, routing algorithms tend to have overhead proportional to the number of links in the network, so it is not advisable to expand a LAN with n nodes into n^2 links (see Figure 12.17).

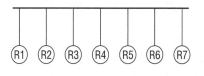

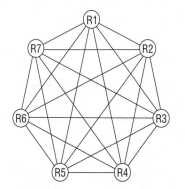

Figure 12.17 Treating a LAN like n^2 links

The alternative, in link state routing, is to consider the LAN itself as a node in the network (see Figure 12.18).

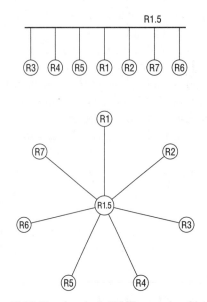

Figure 12.18 Treating the LAN like a node with *n* links

This is done by having the routers on the LAN elect one router to be the *designated router*, through a simple process such as choosing the router with the highest or lowest ID. The designated router names the LAN and constructs an LSP on behalf of the LAN. The name of the LAN is the concatenation of the designated router's ID with an additional field to differentiate among multiple LANs for which that router might be designated.

Each router on the LAN reports only a single link in its LSP for the LAN—that is, a link to the LAN itself (in this case, neighbor R1.5).

R1 issues an LSP for itself claiming a link to R1.5. R1 issues an additional LSP on behalf of the LAN, which lists all the nodes on the LAN, including the endnodes, in the case of CLNP (in IP, information about endnodes is not propagated). Thus, the LAN specific information appears in only a single LSP rather than being listed in the LSPs of all the routers on the LAN.

12.7.2 Disseminating Routing Information

It is more efficient to disseminate routing information by taking advantage of the capabilities of the LAN. However, the LAN service is datagram (especially if the LAN's multicast capability is exploited).

The most obvious thing a router should do on a LAN is to multicast routing information (such as LSPs or distance vectors) to a multicast address listened to by all the routers rather than to transmit individual copies to all the neighbor routers. But routing information must be delivered reliably. There are various methods for ensuring reliable delivery.

1. Have each router transmit an acknowledgment to the router that multicasted a routing message.

    If multicast were not exploited, the source router, R, would have sent an individual message to each of the other routers. Assume that there are n routers on the LAN. Then R would transmit n-1 messages and receive n-1 acks, resulting in $2n$-2 messages for each routing message. If R instead multicasts the message but still collects acknowledgments, then there are n messages: the single multicast by R and the n-1 acks.

    This scheme is similar to the one chosen by OSPF ("open shortest path first"), a link state routing protocol for IP. (OSPF is discussed in more detail in Chapter 14.)

2. Have each router retransmit each routing message fairly frequently. The period between retransmissions should be about equal to the amount of time that a router would have waited, in the absence of having received an ack, before retransmitting.

    This is a reasonable scheme for distance vector routing, in which each router has only a single piece of routing information to transmit. It would not work at all well with link state routing, in which each router has an LSP from each other router in the network.

    The reasoning behind this approach is that it is simple. If the amount of routing traffic is modest (in distance vector routing, with 10 routers on the LAN, each retransmitting a distance vector every 10 sec, the overhead is tolerable), then this scheme cannot be faulted for generating too much overhead. It also does not necessarily consume more bandwidth than a scheme involving explicit acks. If there are n routers on the LAN and if the information changes more frequently than n times the periodic retransmission time, then this scheme actually takes *less* bandwidth than an explicit-ack scheme. Most likely, the information changes less frequently than that, but we must keep in mind that elimination of the acks offsets things somewhat.

    Also, periodic transmissions in the absence of anything useful to say do less harm than a scheme that requires a lot of packets while topology is changing. So again, the periodic-transmission scheme is attractive because its "nonessential" use of bandwidth takes place during times when there would have been no control traffic anyway.

    Furthermore, this approach cannot be faulted for being less reliable than a scheme involving acknowledgments provided that the retransmission timer is the same as the periodic timer. In other words, in an explicit-acknowledgment scheme, if a message is missed, some time will elapse before the transmitter notices the lack of an ack and retransmits. If that time is, say, 10 sec, then a scheme requiring periodic transmissions every 10 sec will recover from lost messages just as quickly.

This scheme was used in Phase IV DECnet, a distance vector routing protocol.

3. Provide periodic database summaries.

In a link state scheme, an alternative to explicit acknowledgments of individual LSPs is the scheme devised for Phase V DECnet (and adopted by ISO in IS-IS). A special packet, known as a *sequence numbers packet*, or SNP, is periodically transmitted by the designated router. It contains the latest sequence numbers of all the LSPs. If, based on receiving an SNP, a router R detects that it has missed an LSP, it can explicitly request the LSP from the designated router. If R detects that the designated router has missed an LSP (because the LSP is not mentioned in the SNP or one with a smaller number from that source is mentioned), then R knows that it should retransmit the LSP.

As with the frequent-retransmissions scheme, if the period with which SNPs are broadcast is the same as the retransmission time that would be used with an explicit-acknowledgment scheme, the SNP approach is as robust and responsive as an explicit-acknowledgment scheme.

Again, as with the frequent-retransmissions scheme, the extra bandwidth consumed by the periodic transmission of SNPs is offset by the elimination of the explicit acknowledgments. It is also bandwidth better spent because it involves having a constant low level of traffic instead of having all the control traffic bunched around the time topology changes occur.

A disadvantage of the SNP scheme is the processing required of the routers that receive an SNP. Each time an SNP is received, the link state database must be checked against the information in the SNP. When no LSPs have been recently transmitted, the check merely verifies that the databases remains synchronized. This may not be a significant disadvantage because if no LSPs have been recently transmitted, the router should have processing cycles to spare. Also, it might be an advantage to periodically compare databases in the event that somehow the databases have become corrupted.

12.8   Types of Service

The term *types of service* has been defined in various ways. This section discusses some of the things that people mean when they use this term.

12.8.1   Handling Directives

A *handling directive* is a special way that the user would like a packet handled, but it does not involve a specially chosen route. An example of a handling directive is *priority*, in which the user requests preferential treatment in terms of placement in queues and perhaps selection of the priority field in the data link header when the packet is forwarded. Other examples are *don't fragment* and *error report requested.*

Any number of handling directives can be implemented, but they must be predefined before the router is implemented. There must be a way of specifying each one in the packet header, and the algorithms for dealing with each one must be implemented. If two or more handling directives are selected on a particular packet, the algorithms for each one must be executed.

12.8.2 Multiple Metrics

If one set of metrics cannot satisfy all users, links could be assigned a set of costs—for example, one for bandwidth and another one for delay. An example of a metric that is very different from delay or bandwidth is money. Some links cost money per packet. Others are "free." Now, as we all should realize, there's no such thing as a free link—it's just a matter of who pays. But some users might want to minimize the money spent, and they might be willing to use an otherwise undesirable path if it costs less money. Routing would be calculated independently for each type of cost, and the forwarding decision would be based on destination address and chosen metric.

What happens if someone wants to consider more than one of the orthogonal characteristics of the link? For example, suppose that someone wants to optimize delay and bandwidth but is not concerned about other types of costs. What is the cost of a link when two or more independent metrics are supposed to be simultaneously optimized? Should the costs of the chosen metrics be combined? What sort of combination should be chosen? It could be the sum, the product, or some weighted quantity assigning more weight to one characteristic than another. It could be that the user considers one characteristic much more important, and a second chosen characteristic is to be used only as a tiebreaker among paths whose cost is equal according to the first chosen characteristic.

Another possibility is to consider each combination of characteristics as a separate metric. This method gives the maximum flexibility in choosing the most sensible method of combining the values but is more costly if characteristics are often combined. That's because n characteristics become 2^n possible combinations of characteristics, yielding 2^n different metrics, which must be manually assigned per link and for which routing must be computed and forwarding databases kept.

The way multiple metrics are specified in IS-IS, there is one metric known as the *default metric*. Every router must implement the default metric, and every link must carry a cost according to the default metric.

Implementation of other metrics is optional. Each router specifies a set of (metric number, cost) pairs for each link. It is possible for a router to report a different set of metrics on different links, but every link must report a value for the default metric. A router that does not report a particular metric on any of its links does not need to compute routes according to that metric. If a router reports a value only for the default metric on each of its links, it computes only a single set of routes.

When a user requests routing according to a metric other than the default metric, a route with that metric (one that traverses only routers and links that support that metric) is chosen if such a route is available. Otherwise, the route calculated according to the default metric is chosen. With this strategy, routers that have not implemented different metrics will work with routers that have implemented them.

The implications of the use of multiple metrics should be considered carefully. A route computed according to a metric other than the default metric is constrained, somewhat arbitrarily perhaps, to use certain links (those supporting the requested metric). The computed route may be wildly nonoptimal because it is restricted to an arbitrary subset of the links and routers.

An amusing scenario, suggested by Ross Callon, involves use of the "money" metric. Suppose that most of the links do not support the money metric, but some of the links cost significant amounts of money to use. Therefore, the managers of the routers attached to those links regard it as important to report the money metric for those links and thereby warn users that the links are expensive. The links that are "free" do not bother reporting a money metric cost. Then someone wants to save money and selects the money metric. The route computed will be a circuitous one that visits enough of the expensive links to reach the destination. In this case, the money spent will be maximized.

The type of service that can be specified in an IP header consists of a 3-bit **TOS** field, where **delay**, **throughput**, and **reliability** each has 1 bit. According to the IP router requirements, this specifies eight different metrics. If a user specifies both delay and reliability by setting both bits and if there is at least one route where every link in the path reports a cost according to the metric of delay plus reliability but not throughput, then the packet is routed according to the best of those routes. If no such route exists the packet is routed according to the default metric—the one in which none of the 3 bits is set in the **TOS** field.

The **TOS** field in CLNP is an option and, as such, might not appear in a packet header. If it does not, the packet is routed according to the default metric. If it does, it might specify "source-specific" or "destination specific"—in which case, the standard does not specify the meaning, and the default metric is used. If the packet contains the globally specified quality of service, there are three relevant bits:

1. **E/C:** "Residual error probability versus cost"

2. **E/D:** "Residual error probability versus delay"

3. **D/C:** "Transit delay versus cost"

Four metrics are defined by default (intended to be bandwidth, delay, money, and error rate). If you're using CLNP, how do you encode which of the four metrics you want using the three bits **E/C, E/D,** and **D/C** provided in CLNP? The metric chosen for each setting of the CLNP bits is specified in IS-IS as shown in Figure 12.19.

E/C	E/D	D/C	metric
0	0	0	money
0	0	1	delay
0	1	0	money
0	1	1	default
1	0	0	default
1	0	1	delay
1	1	0	error rate
1	1	1	error rate

Figure 12.19 Mapping CLNP TOS bits to metric

I dislike the added complexity of multiple metrics, especially as implemented (not all metrics are reported for each link). Any potential gains in terms of better routes is more than offset by the overhead and by the likelihood of extreme suboptimality caused by misconfiguration or misunderstanding of the way multiple metrics work.

12.8.3 Policy-based Routing and Policy-based Constraints

When people say *policy-based routing* or *policy-based constraints*, they mean routing in which the use of certain links and routers is outlawed. This is different from optimizing a metric, in which no paths are outlawed but some are preferred to others. Constraints are motivated by the following.

1. Assumptions that there is not really a giant network to which you attach and then become part of it but rather that there are numerous autonomous routing domains, and the administrators agree to connect to a few other routing domains.

    For example, if nets A and B decide to connect and if B and C decide to connect, it does not give A permission to route traffic to C. Traffic will flow from A to C only if networks A and B explicitly agree to connect to each other, B and C agree to connect to each other, A and C agree to send traffic to each other through B, and B agrees to carry transit traffic between A and C.

2. Laws in various countries, or policies corresponding to the applications running, which might constrain the legal routes. For example, Canadian law requires traffic originating and terminating in Canada to be routed solely within Canada, so a route that entered the United States and then returned to Canada would be illegal.

    These laws are sufficiently complex, and sufficiently likely to change, that a particular law should not be built into the routing algorithm. Rather, routing should somehow be parameterized so that any policy could be entered manually.

3. Policies of certain networks, which might restrict the types of traffic they will carry. For example, the ARPANET was supposed to be used only for government business.

Providing different routes for different types of traffic makes routing almost intractable.

People would like to have the route to destination DEST depend on any combination of the following:

1. Source routing domain

2. Source node

3. Application

4. Content of the message (for example, a mail message regarding government business is allowed to traverse the ARPANET, but not a message recommending science fiction books)

5. The route the packet has traversed so far

I'm sure there are other factors that people will think should be considered in a routing decision. Obviously, the more such criteria, the more difficult routing becomes, especially if it is deemed important for routers to forward packets quickly.

There are several general methods for attempting to deal with these issues, none of them completely satisfactory. Most of the work in this area involves interdomain routing because the assumption is that within a domain, any route should be legal. There was a working group called IDPR (interdomain policy routing), which for the most part had the right approach. It developed a link state routing protocol that passed around the characteristics of links and computed a path, but allowed you to set up a custom-calculated path if the default one calculated by the routing protocol didn't meet your constraints. The link state information gave enough information for a source or a router near the source to calculate such a path. But the working group never completed anything.

The competing protocol to IDPR (at the time) was BGP (border gateway protocol) (see Section 14.5.3) for IP, with an ISO version of BGP called IDRP (interdomain routing protocol). I find BGP scary. It is configuration-intensive. Routes can be permanently unstable. It solves only whatever it happens to solve rather than providing a general-purpose solution. But we're stuck with it.

Here I discuss the generic approaches to providing policy-based routing without concentrating on a specific protocol. For the Internet, for the foreseeable future, we're stuck with BGP.

12.8.4 Static Routes

Static routing is the conceptually simplest solution. Humans can consider whatever they want in determining the desired routes. The main problems with static routes are the hassle of manual configuration, the fact that this approach does not work unless all routers are configured properly and compatibly, and the inability of static routes to adapt to topological changes.

12.8.5 Filters

A filter is an additional algorithm executed in a packet switch that decides which packets it will forward and which it will refuse to forward. For example, a filter could reject packets from a particular source address or source routing domain.

Filters can be useful, and indeed essential, to enforce restrictions on access to resources, but they do not solve the general problem because a packet that is not allowed to use one route to a particular destination might have another, perfectly legal route to that destination. There must be a way to ensure that the packet will traverse a legal route when one is available rather than penalize the user because the network happened to decide to route the packet on a restricted route.

12.8.6 Source Routing

The theory behind source routing is that the source can have any policy it wishes and merely specify the route in the packet header. Source routing has two main problems as the solution to providing policy-based routing. First, the source must have access to a current topological map to select a route that is not only desirable but also works. Second, there must be a way for the source to know the characteristics of other routing domains, links, and switches (whatever criteria it is using for selecting a route). Assuming that it is not a human calculating a path, the computer must be given enough information so that if a new routing domain, switch, or link is attached to the network, the algorithm will know the relevant characteristics.

12.8.7 Routing-domain-specific Policy

Routing-domain-specific policy is the approach taken by BGP/IDRP. The assumption is that routing constraints apply equally to all links and routers within a routing domain. Thus, any policy restrictions can be expressed in terms of the routing domains in the path. Each *border gateway* (a router connecting two routing domains) has a set of policies that it uses to choose a route to a particular destination. Here are some examples of such policies.

- Never use routing domain X for any destination.

- Never use both routing domains X and Y in any particular route.

- Don't use routing domain X to get to a destination in routing domain Y.

- Don't use routing domain X unless you are also using routing domain Y.

- Don't use routing domain X unless no alternative path exists.

- Don't use routing domain X unless the next best alternative path is at least cost C worse.

BGP is a distance vector routing protocol in which each entry in the distance vector gives the sequence of routing domains in the path to the destination. Distributing the sequence of routing domains has two purposes.

1. It solves the counting-to-infinity problem.

2. It allows policy decisions to be made based on the routing domains in the path.

When a border gateway makes a decision regarding the path to a destination, it considers all the routing domain sequence routes it has learned from its neighbor border gateways. It first discards all the routes that are precluded by policy and then uses an algorithm to calculate the *preference* of the remaining routes. The route with the highest preference is advertised in its distance vector.

This approach allows routes to be computed for some policies but certainly not all. After a border gateway makes a route choice, the other routes are not available to border gateways farther from the destination. For example, assume the topology shown in Figure 12.20.

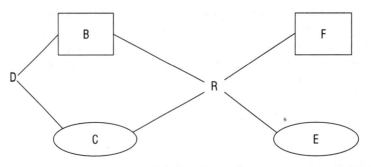

Figure 12.20 Policy dictates routes

Suppose that F and B are routing domains that only U.S. citizens are allowed to use; C and E are routing domains that only French citizens are allowed to use. With these rules, when E wants to transmit to D, it must travel route E–C–D. When F wants to transmit to D, it must travel F–B–D. However, R will make a choice as to its route to D. If it chooses C–D, it will make F unhappy because D will become unreachable to users within F. If it chooses B–D, it will make E unhappy because D will become unreachable to users within E. Source routing allows things to work, but it is unfortunate to require users within E or F to know that source routing is needed and to know a set of source routes that might work. (There could be multiple legal paths, but not all of them may be functional at any moment because links or routers might be down.)

12.8.8 Service-class-specific Policy

Suppose that a link had a small number of independent characteristics—for example, whether the link crossed national boundaries, whether it was commercial or military. In that case, each router could advertise the characteristics of each of its links as a set of flags, one for each characteristic.

A packet would contain a list of characteristics that all the links in the path must meet. If link state routing is used, a route can be computed when a new set of characteristics is seen. A route meeting characteristics i, j, and k can be computed by rejecting all the links that don't have the i, j, and k flags set. If a router has sufficient processing power, it can compute a route every time it forwards a packet. More realistically, it is improbable that a very large number of different combinations of characteristics would be requested during any particular time interval, so a router could compute for a few combinations known to be popular and then compute and cache for others as seen. The overhead to support this sort of service class is not odious because it involves only a bit vector of perhaps 30 flags, for each link in the net, and cached routes for the combinations that are actually requested.

This type of service class is clean and general, but it assumes that the characteristics can be reasonably well defined. This is not the approach being taken in any of the emerging routing standards.

12.9 Partition Repair: Level 1 Subnetwork Partition

Suppose that some links break in a level 1 subnetwork, thereby partitioning the subnetwork into two or more pieces. If one of the pieces has no other connections, it becomes a separate network. Nodes within that piece can talk only to nodes within that piece. Nothing, short of repairing the links connecting that piece with the rest of the network, will restore communication between that piece and the rest of the network.

However, if each partition contains a level 2 router and if the level 2 router has level 2 links to the rest of the network, there can be a path from one partition to the other partition through the level 2 network.

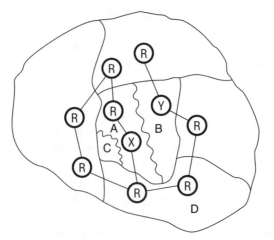

Figure 12.21 Partitioned level 1 subnetwork

A subnetwork partition presents several problems (see Figure 12.21).

1. A cannot talk to B even though there is a physical path, because A's address and B's address look to level 1 routers as if they reside in the level 1 subnetwork. The level 1 routers will attempt to deliver the packet via level 1 routing, fail, and declare the destination unreachable.

2. C cannot talk to anyone. No routing protocol can solve this because there is no physical path out of C's partition.

3. D may or may not be able to communicate with B. Packets for B from D might get routed by the level 2 network toward B's partition, or they might get routed toward A's partition.

This partition problem is a serious annoyance because it can create strange symptoms, in which some nodes can communicate and others cannot. Also, depending on the topology of a given level 1 subnetwork, a single failure can partition the subnetwork, and partitions can happen frequently.

The best solution known for dealing with subnetwork partitions is documented in IS-IS.

1. Level 2 routers residing in level 1 subnetwork FOO identify the partition of FOO in which they are located (this may be all of FOO if FOO is not partitioned). They accomplish this by finding the level 2 router, X, having the lowest ID within the partition. This distinguishes one partition from another because X cannot reside in multiple partitions of FOO or else FOO would not be partitioned. X is known as the "partition-designated level 2 router." The level 2 router that is elected partition-designated level 2 router is responsible for noticing and repairing partitions.

2. Level 2 routers report the name of the partition in which they reside in their level 2 link state packets. For example, a level 2 router in FOO will report in its level 2 LSP that it resides in FOO, partition X.

3. Level 2 router X checks to make sure that all level 2 routers reporting that they reside in FOO also report X as the partition name.

4. If some level 2 router reports attachment to FOO, partition Y, then X concludes that FOO is partitioned.

5. Level 2 router X and level 2 router Y have the task of repairing the partition. X and Y establish communication over the level 2 path connecting them (there must be a level 2 path connecting them because the level 2 LSPs listing X reach the routers that know about Y and vice versa). X and Y treat the level 2 path as a virtual level 1 link.

6. X and Y report, in their level 1 LSPs, that they have a level 1 link to each other. They report this as a virtual link, but it is treated by level 1 routing as an ordinary link. LSPs are exchanged over the link, and data traffic is forwarded over the link.

7. X and Y use the level 2 path as a level 1 link. This is accomplished by encapsulating every packet that must be sent over the link in an extra network layer header, with the source and destination network layer addresses being X and Y (or vice versa).

At this point, FOO is no longer partitioned (see Figure 12.22). When A transmits a packet for B, the packet travels, via ordinary level 1 routing, to B. The only unusual thing is that one of the links used in the path is the virtual link between X and Y.

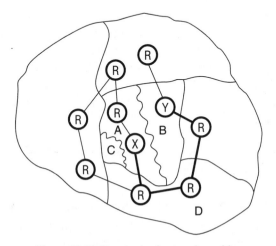

Figure 12.22 Repaired subnetwork partition

When choosing the partition-designated level 2 router, it is important that level 2 routers within FOO consider only level 2 routers reachable via nonvirtual links. Otherwise, as soon as X and Y establish communication, either X or Y would be elected partition-designated level 2 router. They would both conclude that FOO was no longer partitioned, whereupon they would bring down the virtual link (thereby reestablishing the partition).

Homework

1. With standard LSP distribution, each LSP gets transmitted over each link no more than twice. An alternative is to have routers run the bridge spanning tree algorithm and transmit LSPs over the resulting spanning tree. What are the pros and cons of such an LSP distribution scheme? Consider such factors as how quickly an LSP reaches all routers and how many packet transmissions it takes for the LSP to reach all routers.

   Would using the bridge spanning tree violate the principle that the protocol for distributing routing information must not rely on the routing information?

2. Under what circumstances is it possible for router A to forward packets for router B through router C even though routers A and B are neighbors?

3. People generally understand that distance vector protocols behave badly on "bad news"—that is, when a link goes down. However, they can behave badly on good news, too! What is the worst-case number of distance vector messages that might be generated as a result of a single node's coming up in a network? Remember, you can postulate any topology, any assignment of link costs, and any timing of message generation and delivery.

4. Assume a distance vector protocol in which distance vectors are reported every minute (not when they change) and that information is thrown away if it is not refreshed within 3 minutes. Also assume that an unreachable destination is simply not reported, as opposed to reported with a distance of infinity. In the network shown in Figure 12.23, how long will it be from the time D dies to the time R6 knows that D is unreachable if split horizon is used? How about if split horizon is not used?

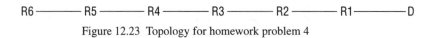

Figure 12.23 Topology for homework problem 4

5. Suppose that A and B are neighbors, but A thinks the cost of the link to B is x, whereas B thinks the cost of the link to A is y. Will this cause any problems with distance vector routing? How about with link state routing?

6. Give a topology in which a single link can change many routes. Give a topology in which there is a link that can go down without disrupting any routes.

7. Consider the following variant of split horizon. In traditional split horizon distance vector routing, R tells neighbor N that R considers D unreachable (or R does not report anything about D to N) if N is the neighbor R uses when forwarding packets to D. Modify the rule so that R informs all neighbors N for which N's distance to D is less than R's that D is unreachable. Will this modification work? How does this compare with traditional split horizon?

   Suppose the rule is modified so that R informs all neighbors N for which N's distance to D is less than *or equal to* R's that D is unreachable. Will this modification work? How does this compare with traditional split horizon and the modification in the first half of this problem?

8. In link state routing, the designated router names the LAN using its ID as part of the name. Why is the DR's ID part of the LAN ID?

9. Consider two mechanisms for reacting to congestion. In the first mechanism, link costs vary according to congestion. In the second mechanism, link costs remain constant, but additional congestion information is passed around in the routing algorithm to help a router choose between equal cost paths. Assuming that no links go up or down and that the only changes are due to congestion, why can the first mechanism cause transient loops, whereas the second mechanism does not?

10. Suppose you wanted to implement a link state distribution scheme with no periodic retransmission of LSPs (LSPs only sent when the information in them changes). Would you still need an age field? How could you garbage-collect LSPs issued by dead routers?

Chapter 13
Fast Packet Forwarding

There is more to life than increasing its speed.
—**Mahatma Gandhi**[1]

In this chapter I talk about various tricks for speeding up packet forwarding. First I explain schemes that add extra headers. Then I talk about two families of address lookup algorithms—Trie and binary search—together with some variants.

13.1 Using an Additional Header

In this section I describe schemes devised to allow routers to make a forwarding decision based on a small header with small addresses rather than IP addresses, on the assumption that it would be prohibitively expensive to build a really fast router that made forwarding decisions based on the regular IP header. The disadvantage of these schemes is that they require adding more information onto the header. IP would probably be a better protocol with this information, but schemes such as the ones described in Sections 13.3 and 13.4 make these schemes less necessary, at least for the purpose of fast packet forwarding.

All the schemes are conceptually similar. One scheme, known as *threaded indices*, was invented by Chandranmenon and Varghese.[2] Another is specific to IP and ATM. One team that developed this sort of approach was Newman, Minshall, and Huston.[3] Another was Parulkar, Schmidt, and Turner.[4] Within the IETF, this sort of scheme, known first as *tag switching*, is now called MPLS (multiprotocol label switching). Originally, these

---

[1] Quote 29 from Byrne, *1911 Best Things,* 11.
[2] G. Chandranmenon, and G. Varghese, "Trading Packet Headers for Packet Processing," *IEEE/ACM Transactions on Networking*, April 1996.
[3] P. Newman, G. Minshall, and L. Huston, "IP Switching and Gigabit Routers," *IEEE Communications*, January 1997.
[4] G. Parulkar, D. Schmidt, and J. Turner, "IP/ATM: A Strategy for Integrating IP with ATM," Sigcomm '95.

schemes were designed to make it possible to build fast routers, but then, using techniques such as those described in Sections 13.3 and 13.4, people built routers fast enough on native IP packets. So now MPLS is thought to be mostly a technique for classifying the type of packet for quality of service or for assigning routes for *traffic engineering* (the ability to control what the routes are rather than have routing simply compute whatever it wants).

These schemes involve something that looks like having an ATM header on your IP packet. But with ATM, you must set up a route first before you can send data. With these techniques, suppose that router R2 receives a packet from R1 for destination D. Without the extra header, or with a header with a label of 0, R2 makes a *slow path* forwarding decision based on the IP header. R2 may, if it wants, tell R1 what to put into the packet to save R2 time in the future. There are two strategies for this.

- Tell your neighbors your desired label as part of the routing protocol. For example, in a distance vector protocol, announce not only your distance to a destination but also the label you'd like someone forwarding to you to use for that destination.

- Do it after receiving data that needs to go through the slow path. As a result of this, send a message to the node that sent you the packet telling it a label to use in the future.

The second scheme has more latency for the first packet because it must go through the slow path until the downstream router can be notified of the label, but it allows a smaller label space because only labels for currently active flows through the router need to be assigned.

In the IP/ATM schemes, the label is an ATM VCI. In the threaded indexing scheme, the label is whatever would be convenient for R2. After the labels are set up, the packet forwarding looks just like ATM, but with large packets. But packets can still be routed even if labels aren't set up at all, or set up only on parts of the path, because the labels are an optimization.

The protocols being developed by the MPLS working group are currently subject to change. There are no RFCs, and only a lot of Internet drafts. But the group seems to be converging on basically reinventing ATM. There would be a backbone that routes based on "labels" rather than IP headers. The ingress router would assign the packet to a "forwarding equivalence class" (in other words, a VC) and label it appropriately. Within the backbone, routing would be based totally on the label. You look at the input port and label, and you find it in a table that tells you the proper output port and label.

I think this is a fine way to do things. The main thing I dislike about ATM is the small cell size. MPLS takes all the rest of the ideas of ATM but uses IP-sized packets.

13.2 Address Prefix Matching

Address matching is the most critical part of making a high-performance router because a router's performance is based on how quickly it can forward a packet. To forward a packet, a router must extract the destination address from the packet and find the matching forwarding database entry.

In layer 2 (bridge) forwarding and in CLNP and DECnet level 1 routing, routing is based on exact matches. For example, in CLNP, the **ID** field is the field on which level 1 routers make their routing decisions. A CLNP level 1 router must have an entry in the forwarding database exactly matching the ID portion of the destination address in the packet. In IP, finding the proper entry in the ARP cache involves essentially the same problem. There are hashing algorithms to find exact matches.

In contrast, in IP, IPX, and routing on the area field of CLNP, there might be several forwarding database entries that match a particular destination address, and it is the most specific or longest address that must be found.

For example, in IP, each entry in the forwarding database corresponds to a 32-bit address and a 32-bit mask. The destination address field in a packet contains a 32-bit value. The router must find the forwarding database entry that has the mask with the most 1's that matches that destination address. All the following examples match destination address 11001111 01011100 00000000 10000111:

1. Value: 11001111 01011100 00000000 10000111
    Mask: 11111111 11111111 11111111 11111111

2. Value: 11001111 01011100 00000000 00000000
    Mask: 11111111 11111111 00000000 00000000

3. Value: 11001111 01011100 00000000 00000000
    Mask: 11111111 11111111 11100000 00000000

In the preceding examples, it is the first item that should match the destination address because the mask is the most specific. However, as IP was originally specified, there can be ambiguities if noncontiguous subnet masks are used. For example, suppose the following two entries were in the forwarding database:

1. Value: 11001111 01011100 00000000 00000000
    Mask: 11111111 11111111 11111110 00000000

2. Value: 11001111 01011100 00000000 00000111
    Mask: 11111111 11111111 00000000 01111111

Both masks have the same number of 1's, and both match the destination address. No standard ever specified which entry, in this case, should be considered a match. If one router chose the first entry and another chose the second, a routing loop could result.

As discussed in Chapter 6, noncontiguous subnet masks are not particularly useful. They are extremely confusing, and they make it difficult to build efficient routers. If subnet masks are contiguous (that is, if they have the property that no 1 bit appears to the right of any 0 bit), then the longest-matching-address-prefix algorithms (described in Sections 13.3 and 13.4) can be used to efficiently find the forwarding database entry for a particular destination.

Because nobody believes in noncontiguous masks, IPv4, IPv6, IPX, and CLNP all route based on the longest matching address prefix. If noncontiguous subnet masks are allowed in IP, it is possible in the general case that no efficient algorithm exists. Trying every mask in the forwarding database might be the best algorithm.

In address-prefix-matching algorithms, the forwarding database consists of a *dictionary* of address prefixes. The problem is to find the longest initial substring of the destination address that is included in the forwarding database.

13.3 Longest Prefix Match with Trie

The Trie algorithm is described by Knuth.[5] The addresses in the forwarding database are put into a tree data structure. Each vertex represents a prefix. The root consists of the zero-length prefix (which matches any address). There are two pointers from each vertex: a "1" and a "0." If no string in the dictionary contains the vertex's string plus the extra bit value, that pointer either is missing or points to a vertex indicating failure.

Each vertex also has a flag associated with it, which indicates whether that string, terminated there, is in the dictionary. In Figure 13.1 the flag is indicated with an asterisk.

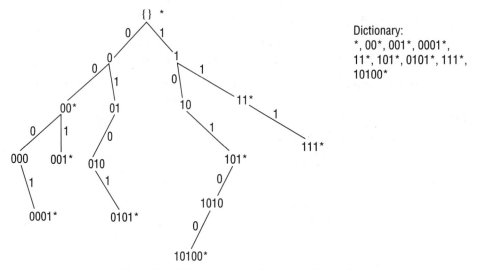

Dictionary:
, 00, 001*, 0001*,
11*, 101*, 0101*, 111*,
10100*

Figure 13.1 Trie structure for longest prefix match

---

[5] Donald E. Knuth, *Sorting and Searching*, vol. 3 of *The Art of Computer Programming* (Reading, Mass.: Addison-Wesley, 1973), 481–500.

Assume that we have the destination address 10101101. We'd use the Trie structure in Figure 13.1 by starting at the top and traversing the path indicated by the destination address, remembering the last time we saw a flag (an asterisk). Starting at the top, the zero-length prefix has a flag. The first bit of 10101101 is 1, so we go to the right and get to the node with the name "1." No asterisk, so { } is still the longest prefix matched so far. The second bit of 10101101 is 0, so we go to the left, to the node 10, and still no asterisk. The third bit is 1, so we go to the right to node 101*. Aha! An asterisk. So 101 is the longest prefix matched so far. We continue. The next bit is 0, and we get to node 1010. The next bit is 1. But there's no pointer marked 1 out of node 1010, so at this point we know that the longest prefix matching 10101101 is 101.

Maintaining the data structure is not difficult. To add an entry, say 1011, follow the pointers to where 1011 would be in the tree. If no pointers exist for that string, they should be added. If the vertex for the string already exists—say, in adding the prefix 01—the vertex merely needs to be marked as being in the dictionary, that is, an asterisk must be added. To delete an entry that has children, the vertex associated with the string is simply unmarked as a legal termination point (the asterisk is removed). To delete an entry that has no children, the vertex and the pointer pointing to it are deleted, and the parent vertex is examined. If it has other children or is marked as a legal termination point, it is left alone. Otherwise (it is not a legal termination point and there are no remaining children), that vertex, too, is deleted, and so on up the tree until a vertex that has other children or is marked as a termination point is found.

This algorithm requires lookup time proportional to the average length of the strings in the dictionary, regardless of how many entries the dictionary contains.

In the case of CLNP, prefix lengths are specified in terms of numbers of nibbles (4-bit chunks), so instead of two pointers from each node, there might be 16. And the search would be faster because 4 bits at a time would be searched.

The following sections describe improvements to Trie.

13.3.1 Collapsing a Long Nonbranching Path

If there is a path in the Trie structure that does not branch and has no asterisk, then you can collapse it so that the entire substring can be found in one probe. For example, in Figure 13.2, you can remove the nodes 01 and 010 by noting that in order to take the "1" branch out of node 0, you must match the three subsequent bits 101.

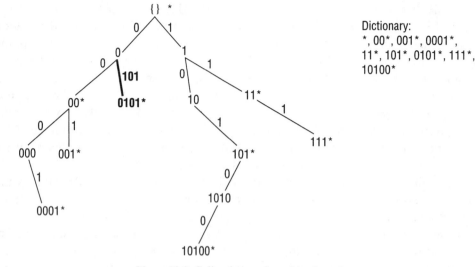

Figure 13.2 Collapsing nonbranching branches

13.3.2 Trading Memory for Search Time

Even though IP prefixes can be any number of bits, Srinivasan and Varghese showed that it is not necessary to search a bit at a time.[6] The idea is simple. Suppose you decide that you want to search 4 bits at a time. You simply expand a prefix that isn't of length 0, 4, 8, 12, 16, 20, 24, 28, or 32 into several prefixes (8 for prefixes 1 more than a multiple of 4, 4 for prefixes 2 more than a multiple of 4, and 2 for prefixes 1 more than a multiple of 4). So, for example, the prefix 10 would expand into 1000, 1001, 1010, and 1011. Any address that matched the prefix 10 would have to match one of {1000, 1001, 1010, or 1011}.

Of course there are subtleties. For example, suppose you have prefixes 1, 10, 100, and 1000. When you expand the prefix "1," you add prefixes 1000, 1001, 1010, and so on. When you expand "10," you get 1000, 1001, and so on. When you expand 100 you get 1000, 1001, and so on. And you already have prefix 1000, which happens, conveniently, to be 4 bits long. The authors call this *prefix capture*. What should you do? Keep all the prefixes? If not, which ones do you discard—the ones padded from smaller prefixes or the ones from larger prefixes? (See homework problem 2.)

Also, the scheme does not require always searching the same number of bits, although at each node you search a fixed number of bits. So, for example, you could at the top level search 4 bits, but then under the node 1101 you could search the next 6 bits and under the node 1110 you could search 2 bits.

---

[6] V. Srinivasan and G. Varghese, "Faster IP Lookups using Controlled Prefix Expansion," ACM Sigmetrics '98, *ACM Transactions on Computer Systems*, March 1999.

If you decided to do this scheme in a straightforward way but use prefix lengths that were, say, multiples of 16 bits, then the 64,000 multiplier for memory would get annoying. Degermark et al.[7] published a clever scheme for data compression for expanded prefixes. It was called Lulea (the university of the inventors of the scheme). It is very difficult to understand and I include it here because the paper is often cited. But it's not necessary to understand this in order to understand the rest of this chapter, so you could skip to Section 13.3.3.

Assume that you want to expand prefixes to lengths that are multiples of 16 bits. You will wind up with 2^{16} child nodes. If you really had all those prefixes, there's no way to save memory. But suppose you really had only a small fraction of the 2^{16} combinations that were "real" prefixes. Most of the nodes would then be the result of expanded smaller prefixes, and you'd be wasting a lot of memory. The Lulea scheme allows you to do data compression in this case.

Imagine that you are searching the next 16 bits after some string X (see Figure 13.3).

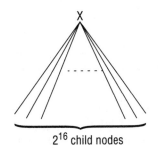

2^{16} child nodes

Figure 13.3 Lulea scheme looking at the 16 bits following X

We're looking at the portion of the address beyond X. For clarity, I'll simply call the prefix X01 "01" and ignore the fact that the prefix actually starts with the string X. So starting with X we have a set of prefixes, and we're going to expand them to 16 bits. The prefix 01 would wind up getting expanded into 2^{14} child nodes, one for every possible combination of the bottom 14 bits (all the child nodes between 0100 0000 0000 0000 and 0111 1111 1111 1111). But it saves space to keep track only of the endpoints of ranges rather than listing all the 2^{14} nodes.

The straightforward way of having 2^{16} child nodes is to have an array 2^{16} wide. To look at the node for the prefix 1101 0100 1000 0001, you'd index into the array by 1101 0100 1000 0001. Each item in the array would have to be fairly large to carry other information you'd like to keep, such as a pointer to the next array representing the children of that node and the number of bits to be searched after that node.

But Lulea wants to keep really minimal storage. Let's call the array that has one element for each of the 2^{16} child nodes the *child-array*. Assume for now that there's only a

[7] M. Degermark, A. Brodnik, S. Carlsson, and S. Pink, "Small forwarding tables for fast routing lookups," Sigcomm '97.

single bit at each location in the child-array (see Figure 13.4). The rule is that if that child node is the result of a 0-padded prefix or exact match, then that bit is set. Also, if it's the entry immediately following a 1-padded prefix it's set. Otherwise, it's zero. Note that in some cases the entry immediately following a 1-padded prefix might already be set because it is a 1-padded prefix. That would occur, for example, with prefixes 0* and 1* because the value immediately to the right of the end of the 0* range is the left side of the 1* range.

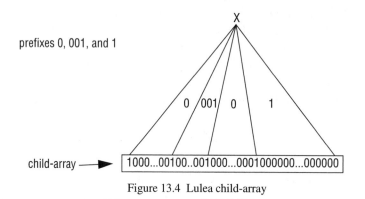

Figure 13.4 Lulea child-array

All the entries with a 0 in the child-array have the same information as the closest entry (on the left) with a 1-bit. There's another array, which I'll call the *info-array*, that contains the real information you want (such as the pointer to the array representing the next generation for the Trie structure, or the forwarding information), but with a single element representing all the nodes in a range (see Figure 13.5). The challenge is to know the proper index into *that* array. For example, assume that the prefixes are 0, 1, and 001. Then the child-array elements at 0000 0000 0000 0000, 1000 0000 0000 0000, and 0010 0000 0000 0000 (representing the small end of a range) will be set. And the child-array element 0100 0000 0000 0000 (which is 1 more than 0011 1111 1111 1111) will be set because it represents the end of the range of addresses covered by 101. There is no bit set for the end of 1* (because it falls off the right end). And there is no bit set for the end of 0* (because it's already set in this case because of the left end of 1*).

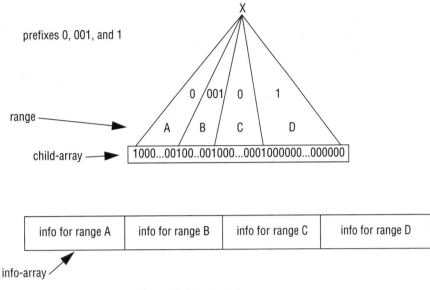

prefixes 0, 001, and 1

Figure 13.5 Lulea info-array

Referring to Figure 13.5, the info-array has only four elements. All the addresses in range A and C match prefix 0. The addresses in range B match 001. And the addresses in range D match 1. The addresses in range A need to access the first element in info-array. The addresses in range B need to access the second element in info-array, and so on.

The straightforward method for knowing which entry in info-array to access is to count the number of 1 bits to your left. But that would be slow. So Lulea takes extra space in the child-array—say, every 64 bits—to store the number of 1 bits to the left. You need to access that number and count the number of 1's to the left of you in your own 64-bit chunk. The total will be your index into info-array.

13.3.3 Binary Search on Prefix Lengths

This idea was invented by Waldvogel, Varghese, Turner, and Plattner.[8] The idea is to do a binary search on prefix lengths. Suppose you don't bother with the prefix expansion in the preceding section. This means that there are 32 possible prefix lengths in your dictionary. First, you do a hash on the first 16 bits of the destination address to see whether it matches any of the prefixes of length 16. If it does, you look for a longer prefix, so (by binary search rules) you search for a prefix of length 24. Not there? Now check against 20, and so forth.

Well, this doesn't quite work. Consider the prefix 0011 1011 0000 1111 101. That's a length of 19. Suppose we have an IP address that matches that prefix. When we check

[8] M. Waldvogel, G. Varghese, J. Turner, and B. Plattner, "Scalable High Speed IP Routing Lookups," Sigcomm '97.

against the prefixes of length 16, we must make sure that we know we must search for longer prefixes. If we did the most straightforward thing and if the prefix 0011 1011 0000 1111 didn't happen to be in the dictionary, we'd think we had failed! So, we must be a little more clever.

What needs to happen is that for all prefixes larger than 16, we must put a *marker* into the prefixes of length 16. The marker indicates there is a longer prefix that begins with the found 16-bit prefix. In this case, we'd put 0011 1011 0000 1111&, where "&" indicates that a longer prefix exists. And just in case the destination address matches those 16 bits but not the actual prefix (say, if the address were 0011 1011 0000 1111 0101 1100 0000 1110), we also must keep the *longest prefix matched so far*. So for each prefix in the table of prefixes of length 16, we keep

- The 16-bit value

- The "&" flag that indicates whether there's actually a longer prefix

- The size of the longest prefix so far (if these 16 bits match)

For example, if 0011 1011 is in the database but there is no longer prefix until the 19-bit prefix 0011 1011 0000 1111 101, then the entry in the prefixes of length 16 would contain

- 0011 1011 0000 1111 (the 16-bit prefix)

- & (indicating a longer prefix exists)

- The value 8, indicating that if searching for a longer prefix fails, the longest match will be the first 8 bits of 0011 1011 0000 1111, or 0011 1011

For example, if the prefix 0011 1011 0000 1111 exists and a longer one also exists starting with the same 16 bits, then there would be an entry in the table of prefixes of length 16 that would contain

- 0011 1011 0000 1111 (the 16-bit prefix)

- & (indicating a longer prefix exists)

- The value 16, indicating that if searching for a longer prefix fails, the longest match will be 0011 1011 0000 1111

I think that's really cool! There are many other subtleties, such as making a good hash at each stage of the search. If the hash isn't good, it might take several probes at each stage to find the matching prefix.

An approach to finding a good hash is to calculate a custom-made hash for each prefix length, given the prefixes that happen to be in the database. For example, there might be a hash algorithm that can take a seed value. You try various seed values until you find one that never has more than, say, three items that collide. Then you triple the size of your fetch so that you retrieve all three values and never require more than one probe.

Another subtlety is that you don't need to put in all shorter prefixes for a prefix. You need only put in prefixes in the spots that binary search would search. For example, in the case of a 19-bit prefix, you put in a marker for that prefix only at length 16. Next, you'd probe 24 (and fail, so you must search for a shorter prefix). Then you'd probe 20 (and fail, so you must search for a shorter prefix). Then you'd probe 18 (and find another marker, so you must search for a longer prefix). Then you'd find it at 19. If the prefix were of length, say, 30, you'd need markers at 16, 24, and 28. (See homework problem 5.)

13.3.4 Exploiting Parallelism with Special Hardware

This approach to speeding up prefix matching is mine, from work done around 1997. It does not require additional memory, as do the schemes in Sections 13.3.2 and 13.3.3. However, it requires a special-purpose lookup engine consisting of k *registers*. Each stage of the lookup compares a portion of the destination address against all k registers simultaneously, with the "winner" being the register with the longest match. The winning register points to a data structure that will hold the bit patterns that the registers will compare at the next stage.

We must look at all the prefixes in the dictionary to prepare the data structure for use by the lookup engine. This process does not need to be fast because it only prepares for fast lookup and is not invoked when an actual packet is forwarded. The second step involves the actual lookup procedure.

13.3.4.1 Preparing the Data Structure for the Lookup Engine

The special-purpose hardware has k registers. For concreteness, let's use the value $k = 13$. After the hardware is built, k is fixed. The larger k is, the faster the lookup will be and the more expensive the special-purpose hardware.

The goal is to divide all the prefixes in the dictionary into k hash buckets. Instead of matching to a fixed number of bits in the prefix, we match to the maximal number of bits possible with the particular prefixes in the forwarding database. Start by naming three of the registers 0, 1, and *. Divide the items in the dictionary into those three hash buckets. The ones that start with 0 go into the bucket called "0." The ones that start with 1 go into the bucket called "1." The zero-length prefix (if it exists in the dictionary) goes into the bucket called "*."

Next, get rid of any buckets that have no prefixes assigned. For example, if none of the prefixes in the dictionary starts with 1, get rid of the bucket called 1.

Next, expand the name of the prefix to be as long as possible. If all the prefixes in a particular bucket start with the same string, expand the name of that bucket to be that common prefix. For example, if all the prefixes in the bucket labeled 0 actually start with 0010 1, rename that bucket 0010 1 (see Figure 13.6). (Note that the spaces are there only for readability; 0010 1 is actually 00101.)

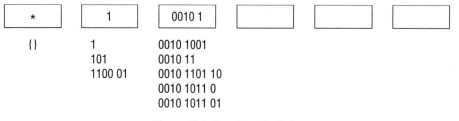

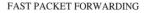

Figure 13.6 Creating *k* buckets

If fewer than *k* hash buckets are being used at this point, find the hash bucket with the largest number of prefixes and divide that. For example, if the bucket named 0010 1 has the most prefixes, divide it into three hash buckets: 0010 10, 0010 11, and 0010 1* (see Figure 13.7). Take the prefixes formerly assigned to the bucket 0010 1 and put them into the appropriate bucket 0010 10, 0010 11, or 0010 1* depending on whether the next bit in the prefix is 0 or 1 or the prefix ends after 0010 1.

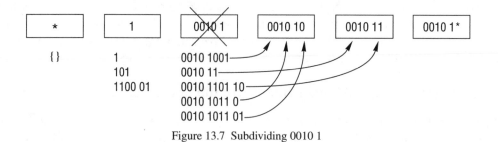

Figure 13.7 Subdividing 0010 1

Then repeat the steps of getting rid of empty buckets, expanding the names of buckets, and then, if fewer than *k* buckets are still in use, divide the bucket that has the most entries.

To divide a bucket in this way requires two additional buckets. But suppose there's only one extra bucket, and every bucket named X contains prefixes X0, X1, and X*. X can be divided by using only buckets X0 and X*. The prefixes starting with X0 will benefit from an extra bit searched during that iteration, but the prefixes starting with X1 can be searched only through the string X. At the next iteration (if X* wins), there will need to be a bucket for *, and all the other bucket names will begin with "1."

The data structure for the first search lookup consists of the values to be loaded into the *k* registers. The data structure has *k* entries that contain

- The number of bits in the name of the hash bucket

- The name of the hash bucket (the set of bits to compare against the destination address)

- LNGST, which equals the number of bits in the longest matching prefix so far

- A pointer to the data structure for the next stage of lookup if this register wins, where "wins" means it is the longest match to the destination address

We keep LNGST in case the lookup ultimately fails. For example, if the database contains prefixes 01 and 0111 1111 1111 111 (along with lots of others, of course) and if the destination address is 0111 1111 1111 1101 1010, it is possible for the first iteration to search up to 0111. At that point LNGST would return 2 bits, because 01 is a prefix in the dictionary and we assume that 011 and 0111 are not in the dictionary. At the next stage, a further 6 bits might be matched, with a register containing 1111 11. Still, LNGST would return 2 because there are still no matching prefixes longer than 01. At the next iteration all registers might fail, in which case LNGST will equal 2, and the answer is the prefix consisting of the first 2 bits of the destination address.

The data structure for the next search lookup is prepared exactly like the previous one, but it looks at the value of the prefixes starting where the preceding stage left off. For example, if the register with value 0010 110 wins and the destination address is 0010 1101 1110 10..., then the lookup will be based on starting from the eighth bit in the destination address. At the next stage, even though all the prefixes in the dictionary that have not yet been eliminated as matches for the destination start with 0010 1, the names of the buckets will omit the 0010 110 and will be named based on the bits following 0010 110.

This procedure winds up examining a maximal number of bits rather than being constrained to look at a fixed number of bits at each lookup stage. In addition, it allows k comparisons in parallel, where each of the comparisons looks at the appropriate number of bits.

The worst-case performance of this algorithm occurs when each time a bucket with n prefixes is split, it results in two buckets, each with one prefix, and the remaining bucket with $n - 2$ prefixes. However, that bucket will have a name of length at least $k/2$. With straightforward Trie with k comparisons, you could look at $\log_2 k$ bits. So this allows exponentially greater numbers of bits to be compared at each iteration, even in the pathological worst case: the prefixes look like *, 0, 1*, 10, 11*, 110, 111*, 1110, 1111*, 11110, ..., where in each case there is only a single prefix in any of the buckets that end in a 0 (or *).

If you are troubled by the pathological case, we can modify the program to improve the worst-case performance. If, for example, the majority of the prefixes wind up in the bucket 11110 and we want to go deeper into the address on that lookup for the vast majority of prefixes that begin 1111 0, then all the prefixes in *, 0, 1*, 10, 11*, 110, 111*, 1110, 1111* can be compressed into the single bucket *, which will match all destination addresses that start with anything other than 1111 0. Then 1111 0 can be divided again to make use of the remaining $k - 1$ registers. It means that for prefixes that start with anything other than 1111 0, that stage of the lookup will make no progress because the address lookup will not search past where it searched in the preceding stage. However, because there are so few prefixes this is not a problem. For example, if there are fewer than k prefixes in the buckets that got combined into *, the next search is guaranteed to find the answer for those prefixes.

13.3.4.2 Doing a Lookup

The first stage of an address lookup (see Figure 13.8) consists of loading the k registers from the initial location, which contains k items. Each item consists of the number of bits to compare against, the value of the bits to compare against, and a pointer to the data structure to be loaded if this is the winning register.

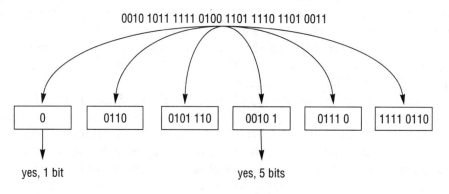

Figure 13.8 Doing a lookup

The destination address is compared against all registers in parallel. The winning register is the one that contains the largest number of bits that match the destination address. The output is a pointer to the data to be loaded into the registers for the next iteration of the lookup, or an indication that this is the end of the search. If the search is not over, the registers are loaded from the indicated location, and the next step of the search starts after the preceding search leaves off. For example, if the preceding step started at bit 11 and the winning register matched 8 bits, the next stage would start comparing at bit 19 in the destination address.

If the search is over—meaning that there is no pointer to a next iteration—the answer is indicated by LNGST, which gives the number of bits in the destination address that form the longest matching prefix.

13.3.4.3 Optimizations

Ideally, the data structure would be on the chip so that the data would not need to be loaded across a potentially small bandwidth pipe to the k registers. If the information must be transmitted at each stage of the lookup, ironically the search time can increase with larger k because the time to transfer the data onto the chip is proportional to k, assuming a serial interface for transferring the data. If the transfer time is sufficiently large, that will dominate the search time rather than the number of probes. So it is a good idea to minimize the amount of information that must be transferred at each stage of the lookup in the case that the memory that holds the database is off the chip. If the search chip contains storage for the data structure, these optimizations are not necessary.

If the register loader can be intelligent, it can load the needed number of bits for each register. Otherwise, the bit string must be padded to be a constant length. If you want to avoid loading the chip with the pointer to data to be loaded for the next stage of the search, you can have the output of the comparison be the register number, with some off-chip location using that output as an index into a table of pointers.

We can save money on the registers, and on data transfer time, by not building each register with the ability to store or compare a full-length address into the prefix. For example, we could limit the number of bits to be searched each time to one-fourth the size of an address. This might result in an address lookup step in which the number of prefixes has not been reduced, but the number of bits matched in the address after that iteration will be one-fourth the size of the address, and that is still very good compared with any of the existing Trie-based schemes.

13.4 Binary Search

Ordinary binary search when you're doing longest prefix matching does not quite work. However, with a few enhancements, a binary search scheme can work. This scheme was originally suggested by Butler Lampson. The idea is to think of a prefix 01* as a *range* of values from 01000000000000000 to 011111111111111111. If all the prefixes are padded—once with 0's and once with 1's—and then sorted, a binary search will determine into which range the destination address belongs. There are subtleties. The prefix 10 padded with 0's looks just like the prefix 1000 padded with 0's, and the prefix 1101 padded with 1's looks just like the prefix 110 padded with 1's.

Start by padding each of the prefixes in the dictionary to a length equal to 1 bit greater than the length of an address. For each padded prefix, note the size the prefix was before it was padded. The reason for this padding is to handle the case of a prefix that is equal to the size of an address, so that it, too, will appear as two padded prefixes and there does not need to be a special case to handle it.

13.4.1 Sort the Prefixes

Next, sort the padded prefixes. Note that both of the padded prefixes 101 and 1010 result in a padded prefix equal to 1010 0000.... When you're sorting padded prefixes that end in 0, sort prefixes in which the unpadded prefix is a smaller number of bits as being smaller. (Note: For clarity I write the pad in a smaller type size and also put spaces after every 4 bits when the number is longer than five digits, again for readability.) For example, prefix 1010 0000 would be considered smaller than 1010 0000. With padded prefixes that end in 1, do the opposite, so that prefix 1011 1111 would be considered larger than 1011 1111. Do this even though numerically, of course, 1010 0000 is equal to 1010 0000.

13.4.2 Add Prefix Length to 1-padded Prefixes

The padded prefixes are equivalent to the beginning address (the 0-padded address) and ending address (the 1-padded address) of address ranges. The idea is to find the address range in which the destination address resides. We must indicate, when the destination address fits to the right of a 1-padded prefix, how many bits of the prefix should be matched. For example, Figure 13.9 shows the ranges if the prefixes in the database are {}, 1, 10, 100, 101, 1110.

```
                        00000-11111
_____
                        10000-11111
       _____
         10000-10111                   11100-11101
       _____      _____
         10000-10011    10100-10111
       _____    _____
```

Figure 13.9 Address ranges for binary search

This can be thought of as nested parentheses, as shown in Figure 13.10.

```
00000  10000  10000  10000  10011  10100  10111  10111  11100  11101  11111  11111
 (      (      (      (      )      (      )      )      (      )      )      )
```

Figure 13.10 Address ranges as nested parentheses

If the destination address we search for fits to the right of a left parenthesis, the prefix represented by the left parenthesis is the longest match. If, however, it fits to the right of a right parenthesis, we must find the matching left parenthesis to indicate the longest match. Consider the destination address 1100. That would fit in the place shown in Figure 13.11.

```
00000  10000  10000  10000  10011  10100  10111  10111  11100  11101  11111  11111
 (      (      (      (      )      (      )      )      (      )      )      )
                                                  ▲
                                                  |
                                                1100
```

Figure 13.11 Fitting 1100 into the ranges

This means that 1100 is outside the range 10000 to 10111. But what would it actually match? The way to discover the matching left parenthesis is to work backward, incrementing for each right parenthesis and decrementing for each left parenthesis until the count reaches −1. That prefix is the one that matches for destinations that fit after the right parenthesis. So, for example, in the preceding example, we'd count as shown in Figure 13.12.

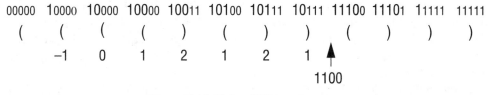

Figure 13.12 Fitting 1100 into the ranges

Because the prefix 1 padded with 0's is the place where we reach −1, that is the prefix that matches any address falling between 10111 and 11100. So the prefix length for 10111 is listed as 1 bit, meaning that addresses falling in the range just to the right of it match the 1-bit prefix "1."

13.4.3 Get Rid of Duplicate Padded Prefixes

Now get rid of duplicate padded prefixes, such as 10000, 10000, and 10000. When the padded prefixes are numerically the same, take the rightmost padded prefix and delete the ones immediately to the left. For example, keep 10000 and delete 10000 and 10000. This ensures that something that fits after 10000 matches the longest prefix of 100 rather than 10 or 1. Note that 10011 will be included in the sorted prefixes, so the destination address cannot fit immediately after 10000 unless it matches 100 because if it starts with 101 it will be to the right of 10011. Similarly, with 1-padded prefixes we keep the rightmost and delete the ones to the left. That is because it is impossible to be greater than 10111 without also being greater than 10111. We keep the duplicates around in order to make the parenthesis counting work out. However, when the parenthesis counting is completed, the duplicates can be removed so that there are fewer padded addresses to search.

13.4.4 *K*-ary Search

The idea of doing *k*-ary search in software was introduced by Lampson, Srinivasan, and Varghese.[9] The idea is to notice that memory accesses are much slower than extra instructions (for example, 50 instructions for one memory access). So if the memory bus allows, say, loading six child pointers simultaneously, then each stage of the branch can

---

[9] B. Lampson, V. Srinivasan, and G. Varghese, "IP Lookups using Multiway and Multicolumn Search," *IEEE Infocom*, 1998.

be a 6-ary tree rather than a binary tree. In CPU it is still necessary to do a binary search among the six selected values, but that time is dwarfed by the savings in memory accesses.

Independently, I developed k-ary search designed for hardware. It is easy to build a special-purpose k-ary search engine similar in principle to the scheme in Section 13.3.4. This was inspired by Ravi Sethi's comment that the worst-case performance for the scheme in Section 13.3.4 occurs when the prefixes get split unequally. With k-ary search, you can ensure equal splits each time. But you are searching twice as many prefixes and taking twice the space as the parallel Trie scheme in Section 13.3.4.

Arrange the condensed padded prefixes for k-ary search by picking the padded prefixes at locations m/k, $2m/k$, ... $(k-1)m/k$ and putting them into a data structure for loading into the registers for the first iteration. Also keep a data structure of $k+1$ entries, each with a pointer to a data structure for the next iteration. The jth entry indicates the prefixes to be compared if the jth register is the largest value still smaller than the destination address (that is, the destination address fits between the value in the jth register and the value in the $j+1$st register). The 0th entry indicates the prefixes to be compared if none of the registers is smaller than the destination address (that is, the destination address lies within the first chunk of $1/k$ prefixes).

The first iteration will narrow down the potential prefix matches to $1/k$ of the original. For each of the $k+1$ ranges where the destination can be, after k comparisons, another data structure is prepared with the prefixes at $1/k$, $2/k$, $3/k$ ... of the prefixes in that range. This is continued until there are $k+1$ or fewer prefixes remaining, in which case the next iteration will find the answer.

13.4.5 Doing a Lookup

Now assume that our program has been written and it looks very similar to the parallel Trie algorithm of Section 13.3.4. The first stage of an address lookup consists of loading the k registers from the initial location, which contains addresses to compare against for the first iteration.

The destination address is compared against all registers in parallel. The winning register is the largest one that is smaller than the destination address. The output is the register number of the winning register, or 0 if the destination lies to the left of the smallest register. The output is used as an index into pointers for the data to be loaded for the next iteration. The final iteration has narrowed the search to the exact prefix, so the final table is a table of matching prefixes, indexed by register numbers.

Homework

1. Continue collapsing Figure 13.2 as much as possible, as recommended in Section 13.3.1.

2. Assume you're doing prefix expansion to multiples of 4 bits as specified in Section 13.3.2. Which prefixes should you keep when prefix capture occurs? For example, assume packets matching 10* should go to neighbor N1, and packets for 100* to neighbor N2, and packets for 1000* to neighbor N3. 1000 will result from expanding 10, and from expanding 100, as well as from the prefix 1000. Which forwarding information should be stored for 1000?

3. Update the structure in Figure 13.1 assuming the following changes to the dictionary. Add prefix 1000. Add prefix 1. Delete prefix 101. Then delete prefix 10100.

4. Consider the IP prefix-matching algorithm of Section 13.3.2. What is the worst-case memory expansion required for searching 4 bits at a time?

5. Consider the IP prefix-matching algorithm of Section 13.3.3. What prefix length would require adding the most marker prefixes at smaller lengths? What prefix length would require adding the fewest marker prefixes?

6. Consider the IP prefix-matching algorithm of Section 13.3.3. What is the worst-case additional memory required?

7. Modify the IP prefix-matching algorithm of Section 13.3.3 by checking only for prefix lengths that actually exist. The basic idea is to include a bitmask with each prefix. This bitmask indicates all longer lengths of prefixes in the database that include that matching prefix as the initial string.

Chapter 14
Specific Routing Protocols

The shortest distance between two points is usually under repair.

—Anonymous

This chapter covers the specifics of several routing protocols. I start the discussion of each protocol by describing some of the concepts you need in order to understand the protocol. Then I show the specific packet formats.

The discussion begins with intradomain protocols. The distance vector intradomain protocols are RIP (IP), RTMP (AppleTalk), RIP (IPX), and DECnet Phases 3 and 4. The link state intradomain protocols are IS-IS (IP, CLNP), NLSP (a version of IS-IS for IPX), OSPF (IP), and PNNI (ATM).

The interdomain protocols are static routing, EGP (the old interdomain IP protocol), and BGP (the current interdomain IP protocol).

14.1 A Brief History of Intradomain Routing Protocols

The first routing protocols used distance vector routing. They included DECnet, the "old" ARPANET routing protocol, and RIP (routing information protocol, RFC 1058). RIP's popularity was due to the fact that it distributed free.

The first link state protocol was the ARPANET "new" routing protocol.[1] The next one was DECnet Phase V's routing algorithm, which I designed around 1985. It was

---

[1] J. McQuillan, I. Richer, and E. Rosen, "The New Routing Algorithm for the ARPANET," *IEEE Transactions on Communications*, May 1980.

adopted by ISO around 1988 and named IS-IS.[2] The contributions in IS-IS include the notion of Designated Routers to make efficient use of LANs[3] (see Section 12.7.1), database overload protection, and self-stabilizing and more efficient link state distribution. The latter was originally done in 1983,[4] but I improved it further for IS-IS (see Section 12.2.3.4), and the result was adopted by all the modern link state protocols.

The IETF wanted a similar protocol for IP and set out to design a link state protocol for IP to be called OSPF (for "open shortest path first," where the phrase "shortest path first" is a synonym for link state). The most recent RFC for OSPF is RFC 2328. It adopted a lot of the ideas from IS-IS but did some things a little differently, which I talk about later in this chapter. Ross Callon[5] pointed out that IS-IS, already implemented and quite stable (in fact it hasn't changed significantly in 10 years), could be easily extended to carry IP addresses as well as any other layer 3 addresses that the network might need to support (such as IPX). Using a single routing protocol for multiple layer 3 protocols is known as *integrated routing*, and IS-IS for IP is in general referred to as "integrated IS-IS" even if the only protocol it is routing is IP. Extending IS-IS for IP was much simpler and cheaper than designing a "new" protocol. Getting IETF to accept a protocol that had been adopted by ISO (even though ISO didn't design it) was a hard sell, so the IAB declared OSPF the winner.

I assumed this meant the death of IS-IS, but it took years to debug the design of OSPF and deploy it. So *Internet service providers (ISPs)* wound up for the most part deploying IS-IS, whereas customers lived with RIP until OSPF was ready, not even aware that IS-IS was a viable alternative. In general, most current customer sites run OSPF (or RIP), and most ISPs run IS-IS. At this point, these protocols are very similar. Routing vendors wind up having to implement both because there is no incentive, if someone has deployed one, to switch. If vendors want to sell to a customer that has deployed OSPF, their box must support OSPF. If they want to sell to a customer that has deployed IS-IS, their box must support IS-IS.

Indeed the rivalry between the protocols increased the quality of both. Although IS-IS hasn't changed significantly in 10 years, recently (1998) the IS-IS working group was revived at IETF. It will make a few changes, such as increasing the size of the metric field, allowing arbitrary levels of hierarchy, using cryptographic authentication, and allowing level 2 information to be sent into level 1 for optimal routing.

---

[2] The name IS-IS comes from "intermediate system to intermediate system." It is defined in ISO 10589, known (by very few people) as "Intermediate system to Intermediate system Intra-Domain routing information exchange protocol for use in Conjunction with the Protocol for providing the Connectionless-mode Network Service." That's why people just call it IS-IS.

[3] Radia Perlman, "Incorporation of Multiaccess Links into a Routing Protocol," Eighth Data Communications Symposium, 1983.

[4] Radia Perlman, "Fault-Tolerant Broadcast of Routing Information," *Computer Networks*, 1983.

[5] Ross Callon, "Use of OSI IS-IS for Routing in TCP/IP and Dual Environments," RFC 1195, December 1990.

14.2 RIP

RIP is a very simple distance-vector-based routing protocol. The specification of version 1 (RFC 1058) was written after the protocol was widely deployed in various implementations. Although the implementations differ in subtle details, distance vector routing is so simple and robust that compatibility between RIP implementations is not a significant problem. Version 2 (RFC 2453) added subnet masks.

A distance vector protocol has each router transmit (destination address, cost) pairs to that router's neighbors (see Figure 14.1). In RIP there are two types of packets: request and response.

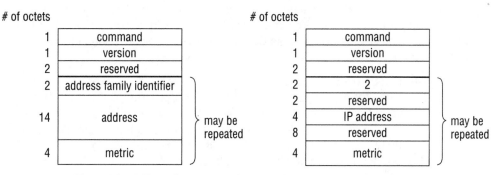

Figure 14.1 RIP version 1 packet format (left) and as used with IP (right)

The portion of the packet starting from **address family identifier** and ending with **metric** can appear as many as 25 times in one packet. This means that as many as 25 destinations can be reported in a single packet.

Command distinguishes *requests* (which equal 1) from *responses* (which equal 2). A request might be transmitted by a router that has only recently come up or by a router that has timed out information about a particular destination. A request asks for information about either all destinations or only some specific destinations. If the request does not specify any destinations, it implies that the requester is asking for information about all destinations. Responses are the messages that actually contain (destination address, cost) pairs. They are sent for one of three reasons.

1. Periodically. If a distance for a particular destination has not been reported by a particular neighbor for some time, the information is discarded. Thus, each destination must be reported to each neighbor periodically. The period given in the RIP spec is once every 30 seconds.

2. In response to a query.

3. Optionally, when information changes. If the cost to destination FOO as reported to neighbor X has become different from the most recent cost to FOO reported to X, it is a good idea to transmit the updated information to X immediately. However, not all RIP implementations do so.

Version equals 1 or 2 (for RIP version 1 or RIP version 2). Notice the field **address family identifier**, which equals 2 for IP. RIP was the first integrated routing protocol!

An implementation that does not support the address family identifier for a particular destination ignores that destination and processes the remainder of the RIP message. If the address family identifier equals anything other than 2, the 14 octets following the address family identifier are used as defined for that address family. Today, RIP is only used for IP.

In RIP version 1, **IP address** is the 4-octet IP address. There is no provision for passing around a mask. The mask must be inferred based on whether the address is class A, class B, or class C. In the following special cases the inferred mask differs from a class A, B, or C standard mask.

1. RIP can be used with subnets, but the routers must be aware of the subnet mask for a particular network number. For example, if class B network number 168.29.*.* is known by router R to be subnetted, with mask 255.255.252.0, then a destination address with the top 2 octets equal to 168.29 will be assumed to refer to a subnetwork specified by the value of the top 22 bits of the destination address.

2. If bits are set in what the router regards as the "host" portion of the address, then the address is assumed to refer to a host and to have a mask of 255.255.255.255.

    The host portion of the address is the part other than the "network" number, which is inferred based on whether the address is class A, B, or C. In the case of preconfigured knowledge of subnets, the host portion of the address is the part in which the preconfigured subnet mask has 0's.

3. If the address reported in a RIP update is 0.0.0.0, it is considered a *default* destination, with a mask equal to 0.0.0.0. All destination addresses match. If a destination address was not known to be reachable based on all the other reported destinations in RIP, the packet would be routed toward the destination 0.0.0.0.

Terminology note: The IP community refers to a destination reported in a routing message as a *route*. It refers to 0.0.0.0 as the *default route*, and a destination with a mask of 255.255.255.255 is known as a *host route*. I wish the IP community wouldn't do that. People already find names, addresses, and routes sufficiently confusing. Then again, terminology doesn't affect performance, robustness, or anything that really matters.

Notice that 32 bits are allocated for the **metric** field, which has a maximum value of 16 in RIP! The number 16 was chosen because of the counting-to-infinity behavior of distance vector protocols. Given such a small value of maximum path cost, most implementations use a simple hop count as the cost metric because anything else would quickly add up to more than 15. The reason 32 bits are allocated for the field is so that important fields in the message are conveniently aligned on 4-octet boundaries.

As a result of RIP's not having been documented until after several implementations were deployed, there are subtle differences between implementations. For example, some implementations do the split horizon and poison reverse optimizations and others don't.

RIP can take a surprisingly long time to converge. In Figure 14.2, imagine what happens when R1 notices that D is down, and assume the most primitive implementation of RIP (no poison reverse, for example). R1 will stop reporting that it can reach D, but, without poison reverse, it will take R2 180 seconds to time out its path to D through R1. Then R2 will stop reporting its path to D, and R3 will take an additional 180 seconds to notice it can't reach D. Routers n hops away will take 180 seconds $* n$ to realize that D is unreachable and stop reporting their distance to D.

D ———— R1 ———— R2 ———— R3 ———— R4 ———— R5

Figure 14.2 RIP slow convergence

So RIP takes a long time to converge and uses a lot of bandwidth because it retransmits all the routing information every 30 seconds. With any luck, one of these days a different acronym will apply to RIP.

> **Every one to his taste, as the woman said when she kissed her cow.**
> **—Rabelais, *Pantagruel*** [6]

14.2.1 RIP Version 2

RIP version 2 (RFC 2453) adds support for subnet masks, authentication, a *route tag* (perhaps to distinguish destinations learned outside the domain, or for future uses), and the ability for one router to announce routes on behalf of another router. It uses the 10 reserved bytes in a route announcement for a mask (4 bytes), a route tag (2 bytes), and the address of a different router (4 bytes) when the RIP announcement is on behalf of a different router.

Authentication, if it is present, must be the first entry in the RIP message. To identify it as an authentication field rather than a real destination, you use address family identification 0xFFFF. So a RIP version 2 message, including authentication, would look like Figure 14.3.

_____

[6] *The Pocket Book of Quotations* (New York, Pocket Books, 1952), 390.

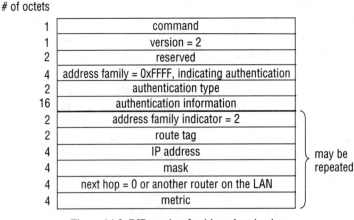

Figure 14.3 RIP version 2 with authentication

14.3 RTMP, IPX-RIP, and DECnet

RTMP and IPX-RIP are both very similar to RIP. In IP-RIP, distances are reported every 30 seconds and timed out after 180 seconds. In RTMP reports occur every 10 seconds and are thrown away after 20 seconds (with clock skew, this can cause disruption if only a single message is lost). In IPX-RIP, reports occur every 60 seconds and information is thrown away after 180 seconds.

RTMP and IPX-RIP mandate split horizon, whereas some implementations of IP-RIP (especially early implementations) don't implement it. IPX-RIP specifies triggered updates and poison reverse.

IPX-RIP and DECnet use the trick described in Section 12.1.1.4 of using two metrics: hops to count to infinity quickly, and a metric with more range to choose the best path.

DECnet is not a periodic distance vector protocol. Instead, information is sent reliably over point-to-point links. When the cost to D changes, only that information (and not the entire distance vector) needs to be transmitted to a neighbor. However, on LANs, we decided not to bother with acknowledgments. Instead, the distance vectors are sent periodically (the default is 10 seconds). However, DECnet's periodic advertisements on the LAN are different from RIP periodic advertisements. In DECnet the distance vector is not timed out. A separate hello message, sent periodically, determines whether the neighbor is up. If you fail to receive hellos, you discard the distance vector from that neighbor. In DECnet the only purpose for the periodic transmission of distance vectors on LANs is to avoid the need for acknowledgments on the LAN. And as stated earlier, on point-to-point links the information is sent reliably and not sent periodically.

Another way in which DECnet differs from the RIP-like protocols is that in DECnet you store the distance vectors from all your neighbors. If a neighbor goes down or reports that it can no longer reach a destination, you have all the information you need to compute your next best path.

14.4 IS-IS, OSPF, NLSP, and PNNI

Most of the concepts involved in building a link state protocol are discussed in Section 12.2. In this section I discuss the interesting ways in which link state protocols can differ. These protocols are largely similar because there's not very much to a link state protocol. There's the notion of flooding information about your neighbors and computing routes based on Dijkstra, which comes from the ARPANET routing algorithm. Flooding it in a self-stabilizing way and making efficient use of LANs comes from IS-IS.

But there are some differences. One annoying difference is terminology. Everyone who lays out packet formats in a slightly different way seems to feel compelled to invent totally new terminology for everything.

What are all these protocols? I explain the history of IS-IS and OSPF in Section 14.1. PNNI (private network-to-network interface)[7] is a link state protocol for ATM. NLSP (NetWare Link Services Protocol) is an IPX-specific version of IS-IS.

I discuss NLSP here because it made a few interesting enhancements to IS-IS that are worth learning about. I would have preferred that the NLSP developers only define the IPX-specific fields and keep the protocol IS-IS, meaning that they should use the same layer 2 protocol type and have the link state packets simultaneously carry IP and IPX information. Even though the packet formats in NLSP are identical to those in IS-IS, the developers did not do this. As a result, if you had a network running both IP and IPX, even if you were using IS-IS for IP you'd have twice the routing traffic because you'd have NLSP hellos, LSPs, and so on in addition to IS-IS hellos, LSPs, and so on.

But the developers of NLSP couldn't just define IPX-specific fields and implement them. Theoretically, they'd have to submit them to ISO and wait years to find out whether ISO approved the fields as is or modified them. Because the developers wanted to implement NLSP immediately, they felt they had no choice but to call it their own protocol. They are probably right about the official process, but I think it hastened the demise of IPX because it needed its own routing protocol.

Sections 14.4.1 through 14.4.7 compare interesting aspects of these link state protocols. Section 14.4.9 discusses the remaining details of IS-IS, and Section 14.4.10 discusses the remaining details of OSPF.

---

[7] If it were up to me I wouldn't have expanded the acronym PNNI because none of the words *private*, *network*, or *interface* give me a clue that it's a link state routing protocol for ATM. Although I don't like its name, it's otherwise a fine protocol.

14.4.1 Hierarchy

Originally, the philosophy of IS-IS was to not bother with optimal interarea routes, instead routing interarea traffic to the nearest level 2 router, whereas OSPF chose to inject enough information to ensure optimal routes. But both protocols evolved to be more flexible, so that in either case they can be configured for either extreme or any point in between. One extreme is to inject a default route, in which case traffic is sent to the nearest border router. At the other extreme, all destinations are reported by all border nodes, and optimal paths are always chosen. By configuring prefixes, you can control the trade-off between memory and optimal routes.

So at this point there is no difference between OSPF and IS-IS in terms of making trade-offs between optimality of routes versus amount of routing information. But the hierarchy rules are different. OSPF allows only two levels, whereas IS-IS allows multiple levels in a tree topology, with a path being able to take a single shortcut rather than going all the way up through the levels. NLSP and PNNI allow an arbitrary mesh of areas.

14.4.1.1 IS-IS Hierarchy

IS-IS was originally designed for CLNP, in which there really are two types of routing:

- Exact match of the bottom 6 bytes of the address ("level 1")

- Longest prefix match of the top part of the address ("level 2," but really multilevel)

So for CLNP, the concept of "level 1 routing" and "level 2 routing" makes sense, but "level 2" should be multilevel. For IP, there should not be a "level 1 routing," and there should be only the multilevel address-prefix routing. IS-IS as originally specified does not inject any level 2 information into level 1, so no effort is made to find the best exit from the area for a particular destination. With CLNP it would have been somewhat difficult to inject level 2 information into level 1 because it would involve a totally different type of routing (prefix rather than exact match). And it was assumed that for destinations outside the area, the route would not be very suboptimal if traffic exited the area at the nearest point (the nearest level 2 router).

The IS-IS working group recently added an LSP option for injecting IP information into level 1. It also increased the size of the metric from 6 bits to 4 bytes. And IS-IS plans to support as many as eight levels. It has the topological restriction that routing information that has traveled down the hierarchy, or across from an area of one level to another area of the same level, cannot be propagated upward. A flag in the reachability information for an IP prefix starts at 0 and is set to 1 if the information is being introduced into a lower-level area or another area of the same level. After the flag is set, the information is not allowed to be injected higher in the hierarchy again.

This option gives almost as much flexibility as the NLSP hierarchy (see Section 14.4.1.2), with less ability to create topologies that might exhibit distance-vector count-to-infinity behavior in the routing protocol when destinations become unreachable.

14.4.1.2 NLSP Hierarchy

NLSP allows arbitrary interconnection of areas, and not just arbitrary numbers of levels, but arbitrary interconnection between areas. An area is defined as the range within which an LSP propagates. To connect two areas you connect a router to both (see Figure 14.4).

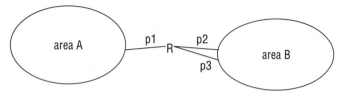

Figure 14.4 Connecting two areas with NLSP

The router must be configured with the mapping of ports to areas, so it must be told that port p1 is area A and that ports p2 and p3 are in area B. This means that if it receives an LSP on port p2, it should forward it to p3 but not to p1. R must keep two separate LSP databases, one for each area. However, R will inject information into the LSP it injects into area B for the address prefixes reachable in area A, and vice versa.

To do this, R is configured with filtering and summarization information. The filtering information indicates which addresses should not be exported or imported. The summarization information consists of address summaries that will be passed from one area into the other. So R might be told that area A's summaries are 58* and 923*. R, in the LSP that it generates in area B, will list 58* and 923* as addresses that R can reach. If R is configured with the summary 21* for area B, it will inject reachability to 21* in the LSP it generates in area A. This rule allows arbitrary interconnection of areas and arbitrary numbers of levels.

In Figure 14.5, R5 might be configured to inject 57* into the area shown in the upper circle and to inject * into the lower circle. R3 might be configured to inject * into the lower circle and 579* into the upper circle. R8 can inject 35* into the lower circle and 5743* into the upper circle.

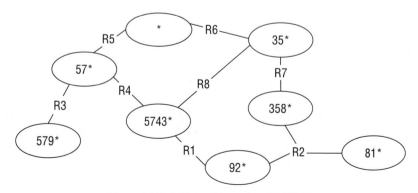

Figure 14.5 Arbitrary hierarchy with NLSP

Now suppose that R1 injects 92* into its upper circle. Assume that the circle marked 5743* contains all addresses within that summary. But because R1 will have also injected the summary 92*, R8 will discover 92* along with the addresses reachable in the circle marked 5743*. Should R8 pass this information on to its other circle (the one marked 35*)? NLSP allows you to choose either behavior. In NLSP, when you configure a summary, you also configure *area-hops*, which is the number of areas the information can be passed along. This allows, for example, two organizations to interconnect their areas without letting the rest of the Internet know about the connectivity and thereby letting it use the path.

Another reason for limiting the spread of routing information with area-hops is to reduce count-to-infinity behavior. The information leaking from area to area resembles a distance vector protocol. Long-lived loops will not exist provided that each time a summary is passed from one area to another the prefix gets shorter or the metric gets larger. But the potential for slow convergence (standard distance vector protocol behavior) if the topology has a lot of loops of areas made the IS-IS working group prefer the more constrained topology. It still allows arbitrary levels, but each area is known to be a parent, child, or peer, and information cannot pass up in the hierarchy after it has passed down.

14.4.1.3 OSPF Hierarchy

OSPF is a strict two-level hierarchy. There is a backbone area (level 2), and packets traveling from one area to another area must go via the backbone area (see Figure 14.6).

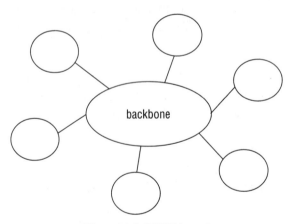

Figure 14.6 OSPF hierarchy

In IS-IS and NLSP, each area border router calculates its cost to a destination and injects that into the area. In OSPF, IP prefixes outside the area but within the domain are reported by area border routers just as in IS-IS and NLSP. However, OSPF reports IP destinations outside the domain differently.

In Figure 14.7, R1, R2, and R5 are area border routers. D1, D2, D3, D4, and D5 are destinations (IP prefixes) outside the AS (OSPF uses the terminology AS for domain). R4 and R5 are AS border routers. In IS-IS, each area border router would calculate its costs to D1, D2, and so on and inject that into the area (if configured to do so rather than simply injecting default). In OSPF, the area border routers inject link state information about their distance to the AS border routers (for example, R1 indicates its cost to R3 and its cost to R4). The AS border routers report their cost to destinations D1, D2, and so on (with configuration as to which summaries to report). The link state information generated by the AS border routers is passed into the area.

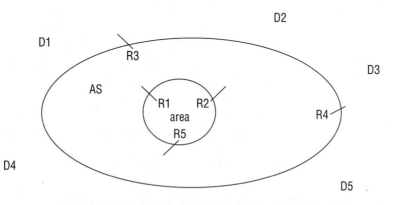

Figure 14.7 OSPF reports of IP destinations outside the AS

If there are fewer AS border routers than area border routers and if the majority of the information consists of IP prefixes reachable outside the AS, this method yields a smaller database than having the area border routers calculate their distance to the destinations and report that directly.

OSPF allows an area to be configured as a *stub* area, which means that the link state information generated by the AS border routers would not get flooded into the area. This is a way of using less memory and bandwidth for routing at the expense of less optimal routes.

14.4.1.4 PNNI Hierarchy

PNNI calls an area a *peer group*. Although there is a hierarchy of peer groups, interconnection between peer groups is arbitrary. A link state protocol is carried out at each level of the hierarchy, and a router knows the link state information for its own peer group and every ancestor peer group (defined in a moment). At the lowest level, "nodes" in the link state protocol are individual routers. At higher levels, a "node" is a peer group. Each peer group elects a leader (as with a LAN Designated Router election). The peer group leader issues the link state information on behalf of the peer group.

A peer group name is a string. A peer group with a name such as ABC is an ancestor of peer group ABCD, because "ABC" is a prefix of "ABCD." The peer group AX is not an ancestor of ABCD. A router in ABCD knows link state information for ABCD and link state information for all ancestors of ABCD, such as ABC, AB, A, and even the zero-bit name { }.

PNNI assumes that paths are selected by the source router. A router specifies the path in a hierarchical way; the path at the lowest level consists of individual routers, but at higher levels it is a sequence of peer group names. If a router in ABCD is connected to AX, it means that peer groups AB and AX are neighbor nodes in the link state protocol carried out within peer group A. In Figure 14.8, the dotted lines indicate where two routers are physical neighbors.

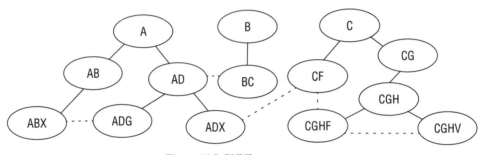

Figure 14.8 PNNI peer groups

The result of this connectivity is the logical connectivity of peer groups as shown in Figure 14.9.

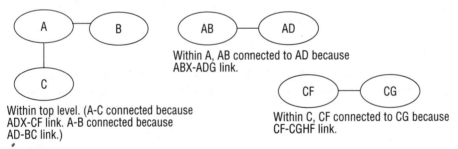

Figure 14.9 Connectivity of peer groups

The only flexibility that NLSP provides that PNNI does not provide is the ability to limit routing information propagation with area-hops. In NLSP, you can create a link between two areas and allow it to be used only for traffic between those two areas by advertising the injected summaries with area-hops of 1. With PNNI, if there is a connection between ADX and CF, all traffic between A and C can flow through that link. Indeed any nodes might wind up with a path that includes at the top level the link A-C, and they will use the link between ADX and CF.

Information learned externally to PNNI is advertised without a metric and as such would wind up with loops if allowed to be advertised with no restrictions. So PNNI restricts advertisement of such information in the same way IS-IS does—namely, that it is allowed to go down in the hierarchy but not up.

Because PNNI is a link state protocol at every level of the hierarchy, it is not susceptible to count-to-infinity behavior as NLSP can be.

14.4.2 Area Addresses

14.4.2.1 IS-IS Area Addresses

An area address in IS-IS is a variable-length quantity. When used for routing CLNP, it is the prefix of the CLNP address shared by all the nodes in the area (the "area" portion). When IS-IS is used for IP, the area address serves only to ensure that two areas don't inadvertently get merged. It's only a name for the area. A router is configured with its area address, which it tells its neighbor in its hello message. If the routers are level 1 routers and the area addresses don't match, they don't talk to each other.

It's not quite that simple, though: an area can have multiple area addresses. This serves to allow migrating an area from one address to another, merging two areas, or splitting an area into pieces.

If an area has three area addresses—say, A1, A2, and A3—a CLNP packet is routed via level 1 routing if the area field in the destination address matches any of these three addresses. But for routing IP, the area address is used only so that routers can make sure that the router it is connected to is supposed to be in the same area.

The set of area addresses configured in a router is known as its *manual area addresses*. A level 1 router R considers an adjacent router S to be a neighbor if R's and S's manual area addresses overlap. The hello messages that R and S send each other include their manual area addresses. If at least one of the area addresses reported by S matches at least one of the area addresses reported by R, they are neighbors.

In addition to including its manual area addresses in its hello messages to its neighbors, a router includes its manual area addresses in its LSP. All level 1 routers take the set union of all the area addresses reported in the area's LSPs to find the complete set of area addresses for the area. In CLNP, if the area portion of the destination address of a packet to be forwarded matches any of the area addresses reported in LSPs within the area, then the packet is routed by level 1 routing. Again, for routing IP, the only purpose of the area addresses is to make sure areas don't inadvertently get merged.

There is a limit to the number of area addresses for an area. Originally the limit was fixed at three, but ISO (unfortunately, in my opinion) modified it to be a parameter, *maximum area addresses*. This seemingly innocent change creates a lot of complexity. Routing would be disrupted if different routers in an area had different values for that parameter. To ensure that all routers in an area agree on the value of maximum area addresses, the parameter value is inserted into the header of IS-IS control packets. For backward compatibility with implementations that were built to the previous version, in which the value of three was fixed, a value of zero for maximum area addresses means three. The header field where maximum area addresses are written was a reserved field in the earlier version of the IS-IS spec. Therefore, implementations built before the change set the value to zero and ignore it upon receipt.

If the number of different area addresses in the union of all the sets of area addresses reported in level 1 LSPs exceeds x, where x is the value of maximum area addresses, then the x area addresses that are numerically lowest are considered to be the area addresses of the area.

To merge area A into area B, the procedure shown in Figure 14.10 is employed.

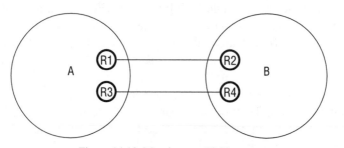

Figure 14.10 Merging two IS-IS areas

Area address B is added to R1's configured set of area addresses (which is now the set {A, B}). As soon as R1 is configured, R1 and R2 become neighbors and exchange LSP databases. R1 passes all of area B's LSPs into area A. All routers in area A accept both "A" and "B" as the name of the area, and the two smaller areas are merged into one big area with two area addresses: A and B.

One-by-one, all the routers in A are configured to accept B as an additional address for their area. After all the routers in the original area A are so configured, they can be reconfigured one-by-one to have only address B configured. Even when there remains only a single router with {A, B} as the set of area addresses, the entire area still has two addresses. When that router is reconfigured to have only address B configured, then the area reverts to having a single area address—namely, B.

14.4.2.2 OSPF Area Addresses

In OSPF each area has only a single ID, which is a 4-byte quantity. The value 0.0.0.0 means "level 2." Therefore, OSPF does not have the ability to merge and split addresses dynamically as IS-IS has.

14.4.2.3 NLSP Area Addresses

NLSP is of course similar to IS-IS except that the area addresses are IPX address prefixes. The area addresses aren't just to name the area to prevent merging, but rather they are used by area border routers as the default address summaries to export from the area.

14.4.2.4 PNNI Peer Group Names

In PNNI a peer group name is a string from 0 to 13 octets in length. A peer group X is contained in peer group Y provided that the string X is a prefix of the string Y. So, for example, peer group ABCDE is contained in peer group ABC but not contained in AFC. In the upper layers of the hierarchy, a peer group is represented as a single node. In that case the name of the node is the peer group name concatenated with the 6-byte unique ID of the router elected peer group leader.

14.4.3 LANs and Designated Routers

The purpose of a Designated Router (DR) is to allow the LAN to be treated like a node; n routers on the LAN look to the routing algorithm like $n+1$ nodes with n links, rather than n nodes with n^2 links. The DR issues the link state information on behalf of the LAN, gives a name to the LAN, and ensures reliable propagation of link state information on the LAN. PNNI is designed for ATM and therefore has only point-to-point links. It does not have (nor need) algorithms for this aspect of routing.

14.4.3.1 IS-IS Designated Router Election

In IS-IS the Designated Router election is deterministic, meaning that given the same set of alive routers, the same router is chosen Designated Router. The hello messages contain each router's 6-byte ID and a 1-byte priority. The router advertising the numerically highest priority wins, with numerically highest ID breaking ties.

14.4.3.2 OSPF Designated Router Election

In OSPF the Designated Router election is *sticky*, meaning that after a router has been elected, nobody can usurp the position unless that router goes down. Immediately after the Designated Router fails, the election is similar to that in IS-IS: election is based on priority and ID. But after a router is elected, nobody else takes over.

I prefer the sticky behavior over the deterministic behavior because it is disruptive to have a new DR. In IS-IS the name of the LAN changes, so all the routers on the LAN must change their LSPs to account for their new neighbor, the newly named LAN. In OSPF it's disruptive to have DR changes because the DR keeps track of which nodes have acknowledged which link state information.

But some people say that deterministic behavior is preferable, and others prefer being able to choose the DR by setting the priorities. So the best solution is the one implemented by NLSP. An IS-IS router can implement the NLSP optimization and remain compatible with routers that do not implement it. I would recommend implementing it.

14.4.3.3 NLSP Designated Router Election

In NLSP the election looks like that of IS-IS except that after a router has been DR for a minute it increases its priority by 20. In that way, if you want the deterministic behavior of IS-IS you set priorities to be at least 21 apart. If you want the OSPF behavior, you set all the priorities to be within 20 of each other. You can also get something in between. For example, suppose there is a set of powerful routers, and if one of them is up you'd like it elected. But you want sticky behavior among that group, and you'd like to elect one router of a second most powerful group, but only if all the powerful routers are dead. In that case, you set all the priorities in the most powerful group to be 21 more than the priorities of any of the other routers.

14.4.3.4 PNNI Peer Group Leader Election

In PNNI, one router is chosen in the peer group to represent the peer group to the next level of routing. This concept is very similar to a LAN Designated Router. PNNI's election is the same as NLSP's. Election is based on configured priority and ID, and after a router is elected it increases its priority by 50.

14.4.4 Reliable Propagation of LSPs on LANs

As stated in Chapter 12, the most straightforward method of reliably distributing LSPs on LANs would consist of having each router transmit an explicit acknowledgment for each LSP. Every router would have to ensure that every other router on the LAN received every LSP. Again, PNNI is not mentioned in this section because it does not deal with LANs.

14.4.4.1 IS-IS and NLSP Link State Information Propagation

The scheme chosen by IS-IS requires no explicit acknowledgments on a LAN. Instead, a router that transmits an LSP on the LAN transmits it once, to a multicast address to which all the routers listen, and assumes the transmission was successful.

Periodically, the DR summarizes the state of its LSP database by multicasting to all the routers on the LAN a packet consisting of the IDs and sequence numbers of all the LSPs in the database. This packet is known as a *complete sequence numbers packet* (CSNP). If a router R detects, based on the received CSNP, that the DR has missed an LSP that R has, R transmits that LSP on the LAN. R detects that the DR has missed an LSP because the LSP either was not listed in the CSNP or was listed with a lower sequence number. If R detects that the DR has a more recent LSP than R, R explicitly requests the missing LSP. R does so by using a *partial sequence numbers packet* (PSNP), which is similar to a CSNP except that the PSNP does not claim to include all LSPs in the database. A PSNP can be used either to explicitly request transmission of a specified set of LSPs or to acknowledge a set of LSPs.

14.4.4.2 OSPF Link State Information Propagation

In OSPF, the designated router is responsible for collecting explicit acknowledgments for each LSA (link state advertisement, OSPF's terminology for LSP) from the other routers.

Because the DR in OSPF keeps a lot of state regarding which routers have which LSAs, it would require a lot of time and protocol messages for another router to take over in the event that the DR crashed. Therefore, OSPF elects not only a DR but also a *backup designated router (BDR)*. The BDR also listens to all the explicit acknowledgments and keeps track of which routers have received which LSAs (see Figure 14.11).

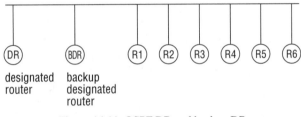

Figure 14.11 OSPF DR and backup DR

When a router R has an LSA to propagate on the LAN, R does not multicast the LSA to all the other routers (as it would in IS-IS). Instead, R transmits it to the DR. But rather than send the LSA to the DR's personal data link address, R transmits it to the multicast address ALLDROUTERS, to which both the DR and the backup DR listen. When the DR receives the LSA, the DR multicasts the LSA to ALLSPFROUTERS. Then the DR collects acks for that LSA, which are transmitted to the multicast address ALLDROUTERS. If the DR does not receive an ack from a subset of the routers, it sends explicit copies of the LSA to each router in that subset.

The protocol is as follows.

1. R3, say, receives an LSA and needs to forward it onto the LAN.

2. R3 multicasts the LSA to ALLDROUTERS.

3. DR and BDR receive the LSA.

4. DR multicasts the LSA to ALLSPFROUTERS.

5. Assume that all the routers receive the LSA correctly.

6. BDR, R1, R2, R3, R4, R5, and R6 all send an explicit ack to the multicast address ALLDROUTERS.

7. Assume that DR does not receive acks from R2, R5, and BDR within the timeout.

DR retransmits the LSA three times: once to R2's data link address, once to R5's data link address, and once to the BDR's data link address (and waits for acknowledgments).

14.4.4.3 Comparison

I think either method is fine in practice, but it's interesting academically to compare them. The OSPF method causes extra latency for disseminating routing information. In OSPF, if a router other than the DR is the first to receive an LSA, the LSA cannot immediately be multicast on the LAN to the other routers. Instead, it must first be transmitted to the DR (and backup DR) and then forwarded to the other routers on the LAN. In IS-IS, the first router on the LAN that receives the information immediately multicasts it on the LAN to the other routers.

If there are no changes to the link state information, the IS-IS method requires a constant background overhead of CSNPs, whereas the OSPF method, after all acknowledgments are received, has no further overhead. If there is a lot of routing information and a lot of routers on the LAN, the IS-IS method has lower overhead because there is no need for acks from all routers. The CSNP is similar to having only a single router (the DR) send acks. It's probably more important to optimize the case when there are a lot of routers and a lot of information to be transmitted rather than opposite; when there's no routing information to transmit, the background overhead is low and there's nothing else to do anyway.

People who are familiar with both OSPF and IS-IS in operation say both schemes are fine in practice.

14.4.5 Parameter Synchronization

In certain cases parameters cannot be a unilateral decision. For example, you can't decide to send hello messages every minute if your neighbor thinks you are sending them every second and will declare you dead if you haven't said anything for 5 seconds. Recall that in the bridge spanning tree algorithm everyone uses compatible parameters because whoever is elected Root informs all the other bridges, in the spanning tree messages, which settings to use. When parameters are an issue only between neighbors and need not be coordinated across all routers, then the proper place to put parameter values is in hello messages so that you can coordinate with your neighbor. For parameters that must be coordinated across the entire area, the LSP works because the LSP will be flooded throughout the area.

14.4.5.1 IS-IS Parameter Synchronization

An IS-IS router R reports *holding time* in its hello message, which determines the length of time between the last hello a neighbor of R receives from R and when the neighbor declares R dead. It's useful to allow holding time to differ for each node. In some cases it is more important to detect quickly that a router is down, and it's worth the overhead of more-frequent hello messages from that router, for example when there are several routers in parallel connecting the LAN to the rest of the world. But in other cases, such as when a router is the only path to a portion of the net, it is not important to discover whether it's up or down. If it's down, there is no alternate path anyway.

I was surprised, when rereading the IS-IS spec for the revision of this book, that holding time is specified to be 10 times the hello time. I'd have either made two parameters (holding time and hello time) or set holding time to be a little more than twice or perhaps three times hello time. I think 10 is excessive. When I asked IS-IS implementers, they said that they ignore that part of the spec, so they either have two parameters or use a smaller multiplier for holding time. Because holding time is all that gets reported, there is no problem with interoperability.

There are two parameters that must be agreed upon by all routers in the area. One is the maximum number of area addresses, and the other is the size of the ID field in LSPs. I'd have left these as constants equal to 3 (for max area addresses) and 6 bytes (length of ID), as they were in the original. But given that the committee wanted to make them variable, they are carried in the fixed part of the header of all IS-IS packets—with the historical quirk that the value 0 in both cases is the original value (because the ability to make these variable was added after implementations that assumed they were constants were deployed). So max addresses = 0 means the same as max addresses = 3, and ID length = 0 means the same as ID length = 6.

14.4.5.2 OSPF Parameter Synchronization

OSPF reports two parameters in its hellos: HelloInterval and RouterDeadInterval. However, unlike IS-IS, in OSPF these parameters must match exactly or else the routers cannot be neighbors. I think this requirement is a serious disadvantage. There is no reason to force all routers on a LAN to have exactly the same timers configured. The flexibility of allowing different values at different routers is important. And even if you don't care about that and are willing for all routers on a LAN to have the same values, it makes it difficult to migrate a LAN from one value of the parameters to another. While you are changing the values at the routers, one-by-one, you partition the LAN because the routers with the old values will refuse to talk to the routers with the new values.

> **Can't we all just get along?**
>
> **—Rodney King**

14.4.5.3 PNNI Parameter Synchronization

PNNI uses the IS-IS scheme, which is that each node has its own timer and tells its neighbor the value of the timer. There is no "incompatibility" if neighbors use different times as long as each one knows what to expect from its neighbor.

14.4.6 Destinations per Packet

The externally reachable IP destinations are reported differently in IS-IS and OSPF. In IS-IS many destinations can be reported in a single LSP fragment. In OSPF each LSA reports only a single destination. Each approach has interesting advantages and disadvantages. Because each LSA requires its own sequence number and age, the total OSPF database will be about three times the size of the IS-IS database required for the same information. However, when a single destination changes, IS-IS requires that the entire fragment containing the changed information be retransmitted, whereas OSPF can update just the single piece of information that changed.

PNNI is somewhat similar to the IS-IS scheme in that multiple destinations can be reported in a single advertisement. However, there are categories of information: node information that gives information about you (or about your peer group if you are a peer group leader and representing the peer group as a node in a higher-level peer group), link information describing the node on the other side, or reachability information describing externally reachable prefixes. Each class of information carries its own sequence number and age, but within a class you can carry as much information as fits.

14.4.7 LSP Database Overload

A router is configured based on an assumption regarding the size of the network it must support. There are two reasons that the assumed network size might be incorrect.

1. *Static overload:* In this case, either the router has been underconfigured, or the area has grown illegally large. Until nodes are disconnected from the network, the router will not be able to participate as a router.

2. *Temporary overload:* In this case, the router is properly configured for the size of the area, but a temporary situation has caused the LSP database to be larger than expected. For example, suppose that the designated router, R1, on a LAN goes down, and another router, R2, takes over. R1 will have issued an LSP on behalf of the LAN, with the LAN having an ID of R1.x. Then R2 will issue an LSP on behalf of the LAN, with an ID of R2.y. Until the R1.x LSPs age out and can be removed, twice as much room will be occupied by the LAN information.

Most routing protocols do not specify what a router should do when memory for the routing database is exceeded. Traditionally, implementations have done one of the following.

1. *Crash:* This is OK but rather inelegant. It makes it difficult to use network management to reconfigure the router because the router will not be reachable via the network. Also, if the overload is only temporary, it is inconvenient to have to manually restart routers.

2. *Work with the random subset of routing information that happens to fit:* This is not OK. A single router that is routing based on incomplete information can cause global routing disruption.

14.4.7.1 IS-IS Database Overload

When the IS-IS routing database exceeds its allocated memory, a router that cannot fit a new LSP into its database simply refuses to acknowledge the LSP. The neighbor continues trying to transmit the LSP. If the overload is a temporary problem, the router will eventually be able to accept it.

A router that is forced to refuse an LSP sets a flag in its LSP indicating that its LSP database is overloaded. Other routers use paths through that router only if no path through non-overloaded routers exists. Because a refused LSP will be retransmitted within a few seconds, a router that has not needed to refuse an LSP for a time longer than the LSP retransmission time clears its flag, indicating that it is no longer overloaded.

This behavior means that a temporary overload situation heals itself without human intervention and with minimal disruption in the meantime. A static overload causes less disruption to the network than having the underpowered router crash. While the router is overloaded, the overloaded router cannot cause routing loops in the portion of the network consisting of non-overloaded routers. The router is available to be managed across the network, and any nodes that can be reached only through that router will still most likely be reachable through that router.

14.4.7.2 OSPF Database Overload

A capability to deal with database overload was recently designed for OSPF, and it is documented in RFC 1765. It is not, however, included in the most recent OSPF RFC (2328). So this is an optional feature and not officially part of OSPF.

In OSPF, overflow is even more likely to happen than in IS-IS. The area has no control over the amount of information inside the area because the type 5 LSAs (see Section 14.4.10.7) get flooded into the area but are externally generated. For most of the lifetime of OSPF, the issue was ignored. Most implementations that couldn't handle the link state database simply didn't acknowledge information that didn't fit. They continued routing with the subset of the data that they happened to have.

RFC 1765 deals only with the external (to the AS) link state information. There is a parameter that specifies the maximum amount of such information. It is supposed to be set identically in all the routers in the AS. But it's not exchanged in protocol messages, so either network management must check up or you must trust the network administrators.

If the database gets exceeded, then presumably all routers are in overflow state (because presumably all of them have the same capacity and the same parameters). Routers in overflow are supposed to purge the external information they have initiated. That can cause "binge and purge" behavior. They'd all purge their information. They'd all exit overflow state, reinsert the information, and so forth.

OSPF could not easily have implemented the IS-IS method because the IS-IS method requires all routers to understand the **overloaded** flag in LSPs. This was not a problem for IS-IS because the overload feature was designed in from the start.

OSPF has no method for dealing with overflow of information other than external information.

14.4.7.3 PNNI Database Overload

Because PNNI is designed for ATM, where paths are selected by a source node, database overload is a less serious matter. If a node knows how to reach its neighbors, it can be a full participant in a path even if it can make no decisions beyond its neighbors. If router R knows only how to reach its neighbors R2 and R3 and it receives a call setup packet from R3 saying that it should set up a path to D via R2, then R need only forward the call setup packet to R2 and remember the VC information. So PNNI allows an overloaded router to continue operating but places some restrictions on it. For example, it is no longer allowed to participate as a peer group leader or a border node because a border node must fill in the details of the path inside its own peer group. As in IS-IS, the overloaded PNNI router sets a flag in its advertisement so that the rest of the peer group will know it is overloaded.

14.4.8 Authentication

The original version of OSPF had a field called **authentication**, which was just a cleartext password. This offered no real security, yet IS-IS was criticized at the time for being less secure than OSPF. So IS-IS added a cleartext password authentication field because it seemed easier to add it than to argue that without cryptography an authentication field doesn't make things more secure.

Today both protocols have true cryptographic authentication, although there are interesting differences between the IS-IS authentication and the OSPF authentication.

In cleartext password authentication in OSPF, there is only a single password per link. In contrast, in IS-IS there is a transmit password and a set of receive passwords for each link. Having a single password per link creates two problems.

1. It makes it difficult to migrate a link from one password to another.

2. It makes things less secure on a point-to-point link. To determine the password, an intruder need only listen for a message from the other node on the link. (Imagine two spies. "Tell me the password." "No, you tell me first.")

The cryptographic authentication for OSPF (and IS-IS) was done correctly, however, in that there are multiple acceptable secrets per link so that it is possible to migrate from one secret to another.

Authentication in LSPs is handled differently in the two protocols. In IS-IS, the router that originally generated the LSP puts in the authentication field. In OSPF, the LSP itself does not contain an authentication field. Instead, the authentication field is in the header of a link state update packet, and inside there are one or more LSAs. The authentication field in OSPF is added by a router that is forwarding the information to a neighbor; in contrast, in IS-IS the original router that generated the LSP inserts the authentication field. This may make configuration of passwords easier in OSPF because a password is a local phenomenon. It also makes it less likely in OSPF for a misconfigured password in a router to cause global disruption, as it can in IS-IS when an LSP is accepted by some routers and rejected by others. However, the OSPF method is less secure because any router can corrupt another router's link state information. IS-IS would be a more suitable base for building the sabotage-proof routing described in Chapter 16.

14.4.9 IS-IS Details

The previous sections discussed areas in which there are interesting differences between OSPF, IS-IS, NLSP, and PNNI. This section discusses remaining details of IS-IS.

14.4.9.1 IS-IS for IP

RFC 1195 defines the extra fields needed for IS-IS to support IP. The hello messages and LSPs have a field to say which protocols you support. Assuming that not all routers support every protocol suite that can be supported with integrated routing, it is necessary for routers to announce which protocol suites they support, thereby preventing data packets in a foreign format from being transmitted to a router that does not handle that protocol. The protocols supported must be announced in hello messages so that routers know the capabilities of their neighbors. The protocols supported are also announced in LSPs, for two reasons. One is to detect misconfiguration if mixing of X-only and Y-only routers in the same area is prohibited. The other is to give sufficient information so that a router that supports both X and Y can encapsulate an X protocol packet in a Y header when forced to forward the packet through a Y-only neighbor. Router mixing can be solved with encapsulation, but it is complex.

The next piece of additional information for IP is the router's IP interface. This is required in hello messages because, in IP, it is necessary to know the IP address of a neighbor router in order to generate ICMP redirects (which include the IP address of the router toward which the endnode is being redirected). An IP address of a router is also included in the router's LSP. It is useful if encapsulation is used either for mixing of X-only and Y-only routers or on virtual links.

The final piece of additional information is known as *interdomain routing protocol information* (IRPI). It is included in level 2 LSPs and serves any function that might be served by the **tag** field in OSPF (see Section 14.4.10.8), but it is more flexible because it is a variable-length field. The IRPI field is intended to be useful to the interdomain routing protocol and is ignored by the intradomain routers. Possible uses of the IRPI field (beyond the uses of the OSPF tag field, which could also be supported) include the following.

1. The IRPI field could allow interdomain routers to find each other. The interdomain routers within a routing domain could discover which of the level 2 routers within the domain were also interdomain routers with a flag in the IRPI field in the level 2 LSPs.

2. If there were many interdomain routers within a domain and if they wished to share information with all the other interdomain routers within the domain, they could include the information in the IRPI field in the level 2 LSPs, which automatically get flooded to all the level 2 routers in the domain. The alternative is for each interdomain router to individually transmit the information to each other interdomain router. The latter mechanism is more efficient if there are only a small number of interdomain routers. It does not require carrying an extra field in the level 2 LSPs that must be stored (although ignored) by all the level 2 intradomain routers.

In RFC 1195, the format of IP address reachability is specified as shown in Figure 14.12.

# of octets

1	R	I/E	default metric
1	S	R	delay metric
1	S	R	expense metric
1	S	R	error metric
4	IP address (4 bytes)		
4	mask (4 bytes)		

Figure 14.12 IP address reachability option in IS-IS LSPs

The **IP address** and **mask** fields are obvious, although it would have been more efficient to encode the address (as a prefix length, address) instead. The **I/E** flag (internal/external) indicates whether the default metric is comparable to internal metrics (so that it can just be added into a path) or incomparable (external). **R** stands for "reserved," meaning that those bits are unused. The **S** bit in the other metrics indicates whether that router supports that metric. Today nobody cares about anything except the default metric, so 3 of those bytes are wasted.

The IS-IS working group in IETF is changing this to allow a larger metric and inclusion of other information for traffic engineering. It's still at the Internet draft stage, but Figure 14.13 shows what it will look like.

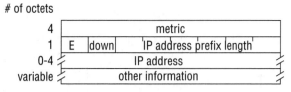

Figure 14.13 New IP address reachability option in IS-IS LSPs

Other information includes maximum reservable bandwidth, the amount of bandwidth that is currently reserved, and an alternative metric for traffic engineering purposes. The **E** flag indicates the presence of other information. This encoding eliminates the 6-bit metric restriction, avoids the overhead of carrying around the metrics that people are no longer interested in, and compacts the information by specifying the IP address as (length, prefix) rather than (address, mask).

14.4.9.2 LAN Designated Router

One router—say, R5—on a LAN is elected Designated Router. It gives the LAN a unique 7-byte ID by taking its own ID and concatenating an extra byte to differentiate that LAN from other LANs that R5 might be DR for (see Figure 14.14).

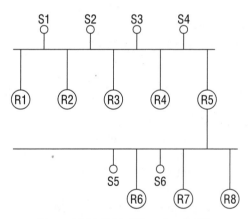

Figure 14.14 R5 is DR on two LANs

Assuming that R5 was elected DR on both LANs, it might name the top LAN R5.1 and name the bottom LAN R5.21. Figure 14.15 shows what the link state information for the routers on the two LANs would look like.

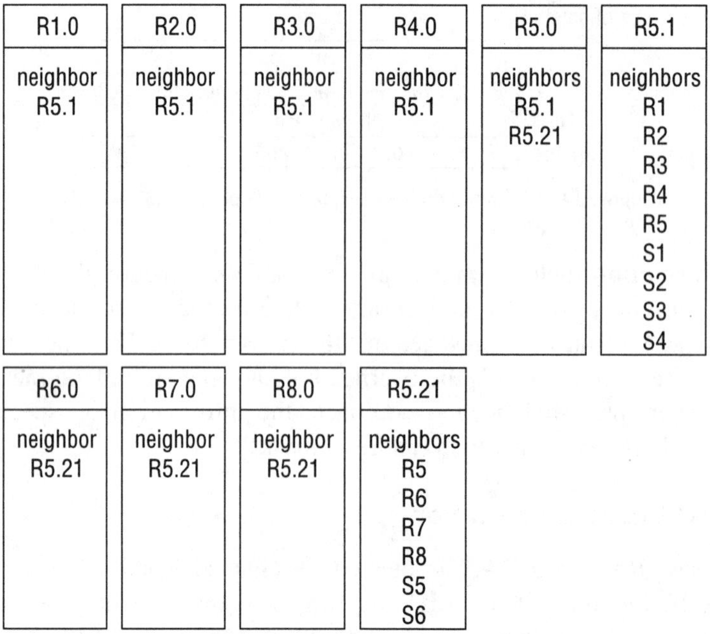

R1.0	R2.0	R3.0	R4.0	R5.0	R5.1
neighbor R5.1	neighbor R5.1	neighbor R5.1	neighbor R5.1	neighbors R5.1 R5.21	neighbors R1 R2 R3 R4 R5 S1 S2 S3 S4

R6.0	R7.0	R8.0	R5.21
neighbor R5.21	neighbor R5.21	neighbor R5.21	neighbors R5 R6 R7 R8 S5 S6

Figure 14.15 Link state information for LANs from Figure 14.14

IS-IS calls the LAN a *pseudonode*. The LAN is treated just like any router. It generates an LSP (although the DR does it on the LAN's behalf). It has links to routers, and routers have links to it.

14.4.9.3 Big Packets

It is possible for LSPs and CSNPs to be so large that they cannot fit into a single packet as transmitted on a link. The same sort of fragmentation and reassembly could be performed on LSPs and CSNPs as would be performed on data packets. Instead, IS-IS has two different mechanisms—one for CSNPs and one for LSPs—that avoid fragmentation and reassembly.

There are two problems with using standard fragmentation and reassembly.

1. *Wasted bandwidth:* If a single fragment is lost, all the fragments must be retransmitted.

2. *Slower than necessary propagation of LSP information:* A fragment of an LSP cannot be propagated until all the fragments have been received and reassembled.

IS-IS avoids these problems by using the following mechanism for keeping control packets small enough that they don't need hop-by-hop fragmentation. The LSP's **source** field consists of 8 octets. The first 6 octets are the ID of the router that issued the LSP. The seventh octet is zero when the router issued the LSP on its own behalf. The seventh octet is nonzero when the router is the DR on a LAN and the router issued the LSP on behalf of the LAN. The eighth octet can be considered the "fragment number."

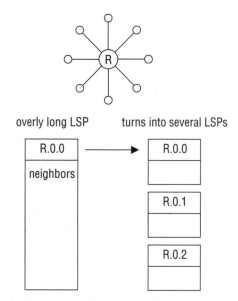

Figure 14.16 Router's LSP broken into fragments

Suppose that router R's LSP is so large that it must be divided into three packets (see Figure 14.16). R generates three LSPs: one from source R.0.0, one from source R.0.1, and one from source R.0.2. If R is generating an LSP on behalf of a LAN for which R is DR and if R has named the LAN R.5, then the LAN's LSP will come from "source" R.5.0. If the LAN's LSP is large enough to require four packets, then there will be four LSPs—from R.5.0, R.5.1, R.5.2, and R.5.3 (see Figure 14.17).

For the purposes of propagating the LSPs, R.x.i and R.x.j are totally different sources and have totally independent sequence numbers. If a single fragment is lost, only that fragment need be retransmitted. And any fragment can be forwarded as soon as it is received. It is only when routes are computed that a router combines all of R.x's LSP fragments into one logical LSP. If a link changes, only the LSP fragment that has changed as a result of that link change must be reissued by the source router.

The scheme for avoiding fragmentation and reassembly of CSNPs is that a CSNP includes an address range for the LSPs reported within the CSNP (see Figure 14.18). If an LSP's ID fits within the address range and it is not reported in the CSNP, it is assumed to be missing from the CSNP transmitter's database. The receiver of a CSNP makes no assumption about LSPs that do not fall within the address range. The transmitter of an overly large CSNP can transmit CSNP pieces in any order and even with overlapping address ranges. The only requirement is that for any possible address, the DR must eventually (in a timely fashion) transmit a CSNP that includes that address in the address range.

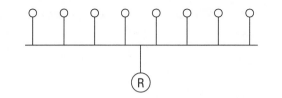

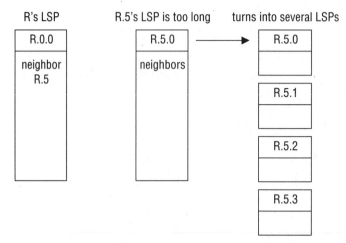

Figure 14.17 Pseudonode's LSP broken into fragments

address range 27.3.0 to 35.0.5	
27.3.0	sequence number 22
27.3.1	sequence number 5
31.0.0	sequence number 291
31.5.0	sequence number 102
31.5.1	sequence number 92
31.5.2	sequence number 61
31.5.3	sequence number 153
31.7.0	sequence number 22
35.0.0	sequence number 6
35.0.1	sequence number 17
35.0.2	sequence number 17
35.0.3	sequence number 3
35.0.4	sequence number 14
35.0.5	sequence number 22

Figure 14.18 CSNP

14.4.9.4 Partitioned Areas

Partitioned area repair is an optional feature in IS-IS. If area FOO is partitioned, it means that FOO has broken into two or more pieces, and level 1 routing cannot route between the pieces. Each piece is called a *partition*. If FOO is not partitioned, it consists of a single partition. The idea is to automatically assign each partition a unique name so that level 2 routing can recognize that the area is partitioned and heal it by having two level 2 routers— R1 and R2—create a virtual wire between the partitions consisting of the level 2 path between R1 and R2.

Level 2 routers examine the level 1 LSP database to find the set of level 2 routers in the partition. They elect (based on ID) a single level 2 router to be the *partition-designated level 2 IS*. (Sorry—I tried unsuccessfully to come up with a shorter, but still descriptive, name for it.)

Assume that X is the partition-designated level 2 IS. Each level 2 router in FOO reports in its level 2 LSP that "X" is FOO's partition-designated level 2 IS. If some level 2 routers claim to reside in FOO and have X as the partition-designated level 2 IS and if others claim to reside in FOO and have Y as the partition-designated level 2 IS, then FOO is partitioned. It is the responsibility of level 2 routers X and Y to "repair" FOO by using the level 2 path between X and Y as a level 1 *virtual link* in FOO. After they establish communication over the virtual link, the virtual link is reported by X and Y in their level 1 LSPs within FOO. Level 1 routers treat the virtual link as a normal link and compute routes that might include the link (see Figure 14.19).

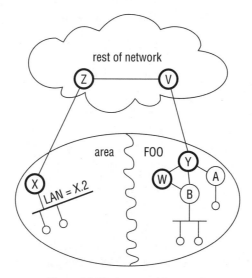

Figure 14.19 Area partition repair

The only subtlety is that level 2 routers must be sure that the partition-designated level 2 router is a router that can be reached via "real" level 1 links and not "virtual" links. Otherwise, as soon as the partition is repaired, X and Y will conclude that the area is no longer partitioned and turn off the virtual link, thus repartitioning the area. This means that the level 2 routers in FOO must first run the routing algorithm to calculate paths within FOO without the virtual links in order to determine which of the level 2 routers are reachable within the partition. Figure 14.20 shows the LSP database of the network in Figure 14.19 before partition repair. Figure 14.21 shows the LSPs that change after the partition is repaired.

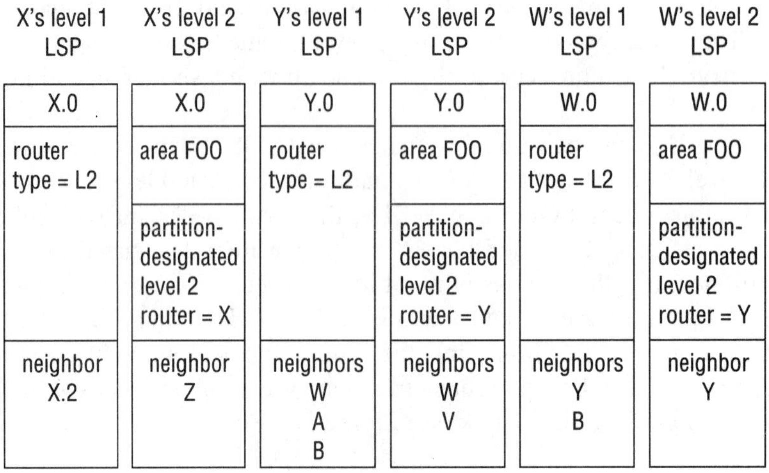

X's level 1 LSP	X's level 2 LSP	Y's level 1 LSP	Y's level 2 LSP	W's level 1 LSP	W's level 2 LSP
X.0	X.0	Y.0	Y.0	W.0	W.0
router type = L2	area FOO	router type = L2	area FOO	router type = L2	area FOO
	partition-designated level 2 router = X		partition-designated level 2 router = Y		partition-designated level 2 router = Y
neighbor X.2	neighbor Z	neighbors W A B	neighbors W V	neighbors Y B	neighbor Y

Figure 14.20 Before partition repair

X's level 1 LSP	Y's level 1 LSP
X.0	Y.0
router type = L2	router type = L2
neighbors X.2 Y (via virtual link)	neighbors W A B X (via virtual link)

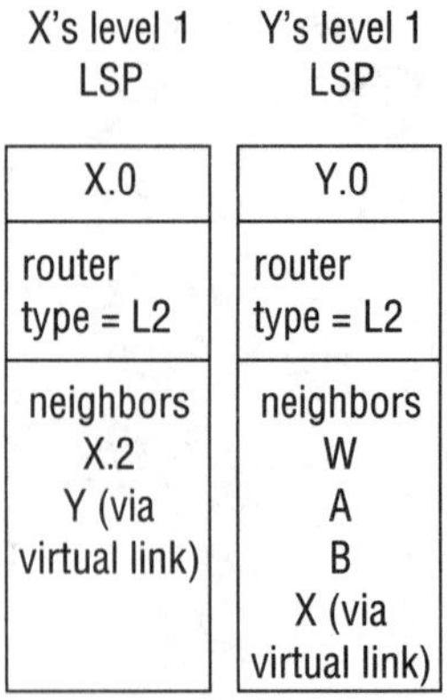

Figure 14.21 LSPs that change after a virtual link between X and Y is established

Partition repair is optional in IS-IS. A level 2 router indicates its support of partition repair in its LSPs. As long as at least one level 2 router in each partition implements the partition-repair capability, the area partition will be repaired.

14.4.9.5 Partitioned Level 2 Network

The network consisting of level 2 routers must be connected. IS-IS does not attempt to automatically repair a partitioned level 2 network by using a level 1 path (see Figure 14.22). However, you could accomplish it by promoting routers along the desired path to level 2 routers, which would again connect level 2.

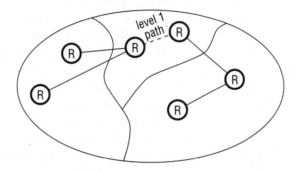

Figure 14.22 Using level 1 to repair level 2

14.4.9.6 Multiarea Bridged LANs

Routers keep track of neighbor routers by periodically sending IS-to-IS hello messages. They are similar in function to the ESH and ISH messages in the ES-IS protocol. Level 1 routers listen to the multicast address ALL LEVEL 1 ISs. There is a separate multicast address for ALL LEVEL 2 ISs. The reason for having different addresses for level 1 versus level 2 ISs is to allow LANs in different areas to be connected via bridges without merging the areas. The connection is made solely as a means of creating connectivity between the level 2 routers.

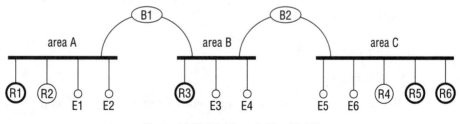

Figure 14.23 Multiarea bridged LAN

According to the ES-IS protocol, routers transmit IS hellos to the multicast address ALL ESs. Routers also transmit IS-to-IS hellos to the multicast address ALL LEVEL 1 ISs. Level 2 routers additionally transmit level 2 IS-to-IS hellos to the multicast address ALL LEVEL 2 ISs.

The bridges in a multiarea bridged LAN are manually configured to filter traffic with the destination addresses ALL LEVEL 1 ISs and ALL ESs, but to forward traffic with the destination address ALL LEVEL 2 ISs. In this way, the endnodes autoconfigure the correct area address. If the bridges forwarded the IS-to-ES hellos, then ESs in area A would see the ISHs from areas B and C as well and would not know the correct area address. They also might choose an IS in area B or C for forwarding off the LAN, and that would probably be less optimal than choosing a router that is closer.

The level 2 routers see each other as neighbors and can forward traffic between each other, but the level 1 routers do not see the IS-to-IS hellos from other areas.

When E1 wishes to communicate with E6, it transmits a data packet to one of the routers it knows about—namely, R1 or R2 (see Figure 14.23). Suppose it chooses R2. R2 forwards the packet to the nearest level 2 router—in this case, R1. Because R2 is forwarding the packet onto the same link from which the packet arrived, R2 transmits a redirect message to E1, redirecting E1 to R1's data link layer address on the LAN.

R1 forwards the data packet to R5. Although R1 forwards the packet onto the same link from which it arrived, R1 does not send a redirect to R2 because it knows that R2 is a router neighbor and a redirect would be ignored. R5 then forwards the packet to E6. Again, although R5 is forwarding the packet onto the same link from which it arrived, R5 does not transmit a redirect to R1 because R5 knows that R1 is a router neighbor.

When E1 transmits the next data packet, it transmits the packet to R1 because of its having received a redirect from R2. R1 forwards the packet to R5. This time, R1 sends a redirect to E1, pointing toward R5's data link layer address. R5 forwards the packet to E6 without issuing a redirect to R1.

When E1 transmits the third data packet, it transmits the packet to R5. R5 forwards the packet to E6 and issues a redirect to E1 because R5 knows that E1 is not a router neighbor. R5 in this case doesn't know for sure that E1 is an endnode because the bridge does not forward E1's ESHs. But the rule is that R5 transmits a redirect unless it knows that it shouldn't.

When E1 transmits the fourth data packet, it uses E6's data link layer address, and the packet is not forwarded by any routers.

14.4.9.7 Packets Used by IS-IS

There are three basic types of packets.

1. *IS-to-IS hello:* This packet allows neighbor routers to keep in touch with each other.

2. *LSP:* This packet includes information about a router's neighbors and is broadcast to all the routers.

3. *SNP (sequence numbers packet):* This packet is transmitted by router R to inform R's neighbors about the sequence numbers of LSPs R has received. It can serve as an acknowledgment to individual LSPs, as a method of requesting infor-

mation upon start-up, or as a method of ensuring that neighbor routers have identical LSP databases. It allows LSP distribution on a LAN without individual explicit acknowledgments.

There are two types of hello: one for LANs and one for point-to-point links. There are two types of SNP: the *complete* SNP and the *partial* SNP. Noninclusion of an LSP in the CSNP means that you do not have it in your database. No such conclusion can be made about the PSNP. The CSNP is used on LANs to make sure that LSP databases of the routers are in sync. PSNPs are used to acknowledge one or more LSPs.

All the IS-IS packets start with the fields shown in Figure 14.24, each 1 octet long. They are formatted like the data packet in CLNP.

# of octets

1	protocol identifier
1	header length
1	version
1	ID length
1	packet type
1	version
1	reserved
1	maximum area addresses

Figure 14.24 Common fixed header of IS-IS packets

Protocol identifier: A constant, equal to 131 decimal.

Length: Length of the fixed header—a useless field with useless information, but included so that the IS-IS packets wouldn't be self-conscious about looking too different from CLNP data packets.

Version = 1. (See also the sixth field on this list.)

ID length: The size of the ID portion of an NSAP. If it's between 1 and 8, inclusive, it indicates the size of the ID portion; if it's 0, it means that the ID portion = 6 octets; if it's 255, it means that the ID portion = 0 octets.

Packet type: Tells the type of packet (level/LSP, Hello, CSNP, PSNP).

Version = 1. (Yes, it's redundant. I suspect I had two **Version** fields in DECnet Phase V for major version (to be incremented for incompatible changes) and minor version (to be incremented for compatible changes) and that it got lost in translation when ISO adopted the protocol for IS-IS and rewrote it into ISO-eze.)

Reserved: Transmitted as 0; ignored on receipt.

Maximum area addresses: Number of area addresses permitted for this area. If the field is 0, the number is 3. Otherwise, the field is the number of area addresses allowed for the area.

I refer to the aforementioned fields as the *common fixed header* in the description of the IS-IS packet formats.

Each type of packet has some more of the "fixed" part of the header—fields that are always present—followed by a "variable" part of the header, with multiple fields TLV (type length value) encoded.

IS-to-IS Hello

The purpose of the IS-to-IS hello is to enable routers to coordinate with their router neighbors. On point-to-point links, it is very similar to an ES hello or an IS hello (see Section 11.2.1). It basically gives the IS's network layer address, together with the holding time, which is how long the receiver of the IS-to-IS hello should hold the information before assuming the router is down. There is a network-management-settable parameter *hello timer*, which is the interval between transmission of hellos. The holding time transmitted in the IS-to-IS hello should be about three times larger than the hello time so that a few lost hellos will not cause false assumptions about the neighbor's death. A small hello timer value allows the routing protocol to recover from failures faster because a router death will be detected quickly, but it involves more overhead because it requires more frequent transmission of hellos.

There are two main types of IS-to-IS hellos: one for transmission on point-to-point links and the other for transmission on LANs. The IS-to-IS hello on a LAN contains additional information, such as the ID of other routers on the LAN, that helps to ensure that connectivity between neighbors is bidirectional.

The point-to-point IS-to-IS hello is packet type 17. The first 8 octets (the portion of the IS-IS packets that is common to all the IS-IS packet types) are defined in the preceding subsection. The remaining part of the fixed portion of the point-to-point IS-to-IS hello is shown in Figure 14.25.

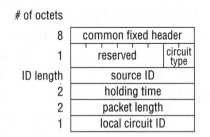

Figure 14.25 Point-to-point IS-IS hello, fixed portion

Circuit type is one of the following:

1 = level 1 only.

2 = level 2 only. The transmitter is a level 2 router that has been manually configured to use this circuit only for level 2 traffic. Such a router does not

transmit an IS-to-ES hello on a LAN. The purpose of transmitting this parameter in IS-to-IS hellos is to detect misconfiguration.

3 = both level 1 and level 2. The transmitter is a level 2 router that is allowed to use the circuit for both level 1 and level 2 traffic.

Source ID: The ID portion of the transmitting router's network layer address.

Holding time: The time at which neighbors can legally declare this router dead if they haven't gotten a hello from it.

Packet length: The length of the entire IS-to-IS hello message, in octets.

Local circuit ID: An identifier for this interface; it is unique relative to the transmitting router's other interfaces. For network management purposes, it is sometimes useful to have a unique "name" for a link in the network. The unique name of a point-to-point link is the concatenation of the ID of the router whose ID is lower with the local circuit ID that that router assigned to the link. Suppose that a point-to-point link connects routers 492 and 581; router 492 assigns the link the ID 12; and router 581 assigns the link the ID 3. The link would be known as 492.12.

The variable-length fields in a point-to-point IS-to-IS hello are as follows.

Area addresses: Type = 1 (see Figure 14.26). This is the set of area addresses manually configured into this router. The data consists of maximum area addresses, each preceded by an **address length** octet.

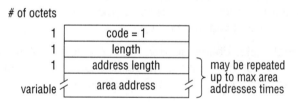

Figure 14.26 Area addresses field in IS-IS

Padding: Type = 8. This allows the packet to be padded to any length. The padding can contain any arbitrary values and is ignored by the receiver.

Authentication: Type = 10. The value contains two fields. The first octet is the type of authentication. The most useful one is HMAC-MD5, type = 54, which contains the 16-byte message digest of the combination of a secret shared by the routers and the message, computed according to the HMAC algorithm defined in RFC 2104. The original one was cleartext password, type 1.

The level 1 LAN IS-to-IS hello is packet type 15. The level 2 LAN IS-to-IS hello is type 16. Both levels of LAN IS-to-IS hello have the same fields. Figure 14.27 shows the contents of the fixed part of the header.

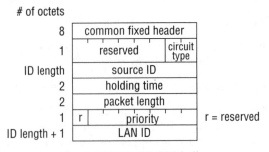

Figure 14.27 LAN IS-IS hello

Circuit type, source ID, holding time, and **packet length:** Same as defined for the point-to-point IS-to-IS hello.

Priority: The transmitting router's priority for becoming designated router on the LAN, with higher numbers having a higher priority.

LAN ID: The name of the LAN, as assigned by the designated router. It can be any 7-octet (ID length plus 1) quantity, as long as the last octet is non-zero, and the entire 7-octet quantity is unique within the area. A common method of assigning the LAN ID is for the designated router to use its system ID as the first 6 octets, and append an extra octet to differentiate among LANs for which it is designated router.

The variable-length fields defined for level 1 LAN IS-to-IS hellos are shown in the following list. In the first three cases, the definitions are the same as shown earlier in this subsection for point-to-point IS-to-IS hellos.

Area addresses: Type = 1.

Padding: Type = 8.

Authentication: Type = 10.

IS neighbors: Type = 6. This is a list of the other routers on the LAN from which the transmitting router has recently heard IS-to-IS hellos. The data consists of a sequence of 6-octet IDs. In this case, it is OK to assume that the ID is exactly 6 octets because this really is defined for 802 LANs. For example, if there were a new kind of LAN with 8-octet IDs, then a new kind of IS-to-IS hello would be defined for use on that new type of LAN.

LSP

There are two types of LSP: level 1 and level 2. A level 1 LSP is packet type 18. The remaining fields in the fixed part of the header are shown in Figure 14.28.

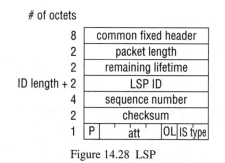

Figure 14.28 LSP

Packet length: The length of the entire LSP.

Remaining lifetime: The "age" field, as discussed in Section 12.2.3.

LSP ID: If the LSP is generated by a router on behalf of itself, the first six (ID length) octets are the system ID of that router, and the next octet is 0. If the LSP is generated on behalf of a LAN, the first 7 octets (ID length plus 1) consist of the LAN ID as described in the LAN IS-to-IS Hello message. The next octet is the fragment number, which is used when an LSP is so large that it must be broken into pieces.

Sequence number: Discussed in Section 12.2.3.

Checksum: Computed as in a data packet. It starts with the LSP ID field and goes to the end. The remaining lifetime field is purposely omitted from the checksum computation so that intermediate routers will never legitimately modify the checksum as computed by the router that originally generated the LSP.

P: A flag that indicates whether the router that generated the LSP supports partition repair. This is relevant only if the LSP was generated by a level 2 router.

Att ("attached," indicating that this level 2 router can reach other areas): A 4-bit field consisting of the four flags shown in the following list. It is relevant only if the level 1 LSP was generated by a level 2 router. Each flag indicates whether this level 2 router can reach at least one other area according to the specified metric.

bit	specified metric
4	Default metric
5	Delay metric
6	Expense metric
7	Error metric

OL (overloaded): Bit 3, if set, indicates that the router that generated the LSP has run out of room in its LSP database. (See Section 14.4.7.1)

IS type: A 2-bit field for which only two values are defined:

value	
1	level 1 router
3	level 2 router

The variable-length fields defined for the level 1 LSP are as follows.

Area addresses: As defined for previous packets.

Authentication: As defined for previous packets. In the case of LSPs, authentication must be implemented carefully. It is not desirable for some routers to accept an LSP and others to discard it because routing depends on routers using the same LSP database. So to be safe, all routers in the area must support authentication if it is being used.

IS neighbors: Type = 2 (see Figure 14.29). Multiple router neighbors can be listed in one occurrence of this field provided that the links to those neighbors have identical costs and flags. If the links to different router neighbors have different costs, this field appears multiple times.

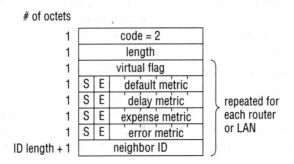

Figure 14.29 IS neighbors

Virtual flag: Indicates whether the link is a true level 1 link or a path through the level 2 network used as a level 1 link to repair a partitioned area.

S: Indicates whether the metric in question is supported. A value of 0 for the flag indicates that the metric is supported. **Default metric** must have this bit clear because it must always be supported.

E: A flag indicating whether the metric is *internal* (has meaning within the routing domain) or *external* (the destination's reachability was learned through an interdomain routing protocol that had no metrics or whose metrics were impossible to combine with the routing domain's metrics for some reason).

Note: Ideally, this bit would never be used. It is extremely inconvenient not to be able to compute the metric on an interdomain path. The metrics need not have the same meaning. The only important thing is that the path cost always increase at every hop.

There are two types of protocols that inspired the need for this bit. One is EGP, which does not provide a metric. The other is RIP, which provides a metric but has a maximum value of 15, which is much smaller than allowed by most other protocols. It is extremely dangerous in a routing protocol to permit the cost of a path to decrease along the way. If part of the path is computed with IS-IS, the accumulated path cost to the destination would almost certainly need to be mapped down into a very small number so that the information could be fed into RIP.

The terms *external* versus *internal* are not exactly correct for this bit. Instead, the terms *comparable* versus *incomparable* should really be used.

Neighbor ID: The ID of the neighboring router, plus a zero octet, or the LAN ID of the neighboring pseudonode.

CLNP ES neighbors: Type = 3. This field (see Figure 14.30) is encoded similarly to router neighbors except that it is assumed that many endnodes might be neighbors on a common link, and thus, the cost to all the endnodes will be the same. Therefore, this field reports the costs according to all the metrics once and then lists all the endnode neighbor IDs for which those costs apply. If the links to different endnode neighbors have different costs, the endnode neighbor field appears multiple times. This field is used only to report CLNP neighbor endnodes.

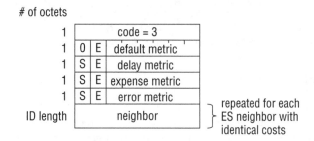

Figure 14.30 CLNP ES neighbors

The level 2 LSP is packet type 20. The only difference between the encoding of a level 1 LSP and that of a level 2 LSP is that the level 2 LSP does not contain a field for endnode neighbors. Instead, it contains a field for *prefix neighbors*, which are the equivalent of endnodes for level 2 routers.

Prefix neighbors: Type = 5. This field is encoded like endnode neighbors in a level 1 LSP except that instead of neighbor ID with a length of ID length, it is a sequence of (**address prefix length**, **address prefix**) pairs (see Figure 14.31). The address prefix length is in units of semioctets. This means that an address prefix need not be an integral number of octets.

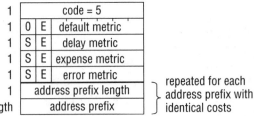

Figure 14.31 Address prefixes

Interdomain routing protocol information (see Figure 14.32).

```
# of octets
        1  |      code = 131        |
        1  |        length          |
        1  |  interdomain info type |
  variable |      information       |
```

Figure 14.32 IS-IS's IRPI field

Interdomain info type: This field indicates the interdomain routing protocol for which the field contains information. For example, it might be BGP information or information for some other interdomain routing protocol.

Information: This field itself is ignored by intradomain routing and is used only by the specified interdomain routing protocol.

Sequence Numbers Packet

A sequence numbers packet describes the LSPs in the LSP database in a compact format so that neighbor routers can ensure that their databases stay consistent. A sequence numbers packet is never forwarded. It is transmitted only between neighbors.

There are two main types of sequence numbers packets. A CSNP (complete sequence numbers packet) includes every LSP in the database. Because a CSNP may not fit into a single packet, a CSNP actually contains an *address range*, and all LSPs within that range are considered to be included.

A PSNP (partial sequence numbers packet) contains some subset of the LSPs. Nothing can be inferred about LSPs that are not included in a PSNP. A PSNP is primarily used to acknowledge one or more LSPs. It can also be used to request transmission of a specific LSP.

Because there are two LSP databases—level 1 and level 2—there are CSNPs and PSNPs for each of the levels. That makes four explicit types of SNPs. Except for the address range, which consists of the two fields **start LSP ID** and **end LSP ID** and is included in CSNPs but not in PSNPs, the encoding of all the SNPs is the same (see Figure 14.33).

# of octets

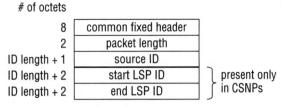

Figure 14.33 SNP

The packet types for SNPs are

- Level 1 CSNP = 24

- Level 2 CSNP = 25

- Level 1 PSNP = 26

- Level 2 PSNP = 27

The **source ID** field is the ID of the router that generated the SNP. Note: This field can be only ID length octets long because it is generated by a router and not on behalf of a LAN. The extra octet is transmitted as 0.

The **start LSP ID** and **end LSP ID** fields are ID length + 2 because an LSP on behalf of a LAN is ID length + 1, and a fragmented LSP requires an extra octet to indicate the fragment number.

The variable-length fields in SNPs are as follows.

LSP entries: As shown in Figure 14.34.

# of octets

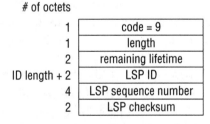

Figure 14.34 LSP entry in SNP

Figure 14.34 summarizes the state of a particular LSP. The **checksum** is included in case the same source generates two different LSPs with different data but the same **sequence number**. This can happen because of faulty behavior on the part of the source, corruption of LSP data, or a source's crashing and then restarting with a duplicate sequence number. The checksum is an inexpensive method of checking for this problem with a high probability of catching it.

Authentication: As described earlier.

14.4.10 OSPF

IS - IS = 0

—T-shirt distributed at an IETF meeting. (Note: I do not agree
or approve, but I concede that the T-shirt was clever.)

OSPF stands for "open shortest path first." *Open* implies that the protocol is not proprietary. *SPF* is the phrase some people use to refer to link state routing algorithms. OSPF
is very similar to IS-IS, in part because there are only so many ways one can build a link
state routing algorithm and in part because a lot of the ideas came from IS-IS.

14.4.10.1 General Packet-encoding Issues

OSPF does not have variable-length fields in the protocol packets, nor does it have any
provision for adding fields that will be ignored by previous-version routers. This arrangement permits compact encoding and faster processing of packets but limits extensibility.
For example, addresses in OSPF are exactly 8 octets (IPv4 address plus mask).

OSPF runs "on top of" IP. This means that an OSPF packet is transmitted with an IP
data packet header. The **protocol** field in the IP header (which is set to 89 for OSPF)
enables OSPF packets to be distinguished from other types of packets that use the IP
header.

14.4.10.2 Terminology

OSPF uses different terminology than IS-IS. The *backbone* in OSPF is what I have been
referring to as the level 2 network. A *backbone router* in OSPF is a level 2 router. An
area border router is a router that connects the area to the backbone. An *internal router*
is a level 1 router. An *AS boundary router* is a router that attaches to routers from other
autonomous systems—that is, an interdomain router. (The IP community refers to a
"domain" as an *autonomous system*. I don't like the term *autonomous system* because I
visualize a single computer when I hear the word *system*.) OSPF refers to link state information as link state advertisements, or LSAs. LSAs are functionally equivalent to the
IS-IS LSPs.

14.4.10.3 Area Partitions

In OSPF, level 2 routers are configured to report address summaries that include all the
IP addresses reachable within the area. For example, if one LAN in the area contains
addresses having the form 5.7.*.* another contains addresses having the form 5.12.*.*,
and it is known that no addresses outside the area have the form 5.*.*.*, then the level 2
router can report that "5.*.*.* is reachable in this area."

OSPF has no automatic mechanism for repairing area partitions. A human could
reconfigure the address summaries after an area partition, and routing would start working again. Or, the theory goes, if one is worried about area partitions, then the level 2

routers need not be configured with summary addresses; instead, they can report each individual IP address reachable within the area. In that case, a partitioned area would automatically break into two areas. However, if summary addresses are not used, there is no routing hierarchy.

14.4.10.4 Level 2 Partitions

Although it is probably preferable for the level 2 network to be connected via "real" backbone links, it is possible for a human to configure two level 2 routers to be endpoints of a *virtual level 2 link*. The purpose of configuring such a link is to repair a partition of the level 2 network. OSPF does not have any method for routers to automatically notice either that a virtual level 2 link is required or that such a link is no longer required. All this is managed by humans.

As indicated in Section 14.4.10.1, OSPF routing messages are carried inside an IP header. When an OSPF routing message is transmitted between level 2 routers X and Y, the destination specified in the IP header is Y and the source in the IP header is X. However, when X forwards a data packet with source A and destination B over the virtual link to Y, the data packet already has an IP header, which contains as the source the ultimate source of the data packet (A) and the ultimate destination of the data packet (B). For it to be possible to forward a data packet between X and Y, the level 1 routers along the virtual link must recognize that packets for out-of-area destination B must be forwarded toward level 2 router Y (see Figure 14.35).

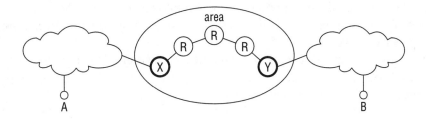

data packet between X and Y with OSPF (no encapsulation)

IP header		data
destination = B	source = A	data

data packet between X and Y if encapsulation were used

encapsulation IP header		IP header		data
destination = Y	source = X	destination = B	source = A	data

Figure 14.35 Data packet with and without encapsulation

An alternative strategy (not used by OSPF) uses *encapsulation*. Level 2 router X receives a data packet with IP source A and IP destination B. X determines that the packet should be forwarded through level 2 router Y over the virtual link between X and Y. X puts an additional IP header on the packet, which specifies X as the IP source address and Y as the IP destination address. Because Y resides in the same area as X, the level 1 routers in the area have no problem forwarding the packet to Y. When Y receives the data packet, it removes the outer IP header added by X and continues forwarding the packet.

The OSPF approach requires level 1 routers to have level 2 information because they must know how to forward a packet destined for another area. The disadvantage of the encapsulation approach (which would not require level 1 routers to have level 2 information) is that encapsulation presents some complications. If the encapsulated packet is too large it must be fragmented, and this, in turn, requires that Y be able to perform reassembly.

14.4.10.5 Finding the Right Level 2 Router

OSPF feeds a summary of the level 2 destinations into the area so that internal routers can choose a more optimal exit point out of the area—that is, take into account the distance from the level 2 router to the destination.

If feeding the level 2 information into some area turns out to be too expensive, you can configure the area as a *stub area* by individually configuring each router in the area. In a stub area, the level 2 routers announce *default route* as the summary of all the IP destinations reachable outside the AS. Information about IP destinations that are outside the area but still within the AS continues to be fed into an area even if it is configured as a stub area. The reasoning given is that the level 2 routing information inside the AS is unlikely to be extensive.

If an area is configured to be a stub area, the routes out of the area to destinations outside the AS become the same as the routes used by IS-IS, and it becomes impossible to configure virtual links through the area.

14.4.10.6 Neighbor Initialization

When a link between two neighbor routers comes up, OSPF has a protocol for synchronizing their link state databases. It is functionally similar to the exchange of CSNPs upon startup that IS-IS does.

First, OSPF determines which of the neighbors will be the *master* in the initialization protocol and which will be the *slave*. This is determined based on ID. The one that is chosen master then sends a description of its link state database (similar to an IS-IS PSNP) by transmitting *database description* (DD) packets, each one containing a portion of the database (it is assumed that the entire database description will not fit into a single packet) and each having a sequence number. The slave acknowledges each DD packet by sending a DD packet with the same sequence number containing information about the slave's LSAs. When the master receives a DD packet from the slave with the same sequence number as the last one the master transmitted, the master sends the next group of information in a DD packet with a sequence number that is 1 higher than the preceding sequence number. The master continues sending DD packets in this manner until it has described all the LSAs in its database, indicating the last packet by clearing the **M** bit in the DD packet.

If the slave requires more DD packets than the master in order to describe the LSAs in the slave's database, the master knows that the slave is not finished because the **M** bit is set in the slave's DD. At this point, the master must continue sending empty DD packets until it eventually receives one from the slave with the **M** bit clear.

When router R1 discovers, as a result of receiving DD information from neighbor R2, that R1 is missing some information, R1 sends *link state request packets* to obtain the missing information from R2. If R1 discovers that R2 is missing some LSAs, R1 transmits those LSAs to R2.

If OSPF had defined the sequence of DD packets to be the equivalent of IS-IS's CSNP (complete sequence numbers packet) rather than IS-IS's PSNP (partial sequence numbers packet), then only one of the two routers would have had to inform the other of the LSAs in the database.

In contrast, in IS-IS, when a point-to-point link comes up between neighbor routers R1 and R2, each router assumes that the other router has no LSPs and marks all LSPs as needing to be transmitted to that neighbor. Additionally, each neighbor transmits a CSNP. If R2 receives R1's CSNP, then R2 notes that R1 already has the LSPs indicated in its CSNP and clears the transmit flags for those LSPs. The CSNP in IS-IS is merely an optimization. In IS-IS, when a new neighbor router comes up on a LAN, no special protocol is required. The designated router's periodic CSNP will keep the LSP databases in all the routers on the LAN synchronized.

14.4.10.7 Types of LSAs

There are five basic types of LSAs in OSPF.

1. *Type 1—router links advertisement:* This is very similar to an IS-IS LSP. It is flooded only within the area and contains information about the router's neighbor routers (via point-to-point links) and the LANs to which the router is attached. It can also be generated by a backbone router and flooded within the backbone—in which case, it is equivalent to an IS-IS level 2 LSP.

2. *Type 2—network links advertisement:* This is similar to an IS-IS LSP generated on behalf of a LAN. The OSPF network links advertisement is generated by the designated router on a LAN, lists all the routers on the LAN, and is flooded only within the area (or within the backbone, if it is level 2).

3. *Type 3—network summary link advertisement:* This is level 2 information that is injected into an area to describe networks that are reachable outside the area (see Figure 14.36). It is generated by an area border router (a level 2 router that is connected to more than one area) and is flooded into an area. An area border router

attached to both area 1 and area 2 generates a different network summary link advertisement for distribution within area 1 than for distribution within area 2.

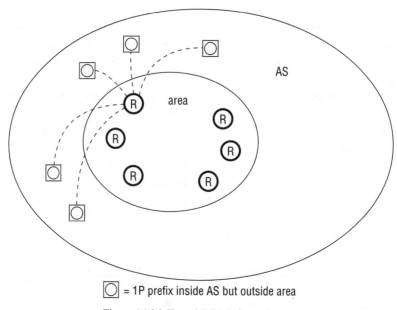

☐ = 1P prefix inside AS but outside area

Figure 14.36 Type 3 LSA information

A type 3 LSA is also used by area border routers to summarize the destinations within the area to the backbone. When the contents of the type 3 LSA contain information about an area, it is flooded to the backbone.

Note that a type 3 OSPF LSA can report only a single IP destination. Therefore, an area border router generates many type 3 LSAs. For each area A to which it has a link, it generates one type 3 LSA for each IP destination outside A within the AS. It also generates one for each IP prefix within A and floods that to the backbone.

4. *Type 4—AS boundary routers summary link advertisement:* This is more level 2 information injected into an area (see Figure 14.37). It describes the cost of the path from the router that generated the type 4 LSA to an AS boundary router. As with type 3, type 4 LSAs carry only a single destination.

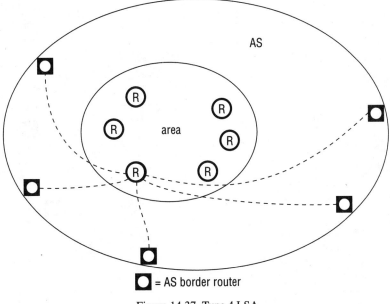

= AS border router

Figure 14.37 Type 4 LSA

5. *Type 5—AS external link advertisement:* This is also level 2 information that is flooded to all the routers throughout the entire AS. It describes the cost from the AS boundary router that generated the type 5 LSA to a destination outside the AS (see Figure 14.38). As with type 3 and 4 LSAs, because the type 5 LSA carries only a single destination, an AS boundary router generates many type 5 LSAs.

The combination of type 4 and type 5 LSAs informs level 1 routers about IP destinations reachable outside the AS. Assume that there are k level 2 routers in some area, j AS border routers in the AS, and n IP destinations reachable outside the AS. With the OSPF scheme, each of the k level 2 routers reports the cost of the path from itself to each of the j AS border routers. Level 1 routers also receive the LSA generated by each of the j AS border routers, each one reporting at least some of the n externally reachable IP destination addresses.

OSPF could have had each area border router report the distance from itself to each of the n externally reachable IP prefixes rather than the chosen scheme, which has each area border router report its distance to each AS border router and then has the AS border routers report the distances from themselves to each externally reachable IP destination. OSPF is based on certain topological assumptions under which the OSPF scheme uses less memory than the variant scheme. (See homework problem 9.)

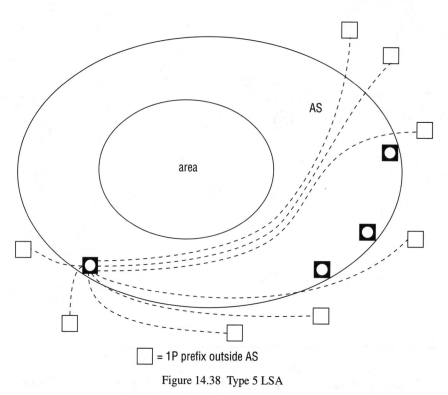

Figure 14.38 Type 5 LSA

14.4.10.8 Packet Encoding

All OSPF packets start with the 24-octet header shown in Figure 14.39.

# of octets

1	version
1	packet type
2	packet length
4	router ID
4	area ID
2	checksum
2	authentication type
8	authentication data

Figure 14.39 Common portion of OSPF header

Version: 2

Packet type: As shown in Figure 14.40.

value	packet type
1	hello
2	database description
3	link state request
4	link state update
5	link state acknowledgment

Figure 14.40 Packet type field values

Packet length: Number of octets in the OSPF packet.

Router ID: The IP address of the router that generated the packet.

Area ID: The ID of the area to which the packet belongs (or 0 if it is a level 2 packet).

Checksum: The same checksum algorithm as for an IP data packet.

Authentication type: As shown in Figure 14.41.

value	authentication type
0	no authentication
1	cleartext password
2	crytographic (keyed message digest)

Figure 14.41 Authentication type field values

Authentication data: 8 bytes. But when cryptographic authentication is used, the authentication data includes only the key ID, the length of the authentication data, and a sequence number. The actual integrity check data is appended to the end of the message.

Hello Packets

Hello packets are similar to the IS-to-IS hello packets (see Figure 14.42). They are transmitted between neighbors and never forwarded.

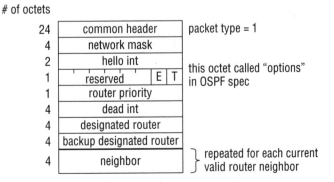

Figure 14.42 OSPF hello

Network mask: The mask for the link configured in the router generating the hello. If this field does not match the receiving router's mask configured for the link, the receiving router rejects the hello and does not accept the transmitting router as a neighbor.

Hello int: The number of seconds between this router's hello packets. As discussed in Section 14.4.5.2, a receiving router will reject the hello and refuse a transmitting router as a neighbor if the receiving router's configured **hello int** on that link is not identical to the transmitting router's **hello int**.

Options: Only the bottom 2 bits are defined. The bottom bit is **T,** which indicates whether the router supports multiple routing metrics. This means that a router must either support exactly one metric (the default) or support all of them (eight metrics, which is all possible settings of the three types of service bits in a data packet header).

The next bit is **E**, which indicates whether the router considers the area to be a stub area. If the receiving router has not been configured identically with the transmitting router, the hello is rejected.

Router priority: Used in the election of designated router and backup designated router. A router with a higher number is more likely to become designated router. A priority of 0 means that the router will never become designated router or backup designated router even if no other routers are up.

Dead int: The number of seconds before a router declares a neighbor router dead if no hellos have been received. As with **hello int**, if this time doesn't exactly match the configured time in the receiving router, the receiving router rejects the hello.

Designated router: The ID of the router that the transmitting router thinks is the designated router (or 0 if the transmitting router thinks there is no DR).

Backup designated router: The ID of the router that the transmitting router thinks is the backup designated router (or 0 if the transmitting router thinks there is no backup DR).

Neighbors: The list of 4-octet IDs of routers from which hellos were received on the link within **dead int** seconds.

Database Description Packets

When a link first comes up between two routers, R1 and R2, one of the routers (the one with the higher ID) becomes master and the other becomes slave. After the identity of the master is known, the master transmits a sequence of database description packets (as many as necessary to include all LSAs in the database). Each fragment of the database description packet contains a sequence number (see Figure 14.43). The slave acknowledges each fragment, and only after fragment number n is acknowledged does the master transmit fragment number $n+1$.

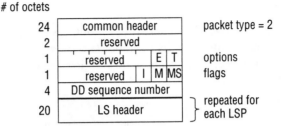

Figure 14.43 OSPF database description packet

Options: The **E** and **T** bits, as described in the preceding subsection.

Flags: Bit 8 (least significant)—**M/S** ("master/slave"). If set, this bit indicates that the transmitting router is the master. If not set, it indicates that the transmitting router is the slave.

Bit 7—**M** ("more"). If set, this bit indicates that this is not the final database description packet.

Bit 6—**I** ("init"). If set, this bit indicates that this is the first in the sequence of database description packets.

Database description packet sequence number: The sequence number of the database description packet. The beginning value should be chosen to be unique to minimize confusion with previously transmitted database description packets.

LS headers list: For each LSA advertised, as shown in Figure 14.44.

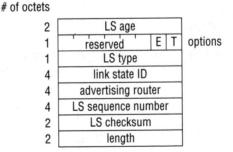

Figure 14.44 OSPF link state header

Link State Request

A link state request packet (OSPF packet type 3) contains a description of one or more LSAs that a router is requesting from its neighbor (see Figure 14.45). A router discovers that it needs LSAs after exchanging database description packets with the neighbor.

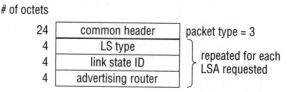

Figure 14.45 Link state request

Link State Update

Link state update packets are OSPF packet type 4 (see Figure 14.46). They contain one or more link state advertisements.

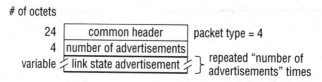

Figure 14.46 OSPF link state update

Link State Acknowledgment

Link state acknowledgments are OSPF packet type 5 (see Figure 14.47). They contain one or more link state advertisement headers, each of which is 20 octets long.

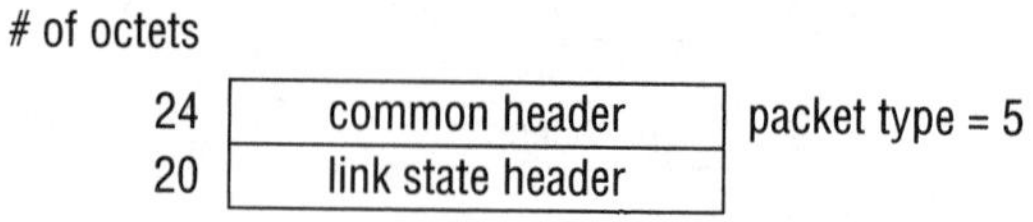

# of octets

24	common header	packet type = 5
20	link state header	

Figure 14.47 Link state acknowledgment

Link State Advertisement

All five types of LSA in OSPF start out with the 20-octet header shown in Figure 14.48.

# of octets

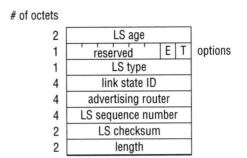

Figure 14.48 OSPF link state advertisement

LS age is an estimate of the number of seconds since the LSA was generated.

Options, carries the **E** bit (meaning that the router believes the area is a stub area) and the **T** bit (meaning that the router can handle multiple types of service).

LS type is one of those shown in Figure 14.49.

value	LS type
1	router links
2	network links
3	reachable IP prefix inside AS (outside area)
4	reachable AS border router
5	reachable IP prefix outside AS

Figure 14.49 LS types values

Link state ID is defined according to the type of LSA (see Figure 14.50).

value	link state ID definition
1	ID of router that generated the LSA
2	IP address of LAN's DR
3	The IP address of the link being reported as an IP destination (mask later in LSA)
4	reachable AS border router's IP address
5	The IP address of the link being reported as an IP destination (mask later in LSA)

Figure 14.50 Link state ID definitions values

Advertising router is the ID of the router that generated the LSA.

LS sequence number is the sequence number of the LSA.

LS checksum is the Fletcher checksum of the complete contents of the LSA. (For details on computation of a Fletcher checksum, see Annex C of ISO 8473, the CLNP specification, or Annex B of RFC 905, the ISO transport specification.)

Length is the number of octets in the LSA.

Router Links Advertisement

A router links advertisement is a type 1 LSA (see Figure 14.51).

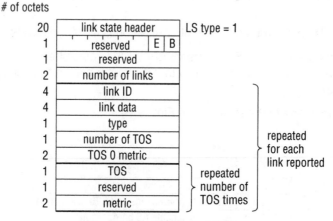

Figure 14.51 OSPF type 1 LSA

When set, bit **E** (which stands for "external") indicates that the router that generated the LSA is an AS boundary router.

When set, bit **B** indicates that the router is an area border router.

Number of links is the total number of links that the router that generated the LSA has in the area.

Link ID identifies what is connected to the router via the link being reported. For each type of link, the link ID is as shown in Figure 14.52.

type of link	contents of link ID field
1	ID of neighbor router
2	IP address of LAN's DR
3	IP address of the LAN
4	ID of neighbor router

Figure 14.52 Link ID

Link data consists of the subnetwork mask when the link is type 3 (stub LAN). Otherwise, it is the IP address of the router that generated the LSA on the advertised link.

Type is the type of link, which is one of those shown in Figure 14.53.

value	link type
1	point-to-point link to another router
2	connect to a "transit" LAN
3	connection to a "transit" LAN
4	virtual link

Figure 14.53 Link types

Number of TOS specifies the number of costs ("types of service") reported for the link, not counting TOS 0, which is required. This is here only for backward compatibility with earlier versions of OSPF created when people thought that having multiple metrics in IP was useful. Today's OSPF implementations always set this field to 0 and do not include any metrics other than default metric. It is legal, however, to allow multiple TOS. In that case, each TOS is the same as the **TOS** field in an IP data packet header, but without the precedence bits, and is followed by the metric for that TOS.

Network Links Advertisement

A network links advertisement is a type 2 LSA (see Figure 14.54).

# of octets

20	link state header	LS type = 2
4	network mask	
4	attached router	} repeated for each attached router

Figure 14.54 Network links advertisement

Network mask is the mask for the LAN's IP address.

Attached router is the ID of a router on the LAN that is a neighbor of the DR.

Summary Link Advertisement

A summary link advertisement (LSA type 3 or 4) is generated by an area border router and flooded into the area. Type 3 reports the cost to an IP prefix outside the area. Type 4 reports the cost to an AS border router (see Figure 14.55). A summary link advertisement reports only a single destination.

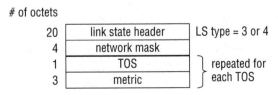

# of octets

20	link state header	LS type = 3 or 4
4	network mask	
1	TOS	} repeated for each TOS
3	metric	

Figure 14.55 OSPF type 3 or 4 LSA

The **network mask** is relevant only for type 3 LSAs. For type 4 LSAs, it is set to 0.

AS External Link Advertisement

An AS external link advertisement is a type 5 LSA (see Figure 14.56). These LSAs are generated by AS boundary routers and flooded to the entire AS, except for stub areas. Like type 3 and 4 LSAs, each type 5 LSA can report only a single destination. Thus, if n subnetwork numbers are reachable outside an AS, each AS boundary router generates n LSAs (unless configured otherwise).

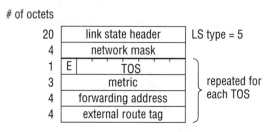

Figure 14.56 OSPF type 5 LSA

Network mask is the mask for the advertised destination.

E is a flag indicating whether the metric reported can be considered comparable to the metric for that TOS used within the AS. If it is comparable (**E** = 0), the total cost to the advertised destination can be calculated by summing the cost to the AS boundary router with the cost that the AS boundary router reports to the advertised destination. If it isn't comparable (**E** = 1), there is no way to compare the internal cost to the external cost. Therefore, the AS boundary router advertising the smallest distance to the destination is chosen, and the cost to the AS boundary router is ignored.

TOS is the same as the **TOS** field in an IP data packet header but without the **precedence** bits.

Metric is the advertised cost to the destination.

Forwarding address is used to optimize the final hop. If the advertising AS is advertising a destination that can more optimally be reached by a different router on the same LAN, then the advertising AS puts that router's address into the forwarding address field. Otherwise, it leaves the field 0. Without this field, in certain topologies, a route might traverse an extra LAN hop.

External route tag is 4 octets of information that might be useful to an inter-domain routing protocol, but the OSPF spec does not specify what that field contains. One idea for information that could be carried in this field is the *autonomous system number* of the next AS hop on the path to the advertised destination. An AS number is a 16-bit quantity that is globally administered by the same authority that administers IP addresses. The AS number is not part of an IP address. It was invented for the EGP protocol. Other interdomain routing protocols may also use the AS number for whatever purpose might be found for it.

Although the purpose of the OSPF external route tag field is not clearly defined, the following reasons were given for providing it.

1. The tag might contain the IP address of the interdomain router that advertised the destination. In theory, an interdomain router R1 that wishes to forward a packet through the domain to interdomain router R2 could use this information to determine whether the intradomain routing protocol (OSPF) has stabilized. R1 could then route the packet toward R2. In my opinion, because routing algorithms always take some time to converge, there is no reason for performing a special check in this situation.

2. The tag might contain the number of the autonomous system from which the information about that destination address was learned. This information might be of use to the obsolescent EGP protocol because EGP requires that information learned from AS 1 not be transmitted back to another EGP router from AS 1. When EGP is replaced by BGP, however, this field is no longer useful for that purpose.

3. It might allow the interdomain routing protocol to pass information to other interdomain routers in the same domain without requiring them to communicate directly. Although this might be more efficient than n^2 pairwise links between the n interdomain routers in a domain, it requires that all the intradomain routers store information they will ignore. It is useful only if the amount of information that the interdomain routers wish to transmit to each other is no larger than 4 octets per destination address. This amount of information might be sufficient for EGP, but it is not sufficient for BGP.

14.4.11 PNNI Details

14.4.11.1 Path Setup

The most radically different thing about PNNI from other routing protocols discussed in this section is that PNNI assumes connection-oriented path setup because it was designed for ATM.

Recall from Section 14.4.1.4 that a PNNI router has the link state database for its own peer group and for each ancestor peer group. However, the "nodes" in the parent peer groups are not individual routers but instead are peer group names. Thus, except for the lowest level of routing, a PNNI router cannot calculate the complete path. Instead, for those levels of routing it specifies a sequence of peer groups.

Suppose a router wishes to compute a path to Dest in peer group CGHV (see Figure 14.57). From the top level of routing, R1 knows it must go from A to C. From the next level of routing, it knows that to get to C the path is AB, AD. PNNI specifies the route as a separate sequence for each hierarchical level, with a position pointer at each level. So the path that R1 will specify is the sequence of routers within ABX that will reach AD—say, R1, R2, R3. So the path will look like [R1, R2, R3] [AB, AD] [A, C].

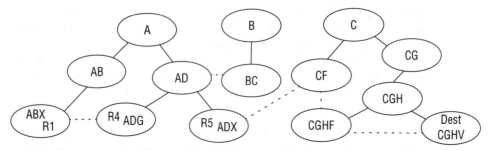

Figure 14.57 PNNI hierarchical path setup

When the path setup packet reaches the first router in AD (R4), R4 replaces the initial portion of the path (R1-R2-R3) with "AB." It also replaces the portion "AD" with the specifics of how to reach C, which is a path with final hop the node ADX. When the path setup reaches R5, it replaces the portion called ADX with the specific route to C.

When the path setup reaches Dest, the route will look like [CGHF, sequence of routers to get to Dest within CGHV] [CF, CG] [A, C].

14.4.11.2 Area Partitions

PNNI's peer group leader election is similar to IS-IS's partition-designated level 2 router election. And like IS-IS, PNNI gives a partition a unique name by taking the peer group name and appending to it the peer group leader's ID. The only difference between PNNI's mechanism and IS-IS's mechanism is that PNNI does not attempt to heal the area by creating a virtual link. Instead, it treats the two partitions as two separate peer groups.

The only issue with doing that (rather than healing the peer group) is that typically routers are configured with summary addresses for advertising into the higher layers of routing. So if a peer group is partitioned, there will be two peer groups advertising the same address prefixes.

This does not create problems for paths going through a peer group, but it creates problems for paths in which the destination is in the partitioned peer group. With traditional hop-by-hop routing, this would be a fatal problem because there is no way to control which partition a packet will be forwarded to by subsequent routers on the path. However, PNNI does source routing, and when a path setup fails there is a crank-back procedure in which the path setup is backed out until there is a router that can make a different decision.

As a result, the router that noticed that there were multiple peer groups in which the destination might reside could at that point attempt a path to a different partition.

Once a path setup succeeds, the fact that the peer group is partitioned is not a problem.

14.5 Interdomain Routing Protocols

Interdomain routing works between domains, and intradomain routing works within a domain. That's a nice definition until you wonder what a domain is. I'm rather a heretic in that I think it was only a historical accident that we wound up with domains rather than a single routing protocol that could scale to arbitrarily many levels.

Interdomain routing protocols are considered different from intradomain routing protocols only because it is assumed that domains don't really want to be combined into one big happy melting pot of a network. Routing domains are independently funded. When a domain routes transit traffic, resources are being consumed. Therefore, some domains might be willing to route some sorts of traffic and not others. Some domains might have different charging policies, and users might wish to control the route to optimize monetary cost. Routing domains don't trust one another. They don't trust the routing algorithms running in other domains to be implemented properly, and they don't want bugs in other domains or in the interdomain routing protocol to affect the routing within the routing domain. And it is assumed that all sorts of administrative rules will restrict the legal routes. Within a routing domain, if you can physically travel a particular path, it is legal. Between routing domains, it might be that the only legal paths are ones for which bilateral agreements have been made between the owners of the domains. Or laws within a country might restrict the legal routes (for example, Canadian traffic must not exit and then reenter Canada). Or network X might agree to be a transit network only for military business.

People claim that having intradomain as well as interdomain routing gives us the flexibility of multiple routing protocols and lets us change routing protocols over time because each domain can run its own intradomain routing protocol. The problem with this reasoning is that there is no such flexibility in interdomain routing. You get only one.

The world would certainly be simpler with a single routing protocol rather than an interdomain one and an intradomain one. To believe that you need two different types of protocols you must believe the following three things.

1. Policy-based routing (choosing paths not based on minimizing a metric but on arbitrary policies) is essential for interdomain routing.

2. Policy-based routing is never important within a domain.

3. A routing protocol capable of handling policies would be too inefficient to be an acceptable solution in the simple world where the only policy is to minimize a metric.

It is hard to believe all three things at once or to believe the third at all. If a routing protocol can't handle the simplest case, surely it would be really horrible in the more complex cases. But at this point the world believes we need two types of protocols and that BGP will be the interdomain protocol.

In this section, I describe three interdomain routing protocols. The first, static routing, is not really a protocol at all. The second is EGP, the IP community's first interdomain routing protocol, which was documented in RFC 827. The IP community refers to an interdomain routing protocol as an "EGP" (for "exterior gateway protocol"). Because I find it confusing to discuss EGP as an example of an EGP, I use the term *interdomain routing protocol* generically and use EGP only when discussing the specific protocol documented in RFC 827. The third protocol is BGP (for "border gateway protocol").

14.5.1 Static Routing

Static routing means that information is manually configured into routers that directly connect to other routing domains. Ordinarily, manual configuration is to be avoided whenever possible. But in interdomain routing, static routing has five attractive features.

1. Often, links between routing domains are expensive to use, and there are long periods of time during which no data traffic needs to flow on the links. Thus, it is attractive not to require any routing control traffic on such links.

2. Security often requires that you have some sort of sanity check on the information because it is easy to disrupt the Internet by advertising that you can reach addresses that you can't really reach.

3. Even a routing algorithm requires a lot of configuration, such as for introducing address summaries.

4. Highly complex policies can be accommodated.

5. Because no interdomain routing protocol is operating, there is no possibility of global disruption caused by faulty interdomain routers in another domain.

The chief disadvantages of static routing are as follows.

1. It does not adapt to changing topologies. Inconsistent manually configured databases can cause looping of interdomain traffic.

2. Manual configuration requires a lot of effort.

Remember that all routing protocols, especially BGP, require a lot of configuration. The Internet has evolved from its research roots, when all participants could be trusted not to do anything intentionally disruptive. Static configuration must play an important role in interdomain routing. An ISP does not, in general, trust a customer network to report its reachable addresses. Instead, the ISP statically configures the information it would have received from the customer.

There are various gradations of static configuration. Certainly today there is a lot of configuration: how to summarize the routing information, what your area address is, what your AS number is. And in many cases, particularly between the customer net and the ISP, the ISP simply configures the addresses reachable from the customer rather than trusting the customer to report them. Tunnels are also configured in order to enforce policies such as that one customer of an ISP wants to use one long distance carrier and another wants to use a different one. So the ISP is statically configured to add an IP header and send the traffic to the desired long distance carrier.

A major form of configuration would be to configure the entire path and allow someone along the path to specify and set up the desired path from source to destination. This is similar to a connection-oriented network such as ATM. Having multiple paths configured would tolerate topology changes because an alternate path could be tried if the primary one did not work. Originally this could have been done with IP only with source routing or repeated encapsulation, and that would have made the header very large. But the concept of MPLS, which adds an ATM-like header to IP and sets up paths as with ATM, makes this possible.

As I discuss in Section 14.5.3, BGP has some alarming properties. Chief among them is that people do not think about whether it is the right solution. It's just there, and nobody has suggested any alternatives. But it would be valuable to study the difference in configuration overhead, robustness, memory and bandwidth overhead, and flexibility of supported policies between BGP and static routing.

14.5.2 EGP

EGP was the first interdomain routing protocol. Nobody likes it, but something was needed. And despite EGP's problems, the Internet limped along with it for many years.

The EGP protocol has three aspects:

1. Neighbor acquisition

2. Neighbor reachability

3. Routing information

14.5.2.1 Neighbor Acquisition

The EGP spec says nothing about how routers decide to become EGP neighbors. An *interior EGP neighbor* is a router within a particular AS with which EGP information is exchanged. An *exterior EGP neighbor* is a router in another AS with which EGP information is exchanged. Theoretically (according to the EGP spec), an EGP neighbor must be a single IP hop away. However, the single IP hop can be over a WAN. If the WAN is a CLNP network, for example, the EGP protocol messages would be transmitted inside a CLNP network layer header. There is no reason that the WAN cannot be running IP as the network layer; then the EGP packet would be contained inside an IP header.

Anyone who isn't confused about when routers become EGP neighbors and what the rules are for configuring routers to initiate being EGP neighbors does not understand EGP.

If router A has been configured to initiate a neighbor relationship with router B, then A transmits a *neighbor acquisition* message to B. If B has been configured to accept a neighbor relationship with A, it transmits a *neighbor acquisition reply*. Otherwise, it transmits a *neighbor acquisition refusal*. If one of the routers wishes a *divorce*, it transmits a *neighbor cease* message, to which the other router replies with a *neighbor cease acknowledgment*. Figure 14.58 shows an EGP neighbor acquisition packet.

```
                    # of octets
                        1   | version number = 1 |
                        1   |      type = 3       |
                        1   |        code         |
                        1   |        info         |
                        2   |      checksum       |
                        2   |     AS number       |
                        2   | identification number |
```

Figure 14.58 EGP neighbor acquisition packet

Version number is 1.

Type is 3, designating this as a neighbor acquisition message of some sort.

Code is one of the following:

value	code
0	neighbor acquisition request
1	neighbor acquisition reply
2	neighbor acquisition refusal
3	neighbor cease
4	neighbor cease acknowledgment

Info depends on the message type. For a refusal message, 1 indicates that the transmitter is out of table space, and 2 indicates that there is an administrative prohibition against becoming neighbors. For a cease message, 1 indicates that the transmitter is planning to go down soon, and 2 indicates that the neighbor relationship is no longer needed.

Checksum is the 16-bit 1's complement of the 1's complement sum of the EGP message starting with the EGP version number field.

AS number is the AS number of the router that generated the message.

The **identification number** aids in matching requests and replies.

14.5.2.2 Neighbor Reachability

The neighbor reachability aspect of EGP consists of two routers that are neighbors with each other sending messages back and forth to ensure that they are still alive and able to communicate (see Figure 14.59). Each router periodically sends a hello, and the other responds with an "I heard you" message.

# of octets

1	version number = 1
1	type = 5
1	code
1	status
2	checksum
2	AS number
2	sequence number
1	minimum polling interval
1	reserved
2	last poll ID number

Figure 14.59 EGP hello/I heard you

Type is 5.

Code is 0 for "hello," 1 for "I heard you."

Status is one of the following:

value	status
0	No status given.
1	"You appear reachable to me."
2	"You appear unreachable to me due to neighbor reachability information."
3	"You appear unreachable to me due to network reachability information."
4	"You appear unreachable to me due to problems with my network interface."

The **sequence number** aids in matching requests and replies.

Minimum polling interval is the minimum number of minutes that the transmitting router would like the receiving router to wait between hello messages.

Last poll ID number gives the identification number of the most recent routing update message received from the router to which this *hello* or *I heard you* is being transmitted.

14.5.2.3 Routing Information

EGP is similar to a distance vector routing protocol, but there is one astounding differ-ence. Instead of specifying the cost to a destination, a router merely reports whether or not the destination is reachable. EGP was designed for a specific topology—namely, the assumption was that there was a "core" system to the Internet, which was the ARPANET, and that various routing domains attached to the core, usually with a single router (see Figure 14.60).

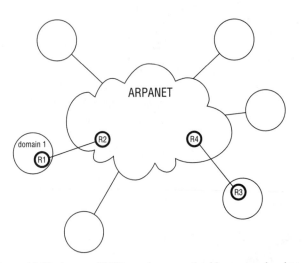

Figure 14.60 Assumed EGP topology: one backbone, two-level tree

R1 discovers, through the intradomain routing protocol operating in domain 1, which IP network numbers are reachable inside domain 1. R1 informs R2 of that list of network numbers. R2 informs the other routers in the core domain so that they will route traffic for any of the network numbers in domain 1 toward R2. R2 also informs R1 of all the network numbers reachable outside domain 1.

Note that this protocol does not work if there are any loops in the topology. For example, consider Figure 14.61.

Assume that IP network number 5 is reachable in domain 1. R1 informs R2 that 5 is reachable via R1. R2 informs R3 that 5 is reachable via R2. R3 informs R4 that 5 is reach-able via R3. R4 informs R5 that 5 is reachable via R4, and R5 informs R6 that 5 is reachable via R5. Meanwhile, in the other direction, R6 informs R5 that 5 is reachable via R6, and so on.

When the core has a packet for network number 5, it has a choice. It sends the packet via either R2 or R3. If it sends the packet to R2, R2 has a choice. It knows it can send the packet to either R3 or R1. If it sends the packet to R1 and if R1 is sensible, then R1 deliv-ers the packet to domain 1 because it should prefer reaching a destination it knows is reachable in the domain via intradomain routing. If, however, R2 sends the packet to R3, then R3 has no reason to prefer the "clockwise" direction in which the packet has been

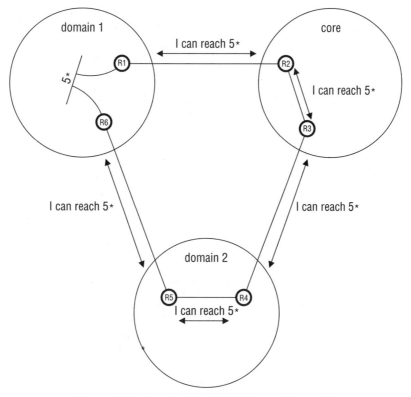

Figure 14.61 Topology in which EGP would not work

traveling and is equally likely to send the packet back to R2. The packet does not keep a diary of its travels. It will eventually be dropped when the TTL field becomes 0. Until then, the Internet will have no idea which way to send the packet, and it is as likely to loop as to get delivered.

Surprisingly, the EGP routing update message includes a metric when reporting the reachability of a destination. But the EGP designers explicitly preclude making routing decisions based on the metric, on the theory that metrics in different domains might be incomparable. For example, RIP allows a metric only as large as 15. Other routing protocols would probably allow much larger metrics. Suppose that a router wishes to report the reachability of a destination having cost 59 with one metric and must translate it into the RIP metric to pass the information across an IP routing domain routed with RIP. In that case, the metric would somehow have to be compressed into a much smaller number. The decision was to deal with incomparable metrics by mandating a loop-free topology and ignoring the metrics.

Another subtlety of EGP is that a routing message includes the IP addresses of other routers, and, for each router listed, there is a list of destinations. The purpose is to allow a single router on a LAN to speak on behalf of other routers on the LAN. Otherwise, each pair of routers on the LAN would need to exchange EGP information. It is more efficient to funnel routing information through one router, which gathers information from all the other routers and keeps all the other routers informed.

If the router with which all the other routers communicate simply advertised the set of all destinations it has learned about through the other routers on the LAN, then all traffic for the advertised network numbers would be sent to the transmitting router. An extra hop might be required on the LAN (see Figure 14.62).

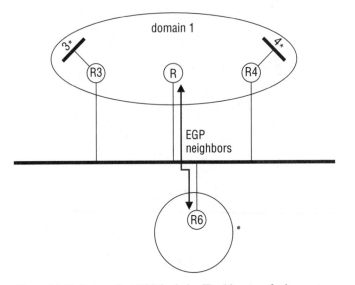

Figure 14.62 Reason that EGP includes IP addresses of other routers

Suppose that R is an EGP neighbor of all the other routers, and no other routers are neighbors with each other (which is a legal configuration). This might be desired instead of having all the routers communicate in a pairwise fashion. If R simply advertised reachability of all the network numbers to R6, then R6 would send traffic for network 4 to R, which would forward it to R4. To eliminate the extra hop, R does not simply advertise reachability of network 4 but rather advertises that network 4 is reachable via router 4.

EGP network reachability messages can be transmitted in response to a poll or on the initiative of the transmitter. What would initiate transmission of an unsolicited network reachability message is not defined, but, presumably, such a message is sent either periodically or when the information changes.

Figure 14.63 shows what a network reachability poll looks like.

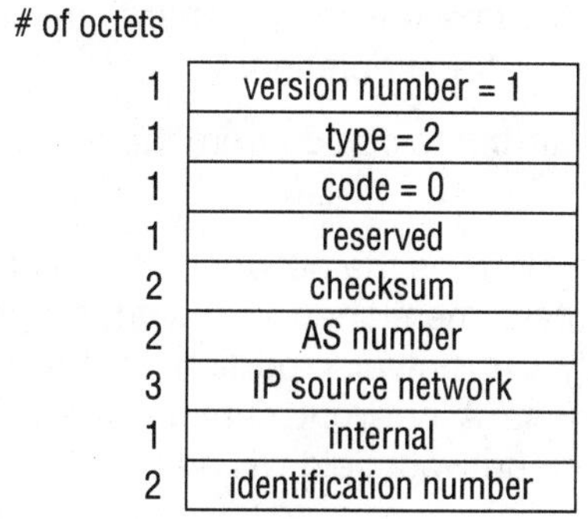

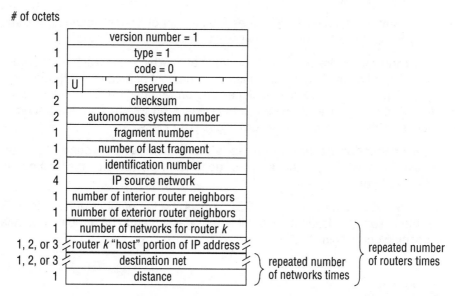

Figure 14.63 EGP network reachability poll

Figure 14.64 shows what the EGP network reachability packet looks like.

Figure 14.64 EGP network reachability packet

The **U** bit indicates whether the routing message is being sent in response to a poll (0) or is being sent unsolicited (1).

The **autonomous system number** is a globally unique 16-bit number identifying the autonomous system (the routing domain). It is globally unique because each IP routing domain is supposed to acquire an AS number from the IP addressing authority.

The **fragment number** is used in case a routing message does not fit into a single packet. If the routing message does fit, the field is set to 0.

The **number of last fragment** is the number of the final fragment, or 0 if the message did not require fragmentation.

The **identification number** is copied from the poll so that responses can be matched to polls.

The **IP source network** gives the network portion of the address of the LAN on which all the routers mentioned in the message reside. The field is 4 octets long, but only the network portion of the address is nonzero. For example, if it is a class A network number, the second, third, and fourth octets of the IP source network field will be 0.

The sum of the next two fields (**number of interior router neighbors** and **number of exterior router neighbors**) indicates the number of routers on behalf of which the transmitter of this routing message is including reachability information. Interior routers (those in the same AS as the EGP transmitter) are listed first.

The **number of networks** indicates the number of IP destination addresses reported on behalf of the router—say, R—listed in the next field.

The **router IP address** is the IP address of R, which can reach the network numbers advertised next. It includes only the host portion of the IP address. Therefore, it is 1, 2, or 3 octets, depending on whether the IP source network field at the beginning of the packet is class A (in which case, the bottom 3 octets of R's IP address are listed), class B, or class C.

The **destination network address** is the IP address of a destination network. The field is 1, 2, or 3 octets, depending on whether the address is class A, B, or C.

The **distance** is claimed in the EGP spec to be the number of hops from R to the advertised destination, but it is really assumed to be a metric that has meaning only within R's AS.

14.5.3 BGP

BGP, a replacement for EGP, is called a *path-vector* protocol. It's similar to a distance vector protocol, but instead of being told a distance to a destination, you are told a path to the destination (a sequence of AS numbers). Based on your neighbors' reported paths, you choose your preferred path and report that to your neighbors. Because the entire path is enumerated, you do not get the count-to-infinity behavior of ordinary distance vector routing.

When you're minimizing a number, it's easy to compute routes. Because BGP doesn't use metrics, you must configure the routers with route preferences, as described in Section 12.8.3. There are several ways you can configure a router that affect which routes get computed:

- Route preferences—for example, don't use any path that goes through AS 73

- Which destinations should not be reported to which neighbors

- How a path should be edited when passed to a particular neighbor

Path editing usually takes the form of adding additional AS numbers into the path to discourage, but not completely prevent, your neighbor from routing to the destination through you. This assumes that your neighbor will be using path length (number of ASs in the path) as a criterion for route selection.

Although we're probably stuck with BGP forever, I've never been convinced it is the right approach. I think the only way to solve the general case of policy-based routing is with a link state protocol plus source-specified routes, where "source" can be the actual source, the first router, or the first interdomain router. The reason link state routing is important is that it gives you complete information. ASs can report their characteristics, and you can supplement or override that information with locally configured information or information read from a trusted location. In that way, you can construct whatever paths you want for whatever exotic policies you need.

To prevent transit traffic with a link state scheme, instead of influencing the routes by not advertising some information to some neighbors, routers would be configured to drop traffic that they do not want to carry. This leaves the problem to the source to compute a path that will work.

With a distance vector protocol, it would require cooperation of all routers to compute a path according to a particular policy. There are unlimited numbers of potential policies, so BGP gives less functionality than would be possible with a link state scheme. A BGP router makes a choice according to its own policies, and everyone on the other side of that router is stuck with that router's choice. And not divulging routes to neighbor N does not prevent N from sending traffic to you. If N is clever enough to assume that you know how to reach a destination, it can send such traffic to you anyway.

BGP has another problem as well. Routing can't really work if every router has its own policy and you don't have one router select the entire path (as you would with PNNI). You can wind up with policies that do not converge. This means that router R1 makes a decision based on information it hears from R2 and R3, and when R1 reports its information, it causes R2 and R3 to change their minds, and so on. Timothy Griffin and Gordon Wilfong showed the following.[8]

- There are policies that never converge. That is, routers will keep changing their minds about routes based on what they're hearing, causing other routers to change their minds, and so on.

---

[8] Timothy Griffin and Gordon Wilfong, "An Analysis of BGP Convergence Properties," *Sigcomm* 1999.

- There are policies that may converge depending on the ordering of messages.

- There are policies that will converge but will become nonconvergent if a link goes down.

- If you could collect all the routers' policies and know the complete topology, it is computationally infeasible in general to decide whether the policies will converge. (For you math types, it's NP-complete.)

So BGP is configuration-intensive. It is likely to break in mysterious ways. It doesn't solve the general problem.

Another thing I find frustrating about BGP is that it was designed without a careful study of the problem to be solved. Every time I suggest that people carefully document all the policies that they think they couldn't do without and those that would be nice but not essential, they think it would be a great idea to do that, but nobody has yet done it. So BGP was deployed, and new hooks were added. People are now used to it and are not enthusiastic about moving to anything else.

For more details about BGP, read RFC 1771, or read *BGP4: Inter-Domain Routing in the Internet*, by John W. Stewart III.

14.5.3.1 BGP Neighbors

A BGP router communicates with neighbor BGP speakers in other ASs, and it communicates with other BGP speakers in its own AS. The common terminology for communication with a neighbor in a foreign domain is E-BGP, and within a domain I-BGP. To prevent loops, an I-BGP speaker is not allowed to pass information it hears from one I-BGP peer to another. This means that I-BGP must be fully connected, that is, each BGP speaker in the AS must be in direct communication with each of the other BGP speakers. They don't have to be physical neighbors. Instead, they maintain a TCP connection because BGP depends on reliable transport of information.

Because fully connected I-BGP causes scaling problems, two mechanisms were introduced. One is *route reflection* (RFC 1996). With route reflection, some BGP speakers in the AS are allowed to collect BGP information and forward it within the domain. These speakers are known as *route reflectors*. The other solution is *confederations* (RFC 1965). It was originally designed to allow aggregation of many ASs within a big super-AS, but it can also be used to subdivide an AS.

14.5.3.2 BGP Attributes

A BGP update message describes the route from the BGP router R that generated the update message to a particular destination D. As part of the description of the route to D, R includes some number of fields, each of which is called an *attribute*. BGP has defined some terms that apply to attributes. Note that the definitions of the words in the following list apply only to BGP. I find the BGP terminology confusing, and I hope that the way these words are used by BGP does not propagate beyond BGP.

1. *Well-known versus optional:* A *well-known* attribute is one that all BGP implementations must recognize—that is, be able to understand when received. The term BGP uses to describe the opposite of well-known is *optional*. An optional attribute is one that need not be recognized by all BGP implementations.

2. *Mandatory versus discretionary:* A *mandatory* attribute is one that must appear in the description of a route. A *discretionary* attribute need not appear.

3. *Partial:* An attribute marked as *partial* has been passed along, unmodified, by a BGP router that has not implemented the attribute. BGP has not invented a word for the opposite of partial.

4. *Transitive versus nontransitive:* A *transitive* attribute is one that can be passed along unmodified by a BGP router that has not implemented the attribute. After this occurs, the attribute is marked as partial. A *nontransitive* attribute is one that must be deleted by a BGP router that has not implemented the attribute.

Most combinations of these attributes make no sense. For example, if an attribute is mandatory, it must be well known because a BGP router must include a mandatory attribute in every route it describes. If an attribute is well known, then the distinction between transitive and nontransitive makes no sense. All BGP routers along the path will have implemented the attribute—in which case, there is no reason to specify what a BGP router that has not implemented the attribute should do with it. The combinations that "make sense" are well-known mandatory, well-known discretionary, optional transitive, and optional nontransitive.

The attributes currently defined by BGP are as follows.

1. *Origin:* This has one of three values.

   a. "IGP" means that the information was originally learned from the routing protocol operating within the AS in which the destination resides and is therefore assumed to be trustworthy.

   b. "EGP" means that the information was learned from the EGP protocol. As stated earlier, EGP does not work in the presence of topological loops. Therefore, if the origin field on a route is equal to EGP, the route would probably be less preferred than a route whose origin is equal to IGP.

   c. The third value of origin is named "incomplete." It seems to have two uses. One is to indicate that the path was learned through some means other than EGP or IGP. For example, it might have been learned through static configuration. The other use is to mark an AS path that has been truncated because it is associated with a destination that is now unreachable. Because the AS path is classified as a mandatory attribute, it must appear even though the destination is being reported as unreachable.

      The origin attribute is classified as well-known and mandatory.

2. *AS path:* This is an enumeration of the autonomous systems along the path to the destination. An AS is identified by a 2-octet number.

   This attribute is classified as well-known and mandatory.

3. *Next hop:* This is the IP address of a router R2 on the same subnet as the BGP speaker R1 that is announcing the route to destination D. This attribute is included because it is sometimes better to have R1 announce routes on behalf of R2. If the next hop attribute were not present, the packet would actually be forwarded through R1. The presence of the attribute indicates that although R1 is announcing the route, it is actually R2 toward which packets should be forwarded.

   Next hop is classified as well-known and mandatory. (Note: It really should be well-known and discretionary, but when I pointed that out to one of the BGP designers he agreed and said, "Oh, well." No real harm done; it just means the attribute must always be reported even though it is often not useful for anything.)

4. *Unreachable:* This attribute, if present, indicates that a formerly advertised route is no longer correct.

   Unreachable is classified as well-known and discretionary.

5. *Inter-AS metric:* This attribute allows a BGP speaker in AS 1 to announce its intra-AS cost to a destination within AS 1. This information can be used by BGP routers within an AS bordering AS 1 to select a more optimal entry point into AS 1 to reach the destination. However, this metric is not allowed to be propagated by BGP speakers in an AS bordering AS 1 to ASs farther away.

   Note: I think the name *intra-AS metric* would be more appropriate for this attribute.

   Inter-AS metric is classified as optional and nontransitive.

6. *Community:* This attribute (defined in RFC 1997), if present, indicates a group to which the destination belongs so that policy can be configured by community rather than individual prefixes. The community is a 4-byte value. To allow independent organizations to define values without danger of picking the same 4-byte value, the first 2 bytes are an AS number, and the second 2 bytes are chosen by someone empowered to do so by the owner of that AS number. Some well-known values are defined in RFC 1997: NO_EXPORT (0xFFFFFF01), indicating that a route so marked should not be advertised outside the confederation boundary; NO_ADVERTISE (0xFFFFFF02), indicating that a route so marked should not be advertised to any other BGP peers; and NO_EXPORT_SUBCONFED (0xFFFFFF03), indicating that a route so marked should not be advertised to other ASs.

   Community is classified as optional and nontransitive.

There is no defined attribute that is optional and transitive.

14.5.3.3 BGP Policies

A policy in BGP is manually configured information that can enable a BGP router to rank routes according to preference. Most routing protocols associate an integer with a path to a destination, which is known as the *cost* to the destination. With an integer, it is easy to rank routes. The route with the smallest cost is the preferred route.

Because BGP does not advertise a cost to a destination, some other means must exist for a router to determine which of several routes it should choose. BGP allows very complex policies. It assumes that there is a local method of managing a BGP router to construct a function that will take as input all the information advertised in a BGP update message about a particular destination, and output a number. After different possible routes are mapped to numbers, the routes can be compared. The preferred route is the one that maps to the smallest number.

14.5.3.4 Confederations

Confederations were originally designed for IDRP, which was basically BGP as defined by ISO (originally for CLNP and then for multiprotocol operation). As interest in a BGP-like protocol for any network layer other than IP waned, IDRP has pretty much gone away. IDRP had a somewhat fancier form of confederation than implemented for BGP. BGP confederations are described in RFC 1965.

A *confederation* is a group of ASs that appear to the routers outside as a single AS. The chief reason for inventing the concept of confederations is to accommodate larger networks by aggregating information. Without confederations, the complete list of ASs along the path to a destination must be reported in the routing update message. With confederations, if several ASs in the path are all in the same confederation, only the confederation need be listed. Confederations also simplify configuring policies because it is easier to configure a policy such as "Don't use routes that go through confederation X" than to list a separate "Don't use routes that go through AS Y" policy for each of the ASs in confederation X. The belief is that people will not aggregate ASs into a confederation unless there is no need for policies to treat the aggregated ASs differently.

As is always the case when hierarchy is added, confederations trade off storage and other protocol overhead for optimal routing. When information is aggregated, routes become less optimal.

A confederation is assigned an AS number and looks to systems outside the confederation like an ordinary AS.

Clumping ASs into a confederation restricts the number of possible routes because BGP enumerates the ASs along a path. If a path were to exit and then reenter the same confederation, it would appear to have a loop. A confederation cannot be listed in a route twice. For example, consider Figure 14.65.

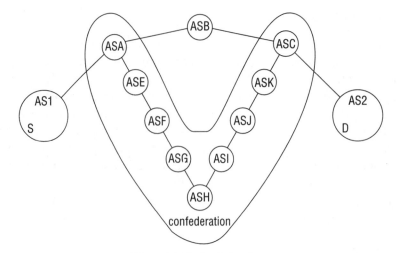

Figure 14.65 Confederations

In Figure 14.65, the path AS1–ASA–ASB–ASC–AS2, which is clearly preferable, cannot be used because a route cannot exit and then reenter a confederation. The only route BGP can find is AS1, ASA, ASE, ASF, ASG, ASH, ASI, ASJ, ASK, ASC, AS2.

A route is a sequence of AS numbers. Therefore, any of the ASs in a route can actually be a confederation. After a group of ASs has been assigned to be in a confederation, the AS numbers of the ASs within that confederation are no longer visible outside the confederation. Routers within the confederation report the AS numbers of ASs within that confederation to other BGP speakers within the confederation. But after the route is reported to a BGP speaker outside the confederation, all AS numbers of ASs internal to the confederation must disappear in the route and must be replaced with the confederation identifier.

The protocol for accomplishing this involves the following.

1. Each BGP speaker is configured with the AS number of the AS to which it belongs as well as the AS numbers of any confederations to which it belongs.

2. Each BGP speaker exchanges information about ASs and confederation membership with each neighbor. In this way, each BGP speaker knows when it is on the boundary of an AS or a confederation.

Routes to a particular destination accumulate outward from the destination (this is just ordinary distance vector routing). When A receives a route from B and A knows that A is in confederation X and B is not, A makes a note in the route that the route is now entering confederation X. Within X, the route accumulates ASs for the ASs in X. Finally, the route may get reported to some BGP speaker on the other side of X. The router on the boundary must get rid of all AS numbers within X before reporting the route to the router outside X. The boundary router accomplishes this by searching the route backward until it encounters the marker noting that the route entered X. The boundary router then deletes that entire section of route and replaces it with the single AS number "X."

14.5.3.5 Message Types

BGP has four types of messages:

1. Open

2. Update

3. Notification

4. Keepalive

The *open* message is the first message transmitted when a link to a BGP neighbor comes up. The *update* message contains routing information. The *notification* message is the final message transmitted on a link to a BGP neighbor, just before the link is disconnected. The *keepalive* message is used to reassure a neighbor, in the absence of routing news, that the transmitter is still alive.

14.5.3.6 Message Formats

All messages start with the fields shown in Figure 14.66.

```
# of octets
       16 | marker |
        2 | length |
        1 |  type  |
```

Figure 14.66 BGP common header

The **marker** field is used for authentication. As with authentication in the other routing protocols, it is only a placeholder that was created on the assumption that someone would someday invent a reasonable authentication scheme. As of the writing of this book, the only authentication scheme defined in the BGP spec is the null authentication scheme, which requires that the **marker** field be set to all 1's but undoubtedly cryptographic authentication similar to what was defined for other routing protocols will be added.

The **length** field is the number of octets in the BGP message, including the header.

The **type** field is one of the following:

value	type field
1	open
2	update
3	notification
4	keepalive

Open Message Format

The open message contains the fields shown in Figure 14.67.

# of octets

19	common header
1	version
2	my AS
2	hold time
4	BGP identifier
1	optional parameters length
variable	optional parameters

Figure 14.67 BGP open message

Version is 3.

My autonomous system gives the AS number of the transmitter.

Hold time indicates how long the receiver should wait before assuming that the transmitter is dead. The transmitter agrees to transmit a keepalive and/or an update and/or a notification message before the hold time elapses.

BGP identifier is an IP address of the transmitter. A BGP router picks an IP address as its identifier and uses that in all its messages.

Optional parameters length indicates the length of the data in the following field, which is actually a collection of TLV-encoded options. The only one defined is authentication, type = 1, which is defined as follows.

Authentication code defines the authentication mechanism.

Authentication data is a field whose length and contents are defined according to the type of authentication being used.

Update Message Format

Figure 14.68 shows the format of the update message.

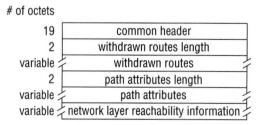

# of octets

19	common header
2	withdrawn routes length
variable	withdrawn routes
2	path attributes length
variable	path attributes
variable	network layer reachability information

Figure 14.68 BGP update message

Withdrawn routes contains a list of IP prefixes that are no longer reachable, specified as a 1-byte length followed by the smallest number of octets needed to specify that length of prefix.

Path attributes is a sequence of fields, each describing one attribute, and is encoded as shown in Figure 14.69.

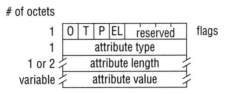

Figure 14.69 BGP path attributes

The **Flags** field contains the following.

O, if set, indicates "optional."

T, if set, indicates "transitive."

P, if set, indicates "partial."

EL ("extended length"), if set, indicates that the length field is 2 octets; if clear, it indicates that the length field is 1 octet.

Attribute type is one of the following.

1 = "origin"; length: 1 octet.

2 = "AS path"; variable-length, consisting of TLV-encoded *path segments*. There are four defined types of path segments:

value	path segment type
1	AS set (unordered set of ASs, which would be the case, for example, when you're summarizing several more-specific prefixes with different routes into a shorter prefix)
2	AS sequence (ordered set of ASs)
3	AS confederation set (unordered set of ASs within a confederation)
4	AS confederation sequence (ordered set of ASs within a confederation).

3 = "next hop"; length: 4 octets.

4 = "unreachable"; length: 0 octets.

5 = "inter-AS metric"; length: 2 octets.

8 = "community"; length: 4 octets.

Notification Message Format

A notification message is an error message sent by router R1 to explain to BGP neighbor router R2 why R1 is closing the connection to R2. The notification message contains the fields shown in Figure 14.70.

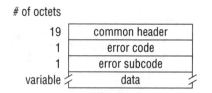

# of octets

19	common header
1	error code
1	error subcode
variable	data

Figure 14.70 BGP notification message

Basically, every field in every message that could contain a value that the receiver might reject is covered in the various codes. The **data** field contains the offending field.

The **error codes** are as follows:

1 = *message header error*, for which the subcodes are

value	
1	unacceptable marker field value
2	unacceptable message length
3	unacceptable message type

2 = *problem with "open" message*, for which the subcodes are

value	
1	unsupported version number
2	unacceptable AS number
3	unacceptable IP address
4	unsupported authentication code
5	authentication failure (authentication type supported, but marker field is the wrong value)

3 = *problem with update message*, for which the subcodes are

value	
1	malformed attribute list (for example, an attribute appears twice)
2	unrecognized well-known attribute
3	missing mandatory attribute (actually, the BGP spec calls this "missing well-known attribute," but that's not what it meant)
4	attribute flags error, meaning that there was a conflict between the receiver's notion of what kind of attribute a particular attribute was and what was flagged by the transmitter of the update message (for example, the receiver thought that attribute number X was optional, but the transmitter set the flag claiming that it wasn't)
5	attribute length error
6	invalid origin attribute
7	the specified AS path has a loop in it
8	invalid next hop attribute
9	optional attribute error, meaning that the receiver understood the attribute and was able to check the value and discover that it was incorrect
10	invalid network field. BGP does not pass along a mask when it refers to a destination. Instead, it expects that the reported destination will be a network number rather than a subnetwork number. If any unexpected bits are set in the destination address in an update message, then this error is reported. For example, this error is reported if the destination address is a class B network number and any bits are set in the final 2 octets

4 = *hold time expired*, during which no BGP messages were received from the BGP neighbor.

Keepalive Message Format

There is no information in a keepalive message other than the standard BGP header. A keepalive message is sent when it has been so long since the preceding BGP message had to be sent that the hold timer might expire unless something were transmitted.

Homework

1. Give an algorithm for computing the mask for a particular destination reported in a RIP message.

2. In RIP, assume that a router R does not keep the latest distance vector from each neighbor and that it discards information about destination D after 180 seconds.

    Assume that the path R has for D is through neighbor N. What should R do in the following events: information about D times out; neighbor M advertises a shorter path to D through M; N advertises a longer path to D than the one R has stored through N?

3. Give a procedure for IS-IS for changing the area address of an area from A to B, with routers being configured one-by-one so as to cause minimal disruption to the area.

4. Give a procedure for IS-IS for splitting an area with area address A into two areas: one with area address A and one with area address B. Routers are configured one-by-one to cause minimal disruption to the area.

5. Design an automatic mechanism for detecting and repairing level 2 network partitions in IS-IS.

6. Suppose that in IS-IS it were impossible to manually configure more than two area addresses into any single level 1 router. Would it then be possible for the area to have more than two area addresses?

    Now suppose that it were impossible to manually configure more than one area address into any single level 1 router. Would it then be possible for the area to have more than one area address?

7. In IS-IS, after all LSPs have been propagated through an area, is it possible for two level 1 routers in the area to have different opinions regarding the legal CLNP area addresses for the area? In other words, is it possible for one of the level 1 routers to think that a particular CLNP address is outside the area and must be routed to a level 2 router and for another level 1 router to think that that address is inside the area?

8. In IS-IS, why is it necessary for all routers to agree on the value of maximum area addresses? When there are too many area addresses, why is it necessary to specify which subset of the area addresses a router should use?

9. In certain topologies it would require less memory to store information about external IP addresses with a scheme in which the level 2 routers report their own distance to each externally reachable IP address instead of the scheme in OSPF, in which the combination of type 4 and type 5 LSAs is used. Which topologies are they?

10. Consider this variant of NLSP's Designated Router election. Instead of always increasing the priority by 20, a router is configured with two priorities: one for when it's not DR, and one that it switches to after being DR for a minute. (This is the same as NLSP's scheme if the second priority is 20 greater than the first priority.) Is there anything you can do with this variant that you can't do with the NLSP scheme? Also, suppose this were implemented and someone configured the second priority to be *smaller* than the first priority in some router. What might happen as a result?

11. Compare the LAN LSP distribution mechanisms in IS-IS and OSPF. Under what conditions would OSPF use less bandwidth? Under what conditions would IS-IS use less bandwidth?

12. Compare the memory requirements for storing link state information about IP destinations in OSPF and IS-IS, assuming that the information is reported in IS-IS using maximum-sized fragments.

13. Let routers R1 and R2 be neighbors. In OSPF, when the link between R1 and R2 first comes up, R1 must send R2 a complete database description, and R2 must send R1 a complete database description. As stated in Section 14.4.10.6, if DD packets were functionally equivalent to IS-IS CSNPs rather than being functionally equivalent to IS-IS PSNPs, then it would be necessary only for R1 to send R2 a complete database description. Why? How would processing of DD packets differ if the sequence of DD packets were treated as a CSNP?

14. An EGP network reachability packet contains only the "host" portion of a router address. What would the router's complete address be? (How can the router receiving this EGP packet know the complete address?)

15. Come up with a potential BGP attribute that it would make sense to classify as optional and transitive.

16. In BGP, come up with an example topology and confederation membership in which there is no legal path between some pair of ASs. In other words, physical connectivity exists between the two ASs, but because of the way confederations have been assigned, there is no path that BGP can find. Give an example involving a single confederation. Give an example involving two confederations, with the constraint that the confederations must be physically intact.

17. Invent a protocol for making distance vector routing reliable when it runs on top of a datagram service. BGP does it by running on top of TCP. IDRP does it by inventing its own reliable end-to-end protocol. Your protocol should ensure that the latest information gets through without requiring that earlier, outdated information be received. Also, you cannot assume that all destinations are reported in each update. Instead, assume that there are many more destinations than can fit in a single update and that, in general, only the destinations for which the path has

changed are transmitted in an update. For any particular destination whose path has changed, the update is transmitted and then later retransmitted if an ack has not been received for that destination within some amount of time—say, 10 sec.

18. Compare the hierarchies in IS-IS, PNNI, OSPF, and NLSP in terms of costs and benefits.

19. Why is database overload less serious for PNNI than for other link state protocols?

20. Research problem: Investigate interdomain routing. Compare BGP; a link state scheme combined with source-specified routes; and static routing with alternate paths and source-specified routes. Evaluate them in terms of attributes such as ease of configuration, likelihood of global disruption in the face of malicious or unintentional misconfiguration, range of useful policies that can be supported, bandwidth and memory overhead, and so on.

Chapter 15
WAN Multicast

15.1 Introduction

This chapter discusses layer 3 multicast. Sometimes people like to use the term *broadcast* as if it were conceptually different from multicast. I don't think we need the word *broadcast*, and the fewer jargon words the better. In layer 2, broadcast is supposed to mean "everyone," but because "everyone" doesn't have to listen, it simply means "everyone listening to the broadcast address," which is no different from multicast. In layer 3 when people try to define broadcast and multicast, they sometimes define them as follows.

- *Broadcast:* deliver data to every link, perhaps within a specified range.

- *Multicast:* deliver data only to links on which there are receivers.

Sometimes it's still considered broadcast if data gets sent to all the routers within a specified range, even though the routers might know not to forward onto the final link if there are no receivers there. It seems to me that a constant range of optimizations is possible. Trying to pick a point and define things on one side as broadcast and things on the other side as multicast is not terribly helpful, so I refer to all of it as multicast.

15.1.1 Layer 2 Multicast

The concept of multicast was invented with the Ethernet, where the shared-medium technology made the ability to multicast convenient and (deceptively) inexpensive. With a shared medium, multicast is convenient and inexpensive for the transmitter, which can transmit a single copy of a packet and reach multiple recipients. It is also convenient for the medium because a single copy of the packet reaches all recipients anyway. However, multicast is not so inexpensive for the receivers. Because it is difficult for the hardware to do perfect filtering of many addresses, a receiver that wishes to receive any multicast addresses winds up processing software interrupts for "wrong numbers"—destination addresses it is not interested in receiving.

Multicast is used on LANs chiefly for autoconfiguration—helping peers or clients and servers to find each other. The two models are *solicit* and *advertise*. In soliciting, a node multicasts a packet asking for responses—for example, when a client queries for a server. In advertising, a node multicasts packets announcing its presence, and anyone that wants to find out about such nodes listens to the multicast address.

With the emergence of bridges and "switched LANs" (which are really just bridged topologies), multicast was no longer "free" for the medium. In bridged LANs, multicast packets are transmitted along the spanning tree to all portions of the *broadcast domain*. In a shared-medium LAN, even if there were only one recipient, it would require no more bandwidth to transmit a multicast packet than a unicast packet. However, in a bridged extended LAN, if there were indeed only a small number of recipients of a multicast packet or if all the recipients resided on a small subset of the ports in the extended LAN, it could take a significant amount of extra bandwidth to transmit a multicast packet (which is delivered and broadcast everywhere in the extended LAN) rather than multiple unicast packets, one to each recipient. (See homework problem 2.)

15.1.2 Reasons for Layer 3 Multicast

When people got used to the capability of layer 2 multicasting, it was natural to ask why it could not be provided in a wide area network. There are several potential applications for layer 3 multicast, as indicated in the following list, and it was argued that others might emerge, given the opportunity to experiment with the technique.

1. Advertisement by servers.

2. Solicitation of servers by clients.

3. Conference calls, in which a conversation is taking place among a group of individuals. Rather than require the source of each packet to make individual copies for each recipient, the network could provide a multicast address for the conversation. All the packets of the conversation could be addressed to the multicast address, and the network would deliver the multicast packets to all recipients.

4. Multiplayer distributed games, in which players in different locations cooperate or compete in an interactive game.

5. Dissemination of datagram information (such as weather reports or stock market prices) of potential interest to many recipients, who can "tune in" to hear the information.

6. Data collection, in which a bunch of sensors transmit results to a bunch of data collection sites.

7. Dissemination of information that must be reliably delivered to many recipients—for example, software distribution.

To evaluate the best method of providing layer 3 multicast, it is important to keep in mind its potential applications.

Note that although most uses of layer 2 multicast are low-bandwidth, much of what people want layer 3 multicast for is high-bandwidth applications. Many people then assume that multicast uses up bandwidth. But if the alternative is to send the same data n times with unicast, multicast *saves* bandwidth. And indeed, the main purpose of layer 3 multicast is to save bandwidth when the same data must be delivered to multiple recipients.

15.1.3 Dimensions to Consider

> We want to make multicast so scalable and easy to use that
> people can create groups and send multicast data with as little
> thought as they do unicast.
>
> —Steve Deering

What might multicast be expected to support? Following are some variables to consider.

- *Number of sources:* Some people argue that the only "real" applications, the ones people will pay money for, involve a single sender. If there are multiple senders, are we talking about tens, hundreds, or millions?

- *Number of receivers:* Does multicast need to scale to trillions of receivers? If there's a very small number of receivers, unicast might be a better choice. (Yes, there's a large range between "trillions" and "very small.")

- *Amount of data:* If the bandwidth requirements are small enough, unicast would solve the problem.

- *Amount of data in a burst:* Some proposed solutions create a tree for each source. Assuming that a per-source tree (a tree with that source as root) yields better traffic patterns, will there be enough data from that source to warrant creating a per-source tree?

- *Length of quiet periods between bursts:* Is it worth keeping state about the tree during quiet periods, or should a new tree be created for the next burst?

- *Number of simultaneous groups expected:* How many groups is a router likely to need to support simultaneously?

- *Amount of time during which the group exists:* If this is a very short time, is it worth the overhead of creating a tree?

- *Topological distance between members of the group:* Clearly, a flooding solution is not good for delivering data to a group of five participants when the members are topologically distant from each other.

- *Denseness of members:* If most of the nodes within a particular space are likely to want to receive the data, then flooding may be a better solution. Maybe there are two kinds of applications: those for which almost all links contain receivers and those for which this is not true. Maybe two mechanisms are appropriate, selectable on a per-application basis: one with a flooding or single spanning tree solution for sending data to all links, and another for optimized delivery when membership is sparse.

- *Volatility of membership:* How frequently do members join and leave?

15.1.4 Multihop Multicast (other than in IP)

Section 11.3.2 discusses algorithms for providing multicast in bridges, ATM, IPX, and SMDS. Here, I review the one for ATM because I compare it with the various solutions to IP. In ATM, each multicast group has one node N in charge, which adds members by sending a special *add member* control packet toward the address of the member being added. The result is a tree with N as the root.

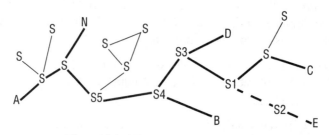

Figure 15.1 ATM multicast tree formation

    In Figure 15.1, the dark lines indicate the ports that are in the tree formed when N creates a multicast group by adding members A, B, D, and C. If at this point N launched an "add E" message, the "add E" packet would travel from N to S1 and then to S2 and E, and the two links with dark dotted lines would get added to the group's tree.

    Currently, ATM multicast VCs are point-to-multipoint, meaning that N is the only sender allowed in the group. It would be nice to allow the same tree to be used with multiple senders. For example, if D were to transmit a cell on the VC, S3 should be able to accept it from D and forward it to S1 and S4. S4 should forward it toward S5 and B, and so on. The only issue is the cell interleaving problem, but as you saw in Section 11.3.2.3, that problem is solvable, and rumor has it that multipoint-to-multipoint VCs will be introduced into the ATM standard.

15.2 Multicast in IP

> Solve 90% of the problem as simply as you can, and then remove
> the other 10% from the problem requirements.
>
> —Marshall Rose

It has been proposed that IP multicast should look just like multicast on a LAN. You should be able to join and leave groups at any time, without the rest of the members nor any central node, knowing who is listening. The proposal also claims that you should be able to transmit a packet with a particular multicast address without listening to packets transmitted to that multicast address.

Although the IETF has been working on this problem for more than 10 years, it is still attempting to come up with protocols to support this style of multicast. Certain pieces of the problem, however, have been standardized. (I would have waited for a plausible proposed solution to the whole problem before standardizing pieces of the problem, or at least be willing to modify those pieces if necessary to make the rest of the problem tractable.) The following parts were standardized early on.

1. A convention was defined for recognizing a particular network layer address as being a multicast address. These addresses are known as *class D* IP addresses and have the top 4 bits = 1110.

2. A convention was defined for mapping a network layer multicast address to a LAN data link layer address—at least, for 802 LANs. (See Section 15.2.3.)

3. A protocol was defined (Internet Group Management Protocol, or IGMP; see Section 15.2.4) in which endnodes inform their adjacent routers about the network layer multicast addresses they wish to receive. Version 1 of IGMP was defined a long time ago, but it has undergone major revisions. Currently, version 3 is being defined.

15.2.1 Centralized versus Decentralized Multicast

Is it better for a group to be managed by a central node (ATM-style) or for members to be able to come and go without permission (IP-style)? There are certainly arguments for both points of view. I'll call the two styles *centralized* and *decentralized.* Arguments for the centralized approach are as follows.

*   A central node can control who joins. Even though traffic can be encrypted to keep the contents from unauthorized receivers, joining a group forces the Internet to expend bandwidth and state in order to deliver data.

*   A central node can know the membership. In many cases it is desirable to have an easy method of knowing all the members.

- The solutions based on this model seem to be simpler and require less overhead.

Arguments for the decentralized approach are as follows.

- There is no single point of failure (the central node that adds, deletes, and keeps track of members).

- When a member is joined to a large group, the join message might go many hops before branching off into new territory. For example, referring to Figure 15.1, if N sends a "join member E," the join must travel all the way from N to S1 before it creates new state by being forwarded to S2 and then E. In contrast, with the join going "the other way," as it would with a protocol such as CBT (see Section 15.2.9), if E sends the join toward N, the join stops at S1.·

- There might be groups that are so large that it would be impractical to keep track of all the members in any one place.

My guess is that for applications that need security, a member will need to register with some central place anyway—to prove authorization to join the group and obtain the necessary encryption keys—so that central place might as well send the join message. Also, network managers often prefer the ability to control things and would prefer not having endnodes join and leave groups without informing a central node. As for the scalability concern with the centralized model, I think it can be solved with a hierarchy of *central nodes* (see Figure 15.2).

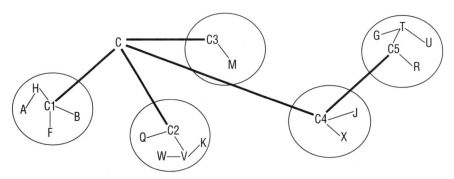

Figure 15.2 Hierarchy of central nodes

In Figure 15.2, C is the top-level central node for a very large group. The members that it has joined are C1, C2, C3, C4, and C5. C5 is managing the subgroup within its circle and has added nodes T, G, U, and R.

This hierachical structure answers the scalability concerns associated with the centralized model, and there are also possible methods for providing backup for the central node. As for the simplicity argument, a slight modification to the IP model would allow multicast that is as straightforward and low overhead as the centralized model (see Section 15.2.14).

15.2.2 Could We Do Without Layer 3 Multicast?

Suppose we gave up on layer 3 multicast. Could we do without it? Here are some suggestions.

- For finding the nearest server of some type, say a "FOO server," use anycast. Have a well-known address (an IP address with a 32-bit mask so that it is link-independent) that is injected into the routing protocol by every FOO server. Anyone that sends a packet to that address reaches the nearest FOO server.

- For finding all the FOO servers, use a Yellow Pages–type naming service.

- For a conference call with a small number of participants, use unicast.

- For high-volume data distribution, use relays at the application layer. Use small enough fan-out and carefully planned locations of relays so that data distribution would not be very suboptimal even though layer 3 provided only unicast.

15.2.3 Mapping NL Multicast to DL Multicast

When the network layer (NL) destination address is a multicast address and the packet is transmitted onto a LAN, what should the data link layer destination address be? Before I answer that, it is important to realize that some applications being considered for NL multicast would be high-traffic. Previous use of data link layer broadcast attempted to minimize the amount of traffic. But the NL multicast is being designed assuming high-bandwidth applications such as video teleconferencing.

One possibility for choosing a data link layer address for transmitting IP multicast messages is to always transmit such messages to the data link layer broadcast address. This method would not be very "socially responsible," though, because there are protocols that require conforming nodes to listen to packets addressed to the data link layer broadcast address. Increasing the number of protocols that use the broadcast address would increase the number of software interrupts. This problem could be alleviated if hardware were extended to filter packets based on the protocol type, but with 2^{47} layer 2 multicast addresses, there's no reason to be using the broadcast address.

Another possibility is to use the data link layer multicast address for "all IP hosts." Although this approach at least does not bother non-IP hosts, it does require IP hosts to deal with a potentially lethal dose of software interrupts.

So instead of having all IP multicast transmitted on the same layer 2 multicast address, it would be nice to have a different layer 2 multicast address for every layer 3 multicast address. Because there are 28 bits of IP multicast address (as noted in the preceding subsection, the top 4 bits of the 32-bit IP address are the constant "1110"), this would require 20 bits of high-order constant in order to leave 28 bits free to specify the layer 3 multicast group. An ordinary block of addresses that one might obtain for an 802 LAN gives 24 bits of high-order constant. If 16 consecutive address blocks could be obtained, then the IP community would have its 28 bits in the layer 2 address, allowing a unique layer 2 multicast address for each IP multicast address (see Figure 15.3).

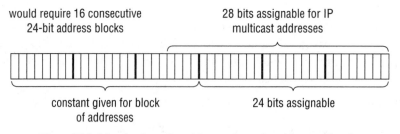

would require 16 consecutive   28 bits assignable for IP
24-bit address blocks   multicast addresses

constant given for block   24 bits assignable
of addresses

Figure 15.3 Mapping layer 3 multicast to layer 2 multicast, uniquely

It was considered impractical economically and politically to obtain 16 consecutive address blocks for IP multicast. Economically, it would have cost $1,000 per block, and the IETF was used to everything being "free." Politically, it was impossible because the IEEE does not want people asking for lots of blocks and has a policy against granting consecutive blocks to one organization in order to discourage schemes such as this. So instead, the IP community decided to reserve half the multicast addresses in its single address block (01-00-5E-00-00-00) for mapping class D IP addresses to layer 2 multicast addresses. That yielded only 23 bits for IP multicast, but that was workable. It simply meant that the mapping is done by copying only the bottom 23 bits of the IP multicast address into 01-00-5E-00-00-00. Thus, 32 different IP multicast addresses will map to the same data link layer multicast address if the bottom 23 bits are the same in all 32 addresses. It is an example of imperfect multicast filtering, which is already the case with the standard chips.

15.2.4 IGMP Protocol

The IGMP version 1 protocol contains two types of messages: *host membership query* and *host membership report* (see Figure 15.4). The query is transmitted by a router. When it is transmitted on a LAN, the data link layer multicast address "all IP endnodes" is used. The response is transmitted to the multicast address derived from the group address being advertised.

Note that because a router must be able to receive all the responses, IGMP requires a router to be able to receive all the 2^{23} possible data link layer multicast addresses derived from IP host group addresses. This requires routers to listen promiscuously to all LAN multicast traffic.

# of octets

1	version	type
1	reserved	
2	checksum	
4	group address	

Figure 15.4 IGMP version 1 message

The **version** is set to 1. The **type** is either 1 (for a host membership query) or 2 (for a host membership report). The **checksum** is the usual IP checksum calculated on the 8 octets defined in Figure 15.4. When transmitted in a query, the **group address** is 0, and when transmitted in a host membership report, it is the 4-octet address of the host group being reported.

IGMP version 2 added the ability to instantly resign from a group. However, a router can't stop sending traffic for group M onto the LAN if the router gets a message from a node on the LAN saying "I'm leaving group M" because there might be another listener on the LAN. So when a router gets the IGMP message "I'm leaving group M," the router must send a *group-specific IGMP query* asking whether anyone is still listening to M. So the leave still can't be immediate because there must be time for the router to query, perhaps several times in case the query got lost or the response got lost. I wouldn't have bothered with this optimization, especially because it caused backward-compatibiliy problems. Routers that are version 2-capable must be configured to use version 1 if any version 1 routers are on the LAN. So IGMP version 2 added configuration requirements (with added possibility for misconfiguration) as well as protocol complexity to gain the optimization of a somewhat quicker group leave.

Version 3 added the ability to join group M with only a specified set of senders. You can say, "I'd like to join multicast address M, but I want to receive only from source S1 and S2" or ". . .but I want to receive traffic from all sources *except* S3, S4, and S5." Version 3 also changed the layer 2 address that an endnode uses when sending an IGMP reply. In earlier versions it was sent to the layer 2 multicast address derived from the layer 3 multicast address, on the theory that endnodes should listen to responses to groups they belong to, in case someone else responds. However, with version 3, the decision was to send all IGMP replies to a single layer 2 multicast listened to by the switch, for several reasons.

- Most LANs now are switched rather than shared media, so it's cheaper not to forward the IGMP replies to lots of ports—even if forwarding the IGMP reply would suppress creation of other IGMP replies. With the IGMP reply sent to the switch, even if zillions of endnodes send the same reply, the replies are absorbed by the switch.

- With IGMP snooping (see Section 15.2.5), switches want every endnode to send a reply so that the switch can know which ports to forward which multicast packets on.

- Having the IGMP reply go to the derived multicast address requires the switch to listen promiscuously to multicast. If the reply is addressed to the switch, then the switch doesn't have to process IP data multicast messages.

- With the new proposal of every endnode requesting a customized list of senders for the group, it would be expensive for an endnode to figure out from other replies whether all the senders it was interested in were already requested by some other endnode.

In my opinion, it's unlikely that the feature of requesting or excluding specific senders will be used. I can't quite imagine how a user would know which senders to include or exclude and what the user interface would be for informing the workstation to add them to the list. And it expands the amount of state and complexity of the forwarding decision for the switches. I can't believe it's worth the implementation bother or the bandwidth and state overhead. But I do agree with sending the replies to the switch's layer 2 address rather than the layer 2 multicast address derived from the IP multicast address.

15.2.5 IGMP Snooping

When a "LAN" is really a bunch of point-to-point links interconnected with a layer 2 switch, it's wasteful to send all IP multicast traffic on all ports and have the endnode do the filtering. So some switches look at IGMP traffic to decide which ports want to receive which multicast addresses. This is known as *IGMP snooping*. Exactly how to do this has never been written down.

For the switch to know all the ports that want to receive a particular multicast address, it is important that all members send an IGMP reply, something they don't do (in version 1 and 2 of IGMP) if they hear another reply. So it's important for the switch not to send the IGMP reply on ports with other endnodes. One possibility is for the switch to forward IGMP replies only onto the port from which it received the IGMP query. This sort of works, except it's better if all the routers hear the IGMP replies. So what's typically done is for switches to know which ports contain other switches or routers and forward IGMP replies only on those ports. These ports can either be configured or learned through a switch-to-switch handshake when the port is brought up.

Then when IP multicast data arrives, the switch can send the traffic only to the ports that have asked for it. Most switch vendors have the switch make the decision based on the layer 2 multicast address. But it's possible for as many as 32 IP multicast addresses to map to the same layer 2 multicast address. Thus, the switch could, if it wanted to be really clever, look at the layer 3 header and make forwarding decisions based on the layer 3 multicast address learned through IGMP snooping.

15.2.6 Reverse Path Forwarding

Reverse path forwarding is a concept introduced by Yogen Dalal.[1] It is an optimized form of flooding. In ordinary flooding, a packet is transmitted to all neighbors except the one from which it was received. Reverse path forwarding accepts a packet from source S via neighbor N only if N is the neighbor you would forward to in order to reach S. This simple technique reduces the overhead of flooding dramatically. Because a router accepts a packet only from one neighbor, it floods it only once. The result is that (assuming all point-to-point links) each packet is transmitted over each link once. An enhancement introduced by Dalal and Metcalfe[2] has router R figure out which of its neighbors forward to S through R; then R forwards packets from S only to those neighbors. An enhancement introduced by Steve Deering[3] has routers, based on the IGMP protocol, refrain from sending multicast packets across the final hop to a *leaf network* if there are no listeners on that leaf network for that group.

15.2.7 Distance Vector Multicast Routing Protocol

Distance Vector Multicast Routing Protocol (DVMRP) is documented in RFC 1075, although there is an Internet draft that will almost certainly become an RFC and supersede it. Here I describe the version of DVMRP documented in the most recent Internet draft, on the assumption that it will become an RFC and because it's closer to the currently deployed implementations than what is described in RFC 1075. The basic ideas are as follows.

- Allow incremental deployment by creating a DVMRP-capable subset of the Internet consisting of routers that support DVMRP. Configured tunnels between DVMRP routers allow skipping over non-DVMRP routers.

- Have DVMRP routers do a routing protocol (over the configured tunnels) using a distance vector protocol similar to RIP. DVMRP uses a *hold-down* mechanism to attempt to avoid the count-to-infinity behavior. After your best path to D goes away, you advertise your cost to D as infinity for some amount of time. The hope is that this technique will give the network a long enough time to purge all nodes of knowledge of the broken path so that after the hold-down timer expires, route computation will be based on links that are up. (In my opinion, and as experience with this mechanism in the ARPANET indicated, this mechanism does not always prevent count-to-infinity behavior. Also, it often slows convergence because progress cannot be made until the hold-down timer expires.)

---

[1] Yogen Dalal, "Broadcast Protocols in Packet Switched Computer Networks," Digital Systems Laboratory, Dept. of Electrical Engineering, Stanford University, 1977.

[2] Yogen Dalal and Robert Metcalfe, "Reverse Path Forwarding of Broadcast Packets," *Communications of the ACM,* December 1978.

[3] Steve Deering, "Multicast Routing in Internetworks and Extended LANs," SIGCOMM Summer 1988 Proceedings, August 1988.

- Use reverse path forwarding based on the information discovered through DVMRP to decide whether you should accept a packet from neighbor N with source S. (You should accept a packet with source S from neighbor N if N is the neighbor that DVMRP computes as the next hop from you to S.)

- If N is the best path from you to S, report distance to S as infinity (32) more than the actual cost when reporting to neighbor N. (This allows implementation of the Dalal/Metcalfe optimization of forwarding only to neighbors that consider you their best path to S.)

- Forward a packet from S only to neighbors that have reported to you a cost of more than 32 to S. (As just explained, reporting a cost to S of more than 32 to neighbor N indicates to N that it is your best path to S.)

The next level of detail involves prunes and grafts. *Prunes* tell the neighbor from whom you are receiving traffic for group M from source S that you do not want traffic for (S,M). The hope is to wind up with a data distribution tree for (S,M) packets that is not much larger than an explicitly created shortest-path tree such as what would be created with the ATM algorithm (see Figure 15.1).

Grafts are used to "change your mind" about a prune. If someone joins M after you've sent a prune, you must undo the prune, which might have been passed many hops away, or else the new member won't receive traffic until the prune expires. This means that you must remember all the prunes you sent for at least as long as your upstream neighbor will remember that you sent a prune.

For example, referring to Figure 15.5, suppose S transmits a packet with destination address M before A has joined. R4 forwards it to R2 (because R4 is R2's best path to S). R2 forwards it to R1 (because R2 is R1's best path to S). R1, however, has learned through IGMP that nobody on the LAN is listening to M (or, to be obnoxiously precise, R1 has *not* learned through IGMP that anyone *is* listening to M). So R1 sends a prune (S,M) to R2. Now all of R2's downstream neighbors with respect to S have sent a prune (S,M), so R2 sends a prune (S,M) to R4. The next time S transmits, R4 does not forward the packet.

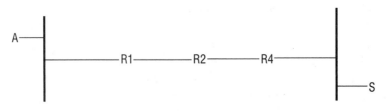

Figure 15.5 Reason for graft message

Now let's say that A joins, and R1 learns this through IGMP. Now R1 must tell R2 to forget the prune, and then R2 must tell R4 to forget the prune.

The details are as follows.

- If you receive an "unwanted" packet for multicast address M from source S via neighbor N, send N a prune message for (S,M). The packet is unwanted if you have no place to forward the packet because on your other links you've either received prunes for (S,M) or because IGMP says there are no listeners. The prune message contains a lifetime, which you set to the default (about 2 hours) or to the minimum lifetime received in a prune for (S,M).

- Remember all the (S,M) prunes you have sent on each link for a relatively long time (about 2 hours).

- Remember all the (S,M) prunes you have received from each link, and don't send traffic for (S,M) on those links.

- If you receive data for M from S despite the fact that you sent a prune (S,M), then send another prune, each time doubling the interval with which you send the prune.

- If IGMP indicates that someone has joined M, check to see whether you have sent any prunes for M. If you have, send a "graft (S,M)" on each link on which you sent a prune (S,M) (for all S's for which you've sent [S,M] prunes).

- If you receive a graft (S,M), send a graft (S,M) on each link for which you sent a prune (S,M).

- Grafts must be acknowledged. If you don't get an ack to your graft, retransmit.

DVMRP has two scaling problems. One is that data is periodically transmitted through the entire Internet, just in case someone far away is interested. Prunes help, of course, but traffic still must be periodically sent all over the Internet. The other scaling problem is the prune state. Each router in the Internet must keep track of (S,M) pairs for all groups that are not of interest to each of their links. Imagine if multicast got truly popular and there were millions of conference calls going on simultaneously! Not surprisingly, people now realize that DVMRP is not a solution to providing Internet-wide multicast. However, I believe there are cases in which a flood-and-prune solution is reasonable: when the amount of data is so low that it's not worth creating the state necessary to optimize its distribution, or the density of receivers is so large that flooding isn't very far from optimal.

15.2.8 Multicast OSPF

OSPF was enhanced to provide support of multicast, and OSPF with the multicast extensions is known as MOSPF and is documented in RFC 1584. The basic ideas are as follows.

- Have the Designated Router on a LAN, based on information learned through IGMP, flood link state information about groups (multicast addresses) for which there are members on the LAN.

- When router R receives a packet from source S with destination address M, if R has already calculated a tree for (S,M), then forward along that tree. However, if it has not seen a packet for (S,M), it must calculate the tree for (S,M). This is done as follows.

    a. Do the Dijkstra calculation with S as the Root.

    b. Find yourself (R) in the tree.

    c. For each subtree under R, if there are members in that subtree, then the link to that subtree is put into the forwarding database for (S,M). Also, R's parent link in the Dijkstra tree rooted on S is in the tree.

- If routing information changes (new group members, links go up or down), throw away or recalculate all the (S,M) forwarding state because it may have changed.

MOSPF has scaling problems that make people generally concede (as with DVMRP) that it would not work as an Internet-wide solution. It requires passing around and storing knowledge of all group members for all groups. It requires a separate Dijkstra calculation for every (S,M) pair. When a source that has not recently transmitted a packet to G sends a packet, there is a large computational burden on the routers because they must calculate Dijkstra and create forwarding state before they can forward the packet.

One strategy for interarea groups is to have the routing protocol pass the group membership information everywhere; into level 2, from there into all the other areas, and also passed between domains. This would enable optimal forwarding of data, but at the cost of a lot of control traffic (passing around group information globally), a lot of computation (calculating all the (S,M) trees), and a lot of storage (all the (S,M) information).

Another strategy saves control traffic and state, but at the expense of extra data traffic. This strategy is similar to using default route in unicast routing. In unicast routing, if a router R claims to be able to reach "*," then all traffic for all unknown destinations is sent to R. Traffic for unreachable destinations does not get dropped until it reaches R. If instead R advertises only the destinations it can reach, then traffic for unreachable destinations can be discarded earlier, saving the network the bandwidth of delivering the data to R. It's a trade-off between carrying extra data traffic and carrying extra control traffic and state.

The analogous strategy for the default route in MOSPF is called a *wildcard multicast receiver*. All data for all groups is sent to that router. For example, the area border router would be the wildcard multicast receiver, and all multicast traffic originated in the area would get sent to that router. Then within the level 2 area (the backbone), all multicast traffic would have to be sent to the area border router for each area, because without knowledge of group membership information, the backbone could not know which areas needed the multicast data and would therefore have to send the data to all areas. The choice is to send the group membership information about all members or to send the data.

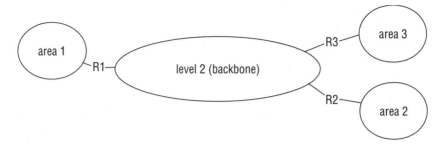

Figure 15.6 Wildcard multicast receivers

Referring to Figure 15.6, R1, R2, and R3 would all be wildcard multicast receivers within their area and within the backbone. If any source transmitted to any multicast group within area 1, the multicast traffic would be delivered to R1. If R2 and R3 broadcast the group memberships of their areas within the backbone, then R1 might be able to drop the multicast traffic if it was not of interest to anyone outside area 1. However, MOSPF does not transmit group information into the backbone, so the multicast traffic R1 receives must be sent across the backbone to R2 and R3, who can drop it if there are no interested members in their area because group information is flooded within the area.

A recent proposal is to reduce the bandwidth wasted with wildcard multicast receivers by using a prune mechanism as in DVMRP to stop unnecessary data leaking. With this mechanism, if S (within area 1) is transmitting on a group that has receivers only in area 1, R2 and R3 could send prunes across the backbone when they receive the multicast data for that group, eventually reaching R1. And then R1 could send a prune into area 1.

15.2.9 Core-based Trees

One version of core-based trees (CBT) has been published as RFC 2189, but it has been superseded by an Internet draft and is still undergoing changes.

The basic idea of CBT was first proposed by Jon Crowcroft, Tony Ballardie, and Paul Francis in 1992. The idea is similar to the ATM style of group formation, only backward. Instead of the central node sending joins outward to each member, each member instead sends joins toward the central node.

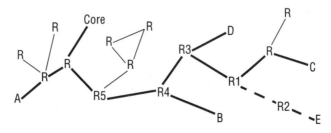

Figure 15.7 CBT

In Figure 15.7, A, B, C, and D have transmitted joins for group (Core,M). The join contains the IP address "Core," and it gets routed toward the core, creating state in the routers along the path. When E sends a join for group (Core,M), it gets sent to R2, which now stores state for group (Core,M), and forwards it to R1. Because R1 already has state for (Core,M) it only needs to add the port to R2 into its existing state for (Core,M) and does not forward the join further.

The result is a single bidirectional tree to support a multicast group; the only routers with any knowledge of the group are the ones that need to know about the group because they are on the tree. And data does not get leaked outside the tree.

Unlike ATM point-to-multipoint trees, in CBT data does not have to originate at the core. For example, if D transmits a packet for M, it gets received by R3 and forwarded by R3 toward R1 and R4. R4 forwards it to B and R5, and so on. In other words, the core is not a bottleneck. Indeed, it has no particular special function after the tree is formed. It's just like any other member. It does not even have to be a router. It does not need to forward data packets (except perhaps for forwarding packets tunneled to it by nonmember senders).

I like CBT as it was proposed in 1992. However, it has since evolved to not specifically choose the core; instead, it expects all routers in the Internet to figure out, based solely on M, who the core is. This leads to complexity and to scaling problems. The two suggested methods in the current CBT draft are as follows.

- Manual configuration of (core, group) mappings in routers adjacent to potential members or senders (which would wind up being most routers).

- A protocol in which various routers volunteer to be cores. They advertise throughout the AS, use a distributed election protocol, and have the elected router flood information about the current set of potential cores throughout the AS. Routers perform a hash of the group address M to select the core for M from the set of potential cores.

The only scaling problem I see with CBT is as a result of the core selection. The manual configuration method would be much too expensive. The other method is bandwidth-intensive because of the AS-wide advertisements of potential cores. It also is likely to result in highly suboptimal trees because an arbitrary router is chosen to be the core, and it might not be close to any of the members of the group.

15.2.10 PIM-DM

PIM-DM stands for protocol-independent multicast, dense-mode. "Dense-mode" means that you're assuming there are enough receivers around that it isn't worth creating a tree. A protocol such as CBT would be known as a "sparse-mode" protocol.

PIM-DM evolved from, and is very similar to, DVMRP. However, instead of having a separate routing protocol run specifically for multicast, PIM-DM uses the forwarding information that is already computed by whatever unicast routing protocol is being run.

After all, the only routing information a router running a DVMRP-like dense-mode multicast protocol requires is the preferred link to S so that it can do reverse path forwarding (where router R2 accepts a packet with source S from R1 only if R2 would forward a packet destined for S through R1).

DVMRP also gives enough information so that router R2 can know which routers consider R2 their preferred next hop to S. In this way, it can do the Dalal/Metcalfe optimization of having R2 forward only to those neighbors. PIM-DM does not assume that it can receive this information from the routing protocol. In theory it could make that assumption if the protocol were a link state protocol such as OSPF or IS-IS. However, RIP does not give this information. So PIM does not bother with that optimization. Instead, R2 forwards a packet from source S to all links except its own choice for forwarding to S. Given that anyone who didn't want the packet will send a prune, the PIM-DM implementers decided not to bother with the optimization.

DVMRP also attempts to have lower overhead of prune messages and leaked data messages. It holds prune state for about 2 hours. This requires careful mechanisms to ensure that state isn't ever incorrectly in the pruned state. PIM-DM uses the simpler strategy of holding state for only about 3 minutes, something that results in more-frequent flooding of data packets.

PIM-DM has the same scaling problems as DVMRP, and they preclude it from being a solution to Internet-wide multicast. Data periodically gets sent everywhere, certainly when a source that has not recently transmitted sends a packet, and too much state is required because routers must keep track of all the (source, group) pairs for all groups and not only those for which the router must forward traffic.

15.2.11 PIM-SM

The most recent version of PIM-SM (protocol-independent multicast, sparse-mode) is documented in RFC 2362. It uses the tree-building mechanism of CBT but calls the core a *rendezvous point* or RP. In addition to the shared tree rooted at the RP for group G, routers join an (S,G) tree rooted at S if, in their opinion, the volume of traffic from S makes it worth it. To prevent loops, with some nodes receiving traffic from S on the tree rooted at RP and others receiving it on a tree rooted at S, the shared tree (known as the (*,G) tree) is *unidirectional*. For someone other than RP to send on that tree, the data must be tunneled to the RP before it can be multicast to the participants.

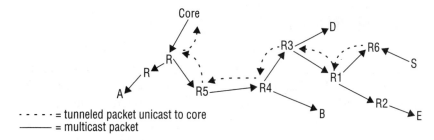

= tunneled packet unicast to core
= multicast packet

Figure 15.8 Unidirectional tree: packet transmissions when S transmits

In Figure 15.8, when S transmits a packet, R6 tunnels it to the RP (by adding an IP header specifying the destination as the RP). Then the RP sends it on the multicast tree. So the packet incurs delay by first having to be sent to the RP before being distributed, and the links between R6 and the RP wind up having the packet appear twice.

PIM-SM also defines a method for routers to determine who the RP is for group G.

- One router is elected bootstrap router (BSR): all routers that are configured to be bootstrap routers flood advertisements throughout the domain (using reverse path forwarding to make the flood less expensive). The one with the highest priority/ address is elected BSR.

- Routers that are configured to be RPs unicast their aliveness and willingness to be RPs to the BSR.

- The BSR floods the list of candidate RPs.

- Candidate RPs might be configured to serve as RPs only for a subset of the multicast addresses. In that case their announcement to the BSR will indicate the range of multicast addresses they are willing to be RP for, and the BSR's list of candidate RPs will list the ranges of addresses for each candidate RP.

- A hash function is defined that takes as input the group address G and the set of qualified candidate RPs and selects from that set the one that will be the RP for G. All routers in the domain must make the same decision.

PIM-SM also has scaling problems that preclude it from being a true Internet-wide multicast solution. The protocol for mapping G to RP is expensive because it involves flooding of the BSR announcements. Also, it would be undesirable to wind up with an RP in, say, Tibet, if all the members of your group are in, say, California.

Also, in my opinion, the overhead of creating a new tree for each source is not worth the overhead. In PIM-SM, the shared tree is likely to be suboptimal for two reasons: the RP selection does not take into account the location of group members in selecting the RP, and the shared tree is unidirectional (packets must be unicast to the RP before being multicast to the group). PIM-SM suffers from a problem known as the *bursty source* problem because of the necessity to create a tree and prune off from the shared tree when a source that has not transmitted recently starts transmitting. The tree rooted at S times out and gets forgotten if S is quiet for some amount of time.

15.2.12 BGMP/MASC

BGMP stands for Border Gateway Multicast Protocol and depends on MASC, which stands for Multicast-Address-Set advertisement and Claim mechanism. At the time of the writing of this book, the design of MASC is far from being finished even though it is the mechanism the IETF working group claims will allow Internet-wide multicast groups to be supported. It is sufficiently far from being viable that a totally different mechanism (MSDP; see Section 15.2.13) is being designed as an "interim measure until BGMP/ MASC is ready."

BGMP involves creating a single bidirectional tree to support a group (so far so good!), just as with CBT. The tricky part is to determine the core for the tree. The basic idea is as follows.

- Each domain dynamically acquires a block of multicast addresses through the MASC protocol.

- The multicast address blocks are advertised throughout the Internet through BGP.

- A join message for group G is sent toward the domain that has acquired the block of multicast addresses that includes G.

- After the join message is inside the domain, a mechanism such as PIM's bootstrap mechanism selects the exact core/RP.

I do not think this approach will work. The proposed MASC protocol is complex and expensive. It's more difficult than expecting the entire Internet to autoconfigure its IP addresses. With IP addresses, you know approximately how many you'll need. Multicast groups are highly dynamic. How many multicast addresses will your domain need? What happens if you underestimate? Then the multicast address space gets fragmented as you go back for extra blocks, increasing the burden on the interdomain routing protocol to pass around all the allocated multicast address blocks. And what happens if everyone overestimates? You'll run out of addresses. A total of 2^{28} addresses might sound like a lot, but not for something in which every domain is attempting to acquire a block of them before they are needed, as opposed to obtaining them one-by-one on an as-needed basis.

And in case we think there are enough addresses, there are proposals for using different parts of the multicast address space to encode information such as the type of group. For example, one proposal is for copyright-sensitive groups. Because some countries don't respect copyright law, you might want to ensure that your multicast data does not leak into a domain that does not respect copyright law. So the idea is to reserve some set of addresses for multicast groups that are copyright-sensitive, and another set for those that aren't worried about the issue. Configure routers on the boundary of copyright-violating domains to know which multicast address ranges are allowed to be sent into such domains. If copyright were the only policy we wanted to encode in this way, this would multiply the number of blocks required by each domain by 2 because each domain might want to acquire a block from the copyright-sensitive as well as a block from the copyright-insensitive multicast address blocks. But how many policies might be wanted? Domains into which pornographic information should not be sent? Sets of countries that don't like other sets of countries? If we want to support policy by partitioning the multicast address space, we require each domain to acquire a block for each possible policy it might need to support.

15.2.13 Multicast Source Distribution Protocol

Multicast source distribution protocol (MSDP) is supposed to be a proposed interim solution to allow interdomain multicast groups until BGMP/MASC gets designed, implemented, and deployed. (This need to design and deploy MSDP, a brand new interim solution, is usually stated in the same speech in which someone also claims that IP multicast has been complete for years and is stable and that everyone loves it.) The basic idea is that tunnels are configured between RPs in various domains, hopefully enough tunnels so that there is a connected mesh even when some RPs are down. The RPs involved in the tunnels speak the MSDP protocol to each other.

Within each domain, the PIM-SM bootstrap mechanism assigns an RP to a multicast address G. If there are members in multiple domains, you wind up with a tree for each domain, each rooted on an RP in that domain assigned to handle address G.

Now let's assume that source S transmits a packet with destination address G. The MSDP speaker(s) in S's domain must flood across the mesh of MSDP tunnels the information that there is traffic from source S for address G. An MSDP speaker in each domain that has members that have joined G now joins a tree rooted on S. In this way, its members can receive traffic for (S,G).

The scaling problem for MSDP is the necessity to pass around information about all (S,G) pairs active in the Internet, throughout the Internet. It also is configuration-intensive. To get resiliency against link or router failures, there must be a great many configured tunnels. And the more tunnels there are, the more expensive the flooding is to distribute the (S,G) information for all active groups in the world.

15.2.14 Simplifying Multicast

> **There are two ways of constructing a software design: One way is to make it so simple that there are obviously no deficiencies, and the other way is to make it so complicated that there are no obvious deficiencies.**
>
> **—C. A. R. Hoare**

For several years I've been proposing the following two suggestions for simplifying multicast.

- Avoid requiring all routers to be able to figure out the core/RP address from the multicast address. Instead, have the core address be part of the identity of the group. In other words, the group is not known simply by the 4-byte class D address G but instead by the pair (C,G). The address G does not need to be globally unique. It need only be unique with respect to C because only the 8-byte quantity (C,G) needs to be unique.

- Don't bother with dynamically created per-source trees. Instead, just live with a single shared (preferably bidirectional) tree for the group.

Making these modifications would be fairly easy, and it would make multicast quite straightforward with low overhead. More and more people are coming to the same conclusion. These suggestions vastly simplify multicast address administration (because the multicast address must be unique only with respect to the core and need not be coordinated to be unique across the Internet). These changes would also create lower overhead in routers and would create a protocol simple and scalable enough that a single mechanism would support both intra- and interdomain groups. The alternative is to deploy nonscalable mechanisms within domains and then invent another mechanism for gluing the domains together.

Any of the tree-creating protocols (CBT, PIM-SM, or BGMP) could easily be modified as per the preceding suggestions. However, after several years this was not happening, so a protocol called Simple Multicast[4] was designed. Independently, Hugh Holbrook and Dave Cheriton from Stanford developed a proposal, called Express, that is extremely similar in spirit to Simple Multicast. The difference between Express and Simple is that Express proposes only unidirectional per-source trees, whereas Simple proposes bidirectional trees. Both proposals have the effect that a group is known by an 8-byte ID. In the case of Express it's (Source,G). For Simple it's (Core,G). In either case, address allocation is trivial, and there is no need for routers to do mappings from G to Core.

15.2.14.1 Creating a Group in Simple Multicast: Choosing C

The first step in creating a group is to choose a core C. Allowing the group creator to specify the core (instead of having one arbitrarily selected by a method such as the PIM bootstrap mechanism) allows more control and better trees. In most cases the choice of the core is obvious. For applications in which most of the traffic is from a single source S, then S should be the core.

For conference-call-type applications, any member of the group, or any node near any member of the group, will result in a good tree. Even if the majority of the members are in New York, one member is in Tasmania, and the Tasmanian member is chosen as the core, the tree will still be a good tree provided that the suggestion in Section 15.2.14.3—selecting a single exit point from the domain (for that group)—is followed.

There is no problem if S is an endnode. An endnode on a tree does not need to forward packets. The forwarding rule on a tree is that you forward data on every interface except the one from which the packet was received. If you have only one link in the tree, there are never any "other interfaces" to forward onto.

---

[4] Tony Ballardie, Radia Perlman, Cheng-Yin Lee, and Jon Crowcroft, "Simple Scalable Internet Multicast," UCL Research Note RN/99/21.

15.2.14.2 How Do Endnodes Discover C?

The idea is that the endnodes know both C and G instead of only G. How would they know that? The answer is, "However they would have figured out G." How would you find out that you wanted to join a particular multicast group G? It depends on the application. Some groups might get registered and advertised in a directory. In this case the group would have a name, and instead of looking up the name to find G, you'd find both C and G. It's like looking up an 8-byte address instead of a 4-byte address. Other groups might be more private. You might create a conference call and send email to the 10 invited participants telling them the address of the group, in this case an 8-byte address. Or someone might advertise some sort of information distribution service on a Web page and invite you to join by clicking on something that would tell your workstation the 8-byte address to join. Basically, the endnode already has to discover G, so it's not any harder to also find out C. It's just finding 8 bytes of information instead of 4.

15.2.14.3 Isn't a Shared Tree Suboptimal?

Assuming a reasonably placed core, a shared bidirectional tree is as optimal as a tree rooted on source S, in terms of cost to the network to deliver the data. And indeed, a bidirectional tree can be thought of as rooted at any node.

There is a persistent myth that in a bidirectional tree the core is a bottleneck. This is not true. Nor do the links near the core get any more traffic than any other link in the tree. Each multicast packet traverses each link in the bidirectional tree exactly once. Each node, including C, receives each packet once.

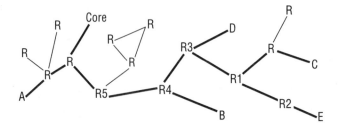

Figure 15.9 Bidirectional tree

In Figure 15.9, although the tree was formed by joining to the Core, if D transmits a packet, the distribution tree for that packet looks the same as if there were a tree with D as the root.

With a bit of care, you can ensure that the bidirectional tree is constructed so that members near each other in the network are near each other in the tree. The trick is to have the routing protocol select a single exit point from a domain or from any region connected to the rest of the network through expensive links.

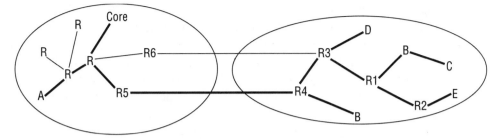

Figure 15.10 Creating a good tree: select one exit point from domain to reach C

In Figure 15.10, R4 is selected as the exit point from the domain for reaching the IP prefix in which Core's address resides. Otherwise, it would be possible to create the tree shown in Figure 15.11.

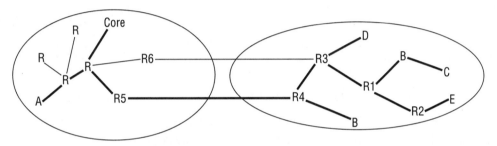

Figure 15.11 A tree that might be created without the one-exit-point optimization

Let's assume that the interdomain links are expensive and that the intradomain links are cheap, fast, and in general more desirable. The tree created in Figure 15.11 is suboptimal for two reasons. One is that each data packet on the group requires traversing two expensive links (R3-R6 and R4-R5). The other is that member B receives packets from D via a long path involving two expensive links, whereas with the single-exit-point optimization, the path between D and B is confined to the domain.

Note that even with a per-source tree (such as if "core" were the source) it is possible (and undesirable) to get the tree in Figure 15.11 unless the single-exit-point rule is followed. It is an undesirable tree because of the total cost to the network of delivering the data from the core to every recipient.

15.2.14.4 Single Point of Failure?

If the core's IP address is part of the identity of the group, wouldn't it represent a single point of failure? There are several answers to this question.

Many applications (probably the vast majority) consist of a single source distributing data. If that source is the core and the core dies, the group is dead. But in this case the group should die because the source is dead.

One simple mechanism to provide redundancy for a multisender application is for the application to create two groups (C1,M1), and (C2,M2). Members join both trees but transmit on only one. The core periodically sends *heartbeat* messages, which get multicast along the tree so that members can transmit on a tree known to be alive.

Another mechanism is the concept of a *distributed core*. Several candidate cores can communicate with each other to elect one—say, R. R would inject a host route C1. If R dies, a different candidate core is elected, and it injects the host route C1. To the rest of the network this is transparent. With (C1,G) as the address of the group, if the core dies, the core automatically moves to a new location and the tree adapts. This sounds similar to the RP selection mechanism of PIM, but it's actually less expensive because the only nodes that need to participate in the election mechanism are the several candidate C1s and not the entire domain. In PIM-SM, the bootstrap messages get flooded throughout the domain. With this mechanism, only the candidate C1s need to exchange control traffic.

And of course another possible mechanism is the PIM bootstrap mechanism, which, although it does not work Internet-wide, works well enough within a domain. The "core" address could be a unicast prefix owned by the domain, and the PIM bootstrap mechanism could find the exact core after the join message or the data message arrived at the domain that owns the unicast prefix.

15.2.14.5 Controlling Who Can Send

In a unidirectional tree, the core can be configured with the set of allowed or disallowed senders and can refuse to forward a packet from unauthorized senders. How can this be provided with a bidirectional tree?

The core periodically sends heartbeat messages to let the members of the group know that the core is alive and to convey any group-specific information to the members. Access control information is just the type of information that can be carried in the heartbeat message. The access control information consists of allowed or disallowed address ranges. If either set is too large, it can be added to as needed. For example, the set of allowed senders can start out null (meaning only the core is allowed to send). If you are not listed in the set of allowed senders, you must transmit by tunneling to the core. If the core decides you are authorized, it forwards your packet and starts advertising your address in the heartbeat message as an authorized sender.

Similarly, the set of unauthorized senders advertised in the heartbeat message can start out empty. This enables an unauthorized sender to send a few packets until the core notices and starts advertising that sender as unauthorized. In that case, all the routers on the tree will refuse to forward packets for that sender.

15.2.14.6 Policy

As described in Section 15.2.12, there are proposals to support various types of policies by partitioning the multicast address space for each type of policy. For example, half the addresses could be allocated to a group that are allowed into copyright-violating domains; the other half would imply that data for that group should not be allowed into copyright-violating domains.

If indeed this were important to support, it's easier to support with Simple Multicast. The heartbeat can specify the "group type" rather than partition the multicast address space.

15.2.14.7 Specifying C in Join Messages

One variant of Simple Multicast is closest in spirit to the original proposal for CBT and involves only a minor modification to CBT: having the endnode that joins group (C,G) tell the router what the mapping between G and C is. Either the endnode sends the join message (rather than participate in IGMP), or the endnode specifies C as well as G in the IGMP reply. Given that the proposal for IGMP v3 has endnodes specify not only the address of the group they're joining but also the list of sources they want to receive traffic from, it's certainly not a bigger change to have an endnode specify C. Let's call this *specified-core CBT*. With this variant, multicast addresses must be chosen so that two groups with the same class D address G don't intersect. This is a simpler problem than getting aggregatable multicast address blocks (required by BGMP/MASC) because the addresses must only be unique and be obtained on an as-needed basis; they do not need to be advertised through BGP. However, it would be far better to use the variant in Section 15.2.14.8 so that multicast addresses need not be globally unique—especially because it's not clear what a router should do if it receives a join for (C2,G) after it's already received a join for (C1,G). Two possibilities are as follows.

- Have the second join fail and send back an error report on why it failed (conflicting core address for G).

- Merge the two groups by choosing, say, the core with the lower address as the core for both groups.

At any rate, the variant in Section 15.2.14.8 avoids this issue.

15.2.14.8 Specify Both C and G in Data Messages

Another variant is to specify C and G in data messages as well. The advantage of including both C and G in data packets is that multicast addresses no longer have to be coordinated across the Internet to avoid simultaneous use of an address by topologically overlapping groups. The address G need be unique only with respect to the core C. To create a group, you select a core and then ask that core for an address it has not recently assigned to another group. That makes the multicast address space virtually inexhaustible because every core has the full range of multicast addresses (minus a few reserved ones) at its disposal.

Where in a data packet can we put C? Various options are as follows.

- Define a new IP option and include C in that option when a node other than C sends a packet to the group.

- Define a new layer 4 header, maybe called MUDP (for Multicast UDP), and include C in that header (again, this is only needed on packets originated by a node other than C).

- Use the destination address in the IP header as if it were an ATM virtual circuit identifier that has only link-local significance. In other words, when R1 sends a join (C,G) to R2, R2 replies join-ack (C,G). Use X. When R1 forwards a data packet for group (C,G) to R2, it replaces the destination address with "X," and forwarding is similar to forwarding in ATM. R2 will know that X means (C,G).

A disadvantage of having the destination address be link-local is that it requires a router to overwrite the destination address as it forwards a packet. In IPv4 this is reasonably expensive because of the header checksum. Some effort could be made to keep the destination address constant, changing only when necessary—that is, when two groups with the same low-order 4 bytes intersect at a router. If, for example, the G is selected at random, then for most groups the quantity "G" would work as the link-local identifier of (C,G). Only when a router has seen a join for (C1,G) and then sees a join for (C2,G) would the router need to assign a link-local address other than G to (C2,G).

Another disadvantage claimed for link-local addresses is that it does not support the ability to transmit to a group without signaling first, which some people consider important (I don't). A way of supporting something that wishes to transmit to the group without receiving the data from the group is to allow *sender-only* joins. The sender-only node would send a join message, specifying that it wanted to transmit to (C,G) but did not wish to receive data for that group. Just as with a "normal" join, it would be told what the link-local address for group (C,G) would be. Another method of allowing S to transmit to (C,G) without joining the group is for S to tunnel the packet to C.

15.2.14.9 Dense-mode Groups

A feature that is easily provided by this form of multicast is the ability to select dense-mode. If the volume of data is sufficiently low or if the density of receivers is sufficiently large within the specified scope of the multicast, then it is not worth the overhead of creating an optimal distribution tree. With Simple Multicast, dense-mode can be specified with the convention of specifying core = FF:FF:FF:FF.

With PIM-DM and PIM-SM you do not get a choice, on a per-application basis, whether dense or sparse is appropriate. Rather, a domain runs one or the other. It makes more sense to be able to select the appropriate delivery mechanism on a case-by-case basis. However, some people worry that if an application is allowed to select dense-mode, it might abuse the privilege and create too much traffic.

15.2.14.10 Express

In Express, a group is the pair (S,G). Again, multicast addresses do not need to be coordinated across the Internet. They need be unique only with respect to a source S. Trees are unidirectional. Only S is allowed to transmit. If there is a group with more than one sender you have two choices. One is to create multiple groups, one per source. The other is to have senders other than S tunnel their packets to S and have S distribute the packet. The Express proposal is basically the same as point-to-multipoint ATM. The Express designers claim that the only applications that really require multicast are single source. However, some reliable multicast protocols require bidirectional trees so that receivers can multicast naks or acks, or find nearby repair nodes.

15.2.14.11 What Is Simpler About Simple Multicast?

Simple Multicast has the following advantages over the "current" approaches to multicast:

- Multicast address assignment is simplified. In the proposal in Section 15.2.14.7, multicast addresses still must be coordinated across the Internet, but they can be allocated on a one-by-one, as-needed basis because they need only to be unique and not aggregatable. In the proposals in Sections 15.2.14.8 and 15.2.14.10, address assignment becomes trivial because addresses need be unique only with respect to a particular node. And multicast addresses become plentiful.

- It eliminates the overhead of protocols to allow all routers in the Internet to be able to figure out the core address from the multicast address.

- Multisender groups can be supported with far fewer trees (assuming bidirectional trees).

- Because there are no scaling issues, a single protocol can be used both inter- and intradomain, and it can replace all of DVMRP, MOSPF, CBT, PIM, MSDP, BGMP, and MASC.

- There are no bursty source problems. Trees are created and maintained and ready for data, regardless of who sends the data, until they are consciously torn down when the session is finished.

The primary objection to Simple Multicast/Express is that it's "too late," and there's "too much momentum" behind the current designs. The same thing was said several years ago, and perhaps the same thing will be said years from now when people again notice that multicast is getting ever more complicated and expensive.

> **It is always the right time to do the right thing.**
> **—Martin Luther King**

Homework

1. Suppose you have a LAN consisting of a single collision domain (that is, a multi-port repeater). Assume that the hub has 10 ports, each 10 Mbit. Compare the maximum total aggregate bandwidth if everyone transmits all packets to a multicast layer 2 address rather than using unicast layer 2 addresses. Now assume that you replace the repeater with a store and forward switch. What is the maximum aggregate bandwidth if everyone is sending unicast packets versus multicast packets?

2. Make the following assumptions.

   a. The topology consists of a single switch with a bunch of ports, all in the same broadcast domain.

   b. The switch does not filter packets sent to layer 2 multicast addresses; it forwards all such packets to all ports.

   c. Source S has a high volume of data to send to n recipients.

   Compare the strategy of having S send n unicast packets, one to each of the n recipients, versus sending a single multicast packet for each data packet in S's data stream. How does multicast affect maximum aggregate bandwidth (considering all conversations going on in this LAN and not just S's data)? How does multicast affect the maximum bandwidth that S's data stream can achieve? (Hint: consider the case when n is small, as well as when n is large.)

3. What are the trade-offs of sending IGMP reply messages to the layer 2 multicast address corresponding to the layer 3 multicast group versus sending the IGMP reply message to a multicast address listened to only by routers?

4. Assume that a switch has learned through IGMP snooping which ports want to receive IP multicast address G. What are the trade-offs of having the switch forward based on the layer 2 multicast address derived from G versus looking at the layer 3 header and forwarding based on G?

5. Compare the overhead of multicast data delivery and the control traffic overhead necessary to support the following.

   a. Simple flooding (send each packet over each link except the one from which it was received, and delete when the hop count expires)

   b. "Source route bridge style" (use flooding, but keep a list of routers visited in each copy of the packet, and router R drops a received packet if R is listed)

   c. Spanning tree (a single spanning tree for all multicast traffic, as with transparent bridges)

d. Reverse path forwarding

e. Reverse path forwarding with the optimization of forwarding a packet from S to neighbor N only if N forwards traffic destined for S to you

6. Compare DVMRP, MOSPF, CBT, PIM-SM, MSDP, BGMP/MASC, and the variants of Simple Multicast (including Express) in terms of bandwidth, state, reliability, and so on.

7. In DVMRP, what is the purpose of remembering that you received an (S,M) prune from neighbor N? What is the purpose of remembering that you sent an (S,M) prune to neighbor N?

8. In DVMRP, prunes specify the source, as in "prune (S,M)," and not just "don't send me packets for M." One obvious reason for specifying S in the prune is that in IGMP v3 you can join M with only a subset of sources. However, assume that joins are only for M (as was the case in IGMP v2). Would the following protocol work?

a. Prunes specify only M.

b. Send a "prune M" to neighbor N if N sent you a packet with (destination M, source S), N is your path to S, and you had nowhere to forward it to (because all of your neighbors that would accept a packet from you from S based on RPF have sent you "prune M."

Chapter 16
Sabotage-proof Routing

When people think of a network component failing, they generally assume that it fails in a *fail-stop* manner—that is, it reverts instantaneously from working properly to stopping completely. But a different sort of failure can and does occur, in which a node continues operating but functions incorrectly. This can result from software bugs, hardware faults, or even sabotage. For example, a router might lie in its routing messages, misroute packets, reset the hop count, corrupt the data, perform perfectly except consistently trash packets from one source, or flood the network with garbage.

This sort of fault is known as a *Byzantine failure.* In this chapter, I sketch how a network can be designed to be resilient to Byzantine failures. Such a network continues operating even if someone with thorough knowledge of how the network works has reprogrammed some of the routers to be as malicious as possible. The resilient network guarantees that data will continue to be transmitted from a properly functioning source to a properly functioning destination, provided that at least one path of properly functioning routers and links connects the source and the destination.

Causing the network to malfunction is known as a *denial of service attack.* In this chapter I describe a method of designing network protocols that will withstand denial of service attacks.[1] The design is practical in the sense that the CPU, memory, bandwidth, and management requirements are not much greater than those for conventional networks. None of today's networks is built this way. Although they provide authentication fields in routing messages, this only prevents nonauthorized nodes from injecting routing traffic. It does not protect against a faulty router. Networks using the techniques in this chapter may become popular in the near future as society depends more on the robustness of networks and as the cost of cryptography decreases.

> **All roads lead to Rome.**
>
> **— A clearly confused router**

---

[1] This chapter summarizes the results first presented in R. Perlman, "Network Layer Protocols with Byzantine Robustness" (Ph.D. dissertation, Massachusetts Institute of Technology, 1988).

16.1 The Problem

The goal is to design a network that guarantees that a packet transmitted between two nonfaulty end systems A and B will have a high probability of being delivered, provided that at least one path consisting of nonfaulty components connects the two end systems. No guarantee is made that all messages sent by A for B will arrive at B—only that each packet independently has a high probability of reaching its destination. Node A can compensate for lost packets by using acknowledgments and retransmissions at a higher layer. The network layer makes no attempt to keep conversations private. If privacy is necessary, encryption must be done at a higher layer. Also, the network layer need not certify data that it delivers. For example, it is possible for some malicious node C to generate data, get it delivered to B, and claim that the data was from A. It is up to the higher layer in B to differentiate between corrupted or counterfeit data and real data by using known cryptographic techniques.

16.2 All You Need to Know about Cryptography

The solution to the problem posed in the preceding section involves cryptography. In this section, I describe all the fundamentals you need in order to understand the solution. If you like this book and want a book with a similar style and technical level that explains cryptography and network security protocols, let me recommend *Network Security: Private Communication in a Public World*, (Prentice Hall), by Charlie Kaufman, Radia Perlman (yes, that's me), and Michael Speciner.

There are two basic types of cryptography. In *secret key cryptography*, a magic number known as the *key* is shared by two or more parties. To encrypt a message, you apply a mathematical function that takes the message and the key as inputs, generating an *encrypted* message, otherwise known as *ciphertext*. The reverse operation, *decryption*, requires the use of the same key (see Figure 16.1). So the operations encryption and decryption are inverses of each other, similar to division by the key being able to reverse the operation of multiplication by the key.

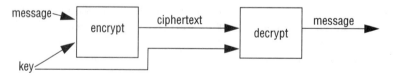

Figure 16.1 Secret key encryption

A second type of cryptography is known as *public key cryptography*. In public key cryptography, two magic numbers are associated with each user. The first number is known as the *private key*, and the user must keep it secret. The other is known as the *public key*, and the user can advertise it widely. The two numbers are mathematically related—they are inverses of each other—but the mathematical techniques are such that knowledge of one of the numbers does not enable you to calculate the other. Keys are typically hundreds or thousands of bits long. If you knew someone's public key and were able to guess the private key, you could verify that the number you guessed was indeed the private key. But because there are no techniques for finding the private key (given only the public key) that are significantly better than guessing numbers at random or trying all possible numbers, finding the private key is computationally infeasible.

Encryption of a message for user "Alice" is done with Alice's public key. The decryption operation, which is the inverse of the encryption operation, cannot be done with the public key; it requires the use of the private key. Thus, anyone with knowledge of Alice's public key can encrypt a message for Alice, but only Alice can decrypt the message (see Figure 16.2).

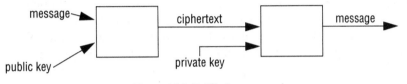

Figure 16.2 Public key encryption

You do not need encryption to design a super-robust network, but you need a concept known as a *digital signature*. A digital signature is a number associated with a message; it is similar to a checksum. In public key cryptography, Alice can generate a signature for a particular message using her private key. The public key is used to verify the signature. Thus, only Alice can generate a signature, but others can recognize Alice's signature. Note that the signature is a function of both the private key and the data. If any of the data is modified, the old signature is no longer valid. This method is comparable to the operation of a checksum. If a message is modified, the checksum is no longer valid (see Figure 16.3).

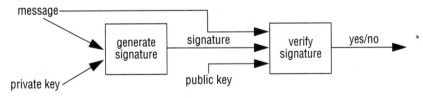

Figure 16.3 Public key signatures

Given that anyone with knowledge of the public key can verify a signature, theoretically someone could forge a signature by trying all possible numbers and then checking to see whether each number satisfies the verification procedure. However, because the numbers are so long, the probability is essentially zero that someone would be able to guess the signature within a reasonable time.

Malicious routers can do anything physically possible, but they cannot do anything supernatural. It is safe to assume that a malicious node cannot guess a legitimate node's private key or forge a signature.

16.3 Overview of the Approach

In Section 16.3.1, I describe a method of robustly delivering a packet to every possible destination in a network (*robust flooding*). Although robust flooding is not very efficient for delivery of data, which is usually supposed to be delivered only to a single destination, it is efficient for information, such as LSPs, that should be delivered to all the routers. Although robust flooding could be used for extremely reliable delivery of data packets, it would likely be used only for delivery of control information that must be broadcast. In Section 16.3.2, I describe how to use the control information (that is robustly delivered through robust flooding) to calculate single destination routes for data packets.

16.3.1 Robust Flooding

First, let's look at a design for robust packet delivery based on flooding. With flooding, if a source emits a packet, the packet is theoretically guaranteed to reach the destination if any correctly functioning path to the destination exists. However, the problem is that resources are finite. For a packet to successfully travel from one node to the next, link bandwidth must be available, and the next node must have both sufficient processing available to receive the packet and sufficient buffer space available to store the packet until it can be transmitted on the next link.

The key to robust flooding is to enforce fair allocation of resources.

- Structure packet buffers so that every source is guaranteed resources. You do this by allocating a buffer for each source, using digital signatures so that only the source can use its reserved resources, and using sequence numbers to avoid problems with replaying of old packets.

- Use link bandwidth fairly by going round-robin through the packet buffers, ensuring that each source's packet will get transmitted on the link.

To verify signatures, all the nodes must know the public keys of all the other nodes. Theoretically, you could do this by manual configuration, but that would be so inconvenient as to render the entire scheme infeasible. Instead, a special node known as the *public key distributor* distributes a special packet containing the public keys of all the nodes. To guard against Byzantine failure of the public key distributor, there can be multiple public key distributors (see Section 16.4.1.3).

This form of robust flooding turns out to be remarkably similar to LSP distribution, as described in Chapter 12. (In fact, after I designed sabotage-proof flooding I noticed to my embarrassment that if the cryptography were removed from the design, the resulting protocol was simpler than what I had recommended for LSP distribution in my 1983 paper[2] and which was implemented in IS-IS and OSPF. I modified the LSP distribution protocol to the protocol described in Section 12.2.3, and the result was implemented in IS-IS, OSPF, and PNNI.)

16.3.1.1 Summary of Robust Flooding

The technique outlined in the preceding subsection guarantees that packets are delivered, provided that at least one nonfaulty path connects source with destination. It is not as efficient as traditional networks because every packet is delivered to all nodes. It is not absurdly inefficient, though, because a packet travels over each link only once. This makes the algorithm n^2, in the worst case, because there can be at most n^2 links with n nodes. In contrast, transparent bridges deliver a packet to every destination in O (n), and source routing bridges deliver an *all paths explorer packet* in $O((b^{13}) * (p^{13}))$, where $b+1$ is the number of bridges per LAN and $p+1$ is the number of ports per bridge. So robust flooding is less efficient than broadcast using transparent bridges but far more efficient than broadcast using all paths explorer packets with source routing.

16.3.2 Robust Routing

Robust flooding is not very efficient when used for data packet routing because every packet is delivered to every node. It is useful for broadcasting the public key distributor's information and LSPs because those packets must be delivered everywhere. But data packets need to be delivered only to one destination.

To make the resilient network nearly as efficient as a conventional network, use robust flooding only for LSPs and public key information. After every node has a database of LSPs from every other node, have the source node calculate the entire path that it would like to use to the destination.

In traditional network packet forwarding, each router independently makes a decision about the next hop. This form of routing works only if all the routers along the path have consistent LSP databases and compatible path-computation algorithms. Allowing the source to compute the route offers the following advantages.

---

[2] R. Perlman, "Fault Tolerant Broadcast of Routing Information," *Computer Networks*, December 1993.

1. All the routers along the path need not have consistent LSP databases. Only the information at the first router must be reasonably accurate so that that router can find a correct path.

2. The router that computes the route can use an arbitrarily complicated algorithm, such as computing routes that avoid certain routers that the source router is suspicious of, perhaps because of previous unsuccessful attempts to route through those routers.

After the source router chooses a route, it sets up the route by launching a special *route-setup* packet, which lists the route. The route-setup packet is cryptographically protected (digitally signed) and travels along the route that the data packets will traverse. The routers along the path examine the route-setup packet and record the information that packets from source S to destination D should arrive from a specified neighbor and be forwarded to a specified neighbor. After a path is set up, data packets travel along it. Data packets do not need to be cryptographically protected. If the path consists of correctly functioning nodes and links, the data packets will get delivered properly. If the path is not correct, it is left to a higher layer to notice the problem and inform the network layer that it would like a different path chosen.

The function that most needs to be efficient is data packet forwarding. Using this approach, the work to forward a packet is not significantly more difficult than with a conventional network. The only extra work to forward a packet is to check that it arrived from the expected neighbor.

16.4 Detailed Description of the Approach

In this section I describe the details of the design for robustly delivering a packet from a single source to all destinations. I describe the various packet types that are required, the databases, and the amount of information that must be manually configured, as well as the protocols involved.

16.4.1 Robust Flooding Revisited

Two types of packets are flooded through robust flooding. The first type is a *public key list* packet, which lists all the public keys of all the nodes. It is generated by one of a few public key list distributor nodes. The second type is an LSP (link state packet).

16.4.1.1 A Priori Information

Each node must be configured with the following information:

1. Its own ID

2. Its own public and private key

3. N, an upper limit on the total number of network nodes

4. The identities of, and public keys for, each of the public key distributor nodes

5. The size of the maximum-size LSP

The public key distributor must also be configured with the IDs and public keys of all the nodes in the network.

16.4.1.2 Dynamic Database

Node R keeps the following: For each public key distributor node for which R has been configured with a key, R sets aside a buffer large enough to hold a packet listing N public keys. Additionally, for each buffer, R keeps a flag for each of its neighbors. The flag can contain three values: *OK*, meaning that no action needs to be taken for this public key list packet; *transmit*, meaning that this public key list packet needs to be forwarded to this neighbor; or *ack*, meaning that an ack for this public key list packet needs to be sent to this neighbor.

For each node reported in a public key list packet, R also reserves a buffer for an LSP and a flag for each neighbor. The flag has the same three possible values: OK, transmit, or ack (see Figure 16.4).

16.4.1.3 Dealing with Multiple Public Key Distributors

Two strategies can be used for dealing with multiple public key distributors. The first is the *majority rules* strategy, in which a buffer is set aside for a node only if a majority of the public key distributors list that node, with the same public key. The second is the *believe everything* strategy, in which a buffer is set aside for every reported (ID, key) pair. If two public key distributors disagree about node X's public key, with one of them reporting (X, key 1) and the other reporting (X, key 2), then two buffers are set aside for X. One buffer is reserved for an X that uses key 1; the other is reserved for an X that uses key 2.

	Neighbor 1	Neighbor 2	. . .	Neighbor k
PKL source = PKD1	OK	OK		ack
PKL source = PKD2	transmit	OK		ack
PKL source = PKD3	OK	OK		OK
LSP source = R1	OK	ack		ack
LSP source = R2	transmit	transmit		ack
LSP source = R3	ack	OK		OK
LSP source = Rn	OK	OK		transmit

Figure 16.4 Database of packets to be robustly flooded

16.4.1.4 Packets

Table 16.1 shows the contents of the packets.

Table 16.1 Contents of Packets in Robust Flooding Approach

Packet	Contents
Public Key List	ID of source Sequence number List of (ID, public key) pairs Signature
LSP Packet	ID of source Sequence number LSP data Signature
Public Key List Ack	ID of source (of public key list packet being acknowledged) Sequence number Signature copied from public key list packet being acknowledged
LSP Ack	ID of source (of LSP being acknowledged) Sequence number Signature copied from LSP

16.4.1.5 Distribution of Public Key List Packets

Assume that node R receives a public key list packet from neighbor P. First, R verifies the signature in the packet. If the signature is not valid (based on the configured public key for the public key distributor node that is the packet's source), the packet is dropped. If the signature is valid, the sequence number in the packet is checked against the sequence number of the packet in memory.

1. If the sequence number of the received packet is greater than that of the one in memory, then the packet in memory is overwritten. For that packet, the flag for neighbor P is set to the *ack* value, and the flags for all the other neighbors are set to the *transmit* value.

2. If the sequence number is equal to that of the packet in memory, then for that packet, the flag for neighbor P is set to the *ack* value.

   As a subtle robustness enhancement, the signature in the received packet should be checked against the signature in the stored packet. If the signatures are different, it means that two different packets have been generated that have valid signatures but the same sequence number. This can happen. For example, it is possible for the source to crash, restart without knowledge of the sequence number it used before the crash, and issue a new packet with a reused sequence number.

In this case, R should use the numerical values of the signatures as a tie-breaker and treat the packet with the numerically larger signature as if it had the larger sequence number.

3. If the sequence number is less than that of the packet in memory, the flag for P is set to the *transmit* value.

Memory is scanned round-robin. When a link to neighbor P is available, memory is scanned for the next public key list packet that has a flag equal to *ack* or *transmit*. If the flag is set to *ack,* then an *ack* for that packet is transmitted and the flag is set to *OK*.

16.4.1.6 Distribution of LSPs

LSPs are distributed in the same way as public key list packets. The only difference is that the list of nodes is obtained from the data in the public key list packets instead of being manually configured.

16.4.1.7 Receipt of Acks

If an ack is received from neighbor P, the signature and sequence number are compared with those of the packet in memory. If the signature and sequence number match, the *transmit* flag is cleared for that neighbor, for that packet.

16.4.1.8 Running Out of Sequence Number

If the sequence number is very large (say, 32 bits or even 64 bits), it will never reach the maximum value except as the result of a Byzantine failure on the part of the source. In this case, it is reasonable for that node to be disabled until manual intervention occurs. The manual intervention required is to change the public key of the node and reregister it with the public key distributor node(s). At that point, the node becomes, in essence, a brand-new node, starting at the lowest sequence number. The network discards all state about the previous incarnation of that node because its old public key is no longer advertised by the public key distributor.

16.4.2 Robust Data Routing

Robust flooding is used for distribution of LSPs and public key list packets. Data packets are routed on a specific route. The source router generates a route based on its LSP database. After a route is chosen, the source generates and signs a route-setup packet, which lists the specified route and travels along that route. Intermediate routers verify the signature, and if valid, store the source and destination IDs, along with the link from which the packet should arrive and the link onto which the packet should be forwarded.

16.4.3 Additional Dynamic Database

For each possible source-destination pair, the following memory is kept:

1. A buffer reserved for a route-setup packet

2. A buffer reserved for the most recently received data packet for that source-destination pair

3. An **RS-ack** flag, which, if set, indicates that an ack should be sent for that route-setup packet

4. An **RS-transmit** flag, which, if set, indicates that the route-setup packet should be forwarded to the next neighbor in the path

5. A **data-transmit** flag, which, if set, indicates that the data packet should be forwarded to the next neighbor in the path

This is a lot of storage (n^2) because room is reserved for every source-destination pair. If each source is limited to a constant number of destinations with which it can be in communication simultaneously, some storage can be saved. Instead of setting aside a buffer for each source-destination pair, you can set aside a fixed number of buffers for each source. In practice, an even smaller number of buffers can be reserved. A router can refuse route requests when no resources are available, as would be done in ATM or any connection-oriented network.

16.4.3.1 Additional Packets

Table 16.2 shows the contents of the additional packets.

Table 16.2 Contents of Additional Packets

Packet	Contents
Route-Setup Packet	Source Sequence Number IDs of the nodes in the route Signature
Route-Setup Ack	Source (of route-setup packet being acknowledged) Sequence number (of route-setup packet being acknowledged) Signature (of route-setup packet being acknowledged)
Data Packet	Source Destination Data

16.4.3.2 Receipt of Route-setup Packets

If the route-setup packet's signature is valid and if its sequence number is greater than the sequence number of the stored route-setup packet (if any) for that source-destination pair, then the stored route-setup packet is overwritten and the **RS-ack** and **RS-transmit** flags are set.

16.4.3.3 Receipt of Data Packets

If a data packet is received from neighbor P, with source S and destination D, the route-setup database is scanned for a route for S–D. If such a route exists and if it indicates that packets from S to D should arrive from P, then the data packet is accepted and stored in memory and the **data-transmit** flag for that packet is set.

Note that no cryptographic check is made on the packet, and no sequence number is checked. If the route consists of correctly functioning routers, there is a very high probability that the most recently received packet is the uncorrupted packet most recently generated by the source for that destination. If the route contains a faulty router, it does not matter what happens because data cannot be guaranteed to flow along a faulty route. The source must detect that the route has become faulty and select a different route.

I have chosen not to acknowledge each data packet but rather to transmit the data packet once to the next neighbor. Assuming that a simple, reliable data link protocol is used (any standard data link protocol will do), there is a high probability that the data packet will be delivered with one network layer transmission.

The protocol could also include acknowledgments for data packets, but then some identification other than source and destination address must be added to the data packet so that an ack can be matched with a specific packet. It should not be a strict sequence number because a corrupted sequence number early in a conversation should not stop the flow of subsequent packets. Instead, something like a packet identifier could be used. It would be treated as a unique identifier rather than having any numeric significance.

16.4.3.4 Nonfunctioning Routes

The robust flooding technique guarantees that if a single functional path exists between S and D, packets will flow along that path. The robust routing technique does not make that guarantee. Although the source is armed with a robustly delivered LSP database, there is no guarantee that a route computed based on that LSP database will consist of correctly functioning routers. For example, a router could perform all protocols correctly but then drop data packets. It could drop all data packets, or it could discriminate against certain sources or destinations.

Based on complaints from the higher layer, the source can detect that a route is not working. The source can then choose one of several strategies.

1. Select a new route, avoiding as many of the routers in the previous route as possible.

2. Keep track of routers on previously nonworking paths, avoiding them insofar as possible when choosing routes.

3. Attempt to find the bad routers by collecting management data.

4. Fall back on robust flooding as a routing technique when the chosen route does not work.

16.5 Summary

With the design described in the preceding section, forwarding of data packets is as efficient as in a conventional network. Forwarding of route-setup packets, LSPs, and public key list packets is more CPU-intensive than forwarding of data packets because a public key signature must be verified. It is possible with some public key signature schemes—in particular, the RSA (Rivest, Shamir, Adleman) algorithm—to make signature verification much less expensive than signature generation. Signature verification efficiency is much more critical than signature generation efficiency because signature verification happens so much more frequently.

Byzantine failure of routers in a network should be a very rare event. If that is indeed the case, routes chosen by the source almost always function properly. If there were to be a Byzantine failure in a router, most probably very few such failures would occur simultaneously in the network. In this case, again, most routes will work, and it should be possible to find alternate routes quickly. If it is expected that many Byzantine failures might occur simultaneously, then allowing the fallback strategy of flooding data packets will ensure that data packets (such as LSPs and public key list packets) will be delivered even if only a single functional path connects the source and destination.

16.6 For Further Reading

For understanding cryptography and network security protocols, I recommend the following: C. Kaufman, R. Perlman, and M. Speciner, *Network Security: Private Communication in a Public World*, Prentice Hall, 1995.

For the original paper that launched public key cryptography, see W. Diffie and M. Hellman, "New Directions in Cryptography," *IEEE Transactions on Information Theory* IT-22 (Nov. 1976): 644–654.

For the original paper on the RSA algorithm, see R. L. Rivest, A. Shamir, and L. Adleman, "On Digital Signatures and Public Key Cryptosystems," *Communications of the ACM* 21 (Feb. 1978): 120–126.

For a description of the famous computer science problem known as the "Byzantine generals problem," see L. Lamport, R. Shostak, and M. Pease, "The Byzantine Generals Problem," *ACM Transactions on Programming Languages and Systems* 4, no. 3 (July 1982): 382–401.

For more details and more variations on robust routing, see R. Perlman, "Network Layer Protocols with Byzantine Robustness," Ph.D. dissertation, Massachusetts Institute of Technology, Aug. 1988.

Homework

1. What manual configuration is required in order to install a new node in a network? What if the addition of the new node causes the network to grow beyond the configured parameter N? What manual configuration is required to add a new public key distributor to the network?

2. Why is self-stabilization a significant defense against saboteurs even if the network cannot withstand Byzantine failures?

3. Compare the two strategies for dealing with multiple public key distributors ("majority rule" and "believe everything"). Consider such factors as the amount of memory and bandwidth that might be reserved for invalid nodes and the resilience of the network to multiple malicious public key distributor nodes.

4. In robust flooding, suppose that an ack gets lost. What happens as a result?

5. If a public key distributor has a Byzantine failure, what problems can it cause? Can such a failure be detected easily?

6. Suppose that a router has a Byzantine failure in its protocol for robust flooding. What problems can it cause? Can this sort of failure be detected easily?

7. Why does a route-setup packet not require a separate flag for each neighbor, as do public key list packets and LSPs?

Chapter 17
To Route, Bridge, or Switch:
Is That the Question?

This chapter doesn't contain any new information; rather, it's a summary of the rest of the book.

17.1 Switches

I never know what to say when someone comments that switches have replaced bridges and routers. As discussed in Chapter 5, a switch is just a generic term that has come to mean a box that moves data quickly. Some of them (layer 2 switches) are bridges. Others (layer 3 switches) are routers. So this is not a meaningful statement.

17.2 Bridges versus Routers

What is a bridge? What is a router? Without knowing the answers to those two questions, it is difficult to make an intelligent comparison. The ISO terminology makes the distinction very clear: A bridge is a data link layer relay; a router is a network layer relay. Very clear, that is, until you wonder, "What is a network layer? What is a data link layer?"

I think that a data link layer should be designed to carry a packet of information across a single hop. If the data link layer assumes multiple hops, it is hard to imagine what the network layer is supposed to do. With reluctance, I rationalized that transparent bridges operate in the data link layer because the protocol used by the endnodes was designed to work across a single hop. Because source routing bridges were also defined as operating in the data link layer, I was at a loss to devise any definition of a data link layer that would differentiate it from a network layer—until I discovered the true definition of a data link layer: *A data link layer protocol is anything standardized by a committee chartered to standardize data link layer protocols.*

Now that you know what differentiates a bridge from a router, you can ask why bridges and routers should have any functional differences. To discuss this question at all sensibly, I must ignore source routing bridges. In my opinion, source routing bridges should be considered routers. Transparent bridges were designed with the constraint that they fit neatly within the existing data link layer. Source routing bridges were designed by adding protocols more typical of network layer protocols into the end stations. Only because the work was done within a committee dealing with something called a data link layer is source routing (as described in Chapter 4) considered a "bridging function."

The data link layer was designed with the assumption that the nodes communicating via the data link protocol are attached to a common link. The data link header lacks several fields that would be designed into a network layer header—for example, hop count, fragmentation and reassembly information, congestion feedback, and intermediate destination (next hop), in addition to final destination. There is no handshaking protocol (such as ICMP or ES-IS) by which endnodes and routers can become aware of each other.

Another constraint applicable to bridges is that they must work with the 802 addresses. An 802 address cannot be assumed to have any topological significance. Stations are designed so that address assignment is done at the time of manufacture. Transparent bridges must not require that a station's address depend on its location. They must allow a station to attach to any LAN within a bridged network, using its preconfigured 802 address. In contrast, all the civilized layer 3 protocols described in this book assign layer 3 addresses that indicate where the node resides.

Yet another constraint is that bridges not reorder packets from the same source. Protocols designed to work over a network layer expect some packet reordering (or they should; if they don't, they get what they deserve).

Therefore, bridges are operating under constraints that do not apply to routers. Let us examine some of the disadvantages of bridges relative to routers.

1. Bridges can use only a subset of the topology (a spanning tree). Routers can use the best path that physically exists between source and destination.

   This constraint is caused by two factors. The first is that the lack of a handshaking protocol between endnodes and bridges forces bridges to learn the location of stations based on the direction from which traffic is received. The second is that bridges must be transparent—they do not modify the packet in any way. A packet as transmitted by a bridge cannot be distinguished from a packet as transmitted by the source endnode.

2. Bridge reconfiguration after a topological change is an order of magnitude slower than router reconfiguration after a topological change.

   This stems from the transparency constraint that makes bridge loops much more dangerous than router loops. New bridge connectivity cannot be introduced until it is definitely known to be safe. The layer 2 header has no hop count to kill off packets in an infinite loop, and packets can spawn many copies; bridges might forward a packet onto multiple ports, and multiple bridges might pick up a packet transmitted on a shared medium. In contrast, loops are not a disaster with routers, so routers can switch over to new paths as soon as information is received.

3. The total number of stations that can be interconnected through bridges is limited to the tens of thousands. With routers, the total size of the network is, for all practical purposes, unlimited.

   The reason is that network layer addresses contain topological information, and it is possible to summarize a large number of addresses by using a prefix. Bridges cannot use hierarchical routing because the addresses have no routing hierarchy.

4. Bridges offer no firewall protection against broadcast storms.

   This is really an unfair complaint against bridges, but it is one of the major reasons that some users have come to dislike them. Bridges are simply doing their job. They are making multiple LANs appear to the upper-layer protocols as if they were a single LAN. A broadcast storm disables a LAN. When LANs are bridged, they become a single LAN from the point of view of the upper-layer protocols, and the broadcast storm therefore disables the entire bridged set of LANs. Even without pathological situations such as broadcast storms, some protocols (such as ARP with IP) use a lot of layer 2 broadcast traffic. As a result, people want to limit the size of the LAN and instead break a large topology into smaller IP subnets. The IP subnets must be interconnected through layer 3 rather than layer 2.

5. Bridges must drop packets that are too large to forward.

   The network layer header contains fragmentation and reassembly information. The data link layer header does not. Therefore, bridges must drop a packet that is too large to forward. Also, they cannot send an error message back to the source to let it know why the packet was dropped because no such packet is defined in the data link header.

6. Bridges cannot give congestion feedback to the endnodes.

   Layer 3 protocols have mechanisms such as congestion-experienced flags and source quench messages. The data link layer has no similar mechanism.

On the other hand, bridges offer some very attractive features compared with routers.

1. Bridges are really plug and play. Routers require much more configuration. This is a significant advantage of bridges. Although some layer 3 protocols (Apple-Talk, IPX, CLNP) are close to being plug and play and IP is improving, bridges are still much easier to deal with.

(Again, keep in mind that I am discussing only transparent bridging. Source routing bridges are definitely not plug and play because each bridge must be configured with a LAN number for each port, and parallel bridge numbers must also be configured.)

2. Bridges have a better price to performance ratio than routers. The reason is that routers must parse a network layer header, which is more difficult to parse than a data link header (because of such factors as header checksums that must be modified when hop counts are modified, variable-length fields, and potential options such as route recording).

   Routers are getting better; however, bridges are still faster and cheaper.

3. Bridges are multiprotocol. This issue is less important than it used to be because now there are multiprotocol routers, and the world has fewer and fewer layer 3 protocols.

4. Bridges forward even unroutable protocols. Although I wish it were not true, people have designed upper-layer protocols to run directly over the data link layer. Without a network layer, only a bridge can interconnect LANs with respect to such protocols. There is no intrinsic reason that these protocols could not have been designed to run over a network layer. They just weren't. The designers of these protocols believed that nobody would ever want to use them between LANs. As long as these protocols are in use, bridging will be necessary. Maybe someday they will be replaced by equivalent protocols designed to run over a network layer.

   Brouters (described later in the chapter) allow support of such protocols without requiring that other protocols be bridged.

5. Bridges allow an IP node to move within the bridged portion of the topology without changing its IP address. So even if all your nodes run IP, it is useful to build parts of your IP network out of bridges.

17.3 Extensions to Bridges

In this section, I examine various types of features that can be added to bridges to make them more routerlike.

17.3.1 Using More Than the Spanning Tree

Because a point-to-point link between two bridges has no stations attached, it remains idle if it is not selected for the spanning tree. Because of the perceived waste of resources, various strategies such as VLANs have been developed so that bridges can use more than a single spanning tree or use point-to-point links that were not selected by the spanning tree algorithm.

Another strategy is to use parallel links between two bridges. The two bridges can have some sort of local protocol (between the two of them) that makes the bundle of links between them appear to the outside world as a single link. Packets being forwarded across the "superlink" could be sent on any of the links for maximum utilization of all the links, provided that they are put back in order after receipt.

17.3.2 Fragmenting Bridges

Some vendors have various capabilities within bridges that require bridges to look at the network layer header. One example is network layer fragmentation. There are some transparent bridges that check the protocol type, and, if the protocol type is CLNP or IP and the packet is too large to be forwarded, the bridge performs fragmentation.

The IETF (Internet Engineering Task Force) Router Requirements working group attempted to define anything that looked at the network layer header as a router. Given that definition, bridges with features such as IP or CLNP fragmentation would be considered routers and would therefore have to conform to the router requirements document. They would have to do things such as decrement the hop count whenever they forwarded an IP packet and perhaps even support the IP routing protocol. However, the people building such bridges do not consider them to be routers. They view fragmentation as a fairly simple operation that gives their product a lot of functionality and have no interest in providing all the rest of the functionality that would be required in order to turn their product into a full-scale router.

17.3.3 IGMP Snooping

Some bridges look at IGMP packets so that they can know which IP multicast addresses should be forwarded on which ports (see Section 15.2.5). In a bus topology, if anyone wants to receive the packet, it must appear on the LAN. But in a LAN implemented as a multiport bridge, it is highly desirable for the bridge to be intelligent about which multicast messages to send on which ports. IGMP is definitely a layer 3 protocol, so should a box that implements this feature still be called a bridge?

> **What's in a name? That which we call a rose by any other name would smell as sweet.**
>
> **—William Shakespeare**

17.4 Extensions to Routers

In this section, I describe extensions to routers that give them some of the advantages of bridges.

17.4.1 Faster Routers

One of the reasons people prefer bridges is that they are capable of forwarding faster. There were two ways to make routers faster, both of them described in detail in Chapter 13. One is simply to be more clever about forwarding IP packets, such as by doing longest prefix matching more quickly. Another technique is to add an extra header, with small identifiers, which winds up similar to ATM but with arbitrary sized packets.

17.4.2 Multiprotocol Routers

Multiprotocol routers are almost irrelevant in practice today because the world has converged on IPv4. However, some of the issues associated with supporting multiple protocols are interesting, and perhaps the world will again be faced with two protocols when IPv6 gains popularity.

There are two methods of supporting an additional network layer protocol in a router. One method, the integrated approach, involves integrating support of that network layer protocol into a routing protocol already implemented within the machine. Another method involves adding the extra protocol in a "ships in the night" fashion by implementing a complete routing protocol for that protocol.

These two approaches differ only in terms of how routes are computed. After forwarding databases are built up for all the supported protocols, data packet forwarding is similar. A data packet arrives at the router; the protocol type is determined from the data link layer information; and the packet is handed to a module designed to parse that network layer header.

It is possible for some of the protocols to be supported with a ships in the night scheme and others with integrated routing. For example, consider Figure 17.1.

Figure 17.1 Multiprotocol router

This multiprotocol router supports seven different network layer protocols: A, B, C, D, E, F, and G. One integrated routing protocol supports A, B, and C; another one supports F and G. D and E are each implemented with a separate routing protocol.

Mixing routers that support different subsets of the multiple protocols in a network can be complex, especially with integrated routing. If the ships in the night approach is used with each protocol, a separate route gets calculated for each protocol. Because only the routers that support protocol X participate in X's routing protocol, routes for protocol X are guaranteed to go through only those routers that support X. In contrast, with the integrated approach, routers calculate a single set of routes to all the routers. A protocol X endnode is declared reachable from some router R, which supports protocol X (otherwise, R could not have declared in its LSP that the protocol X endnode was a neighbor). However, if any of the routers along the path from the source to R do not support protocol X, then there is a problem. The integrated routing approach could calculate a different set of routes for each protocol, but at least the approach chosen by the integrated IS-IS protocol is to calculate only a single set of routes. In that case, if there really are some routers that do not support all the protocols, there are two choices.

1. Use encapsulation to "hop over" routers that do not support a particular protocol. When router R1 wishes to forward a protocol X packet through neighbor router R2 that does not support X, R1 must encapsulate the packet with a network layer header for some protocol that R2 does support. R1 addresses the packet to a router farther along the path toward the destination that understands both protocols. This latter router removes the encapsulating header and lets the protocol X packet proceed on its way to the destination.

2. Calculate separate paths for each protocol. The Dijkstra algorithm must be run once for each network layer protocol supported. Each time, the only routers considered are those that have advertised in their LSP that they support the protocol for which routes are being computed.

17.4.3 Single-protocol Backbone

This approach will probably play a big part if the world successfully migrates to IPv6. Most likely, IPv6 will start out being deployed in some customer networks and will be carried across an IPv4 backbone. The ISPs are not eager to support IPv6 until there is customer demand.

The multiprotocol routers discussed in the preceding subsection forward packets in *native mode*—that is, each router along the path of a protocol X packet must be able to parse a protocol X header. If a router supports seven protocols, it must be able to parse seven different network layer headers.

In the single-protocol backbone approach, the assumption is that all routers must be able to parse a single type of network layer data packet—say, protocol X. A router R1 that has a protocol Y neighbor must additionally handle all the endnode/router handshaking protocols required of protocol Y and must be able to parse protocol Y data packet headers. When R1 receives a protocol Y packet for forwarding, it figures out which router R2 in the backbone is the appropriate destination router for the protocol Y destination address; constructs a protocol X header with R2 as the network layer destination address; encloses the entire protocol Y packet, including the header, in the newly constructed protocol X header; and forwards the packet toward R2.

R1 has two ways of determining that R2 is the appropriate destination router: It can use either an integrated routing approach or a ships in the night approach. With the integrated approach, the routing protocol used in the backbone would allow each router to advertise all the destinations it can reach, for each protocol (as integrated IS-IS does). Intermediate routers that do not support protocol Y would ignore the portion of R2's LSP that says, "These are the protocol Y destinations I can reach." These intermediate routers will never see a protocol Y data packet because router neighbors of protocol Y endnodes will always enclose protocol Y packets inside protocol X network layer headers.

With the ships in the night approach, the backbone is completely unaware of protocol Y. Protocol Y routers R1 and R2 must have some means of finding each other besides the protocol X routing protocol (for example, manual configuration of each other's protocol X network layer addresses or the use of some sort of multicast capability provided by protocol X). After R1 knows that R2 also understands protocol Y, R1 communicates with R2 as if R2 were an immediate neighbor with respect to protocol Y by encapsulating protocol Y control messages inside protocol X network layer headers. Intermediate routers in the backbone would not distinguish R1–R2 control packets for protocol Y from ordinary data packets.

If protocol Y is indeed confined to a few locations within a network, a single-protocol backbone idea might be attractive because it requires fewer routers to support protocol Y. If protocol Y endnodes exist on almost all the LANs in the network, there is no reason to encapsulate every protocol Y packet inside a protocol X header because virtually all the routers would have to support protocol Y anyway. Encapsulation makes the packets longer. It also requires that the decapsulating router support reassembly, which is messy enough when performed at the destination endnode.

One problem with single-protocol backbones is the perception people have of them. If protocol X is the protocol in the backbone and protocol Y is encapsulated within protocol X, then people who really like protocol Y sometimes get insulted. It seems as if their protocol is treated like a second-class citizen. Protocol X packets are transmitted in native mode (with no extra header). Protocol Y packets must carry the additional protocol X header, and that makes them longer. If reassembly is required at an intermediate router because of the encapsulation, throughput for protocol Y can be severely degraded.

The best solution to supporting all the network layer protocols employed in a given network is to use as few network layer protocols as possible. The ideal number is one.

17.4.4 Brouters

A *brouter* is simply a router that can also perform as a bridge. Assume, for the moment, that the brouter is only a single-protocol router. For example, it supports IP. When a packet arrives at the brouter, the brouter examines the packet's protocol type. If the protocol type is "IP," then the router code handles processing of the packet as if the box were a simple IP router. If the protocol type is anything other than "IP," the bridge code handles processing of the packet as if the box were a simple bridge. In essence, a brouter is a bridge and a router implemented in a ships in the night manner.

A brouter can be a multiprotocol router combined with a bridge (see Figure 17.2).

Figure 17.2 Brouter

It cooperates in the spanning tree algorithm just as an ordinary bridge would. It cooperates in all the supported routing protocols just as an ordinary router would. When it receives a packet whose protocol type is A, B, C, D, E, F, or G, it processes the packet as a router would. If it receives a packet whose protocol type is anything other than A, B, C, D, E, F, or G, it processes the packet as a bridge would.

Chapter 18
Protocol Design Folklore

In this chapter I attempt to capture the tricks and "gotchas" in protocol design learned from years of layer 2 and layer 3 protocols. Interspersed among the text are boxes containing "real-world bad protocols." They share with you the warped way I look at the world, which is to notice and be distracted by suboptimal protocols in everyday life. Sometimes the boxed stories pertain to the subject of the section they are in; sometimes there was no logical place to put them, so they are placed wherever they fit.

This chapter also serves as a review of the rest of the book.

18.1 Simplicity versus Flexibility versus Optimality

> **Making the simple complicated is commonplace; making the complicated simple, awesomely simple, that's creativity.**
>
> —**Charles Mingus**

> **If your protocol is successful, it will eventually be used for purposes for which it was never intended, and its users will criticize you for being shortsighted.**
>
> —**Charlie Kaufman**

The simpler the protocol, the more likely it is to be successfully implemented and deployed. If a protocol works in most situations but fails in some obscure case, such as a network in which there are 300-baud links or routers implemented on toasters, it might be worthwhile to abandon those cases, forcing users to either upgrade their equipment or design a custom protocol for those networks. Various factors cause a protocol to become complicated.

- *Design by committee*: Committees tend to want to put in all ideas so as to make all members feel they have made contributions. When there are technical choices and the committee cannot decide, often the result is to put in all options, even if for all practical purposes any choice alone would have worked well enough.

- *Backward compatibility*: Admittedly, it is difficult to cause old stuff to go away. But years of patching to fix bugs or adapt to technology for which the original protocol was not designed create complexity. It sure would be nice every few years to start fresh, learning from experience. At any rate, backward compatibility shouldn't be the only consideration. It must be weighed against its cost.

- *Flexibility*: People want a protocol to be flexible enough to fit every possible situation. Sometimes flexibility is good because it prevents the need to design something new when technology changes, but sometimes we wind up with a protocol so heavyweight it does not work well in any situation. When the goal of flexibility is carried too far, you can wind up with a protocol with so many choices that it is unlikely that two independent, conformant (to the specification) implementations will interwork. Also, the protocol requires a complex negotiation to find a set of choices that both parties support.

- *Optimality*: Sometimes going after "the optimal" solution increases the complexity of a protocol many fold even though users wouldn't be able to tell the difference between a "pretty good" solution and an "optimal" solution.

- *Underspecification*: Choices are often the result of the inability of the committee to reach consensus. Specifications are so general, and leave so many choices, that it is necessary to hold "implementer workshops" to agree on what subsets to build and what choices to make. The specification isn't a specification of a protocol. Instead, it is a "framework" in which a protocol could be designed and implemented. In other words, rather than specify an algorithm for, say, data compression, the standard may specify only that there will be two fields: **compression type**, and **type-specific data**. Often, even the type codes are not defined in the specification, much less the specifics of each choice.

- *Exotic features*: Sometimes these features come from legitimate, but unusual, cases, and the costs and benefits should be carefully considered before the general-use protocol is complicated for one exotic application. Other times, features come from the creative minds of researchers who are eager for difficult problems about which to write papers. There is nothing wrong with papers, but we shouldn't clutter protocols to solve problems that don't need to be solved. Sometimes there are two competing proposals. Any peculiarity allowed by one of the protocols is considered a "weakness" if not supported in the other, so people keep adding things to their protocol so that there can't possibly be any features provided only by the competing protocol.

18.2 Knowing the Problem You're Trying to Solve

Before we design a solution, it's often useful to define the problem to be solved. The counterargument is that if we do that, we might design something only for the problems we think of, whereas if we design without preconception of the problems, there might be applications we would otherwise never dream of. Although I appreciate the advantages of flexibility and generality, I think it's a good idea to have at least one well-defined problem in mind, perhaps designing the system so that other variants can be supported without making the solution too complicated.

> **Real-World-Protocol**
>
> Sneeze protocol: First you sneeze. Then someone says, "Gesundheit." Then I suppose you must say, "Thank you." Then I suppose you must say "You're welcome." I think, at that point, the protocol terminates. The only problem is, what has it accomplished? I'd say all the messages in the sneeze protocol are wasted messages. In fact, if I involuntarily make an embarrassing noise, the protocol I wish everyone around me would follow is the "pretend they didn't notice" protocol.

An example is policy-based routing. The general problem is easy to state. Some paths are willing to carry only certain types of traffic. Some traffic finds only certain paths acceptable. But nobody ever describes all the known actual customer needs. BGP provides some set of policies but not the general case. For example, a BGP router chooses a single path to the destination without taking into account the source. It's quite likely that packets from different sources would need to be routed differently. So BGP doesn't even solve all the known cases; it solves only what it happens to solve.

Does BGP solve the important cases, or has the world adapted to what BGP happens to solve? If it's the latter, would the world have been satisfied with a more conveniently accommodated subset, or perhaps even without policy-based routing at all?

> **Real-World-Protocol**
>
> Real-life example of "know the problem": When my son was three I saw him in the hallway crying, holding up his hand, saying, "My hand! My hand!" I took his hand lovingly and kissed it a few times and said, "What's the matter, honey? Did you hurt it?" He sobbed, "No, I got pee on it."

18.3 Overhead and Scaling

We should calculate the overhead of the algorithm. For example, the bandwidth used by source route bridging increases exponentially with the number of ports per bridge and bridges per LAN. It is usually possible to choose an algorithm with less-dramatic growth, but most algorithms have some limit to the size network they can support. Make reasonable bounds on the limits, and publish them in the specification.

Sometimes there is no reason to scale beyond a certain point. For example, a protocol that was n^2 or even exponential might be reasonable if it's known that there would never be more than five nodes participating.

Scaling also applies to the low end; it is also good if the technology makes sense with very few nodes. For example, one of the strengths of Ethernet is that if you have only a few nodes, you don't require an expensive specialized box such as a router.

Real-World-Protocol

Post-toast wineglass clicking: This is an n^2 protocol. And some of us do not have arms long enough to reach across a banquet table to the people on the other side. Surely someone can invent something more efficient. I'd do it if I could figure out what problem is supposed to be solved by that protocol. My son claims the purpose is to make sure everyone drinks at the same time in case the wine is poisoned. Is that a good thing? And does this protocol accomplish that?

18.4 Operation Above Capacity

If there are assumptions about the size of the problem to be solved, one of two things should happen. Either the limit should be so large that it would never in practice be exceeded, or the protocol should be designed to gracefully degrade if the limit is exceeded or at the very least to detect that the topology is now illegal and complain (or disconnect a subset to bring the topology within legal limits).

IS-IS is the first routing protocol to have explicit procedures to follow in the case of database overload, and OSPF and PNNI now also have such mechanisms.

Real-World-Protocol

Multiple queue protocol: Whenever I have to choose a queue, I always pick the bank line at which someone in front of me asks to audit all the bank's transactions for the past 15 years, rather than all the other lines where people are just making simple deposits and withdrawals. Because people do not give any hints as to whether they are planning on asking for change for a dollar or negotiating a merger, it is impossible to intelligently choose a queue, and the result is highly unfair. A far better protocol is the single queue/multiple server protocol, in which the next free server serves the next person in line.

The spanning tree algorithm for bridges does not need to consider this problem because the amount of memory required does not grow with the size of the network. A bridge merely keeps the best hello message (a fixed-size message) for each of the bridge's ports. The bridge has only a fixed number of ports.

18.5 Compact IDs versus Object Identifiers

Often, a protocol contains a field identifying something, such as a protocol type. If there is a central authority handing out the numbers, the numbers can be compact because they can be handed out sequentially. Most IETF standards have numbers assigned by the IANA. I'll call this approach "IDs."

An alternative to IDs is an "object identifier," as in ASN.1. Object identifiers are very large but because of their hierarchical structure they have the advantage that it is not necessary to obtain one from a central authority.

Another advantage of object identifiers is that you can get one without telling anyone. A company might want to deploy proprietary extensions without letting anyone know that they are doing this. With an ID approach assigned by a central authority, it is common for the central authority to have a policy that you are not allowed to obtain an ID without documentation of the feature. Sometimes there is the additional requirement that such documentation be publicly divulged.

There are several disadvantages to object identifiers.

- The field is larger and variable-length, and therefore it consumes memory, bandwidth, and CPU.

- There is no central place to look up all the currently used object identifiers, so it might be difficult to debug a network.

- Sometimes the same protocol winds up with multiple object identifiers. This is a result of not having central coordination. Two different organizations might define an object identifier for the same protocol. Then it is possible that two implementations might be in theory interoperable, but because the object identifiers assigned differ, the two implementations would be unable to interoperate.

18.6 Optimizing for the Most Common or Important Case

Huffman coding is an example of this principle. It is a form of compression that encodes each symbol with a variable-length quantity, where the shorter quantities are used to encode more frequently occurring symbols.

In networking protocols the "optimize for most common or important case" principle might be applicable to implementation or to protocol design. An example of an implementation that optimizes for the usual case is one in which a "common" IP packet (no options, nothing else unusual) is switched in hardware, whereas if there is anything unusual about the packet it is sent to the dungeon of the central processor to be prodded and pondered when the router finds it convenient.

An example of this principle in protocol design is to encode "unusual" requests, such as source routing, as an option. This is less efficient in space and in parsing overhead, when such requests appear, than having the capability encoded in a fixed portion of the header. However, in the usual case, when they do not appear, it is far more efficient to have them not appear in the packet at all.

Another interesting example is the IPv6 length extension. The fixed part of the header contains a 2-byte field for packet length. However, if the packet is longer than that, the 2-byte packet length in the header is set to 0; 8 additional bytes are required to carry an option that will carry a 4-byte packet length. When I commented to someone that this seemed like an incredible kludge—and that there should just be a 4-byte length field if people thought 2 bytes was not long enough— someone pointed out that this could be an example to illuminate the "optimize for the usual case" principle. In the normal case, the length field requires 2 bytes of header. In the weird, longer-than-65,000-bytes case, it requires 10 bytes to encode the length, but I suppose with a packet that large you'd never miss the 10 bytes of overhead.

> ### Real-World-Protocol
>
> The "leave a message with my son" protocol. (I have his permission for including this, by the way.) This was more of an issue when my son was about 10. People would call and insist on leaving a message with him. He'd jot it down on a little scrap of paper somewhere, or if he couldn't find a pencil and paper scrap, he'd just intend to remember it. Years later I'd find a telephone number on a scrap of paper, or have him say, "Oh yeah. Someone called the other day. I've forgotten who it was and what it was about."
>
> Surprisingly, the "leave a message with my daughter" protocol seems to work just fine.
>
> Andy Tanenbaum suggested a method of turning this protocol into an "optimize for the most important case." He suggested making up a bunch of sticky notes with the message "your boss called" (assuming that's the most important phone call I might get) and placing them all near the phone. If someone other than my boss called, my son could do his usual thing, but if it was indeed my boss, my son could simply move a sticky note directly onto the phone.

18.7 Forward Compatibility

Protocols generally evolve, and it is good to design with provision for making minor or major changes. Some changes are "incompatible," meaning that it is preferable for the later-version node to be aware that it is talking to an earlier-version node and switch to speaking the earlier version of the protocol. Other changes are "compatible," and later-version protocol messages can be processed without harm by earlier-version nodes. There are various techniques, covered in the next few sections, to ensure forward compatibility.

18.7.1 Large Enough Fields

A common mistake is to make fields too small. It is better to overestimate than to underestimate. It greatly expands the lifetime of a protocol. Following are examples of fields that one could argue should have been larger.

- IP address.

- Packet identifier in IP and CLNP headers (because it could wrap around within a packet lifetime).

- Fragment identifier in IS-IS (because an LSP could be larger than 256 fragments).

- Packet size in IPv6. (Some people might argue that the desire to "optimize for most common case" is the reason for splitting the high-order part into an option in the unusual case where packets larger than 64K would be desired.)

- Date fields.

18.7.2 Independence of Layers

It is desirable to design a protocol with as little as possible dependence on other layers, so that in the future one layer can be replaced without affecting other layers. An example is to have protocols above layer 3 make the assumption that addresses are 4 bytes long.

The downside of this principle is that if you do not exploit the special capabilities of a particular technology at layer n, you wind up with the least common denominator. For example, not all data links provide multicast capability, but it is useful for routing algorithms to use link level multicast for neighbor discovery, efficient propagation of information to all LAN neighbors, and so on. If we adhered too strictly to the principle of not

---

Real-World-Protocol

Wrong medium: At work, during a meeting, the loudspeaker announced, "Urgent. There is a water emergency. Everyone must log out and turn off all computers." I didn't even know there was a loudspeaker. That was the first announcement I'd ever heard in the year I'd worked there. And gee, whatever a "water emergency" was, it sounded really important. So we all rushed off to turn off our machines and finish the meeting. Later we were chatting in the halls, and someone walked by, joined in the conversation, and then said, "Well, gotta get back to work." We said, "But all the machines are down." He said, "Oh no, they're not. They never even went down." We said, "Oh really? We didn't hear another announcement. How did you find out we didn't need to turn everything off?" He said, "They sent email."

making special assumptions about the data link layer, we might not have allowed layer 3 to exploit the multicast capability of some layer 2 technologies.

Another danger of exploiting special capabilities of layer $n-1$ is that a new technology at layer $n-1$ might need to be altered in unnatural ways to make it support the API designed for a different technology. An example is attempting to make a technology such as frame relay or SMDS provide multicast so that it "looks like" Ethernet. For example, the way that multicast is simulated in SMDS is to have packets with a multicast destination address transmitted to a special node that is manually configured with the individual members; that node individually addresses copies of the "multicast" packet to each of the recipients.

18.7.3 Reserved Fields

Often there are spare bits. If they are carefully specified to be transmitted as zero and ignored upon receipt, they can later be used for purposes such as signaling that the transmitting node has implemented later version features, or they can be used to encode information, such as priority, that can safely be ignored by nodes that do not understand it. This is an excellent example of the maxim "Be conservative in what you send, and liberal in what you accept" because you should always set reserved bits to zero and ignore them upon receipt.

18.7.4 Single Version-number Field

One method of expressing version is with a single number. What should an implementation do if the version number is different? Sometimes a node might implement multiple previous versions. Sometimes newer versions are indeed compatible with older versions.

It is generally good to specify that a node that receives a packet with a larger version number simply drop it, or respond with an older version packet, rather than logging an error or crashing. If two nodes attempt to communicate, and the one with the newer version notices it is talking to a node with an older version, the newer-version node simply switches to talking the older version of the protocol, setting the version number to the one recognized by the other side.

One problem that can result is that two new-version nodes might get tricked into talking the old version of the protocol to each other. Any memory from one side

> **Real-World-Protocol**
>
> The "spectacularly bad idea" protocol: I was staying at a hotel where they put the following announcement under my door. "Tomorrow morning we will be testing the emergency procedures. Guests should ignore all alarms and all behavior of the staff during the day tomorrow, as it is only a drill."

that the other side is older causes it to talk the older version and therefore causes the other side to talk the older version. A method of solving this problem is to use a reserved bit indicating "I could be speaking a later version, but I think this is the latest version you support." Another possibility is to periodically probe with a later-version packet.

18.7.5 Split Version-number Field

This strategy uses two or more subfields, sometimes referred to as *major* and *minor* version numbers. The **major** subfield is incremented if the protocol has been modified in an incompatible way and it is dangerous for an old-version node to attempt to process the packet. The **minor** subfield is incremented if there are compatible changes to the protocol. For example, a transport layer protocol might have added the feature of delayed acks to avoid silly window syndrome.[1]

The same result could be applied with reserved bits (signaling that you implement enhanced features that are compatible with this version). However, having a **minor** version field in addition to the **major** version allows 2^n possible enhancements to be signaled with an n-bit **minor** version field (assuming that the enhancements were added to the protocol in sequential order so that announcing enhancement 23 means that you support all previous enhancements).

If you want to allow more flexibility than "all versions up to n," there are various possibilities.

- I support all capabilities between k and n (requires a field twice the size of the *minor* version field and the assumption that it makes sense to implement a range rather than everything smaller than n).

- I support capabilities 2, 3, and 6 (you're probably better off with a bitmask of n bits).

With a version number field, care must be taken if it is allowed to wrap around. It is far simpler not to face this issue by either making the version number field very large or being conservative about incrementing it. One solution to the problem of running out of version numbers is to define the use of the highest numerical value in the version number field to indicate that the actual version number follows, most likely with a larger field. For example, if the original protocol called for a 1-byte version number, the value 255 might mean that the version number extension follows.

18.7.6 Options

Another way of providing for future protocol evolution is to allow the appending of options. It is desirable to encode options so that an unknown option can be skipped. Sometimes, however, it is desirable for an unknown option to generate an error rather than be ignored. The most flexible solution is to specify, for each option, what a node

---

[1] Dave Clark, "Window and Acknowledgement Strategy in TCP," RFC 813.

that does not recognize the option should do, whether it be "skip and ignore," "skip and log," or "stop parsing and generate an error report."

To skip unknown options, the strategies are as follows.

- Have a special marker at the end of the option (requires linear scan of the option to find the end)

- Have options be TLV-encoded, which means having a **type** field, a **length** field, and a **value** field

Note that to skip over an unknown option, L (length) must always mean the same thing. Sometimes protocols have L depend on T—for example, not having any L field if the particular type is always fixed length, or having the L be expressed in bits versus bytes depending on T.

Another way to make it impossible to skip over an unknown option is if L is the *usable length* and the actual length is always padded to, say, a multiple of 8 bytes. If the specification is clear that all options interpret L in that way, then options can be parsed, but if some option types use L as "how much data to skip" and others as "relevant information" to which padding is inferred somehow, then it is not possible to parse unknown options.

To determine what to do with unknown options, there are various strategies.

- Specify the handling of all unknown types (for example, skip and log, skip and ignore, generate error and ignore entire packet) and live without the flexibility in the future of defining an option that should be handled differently.

- Have a field present in all options that specifies the handling of the option.

- Have the handling implicit in the type number—for example, a range of T values that the specification says should be ignored and another range to be skipped and logged, and so on. This is similar to considering a bit in the type field as a flag indicating the handling of the packet.

Priority is an example of an option that would make sense to ignore if unknown. An example of an option in which the packet should be dropped is strict source routing.

Ironically, the 1984 version of ASN.1 (still widely deployed today), although it uses TLV encoding, does not allow you to add new options that are accepted by old implementations of your protocol if you define your structures in the straightforward ASN.1 way. You can define fields in your data structure as optional, but that means only that the implementation is willing for any of those defined fields to appear. Any options that you don't define will cause a parsing error.

18.8 Migration: Routing Algorithms and Addressing

It's hard enough to get one distributed algorithm right, but to get two of them to interoperate is far more difficult. One strategy, for example, when you mix RIP with a link state protocol such as OSPF or IS-IS, is for a router that connects to both a RIP neighbor and an OSPF neighbor to translate back and forth. This is very complicated because the maximum RIP metric is 15. Metrics must be scaled down, and then when they are reintroduced into another portion of the network you can wind up with loops. It doesn't matter what a metric means, but the cost to a destination should always increase as you get further away.

Another strategy for deploying a new routing protocol in an existing network (in which most of the routers don't support the new routing protocol) is tunnels, which is used by DVMRP. People configure DVMRP routers to know about other DVMRP routers that they should be neighbors with. These DVMRP routers are not actually neighbors, so they must communicate by tunneling their packets—routing messages as well as data messages—to each other.

The ARPANET went from a distance vector protocol to a link state protocol by running the two protocols in parallel. There were four stages a router went through:

1. Distance vector

2. Distance vector + link state, but route based on distance vector database

3. Distance vector + link state, but route based on link state database

4. Link state only

So first the network was running distance vector only. One by one, routers started sending link state information but not actually using it for routing packets. After all routers were running both protocols, and the link state database seemed to compute the same routes as the distance vector protocol, the routers were configured, one by one, to switch over to using the link state database for forwarding. Only when all of them were using the link state database could the routers, one by one, be configured to turn off distance vector.

Another strategy when running two protocols is to treat the network like two separate networks. This was done in bridging so that havoc was not created when transparent and source routing bridges were mixed. Transparent bridges were not allowed to forward data packets with the multicast bit in the source address set, and source routing bridges were allowed to forward only such packets.

The most complex strategy is to try to mix routers. An example is multicast protocols, in which there are several protocols deployed. Because none of the current protocols scales to be interdomain, the assumption is that a new interdomain protocol, compatible with all currently deployed protocols, must be designed. An alternative is to keep the protocols separate, as was done with the bridges, by somehow making sure that only one protocol handles a particular packet. This can be done by using a different packet format or by having ranges of multicast addresses handled by each protocol.

There are similar issues with changing addresses. Originally the strategy when moving from DECnet Phase IV to DECnet Phase V addresses was to have Phase-IV-compatible Phase V addresses and translate between them. However, this is very complicated and results in a world that has none of the advantages of the larger address space because all the Phase V nodes need Phase IV-compatible addresses until all the Phase IV nodes go away. A far simpler strategy is *dual stack*, which means that you implement both. You talk to a Phase IV node with Phase IV, and you talk to a Phase V node with Phase V.

For IPv6, many complicated migration strategies were discussed before it was concluded that dual stacks was the one most likely to work.

18.9 Parameters

There are various reasons for having parameters, some good and others bad.

*   The protocol designers can not figure out reasonable values, so they leave it to the user. This might make sense if deployment experience might help people determine reasonable values. However, if the protocol designers simply can't decide, it is unreasonable to expect the users to have better judgment. At any rate, if deployment experience gives people enough information to set the values, it would be nice to make the parameters constants in later versions of the protocol.

*   The values are parameters because there are reasonable trade-offs—say, between responsiveness and overhead—and it is desirable to allow the user to tune the network. In this case, the parameter descriptions should explain the range and the reasons for choosing points in the range.

18.9.1 Avoiding Parameters

In general, it is a good idea to avoid parameters whenever possible because it makes for intimidating documentation that must be written—and, what's more, read—to use the protocol. Sometimes a parameter is an unnecessary frill, and it is possible to pick a value and let everyone live with it. In other cases the parameter can be figured out by the computer rather than the human, and protocols should try hard to make everything plug and play. For example, it is highly desirable for addresses to autoconfigure. Admittedly, autoconfiguration is easier with a protocol such as IPX, but it was well worth the complexity and expense to deploy DHCP to make IP largely autoconfigure.

Another parameter that can autoconfigure is link cost. IPXWAN is a protocol that measures the round trip delay and bandwidth when a link starts up and, from that, calculates a reasonable link cost.

18.9.2 Legal Parameter Setting

It is important to design a protocol so that parameters set by people can be modified in a running network, one node at a time.

In some protocols, parameters can be set incorrectly and the protocol will not run properly. Unfortunately, it isn't as simple as having a legal range for the parameter because one parameter might interact with another, even a parameter in a different layer. In a distributed system it's possible for two systems to independently have reasonable parameter settings but have the parameter settings be incompatible. A simple example of incompatible settings is in a neighbor aliveness detection protocol, in which one sends hellos every n seconds and the other declares the neighbor dead if it does not hear a hello for k seconds. If k is not greater than n, the protocol will not work very well.

There are some tricks for causing parameters to be compatible in a distributed system. In some cases, it is reasonable for nodes to operate with different parameter settings, as long as all the nodes know the parameter setting of other (relevant) nodes.

18.9.2.1 "Report My Values" Method

The *report* method has node N report the value of its parameter, in protocol messages, to all the other nodes that need to hear it. IS-IS uses the report method. If the parameter is one that neighbors need to know, it is reported in a hello message (a message that does not get forwarded and is therefore seen only by the neighbors). If the parameter is one that all nodes (in an area) need to know, it is reported in an LSP. This method allows each node to have independent parameter settings and yet interoperate. For example, a node adjusts its Listen timer (when to declare a neighbor dead) for neighbor N based on N's reported Hello timer (how often N sends Hellos).

18.9.2.2 "Detect Misconfiguration" Method

Another method is the *detect misconfiguration* method, in which parameters are reported so that nodes can detect whether they are misconfigured. For example, the detect misconfiguration strategy makes sense when routers on a LAN might report to each other the (IP address, subnet mask) of the LAN.

An example in which the detect misconfiguration method is not the best choice is the OSPF protocol, which puts the Hello timer and other parameters into hello messages and has neighbors refuse to talk if the parameter settings aren't identical. This forces all nodes on a LAN to have the same Hello timer, but there might be legitimate reasons that the responsiveness versus overhead trade-off for one router might be different from that of another router so that neighbors might legitimately need different values for the Hello timer. Also, the OSPF method makes it difficult to change parameters in a running network because neighbors refuse to talk to each other while the network is being migrated from one value to another.

18.9.2.3 "Use My Parameters" Method

Another method is the *use my parameters* method. In one example (the bridge spanning tree algorithm), the Root bridge reports, in its spanning tree message, its values for parameters that should be used by all the bridges. In this way, bridges can be configured one by one, but a non-Root bridge simply stores its configured value in nonvolatile storage to be used if that bridge becomes Root. The values everyone uses for the parameters are the ones configured into the bridge that is currently acting as Root. This is a reasonable strategy provided that there is no reason to want nodes to be working with different parameter values.

Another example of this method is Apple-Talk, in which the *seed router* informs the other routers of the proper LAN parameters, such as network number range. However, it is different from the bridge algorithm because if there is more than one seed router, they must be configured with the same parameter values.

A dangerous version of this method is one in which all nodes store the parameters when receiving a report. This might lead to problems because misconfiguring one node can cause all the other nodes to be permanently misconfigured. In contrast, consider the bridge algorithm. Although the Root bridge might get misconfigured with undesirable parameters, even if those parameters cause the network to be nonfunctional, simply disconnecting the Root bridge will cause some other bridge to take over and cause all bridges to use that bridge's parameter settings. Or simply reconfiguring the one Root bridge will clear the network.

> ### Real-World-Protocol
>
> The handshake protocol: This is bad enough when there are two people. Invariably I'm carrying things in both hands. Or I've just sneezed (see sneeze protocol). Or I've just come in from outside and my hand is embarrassingly cold (and I'm wishing the protocol were "stick your hand on the other person's neck protocol"). But when there's a group of n people all greeting each other, as with the wineglass protocol, it winds up as n^2. And it takes complex choreography to avoid getting between a pair of handshakers.
>
> To add to the confusion, when I go to a meeting such as an IETF meeting, most people look at least vaguely familiar. Some of them, apparently, I'm supposed to ignore. Others I'm supposed to acknowledge with a vague nod. To others I'm supposed to say "Hi." With others I'm supposed to shake their hands. Others I'm supposed to hug. Then there are some countries in which you're supposed to kiss even the most casual acquaintance on the cheek. And other countries in which you're supposed to kiss both cheeks. I've never figured out how people decide what protocol to use, and I'm always worried about offending people by guessing the wrong protocol.

18.10 Making Multiprotocol Operation Possible

Unfortunately, there is not just one protocol or protocol suite in the world. There are computers that want to be able to receive packets in multiple "languages." Unfortunately, the protocol designers do not in general coordinate with each other to make their protocols self-describing, so it is necessary to figure out a way to ensure that a computer can receive a message in your protocol and not confuse it with another protocol the computer may also be capable of handling.

Because there are several methods of doing this, it can be confusing. There is no single "right" way even though the world would be simpler if everyone did it the same way. I will attempt to explain the various approaches.

- *Protocol type at layer n–1*: This is a field administered by the owner of the layer *n*–1 specification. Each layer n protocol that wishes to be carried in a layer *n*–1 envelope is given a unique value. The Ethernet standard has a protocol type field assigned.

- *Socket, port, or SAP at layer n–1*: This consists of two fields at layer *n*–1: one applies to the source, and the other applies to the destination. This makes sense when these fields must be applied dynamically. However, almost always when this approach is taken, there are some predefined *well-known* sockets. A process tends to *listen* on the well-known socket and wait for a dynamically assigned socket from another machine to connect. In practice, although the IEEE 802.2 header is defined as using SAPs, in reality the field is used as a protocol type. The SAP values are either well known (and therefore the destination and source SAP values are the same), or they are set to the "SNAP SAP" and multiplexing is done with a protocol type later in the header.

- *Protocol type at layer n*: This consists of a field in the layer n header that allows multiple different protocol *n* protocols to distinguish themselves from each other. This technique is usually used when multiple protocols defined by a particular standards body share the same layer *n*–1 protocol type. The ISO layer 3 protocols start with a value known as NLPID to distinguish between CLNP, ES-IS, IS-IS, and so on, all of which use the same layer *n*–1 protocol type.

One could argue that the **version number** field in IP is actually a layer *n* protocol type, especially because "version" = 5 is clearly not intended as the next "version" of IP. The intention for IPv6 was that the version number allow IPv6 to be distinguished from IPv4

Real-World-Protocol

False economy protocol. At one company, in order to "save money" they periodically banned buying supplies. People got used to expecting periods of "famine" and hoarded supplies, wildly overstocking when the ban was lifted. After a few weeks of a ban, the various groups spent a great deal of time and energy bartering supplies. For example, a group with a surplus of toner might be able to exchange toner for printer paper.

and that they could share the same layer 2 multiplexing value. However, some components assumed, based solely on the layer 2 protocol type field, that they were dealing with an IPv4 packet, and so would misparse an IPv6 packet. So IPv4 and IPv6 are actually distinguished by having different layer 2 protocol types. So the multiplexing information might be one field or two (one for source, one for destination), and the multiplexing information might be dynamically assigned or well known.

Multiplexing based on dynamically assigned sockets does not work well with *n*-party protocols or connectionless protocols. In particular, IEEE made the wrong choice when it changed the Ethernet protocol to have sockets (SAPs), especially with the destination and source sockets being only 8 bits long. Furthermore, it defined two of the bits, so there were only 64 possible values to assign to well-known sockets and only 64 possible values to be assigned dynamically. Because of this mistake, the cumbersome and confusing SNAP encoding was invented.

Dynamically assigned sockets are useful at layer 4. How can you do that using something such as Ethernet that has only a protocol type field? The answer is to define one protocol type to be *dynamically assignable sockets layer*, which would be something similar to UDP. Let's call that L2UDP (for "layer 2 UDP"). The layer 2 protocol would indicate L2UDP. The next layer would contain the sockets indicating the source and destination processes. This is really how protocols such as AppleTalk and IPX, which contain both a packet type and destination/source socket numbers, should be used.

18.11 Running over Layer 3 versus Layer 2

Sometimes protocols that work only neighbor-to-neighbor are encapsulated in a layer 3 header—for example, many of the routing protocols for routing IP. Because such messages are not intended to ever be forwarded by IP, there is no reason to have an IP header. The IP header makes the messages longer, and care must be taken to ensure that packets don't actually get routed because that could confuse distant routers into thinking they are neighbors. The alternative to carrying messages in an IP header is to acquire a layer 2 protocol type.

Because the layer 3 header is really wasted bits for messages that are neighbor-to-neighbor, why would people choose to run such protocols over layer 3? There are various practical reasons.

- There might be an API for running over layer 3—so that the application can be built as a user process—whereas there might not be an API for running over layer 2. Therefore, running over layer 2 would require modifications to the kernel.

- It might be bureaucratically difficult to obtain a layer 2 protocol type.

- In the case of IPv4, it lets you do fragmentation without devising some other mechanism. This is being used as a reason for allowing IS-IS to run on top of IP.

18.12 Robustness

One type of robustness is *simple* robustness, in which the protocol adapts to node and link fail-stop failures.

Another type is *self-stabilization*. Operation may become disrupted because of extraordinary events such as a malfunctioning node that injected incorrect messages, but after the malfunctioning node is disconnected from the network, the network should return to normal operation. The ARPANET link state distribution protocol was not self-stabilizing. If a sick router injected a few bad LSPs, the network would have been down forever without hours of difficult manual intervention, even though the sick router had failed completely hours before and only "correctly functioning" routers were participating in the protocol.

Another type is *Byzantine robustness*. The network can continue to work properly even in the face of malfunctioning nodes, whether the malfunctions are caused by hardware problems or by malice.

As society becomes increasingly dependent on networks, it is desirable to attempt to achieve Byzantine robustness in any distributed algorithm such as clock synchronization, directory system synchronization, or routing. This is difficult, but it is important if the protocol is to be used in a hostile environment (such as when the nodes cooperating in the protocol are remotely manageable from across the Internet or when a disgruntled employee might be able to physically access one of the nodes).

> ### Real-World-Protocol
>
> "We'll let you know if there's a problem" protocol. This drives me crazy because it's so popular. It doesn't work because the problem notification message is invariably a datagram and can get lost. For example, at one conference, the person organizing all the hotel rooms for the speakers said, "Don't worry if you haven't gotten a confirmation. We'd let you know if there was a problem getting you a room." Sure enough, at least one of us showed up and had no hotel room.

Following are some interesting points to consider when your goal is to make a system robust.

- Every line of code should be exercised frequently. If there is code that gets invoked only when the nuclear power plant is about to explode, it is possible that the code will no longer work when it is needed. Modifications may have been made to the system since the special case code was last checked, or seemingly unrelated events such as increasing link bandwidth may cause code to stop working properly.

- Sometimes it is better to crash rather than gradually degrade in the presence of problems so that the problems can be fixed or at least diagnosed. For example, it might be preferable to bring down a link that has a high error rate.

- It is sometimes possible to partition the network with containment points so that a problem on one side does not spread to the other. An example is attaching two LANs with a router versus a bridge. A broadcast storm (using data link multicast) will spread to both sides, whereas it will not spread through a router.

- Connectivity can be weird. For example, a link might be one-way, either because that is the way the technology works or because the hardware is broken (for example, one side has a broken transmitter, or the other has a broken receiver). Or a link might work but be sensitive to certain bit patterns. Or it might appear to your protocol that a node is a neighbor when in fact there are bridges in between, and somewhere on the bridged path is a link with a smaller MTU size. Therefore, it could look as if you are neighbors, but indeed packets beyond a certain size will not succeed. It is a good idea to have your protocol check that the link is indeed functioning properly (perhaps by padding hellos to maximum length to determine whether large packets actually get through, by testing that connectivity is two-way, and so on).

> **Real-World-Protocol**
>
> The "unclear on the concept" protocol (contributed by Joshua Simons).
>
> Joshua connected to a Web site with his secure browser and made a purchase (so the credit card information was sent across the network encrypted). The Web site then sent him a confirmation email (in the clear) with all the details of the transaction, including his credit card information.

- Certain checksums detect certain error conditions better than others. For example, if bytes are getting swapped, Fletcher's checksum catches the problem whereas the IPv4 checksum does not catch it.

- Ideally, every packet should be able to be processed at wire speeds. An unauthorized person might not be able to generate correct signatures on a packet, but if it requires more time for a node to do the calculation necessary to realize that the packet is invalid and should be discarded than it takes to receive the packet, a denial of service attack can be mounted merely by sending a lot of invalid packets.

18.13 Determinism versus Stability

The Designated Router election protocols in IS-IS and OSPF differ in an interesting way. In IS-IS the protocol is *deterministic*, which is considered by some people to be a desirable property. "Determinism" means that the behavior at this moment does not depend on past events. So the protocol was designed so that given a particular set of routers that are up, the same one would always be DR. In contrast, OSPF went for *stability* to cause minimal disruption to the network if routers go up or down. In OSPF, after a node is elected DR it remains DR unless it crashes, whereas in IS-IS the router with a "better" configured priority will usurp the role when it comes up.

A good compromise is reached in NLSP. Nodes change their priority by some constant (say, 20) after being DR for some time (say, a minute). Then if you configure all the routers with the same priority, the protocol acts like OSPF. If you configure all the routers with priorities more than 20 apart, it acts like IS-IS. To allow OSPF-like behavior among a particular subset of the routers (such as higher-capacity routers), set them all with a priority 20 greater than any of the other routers. In that way, if any of the high priority set is alive, a high-priority router will become DR, but no other router will usurp the role.

18.14 Performance for Correctness

Sometimes in order to be "correct" an implementation must meet certain performance constraints. An example is the bridge spanning tree algorithm. Loops in a bridged network can be disastrous because packets can proliferate exponentially while they are looping. The spanning tree algorithm depends on receipt of spanning tree messages to keep a link from forwarding. If temporary congestion caused a bridge to throw away packets before processing them, the bridge might be throwing away spanning tree messages. Links that should be in hot-standby would forward traffic, creating loops and exponentially more congestion. It is likely that a bridged topology might not recover from such an event. Therefore, it is highly desirable that bridges operate at wire speed.

A lot of denial of service attacks (such as the TCP SYN attack) are possible because nodes are not capable of processing every received packet at wire speeds.

18.15 In Closing

Well, it's time to end this book. Feel free to contact me with comments, corrections, complaints, and especially compliments. I'm always looking for more quotes, real-world funny protocols, and ideas for topics to cover in future editions. My email address is radia@alum.mit.edu, or I can be reached via the publisher.

Glossary

AAL (ATM Adaptation Layer) — A layer on top of ATM to provide an interface more convenient than 48-byte cells. AAL1 is constant bit rate, AAL2 is variable bit rate, AAL5 is large datagram packets. AAL3/4 was an unsuccessful attempt to provide what eventually was redesigned as AAL5.

AARP (AppleTalk Address Resolution Protocol) — Just like ARP but for AppleTalk.

aggregatable — Addresses that can be summarized easily because all the numerically contiguous addresses are located next to each other in the topology.

anycast — Transmit to the nearest of a set of nodes.

ARP (Address Resolution Protocol) — A protocol for mapping 32-bit IP addresses to 48-bit data link layer addresses, specified in RFC 826.

AS (Autonomous System) — A portion of a network, usually within the control of one organization and usually running a single routing protocol. Routing between autonomous systems is done with a protocol that is defined as being an interdomain or inter-AS protocol or an exterior gateway protocol.

The term *autonomous system* within the IP community is synonymous with the term *routing domain* within the ISO community.

ASN.1 (Abstract Syntax Notation #1) — An ISO standard for data representation and data structure definitions.

ATM (Asynchronous Transfer Mode) — A connection-oriented data transmission technology involving fixed length cells.

ATMARP (ATM ARP server) — The node, specified in RFC 2225 (Classical IP and ARP over ATM), that each node in the LIS registers with and requests IP/ATM address correspondence from.

backpressure — Inform ports with incoming traffic that there is congestion, to cause them to slow down or stop transmitting until the congestion recedes.

bandwidth — The rate of information flow.

BGP (Border Gateway Protocol) — An interdomain routing protocol being standardized by the IETF.

BOOTP (BOOTstrap Protocol) — A protocol defined by RFC 951 to enable a diskless client machine to discover certain information, such as its own IP address.

broadcast — Transmit to "everyone." (In my opinion, this should be the same as multicast, and no need to make a special case if everyone happens to be listening.)

broadcast address — A group address that, by convention, means "everyone." The 802 broadcast address is a bit string of 481's.

broadcast domain — The set of ports between which a bridge forwards a multicast, broadcast, or unknown destination frame.

broadcast storm — A phenomenon of extreme congestion, usually caused by bugs in implementations or ambiguities in protocol specifications.

BSR (Bootstrap Router) — A PIM-SM concept. It's a router that collects announcements from candidate RPs and then floods the set of RPs throughout the domain.

BUS (Broadcast and Unknown Server) — A node in the LANE design that facilitates broadcast within an ELAN by maintaining a point-to-multipoint VC between itself and all LECs in the ELAN.

Byzantine failure — A failure in which a node does not instantaneously halt but rather functions incorrectly, for example by misrouting packets or sending faulty routing messages. (*See fail-stop failure.*)

carrier extension — A mechanism in gigabit Ethernet to ensure that a collision will be detected. Consists of adding a signal after a first packet that is smaller than 512 bytes so that the first packet in a burst will take a complete slot time.

CBR (Constant Bit Rate) — A type of service in which an endnode can transmit or receive data at a constant rate.

CBT (Core-Based Trees) — A multicast routing protocol defined in RFC 2189.

CIDR (Classless InterDomain Routing) — The concept of allowing arbitrary blocks of IP addresses rather than being confined to class A (1-byte mask), class B (2-byte mask), and class C (3-byte mask).

CIP (Classical IP and ARP over ATM) — The acronym for the scheme defined in RFC 2225.

class D IP address — An address in which the top 4 bits are 1110. Class D addresses are defined to be multicast addresses.

CLNP (ConnectionLess Network Protocol) — The ISO protocol, consisting primarily of the data packet format, documented in ISO 8473.

CLNS (ConnectionLess-mode Network Service) — The ISO term for the datagram network layer service.

closed user group — A feature offered by a "cloud" in which there is a subset of the nodes attached to the cloud, and the nodes in that subset can talk only to other nodes in that subset.

collision domain — The set of ports between which a repeater will repeat a signal.

company_id — Really the same thing as an OUI. It's a 3-byte address prefix that you can get from IEEE. Theoretically, the company_id is for EUI-64 addresses rather than IEEE 802 addresses, but this is only terminology. You can request a company_id and use it as an OUI.

confederation — A concept in IDRP that involves grouping several domains and presenting the group to the outside world as if it were a single domain.

connectionless — A service in which data is presented, complete with a destination address, and the network delivers it on a best-effort basis, independent of other data being exchanged between the same pair of users.

connection-oriented — A service in which a connection-setup procedure must be implemented before data can be exchanged between two users.

CONS (Connection-Oriented Network Service) — X.25 is an example of a protocol that provides CONS.

CRC (Cyclic Redundancy Check) — A type of FCS computed by treating bit strings as polynomials with binary coefficients. The CRC is the remainder resulting from division by the CRC polynomial.

CSMA/CD (Carrier Sense Multiple Access with Collision Detection) — A contention scheme for allocating bandwidth on a shared bus. Examples are 802.3 and Ethernet.

CSNP (Complete Sequence Numbers Packet) — An IS-IS link state database summary issued periodically by the Designated Router on a LAN to ensure that all the routers on the LAN have synchronized LSP databases.

cut set — The set of links or nodes that, if broken, would partition the network.

cut-through forwarding — Forwarding a packet as quickly as a decision can be made rather than waiting until the entire packet is received.

datagram — A service in which delivery is on a "best-effort" basis. This term is also sometimes used for a piece of information presented to a network that provides a datagram service.

DCE (Data Circuit-terminating Equipment) — The X.25 term for the device to which an endnode attaches.

DDCMP (Digital Data Communication Message Protocol) — A data link protocol developed by Digital Equipment Corporation.

default route — (I prefer the term *default destination*). The prefix that matches any address, such as the zero-length prefix in longest prefix routing.

DHCP (Dynamic Host Configuration Protocol) — A protocol defined in RFC 2131 to facilitate autoconfiguration of an IP endnode. DHCP is really an extension of BOOTP.

distance vector routing — A type of routing protocol in which each router tells its neighbors its distances to all destinations.

DLS — A Vitalink proprietary enhancement to the transparent bridge standard that, in some cases, allows point-to-point links that are not in the spanning tree to be used by bridges for forwarding packets.

DNS (Domain Name System) — The Internet facility for translating names to IP (layer 3) addresses.

DTE (Data Terminal Equipment) — The X.25 term for an endnode.

DVMRP (Distance Vector Multicast Routing Protocol) — A "flood and prune" protocol for multicast documented in RFC 1075.

EGP (Exterior Gateway Protocol) — A term used in the IP community in two different ways: (1) a class of routing protocol for routing between ASs; (2) the specific protocol documented in RFC 827.

ELAN (Emulated LAN) — A subset of an ATM network that looks like a single LAN. This is a concept in the ATM forum's LANE specification.

encapsulation — Handling protocol A's packets, complete with A's header information, as data carried by protocol B. Encapsulated protocol A packets have a B header, followed by an A header, followed by the information that protocol A is carrying as its own data. Note that A could = B, as in IP inside IP.

ESH (End-System Hello) — Message in the ES-IS protocol, multicast on a LAN periodically by endnodes (ESs) to a multicast address listened to by routers to let the routers know about the endnodes on the LAN.

ES-IS (End System to Intermediate System protocol) — ISO's protocol, as specified in 9542, for handshaking between routers and endnodes and for mapping network layer addresses to data link layer addresses.

Ethernet — The original CSMA/CD LAN invented by Xerox and standardized by Digital, Intel, and Xerox.

Ethertype — The 2-byte protocol type field in the Ethernet header.

EUI-48 — Another name for the 6-byte (48-bit) IEEE 802 addresses.

EUI-64 — An 8-byte address defined by IEEE similar to IEEE 802 addresses.

fail-stop failure — A failure in which a node reverts instantly from correct operation to halting.

FCS (Frame Check Sequence) — A quantity transmitted along with a packet to enable the receiver to detect data corruption.

FDDI (Fiber Distributed Data Interface) — A 100-Mb token ring being standardized by the American National Standards Institute (ANSI).

filter — To selectively discard packets of a certain type.

flow control — Telling the source of data to stop until there are buffers available.

fragmentation — The act of breaking a packet into multiple pieces, hopefully to be followed by reassembly, which is putting it back together again. Done because the packet must be transmitted over a link for which the packet is too large.

functional address — A severely restricted form of multicast addressing implemented by some 802.5 chip sets.

group address — An address to which are sent transmissions intended for receipt by a set of recipients.

HDLC (High-level Data Link Control) — A data link layer protocol.

HIORD — The 4-byte constant AA-00-04-00 used in DECnet to append to a 2-byte DECnet address to find the node's layer 2 address.

hippety — The cost of traversing a node. Instead of just counting the cost of the links on a path, in some cases it is useful to add a cost for traversing a switch. The name *hippety* comes from "hippety-hop."

hold down — A mechanism tried in the old ARPANET that was intended to solve the count-to-infinity behavior of distance vector protocols. The rule is that for a specified time after your best path to D goes away, you advertise your path to D as infinity.

hops — The simplest routing metric in which each link has a cost of 1. This function counts the number of times a packet must be forwarded.

host route — An IP destination with a 32-bit mask advertised in the routing protocol, that is, a destination that is a single node.

hub — The device that acts as the center of a star topology. Usually a multiport repeater, although sometimes the term is used even if the hub does store-and-forward.

IAB — (Internet Architecture Board) People aren't in total agreement on what the *A* stands for. (It is also sometimes expanded to "appeals," "activities," or "advisory.") It also isn't completely clear what it does and what power it has (I'm allowed to say that, having served on the IAB). It is an elected body that both listens to formal appeals and writes architecture documents (because the chair complained that it needs to write such things in order to rate the *A* in the acronym).

IANA — (Internet Assigned Numbers Authority) The organization that hands out blocks of IP addresses and numbers in protocol fields.

ICMP — Internet Control Message Protocol, documented in RFC 792. Provides error messages and other information.

IDPR (InterDomain Policy Routing) — A link state interdomain routing protocol being worked on in the IETF community.

IDRP (InterDomain Routing Protocol) — A distance vector interdomain routing protocol derived from BGP and adapted for ISO.

IEEE (Institute of Electrical and Electronics Engineers) — The standards organization for most of the layer 2 protocols.

IETF (Internet Engineering Task Force) — An organization, open to anyone who wishes to participate, that helps define the protocols used in the Internet.

IGMP (Internet Group Management Protocol) — A protocol in which a router can find out what IP multicast addresses its endnode neighbors are listening to.

IGP (Interior Gateway Protocol) — The IP community's term for the routing protocol used within an AS. The ISO's synonym is *intradomain routing protocol.*

individual address — An address that is intended to correspond to a specific recipient.

integrated routing — Using a single routing protocol to carry information about multiple network layer protocols.

IP (Internet Protocol) — The connectionless network layer protocol in the TCP/IP protocol suite, standardized in RFC 791.

IPng — A term used interchangeably with IPv6. The "ng" stands for "next generation," named in honor of a TV show popular among the people who gather at IETF meetings.

IPv4 — Same as IP, the v4 referring to the fact that in IP the **version** field = 4.

IPv6 — A network layer protocol standardized by IETF as an intended replacement to IP. The v6 refers to the fact that the **version** field = 6.

IPX — (Internetwork Packet Exchange) Connectionless layer 3 protocol with 10-byte addresses.

IPXWAN — Protocol used with IPX on point-to-point links that measures the delay and bandwidth to calculate a cost for the link (for the routing protocol), negotiates things (such as what routing protocol to run), and assigns an IPX address to an endnode.

ISH (Intermediate-System Hello) — Message in the ES-IS protocol, multicast periodically on a LAN by routers (ISs) to a multicast address listened to by endnodes to let endnodes know about router neighbors.

ISO (International Organization for Standardization) — A worldwide federation of national standards bodies from over 100 countries. You might wonder why the acronym isn't IOS, or the expansion of the name isn't International Standards Organization. But they claim that ISO is not an acronym; rather, it is derived from the Greek "isos" meaning "equal."

IS-IS (Intermediate System to Intermediate System protocol) — The ISO standard intradomain routing protocol, documented in ISO 10589.

ISP (Internet Service Provider) — The folks you pay a monthly fee to and who in turn provide you with busy signals.

LAN (Local Area Network) — Usually a shared medium with broadcast capability providing logical full connectivity, typically over a limited geographic area the size of a building or perhaps a campus.

LANE (LAN Emulation) — A scheme devised by the ATM forum for ATM to provide the capabilities of a LAN to any layer 3 protocol.

LEC (LAN Emulation Client) — An endnode in the LANE design.

LES (LAN Emulation Server) — The node in an ELAN that LECs register with so that it can keep a list of all the LECs, introduce LECs to each other, and keep LECs generally informed.

link-local address — An IPv6 address that can be used only on a single LAN and must not be forwarded off that LAN by a router.

link state routing — A type of routing protocol in which each router constructs an LSP listing its neighbors; the LSP is then broadcast to all the routers.

LIS (Logical IP Subnetwork) — A concept defined in "Classical IP and ARP over ATM" (RFC 2225). It's a subset of an ATM network that looks to IP like a single LAN.

LLC (Logical Link Control) — A sublayer of the data link layer defined by the IEEE 802 committee. Part of LLC defines the multiplexing fields; the other part gives optional types of service that can be run over 802 LANs. LLC type 1 is a datagram service. LLC type 2 is a reliable connection-oriented service. LLC type 3 is semireliable.

LSA (Link State Advertisement) — OSPF's terminology for LSP; information that is generated by a router in a link state routing protocol that describes the reachability of something (for example, a router neighbor, an address prefix).

LSP (Link State Packet) — A packet that is generated by a router in a link state routing protocol and lists that router's neighbors.

MAC (Medium Access Control) — A sublayer of the data link layer, defined by the IEEE 802 committee, that deals with issues specific to a particular type of LAN.

MAC address — The layer 2 address on IEEE LANs—for example, the 6-byte Ethernet address.

magic cookie — The 4-byte value 63, 82, 53, 63 (all in hex) placed in the beginning of the vendor-specific field in BOOTP to indicate it is a DHCP message.

MAN (Metropolitan Area Network) — A shared medium bigger than a LAN but smaller than a WAN. An example is 802.6.

mask — The address-sized quantity, configured along with an address, that has 1's for the "link" portion of the address and 0's for the "node" portion of the address.

MPLS (Multiprotocol Label Switching) — Adding extra information to a layer 3 protocol. Motivated originally by the wish to make layer 3 forwarding decisions based on a small header with small addresses but is now thought more useful as a way of marking packets for quality of service or fixing paths for traffic engineering.

MTU (Maximum Transmission Unit) — The largest packet size that can be transmitted between source and destination.

MSDP (Multicast Source Distribution Protocol) — A proposal for configuring a set of tunnels between routers in different domains for the purpose of informing routers in all domains about who the active transmitters are in all active multicast groups. Claimed to be an "interim solution" for groups with members in multiple domains until BGMP/MASC gets designed, implemented, and deployed.

multicast — To transmit information to a group of recipients via a single transmission by the source.

multiplexing — Sharing a communications channel by transmitting messages for multiple destinations with some indication of the intended recipient.

NAPT (Network Address Port Translator) — A device that sits between a private network and the Internet and translates (address, port) pairs to (address, port) pairs.

NAT (Network Address Translator) — An admittedly useful kludge that sits between your network and the Internet and translates network layer addresses so that your intranet can survive without globally unique addresses.

NBMA (Non-Broadcast, Multiple Access) — A kind of "link," such as ATM, that looks like a LAN in that it is multiple access but does not have the multicast capability that allows neighbor discovery.

NET (Network Entity Title) — The ISO term for the identifier of the network layer running at a particular node.

NetBEUI (NetBIOS Extended User Interface) — A protocol used in some PCs. Designed for LAN-only, it is unroutable.

NHRP (Next Hop Resolution Protocol) — The scheme documented in RFC 2332 for getting rid of extra hops on an NBMA network.

NIC (Network Interface Card) — The board that enables a computer to connect to a network.

NLPID (Network Layer Protocol ID) — The first octet of any of ISO's network layer protocols. This octet enables ISO network layer protocols to be distinguished even if they are transmitted over a data link that has no "protocol type" or "SAP" field.

NLPIDs can be assigned to non-ISO protocols. The assigned NLPID can sometimes be a convenient method of identifying protocols.

NLSP (NetWare Link Services Protocol) — Also sometimes referred to as NetWare Link State Protocol. An IPX-specific version of IS-IS.

NSAP (Network Service Access Point) — The ISO term for the quantity that specifies a client of a network layer running at a particular node.

NSP (Network Services Protocol) — The layer 4 protocol in DECnet Phases IV and earlier.

OSPF (Open Shortest Path First) — A link state routing protocol used for routing IP.

OUI (Organizationally Unique Identifier) — The 3 octets assigned by the IEEE in a block of 48-bit addresses.

peer group — PNNI's term for an area.

PIM-DM (Protocol-Independent Multicast, Dense-Mode) — A "flood-and-prune" multicast routing protocol.

PIM-SM (Protocol-Independent Multicast, Sparse-Mode) — A multicast routing protocol defined in RFC 2362.

PNNI (Private Network-to-Network Interface) — A link state protocol similar to IS-IS and OSPF developed for ATM.

poison reverse — The practice, in distance vector routing, of reporting a distance of infinity to D when you lose your path to D rather than just letting your neighbor time it out.

PPP (Point-to-Point Protocol) — A data link layer protocol for a point-to-point link with multiplexing capability standardized within the IP community.

prefix — A way of summarizing a large number of addresses in a compact way. The prefix, which would be at most the length of an address, specifies all addresses that start with that prefix.

promiscuous listen — Having the hardware receive and pass to the upper layers all packets that arrive on a LAN.

protocol type — A multiplexing field that defines the type of packet in which only a single field appears in the packet. In contrast, a SAP type of multiplexing field has a source SAP and a destination SAP, and, theoretically, the two SAP values are numerically unrelated.

provider-based addressing — The strategy of having ISPs give out blocks of addresses to their customers so that addresses reflect the topology and routing tables can be small.

public key cryptography — Also known as asymmetric cryptography. Each user has two keys: one that is kept private and one that is public. The two keys are inverses of each other. For example, generating a signature uses Alice's private key, and verifying the signature uses Alice's public key (see *secret key cryptography*).

PVC (Permanent Virtual Circuit) — A concept in connection-oriented networks such as X.25 and ATM in which a call is administratively set up, with a fixed destination.

QOS (Quality of Service) — A field in the CLNP network layer header that is functionally equivalent to the **TOS** field in the IP header.

RARP (Reverse ARP) — A protocol defined by RFC 903 to enable a diskless client machine to discover its own IP address. BOOTP accomplishes the same goal and is the preferred protocol.

reassembly — The act of combining the fragments of a packet that must be cut into pieces in order to traverse links that cannot accommodate the original sized packet, to hopefully wind up with the original packet.

repeater — A physical layer relay that forwards bits, in contrast to bridges and routers, which forward packets.

reverse path forwarding — A technique for reducing the overhead of flooding, in which a router accepts a packet with source address S only from link L, if L is the link the router would use for forwarding toward S.

RFC (Request for Comments) — The document series maintained by the Internet community that records the protocols within the Internet and gives other information.

RIP (Routing Information Protocol) — A distance vector routing protocol popular for routing IP.

route reflection — An alternative to having all BGP speakers within an AS maintain full connectivity. Route reflectors are BGP speakers allowed to collect BGP information and forward it to other BGP speakers within the AS.

routeing — The spelling of the word *routing* that vigilant members of the ISO network layer committee pointed out was mandated by the ISO rules, which specify the particular edition of the *Oxford English Dictionary* in which that spelling is used.

routing domain — The ISO equivalent of an AS. (See **AS**.)

RP (Rendezvous Point) — A PIM-SM term for the node that is the root of the shared tree for a multicast group.

RPF (Reverse Path Forwarding) — An optimization to flooding invented by Yogen Dalal in which packets from source S are accepted from neighbor N only if N is the neighbor to which you would forward a packet destined for S.

RTMP (Routing Table Maintenance Protocol) — The AppleTalk equivalent of the IP RIP protocol.

SAP (Service Access Point) — A term that can be employed for the address of a user of a service (as in "NSAP"). In 802.2, it is used to describe a field that further defines an address. For example, the destination address plus the DSAP (destination service access point) define the recipient of a packet. It differs from a protocol type in that the assumption is that the SSAP (source service access point) and DSAP are numerically unrelated.

SAP (Service Advertisement Protocol) — A protocol in NetWare version 3 that advertises names and addresses.

SEAL (Simple Efficient Adaptation Layer) — The protocol standardized by the ATM forum as AAL5.

secret key cryptography — Also known as symmetric cryptography, because encryption and decryption use the same key. (See *public key cryptography.*)

seed router — An AppleTalk router configured with the LAN information (network number range and zone information), from which other routers on that LAN learn the information.

self-stabilization — A property of a distributed algorithm in which after any arbitrary bad event such as injection of bad data or corruption of databases, after any malfunctioning equipment is disconnected from the network, the network returns to correct operation without human intervention.

ships in the night — A term given to using two routing algorithms in parallel. The opposite of integrated routing.

SMDS (Switched Multimegabit Data Service) — A public packet-switched network that is connectionless, uses telephone numbers (E.164 addresses), and carries packets up to 7168 bytes of data.

SNAP SAP (SubNetwork Access Protocol SAP) — A particular value of SAP reserved by 802.2 for all protocols that do not have a globally assigned SAP value.

spanning tree — A subset of a network in which exactly one path exists between any pair of nodes.

SPF (Shortest Path First) — The term often used for the Dijkstra algorithm, in which paths to all destinations are computed given complete knowledge of a graph (the LSP database, in the case of a link state routing protocol).

split horizon — A technique for improving the convergence of distance vector protocols, in which you do not report, to neighbor N, that you can reach D, if N is the neighbor you use when forwarding to D.

SR bridge — A bridge that forwards only packets that contain source routing header information.

SR-TB bridge — A bridge that translates between source routing and transparent packets.

SRT bridge — A bridge that forwards both packets with source routing header information and transparent packets.

startup range — The range of AppleTalk network numbers (FF00 to FFFE) reserved for use when no router is on the LAN or when the LAN's network number range is unknown.

SVC (Switched Virtual Circuit) — A concept in a connection-oriented network such as ATM or X.25 in which the connection is set up on demand to a specified destination and is hung up by either endpoint when no longer needed.

switch — Anything that moves data. Somehow the term is applied to imply that the device is fast and cheap. Can be a bridge (layer 2 switch) or router (layer 3 switch), or sometimes used for something that moves ATM cells.

TCP (Transmission Control Protocol) — The reliable connection-oriented transport layer protocol defined in the Internet suite of protocols.

TCP/IP — A term often used to describe the Internet suite of protocols. Although TCP and IP are only two of the protocols within the suite, for some reason it has become popular to call the whole suite TCP/IP.

TLV — (Type, Length, Value) A way of encoding information into a protocol in a flexible and forward-compatible way. New fields can be added by defining new types, and unknown fields can be skipped due to the **length** field.

token — Something that is passed between users. In token-oriented LANs, possession of the token gives the possessor permission to transmit.

token bus — A type of LAN standardized within 802.4.

token ring — A type of LAN standardized within 802.5 and FDDI.

TOS (Type of Service) — A field in the IP data packet header that specifies the criteria that the source wishes the routers to consider when computing a route for this packet.

traffic engineering — Configuring your network so as to control the flow of traffic. Could be done by manually creating PVCs routing based on QOS and constraints.

triggered update — The practice, in distance vector routing, of sending information when it changes (as opposed to only when the periodic timer expires).

tunnel — A synonym for *encapsulation*. See *encapsulation*.

UDP — (User Datagram Protocol) The connectionless layer 4 protocol in the IP protocol suite.

unicast — To transmit to a single recipient (in contrast to *multicast* or *broadcast*).

VCI (Virtual Circuit Indicator) — The field in ATM that indicates which VC a cell belongs to.

VLAN (Virtual LAN) — A set of ports treated by a set of interconnected bridges as a broadcast domain.

VPI (Virtual Path Indicator) — The high order part of the field in an ATM cell that tells what path the VC should be routed on. In a backbone the call mapping database might be based purely on the VPI field so that many VCs can be carried over the same path and state can be per path rather than per VC.

WAN (Wide Area Network) — A term usually applied to networks in which there are packet switches called routers.

ZIP (Zone Information Protocol) — The AppleTalk protocol.

zone — An AppleTalk concept. It's the name of a group of nodes, rather like the name of a directory. To find the address of an AppleTalk node, a search is made within the zone in which that node's name is considered to reside. A zone has no relationship to topology. A particular zone can exist on multiple LANs, and multiple zones can exist on a LAN.

Index

Addison-Wesley Computer and Engineering Publishing Group

How to Interact with Us

1. Visit our Web site

http://www.awl.com/cseng

When you think you've read enough, there's always more content for you at Addison-Wesley's web site. Our web site contains a directory of complete product information including:

- Chapters
- Exclusive author interviews
- Links to authors' pages
- Tables of contents
- Source code

You can also discover what tradeshows and conferences Addison-Wesley will be attending, read what others are saying about our titles, and find out where and when you can meet our authors and have them sign your book.

2. Subscribe to Our Email Mailing Lists

Subscribe to our electronic mailing lists and be the first to know when new books are publishing. Here's how it works: Sign up for our electronic mailing at http://www.awl.com/cseng/mailinglists.html. Just select the subject areas that interest you and you will receive notification via email when we publish a book in that area.

3. Contact Us via Email

cepubprof@awl.com
Ask general questions about our books.
Sign up for our electronic mailing lists.
Submit corrections for our web site.

bexpress@awl.com
Request an Addison-Wesley catalog.
Get answers to questions regarding your order or our products.

innovations@awl.com
Request a current Innovations Newsletter.

webmaster@awl.com
Send comments about our web site.

cepubeditors@awl.com
Submit a book proposal.
Send errata for an Addison-Wesley book.

cepubpublicity@awl.com
Request a review copy for a member of the media interested in reviewing new Addison-Wesley titles.

We encourage you to patronize the many fine retailers who stock Addison-Wesley titles. Visit our online directory to find stores near you or visit our online store: http://store.awl.com/ or call 800-824-7799.

Addison Wesley Longman
Computer and Engineering Publishing Group
One Jacob Way, Reading, Massachusetts 01867 USA
TEL 781-944-3700 • FAX 781-942-3076